SAINT JOSEPH'S UNIVERSITY
PHILADELPHIA 1851
Francis A. Drexel
LIBRARY
Books For College Libraries
Third Edition
Core Collection
SAINT JOSEPH'S UNIVERSITY

UNITED STATES ARMY IN WORLD WAR II

Special Studies

MILITARY RELATIONS BETWEEN THE UNITED STATES AND CANADA 1939–1945

by

Colonel Stanley W. Dziuban

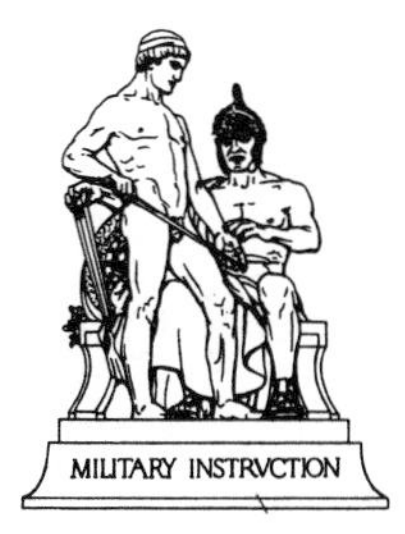

OFFICE OF THE CHIEF OF MILITARY HISTORY
DEPARTMENT OF THE ARMY
WASHINGTON, D. C., 1959

This volume, one of the series UNITED STATES ARMY IN WORLD WAR II, is the fifth to be published in the subseries Special Studies. All the volumes will be closely related, and the series will present a comprehensive account of the activities of the Military Establishment during World War II. A tentative list of subseries is appended at the end of this volume.

Library of Congress Catalog Card Number: 59-60001

Reprinted 1970

For sale by the Superintendent of Documents, U.S. Government Printing Office
Washington, D.C. 20402 - Price $6.75 (cloth)

UNITED STATES ARMY IN WORLD WAR II

Kent Roberts Greenfield, General Editor

. . . to Those Who Served

Foreword

As late as the beginning of 1940, with World War II several months old, military liaison between Canada and the United States was so scant that they had not even exchanged service attachés. Yet the two countries and their armed forces were inevitably brought into extensive and intimate collaboration in the prosecution of World War II. This study is a historical record of the military and politico-military aspects of this collaboration.

The impact of advancing technology since World War II on time and space factors has demonstrated ever more forcefully that the defense problem of the two countries is a continuing one requiring joint solutions. In consequence, the two countries have in recent years been drawn into even closer co-operation.

This study is intended to provide background information to staff officers currently involved in defense planning, to officers on exchange duty with the Canadian armed forces, and to officers in the service schools preparing for such duties. Since many of the current joint problems are similar to those of World War II, these officers should find in the record of World War II experience guidance which will help them achieve the optimum solutions to their current problems.

From the analyses of the politico-military relationships between the two countries, many lessons can be gleaned by Americans of both the military and the diplomatic services, as well as by civilian scholars. The study will perhaps be similarly useful to Canadians. In its broader aspects, the experience recorded herein may be applicable, with interpretation, to similar arrangements between other pairs of neighboring countries or within a multilateral security arrangement.

The author of this volume, Col. Stanley W. Dziuban, began work on it early in 1950 to satisfy the doctoral dissertation requirement of Columbia University, from which he received a Ph.D. degree in 1955. Colonel Dziuban, a 1939 graduate of the U.S. Military Academy, is at present assigned as Deputy Division Engineer, U.S. Army Engineer Division, New England.

The subject of his book was selected upon recommendation of the Office of the Chief of Military History and with the endorsement of the Director, Plans and Operations Division, General Staff. Publication has been delayed because the greater part of the work on the volume had to be done by the author in his off-duty hours and because almost a year was consumed in obtaining the necessary clearances from the authorities concerned.

Washington, D. C.
1 February 1958

R. W. STEPHENS
Maj. Gen., U.S.A.
Chief of Military History

Preface

This study contains a detailed account of how the United States joined with Canada to thwart the Axis threat to North America and how the two nations together cast their resources in the balance to help tip the scales decisively against the Axis Powers. The common effort ranged from the prosaic growing of wheat to the climactic development of the atomic bomb. In the defense of their homelands, North Americans accomplished epic feats and experienced high adventure as they built roads, pipelines, telephone lines, and air bases in the raw Arctic wilderness, in some instances in areas never before penetrated by white man.

Canadian and U.S. armed forces undertook their strategic and logistical operations initially to repel the advance of German and Japanese forces toward North America and subsequently to help drive the enemy to defeat. In executing those operations, Canadians and Americans worked and fought shoulder to shoulder on land and on sea and in the air, and together solved in a spirit of co-operative friendship the countless problems that arose.

Prepared primarily as a doctoral dissertation in the field of international relations, this study also strives to present a rounded military history of the co-operation between the two countries. As a consequence it includes, on the one hand, material such as that in Chapters IX and X which contributes only marginally to an analysis of the politico-military collaboration. It covers, on the other hand, a number of matters normally outside the scope of a military history.

The political and military relationships that evolved between the two North American neighbors are examined, as is the impact of the great disparity between them in size and resources. The influx of U.S. forces into Canada posed many problems, one of the most significant of which was the jurisdictional status of those forces. The need to protect Canadian sovereignty motivated Canada, which had had for decades carefully to nurture that sovereignty, to guard against all encroachments. The two countries worked out a variety of joint mechanisms and arrangements for the joint operations of their forces, the joint construction and utilization of facilities, and the joint control of other enterprises of common interest. In these arrangements, Canada's status as a British Commonwealth nation and the joint U.S.-United Kingdom direction of global war strategy emerge as two basic complicating factors.

As the bibliographical note indicates in detail, the study is based largely on official records. Full access was given the author to the pertinent official U.S. records. Within the limitations imposed by a few gaps in, and by the character of, contemporary documentation, the factual record chronicled can be considered authoritative. Because the source material included documents still classified as secret, the study was submitted for and received military security clearance. The author was not required as a result of that review to make textual changes. Such review constitutes no official endorsement of the study, and where the author sets forth hypotheses, analyses, conclusions, or recommendations, they are presented solely as his own views and upon his own responsibility. They do not and cannot purport to represent the views of the Department of the Army, the Department of Defense, or the U.S. Government.

Acknowledgment is due the Houghton Mifflin Company for permission to reproduce material from *The Second World War* by Winston Churchill, and to Messrs. Joseph C. Grew, McGeorge Bundy, and Henry Morgenthau, Jr., for access kindly provided to, respectively, the Pierrepont Moffat, Stimson, and Morgenthau diaries.

No attempt has been made to use records of the Canadian Government, excepting insofar as they were in the public domain or were to be found in files of U.S. agencies. Even assuming that these records might have been accessible to this researcher, their exclusion would have been dictated by considerations of time and labor. This omission imposes limitations on the study, the full impact of which can be appraised when a comparable study is presented from the Canadian point of view.

Many persons have contributed to the preparation of this study. Helpful review and comment were generously offered by Brig. Gen. Paul M. Robinett (retired), of the Office, Chief of Military History, Department of the Army; Professor W. T. R. Fox and the late Professor J. Bartlet Brebner, of Columbia University; Maj. Gen. Guy V. Henry (retired), U.S. Chairman of the Permanent Joint Board on Defense, Canada-United States; the late Capt. Tracy B. Kittredge, U. S. Navy; Maj. Gen. R. J. Wood and Col. Francis J. Graling, U.S. Army; and Drs. Byron Fairchild and Rose Engelman, of the Office, Chief of Military History. Substantive contributions through correspondence, personal interview, or review of portions of the study were made by many officers who participated in the events chronicled. These officers are listed in the bibliographical note. The author is also grateful for the help of other individuals who must go unnamed.

Dr. Stetson Conn, Deputy Chief Historian of the Office, Chief of Military History, and Helen McShane Bailey, editor of this volume, shared the burden of reviewing and preparing the manuscript for publication in its present form. Margaret E. Tackley, Chief of the Photographic Branch, Office, Chief of Military History, selected the photographs. Franklin F. Marsh and Myrna Thompson prepared the index. The author alone stands responsible, not only for the analyses and conclusion drawn, but also for the scholarship and workmanship of the study as a whole.

STANLEY W. DZIUBAN
Colonel, U.S. Army

Washington, D. C.
1 February 1958

Contents

Chapter | *Page*

I. CHAUTAUQUA TO OGDENSBURG 1
- *Seeds of World War II Co-operation* 3
- *Backdrop for Ogdensburg* 4
- *Initial Canadian Approaches* 13
- *The Ogdensburg Declaration* 22

II. THE PERMANENT JOINT BOARD ON DEFENSE 31
- *Organization and Composition* 33
- Modus Operandi 38
- *Scope of Responsibilities* 46
- *Collaboration Through the Board* 52

III. PARTNERSHIP VERSUS TRIANGLE 55
- *The Roosevelt-Churchill Axis* 55
- *North Atlantic Triangle* 59
- *The Stresses of Partnership* 69
- *Canadian Staff Representation in Washington* 71
- *The Combined Agencies* 77

IV. JOINT DEFENSE PLANNING 86
- *Initial Defense Plans* 86
- *Early Supply Assistance* 90
- *Strengthening the Garrisons* 95
- *ABC-1 and ABC-22* 101
- *Putting Plans Into Action* 106

V. ORGANIZATION AND COMMAND 109
- *Unity of Operational Command* 110
- *Local Command Arrangements* 116
- *Organization for the Logistical Tasks* 126
- *Organizational Chaos* 131

VI. HEMISPHERE DEFENSE PROBLEMS 142
- *The Twenty-second Chair* 143
- *Securing Greenland* 149
- *The Defense of Iceland* 155
- *St. Pierre and Miquelon* 158
- *Summary* 160

VII. OPERATIONS IN THE EASTERN AREAS 162
- *The Lease and Construction of Newfoundland Bases* 162
- *Defending Newfoundland* 170
- *North Atlantic Ferry Operations* 181
- *Sault Sainte Marie* 193

Chapter | *Page*

VIII. ACTIVITIES IN WESTERN CANADA 199
The Northwest Staging Route 200
The American Construction Phase 207
Traffic Along the Staging Route 215
The Alaska Highway 217
The Canol Project 228
Communications and Weather 236
The Prince Rupert Port 238

IX. COMRADES IN ARMS 241
Battle of the Atlantic 242
Securing Alaska Against the Japanese 252
The First Special Service Force 259
Canadian Army Pacific Force 268

X. CO-OPERATION IN OTHER FIELDS 273
Administration and Personnel 274
The Rush-Bagot Agreement 278
Miscellaneous Co-operation 280
Research and Development 284
Arsenals of Democracy 289

XI. PROBLEMS IN JÚRISDICTION 296
Jurisdiction Over Friendly Foreign Forces 296
Airway Traffic Control 301
Military Air Services 306
Maintenance and Control of Bases 313

XII. MISSION ACCOMPLISHED 317
Beginning the American Roll-up 317
The Northern Airfields Settlement 320
Disposals Under the Thirty-third Recommendation 325
Special Dispositions 329
The 12 February 1947 Statement 334
The Lessons of World War II 339

Appendix

A. Recommendations of the Permanent Joint Board on Defense, Canada-United States, 26 August 1940–1 September 1945 347
B. First Report of the Permanent Joint Board on Defense, Canada-United States 366
C. Extract of Journal of Discussions and Decisions for Meeting of Permanent Joint Board on Defense, Canada-United States, on 26 February 1942 370
D. Hyde Park Declaration by President Roosevelt and Prime Minister Mackenzie King Regarding Co-operation in War Production 373
E. The 12 February 1947 Joint Statement on Defense Collaboration 374

BIBLIOGRAPHICAL NOTE 377

Page

CHRONOLOGY OF STATEMENTS IN THE CANADIAN HOUSE OF COMMONS 393

LIST OF ABBREVIATIONS 395

INDEX 399

Tables

No.

1. Membership of the Permanent Joint Board on Defense, Canada-United States: 22 August 1940–1 September 1945 36
2. Meetings of the Permanent Joint Board on Defense: 26 August 1940–31 December 1945 39
3. Combined Canadian-United States Production of Selected Munitions: 1 July 1940–31 August 1945 290
4. United States Lend-Lease Aid: 11 March 1941–31 December 1955 293
5. Canadian Mutual Aid Board Expenditures 294
6. Canada's War Production During the Mutual Aid Period: 1 September 1943–1 September 1945 295
7. Canadian-United States Expenditures on the Northern Airfields, Detailed by Projects 324

Chart

1. United States Administrative and Logistical Organization in Canada and Newfoundland: 1 April 1943 132

Map

1. Canada, Alaska, and Greenland (*National Geographic Society Map*) ..... *Inside back cover*

Illustrations

Members of the Permanent Joint Board Arriving in Newfoundland 40
Quebec Conference, August 1943 67
Meeting at Quebec, August 1943 77
Brig. Gen. C. L. Sturdevant 129
Maj. Gen. W. W. Foster 138
Harbor Camp Area of the Greenland Base Command 153
155-mm. Gun Emplacement 176
Mayor Fiorello H. LaGuardia 185
Flight Strips at the Watson Lake Airport 208
U.S. Army Engineers Constructing a Pioneer Road 220
Sikanni Chief River Bridge 223
Train Plowing Through Deep Snow 226
Retreat Ceremony at Fort William Henry Harrison 261
Canadian and U.S. Soldiers of the First Special Service Force 263

All illustrations are from Department of Defense files.

MILITARY RELATIONS BETWEEN THE UNITED STATES AND CANADA 1939–1945

360-477 O - 70 - 2

CHAPTER I

Chautauqua to Ogdensburg

The twentieth century gave a new turn to the history of U.S.-Canadian military relations. Up until that time the two neighbors had had no occasion jointly to prepare to defend North America against aggression from without. It was not too many years earlier, in fact, that the North American military problems that arose found the peoples of the two countries not partners, but antagonists. The open fighting of the War of 1812 ended in December 1814 with the Treaty of Ghent, but this treaty marked the end only of formal hostilities.

While the Rush-Bagot Agreement, subsequently signed at Washington in April 1817 to provide for naval disarmament on the Great Lakes, has been repeatedly cited as a symbol of the friendly relations which have existed since that date,[1] sporadic border skirmishes and incursions continued for several decades. These eruptions resulted from the mutual rivalries and suspicions that remained alive on both sides of the border.[2] But by the end of the nineteenth century the two peoples had learned to live together peaceably, if not fully to understand each other. In fact, an era of peaceful neighborly relations, unexcelled in the history of any other pair of adjacent countries, was by 1900 well established.

Prussian militarism and World War I first brought the two countries shoulder to shoulder as wartime partners. Although they entered the war for different reasons, and although Canada was then only a partially autonomous dominion of the British Empire, the two countries collaborated directly to meet certain of their war requirements. Canadian recruiting staffs in the United States accepted thousands of recruits for the Canadian Army. Canadian pilots were trained in the southern United States under arrangements made by the British Royal Flying Corps, and some American pilots were trained in the Canadian training establishment. American munitions production

---

[1] For an example, see the 1946 exchange of notes published in Treaties and Other International Acts Series (TIAS), 1836. For an account of the interpretations of the Rush-Bagot Agreement made to meet World War II needs, see below, pp. 278–80.

[2] An excellent account of these border difficulties is given in Charles P. Stacey, "The Myth of the Unguarded Frontier, 1815–1871," *American Historical Review*, LVI (October 1950), 1–18.

helped meet Canadian needs. When the United States entered the war, the expanded Canadian aircraft industry was in turn able to supply some of the training aircraft and flying boats needed to meet American requirements. The value of Canadian munitions deliveries to the United States in World War I totaled $32,785,000, while, as a result of the armistice, contracts in the amount of $145,645,000 were canceled. During 1918 a U.S. Navy air unit, commanded by Lt. Richard E. Byrd, flew antisubmarine escort and patrols from Halifax and Sydney, Nova Scotia, while a Royal Canadian Naval Air Service was being established with American assistance. But after Armistice Day, 1918, many years were to pass before any joint consideration was again to be given to common defense problems.[3]

Despite the foregoing accomplishments World War I relationships were not without their unhappy aspect. From August 1914 until the U.S. declaration of war, bitter feeling in Canada developed because of U.S. neutrality and isolationism. After the armistice, owing to the U.S. attitude on war debts, this feeling increased, but it waned with the passing years.[4]

World War I did provide a demonstration that, by the beginning of the twentieth century, Canada and the United States recognized several fundamental facts as the basis of their military policies. First, Canada shared with the United States the geographic isolation of North America. In the case of Canada, climate and topography heightened the isolation. The Arctic wastes made a surface approach from that quarter virtually impossible. The rugged coast and mountainous littoral of western Canada and the paucity of developed transportation facilities rendered invasion there extremely difficult. On the east coast, dominated by the Labrador headlands, only limited access was possible through the St. Lawrence Valley and the Maritime Provinces.

Second, and more important perhaps than these natural barriers, was the vital concern of the United States in the maintenance of Canadian territorial integrity. This concern had found its basic political expression in the Monroe Doctrine. As early as 1902 a Canadian prime minister, Sir Wilfred Laurier, had acknowledged the Monroe Doctrine as Canada's basic protection against enemy aggression.[5] The Monroe Doctrine in effect amounted to a *de facto* security guarantee by the United States, having as its principal

[3] *Canada at War,* No. 31 (Dec 43), pp. 24–25; G. N. Tucker, *The Naval Service of Canada* (Ottawa: E. Cloutier, King's Printer, 1952), I, 256–60; Richard E. Byrd, *Skyward* (New York: G. P. Putnam's Sons, 1928), pp. 64–76.

[4] Hugh L. Keenleyside devotes a chapter to the development of the Canadian attitude in *Canada and the United States* (Revised edition by Keenleyside and G. S. Brown; New York: Alfred A. Knopf, 1952).

[5] Charles P. Stacey, *The Military Problems of Canada* (Toronto: Ryerson Press, 1940), p. 68. See this work for a full discussion of the pre-World War II strategic position of Canada.

visible evidence during recent decades the U.S. Navy dominating the Pacific. The U.S. Navy, together with the British Fleet similarly dominating the Atlantic, rendered large-scale invasion of North America virtually impossible.

On the political side, the era of peaceful relations and friendly stability had become so well recognized that the prospect of war between the United States and Canada had in reality vanished. This framework of stability was firmly welded to the broader framework of a by now well-established Anglo-American friendship.

Within this strategic and political setting, Canada enjoyed a "privileged sanctuary" position, leaving it free to spring to Great Britain's side in any European war without concern over the need for home defenses and secure in the knowledge that, even if by some remote chance Canada itself should be attacked, the United States would step in to repel the invader.

Seeds of World War II Co-operation

The drums of war, with their portent for the future, had already been heard in Ethiopia and China when, on 14 August 1936, President Franklin D. Roosevelt gave his first public pledge of defense assistance to Canada. Speaking at Chautauqua, New York, he said: "Our closest neighbors are good neighbors. If there are remoter nations that wish us not good but ill, they know that we are strong; they know that we can and will defend ourselves and defend our neighborhood." [6]

The significance of this declaration of defense solidarity was missed by the Canadian public.[7] Yet not long afterward, the first of a number of discussions on mutual defense problems took place between the President and Prime Minister W. L. Mackenzie King. During a visit of King to Washington in March 1937, the two agreed on the need for military staff talks on such problems some time in the future. Staff discussions on Pacific problems took place in Washington in January 1938 as a result of the President's naval visit to Victoria, British Columbia, in the preceding September.[8]

Almost two years to the day after the Chautauqua speech, President Roosevelt gave an even stronger pledge of defense solidarity. On 18 August 1938, while speaking at Kingston, Ontario, he declared: "The Dominion of Canada is a part of the sisterhood of the British Empire. I give to you assurance that the people of the United States will not stand idly by if domi-

---

[6] Department of State *Press Releases*, XV, 168.

[7] F. H. Soward *et al.*, *Canada in World Affairs: The Pre-War Years* (Toronto: Oxford University Press, 1941), p. 107.

[8] Canada, *House of Commons Debates* (Ottawa: King's Printer) (cited hereafter as *H. C. Debates*) 12 Nov 40, p. 55.

nation of Canadian soil is threatened by any other empire."[9] Significantly, this promise was inserted into the speech by the President himself while he was revising a draft prepared by the Department of State.[10]

During this visit to Canada the President again discussed common defense problems with the Prime Minister, with particular reference to Atlantic coastal defense.[11] Two days after Roosevelt's Kingston speech, Prime Minister King, during an address at Woodbridge, Ontario, responded: "We, too, have our obligations as a good friendly neighbor, and one of these is to see that, at our own instance, our country is made as immune from attack or possible invasion as we can reasonably be expected to make it, and that, should the occasion ever arise, enemy forces should not be able to pursue their way either by land, sea or air, to the United States across Canadian territory."[12]

Prime Minister King's visit to Washington in November 1938, on the occasion of the signing of a bilateral trade agreement, furnished another opportunity for discussion of common problems of defense "at length and in a more concrete and definite way."[13] Coincidentally, this discussion followed by only a few days a declaration by the President that the United States intended to make the American continents impregnable from the air and that he believed Canada would co-operate in meeting such an objective.[14]

The outbreak of World War II altered the complexion of such conversations, which acquired new political implications, especially for the United States, in the light of Canadian belligerency and U.S. neutrality. Nevertheless, when the two heads of state again met at Warm Springs, Georgia, in April 1940, a month before the German blitzkrieg, they used the opportunity "for a careful review of the whole situation."[15] The prospect of attacks of any consequence on Canada or of U.S. participation in the war still appeared remote. But the events of the next two months were to move the two countries quickly together into close collaboration in military planning.

Backdrop for Ogdensburg

The outbreak of World War II had found Canada with armed forces comprising active establishments of only 4,500 ground, 1,800 sea, and 3,100 air per-

---

[9] Department of State *Press Releases,* XIX, 124.

[10] Cordell Hull, *The Memoirs of Cordell Hull* (New York: The Macmillan Company, 1948), I, 587–88. For examinations of the pledge in the light of the Monroe Doctrine, see Chas. G. Fenwick, "Canada and the Monroe Doctrine," pp. 782–85, and Lionel H. Laing, "Does the Monroe Doctrine Cover Canada?," pp. 793–96, *American Journal of International Law,* XXXII (1938).

[11] *H. C. Debates,* 12 Nov 40, p. 55.

[12] *Ibid.,* 12 Feb 47, p. 346.

[13] *Ibid.,* 12 Nov 40, p. 60.

[14] *The New York Times,* November 16, 1938.

[15] *H. C. Debates,* 12 Nov 40, p. 60.

sonnel. However, plans were ready for expansion of these forces, and on the very day of Hitler's assault on Poland the Canadian Department of National Defense authorized the organization of two infantry divisions and supporting units. Similar plans for expansion of the Navy and Air Force were rapidly placed in effect.[16]

On 3 September 1939 the United Kingdom declared itself to be in a state of war with Germany. The Canadian Government also acted immediately after the German initiation of hostilities and declared the existence of a state of "apprehended war" as from 25 August. By this step the Canadian Government was able to assume the powers authorized under the War Measures Act of 1914, still in force, which authorized such action when "war, invasion or insurrection, real or apprehended," existed. In keeping with its status as a fully self-governing dominion, Canada then proceeded independently, and unfettered by any automatic commitment to the United Kingdom, to deliberate a declaration of war. With the approval of the Canadian Parliament, a declaration of war on Germany was made on 10 September, a week after the United Kingdom action.

Canada quickly acted to undertake an industrial production program and other economic measures needed to support the planned mobilization effort. The primary objective of the Canadian war program was, through consultation and co-ordination with the United Kingdom, to make the most effective contribution to the conduct of the war. Representations from London indicated that most needed immediately were military and naval matériel, raw materials and industrial goods, air, naval, and technical army personnel, and the preparation of an expeditionary force for later use.[17] While undertaking to meet these requirements, the government also made provision for essential home defense such as the deployment of forces to defend coastal areas and vulnerable points.[18]

In proceeding with the formation of the two infantry divisions, Canada found itself largely unprepared to provide them with modern equipment.

[16] The reader interested in accounts of prewar status and expansion of the Canadian armed forces should consult Charles P. Stacey, *The Military Problems of Canada* and *The Canadian Army, 1939–1945* (Ottawa: E. Cloutier, King's Printer, 1948); Joseph Schull, *The Far Distant Ships* (Ottawa: E. Cloutier, King's Printer, 1950); and Tucker, *The Naval Service of Canada*.

[17] The question of the adequacy of the Canadian voice in the formulation of policy and strategy for the conduct of the war and the use of Canadian resources subsequently became the subject of some debate in Canada. It is discussed by Dawson, *Canada in World Affairs: 1939–1941*, Ch. X, and by C. C. Lingard and R. G. Trotter, *Canada in World Affairs*, III, *September 1941 to May 1944* (Toronto: Oxford University Press, 1950), 238.

[18] Canadian Department of National Defense statement of 20 September 1939, quoted in Robert M. Dawson, *Canada in World Affairs: 1939–1941* (Toronto: Oxford University Press, 1943), pp. 286–89.

Such equipment was not on hand, nor was there production capacity for it since Great Britain had in the past been the source of this material. Expansion of the Air Force was similarly handicapped. Having, however, a substantial industrial base and an adequate supply of raw materials and skilled workers, Canada was able quickly to initiate expansion of its munitions industry from the single ammunition-producing arsenal that was in production at the outbreak of war.

In the succeeding months the production requirements presented by the United Kingdom proved to be much smaller than had been expected. The result was that by May 1940 only a relatively modest expansion of the Canadian munitions industry had taken place, inadequate to meet by itself increased Canadian requirements, let alone other needs, which arose after the fall of France.[19]

United States preparations in the face of the worsened world situation had, before the outbreak of war, also been modest. A Naval Expansion Act approved in 1938 was a first, but small, step toward a powerful two-ocean Navy. In April 1939 legislation was enacted to provide new aircraft and other equipment for the Army and to expand the base of munitions production. The U.S. reaction to the actual outbreak of war was the Presidential proclamation on 8 September 1939 of a limited national emergency. But participation in the war seemed remote and, to most Americans, improbable. No sense of urgency marked U.S. defense preparations.[20]

In this period preceding the German invasion of the Low Countries on

[19] *H. C. Debates*, 22 May 40, p. 128, and 11 Jun 40, pp. 656–57; R. G. Trotter and A. B. Corey (eds.), *Conference on Canadian-American Affairs: Proceedings at Queen's University, 23–26 June 1941* (Toronto: Ginn and Company, 1941), pp. 44–45. Several authorities have stated that fear of postwar competition and the desire to conserve credits motivated the paucity of British orders. See Dawson, *Canada in World Affairs: 1939–1941*, pp. 16–17, 114–17, and H. Reginald Hardy, *Mackenzie King of Canada: A Biography* (Toronto: Oxford University Press, 1949), p. 190.

[20] For accounts of pre-Pearl Harbor military preparations in the United States, see Mark S. Watson, *Chief of Staff: Prewar Plans and Preparations*, UNITED STATES ARMY IN WORLD WAR II (Washington: Government Printing Office, 1950); Wesley F. Craven and James L. Cate (eds.), *The Army Air Forces in World War II*, I, *Plans and Early Operations* Chicago: University of Chicago Press, 1948); Samuel Eliot Morison, *History of United States Naval Operations in World War II*, I, *The Battle of the Atlantic, September 1939–May 1943* (Boston: Little, Brown and Company, 1947); and *The War Reports of General of the Army George C. Marshall, General of the Army H. H. Arnold, and Fleet Admiral Ernest J. King* (New York: J. B. Lippincott Company, 1947). Also related are Maurice Matloff and Edwin M. Snell, *Strategic Planning for Coalition Warfare, 1941–1942*, UNITED STATES ARMY IN WORLD WAR II (Washington: Government Printing Office, 1953), and the forthcoming volume in the same series by Stetson Conn and Byron Fairchild, The Framework of Hemisphere Defense. An account of the development of U.S. foreign policy from 1937 through August 1940 has been written by William L. Langer and S. Everett Gleason, *The Challenge to Isolation* (New York: Harper & Brothers, 1952).

9–10 May 1940, only isolated contacts in the field of politico-military co-operation took place between Canada and the United States. The Roosevelt-King meeting in April has already been mentioned. In August 1939, when the outbreak of war had not yet occurred but appeared imminent, Canadian Minister of National Defense Ian A. Mackenzie and Chief of Air Staff Air Marshal William Bishop had secretly approached the White House and the War Department seeking the purchase of some sixty-five medium bombers, trainers, and flying boat patrol aircraft. Their efforts were fruitless. In January 1940 the Canadian Government asked if there would be U.S. objection to the purchase of yachts for conversion to armed vessels. A negative reply was received, and in the next few months Canada carried out a complicated scheme of purchase by Canadian civilians of suitable yachts that were in turn requisitioned by the government. During this "phony war" period some procurement of military equipment took place by direct contracting between the Canadian Government and U.S. manufacturers.[21]

During the prewar and phony war periods, U.S. Army and Navy officers in Washington took into account in their planning studies the national policy pronouncements of the President calling for defense of the hemisphere from North Pole to South Pole. In these studies, they examined the defense of the contiguous Canadian territory. The need for some sort of collaboration with Canada in this regard was recognized. Nevertheless, these studies did not result in the development of any approved requirements for bases in Canada or in any joint planning with Canadian staffs. The more serious threats to the Americas were viewed as directed toward the Panama Canal, the Caribbean Sea, and contiguous land areas. Emphasis was placed in the planning studies on these areas, with secondary consideration being given to northern North America. Although the planning studies did visualize some need to utilize bases in Newfoundland, no requirement for rights there was established by the War and Navy Departments in their over-all statements of requirements, which did include a number of sites in Latin America and western Atlantic waters.

The German blitzkrieg of May 1940 undoubtedly startled Americans, to whom the war was still a political issue and not a military reality. To Canadians, however, the Nazi successes meant that the war was but one step short of Canada's threshold. By 17 June the German assault begun on 10 May had forced the French to seek an armistice and had left, in the wake of

---

[21] Memo, L. Johnson for President, 25 Aug 39, Roosevelt Papers, Secy's File, Box 42; Cdn Leg *aide-mémoire,* 18 Jan 40, D/S 195.2/3666; Tucker, *The Naval Service of Canada,* II, 25–26.

Dunkerque, a battered British Army evacuated safely, but only after the loss of most of its heavy equipment.

The successful onslaught of the German blitzkrieg brought the Nazi panzers to the English Channel, where they sat poised as if for invasion. Behind them the Luftwaffe girded itself for the aerial assault which, it was hoped, would further cripple England and make easy its subjugation. The Battle of Britain did not start immediately, but it was certain to begin and to rain death and destruction from the skies on the people, homes, and factories of Britain.

In this emergency, and in the face of such a dismal prospect, President Roosevelt and his closest advisers acted without hesitation. From reserve stocks, the United States during June 1940 shipped to the United Kingdom a half-million Enfield rifles with 130 million rounds of ammunition, 975 artillery pieces with a million rounds of ammunition, 80,000 machine guns, and other munitions.[22] Canada, too, hurriedly made available to the United Kingdom such additional military resources as could be scraped together. Beyond this "scraping of the bottom of the barrel," there could be no significant augmentation of supplies of matériel to the English during the following months.

Yet if the major scenes of this Wagnerian tragedy were being played in western Europe, overtones could easily be heard in North America. With the invasion of an all but defenseless Britain seemingly an imminent possibility, to Canadians hardly less than to Britons, great consequences hung on the answers to the questions: Would Hitler invade? Would he be successful? As early as 15 May, British Prime Minister Winston S. Churchill had at least entertained the possibility that the answers to both questions might be affirmative, when he told U.S. Ambassador Joseph P. Kennedy that, even if England were completely destroyed, rather than give up, the government would move to Canada with the fleet and fight on. Again on 4 June, when reporting to the House of Commons on the disasters on the Continent, Churchill, though disbelieving that Germany could conquer Britain, proclaimed that such action would be followed by liberation by "our Empire beyond the seas, armed and guarded by the British Fleet." [23]

Consideration of this dire possibility, with its tremendous implications for Canada, was the burden of a message from Churchill which was deposited

[22] Army Service Forces, International Division, *A Guide to International Supply* (Washington: 1945), p. 4.

[23] D/S 740.0011 EW 1939/2952; Hull, *Memoirs,* I, 765–66; Great Britain, *Parliamentary Debates,* Vol. 361, col. 796.

on Prime Minister King's desk on 5 June. In it Churchill discussed continued U.S. neutrality and alternate courses of action regarding the British Fleet should the United Kingdom be defeated. He also pointed out:

> We must be careful not to let Americans view too complacently prospect of a British collapse, out of which they would get the British Fleet and the guardianship of the British Empire, minus Great Britain. If United States were in the war and England [were] conquered locally, it would be natural that events should follow the above course. But if America continued neutral, and we were overpowered, I cannot tell what policy might be adopted by a pro-German administration such as would undoubtedly be set up.
>
> Although President is our best friend, no practical help has [reached us] from the United States as yet. We have not expected them to send military aid, but they have not even sent any worthy contribution in destroyers or planes, or by a visit of a squadron of their Fleet to southern Irish ports. Any pressure which you can apply in this direction would be invaluable.[24]

The implications for Canada of a German conquest of the United Kingdom were understandably overwhelming. Having sent one of its two partially trained and partially equipped divisions to England the preceding December-January, Canada would find the war at its doorstep without an adequate Army, Navy, or Air Force to defend it, and without a munitions industry adequate to equip and supply such forces had they existed. Naval base facilities and other resources needed to support the British Fleet were insufficient or not available. A seat for the United Kingdom Government would have to be provided, and Canada's modest means would have to support the war effort of both governments. Serious problems concerning the relationship between King's government and Churchill's government-in-exile would arise and have to be worked out.

The Canadian Government and its planning staffs took under urgent study both the immediate and the longer-term problems arising from the impending fall of France. Prime Minister King reaffirmed the policy he had announced when Canada declared war, that of assisting Great Britain by contributing as far as possible to the defense of Newfoundland and the other British and French territories in the Western Hemisphere. In June Canadian Army troops were dispatched to Newfoundland and, at the request of London, to the British West Indies and to Iceland.[25]

The Nazi blitzkrieg also resulted in a disruption of the British Commonwealth Air Training Plan in Canada, to which Canada had been devoting a

[24] The full text of the telegram is given in Winston S. Churchill, *The Second World War: Their Finest Hour* (Boston: Houghton Mifflin Company, 1949), pp. 145–46.

[25] *H. C. Debates,* 20 May 40, p. 47, and 17 Jun 40, p. 854; Stacey, *The Canadian Army, 1939–1945,* pp. 24–25. For an examination of the shifts in emphasis in Canadian defense policy from 8 September 1939 to the end of 1940, see Trotter and Corey (eds.), *Conference on Canadian-American Affairs, 1941,* pp. 40–44.

substantial part of its war effort. In consequence of the urgent need for strengthening the British air defense force, planes and pilots in Canada suitable for that purpose were rushed to England, while the flow of aircraft from England for use in the training program was cut off. In an effort to sustain the training plan, Canada scoured the United States seeking to purchase available used aircraft and supplies. As an alternate means of procuring pilots, British Ambassador Lothian and Canadian Chargé d'Affaires Merchant Mahoney on 27 May 1940 sought an arrangement by which air trainees could be sent to schools in the United States. The request was refused on the grounds that such facilities were being fully utilized to meet U.S. needs and, furthermore, that any such step would violate the Hague Convention.[26]

In the United States, too, the imminent fall of France and the possibility of British defeat gave impetus to urgent actions in the War and Navy Departments.[27] The Joint (Army-Navy) Planning Committee dropped work on other plans and hurriedly drafted RAINBOW 4, a plan based on the assumptions that Britain and France would be defeated and that the United States would face a coalition of Germany, Italy, and Japan. The plan envisaged the defense of North America and the northern part of South America.

The military analyses made by the President and his service chiefs—General George C. Marshall, Army Chief of Staff, and Admiral Harold R. Stark, Chief of Naval Operations—in consultation with Under Secretary of State Sumner Welles, all were based on a primary effort in South America to forestall Nazi subversion or intervention. Such activities were to be countered by occupation of British, French, Dutch, and Danish possessions in the Western Hemisphere.

The planners in the War and Navy Departments had long recognized the need for garrisoning additional bases in the Western Hemisphere as essential to adequate continental defense. However, even under the impact of the fall of France, the staff planners had not until this time seriously considered that a need for military bases in Canada existed and had not envisaged a situation requiring arbitrary action toward Canada. The pre-World War II RAINBOW 1 war plan approved in August 1939, for example set forth a need for bases in British possessions and in Latin American areas but not

[26] Memo/Conv, British High Commissioner Sir Gerald Campbell and Jay Pierrepont Moffat, 15 Jun 40, Moffat Diary; Memo/Conv, Chargé Mahoney and J. C. Green, 4 Jun 40, D/S 711.00111 Lic. Babb, Chas. H./71; Memo/Conv, Mahoney and Moffat, 4 Jun 40, D/S 811.22742/310.

[27] For an account of U.S. Army plans and measures during this period, see Conn and Fairchild, The Framework of Hemisphere Defense, Ch. II.

in Canada.[28] After the major Allied reverses in the Low Countries and France in May 1940, and at the direction of the President, the planners outlined steps to be taken in case Germany demanded cession of the strategically important British, French, and Dutch possessions in the Western Hemisphere. They concluded that, in the event of such demands, the United States should "assert sovereignty" over the possessions, excepting Newfoundland, where they considered co-operation with Canada (which had already garrisoned that island) would be practicable.[29]

The needs for bases in the Western Hemisphere were outlined in a joint Army-Navy estimate that had been requested by President Roosevelt on 13 June 1940. Entitled "Basis for Immediate Decisions Concerning the National Defense," this estimate of the world situation had been prepared and revised through ten editions by 27 June. All editions urged the necessity for maximum co-operation with the Latin American republics and with Canada in the defense of their territories, and recommended initiation of diplomatic action toward that end. The 22 June version of the report was presented to the President by General Marshall and Admiral Stark and was discussed by the three. Although never formally approved by the President or the War and Navy Departments, the conclusions and recommendations of this joint estimate apparently accurately reflected U.S. policies and attitudes during the summer of 1940 as to its continental defense needs.[30]

Major emphasis in the joint estimate was placed on the strengthening of hemisphere defenses through the provision of arms to the Latin American republics and other measures in that area. Such measures had already been considered in the executive departments. On 23 May the President had approved the dispatch of Army and Navy liaison officers to the South American countries.[31] Congress, too, had already considered, and on 15 June 1940 passed, House Joint Resolution 367 authorizing military and naval assistance to the American republics, and planning with these republics for such assistance was started. In the following month the foreign ministers of the American republics met at Havana, Cuba, to consult with respect to security

[28] Tracy B. Kittredge, U.S.-British Naval Co-operation, 1940–1945 (Unpublished monograph, 1947, copy in OCMH), Vol. I, Sec. II, n. 28.

[29] OCNO Memo, OP-12B-MCC, 28 May 40, states that WPD generally concurred, and bears the notation that Under Secretary of State Welles had seen it; see also Watson, *Chief of Staff: Prewar Plans and Preparations,* p. 477, for the more restrained concurrent recommendations of General Marshall's planners for the acquistion or protective occupation of the possessions; Conn and Fairchild, The Framework of Hemisphere Defense, Ch. II.

[30] Watson, *Chief of Staff: Prewar Plans and Preparations,* pp. 110–13; Conn and Fairchild, The Framework of Hemisphere Defense, Ch. II.

[31] Memo, L. Duggan for Welles, 21 May 40, D/S 810.20 Defense/21–3/5; Conn and Fairchild, The Framework of Hemisphere Defense, Ch. VIII.

problems presented by the changed situation in Europe. By the end of July the President had approved the policy for providing arms assistance to the republics.[32]

While the U.S. Army and Navy staffs were placing principal emphasis in planning for hemisphere defense on preparations in the Caribbean Sea, South America, and contiguous areas, the forces that were to bring Canada and the United States into a close defense collaboration were at work. In response to the 5 June request from Churchill, which accompanied his suggestion that the safety of the British Fleet would not be certain, King proceeded in his own way to "apply . . . pressure" on the United States.[33] Shortly after receiving the message, King sent Hugh L. Keenleyside, an officer of the Department of External Affairs, to Washington as a special emissary on a highly secret mission known only to one other person in Ottawa and to five persons in Washington. Keenleyside met with President Roosevelt and Secretary of State Cordell Hull and discussed with them the Churchill telegram of 5 June. The telegram disturbed the President considerably, since in it Churchill had given no assurances that he would not allow the British Fleet to be surrendered and had suggested the possibility of a pro-German administration in the United Kingdom.[34]

King interpreted the Churchill telegram as at least suggesting that his pressure take the form of bargaining for U.S. entry into the war, using the British Fleet as a lever. However, he apparently avoided this tactic and, instead, in replying to Churchill on 17 June, counseled against it on the basis that some feeling was developing in the United States that the United Kingdom was in fact striving for such a bargain. At the same time King pressed Churchill for an examination of the practical problems that would arise if remnants of the British Fleet were to come to North America.[35]

Churchill's reply to Prime Minister King disclaimed any suggestion of a bargain and recommended against dwelling on the possible consequences of the defeat of Great Britain. On the one hand, he saw no need for practical preparations for possible transfer of portions of the fleet across the Atlantic; on the other, he acknowledged that he could not guarantee the course of events if Great Britain were defeated.[36] For the public record, the

[32] Statement, Proposed National Policy re Supply of Arms to American Republics, dated July 1940 and apparently approved and initialed by the President about 29–31 July, D/S 810.24/123–4/21.

[33] See above, pp. 8–9.

[34] Memo/Conv, Moffat and President, 10 Jun 40, and Memo/Conv, Moffat and Prime Minister King, 13 Jun 40, Moffat Diary.

[35] Memo/Conv, Moffat and King, 27 Jun 40, Moffat Diary.

[36] The reply, dated 24 June 1940, is quoted in Churchill, *Their Finest Hour*, p. 227.

possibility of British defeat and surrender of the fleet were denied, as in the forceful and vivid terms of Churchill's speech to the House of Commons on 4 June. Nevertheless, these contingencies found expression in secret discussions involving Prime Ministers Churchill and King, President Roosevelt and Secretary of State Hull, British Ambassador Lothian and Canadian Minister Loring Christie, and the new U.S. Minister in Ottawa, Jay Pierrepont Moffat.[37]

The emphasis on RAINBOW 4 planning testified to the serious consideration given these possibilities by the U.S. staff planners. The Canadian Chiefs of Staff Committee, too, in its plan for the defense of Canada, revised as of 9 July 1940, envisaged the possible loss of British Fleet supremacy in the North Atlantic. In fact, by mid-July advance preparations were actively being made in Canada for the possibility that all or part of the fleet might fall back to base on Canada. These preparations included the installation of anchorages, buoys, and nets and other protective devices.[38] The problem appeared to the Canadian Government to warrant exploration of new solutions.

Initial Canadian Approaches

On 14 June King and U.S. Minister Moffat, whose credentials the Canadian Prime Minister had accepted the preceding day, met and discussed the many practical problems that the possible movement of the British Fleet, or part of it, to Canada would present. King thought the time had arrived for staff talks with the United States but wondered whether the suggestion would embarrass, or be welcomed by, the President. The suggestion had not yet been reported back to Washington two days later, when broader approaches were made. In another meeting, on 16 June, Prime Minister King asked the United States to provide Canada with matériel and training assistance, and to supply troops in the event of an emergency.[39]

Similar approaches were made in Washington the next day, when the Canadian chargé handed Secretary Hull an *aide-mémoire* suggesting staff conferences "with respect to the naval, military and air defense of North America, having particular regard to the defense of the Atlantic Coast."[40] A sec-

[37] Churchill, *Their Finest Hour,* p. 400 *et passim;* Memo/Conv, Roosevelt and Moffat, 10 Jun 40, and Memo/Conv, King and Moffat, 14 Jun 40, Moffat Diary; Memo/Conv, Hull and Lothian, 24 Jun 40, Roosevelt Papers, Secy's File, Box 62; Memo/Conv, L. Christie and A. A. Berle, Jr., 12 Jul 40, D/S 740.0011 EW 1939/4700.

[38] The Canadian plan of 9 July 1940 is at PDB 104-7; Memo/Conv, Moffat and Adm P. Nelles, 13 Jul 40, Moffat Diary.

[39] Ltr, Moffat to Secy State, 16 Jun 40, D/S 711.42/194.

[40] D/S 711.42/195.

ond *aide-mémoire* presented at the same time requested the sale to Canada of forty-eight fighter and forty patrol aircraft.[41]

Coincidentally, a British request for staff talks was received at almost the same time. On 11 June 1940 Ambassador Lothian laid before Secretary Hull the suggestion that naval staff conversations take place. Hull expressed doubts about their need but promised to pass the suggestion on to President Roosevelt. Two weeks later, when Lothian again suggested military staff talks for discussion of policies for future developments, Hull proposed, as an alternative, exchange of information through diplomatic channels.[42]

The Canadian proposals fared only a little better. Secretary Hull's conclusion that it was not yet possible to give a definitive answer was transmitted to King on 27 June by Moffat. However, on the same day Moffat received a letter from Under Secretary of State Welles, in which Welles and Secretary Hull suggested, at President Roosevelt's instance, that Moffat should ascertain in detail what the Canadians wished to discuss and should bring this information to Washington. Welles considered that, after Moffat had reported the information to General Marshall and Admiral Stark, it would be possible for a Canadian officer to come to Washington secretly for "technical conversations." [43]

Two days later, on 29 June, Moffat, at the suggestion of Prime Minister King, met with newly appointed Minister of National Defense J. L. Ralston and Minister of National Defense for Air C. G. Power. The Canadian officials stated that commitments would neither be sought nor given. The agenda would include Newfoundland, where they thought the important air base was vulnerable to air attack; St. Pierre and Miquelon, which they thought should be occupied; and defense problems in the Maritimes, Greenland, and Iceland. They discussed problems Canada faced in connection with the possible transfer of the British Fleet to Canada and with the British Commonwealth Air Training Plan, which had been disrupted by the British failure to supply promised aircraft. United States help was needed to meet critical supply deficiencies, and, insofar as Canada's industry could meet them, Canada would wish to work closely with U.S. industry. Among the additional suggestions that would be advanced for help from the United States were the conduct of reconnaissance flights over the western North Atlantic and

[41] D/S 811.111 Canada/688. The action taken on this and subsequent supply requests is recounted in Chapter IV, below.

[42] Memo/Conv, 11 Jun 40, Roosevelt Papers, Secy's Safe File, Lord Lothian Folder, and 24 Jun 40, Secy's File, Box 62.

[43] Ltr, Hull to Moffat, 25 Jun 40, D/S 711.42/194; Memo/Conv, King and Moffat, 27 Jun 40, Moffat Diary; Transcript of Discussion, Henry Morgenthau, Jr., Marshall, Stark, *et al.*, 3 Jul 40, Morgenthau Diary, Vol. 279, p. 149.

the acquisition and development of air bases in the West Indies and Newfoundland through lease or purchase of land.[44] In a final conversation before Moffat's departure for Washington, Prime Minister King entered an especial plea for favorable action on the outstanding Canadian request for rifles, machine guns, and artillery, without which the troops to be called up shortly could not be equipped, since Canada had sent nearly all such equipment to the United Kingdom.[45]

In Washington, on 2 and 3 July, Moffat met in turn with General Marshall and Admiral Stark, and with Henry Morgenthau, Jr., Secretary of the Treasury, who had been charged by President Roosevelt with the conduct of arrangements for supplying materiel aid to the United Kingdom, France, and others. For these officials, Moffat painted a very dismal picture of the Canadian defense situation. Marshall, while indicating a readiness to receive Canadian staff officers, feared that if they learned the true state of the U.S. supply situation the effect might be more discouraging than helpful. Furthermore, on 2 July an act of Congress was approved which made transfers from remaining stocks even more difficult. Stark, who was somewhat more enthusiastic than Marshall about meeting some senior Canadian officers, suggested that the group could come to Washington ostensibly to consult the British Purchasing Commission but actually to meet at luncheon with their U.S. colleagues. The meeting with Morgenthau brought out the fact that British Commonwealth requests had always been received and acted on as a unit, without questioning the allocations made by the United Kingdom within the Commonwealth. This procedure had apparently worked to Canadian disadvantage.[46]

Morgenthau, Marshall, and Stark met on 3 July to discuss the perplexing problems presented by Moffat, while the U.S. Minister in Ottawa continued his discussions, meeting in turn with Hull and Welles of the State Department. Marshall felt that the U.S. supply situation was already so difficult that, rather than weaken U.S. defense forces further by sending supplies to Canada, a better alternative would be to plan to send U.S. forces to Canada when the situation required it. He mentioned that the President had already asked railroad officials how they would move 300,000 troops to the Maritime Provinces. Apart from the obstacles in the way of furnishing matériel aid to Canada, Marshall, and to a lesser degree Stark, did not see how a meeting

[44] Memo/Conv, 29 Jun 40, Moffat Diary.

[45] Ltr, Moffat to Secy State, 1 Jul 40, Moffat Diary. The Minister of National Defense publicly reported on the difficult supply situation to the House of Commons later in July. (*H. C. Debates,* 29 July 40, p. 2237.)

[46] Moffat Diary.

360-477 O - 70 - 3

with Canadian staff officials could be held to discuss matters of substance, since the basic policy decisions had yet to be taken by the United States with regard to the problems that would have to be examined at such a meeting. For instance, the U.S. military staffs had no policy guidance on what was probably the major problem—the action to be taken if the British Fleet moved to the North American east coast. Morgenthau pointed out, however, that the United States had something to gain from such discussions, for, in the event war came to North American territory, a knowledge of Canadian defense plans and capabilities would be helpful, not to mention the possibility of effecting some co-ordination of those defense plans with U.S. plans. Later the same day President Roosevelt consulted with the officials who had participated in the round of discussions and authorized informal staff talks, which were to be secret and not to involve commitments.[47]

In preparation for the coming Canadian staff visit, the U.S. Army and Navy staffs made a detailed examination of the statements of Canadian requirements that had been presented in Ottawa and Washington. The recommendations of the staff planners were recorded in their hastily prepared report dated 5 July 1940, "Decisions Required If Military Assistance Is To Be Afforded to Canada in the Immediate Future." [48] The report considered the three categories of Canadian requirements: matériel, training assistance, and forces, the last having been requested in the event of emergency. The U.S. planners concluded that the matériel requests, which included over 200,000 rifles, must have been based on the assumption of an attack in force, whereas raids would probably be the largest German capability. The only weapons they felt could be made available were 28,500 Enfield rifles, plus 20,000 earmarked for Eire if the latter were not sent. Ammunition for these rifles would not be available until January 1941. As to training assistance, they felt that the expansion of U.S. programs would require all available training personnel and facilities, although they did feel that 1,200 personnel could be accepted for "on-the-job" training with units.

The planners examined the desirability of immediate deployment of U.S. troops to Canada and Newfoundland, rather than the emergency employment contemplated by the Canadians. The deployment of U.S. troops, they said, would involve the neutral United States in the war. Furthermore, the available forces could not be sent to those locations since they were inadequate even to occupy other Western Hemisphere possessions that might soon need to be garrisoned. The staff planners recommended that troops be sent only when attack was imminent and that planned reinforcements be

[47] Morgenthau Diary, Vol. 279, pp. 145–50; Moffat Diary; Hull, *Memoirs,* II, 834.
[48] The report is filed at WPD 4330–1.

limited to one reinforced infantry division and a composite air group for Newfoundland plus a second reinforced division with supporting corps and army troops for the Maritime Provinces.

The recommendations were not acted upon formally, but they were apparently used as the basis of the U.S. position in the conversations that ensued. On 12 July the Canadian staff officers—Brigadier Kenneth Stuart, Deputy Chief of the General Staff; Captain L. W. Murray, Deputy Chief of the Naval Staff; and Air Commodore A. A. L. Cuffe, of the Royal Canadian Air Force (RCAF) Air Staff—arrived in Washington. The same day they met and discussed Canada's defense problems with Brig. Gen. George V. Strong, Assistant Chief of Staff, War Plans Division, and other officers of the War and Navy Departments.[49]

The discussions were apparently inconclusive and left certain questions incompletely considered. A few weeks thereafter written reviews of these discussions and a restatement of the Canadian estimate of the situation were transmitted to the War Department.[50] They emphasized that reinforcement by Canada of the meager Canadian garrison of one infantry battalion and one flight of patrol aircraft already in Newfoundland would require equipment assistance from the United States, for the Canadian equipment shortage was most serious. The assistance immediately sought was equipment, and not troops. In the event of an emergency need for U.S. intervention, it was estimated that three divisions in the Maritimes would probably suffice. The study also suggested the possibility that it might be desirable for the United States, after its entry into the war, to take over the entire defense of Newfoundland.[51]

The staff discussions in Washington appear to have had no significant impact on the conclusions already reached by the U.S. staff planners in preparing for the 12 July meeting. Matériel assistance capabilities were estimated as before. However, the possibility of having to send reinforcements to the Maritimes and Newfoundland was accepted as sufficiently good to warrant the War Plans Division of the War Department General Staff to request the Intelligence Division to prepare the detailed information on those areas that would be needed in the event troops were actually sent there.[52]

While exploration of this avenue of approach seemed to have reached a dead end, pressures in Canada and elsewhere for some form of defense cooperation between the two countries continued to increase. Canadian pessi-

[49] Memo/Conv, Moffat and J. L. Ralston, 10 Jul 40, Moffat Diary.

[50] Ltr, Brig K. Stuart to Brig Gen G. V. Strong, 5 Aug 40, PDB 104-4.

[51] This suggestion is interesting in the light of the action the Canadian Government took with respect to Newfoundland two weeks later. See below, pp. 29-30.

[52] Memo, 5 Aug 40, WPD 3845-3.

mism as to the future reached its lowest depths in the period after the capitulation of France on 17 June. A week later U.S. Minister Moffat, in summarizing the impressions of his first ten days in Canada, reported to Washington that, as the rush of events had moved the war closer to North America and disrupted the Canadian war program, the conviction was developing among Canadians that some form of concerted action was necessary. When the isolationist Chicago *Tribune* on 19 June editorially advocated a formal military alliance, Canadians were surprised and impressed, and their conviction was strengthened.[53]

A group of influential people within and without the Canadian Government, viewing the quickened preparations of the partially aroused colossus to the south, realized that new problems might present themselves from that quarter, too, unless some means of collaboration on a basis satisfactory to Canada could be established.[54] This group reached conclusions along the following lines: A United States bent on large-scale preparations for its own defense and that of the hemisphere would be determined to take adequate measures wherever they might be needed. If concerned about the inadequacy of the meager Canadian defenses, it might and probably would insist on acting to augment them. Canada would have to co-operate voluntarily or involuntarily. If, in considering the U.S. defense requirements in Canadian territory, Canada unduly emphasized its independence of action, it might provoke the United States to a strong attitude that could threaten loss of Canadian national identity. It appeared that the best way to prevent such a turn of events would be frankly to admit Canadian inability adequately to protect its air, sea, and ground frontiers and to request U.S. co-operation in providing such protection on a continental or perhaps even hemispheric basis.

During the latter part of July Canadian opinion as to British ability to withstand German attack became much more optimistic as a result of the success of the British air defenses, the German failure to launch an assault, and other factors. But public favor in Canada for a consultative arrangement with the United States continued to grow.[55] In the Canadian House of Commons the Prime Minister was asked on at least two occasions if defense arrangements were being co-ordinated with the United States and if a formal defensive treaty could be effected. King, keenly aware of the political implica-

[53] Ott Leg Telg 147, 23 Jun 40, D/S 711.42/193.

[54] On 17–18 July a group of twenty Canadians, including government officials, scholars, and other influential people, met and drafted "A Program of Immediate Canadian Action." The rest of the paragraph in the text reflects the tenor of the group's report. The group included Brooke Claxton, Hugh Keenleyside, Alexander Skelton, R. A. MacKay, R. M. Lower, George Ferguson, and others. This rather remarkable document is filed at WPD 4330.

[55] Ott Leg Desp 176, 26 Jul 40, D/S 740.0011 EW 1939/4900.

tions in the United States of the latter step, pointed out that such a treaty might be received differently in a neutral United States than in Canada, and cautioned that, with the U.S. elections approaching, public discussion in Canada of such a treaty might be inadvisable.[56]

Early in August 1940, when Canadian-U.S. negotiations were at a standstill, other developments moved to the front of the stage. Churchill's efforts since May to obtain a number of U.S. destroyers was by July receiving the support of a group of citizens in the United States who called themselves the Century Group and who, on 11 July, advanced the proposal that the destroyers be traded for bases in the British possessions in the Western Hemisphere. The group widely publicized its proposals, which were circulated in a more detailed form to the President and other officials concerned in the latter part of July.[57]

At a Cabinet meeting on 2 August, the decision was reached by the President and his advisers to seek a workable arrangement for effecting the trade. The preceding day Secretary of the Navy Frank Knox had suggested to British Ambassador Lothian that the British desire for destroyers might be usefully linked with an offer of bases. The suggestion bore fruit, and on 4 August Lothian advised Secretary Hull that Great Britain was prepared to offer to the United States facilities for naval and air bases in the Caribbean and Antilles areas, "as well as the use of the facilities for aircraft in Newfoundland which were constructed by the British Government at a cost of three quarters of a million pounds." A memorandum transmitted the following day amplified the entire offer and stated that "United States aircraft [would] . . . be authorized to make occasional training flights to Newfoundland and to make use of the airport there." [58]

The 4 August conversation was the first specific interjection of a Newfoundland base into the destroyer-bases discussions, and it immediately made the negotiations a matter of concern to Canada. Newfoundland, adjacent to but not a part of Canada, had in 1934 yielded its government to a Royal Commission, appointed in Great Britain, in order to obtain British assistance in solving its financial difficulties. Nevertheless, Canada had always considered Newfoundland of vital strategic importance and counted the defense of the island a major responsibility in the event of war. The day

[56] The questioners were Messrs. M. J. Coldwell (Rosetown-Biggar) and Jean Pouliot (Temiscouata), *H. C. Debates,* 31 Jul 40, pp. 2190–91, and 6 Aug 40, pp. 2539–40.

[57] For detailed accounts of the development of the destroyer-bases deal, see Langer and Gleason, *The Challenge to Isolation,* Ch. XXII, and Conn and Fairchild, The Framework of Hemisphere Defense, Ch. II.

[58] Memo/Conv, Hull, Lothian, and others, 4 Aug 40, D/S 841.34/370–1/2; Ltr, Lothian to President, 5 Aug 40, Roosevelt Papers, Secy's File, Box 59.

before he requested a declaration of war on Germany, Prime Minister King had declared that "the integrity of Newfoundland and Labrador is essential to the security of Canada," and had proposed that Canada aid in its defense.[59] Shortly thereafter Canada sent some Lewis machine guns and rifles to Newfoundland. In June, after the defeat of France, Prime Minister King announced that Canadian armed forces had arrived for duty in Newfoundland, where they were to defend the Newfoundland airport and other strategic areas.[60] In July 1940, when a new Canadian naval command for the Atlantic coast was established, Newfoundland was included within its defense area, as was also done for the Canadian Army Atlantic Command established on 1 August. Thus Newfoundland was for defense purposes affirmed to be a part of Canada.[61]

Elsewhere developments were taking place with respect to British-U.S. collaboration which appear also to have had a bearing on Canadian-U.S. cooperation, although, the extent of this bearing is not clear. Whereas the June Canadian request for staff talks had initially received a more auspicious reception than the concurrent British request, by early August the situation had been reversed. The Canadian-U.S. talks were at a standstill. The British proposals for staff talks, initially rebuffed, were later accepted on a modified basis, and, in August 1940, senior U.S. Army and Army Air officers joined with a Navy colleague already in London in informal talks.[62]

Prime Minister King had been a partner in the efforts to bring about a closer U.S.-United Kingdom collaboration. Churchill, in his 5 June telegram, had specifically asked King to make such efforts.[63] However, it appears likely that Canadian disappointment in the desultory progress of the Canadian-U.S. staff talks was increased by the establishment of British-U.S. staff liaison in London. With the German frontier upon the Atlantic coast, and with some prospect of the war moving even closer to North America, the Canadian Government probably viewed with some concern these developments for collaboration among the three countries. The over-all direction by His Majesty's Government in London of Canada's war effort within a British Commonwealth framework, and in close consultation with Ottawa, was acceptable and desirable when the battles were being fought in Europe. Under

[59] *H. C. Debates*, 8 Sep 39, p. 35. Newfoundland as a political entity comprises Labrador and the island of Newfoundland.

[60] Stacey, *The Canadian Army, 1939–1945*, p. 43; *H. C. Debates*, 18 Jun 40, p. 854. King's earlier statement on 20 May that "our troops are assisting in the defense of strategic areas in Newfoundland" (*H. C. Debates*, p. 43) apparently referred to the matériel assistance provided earlier, and not to a troop garrison.

[61] *H. C. Debates*, 29 Jul 40, p. 2093.

[62] A British-U.S. service liaison had been established as early as December 1937. The best account of its development is given in the Kittredge monograph. A good account may be found in Watson, *Chief of Staff: Prewar Plans and Preparations*.

[63] *H. C. Debates*, 17 Feb 41, p. 813; Churchill, *Their Finest Hour*, p. 146.

the same circumstances, a close British-U.S. liaison was acceptable. But as those battles moved closer to its shores, Canada would understandably want a stronger voice in the war councils and would feel that problems of North American defense should be considered and decided in a Canadian-U.S. forum. The projection of the United States into the Newfoundland defense scheme, together with these developments in collaborative arrangements, apparently increased the Canadian desire to effect a closer defense relationship with the United States and motivated Canada to formalize its defense relationship with the Newfoundland Government.

Subsequent to the decision made at President Roosevelt's 13 August Cabinet meeting to press the destroyer-bases agreement, the detailed U.S. proposals were transmitted to the British Prime Minister. On 15 August Churchill acknowledged their receipt gratefully, and stated: "It will be necessary for us to consult the Governments of Newfoundland and Canada about the Newfoundland base, in which Canada has an interest. We are at once proceeding to seek their consent." [64]

Late on 13 August Loring Christie, the Canadian Minister in Washington, met with Sumner Welles, the Acting Secretary of State, and reported that he was under instructions from his Prime Minister to seek an interview with the President on the U.S.-United Kingdom destroyer negotiations. Welles telephoned the White House to ask for an appointment on the next day so that Christie could deliver an important message from King.[65]

King's message, which Welles delivered to the President on 14 August, apparently included the suggestion that the two heads of government meet in upper New York during a trip the President contemplated.[66] On the

[64] Churchill, *Their Finest Hour,* p. 407. The wording suggests the possibility that Ottawa had approached London in this vein, although the point can be clarified only by consulting the records in Ottawa or London.

[65] Memo/Conv, Christie and R. Atherton, 13 Aug 40, D/S 841.34/370; Memo, Brig Gen E. M. Watson for President, 14 Aug 40, Roosevelt Papers, Secy's File, Box 62. Christie was told that Welles could not be seen before 5:00 P. M. on the 14th, but he pressed the importance of an earlier meeting successfully.

[66] Memorandums by Welles recording the important conversations with Christie on the 13th and the President on the 14th could not be found despite careful search. This gap in the documentation makes it impossible accurately to establish the nature of Prime Minister King's representations and their bearing on the events of the next few days. Welles has stated it is his "strong belief" that King's message included the suggested meeting and that after discussion with the President, he (Welles) informed Christie of the President's willingness to meet with King as well as of the status of the discussions with Churchill. (Ltr to author, 25 Aug 53.) Hugh Keenleyside, who was probably in a position to know, has stated in a manuscript that Prime Minister King took the initiative in suggesting the Ogdensburg meeting. (The Canada-U.S. Permanent Joint Board on Defense, 1940–1945 [cited hereafter as Keenleyside MS], copy filed at PDB 100-2.) If this statement is accurate, Prime Minister King's proposal may well have been made in the message delivered orally to the President on the 14th. Alternatively, it might have been advanced in a telephone conversation between King and Roosevelt, who fairly frequently conversed in this manner. However, this possibility could not be explored since the White House kept no record of such conversations and did not even record what important telephone calls had taken place.

same day Moffat, the U.S. Minister in Ottawa, wrote Welles discussing at length the growing demand in Canada for a joint defense understanding with the United States. According to Moffat, all elements among Canadians were now pressing for such an arrangement, though the Prime Minister realized that any open initiative on his part might cause embarrassment or at least controversy in the United States. Welles sent Moffat's report to the President on 16 August. With Prime Minister King's message and the Moffat report before him, President Roosevelt was ready to act.[67]

Roosevelt was to leave Washington on the evening of 16 August by train to proceed to Pine Camp in northern New York State to see Army maneuvers there the following day. The trip provided an excellent opportunity for a meeting with Prime Minister King, and the President telegraphed King suggesting that he come to Ogdensburg to meet him. On the same day, and before receipt of a reply, Roosevelt acted on one of the points mentioned in Moffat's report. At a White House press conference, he stated that conversations were going forward between the two governments on the defense of the Americas. That evening King's acceptance reached the President aboard his train a half-hour after its departure, and Roosevelt announced the forthcoming meeting to press reporters aboard the train.[68] Afterward he again discussed the impending meeting at a press conference at the maneuver headquarters in Ogdensburg on 17 August before King's arrival. He told reporters that the discussion with King would concern Pan American defense and a specific course of action vis-à-vis Canada involving "greater ties than we have had in the past."[69]

The Ogdensburg Declaration

Prime Minister King arrived in Ogdensburg by automobile shortly before 7:00 P.M. on 17 August. At President Roosevelt's request, Moffat accompanied King from Ottawa. The party boarded the President's train, which

[67] The Moffat letter and Welles' covering note of 16 August 1940 to the President are in the Roosevelt Papers, Secy's File, Box 62.

Mayor LaGuardia of New York City, who was assigned an important position on the board which was to be established by Roosevelt and Prime Minister King of Canada a few days later, met in Washington with the President on 15 August. LaGuardia advised reporters they had talked about problems of civil defense. Although the President may have been contemplating the actions that followed in the next few days, it appears that they were touched off on the 16th by the Moffat letter and that the LaGuardia meeting was a coincidence. The meeting apparently had no greater significance in regard to the Canadian situation than that it perhaps put LaGuardia's name in the President's mind as a candidate for the U.S. chairmanship. When the news of the designation reached LaGuardia a few days later, it was reportedly a complete surprise to him. Unfortunately, as a matter of course no written record was made of the President's White House interviews and consequently this point and many others must remain obscure.

[68] *The New York Times,* August 17, 1940.

[69] Roosevelt Papers, Press Conferences, Box 215.

moved approximately eight miles to Heuvelton, New York, for the night. That evening the President and the Prime Minister, together with Secretary of War Henry L. Stimson, who had accompanied Roosevelt to the maneuver area, dined together and continued to confer until after 11:00 P.M.

Several accounts of the discussions are available. Stimson recorded a first-hand account in his diary. Moffat similarly recorded the account rendered by King during the course of their return drive to Ottawa, and King later gave a summary report on the meeting in the House of Commons on 12 November.[70]

The meeting and discussions were a complete surprise to Secretary of War Stimson. According to his account, President Roosevelt opened the informal meeting by reciting the history of the destroyer-bases negotiations and enumerating the different places in the British possessions where there were to be naval and air bases. Then, according to Stimson, when the President "came to the Canadian matter, he pointed out that of course Canada being a dominion, the negotiation must be with Canada, and that was the purpose of the meeting that night." He went on to suggest establishment of a joint board, composed of representatives from each country, which should discuss plans for the defense of the northern half of the Western Hemisphere, but particularly against attack by way of the St. Lawrence or the northeastern coast of Canada. "He pointed out that he wanted to have a naval base and an air base somewhere in that region. He mentioned specifically some place like Yarmouth, Nova Scotia, or some place further along to the eastward along the Nova Scotia coast."[71]

Additional light is cast on the discussions by Moffat's record of the account given him by King. In describing the destroyer-bases negotiations, Roosevelt indicated that, if Canada wanted any of the ships, this was a matter for United Kingdom-Canadian negotiation. As to the bases needed, these fell into three groups—those to be selected by the United States and Great Britain; those in Newfoundland, where Canada had an interest; and those in Canada, which would be selected by the United States and Canada. King felt that the Canadian base or bases would be granted by the Canadian Government under its war powers and without submission of the matter to Parliament. The practical arrangement would involve a limited free port where the United States would establish docks and facilities. In order to avoid hurting Canadian feelings, the United States would not object to the use of

[70] King was apparently in the habit of writing memorandums recording his conversations with the President, and presumably such a record for the Ogdensburg discussions may be found in Ottawa.

[71] Stimson Diary, 17 Aug 40.

Canadian forces to defend such bases. As to the new board, Under Secretary of the Navy James V. Forrestal had been mentioned as the probable head of the U.S. section, while it was thought tentatively that the other members would be the heads of the armed services.[72]

After spending the night on the train, Roosevelt and King reviewed a display of military aircraft and, it being Sunday attended a military memorial service. On returning to the train at Ogdensburg, the two drafted a joint statement for issue to the press that embodied the agreement reached the preceding day. The release, made shorly before King's departure for Ottawa at 1:00 P.M. on 18 August, the second anniversary of Roosevelt's pledge at Kingston, read as follows:

> The Prime Minister and the President have discussed the mutual problems of defense in relation to the safety of Canada and the United States.
>
> It has been agreed that a Permanent Joint Board on Defense shall be set up at once by the two countries.
>
> This Permanent Joint Board on Defense shall commence immediate studies relating to sea, land and air problems including personnel and material.
>
> It will consider in the broad sense the defense of the north half of the Western Hemisphere.
>
> The Permanent Joint Board on Defense will consist of four or five members from each country, most of them from the services. It will meet shortly.[73]

The outcome of the two-day meeting was eminently gratifying to its participants. Stimson told the others he "felt that it was very possibly the turning point in the tide of the war," and that from then on they could hope for better things. He recorded, too, that King, who "was perfectly delighted with the whole thing," told the President his "courage and initiative in bringing [it] . . . out would be a most tremendous encouragement to the morale of Great Britain and Canada." In reporting on the Ogdensburg meeting to the House of Commons in November, King also called it the most significant development in international affairs since the Parliament had adjourned three months earlier, and said, "in ultimate importance, it far surpasses the formation of the triple axis."[74]

Moffat's subsequent analysis for the State Department noted that the joint statement was the fruition of twenty years of work toward one of King's three major goals, which were the establishment and maintenance of Canadian autonomy, support of the Commonwealth as a policy in the Canadian

[72] Memo/Conv, Moffat and King, 18 Aug 40, Moffat Diary. In his account of the discussion on leased bases, King mentioned that he had suggested such a trade to Churchill two months earlier and regretted that this time had been lost. The reader will recall the similar suggestion by Power to Moffat on 29 June.

[73] Canadian Treaty Series (CTS), 1940, No. 14; Department of State *Bulletin*, August 24, 1940, III, 154.

[74] Henry L. Stimson and McGeorge Bundy, *On Active Service in Peace and War* (New York: Harper & Brothers, 1947), p. 359; Stimson Diary, 17 Aug 40; *H. C. Debates*, 12 Nov 40, p. 54.

interest, and the promotion of a close U.S.-Canadian friendship with the objectives of speeding Canadian development and bringing Great Britain and the United States closer together as the best guarantee of peace. Despite his constant efforts toward this third goal, King had probably not dared hope for an arrangement as far reaching as that completed at Ogdensburg, and it is likely that no one was more surprised by it than he.[75]

Prime Minister Churchill telegraphed King expressing the hope, but not the conviction, that the Canadian public would approve the Ogdensburg action. His estimate proved inaccurate, for with minor exceptions Canadians unanimously acclaimed it. Support from opposition elements included that of the ultraconservative Tories, who saw the declaration as a step toward U.S. alliance with the British Empire. Only minor notes of criticism were heard. These suggested that the United States would exact political concessions from a dependent Canada, or that the step appeared to be a Canadian hunt for cover and a desertion of a Britain facing the possibility of defeat. Nevertheless, these voices were small amidst the general acclaim, and they served principally to evoke, in response, more numerous expressions of approval that served to clear the air.[76]

The general Canadian reaction was matched by the U.S. response, indicated by a November 1940 public opinion poll. Of those queried about the Permanent Joint Board on Defense, 83.8 percent approved its establishment, while only 5.2 percent disapproved.[77] This reaction approximated that of a June 1940 poll, when 81 percent of the Americans interviewed were ready to employ U.S. armed forces to aid Canada if it were attacked. The U.S. attitude of community of defense interest with Canada was markedly divergent from the U.S. reaction to the European war. Months later, in April 1941, over two-thirds of those polled were unwilling to send either Army or Navy units to Europe to help Great Britain.[78]

The arrangement embodied in the Ogdensburg statement was one masterfully designed to meet the needs of both leaders. Limiting the scope of the arrangement to mutual defense problems made it generally acceptable politically in the United States, where public opinion strongly opposed active participation in the war. As if to reject completely any suggestion of aggressive intent, the word "defense" appeared five times in the 109 words of the statement, once in each sentence but the last.

At King's suggestion, according to the President, the Joint Board on

[75] Ott Leg Desp, 21 Dec 40, D/S 842.00 P.R./192.

[76] Memo/Conv, Moffat and King, 13 Sep 40, Moffat Diary; Leg Ott Telg, to Department of State, 20 Aug 40, D/S 810.20 Def/153; Leg Desp, to Secy State, 30 Aug 40, PDB 100-2.

[77] *Public Opinion Quarterly,* V (March 1941), 164.

[78] *Ibid.,* (Fall 1941), 483, 496.

Defense was designated as a "Permanent" one.[79] By indicating a collaborative arrangement designed to outlast the war and to serve the two countries indefinitely, this designation also helped to counter any suggestion that the arrangement would hasten U.S. participation in World War II.

The Permanent Joint Board, the declaration stated, was to comprise service representatives and civilians, and, on 22 August when the membership was announced, the chairman of each of the two national sections was a civilian. The inclusion of civilians raised the Board from the military staff level to a higher politico-military level. This step also appears to have been a concession to the still ardent desire of a neutral United States to avoid actions that might speed its involvement in the war.

The Ogdensburg press release stated that the Board would make defense studies, including problems of personnel and material. These terms of reference highlighted for the Board, as it embarked on its endeavors, two major Canadian problems. The terms also limited the Board to an advisory function, with no executive powers, since the Board's recommendations would be submitted to the two governments for their approval. In the Board the vote of the great United States would count for no more than the vote of Canada with one-tenth as large a population. The arrangement promised to allow full expression of the Canadian view and to give Canada adequate control over the defense measures that might be proposed for northern North America. The President's stated purpose in arranging the Ogdensburg meeting—to obtain for the United States one or more bases in Canada—found no expression in the joint press release. Geographically, the Permanent Joint Board was given broad scope in its mandate to consider "the defense of the north half of the Western Hemisphere." [80]

In establishing the Permanent Joint Board on Defense, President Roosevelt and Prime Minister King followed, be it consciously or unconsciously,

---

[79] Ltr, John D. Hickerson to Lewis Clark, 27 Nov 44, D/S Office of Dominion Affairs file, PJBD Membership.

[80] The use the Board made of the geographic rein given it will be discussed in Chapter II, below.

A few years later an official Canadian publication stated that it was hardly a coincidence that the Ogdensburg statement, with its geographic charter extending across South America to the equator, was made less than three weeks after the meeting of inter-American foreign ministers at Havana. "It also meant that for all practical intents and purposes Canada had underwritten the Monroe Doctrine, a doctrine that had been extended to Canada" by President Roosevelt's Kingston speech in 1938. (Canadian Wartime Information Board, "Canada and the Inter-American System," Reference Paper 34 [Ottawa: 16 Feb 45].) No evidence has been found showing a direct connection between the occurrence of the Ogdensburg meeting and considerations of Pan American defense planning. The foregoing statements should be viewed in the light of the fact that Reference Paper 34, which was published to inform Canadians about the inter-American system, argued strongly in favor of Canadian adherence.

a fairly well-defined pattern for joint collaborative mechanisms between the two countries. They could probably have chosen from a range of military and/or political relationships, varying from something similar to the British-U.S. Combined Chiefs of Staff committee established later to a purely informal and consultative liaison arrangement. Actually, the Board was similar in composition and function to several other Canadian-U.S. agencies already in existence.

In 1909 the United States and Great Britain had signed a treaty relating to boundary problems between Canada and the United States.[81] The treaty provided for the establishment of an International Joint Commission, a full-time body made up of six commissioners, three Canadian and three American. The commission was granted final authority over certain questions relating to boundary waters, and was also to investigate and report upon such other boundary questions as the two signatories might agree to refer to it. The commission had been markedly successful in solving boundary questions, which up to the time of its establishment had been a continuing thorn in the relationships of the two countries.[82]

By 1940 this precedent had been followed in solving several other generally similar problems, all pertaining to jointly used fisheries, although the authority and purposes of the bodies varied slightly in each instance. The International Fisheries Commission performed certain advisory and operating functions for the North Pacific and Bering Sea halibut fisheries; the International Pacific Salmon Fisheries Commission made recommendations for the preservation of the Fraser River salmon fisheries; and a Board of Inquiry for the Great Lakes Fisheries performed similar functions for those waters. It is probably a fair estimate that the successful work of the International Joint Commission and of the other similar bodies suggested to the President and Prime Minister the use of a similar mechanism to study common defense problems.

The actions taken at Ogdensburg in August 1940 have been variously referred to as the Ogdensburg Agreement and the Ogdensburg Declaration. A few weeks after the meeting Prime Minister King, in a letter to the President, made a distinction between the two, expressing the opinion that the "Ogdensburg Agreement" was reached on 17 August during the long evening discussion and should carry that date. The Ogdensburg Declaration,

[81] United States Treaty Series (TS), 548; British Treaty Series, 1910, No. 23.

[82] For a detailed study of the commission, see Chirakaikaran J. Chacko, *The International Joint Commission* (New York: Columbia University Press, 1932). See also A. G. L. McNaughton, "Organization and Responsibilities of the International Joint Commission," *Engineering Journal*, XXXIV (January 1951), 2–4, 12.

made on the 18th, "was merely the statement of terms." King made the same distinction in informing Moffat that he had asked the President for his view, but he acknowledged the merit of using the 18th, which was the anniversary of the President's Kingston speech. The President apparently never responded to King's discussion of the choice between dates, and, in reporting on the meeting to the House of Commons in November, the Canadian Prime Minister stated that "the Ogdensburg Agreement was reached on August 17" and the "joint statement with respect to the agreement which had been reached was, on August 18, released for publication." [83]

On the U.S. side, neither King's distinction nor any views of the President thereon reached the staff levels concerned with implementation of the arrangements. The joint statement of 18 August was published in the official Department of State *Bulletin* without use of a title. That date has been generally accepted by U.S. agencies, and the predominant usage has favored the Ogdensburg Declaration alternate, although the term "Agreement" has also been applied.[84] On the Canadian side, the predominant usage seems to have been the Ogdensburg Agreement.[85]

The importance that each of the parties attached to the declaration can probably not be measured by the degree of formality by which each subscribed to it. Prime Minister King submitted to the Ministerial Committee of the Privy Council his report, dated 20 August 1940, narrating his conversations with the President and recommending that his actions be ratified and confirmed. King's Cabinet Ministers concurred in his recommendations and submitted them to the Governor General, who approved them by a minute of council on 21 August, thus formally ratifying and confirming the establishment of the Permanent Joint Board on Defense.[86] In the United States, the Ogdensburg Declaration was merely published in the Department of

[83] Ltr, King to Roosevelt, 7 Sep 40, Roosevelt Papers, Secy's File, Box 69; Memo/Conv, King and Moffat, 3 Oct 40, U.S. Emb 715/710 Prime Minister; *H. C. Debates,* 12 Nov 40, pp. 54, 57. By coincidence, 17 August (1874) was King's birthday. If this distinction is made, it is interesting to note that the "Ogdensburg Agreement" was actually reached at Heuvelton.

[84] For example, it was used by the President in Samuel Rosenman (compiler), *The Public Papers and Addresses of Franklin D. Roosevelt,* XIII, *Victory and the Threshold of Peace, 1944–45* (New York: Harper & Brothers, 1950), p. 589, and by Secretary of State Hull in his note dated 30 November 1942 published in Executive Agreement Series (EAS), 287.

[85] See the repeated references to the Ogdensburg Agreement by King in his 12 November 1940 report to Parliament, *H. C. Debates,* pp. 54–61; Canada, Dominion Bureau of Statistics, *The Canada Year Book, 1945* (Ottawa: E. Cloutier, King's Printer, 1945), p. 705; and *Canada at War,* No. 25 (Jun 43), p. 57, No. 30 (Nov 43), p. 39, and No. 32 (Jan 44), p. 56. The last publication erroneously states in each instance, "Canada and the United States signed the agreement."

[86] King described the procedure to the Parliament in these terms, which appear to exaggerate the formality of the procedure of obtaining Canadian governmental approval. (*H. C. Debates,* 12 Nov 40, pp. 56–57.)

State *Bulletin.* The President issued no written instruction directing implementation of the declaration, but he indicated this to be his desire during the course of his telephone conversations from Hyde Park on 19 August to the Departments of State, War, and Navy. Soon after its publication, the State Department was queried by Senator Arthur H. Vandenberg as to whether the Ogdensburg Agreement should be submitted to the Senate for its constitutional advice and consent. The Secretary of State replied that the agreement hardly constituted a treaty, since it provided only for the study of defense problems, and was "more properly to be denominated an Executive Agreement." As an executive agreement, the President did not consider it necessary formally to submit the Ogdensburg Agreement to the Senate.[87] The Canadian Government formalized the declaration by publishing it in its Treaty Series.[88] Before taking this action Canada consulted the Department of State as to its intentions regarding the publication of "certain agreements between our two Governments, including the Ogdensburg Agreement."[89] The Department of State replied that parallel U.S. action would not be taken, since only signed or written agreements were printed in the Executive Agreement Series and since the text had already been published in the Department of State *Bulletin.*[90]

On the U.S. side, the Permanent Joint Board on Defense was, it is clear, the personal creation of President Roosevelt. The War and Navy Departments were not consulted as to their views on the need for such a board or on its composition and terms of reference, and were not even aware of the President's intention to set up a board. The President had stated his purpose in meeting at Ogdensburg and in establishing the Board to be the acquisition of one or more bases in Canada which his military advisers had not considered necessary. Indeed, they were loath to contemplate the deployment of forces to eastern Canada, except when attack should become imminent. Nevertheless, the War and Navy Departments proceeded to implement the President's undertaking and to carry out the declared objectives of the Permanent Joint Board on Defense.

Of the chain of events set in motion in early August, one more should be noted. The sudden projection of the United States into the Newfoundland defense picture during the destroyer-bases negotiations apparently motivated Canada not only to join readily in a collaborative arrangement with

[87] *Congressional Record,* Vol. 86, Pt. II, p. 12056.

[88] CTS, 1940, No. 14.

[89] Ltrs, H. Wrong, Cdn Leg, to Hickerson, 25 Jul and 11 Sep 41, D/S 842.20 Def/93 1/2 and/129.

[90] Ltr, Hickerson to Cdn Minister Counselor, 8 Oct 41, D/S 842.20 Def/91.

the United States but also to formalize its defense relationship with the Newfoundland Government. On 18 August Prime Minister King and President Roosevelt issued the Ogdensburg Declaration announcing the intended establishment of the Permanent Joint Board on Defense. On 20 August, two days later and before the first meeting of the Board, an official Canadian mission arrived in St. John's, the capital of Newfoundland. In this interim period the mission carried out its task in St. John's.[91] During its stay on 20 and 21 August the mission, headed by Mr. C. G. Power, Minister of National Defense for Air, and including senior staff officers and commanders, fully considered the problems of Newfoundland defense and reached agreement in broad detail with the Newfoundland Government on all questions of co-ordination of defense measures. Under the arrangements effected Canada assumed responsibility for the security of Newfoundland.[92]

Thus by the eve of the first meeting of the Permanent Joint Board on Defense, Canada could view with satisfaction two important achievements. It had clearly established and formalized its defense interest in Newfoundland, and it had joined with the United States in a collaborative arrangement that promised to assist in meeting urgent Canadian defense requirements on an acceptable basis. For its part the United States, still ostensibly neutral, had entered into a working partnership with a warring democracy.

---

[91] Dawson, *Canada in World Affairs: 1939–1941,* p. 214, conjectures as to whether this coincidence with the Ogdensburg Declaration and the destroyer-bases deal was accident or design.

[92] Montreal *Gazette,* August 21 and 22, 1940. Compare this action with Brigadier Stuart's suggestion sixteen days earlier that, in the event of U.S. entry into the war, it might be desirable for the United States to take over the full defense responsibility in Newfoundland. Later in August, the Canadian Army established a new Atlantic Command, which included Newfoundland as well as the Maritimes and most of Quebec. (Stacey, *The Canadian Army, 1939–1945,* p. 43.)

CHAPTER II

The Permanent Joint Board on Defense

The day after President Roosevelt and Prime Minister King announced their agreement to form the Permanent Joint Board on Defense, the President directed the State, War, and Navy Departments to select members for the Board in order to permit the announcement of their designation on 22 August and an initial meeting early in the week of 25 August. On 20 August the Canadian Minister in Washington suggested to the Department of State that the Board meet initially in Ottawa on 22 August. He also suggested that the agenda for the meeting include discussions of the sea, air, and coastal defenses of Newfoundland and the eastern and western coastal areas of Canada and the United States, and of the problem of procuring armament and ammunition.[1]

The United States was unable to be ready by the early date the Canadian Prime Minister had proposed, and King arranged instead, by telephone conversation with President Roosevelt, for an initial meeting on the 26th. During the conversation King suggested that each section include a recording secretary and indicated he would name Hugh L. Keenleyside of the Department of External Affairs, his special emissary to Washington the preceding June, to that post. Roosevelt responded that he would fill the additional position with a State Department officer of Welles' selection.[2] Later the same day, 22 August, the full membership of the new Board was announced.[3]

The Honorable Fiorello H. LaGuardia, president of the U.S. Conference of Mayors and Mayor of New York City, was named chairman of the U.S. Section. Its senior Army member was Lt. Gen. Stanley D. Embick, who had been commanding the Third Army. Captain Harry W. Hill, assigned to the War Plans Division of the Office of the Chief of Naval Operations,

[1] Ltr, Acting Secy State to SW, 20 Aug 40, PDB 100; *The New York Times,* August 20, 1940.

[2] Keenleyside MS; Memo/Conv, King and Moffat, 22 Aug 40, Moffat Diary.

[3] White House Press Release, 22 Aug 40. Although President Roosevelt during the Ogdensburg meeting had tentatively mentioned James Forrestal of the Navy Department for the chairmanship of the U.S. Section, the designation went to Mayor LaGuardia, who had met with the President on the eve of his departure for Ogdensburg. The three Canadian service designees were those who had participated in the informal staff talks in July. (Memo/Conv, King and Moffat, 18 Aug 40, Moffat Diary.)

360-477 O - 70 - 4

was appointed as the Navy member. Two Air officers, Commander Forrest P. Sherman of the Navy and Lt. Col. Joseph T. McNarney of the Army Air Corps, were assigned to the U.S. Section, and John D. Hickerson, the Assistant Chief of the Division of European Affairs, Department of State, was named secretary.

The Canadian Section was headed by O. M. Biggar, K.C., a distinguished Ottawa barrister and retired Army colonel, as chairman. The Army member was Brigadier Kenneth Stuart, D.S.O., M.C., Deputy Chief of the Canadian General Staff; Captain L. W. Murray, Deputy Chief of the Naval Staff represented the Royal Canadian Navy; and Air Commodore A. A. L. Cuffe of the Air Staff, Royal Canadian Air Force, was appointed Air member. Hugh L. Keenleyside, Counselor of the Department of External Affairs, was named secretary of the Canadian Section.

Since the first meeting of the Permanent Joint Board came almost as precipitately as its establishment, there were few administrative preparations on the U.S. side beyond the formulation of an agenda. Pondering their mission and the broad terms of reference contained in the Ogdensburg Declaration, General Embick, Captain Hill, and Mr. Hickerson met on 23 August to discuss the forthcoming meeting. As preparation for the discussions of military matters, they had before them the record of the informal staff conversations that had already taken place. Puzzled as to the role and specific duties Mayor LaGuardia would have in the military discussions that were anticipated, they concluded that the mayor would probably handle the mutual requirements for materials and production output. Hickerson counseled the members of the U.S. Section to consider the problems before the Board always in terms of reciprocal and mutual measures. If they did so, even though in many instances the necessary resources might be contributed largely or entirely by the United States, such an approach would naturally produce a more favorable reaction on the part of the Canadian Section.[4]

A meeting of the U.S. Section took place the next day with President Roosevelt and Secretaries Stimson and Knox. The meeting, which Mayor LaGuardia joined after the discussions had begun, provided the President an opportunity to present his views on the duties of the Board and the question of defending Canada and the United States from attack. He discussed the action being taken to obtain bases in British territories in return for destroyers and the bearing of this action on the question of getting bases in Canada. There really was no relation, he pointed out, since the problem of securing U.S. bases in Canada was one for discussion with Ottawa, not London.

[4] Summary of Preparatory Conference, PDB 100.

Knowing eastern Canada well, the President had some specific ideas as to where U.S. bases should be located to defend the United States against attack through Canada, and he proceeded to outline his views. With this guidance, the U.S. Section proceeded to Ottawa to meet with its Canadian counterpart.[5]

The initial meetings of the Permanent Joint Board took place as scheduled in Ottawa on 26–27 August 1940 and were most fruitful in terms of formal recommendations. The Board adopted seven recommendations during these meetings, more than one-fifth of the thirty-three made between the time of the Board's establishment and V-J Day. This can be explained in part by the fact that many problems had been urgently awaiting solution and some preliminary work had already been done on them at the earlier military staff talks.

Organization and Composition

The Permanent Joint Board on Defense, Canada-United States, was organized in two national sections, each with its own chairman and physically separate and independent administrative machinery.[6] Only on the occasion of the Board's scheduled meetings did the two sections unite as a single corporate body with but a single purpose—the adequate joint defense of the two countries.[7] At other times the members of the Board operated from the offices of the two sections, located in the respective capitals. At the Board meetings the two chairmen sat side by side, and when meetings were held in Canada the Canadian chairman presided, whereas at meetings in the United States the U.S. chairman did so.[8]

Supplementing the joint meetings of the two sections of the Permanent Joint Board was a continuous and substantial correspondence and telephonic liaison between the pairs of corresponding members of the Board. Through these means the Board followed up implementation of the conclusions and recommendations decided on at its meetings, paved the way for new proposals, and in a variety of ways facilitated the joint defense measures of the two countries.

Officially, the primary mission of the Board was to make recommendations, and its two sections had no executive authority or responsibility within

[5] Stimson Diary, 24 Aug 40.

[6] Although the past tense is used throughout this description of the Board, the organization and functioning described remained substantially unchanged at the time of this writing.

[7] Address by Gen A. G. L. McNaughton, 12 Apr 48, Department of External Affairs, Statements and Speeches, No. 48/18.

[8] Keenleyside MS. Keenleyside was the Canadian secretary from the time of the Board's establishment until 1 September 1945. However, General McNaughton, who assumed Canadian chairmanship in August 1945, has indicated that during his tenure the chairmen had been presiding jointly. (McNaughton address cited above, n. 7.)

their governments. One of the Canadian chairmen has stated that the strength of the Board lay in this fact.[9] Operating problems were, in theory, handled through the military attachés and, after its establishment in 1942, the Canadian Joint Staff in Washington. In practice, the Board did not limit itself to making policy recommendations, and in both Ottawa and Washington the sections of the Board, through their members drawn from the military departments and the Departments of State and of External Affairs, functioned informally and unofficially as executive agencies. Additionally, the substantial volume of correspondence between the two sections of the Board, and between the individual members and their counterparts, formed a major alternate channel between the military and political departments of the two countries.

The responsibility of the sections of the Permanent Joint Board was to the highest level of authority in each country. In the United States, formal recommendations were presented directly to the President, usually by the U.S. chairman or the secretary acting for him. Approval of a recommendation constituted the basis for the necessary implementing action by the appropriate executive departments. The Canadian Section of the Board reported directly to the Cabinet War Committee, over which the Prime Minister presided.[10] Its approval of Board recommendations constituted a directive for their execution.

The two civilian chairmanships of the Permanent Joint Board were filled throughout the war by the men originally appointed. LaGuardia, who was selected as chairman of the U.S. Section by the President personally, retained his post until his death on 20 September 1947, at which time he was the last of the original members still serving on the Board. Less than two months before his designation, he had on 25 June 1940 addressed the U.S. Conference of Mayors in Ottawa. In this speech he had emphasized the importance to the United States of making secure all of the Western Hemisphere seaboard and had pointed out the need for Canadian-U.S. co-operation for this security. Biggar's tenure as chairman of the Canadian Section continued until shortly after V-J Day, although a period of illness beginning about January 1944 forced his absence from subsequent Board meetings except for those held in April 1945. During his absence the Canadian secretary, Hugh Keenleyside, acted as chairman. *(Table 1)*

The Canadian Army, Navy, and Air Force representatives functioned in two capacities—as Board members, and as staff officers dealing with the same types of problems in their respective service staffs. When functioning in

[9] McNaughton address cited above, n. 7.

[10] Organization Chart, *H. C. Debates,* 21 Jun 48, p. 5828.

staff capacities they were, of course, responsible individually to their respective chiefs of staff. Such an arrangement made for close co-ordination between the Canadian Section and National Defense Headquarters.

In the United States, where the Air components were not independent, the War and Navy Departments each furnished a senior non-Air officer. In addition, an Air officer of lesser rank was provided from the war planning staffs of each of the departments to permit inclusion of Air representation without allowing one or the other department a stronger position. *(See Table 1.)* As a general rule, the U.S. senior service representatives sat physically and organizationally outside the War Department General Staff and the staff of the Chief of Naval Operations, although in close proximity thereto. The lack of responsibility to these staffs had some advantages, but it necessitated a continuing liaison effort to insure that staff views were taken fully into account.

The U.S. Section initially outnumbered the Canadian Section by one service member. This situation prevailed for only a few weeks. On 11 September 1940 Prime Minister King, who had intimated at the time of the original announcement of the membership of the Board that an additional Canadian member might be named later, sought and received the concurrence of the President and Secretary of State Hull in such a step. On 11 October the Canadian secretary accordingly advised the U.S. secretary that the Canadian Government had appointed Lt. Col. George P. Vanier as an additional member. When the new member took his place on the Board, the members of the U.S. Section conjectured that the step had also been taken to permit inclusion of a French-Canadian on the Board. When Vanier, then a brigadier, resigned about the end of 1942 to accept a diplomatic post overseas, he was not replaced.[11]

Both secretaries held additional positions in the Departments of State and External Affairs during World War II. The U.S. secretary was immediately responsible for Canadian affairs in the Department of State, and Keenleyside, the first Canadian secretary, was initially a counselor in his department and subsequently Assistant Under Secretary of State for External Affairs.

Appointments of members to the Canadian Section were made by the

[11] Ltr, Cdn Secy to U.S. Secy, 11 Oct 40, PDB 100; Ltr, Christie to Secy State, 14 Oct 40, D/S 842.20 Def/35. At about the time of Brigadier Vanier's resignation, however, the Canadian Army member began to be accompanied by an assistant, who, although not formally designated a member, kept the Canadian Section numerically equal to the U.S. Section. Numerical equality was formally achieved in 1947 when, as a result of the establishment in Washington of a Department of the Air Force, U.S. service representation on the Permanent Joint Board on Defense was limited to three officers, one Army, one Navy, and one Air Force.

TABLE 1—MEMBERSHIP OF THE PERMANENT JOINT BOARD ON DEFENSE, CANADA-UNITED STATES: 22 AUGUST 1940–1 SEPTEMBER 1945

United States Section						
Date	Chairman	Army	Navy	Army (Air)	Navy (Air)	Secretary
22 Aug 1940	F. H. LaGuardia	Lt. Gen. S. D. Embick	Capt. H. W. Hill	Lt. Col. J. T. McNarney	Cdr. F. P. Sherman	J. D. Hickerson
30 Sep 1940				Lt. Col. C. Bissell		
12 Feb 1942			Capt. F. P. Thomas	Lt. Col. R. W. Douglass, Jr.		
30 May 1942					Capt. F. D. Wagner	
— Nov 1942		Maj. Gen. J. P. Smith				
— Dec 1942		Maj. Gen. G. V. Henry				
— Feb 1943			V. Adm. A. W. Johnson	Lt. Col. E. W. Hockenberry	Capt. J. P. Whitney	
— Nov 1943					Capt. R. W. Ruble	
— Dec 1944				Col. C. H. Deerwester		
18 May 1945					Capt. T. P. Jeter	
— Aug 1945			V. Adm. D. W. Bagley			

TABLE 2—MEETINGS OF THE PERMANENT JOINT BOARD ON DEFENSE: 26 AUGUST 1940–31 DECEMBER 1945

Month	1940		1941		1942		1943		1944		1945	
	Date	Place	Date	Place	Date	Place	Date	Place	Date	Place	Date	Place
January	------	------------	20–21	Montreal	20	Montreal	13	New York	13–14	New York	22–23	Montreal
February	------	------------	27	Buffalo	25–26	New York	24–25	Montreal	------	------------	------	------------
March	------	------------	------	------------	------	------------	------	------------	------	------------	------	------------
April	------	------------	16–17	Montreal	7–8	Montreal	1–2	New York	12–13	Montreal	10–11	Ottawa
					27	New York						
May	------	------------	28–29	Washington	26–27	Quebec	6–7	Montreal	------	------------	------	------------
June	------	------------	------	------------	9	Montreal	------	------------	28–29	New York	14–15	New York
July	------	------------	29–30	Montreal	6	New York	3	Vancouver	------	------------	------	------------
							5	([a])				
							14	([b])				
August	26–27	Ottawa	------	------------	------	------------	24–25	New York	------	------------	------	------------
September	9–11	Washington	9–10	New York	1	Montreal	------	------------	6–7	Montreal	4–5	Montreal
					27	St. John's						
October	2	Boston	------	------------	------	------------	------	------------	------	------------	------	------------
	3, 4	Halifax										
	13	San Francisco	10–11	Montreal	3–4	New York	8–9	Montreal	7–8	New York	7–8	New York
November	14	Victoria	------	------------	------	------------	------	------------	------	------------	------	------------
	15	Vancouver										
December	16–17	New York	20	New York	14–15	Montreal	------	------------	------	------------	------	------------

[a] Aboard SS *Princess Norah* en route to Alaska.
[b] Aboard airplane between Winnipeg and Ottawa.

MEMBERS OF THE PERMANENT JOINT BOARD ARRIVING IN NEWFOUNDLAND, *September 1942. Front row from left: Hon. L. E. Emerson, Mr. J. D. Hickerson, Capt. H. DeWolfe, Commodore E. R. Mainguy, Captain Bidwell, Mr. O. M. Biggar, Mr. H. L. Keenleyside (in second row), Brigadier G. P. Vanier, Colonel Jenkins, Group Captain R. S. Grandy, Air Commodore F. V. Heakes, Hon. C. J. Burchell, and Mayor F. H. LaGuardia.*

tions based on studies of the joint defense needs of the two countries. Joint meetings of the two sections of the Board took place at irregular intervals, as frequently as the Board considered them necessary to handle its work. Thus the Board met monthly in 1940, but only eight times in 1941. *(Table 2)* United States entry into the war increased the number of meetings in 1942 to eleven. Thereafter, as the war moved farther from the Western Hemisphere and as fewer hemisphere defense measures were needed, the intervals became greater. Seven meetings took place in 1943, five in 1944, and three in 1945 up until 1 September.

Customarily meetings were held alternately in Canada and in the United States. Except for the initial meetings in Ottawa and Washington, at which there were official entertainment and publicity, Board meetings were not publicized. Efforts to avoid publicity were usually successful except when meetings were held in locations where the presence of the Board drew attention. On such occasions, press reports and speculation resulted from the meetings. Especially during its first year, the Board held meetings at the sites of proposed defense projects so that the members could study problems at close hand. Such meetings were held in Boston, Halifax, San Francisco, Victoria, Vancouver, Buffalo, St. John's, and while en route to and from Alaska. At these and other meetings of the Board, participation by officials concerned in the defense projects gave the Board full opportunity to explore all the ramifications of the problems.[13] In the later World War II years, the Board usually met alternately in Montreal and New York, the latter location apparently as a matter of convenience to Mayor LaGuardia. The meetings themselves were held at a military establishment where one was available, or in a commercial facility, as for example the Hotel Windsor in Montreal and the Waldorf-Astoria in New York.

Meetings were conducted informally. Ordinarily the Board preceded its discussions of new problems by a review of the progress reports (six in all) submitted by each of the services of the two countries. These reports reviewed the progress made on previously approved recommendations of the Board and on other projects of joint defense interest. The Board would then proceed to discuss problems remaining before it for consideration. No voting procedure was used, and each problem was discussed until general agreement was reached. When disagreements did develop, they were more frequently along service lines than along national lines.[14] All formal recommendations made by the Board were unanimously approved.[15]

Problems came up for discussion in a variety of ways. The Board might take up a problem on its own initiative, perhaps as a result of its observation of the need for new action or for changes in a previously approved project. Alternately, an agency of either government might request one of the Board members to present a problem to the Board for its consideration. The request might be in the form of a rudimentary idea requiring detailed study, or in the form of a complete staff study with a specific course of action recommended. One item, the proposed highway to Alaska, had already been approved by the President himself and in part by the Department of External Affairs before it was considered and acted upon by the Permanent Joint Board on Defense.

[13] On 4 October 1940, Messrs. Emerson and Penson, Commissioners of Justice and Defense, and of Finance, respectively, of the Newfoundland Government, took part in discussions in Halifax; on 13 November 1940, the Board meeting in San Francisco, heard Lt. Gen. J. L. DeWitt and Rear Adm. A. J. Hepburn, the senior U.S. Army and Navy commanders in that area.

[14] Keenleyside MS.

[15] The Board did not quite achieve the record claimed by General McNaughton in his address of 12 April 1948 (cited above, n. 7) of having reached *every* conclusion unanimously. At its 10–11 November 1941 meeting, the Board informally agreed "with the exception of the Canadian Air Force member" that certain measures were needed to hasten construction in Labrador of the North West River air base. (Journal, PDB 124.)

In considering a problem or a recommendation, the Board members in theory acted as free agents responsible only to the President and the Prime Minister. Board approval of a recommendation gave it no status except assurance that the governments would consider it. As a practical matter, the members all realized that adoption of the Board's recommendations was usually contingent upon favorable reactions within the Departments of External Affairs and National Defense in Ottawa, and the State, War, and Navy Departments in Washington. To the extent practicable, the members maintained such liaison as would insure their acting in accordance with the views of those departments. However, such concurrence of views was not an essential condition of Board approval of a recommendation.[16] Likewise, the Board members themselves might have doubts about the merits of a particular proposal but would recommend in its favor "for reasons of general policy."[17]

The Canadian defense establishment and cabinet system probably lent themselves to a more methodical processing of the recommendations of the Board than did the U.S. machinery. Before recommendations were considered by the government, the views of the Canadian Chiefs of Staff were obtained.[18] Action by the Cabinet War Committee provided for integration of the views of all the ministers whose departments were concerned.

In the U.S. Government no routine procedure or pattern was followed, and, especially during the initial months of the Board's existence, the recommendations were processed rather haphazardly. A number of them were apparently not submitted to the President at all. LaGuardia forwarded some of them directly to the President without reference to the departments concerned, leaving it to the President to determine the views of those departments if he saw fit. Later, and more generally, the practice was for the members of the Board first to get the concurrence of the interested departments, after which the recommendation was submitted to the President with those concurrences indicated. Approval of a recommendation by both governments in effect constituted the necessary directive to the agencies involved.

Of the thirty-three recommendations adopted by the Permanent Joint

[16] For example, whereas the Twenty-third Recommendation, which envisaged the use of surplus Canadian air training capacity for training Americans, was approved by the Board and the two governments, the War Department opposed any such arrangement. (Ltr, SW to Secy State, 13 May 42, PDB 119-6.)

[17] The Keenleyside manuscript cites this basis for Canadian approval of the Twenty-fourth Recommendation, even though the Canadian Section questioned the strategic value of the proposed Alaska Highway. See also Lingard and Trotter, *Canada in World Affairs*, III, 67.

[18] Statement in "Canadian-United States Defense Collaboration," transmitted on 5 April 1948 by the Canadian Ambassador to the U.S. secretary of the Board, on file in the U.S. secretary's office.

Board before V-J Day, twelve dated from 1940, eleven from 1941, four from 1942, five from 1943, and one from 1944.[19] In addition, on 4 October 1940 the Board approved a First Report and submitted it to the two governments. This report, later approved by both governments, included such portions of the first eight recommendations as related to defensive deployments not yet made. It included also extensive new recommendations for additional deployments to be made, facilities to be provided, and operational responsbilities to be undertaken.[20]

At least within the U.S. Section, procedures for obtaining and recording governmental approval of the formal recommendations were apparently rather loose during the early part of the Board's existence.[21] The incorporation of portions of the first eight recommendations in the First Report tends to confirm that those recommendations had not earlier been acted upon by the governments. This omission is probably accounted for at least in part by the fact that many of the actions recommended could be executed by the services within existing authority and without reference to the governments, and that, in instances where action was required by only one country, officials in the other country probably considered reference to their government for approval unnecessary.

In any event, almost all of the recommendations made by the Permanent Joint Board were approved either tacitly or expressly.[22] The Canadian Government did not approve the Twenty-ninth Recommendation, whereupon the United States, which had actually completed its approving action, withheld report of its approval.[23] Canada also did not approve the Thirtieth Recommendation as such, but it accepted the proposals in part so that the Board was able to agree that the qualified action was a satisfactory response to the original proposal.[24]

When most of these recommendations were made, they naturally con-

[19] Texts of the recommendations are reproduced below, Appendix A.

[20] Text of First Report is reproduced below, Appendix B. There were no further similar reports approved by the Board, although a Second Report was drafted. (See Chapter V, below.)

[21] Until a review of the situation was initiated in 1951, files in the Departments of State and the Army indicated no record of action by either government on the first eleven and certain other recommendations except insofar as parts of the first eight were duplicated in the First Report. Careful search of these files and those of the late President Roosevelt and of the U.S. Section of the Permanent Joint Board revealed no evidence of submission to the President for his approval of the Board's first twenty formal recommendations, except the Sixteenth, which required his consideration of a Reconstruction Finance Corporation loan.

[22] Where express approval does not appear in the U.S. files examined, tacit approval is indicated by the subsequent correspondence concerning the implementation of the recommendations and by the progress reports rendered thereafter on each recommendation and appended to the journals of the Board meetings.

[23] PDB 105-13. See also Appendix A, below.

[24] RCAF Progress Report, at meeting 8-9 Nov 43, PDB 124. See also Appendix A, below.

tained secret or restricted data and received no publicity, as was true of most of the Board's work. A partial exception was the Twenty-fourth Recommendation concerning the highway to Alaska. Not only had there been much interest in such a highway over a period of years but also, by its very nature, information about this project could not remain restricted. The two governments publicized their agreement concerning the construction of the highway in an exchange of notes that quoted about two-thirds of the brief recommendation.[25] The only real exceptions were the Twenty-eighth and Thirty-third Recommendations.[26] Both of these pertained to the terms for the disposition of United States property and installations in Canada, about which there would inevitably be a great public interest, and there was no need for security restrictions.

The policy of maintaining an official silence as to the work of the Permanent Joint Board received a strong impetus within the first few months of its existence. When the First Report of the Board had been approved by both governments in November 1940, President Roosevelt proposed that the action be announced by simultaneous press statements in the two capitals. Prime Minister King demurred on the basis that such an announcement would give rise in Parliament to innumerable questions that he would be unable to answer because of their military nature. The President deferred to this view, and the public remained unaware that such a broad program of joint defense measures had been co-ordinated.[27]

In its five years of life up to the end of hostilities, the Board probably established a record for self-restraint in accumulating files. The total file of records representing agreed documents of the Board as a whole aggregate less than a cubic foot. These records comprise only the Journals of Discussions and Decisions prepared after each meeting, and, appended to the journals, the progress reports rendered to the Board by its members.

The journals are merely brief summary accounts of the discussions and decisions at the meetings. They do not record the various positions taken nor the arguments pro and con, but only the principal considerations involved and the decisions reached.[28] Initially, the journal was drafted at the end of a meeting and circulated and amended thereafter through correspondence. To shorten this procedure, the Board began to draft its journals during the course of a meeting and to agree on its text in detail before adjournment. In a number of instances the substance of the action of meetings lasting many

[25] EAS, 246; CTS, 1942, No. 13. See Chapter VIII, below, for the significance of the omission.

[26] Reproduced in their entirety in EAS, 391, and 444, and in CTS, 1943, No. 2, and 1944, No. 35, respectively.

[27] Ltr, Welles to Roosevelt, 25 Nov 40, Roosevelt Papers, Official File, Box 4090.

[28] A sample journal extract is reproduced below, Appendix C.

hours over a two-day period was recorded on only two or three double-spaced legal-sized sheets of paper. To each journal was appended a series of progress reports, usually six in number, for the Army, Navy, and Air Force of each country. These were prepared before the meeting and submitted to and edited by the Board as a whole. They, too, recorded an agreed understanding of action being taken or scheduled to be taken.

After each meeting the journal and progress reports were circulated within the appropriate agencies of each government. They served the dual purpose of providing information and of pointing the way for further planning. In addition to those records of the Board as a whole, each national section amassed a many times greater volume of intersectional and intracountry correspondence. Some of this was in execution of the Board's primary function, that of study of and recommendation on broad defense problems. Problems under consideration might be the subject of correspondence between the secretaries, or between other pairs of "opposite numbers" who would circulate copies of the exchanges to the rest of the members to keep them advised.

The bulk of such additional correspondence was occasioned by the Board's performing a wide range of operating functions, which apparently had not been intended by its founders. Nevertheless, the channels available through the Board seemed to fill a need and were used extensively for such purposes as handling minor administrative matters not brought before the Board and following up in detail the execution of approved recommendations.

The U.S. Section had no authority as an executive or operating agency within the executive departments of the U.S. Government. Yet in efforts to facilitate joint action the members of this section dealt with agencies of the military departments on the operating and administrative level and, in some cases, arrogated to themselves authority belonging to those departments.[29] Irregular as these procedures might have been, they were tacitly accepted by the War Department and undoubtedly greatly aided the execution of actions of joint interest.

The U.S. Section did not, during World War II, establish any regularized working relationship of note with the Joint Board or the Joint Chiefs of Staff (JCS), the joint organizations of the U.S. services. A few of the matters considered by the Permanent Joint Board were also acted upon by the two U.S. joint agencies, but such instances were by far exceptions rather than

[29] An example of such an action is the SUSAM indorsement, dated 23 June 1945, of a basic letter to the Commanding Officer, U.S. Army Forces in Central Canada, at Winnipeg. Such an action was properly the responsibility of the War Department. Another example is an acknowledgment, dated 2 June 1944, from Office, Chief of Engineers, to SUSAM which stated: "Your instructions to this office require that the transfer of any improvement be cleared through your office."

the rule. A notable exception before Pearl Harbor was the Joint Canadian-United States Basic Defense Plan 2 (ABC-22), on which action followed the same pattern as had the earlier action on the related United Kingdom-United States plan, ABC-1. The ABC-22 plan was reviewed and approved by the Joint Board, by the Secretaries of War and the Navy, and then submitted to the President for his approval. In June 1942 the Joint Chiefs of Staff reviewed the U.S. plan for the North Atlantic Ferry Route CRIMSON bases, which became the Twenty-sixth Recommendation of the Permanent Joint Board. This review, however, was principally incident to Combined Chiefs of Staff examination of the shipping requirements for the plan.[30]

The limited relationship before Pearl Harbor is explained in part by the fact that the Joint Board considered only strategic and operational problems requiring employment of U.S. military resources. The contemporary recommendations of the Permanent Joint Board on Defense often required action only by Canada or were matters within the purview of the service departments. Additionally, the normal procedure of obtaining War and Navy Department approval of the recommendations constituted, in effect, all but formal approval by the Joint Board.

By the time the Joint Chiefs of Staff began to function, joint U.S.-Canadian defense plans had been completed and placed in effect. Similarly, two-thirds of the World War II recommendations of the Permanent Joint Board had already been made, while the remainder pertained mainly to administrative or other problems within the purview of the War and Navy Department staffs. Despite the lack of any formal or regularized link between the U.S. Section of the Permanent Joint Board and the Joint Chiefs of Staff, no serious problem of co-ordination existed. Since the service members of the Board also functioned on, or in close liaison with the planning staffs of the members of the Joint Chiefs of Staff, they were able to assure that their several planning projects were adequately co-ordinated and integrated.

Scope of Responsibilities

In establishing the Permanent Joint Board on Defense, Canada-United States, President Roosevelt and Prime Minister King stated its mission and responsibilities in only the most general terms. The Board was to "consider in the broad sense the defense of the north half of the Western Hemisphere" and to make "studies relating to sea, land and air problems including personnel and material."

Undoubtedly the Canadian Section received from higher Canadian authority some guidance as to what it should seek to accomplish, much as President

[30] See below, Chs. IV and VII.

Roosevelt had oriented the U.S. Section. But the broad charter in the Ogdensburg Declaration was never jointly amplified either by the founders of the Board or on the initiative of the Board itself. When proposing the first meeting of the Board, Canada suggested that initial discussions should bear on the defense of Newfoundland and the Pacific coast and on questions of reciprocal maneuvers and procurement of matériel. At the second meeting of the Board, the Canadian Section made an attempt to clarify the over-all terms of reference. The Canadian Section envisaged the scope of responsibilities of the Board as follows:

a. Disposition of Canadian forces and U.S. matériel needed in Canada and Newfoundland to meet the threat of Axis attack.

b. Preparations needed in Canada and the United States to meet the contingency of U.S. participation in defense against the threat, including (1) physical facilities, (2) troop and matériel dispositions, and (3) plans for co-ordinated action.

c. Long-term plans for the permanent security of North America including (1) military defenses, (2) raw materials stockpiles, (3) integration of the production effort, (4) continuous revision of plans, and (5) research and development co-operation.[31]

The Permanent Joint Board discussed this outline of its major duties but did not consider it necessary to adopt it. Nevertheless, the Board recorded that it "understood that the Canadian Section would use the outline for its own guidance and for submission to the Canadian Government."[32] The Board's views on the outline were not recorded. Points *a* and *b* are reasonable statements of urgent joint defense problems that faced the two countries. Point *c* is somewhat puzzling, and unfortunately the journal for the meeting records no clarifying discussion. It appears unlikely, in the light of the gravity of the Allied situation, that the Canadian Section contemplated that any resources could in fact have become surplus to the requirements of the war against the Axis and available for long-term planning for post-World War II permanent North American security. An alternate possible interpretation is that the offensive phase of World War II and the defeat of the Axis were envisaged as bringing about the permanent security of North America. But the word *defenses* would belie this interpretation. Another alternate perhaps envisaged long-term planning for projects to be undertaken only after World War II was won. Still another possible thesis, in the light of the fall of France and of Dunkerque and of the raging Battle of Britain, is that

[31] Ltr, Cdn Minister to Welles, 20 Aug 40, Roosevelt Papers, Secy's File, Box 77; Journal, 10 Sep 40 meeting, PDB 124.

[32] Journal, PDB 124.

360-477 O - 70 - 5

point *c* was intended to cover the long-term defense requirements that would have to be met if the United Kingdom were occupied. Fortunately, the passing months made this contingency more remote, and the Board was able to address itself to limited scales of Axis capabilities and to the needs of supporting the war overseas.

The President and Prime Minister gave the Board considerable scope geographically. The northern half of the Western Hemisphere to the geographer conventionally includes the area between meridians 20° west and 160° east, north of the equator. This area includes almost all of Greenland, parts of Iceland and Siberia, all of North America, and all or parts of Colombia, Venezuela, Brazil, and other adjacent South American lands. Significant variations on the geographer's Western Hemisphere can, however, be found. President Monroe in the message to Congress in 1823 that enunciated the Monroe Doctrine referred to "this hemisphere" and "the American continents," apparently synonymously. The Treaty of Reciprocal Assistance drafted by the Inter-American Conference in 1947 delineated an area embracing the two continents and Greenland. President Roosevelt, when weighing the need for U.S. Navy patrolling and convoying in the Atlantic in July 1941, delineated for Harry Hopkins a hemisphere that included all of Iceland.[33]

The Permanent Joint Board followed a fairly narrow interpretation of the general geographical bounds enunciated at Ogdensburg. Its first approved over-all review of the defense problems facing it was the First Report of October 1940.[34] This report set forth the preparatory steps and allocation of responsibilities recommended to provide for the defense of what might be described as northern North America. The area embraced Canada, Newfoundland and Labrador, Alaska, and coasts of the United States adjacent to the Canadian border. Greenland and Iceland were excluded, as were the Caribbean islands, Central America, and the United States with the exception of the coastal regions mentioned.

This narrower concept of the geographic scope of the Board's responsibility was also reflected in the Joint Canadian-United States Basic Defense Plan—1940, which was prepared by the service members of the Board, and again in the Joint Canadian-United States Basic Defense Plan 2 (ABC–22), prepared in 1941.[35] This cannot be attributed to the lack of defense tasks

[33] TIAS, 1838; Robert E. Sherwood, *Roosevelt and Hopkins: An Intimate History* (New York: Harper & Brothers, 1948), pp. 308–11.

[34] See Appendix B, below.

[35] The 1940 Plan is in PDB 122. Actually the First Report was based on drafts of the 1940 Plan prepared in September and discussed by the Board then. Large parts of the text were common to both. ABC–22 is reproduced in its entirety in Joint Committee on the Investigation of the Pearl Harbor Attack, 79th Congress, 1st Session, Hearings on Senate Concurrent Resolution 27, *Pearl Harbor Attack* (hereafter cited as *Pearl Harbor Attack*), Pt. 15, pp. 1586–93.

in the areas not included. The United States-British Commonwealth Joint Basic War Plan prepared during January-March 1941 set forth Army, Navy, and Air Force tasks in other parts of the "north half of the Western Hemisphere" and recommended substantial deployments for the execution of those tasks.[36] In fact, the British Commonwealth forces then deployed in those areas included a Canadian infantry battalion at Jamaica.

In effect then, the Permanent Joint Board limited itself to planning the measures and the troop and material resources needed to defend northern North America. It is probable that an approach of this scope was tacitly accepted by both sections of the Board because it best met the needs of the situation. The Canadian Section was able to assure itself that Canada and Newfoundland would be reasonably well protected. It probably had no particular desire to participate in planning concerned with more remote portions of the United States and North America. The United States Section was able likewise to look after U.S. security interests in Canada without having to give the Canadians full access to all the continental and hemisphere defense plans of the United States, which it probably could not have done anyway.

In August 1940 President Roosevelt had made clear to Prime Minister King, and to the U.S. Section of the Board, his desire to obtain a naval base and an air base in the Maritimes, yet the U.S. Section seems to have made no strong effort to carry out his desire. Some measures in that direction were taken, but they fell far short of providing United States bases comparable to those obtained under the destroyer-bases agreement with the United Kingdom. Under the Third Recommendation and the First Report, Canada undertook to develop facilities to permit operation of four squadrons of U.S. patrol aircraft and a composite wing of some 200 additional aircraft. Similarly, Canada undertook to complete the steps necessary to provide defended harbors and "docking, repair and supply facilities capable of accommodating the major portion of the United States or British fleets." Although Canada did proceed to develop the necessary facilities, the United States was to utilize them only when necessary and agreed, and it acquired no legal status thereat. The United States made no use of the air facilities, but it was permitted the use of Shelburne and Halifax as naval operating bases and of Sydney as an emergency base after July 1941, when the U.S. Navy began active convoying between the United States and Iceland.

The explanation of why the United States did not try to obtain more may lie in the fact that the service members of the U.S. Section, reflecting

[36] The plan is Annex III to ABC-1, which is reproduced in *Pearl Harbor Attack*, Pt. 15, pp. 1485-1541.

the views of their services, probably had no real desire to obtain bases in the Maritimes, which might have required commitment of forces that later would have been badly needed elsewhere. In any event, the President on 19 Nobember 1940 approved the more modest arrangements provided in the First Report. By then, British stamina in the Battle of Britain had indicated that the threat to North America was not as great as the prospect may have appeared in August. Viewed in the light of the subsequent discussions in the Permanent Joint Board, it appears to be a reasonable thesis that U.S. effort to obtain lease-type bases in Canada might have met strong resistance and imposed a considerable strain on the collaborative efforts of the Board.

Conspicuously absent from the list of defense problems considered by the Board were those pertaining to Greenland. The islands of St. Pierre and Miquelon also were discussed only briefly in November 1941, just before the minor crisis precipitated by Free French occupation of the islands on Christmas Day, 1941. After this action, the journals were silent concerning any discussion that may have taken place about the islands. Apparently the significant political problems involved in both cases made them patently problems for discussion on the political level. The occupation of Iceland by British Commonwealth forces before the establishment of the Board eliminated the need for consideration of the defense problems of that island. Another notable, but not too surprising, omission was the Great Lakes-St. Lawrence seaway project. President Roosevelt's enthusiasm for the project understandably received no endorsement in the Permanent Joint Board, for Canada did not consider the diversion of the necessary construction resources justified during the war, and the War and Navy Departments had not yet been attracted by the military advantages of the project. Too, it was unlikely that Mr. LaGuardia, mayor of the east coast's largest seaport, would press an undertaking that was opposed by powerful railroad, port, and other interests in his constituency.[37]

As the war progressed and the threat to North America receded farther from it shores, the geographic scope of the work of the Permanent Joint Board narrowed even further. The journals and progress reports indicate that activities in Alaska gradually ceased to be considered. Throughout the later war years, Board consideration was generally limited to projects or activities of mutual concern or interest in Canada and Newfoundland.

Another principle that established bounds for the problems of which the Board took cognizance was the charge to consider only the *defense* of the

[37] See Chapter X, below. In the post-World War II period, the Permanent Joint Board and the U.S. War and Defense Departments actively supported the seaway project on the basis of its military advantages.

northern half of the Western Hemisphere. The Board by and large succeeded in avoiding projects that did not have some relation to joint defense. It is probably this fact that accounts, in part at least, for the absence from the Board agenda of, for example, the First Special Service Force and the Canadian Army Pacific Force, which were organized to fight in Europe and the Pacific, respectively.[38]

On the other hand, several of the Board's recommendations did concern themselves with projects whose primary role pertained to the war overseas, although in each instance there was usually a secondary or partial role relating to joint continental defense. Examples are the Seventeenth and the Twenty-sixth, concerning ferrying operations; the Twenty-third, relating to the meeting of world-wide pilot training requirements; and the Twenty-seventh, which was designed to facilitate the intercountry flow of all war materials whether needed for the continental or world-wide war effort.

This situation became more general as the war receded from North American shores and a short-term defense requirement virtually ceased to exist. Some projects that had been viewed by the Permanent Joint Board as purely defensive measures, as for example the Northwest Staging Route, later played a new and important role in the support of the general global war effort. Toward the end of the war, practically all the joint projects and activities that had been sponsored by the Board were in fact supporting the Allied war effort either in Europe or in the Pacific.

In the area of operating functions the Board's work was necessarily circumscribed by virtue of the existence of service attachés and their staffs in both capitals, and the Canadian Joint Staff in Washington. With three operating channels between the Canadian services in Ottawa and those of the United States in Washington, there was understandably an overlapping of effort and confusion as to responsibilities. Several efforts were made to clarify these responsibilities and to delineate the types of matters which each of the agencies should handle. For instance, an advice to the U.S. Section of the Permanent Joint Board, intended to define the areas of responsibility of the Canadian air attaché and the Air member of the Canadian Joint Staff, stated those of the former to include matters concerning U.S. Army Air Forces (AAF) organization, Royal Canadian Air Force personnel in the United States, visits, and American personnel in the RCAF.[39] Those of the latter included plans and operations, intelligence, communications, and aircraft and other equipment.

[38] See Chapter IX, below, for accounts of these organizations.

[39] Ltr, Air Member, Canadian Joint Staff, to SUSAM, 12 Oct 42, PDB 100-2. The division of duties for the other services was probably comparable.

On several occasions the question of the role of the Board in operational planning and in the direction of operations under the joint defense plan was raised. In one case the head of the War Plans Division of the U.S. General Staff indicated his belief that the Permanent Joint Board was exceeding its competence in attempting to prepare strategic plans. On another occasion the Senior Canadian Army Member pointed out to the Board that its service members, and not the Board itself, had prepared plan ABC-22. Furthermore, the Board had not reviewed the plan, since this review, as well as the execution of the plan, was a responsibility of the chiefs of staff of the two countries.[40] In regard to planning responsibility, it is apparent that, after the Canadian Joint Staff in Washington was established, the Board had no role beyond that of recommending preparation of plans or their revision when necessary. Nevertheless, in its first year the Board clearly functioned in the planning area—witness its First Report, which in effect constituted, in part, a plan for the assignment of operating responsibilities.[41]

Functionally, the principal area in which the Permanent Joint Board operated was in connection with construction of Army, air, and naval bases, and of the auxiliary road, communication, weather, radar, and similar facilities required by the United States in Canada and Newfoundland. Collateral subjects were the supply of materials and construction equipment, utilization of air transport services, the operation of airways for such air traffic, the responsibility for the maintenance and operation of the bases and facilities, and finally their disposition.

The most notable problem of this type not considered by the Board was the Canol Project. The omission was apparently by design on the part of the U.S. secretary, whose initial doubts as to the soundness of the project were later shared by the U.S. Senate's Special Committee Investigating the National Defense Program.[42]

Collaboration Through the Board

The important part played by the Permanent Joint Board on Defense in U.S.-Canadian military co-operation before and after U.S. entry into World War II is indicated by the scope and nature of its formal recommendations. By the time of the Pearl Harbor attack, twenty-one such recommendations

[40] Memo/Conv, Brig Gen G. V. Strong and P. Moffat during latter's Washington visit 6–10 October 1940, Moffat Diary; Note, by Maj Gen M. Pope, CJS, 10 Aug 42, sub: ABC-22 and the PJBD, PDB 135-3. See Chapter IV, below, for an account of the planning under discussion.

[41] See Appendix B, below.

[42] After this committee initiated its searching investigation, the U.S. secretary recalled to Mayor LaGuardia that their hands-off position had been due to his foresight. (Ltr, 29 Dec 43, U.S. Secy's file, PJBD 1943.) See Chapter VIII, below.

had been made that formed the basis for U.S.-Canadian military co-operation throughout the war. Seven December 1941 found, as a result of the Board's work, the requisite force dispositions already made, construction of the necessary bases, installations, and facilities under way, and defense plans complete. Significantly, the Twenty-first Recommendation, the last approved before the Pearl Harbor attack, was concerned with the establishment of arrangements for maintaining facilities provided by one government for forces of the other, as if to mark the ending of the preliminary phase of the joint relationship.

The more important subjects of the pre-Pearl Harbor recommendations were as follows:

a. Exchange of information.

b. Forces and responsibilities for the defense of Newfoundland and the Maritime Provinces.

c. Development of airfields in northwestern Canada for staging purposes.

d. Improvement of communications in the northeastern area, particularly the Newfoundland railroad and road systems.

e. Preparation of joint defense plans.

The entry of the United States into the war occasioned virtually no change in the functioning of the machinery already in motion. It was necessary only for the military chiefs of the two countries to place the previously prepared plans in effect. The volume and tempo of the detailed work of the two sections of the Board increased, but the number of recommendations and new projects diminished.

No real thought had been given to changes in the status of the Permanent Joint Board after the United States became a belligerent. Less than three months before that event, the Canadian view was expressed "that if the United States became a full belligerent the PJBD would go into abeyance, to be resurrected at the end of the war."[43] Such a turn of events never materialized, and the Board continued to have a vigorous and useful wartime life.

After Pearl Harbor a few new projects were needed to meet additional requirements, and recommendations were made accordingly. By and large, however, the pattern of co-operation was well established and the Board's principal effort was devoted to overseeing, expediting, and facilitating in many detailed ways the execution of projects already in hand. The major construction projects occasioned by entry of the United States into the war and recommended by the Board were (a) the highway to Alaska, (b) the northeast ferry routes across the Atlantic, and (c) the expansion of the air

[43] Memo/Conv, Moffat and Norman Robertson, 25 Sep 41, D/S 842.20/204.

staging route to Alaska. The Thirtieth Recommendation, approved by the Board in April 1943, was the last to propose a new operational or logistical project. The remaining three recommendations of the World War II period related to the administration and disposition of facilities.

The Thirty-third and last wartime recommendation (in September 1944) set forth the arrangements for the disposition of U.S. facilities and property in Canada. Questions regarding termination of U.S. activities had arisen as early as 1942 and had occasioned the adoption of the Twenty-eighth Recommendation in January 1943. The arrangements provided for by the modifying Thirty-third Recommendation proved adequate to cover the disposition problem without further revision. But the execution of the disposition arrangements proved to be a substantial and administratively complex task which fully absorbed the capacities of the U.S. Section of the Permanent Joint Board throughout the remainder of the war and for some months afterward.

Even in the spring of 1945, when victory was imminent in Europe and only a matter of time in the Pacific, and throughout the balance of the World War II period, the Board continued to limit its discussions and actions to problems connected with the war. Problems of co-operation for postwar defense were not raised in the Board, which apparently felt impelled to let the pattern of postwar developments point the way to further collaboration. The usefulness of the Board had been proven, however, and, when the two governments began their discussions of postwar security needs, it became apparent that a role for the Permanent Joint Board in meeting those needs would be assured.

CHAPTER III

Partnership Versus Triangle

During the months after the establishment of the Permanent Joint Board on Defense and the initiation at about the same time of informal staff collaboration with the United Kingdom, the U.S. public continued to remain cool to the idea of involvement in the European war. Nevertheless, preparatory measures for continental security were considered legitimate actions in self-defense and had widespread public support. In this setting, the special military relationship between Canada and the United States developed harmoniously without undue involvement resulting from Canada's membership in the British Commonwealth and its participation in the European war.

The Roosevelt-Churchill Axis

The initial development of U.S.-British collaboration may have given some impetus to Canada's desire to join with the United States in a mutual defense scheme. The further development of that collaboration suggested the possibility of even greater impact on the U.S.-Canadian relationship and was therefore watched with interest from Ottawa.

The liaison established between the British services in London and the visiting U.S. staff group in August 1940 became closer during the ensuing months. With utmost secrecy and on an informal basis, the staffs explored the actions the United States would have to take if it entered the war. These were the first real steps in the direction of combined planning.

In the meantime, British Ambassador Lothian had presented to Secretary of State Hull, on 5 October 1940, a proposal for the conduct of formal military staff talks on the Japanese threat in the Pacific. His proposal, which was repeated later in October and again in November after the presidential election, and which contemplated multilateral participation, was not found acceptable in Washington. Yet it was probably this proposal that inspired the broader U.S.-British staff talks that took place in January 1941.[1]

[1] For a discussion of these proposals and some interesting material on their relationship to the elections, see Herbert Feis, *The Road to Pearl Harbor* (Princeton: Princeton University Press, 1950), pp. 126–27. As a matter of fact, after this rejection the Chief of Naval Operations instructed his representatives in London and Manila secretly to explore the problem with the British naval staffs in London and Singapore.

During the autumn months of 1940 the war outlook changed substantially. British successes in defending against German air attacks in the Battle of Britain, together with German failure to attempt the English Channel crossing during the most favorable periods, increased the conviction that Great Britain would hold. In turn, the threat to North America was seen as diminishing. In the War and Navy Departments, emphasis in planning began to shift by the end of October from concern over hemisphere defense toward the concept of supporting Great Britain.[2]

Immediately after President Roosevelt's re-election in November 1940, Admiral Stark, Chief of Naval Operations, recommended that the President authorize secret and exhaustive military talks with the British staffs. General Marshall concurred in the proposal, which the President approved. On 30 November Admiral Stark issued the invitation to the British Chiefs of Staff in his own name.[3]

The staff group sent to represent the British Chiefs of Staff arrived in Washington in January 1941. Between 29 January and 29 March, fourteen plenary meetings with United States staff representatives took place. As stated in the report of the conferees, the conversations had the following purposes:

a. To determine the best methods by which the armed forces of the United States and the British Commonwealth, with its allies, could defeat Germany and its allies, should the United States be compelled to resort to war.

b. To co-ordinate on broad lines the plans for the employment of the forces of the associate powers.

c. To reach agreements as to the methods and nature of military co-operation, including the allocation of principal areas of responsibility, the major lines of military strategy, and the strength of forces that might be committed.[4]

The United Kingdom representatives, on entering upon the talks, presented themselves as the "United Kingdom delegation," which was to represent the British Chiefs of Staff in their collective capacity as military advisers to the War Cabinet of His Majesty's Government in the United Kingdom. Both the British Chiefs of Staff and the War Cabinet were parts of the United

[2] For a detailed account of the transition, see Matloff and Snell, *Strategic Planning for Coalition Warfare, 1941–1942*, Ch. II.

[3] Morison, *The Battle of the Atlantic*, pp. 43–44; Feis, *The Road to Pearl Harbor*, pp. 138–39.

[4] Full text of the report, "United States-British Staff Conversations, Report, 27 Mar 41, Short Title ABC–1," is reproduced in *Pearl Harbor Attack*, Pt. 15, pp. 1485–1541. Accounts of the conduct of the staff talks are to be found in testimony recorded in *Pearl Harbor Attack*, Pt. 3, pp. 991ff., 1053ff. More rounded accounts of the conversations are contained in Watson, *Chief of Staff: Prewar Plans and Preparations*, Ch. XII, and Matloff and Snell, *Strategic Planning for Coalition Warfare, 1941–1942*, Ch. III.

Kingdom Government and not of any Commonwealth machinery. Consistently, the British group was referred to in British papers, and in papers prepared by the joint secretariat that served the conferees, as the United Kingdom delegation.[5] However, the U.S. committee specifically examined the question of nomenclature and concluded that it should refer to the United Kingdom representatives as the "British delegation." This delegation indicated in its initial statement that it understood the object of the conversations to be the co-ordination of plans for the employment of forces of the British Commonwealth, its present allies, and the United States. The records of the conversations do not indicate that the U.S. representatives in any way questioned the authority of the United Kingdom group to speak for the Commonwealth and its allies. The U.S. committee did consider the question of participation of Canadian and Australian officers as observers, and agreed that such participation was undesirable, although those officers could remain available to the British delegation as technical advisers.

The conversations thus proceeded with, at best, only indirect representation through the United Kingdom delegation for Canada, other Commonwealth countries, and other allied belligerents. Despite this fact the British and U.S. representatives in their talks and in the war plan prepared during the talks made world-wide allocations of strategic responsibilities and of the military resources available. The resources of Canada and the rest of the Commonwealth were included and simply enumerated as part of the total British resources. The war plan did take note of existing U.S.-Canadian defense planning by acknowledging that the measures needed for the defense requirements of contiguous land and coastal areas of the two countries would be covered in plans prepared by them. The report of the conversations, dated 27 March 1941 and given the short title ABC-1, made provision for methods of command and staff representation that proved unsatisfactory to Canada. The report had, of course, a considerable bearing not only on the form and substance of U.S.-Canadian co-operation but also on the role of Canada and on the future conduct of the war.

As provided for in ABC-1, the British Chiefs of Staff undertook to secure the concurrence of the dominion governments to relevant portions of the report. They submitted ABC-1 to the Canadian Government for approval but apparently had not yet received it at the end of July, four months after completion of the report.[6] Earlier in July the Department of State had been

[5] Minutes of the plenary meetings and other papers prepared during the conversations are filed in WPD 4402-89.

[6] The 28 July draft of ABC-22 merely states that ABC-1 had been submitted to the Canadian Government for concurrence.

notified that "the United Kingdom Government . . . [was] in general agreement with the report" on the staff conversations except for "certain subsidiary points—such as some of the proposals made in paragraph 6 of the 'Joint letter of transmittal,' " on which London had not yet made up its mind.[7]

In Washington, the Secretaries of War and the Navy approved ABC-1, but the President merely noted it. Roosevelt's approval, tacit if not express, was assumed, and the U.S. services used the plan as the framework for their own global strategic planning.

On 27 May 1941, two months after the conclusion of the staff talks, President Roosevelt declared an unlimited national emergency. This date may be said to mark the transition from the informal liaison in Washington and London into a more-or-less formal and continuing combined U.S.-British planning arrangement. In accordance with the provisions of ABC-1 but in advance of the time specified in it, the United Kingdom had, in early April, already established the British Military Mission (later designated the British Joint Staff Mission) in Washington.[8] On 17 June the first meeting of the U.S. and United Kingdom representatives who were later to become the working members of the Combined Chiefs of Staff committee took place in Washington.[9]

As the United States intensified planning and preparation for possible participation in the war against the Axis and increased collaboration with the United Kingdom, its collaboration with Canada receded in relative importance. The work of the Permanent Joint Board continued unabated and close interservice co-operation expanded. Since the foundations of U.S.-British direction of the over-all war effort had been laid, Canada could but watch the United States move into ever closer collaboration with the United Kingdom.

Not long after Pearl Harbor the White House announced that military staff meetings with the United Kingdom had been taking place regularly in Washington and London. The announcement stated that the machinery for joint planning would soon be expanded to include representatives of the Soviet Union, China, the Netherlands, and other governments engaged in

---

[7] Ltr, Ambassador Halifax to Welles, 4 Jul 41, Roosevelt Papers, Secy's File, Box 74. It appears not unlikely that one or more of the dominions may have objected to this paragraph, which begins: "The High Command of the United States and United Kingdom . . . ." The Canadian Government also indicated its dissatisfaction with the provisions of ABC-1 relating to service liaison between Canada and the United Kingdom and United States in matters relating to ABC-1. (See below, pp. 71-76.)

[8] The ABC-1 report provided for an exchange of missions after the United States entered the war.

[9] Memo, BUS(J)(41)40, 4 Apr 41, WPD 4402-94; Kittredge Monograph, pp. 445-52; Matloff and Snell, *Strategic Planning for Coalition Warfare, 1941-1942,* pp. 42-43.

the war. Secretary of State Hull urged President Roosevelt to establish a supreme war council, with major power representation, along the lines of the body that functioned in World War I. Hull opposed as an unwieldly arrangement the suggestion of Lord Halifax, the British Ambassador, that the dominion governments would probably have to be given the same status in such a council as Great Britain. By early January 1942 the President had concluded that a regional basis for co-ordination was best initially, and the Hull proposal was dropped.[10]

While a supreme war council was being debated, arrangements were being made for Prime Minister Churchill and the British Chiefs of Staff to come to Washington. They arrived in Washington for the ARCADIA Conference, the first of the major U.S.-British politico-military conferences of World War II, on 22 December 1941. Concurrently with the meetings of the political leaders, the chief staff officers of the two countries met and prepared recommendations on military problems for the consideration of Roosevelt and Churchill.[11] No Canadian, or other third power, representatives participated in the military conferences, although Prime Minister King and political figures from other countries participated in the political discussions with Roosevelt and Churchill.

From the ARCADIA Conference emerged the Combined Chiefs of Staff (CCS) committee as a formally constituted body with an elaborate organization of subordinate planning and technical bodies. The U.S. members of the committee were General George C. Marshall, Chief of Staff of the Army; Admiral Harold R. Stark, Chief of Naval Operations; Lt. Gen. Henry H. Arnold, Chief of the Army Air Forces; and Admiral Ernest J. King, Commander in Chief, U.S. Fleet.[12] Since the British Chiefs of Staff could not leave London for any protracted period, the British component of the Combined Chiefs of Staff normally consisted of senior representatives of the British Chiefs of Staff who spoke for and consulted them as necessary.[13]

North Atlantic Triangle

The culmination of the informal British-U.S. staff collaboration in the establishment of the Combined Chiefs of Staff raised for Canada, and for

[10] Department of State *Bulletin*, December 20, 1941, V, 541; Hull, *Memoirs*, II, 1121–24.

[11] For an account of the ARCADIA staff meetings, see Craven and Cate (eds.), *Plans and Early Operations*, pp. 237–45.

[12] Stark, after attending only a few meetings, left Washington in March and Admiral King assumed the duties of Chief of Naval Operations in addition to those of Commander in Chief, U.S. Fleet. Admiral William D. Leahy, when he became chief of staff to the President in the summer of 1942, joined Marshall, King, and Arnold as a member of the U.S. Joint Chiefs of Staff and the U.S.-British Combined Chiefs of Staff.

[13] For an account of the development of the CCS organization and its functioning, see Ray S. Cline, *Washington Command Post: The Operations Division*, UNITED STATES ARMY IN WORLD WAR II (Washington: Government Printing Office, 1951), Ch. VI.

other governments as well, the question of the adequacy of its representation in this new strategic council.[14] Ottawa had already learned that not all arrangements worked out between Washington and London, and involving Canadian matters, accorded with the Canadian desires.

Difficulties had first been experienced in the field of matériel procurement. At the outbreak of war Canada had been obtaining such of the equipment for its armed forces as was procured from the United States by direct purchase from U.S. manufacturers.[15] This procedure gave Canada full freedom of action as to items that were not in short supply. But even before the fall of France, the expanding needs of the United States and Great Britain were competing for an ever-increasing list of products. British and French supply and procurement activities in the United States were being co-ordinated through the Anglo-French Purchasing Board. Canada joined this arrangement, apparently as a means of improving its position in procuring competitive items, and on 5 March 1940 notified the Department of State that the board, then under the chairmanship of Arthur B. Purvis, a Canadian, was "acting for the Canadian War Supply Board in respect of purchases in the United States for Canadian defense service." [16]

The fall of France caused the dissolution of the Anglo-French Purchasing Board and its replacement by the British Purchasing Commission.[17] It also greatly increased both British and American demands on the U.S. output of military matériel. Canada was not completely satisfied with the system of procuring U.S. matériel either through the board or through the commission because the United Kingdom was favored in allocations of the available matériel made by the commission, especially after the fall of France.[18]

Moffat had reported the Canadian difficulties to Morgenthau during his discussions in Washington on 2–3 July 1940, and had informed Prime Minister King, on his return to Canada, that henceforth the United States might break down the Empire requests by country and act on the requests piecemeal. To King, it appeared that such a procedure would make supply to Canada easier, since matériel for Canada would contribute more directly to the defense of the United States.[19]

[14] For a historical survey of the interplay of Canada, the United States, and Great Britain, see John B. Brebner, *North Atlantic Triangle* (Rev. ed.; Toronto: Ryerson Press, 1947). See also J. B. Brebner and R. G. Trotter, "Relations of Canada and the United States," *Canadian Historical Review*, XXIV (1943), 117–35.

[15] Dawson, *Canada in World Affairs: 1939–1941*, p. 220.

[16] Cdn Leg Note 82, to Secy State, 5 Mar 40, D/S 841.24/208.

[17] British Emb Note 315, to Secy State, 9 Jul 40, D/S 851.24/187.

[18] Summary of Meeting of U.S. Section, PJBD, 23 Aug 40, PDB 100–4; Morgenthau Diary, 3 Jul 40, Vol. 279, p. 146.

[19] Memo/Convs, Moffat and Morgenthau, 3 Jul 40, and Moffat and King, 5 Jul 40, Moffat Diary.

Months later, in November 1940, the Canadian Section of the Permanent Joint Board on Defense was trying to improve this situation and proposed to the Board that Canadian matériel needs be divided into two categories: those for North American defense, and those for the European war. Orders for matériel in the latter category, the proposal stated, should properly be placed through the British Purchasing Commission for allocation from the quantities excess to U.S. needs, but matériel requirements for North American defense, the Canadian Section felt, should be met on the same basis as U.S. defense needs and without passing through the British commission.[20]

Another measure apparently designed, at least in part, to improve the Canadian position in the procurement of matériel was the establishment in January 1941 of a British Supply Council in North America to deal with "issues of policy concerning supply, including representations to be made to the United States Administration."[21] Mr. C. D. Howe, Canadian Minister of Munitions and Supply, became a member of the new council. That Canadian efforts in this direction did not adequately fulfill Canadian needs is indicated by the fact that the Canadian Section of the Permanent Joint Board, which had at the November 1940 meeting reported its lack of success in obtaining through the British machinery a number of American flying boat patrol aircraft, had to report two months later that Great Britain had not yet agreed to this urgent Canadian request.[22]

Insofar as practicable Canada continued to purchase equipment directly from U.S. manufacturers. For items in competitive supply, the Canadian requests were placed through the British Supply Council and assigned an agreed priority. In turn, the British Commonwealth requests were considered by the U.S. Joint Army and Navy Munitions Board Priorities Committee, which assigned priorities in relation to U.S. requirements. After U.S. entry into the war, it became necessary for Canada to place virtually all requirements before the appropriate new combined agencies that were established in which allocations were made on the basis of world-wide operational requirements and priorities.[23]

The field of matériel procurement was not the only area in which Canada had experienced difficulties as a result of arrangements worked out between Washington and London. In some instances the United Kingdom and the

[20] Journal, PDB 124.

[21] British Emb Note 22, to Secy State, 14 Jan 41, D/S 841.24/425. The new council had been proposed some weeks earlier and had been discussed in the interim.

[22] Journals, November 1940 and January 1941 meetings, PDB 124.

[23] Dawson, *Canada in World Affairs: 1939–1941*, p. 220; Canada, Department of National Defense, *Report for the Year Ending March 31, 1942* (Ottawa: E. Cloutier, King's Printer), p. 15.

United States took actions in which the Canadian Government felt that it had been inadequately advised or consulted. One such instance was the conclusion, in March 1941, of the leased-bases agreement between the United Kingdom and the United States. During the later stages of the negotiations leading to the signing of the preceding destroyer-bases agreement of 2 September 1940, Prime Minister King had been consulted by both Roosevelt and Churchill, and had approved the arrangements embodied in the preliminary agreement.[24] Although King had apparently expected to be a principal in the negotiation of the detailed agreement relating to the bases in Newfoundland, the negotiations were virtually completed before Canada was invited to participate and, even then, only in the role of observer at the conclusion of the leased-bases agreement, which was signed on 27 March 1941. At Canadian instance the three countries simultaneously signed a protocol clarifying the Canadian interest in the defense of Newfoundland.[25] Prime Minister King felt so strongly about this case of bilateral U.S.-United Kingdom negotiation of a matter of direct concern to Canada that he complained to both the President and the Secretary of State.[26]

A similar situation was to develop within a few months. In August 1941 the first wartime meeting of Roosevelt and Churchill took place aboard ship off Argentia, Newfoundland. Roosevelt, in planning his secret voyage to the rendezvous, considered a route through Ottawa to Quebec, where he would embark on a cruiser. He rejected this route on the ground that it would be difficult either to explain his failure to take Mr. King along, or to take Mr. King, in the absence of the leaders of other interested states, to what became known as the Atlantic Conference. The conferees did discuss questions of over-all policy, such as the Atlantic Charter and the situation in the Pacific. Important decisions concerning the Canadian war role were also taken, yet no Canadian official participated in the discussions.[27]

The establishment of the Combined Chiefs of Staff and other combined United Kingdom-U.S. agencies subsequent to formal U.S. entry into the war

[24] See Ch. I, above; Journal, 27 Aug 40 PJBD meeting, PDB 124.

[25] See Ch. IV, below; Dawson, *Canada in World Affairs: 1939–1941*, pp. 213–17; D/S Telg 973, to London, 22 Mar 41, PDB 107–9; Trotter and Corey (eds.), *Conference on Canadian-American Affairs, 1941*, p. 49.

[26] Memo/Conv. Hull and King, 17 Apr 41, D/S 711.42/214; Memo/Conv, Robertson and Moffat, 12 May 41, Moffat Diary.

[27] "Memorandum of Trip to Meet Winston Churchill, August 1941," 23 Aug 41, prepared by President Roosevelt, Roosevelt Papers, Atlantic Charter meeting file. See Ch. V, below.

According to Dawson, *Canada in World Affairs: 1939–1941*, p. 209, the Argentia meeting was a decided shock to King, who forthwith journeyed to London for several weeks of consultations. The meeting may have been a shock, but it is clear from correspondence in the Roosevelt papers that King had planned his trip to London before he was aware of the Roosevelt-Churchill meeting.

brought new occasions for Canadian dissatisfaction. In addition to creating the Combined Chiefs of Staff committee, Roosevelt and Churchill announced, on 26 January 1942, the establishment of the Munitions Assignments Board, the Combined Shipping Adjustment Board, and the Combined Raw Materials Board. The bilateral membership of these agencies accorded with the Churchillian concept that the "most sure way to lose a war" was to put every power contributing forces "on all the councils and organizations which have to be set up and [to require] that everybody is consulted before anything is done." [28]

President Roosevelt, while agreeing to the creation of the British-U.S. agencies, recognized the need for dominion and Dutch participation in the over-all conduct of the war, particularly in respect to the Southwest Pacific, where dominion and Dutch forces were engaged. Accordingly, the Combined Chiefs of Staff considered outline proposals formulated by the President and accepted the recommendations thereon of the British members. These proposals provided that political questions should be discussed in London, since the principal political representation of the countries concerned was centered there, and that strategic questions should be considered in Washington by the Combined Chiefs of Staff, who would hold the British Joint Staff Mission responsible for evolving a co-ordinated British Commonwealth point of view. Although staff representatives of the participating countries could maintain normal contacts with the U.S. staffs and attend Combined Chiefs of Staff discussions on matters of concern to them, the responsibility for making final recommendations to the British and U.S. Governments was to remain with the Combined Chiefs of Staff since they had to considered "the strategy of the war as a whole, the interests of their two Nations being world-wide." [29]

The British-U.S. organizational arrangements growing out of the ARCADIA Conference left the Canadian Government feeling that the Canadian position relative to the war direction boards was confused and unsatisfactory and that Canada had been pushed aside, even in fields where it had a direct interest. As a result, a Department of External Affairs officer, Lester B. Pearson, was sent to Washington on 19 February to clear up a situation that had apparently developed not only because of the natural desire to keep the directing bodies as small as possible, but also because of Churchill's "personal predilection for speaking in the name of the entire Empire and trying to reverse the process of recent years and integrate it more closely." Canadians felt that

[28] Great Britain, *Parliamentary Debates*, Vol. 377, cols. 610, 616.

[29] CCS 21/1, 3 Feb 42. The CCS recommendations received governmental approval on 10 February 1942.

360-477 O - 70 - 6

Churchill had been ably abetted in this effort by the U.S. services, "whose attitude throughout had been that Canada was a nuisance and had much better be treated as a part of Britain," rather than as an independent country, which was in fact the true status of Canada and the other dominions.[30]

In March Prime Minister King himself came to the United States to discuss Canadian exclusion from the war direction agencies. Although by this time the Canadian Government had accepted its exclusion from the Combined Chiefs of Staff, it still sought representation in the raw materials and munitions assignments agencies. Arrangements were worked out to keep Canadian representatives better informed so that, upon the occasion of King's next visit to Washington in April 1942, he was satisfied to press only for membership on the Munitions Assignments Board.[31]

Nevertheless, the question of Canadian participation in the direction of the war continued to be a vexatious one for Prime Minister King. Self-interest demanded that he vigorously protest cavalier treatment by either Great Britain or the United States and seek a strong Canadian voice in the war councils. Before the United States entered the war it had been his view that Canada had a special role to play in the promotion of British-American friendship and harmony of sentiment. One of the reasons he had given for his unwillingness to sit in an Imperial War Cabinet in London was his belief that his availability for personal contact with President Roosevelt "in critical situations affecting the relations between the United States and British Commonwealth" might easily be more important than any service he could render in London.[32]

Canadians as a whole had taken pride in the Canadian role as connecting link, or hinge, between the two major English-speaking countries. Some of the developments that had taken place might understandably have made Canadians wonder whether at times the role had not more nearly resembled that of a nut between the two jaws of a nutcracker. Nevertheless, King followed a policy of taking such positions in regard to Canadian representation as "would best serve to bring about co-operation among all the governments concerned." He accepted the "arrangement under which the war . . . [was] being carried on, on behalf of the United Nations and which . . . [recognized] at the head as the combined command, the Prime Minister of Great Britain and the President of the United States." Where Canadian interests were likely to be prejudiced, he was prepared to, and did, make strong protests to get

[30] Memo/Conv, Robertson and Moffat, 19 Feb 42, D/S 711.42/237.

[31] Memo/Conv, Welles and Moffat, 3 Mar 42; Notes on conversation between Welles and Moffat during latter's Washington visit 4–11 April 1942; both in Moffat Diary.

[32] *H. C. Debates*, 12 Nov 40, pp. 58–59, and 17 Feb 41, p. 813.

representation. Otherwise, he recognized that the problem of representation by the many nations was only one of the difficulties facing Roosevelt and Churchill and endeavored not to add to an already complex situation.[33]

Arrangements for the strategic direction of the war followed the basic concept established in the ABC–1 report. A U.S.-British high command provided over-all direction, while the earth's surface was divided, with one exception, into three areas of responsibility—the first British, the second American, in which each government provided strategic direction through a senior national commander, and the third comprising the land areas in which joint U.S.-British offensive operations would later be launched under jointly agreed unity of command arrangements. The single exception provided that Canada could assume responsibility for the strategic direction of forces in such waters and territories of the Atlantic Ocean areas as might be defined by joint U.S.-Canadian agreements. The joint U.S.-Canadian defense plan, ABC–22, prepared in correlation with the ABC–1 plan, did provide for such assignments of responsibility to Canada. The net effect was that Canada alone of all the other powers was singled out for such an assignment of strategic responsibility.[34]

Insofar as the rest of the war areas were concerned, Canada and other powers participated in the deliberations of the Combined Chiefs of Staff only when the problems under consideration related to them. This participation comprised in part informal and continuous liaison between Canadian service representatives in Washington and members of the Combined Chiefs of Staff committee and its working subcommittees. Alternately, these representatives were invited to participate in the formal sessions of the Combined Chiefs of Staff. Canadian participation at formal meetings took place on several occasions.[35]

In time, Canada achieved membership on three of the subcommittees of the Combined Chiefs of Staff committee. By the spring of 1944, the United Kingdom half of the Combined Communications Board and the Combined Meteorological Committee had been expanded on a Commonwealth basis to include Canadian and other dominion representatives. In September 1944

[33] *H. C. Debates*, 27 Jan 42, pp. 58–59, 25 Mar 42, pp. 1632–33, and 21 Apr 42, p. 1791. In addressing the President on 16 June 1944 on the relationship of the Canadian Government and armed forces to the CCS, Prime Minister King again stated that Canada had "recognized that the higher direction of the war should be exercised by the Combined Chiefs of Staff, under Mr. Churchill and the President," but he also pointed out that the Canadian Government had never "been requested to recognize the Combined Chiefs of Staff as the source of authority of the Supreme Allied Commanders." (JCS 808/1, 19 Jun 44.)

[34] See Ch. IV, below.

[35] Representatives of third powers participated in approximately 25 of the 200 CCS meetings that had been held by 14 July 1945.

independent Canadian representation on the Combined Civil Affairs Committee was approved, thus making this committee tripartite in nature.[36]

Two of the eight wartime politico-military conferences took place in Canada—QUADRANT (First Quebec Conference) in August 1943, and OCTAGON (Second Quebec Conference) in September 1944. At each of these conferences three general categories of meetings took place—those of the Combined Chiefs of Staff, those of the Combined Chiefs of Staff with President Roosevelt and Prime Minister Churchill, and the political meetings between Roosevelt and Churchill and, when invited, the representatives of other powers. Only the British and U.S. staffs participated in the first two categories of meetings, although informal and formal meetings and discussions did take place between the Canadian Chiefs of Staff, on the one hand, and the U.S. Joint Chiefs of Staff or the British Chiefs of Staff, on the other. The Canadian Chiefs of Staff visited Washington in May 1943 concurrently with the TRIDENT Conference and discussed mutual problems in a similar manner. Mr. King participated in Roosevelt-Churchill discussions at TRIDENT, QUADRANT, and OCTAGON and also met with the President and British Prime Minister separately. Thus, although no formal Canadian participation took place at the Combined Chiefs of Staff meetings, there was frequent opportunity to discuss and concert policies and measures of mutual interest.[37]

The three members of the North Atlantic triangle also participated in other bodies established to provide co-ordinated direction to the war effort. Pursuant to the ARCADIA discussions, Mr. Churchill had, on 27 January 1942, announced the proposed establishment of a Pacific War Council on the ministerial level in London to provide co-ordinated political guidance on the Pacific war to the Combined Chiefs of Staff. It held its first meeting on 10 February, with Great Britain, New Zealand, Australia, the Netherlands, and

[36] CCAC 143, 29 Sep 44, and 143/1, 16 Oct 44.

[37] Winston S. Churchill, *The Second World War: Closing the Ring* (Boston: Houghton Mifflin Company, 1951), p. 66; William D. Leahy, *I Was There* (New York: Whittlesey House, 1950), p. 174; Tucker, *The Naval Service of Canada*, II, 442–44, 466; CCS Conference Books, *passim;* "The Log of the President's Visit to Canada: 16 August–26 August 1943," Roosevelt Papers, H. Hopkins file, Box 24; R. K. Carnegie, "The Quebec Conference," *Canadian Geographical Journal*, XXVII (September 1943), 96–105; Wilson Brown, "The Allies at Quebec," *Queens Quarterly*, LVI (Winter 1949–1950), 465–78; Lingard and Trotter, *Canada in World Affairs*, III, 131n, 238, 257–58; *Canada at War*, No. 25 (Jun 43), p. 17, and No. 41 (Oct 44), p. 11; Samuel Rosenman (compiler), *The Public Papers and Addresses of Franklin D. Roosevelt*, XII, *1943 Volume: The Tide Turns* (New York: Harper & Brothers, 1950), 363–64. For a general account of the international conferences, see Cline, *Washington Command Post: The Operations Division*, Ch. XII. The other international conferences were ARCADIA (Washington, December 1941–January 1942), in which Mr. King participated, SYMBOL (also called ANFA, Casablanca, January 1943), SEXTANT-EUREKA (Cairo-Tehran November–December 1943), ARGONAUT (Malta-Yalta, January–February 1945), and TERMINAL (Potsdam, July 1945).

QUEBEC CONFERENCE, AUGUST 1943. *Seated are the President of the United States, Franklin D. Roosevelt, and the Governor General of Canada, the Earl of Athlone. Standing are Prime Minister Mackenzie King of Canada and Prime Minister Winston Churchill of Great Britain.*

India participating.[38] Subsequently Canada requested, and was granted, representation on the London council. On 30 March President Roosevelt announced establishment of a Washington body with the same name and similar functions and composition. This body, which met first on 1 April 1942 and included representatives of the United States, United Kingdom, Australia, Canada, China, India, the Netherlands, New Zealand, and the Philippine Commonwealth, met frequently during 1942 and 1943. The London council, with somewhat narrower representation, continued to meet, but less frequently. Both bodies furnished a formal forum, on the ministerial level,

[38] Great Britain, *Parliamentary Debates*, Vol. 377, col. 611; *H. C. Debates*, 10 Feb 42, p. 598.

in which the smaller countries could express their views and recommendations.[39]

A parallel staff agency, the Military Representatives of the Associated Pacific Powers, was also established at Washington in the spring of 1942 and included, in addition to the Washington members of the Combined Chiefs of Staff committee, representatives of Australia, Canada, New Zealand, the Netherlands, and China. This body met about once a month. In January 1943 French and Polish representatives were admitted, and in April the word "Pacific" was dropped from the title. Apparently by common consent, meetings of this group, which heard reports and exchanged views on a wide range of military problems, were not held after June 1943.[40]

Thus Canada, after some initial concern as to its role vis-à-vis the United Kingdom-U.S. machinery for the broad policy and strategic direction of the war, succeeded in developing satisfactory relationships which seemed adequate to its needs. In due course Canada also participated to varying degrees in other Anglo-American combined bodies.[41]

Canadian dissatisfaction over participation in the Anglo-American combined organizations was by no means the only occasion for resentment directed at the United States. Numerous incidents occurred on the point of the relationship of Canada to the British Empire that led Canadians to conclude that Americans still considered Canada a nonautonomous part of the Commonwealth. President Roosevelt had in September 1939 set a precedent in this regard that he himself failed to follow on several occasions. The United Kingdom had declared a state of war with Germany on 3 September. The Neutrality Act of 1937 required issuance of a U.S. neutrality proclamation involving an embargo on arms deliveries to belligerent states. Associates of the Secretary of State argued that, since the United Kingdom was at war, the dominions were also, unless they formally seceded from their association under a common sovereign. Hull recommended a contrary view to the President, who immediately telephoned Prime Minister King for his opinion. King stated that he did not regard Canada as being at war. Accordingly, Canada was not included in the U.S. neutrality proclamation of 5

[39] Ltr, L. McCarthy to Welles, 28 Mar 42, D/S 740.001 PW/2190–4/5; Department of State *Bulletin*, January 16, 1943, VIII, 186; *H. C. Debates*, 21 Apr 42, p. 1791; Sherwood, *Roosevelt and Hopkins*, pp. 509–10; *Canada at War*, No. 25 (Jun 43), p. 17; Lingard and Trotter, *Canada in World Affairs*, III, pp. 135–37; Canada, *Annual Report of the Secretary of State for External Affairs, 1943* Ottawa: E. Cloutier, King's Printer, 1944), p. 11.

[40] Papers relating to these meetings are filed in ABC 334.8 M.R.P. (5–26–42). The ninth and last meeting was held on 18 June 1943.

[41] See below, pp. 77–85.

September but in a separate proclamation issued on 10 September, the day of the Canadian declaration of war.[42]

Yet in drafting a proposed list of signatories to the Atlantic Charter in August 1941, the President initially grouped the dominions in a listing under the United Kingdom, although he later revised the list to place all the countries in alphabetical order. In January 1942 the State Department not only proposed a listing of signatories for the Joint Declaration by the United Nations in which Canada appeared as one of a British Empire group of nations, but it also compounded this maladroitness by presenting the document to Canada through the British Embassy, thereby occasioning a formal Canadian objection.[43] Incidents such as these led some Canadians to conclude that both service and civilian elements of the U.S. Government believed Canada to be a nuisance, much better treated as a part of Great Britain.[44]

The Stresses of Partnership

Not all the difficulties that arose in U.S.-Canadian politico-military dealings during World War II can be ascribed to the North Atlantic triangle relationship or to Canada's position in the British Commonwealth. Naturally, in the course of years of close collaboration subsequent to the Ogdensburg meeting, many disagreements developed. Although it was not always possible to reconcile divergent fundamental points of view, representatives of the two countries always succeeded in amicably working out solutions which, if not the solution preferred by both sides, at least met the essential requirements of the situation. Despite the number of disagreements, large and small, disagreement was far from the norm for U.S.-Canadian wartime

---

[42] Hull, *Memoirs*, I, 678–79; Dawson, *Canada in World Affairs: 1939–1941*, p. 6. The proclamations are 2349 (4 FR 3819), and 2359 and 2360 (4 FR 3857). Similarly, in telling King at Ogdensburg of his reasons for wanting a defense board, the President acknowledged the need for negotiating for bases in Canada with Ottawa, since Canada was an autonomous dominion, rather than with London, where the trade of destroyers for leased bases in British territories was being worked out.

[43] Sherwood, *Roosevelt and Hopkins*, p. 452; Memo/Conv, Wrong and Berle, 31 Dec 41 and 1 Jan 42, D/S 740.001 EW1939/18384 and /18454.

[44] Memo/Conv, Moffat and Under Secy State for External Affairs, 19 Feb 42, D/S 711.42/237; Memo, for Secy State, 20 May 43, D/S 711.42/255.

It is interesting to speculate on the extent to which this attitude on the part of U.S. officials was a reflection of the Department of State organization for handling British and Canadian affairs. The Canadian-desk officer throughout the World War II period sat in the Division of British Commonwealth Affairs, which in turn was a part of the Office of European Affairs. In addition to providing a governmental pattern for considering Canada within a British framework, this organization had the effect of placing Canadian problems for review and consideration before one officer whose responsibility was for the British Commonwealth as a whole, and before another whose responsibility was for European affairs. State Department officers queried on the point expressed divergent views to the author as to whether this organizational arrangement did in fact influence the handling of Canadian problems in the State Department.

co-operation. The many great joint wartime achievements deny any such conclusion. The areas of harmonious co-operation far overshadowed those in which disagreements needed to be worked out. Nevertheless, the record of these disagreements is a necessary and useful one, for their existence and causes should be noted and should serve as guideposts in the future.

Often the difficulties were the result of the manner in which the United States consulted and negotiated with Canada. On one occasion a communication to the RCAF member of the Permanent Joint Board in August 1941 tactlessly advised him that, as a result of discussions between the President, Maj. Gen. Henry H. Arnold, and Lord Beaverbrook concerning Atlantic aircraft ferrying, General Arnold desired Canadian authorization for the United States to establish three weather and emergency stations in Canada, and that it was "mandatory that definite decision be received promptly" as delay might defeat the entire project. This message reached a Cabinet War Committee meeting, where it was read and provoked a strong reaction not only to the use of the term "mandatory" (with the flavor of a British-U.S. ukase) but also to the use of military, rather than diplomatic, channels for presentation of the request. Canada promptly approved the request, but the incident was not as promptly forgotten.[45]

Similar lapses occurred on the part of the State Department. To cite an important instance, the United States had, throughout most of 1941, actively discussed with the other Pacific powers questions relating to the possibility of war with Japan. During the summer some consultation with Canada took place, although it was necessary for Canada not only to request that it be kept advised but also that this be done directly and not through the British Government. As the situation regarding Japan became critical, the United States after September 1941 carried on extensive political discussions with Japan in an effort to achieve a *modus vivendi.* During the talks the United States considered itself a trustee for the other governments concerned. On occasion during November, as the situation approached a crisis, the diplomatic representatives of the United Kingdom, China, the Netherlands, and Australia were consulted on the negotiations.[46] Despite the clear Canadian interest in the political and security problems of the Pacific, Canada was not consulted. Mr. King expressed concern and regret on this score, and, al-

---

[45] Memo, Lt Col C. Bissell for Brig Letson, 20 Aug 41, WPD 4262-7; U.S. Leg Ott Desp 1867, to Secy State, 22 Aug 41, D/S 811.9243/27; Memo for Record, by Moffat, 22 Aug 41, Moffat Diary.

[46] U.S. Leg Ott Telg 200, to Secy State, 5 Aug 41, D/S 840.51 Frozen Credits/2882; Telg 203, 6 Aug 41, D/S 701.4294/21; Memo/Conv, Moffat and Robertson, 29 Sep 41, D/S 742.94/13. For accounts of these negotiations and consultations, see Feis, *The Road to Pearl Harbor, passim,* and Hull, *Memoirs,* II, 1073, 1076.

though Pearl Harbor soon made the question academic, for many weeks "the failure to include Canada among the powers invited to discuss the Pacific problems in late November continued, despite all explanations, to rankle."[47]

Many of the difficulties that arose after Pearl Harbor were the result of fundamental differences in the approaches of the two countries to mutual problems. Americans would attack each problem vigorously and impatiently, and in terms of the short-term military need, with only secondary consideration to long-term aspects or to the concurrent impact on other conditions in Canada. Canada, usually the grantor in all the requests presented, was interested, too, in "getting the job done," but it was also prone to give more consideration to the broader implications of the U.S. requests.

The initial U.S. request after Pearl Harbor evoked a response that exemplified this difference in approach. On receiving a U.S. request, transmitted to Ottawa by the State Department on 8 December, the Cabinet War Committee on the next day considered authorizing the United States to establish a radio direction finding installation in British Columbia involving some fifty personnel. The authorization was granted with several conditions relating to the relationship between the detachment and Canadian commanders and financial and procurement provisions that had been recommended by the Canadian Section of the Permanent Joint Board. One of these called for a commitment to leave the radar set in Canada if the U.S. requirement for an installation at that site ceased to exist. State Department officers reacted strongly to these conditions and declared them unacceptable, forecasting major reactions if such conditions were indicative of the Canadian idea of a basis for wartime co-operation. Needless to say, the problem was satisfactorily resolved, as were many others that followed it. As the fundamental points of view on each side became better understood and approached a common denominator, the handling of similar requests became routine and perfunctory.[48]

Canadian Staff Representation in Washington

Until the start of World War II, neither Canada nor the United States maintained service attaché representation in the other country. On Canadian initiative in February 1940, Air Commodore W. R. Kenny was assigned

[47] Memo/Conv, Wrong and Welles, 25 Nov 41, D/S 711.94/2559; Moffat, Notes on Washington Visit, 1–4 December 1941, Moffat Diary. The explanations offered were the great rapidity of the November events, the lack of interest shown by the Canadian Legation in Pacific problems, and Hull's assumption that King was being kept advised by the President during their "constant and close contact." During this period Canada considered itself sufficiently concerned with the Pacific situation to send two infantry battalions to reinforce the British garrison at Hong Kong. They arrived just before Pearl Harbor and shared the defeat of that garrison by Japanese forces. (Stacey, *The Canadian Army, 1939–1945*, pp. 273–88.)

[48] Memo for Record, Moffat, 10 Dec 41, Moffat Diary.

to Washington as the first Canadian air attaché there, and was followed in August and September by Commodore V. G. Brodeur and Col. H. F. G. Letson, as naval and military attachés, respectively.[49] The War Department sent its first attaché, an Air officer who served as both military and air attaché, to Ottawa in April 1940, while the Navy Department first assigned a naval attaché there in August 1940. This nominal and routine attaché liaison was supplemented, after the Ogdensburg Declaration, by liaison through the Permanent Joint Board on Defense.

Two types of liaison between the United States and the dominions were provided for in the ABC–1 report of March 1941: Canada, Australia, and New Zealand were to be represented by their service attachés on the British military mission to be established in Washington, and the United States might exchange liaison officers with the dominions for direct co-operation.[50] These arrangements were not, from the Canadian point of view, enough. Canadian desire for liaison through a mission similar to the British mission, which was established during April 1941, were apparently first indicated in a Canadian working-level draft of an operational plan at the time of the joint drafting of defense plans.[51] The operational plan provided for an exchange of military missions between Ottawa and Washington at the time that it was put into effect. In March, at least on the service working levels, the War Department had seemed willing to accede to the Canadian desire, but Canadian efforts to establish a staff mission in Washington were to travel a rocky road for many months.[52]

The Canadian Government on 1 July 1941, after consulting with the United Kingdom, formally requested U.S. approval of the establishment of a military mission in Washington and stated that it felt "very strongly" that the recommendations concerning Canadian representation in Washington made in the ABC–1 report were inadequate. "Problems of joint action in the western Atlantic and possibly in the eastern Pacific," could, in the Canadian view, "best be handled by the establishment of a separate organization rather than by any method of Canadian representation on the United Kingdom Mission." Pending approval of the Canadian mission, the Canadian Government asked that its service attachés be allowed to attend joint meetings of the British Joint Staff Mission and the U.S. service departments. At

[49] Canada, *Annual Report of the Secretary of State for External Affairs, 1940*, p. 10.

[50] *Pearl Harbor Attack*, Pt. 15, p. 1500; BUS(J)(41)24, WPD 4402–94.

[51] Draft, Joint Operational Plan 1, United States Army-Canada Army and Air Force, 14 Apr 41, PDB 133.

[52] A U.S. Army draft of a joint Canada-U.S. Army defense plan, transmitted to SUSAM on 20 March 1941, provided for liaison between the War Department and Canadian War Office and Air Ministry through the exchange of missions between Washington and Ottawa. (PDB 133.)

such meetings, it was to be understood that "the Canadian Service Attachés . . . [were] acting in their capacity as such, and not as members of the British Mission."[53]

Both the War and Navy Departments in July opposed a Canadian mission on the grounds that representation through the Permanent Joint Board on Defense and the British Joint Staff Mission met all the Canadian needs for liaison, and that an undesirable precedent would be established for similar requests by other dominions and the American republics.[54] The Department of State replied to the Canadian *aide-mémoire* on 25 July, taking the position that, although as a matter of general policy a mission would be welcome, the matter was primarily a military one and the case made by the service departments seemed convincing.[55]

During the period that the United States was considering the formal Canadian request, the service members of the Permanent Joint Board were completing the drafting of the 1941 Canadian-U.S. defense plan (ABC-22). The final draft, dated 28 July 1941, provided for the establishment, when the plan became effective, of officers of each country as representatives of their chiefs of staff vis-à-vis their opposite numbers in the other country. Thus the joint drafters were able to go somewhat further than the provisions of ABC-1 in meeting the Canadian desires but were unable at this time to repeat the War Department's willingness to agree to an exchange of missions, even if their establishment were to await the time when the plan would be put into effect.

Soon afterward, on 18 August 1941, Prime Minister King informed U.S. Minister Moffat that the prolonged refusal of Washington to approve a military mission was the only aspect of U.S.-Canadian relationships that seriously troubled him. King felt not only that Canadian contacts with the War and Navy Departments were being funneled through British channels, but also that the British were consciously sidetracking the Canadians. He accordingly urged that the proposal be reconsidered in the light of its political implications and of the greater confidence that would be engendered in the Canadian public mind by direct military representation at Washington.[56]

While the War and Navy Departments re-examined the request, Moffat discussed with Department of State officers the true significance of the continued Canadian pressure for a military mission. The decision to continue the pressure had been taken at the highest political levels, and was a manifestation of dissatisfaction with the way the Canada-United States-United

[53] Cdn Leg *aide-mémoire*, 1 Jul 41, WPD 4543.
[54] Ltr, Secy Navy to Secy State, 21 Jul 41, PDB 111-6.
[55] Memo/Conv, Hickerson and Wrong, 25 Jul 41, WPD 4543-1.
[56] U.S. Leg Ott Telg 218, 18 Aug 41, D/S 842.20/197.

Kingdom relationship had developed during the preceding year. Although resentment was greatest against the British, there was disappointment that the United States should have allowed Canada to be pushed aside. A solution to the mission problem was psychologically important to prevent a transfer of active resentment to the United States. Moffat also surmised that considerations of domestic politics were a motivating force in the Canadian insistence on a mission.[57]

The political considerations relative to the mission did not weigh heavily in War and Navy Department deliberations. The Chief of Staff and the Secretary of War agreed "that foreign political considerations inimical to our military interests should not be allowed to determine the attitude of the War Department," and they approved a recommendation that the request should again be rejected. The substantially identical responses of the Secretaries of War and the Navy proposed, as an alternate solution, the establishment in Washington of a permanent office for the Canadian Section of the Permanent Joint Board on Defense. This proposal, which had already been explored in informal diplomatic discussions, had been rejected by Canadian officials on the grounds that the subject matter for discussions contemplated did not belong to the Board, and that the personnel making up the Canadian Section were not considered suitable for this purpose.[58]

The reason for the U.S. planners' reversal of position, from their initial working-level acceptance of the idea of a mission to their subsequent opposition when advising their chiefs in connection with the formal Canadian requests, is not clear. The answer may be that the question of command relationships under the 1941 defense plan came under joint discussion in the interim. Despite intermittent U.S. pressure beginning in March 1941, and lasting for over a year, the Canadian Section of the Permanent Joint Board and Canadian service planners vigorously opposed, as a general principle, assignment of parts of Canada and Newfoundland, or of Canadian forces located in either, to U.S. strategic or operational command.[59] This Canadian position may well have led U.S. service personnel to use the mission question as a *quid pro quo.*

United States entry into the war provided the occasion for the next Canadian approach, for no longer would acceptance by the United States of

[57] Ltr, Moffat to Hickerson, 5 Sep 41, D/S 842.20/203; Memo/Conv, Moffat and Robertson, 25 Sep 41, D/S 842.20/204.

[58] Memo/Conv, Moffat and Pearson, 5 Sep 41, PDB 111-6; Ltrs, SW to Secy State, 8 Oct 41, and Secy Navy to Secy State, 30 Sep 41, WPD 4543. Despite the Canadian view on the U.S. counterproposal, Maj. Gen. M. A. Pope, who was designated chairman of the Canadian Joint Staff upon its establishment, had been a member of the Permanent Joint Board on Defense for over a year, and served in the dual capacity for approximately two years.

[59] See Ch. V, below.

a mission from a belligerent necessarily establish a precedent to be followed for nonbelligerent American republics. Action on this renewed Canadian request was apparently delayed pending the outcome of the ARCADIA meetings and the command and liaison arrangements that emerged therefrom. On 10 February 1942 the Combined Chiefs of Staff received the approval of Roosevelt and Churchill on their recommendations for representation of the dominions and other powers. These recommendations envisaged the establishment of "staff missions" in Washington. As an intermediate step and pursuant to a Combined Chiefs of Staff invitation announced in March, Canada notified the United States that Maj. Gen. Maurice A. Pope was being sent to Washington as the military representative of the Cabinet War Committee to maintain, with the aid of alternates from the Navy and Air Force, continuous contact with the Combined Chiefs of Staff.[60]

After making this advance, Canada had not much longer to wait before reaching more important goals. By July 1942 U.S. service views on this and other points at issue had changed. The Canadian Government was able to advise the U.S. Secretary of State that informally it had found officers of his department and of the services in agreement on the establishment of a Canadian Joint Staff mission, and formally to propose this step.[61] Canadian efforts of over a year were at last rewarded with success. Concurrently, the U.S. attitude on the command question had relaxed considerably. By 1 June 1942 the U.S. service members of the Permanent Joint Board had concluded that forcing acceptance of "unrestricted unity of command" not only would be resisted by the Canadian services and Cabinet but also would result in a diminution of Canadian co-operation.[62] This conclusion, in turn, reflected changes wrought by Pearl Harbor. Where close Canadian co-operation had not always been sought before the United States entered the war, Canadian co-operation in making available its strategic resources, be they air-base sites, highway right of way, or something else, to the United States was now essential and to be courted.

The record of negotiations for establishment of the mission, with its undertone of acrimony, is one of the least happy aspects of the U.S.-Canadian World War II relationship. Canadian aspirations were understandable enough. The special geographic and historical relationships of the two countries would seem to have been adequate justification for a mission that

---

[60] U.S. Leg Ott Telg 307, 15 Dec 41, D/S 842.20/206; Cdn Leg Note 203, 25 Mar 42, WPD 4543; CCS 21/1, 3 Feb 42. Pope actually arrived in Washington on 6 March.

[61] Cdn Leg Note 459, 2 Jul 42, WPD 4543. In addition to General Pope as Canadian Army member and chairman, the initial Royal Canadian Navy and RCAF members were Rear Adm. V. G. Brodeur and Air Vice Marshal G. V. Walsh.

[62] Memo, SUSAM for CofS, 1 Jun 42, PDB 135-2.

need not have become a precedent for acceptance of missions from other countries. Too, the desire of a soverign state, both for practical reasons and for political reasons at home, to speak to representatives of another government with its own voice and not through a third party should have been understandable. The importance of considerations of national pride, prestige, and sensitivity should also have been apparent.

Shortly after the Canadian Joint Staff was formally established in Washington, it raised the question of direct exchange of information with the U.S. services. The U.S. Joint Chiefs of Staff approved the principle that the U.S. and Canadian chiefs of staff should deal directly on matters relating to joint U.S.-Canadian forces and spheres of activity, and the U.S. Joint Staff Planners committee was assigned responsibility for maintaining continuous liaison with the Canadian Joint Staff.[63]

The Canadian Joint Staff was the third and last type of wartime Canadian service liaison established with the War and Navy Departments in Washington, the others being liaison through the service attachés and the service members of the Canadian Section of the Permanent Joint Board. The general responsibility of the Canadian Joint Staff was to exchange information and co-ordinate strategic planning, deployments, and joint operational matters with the Combined Chiefs of Staff and its subordinate committees, and with U.S. counterparts in the Joint Chiefs of Staff committees.

The United States never attempted to establish similar representation in Ottawa. In January 1944 the U.S. Section of the Permanent Joint Board considered whether there might be military advantage in adopting the repeated suggestion of the U.S. Ambassador in Ottawa that the military attaché be placed in a position comparable to that of the chairman of the Canadian staff mission. The Senior U.S. Army Member concluded that there would be none. The Canadian mission was useful because the Combined Chiefs of Staff organization was located in Washington. No comparable need existed in Ottawa.[64]

Subsequent to the establishment in Washington of the Canadian Joint Staff, one more development in connection with the problem of representation served further to smooth ruffled waters. On 11 November 1943 Prime Minister King announced that the two countries were raising their diplomatic missions in the respective capitals to embassy status. This step was gratifying to Canadians, and was a logical one in light of Canada's increasingly important international stature.[65]

[63] JCS 82, approved 18 Aug 42.
[64] Memo, Hickerson for SUSAM, 25 Jan 44, and Reply, 29 Jan 44, PDB 109-7.
[65] U.S. Emb Ott Desp 389, 1 Dec 43, D/S 124.42/69.

MEETING AT QUEBEC, AUGUST 1943. *From left: Vice Adm. Lord Louis Mountbatten, Adm. of the Fleet Sir Dudley Pound, Gen. Sir Alan Brooke, Air Chief Marshal Sir Charles Portal, Air Marshal L. S. Breadner, Lt. Gen. Sir H. L. Ismay, Field Marshal Sir John Dill, Adm. E. J. King, Gen. H. H. Arnold, Adm. W. D. Leahy, Lt. Gen. K. Stuart, Vice Adm. P. W. Nelles, and Gen. G. C. Marshall.*

The Combined Agencies

The establishment of the Permanent Joint Board on Defense, Canada-United States, and the initial informal United Kingdom-United States military staff discussions in London in August 1940 were only the first steps in the creation of the complex international co-ordinating machinery for the conduct of all aspects of the war. As the European war expanded, agency after agency was established to meet the unprecedented needs for co-ordination of total war on a global scale. The United States played a major role or participated in practically all of them. Canada also played a role in certain of them, as a member as well as a contributor of resources with which the agencies were concerned. In other instances the direction of agencies had been assumed by the United States and the United Kingdom, and Canada stood outside along with other powers.[66]

When the Combined Chiefs of Staff committee was established in 1942,

[66] Two excellent works bearing on the subject of the U.S.-Canadian role in the British-American agencies are Robert W. James, *Wartime Economic Co-operation: A Study of Relations Between Canada and the United States* (Toronto: Ryerson Press, 1949), and S. McKee Rosen, *The Combined Boards of the Second World War* (New York: Columbia University Press, 1951).

the term "combined" was employed to distinguish this *international* agency and all its subordinate committees from the *national* interservice staff organizations that were called "joint" agencies. The term "combined" was thereafter generally applied to subsequent international co-ordinating war agencies established by the United Kingdom and the United States, whether military or civilian organizations.

President Roosevelt and Prime Minister King had, in the prior naming of the Permanent Joint Board on Defense, Canada-United States, established a contrary pattern, which was followed for most of the U.S.-Canadian co-ordinating agencies established thereafter. Both Canadian and U.S. officers who served in the various Canadian-U.S. agencies have indicated that a certain amount of confusion resulted from the "joint" terminology. Working-level proposals for adjustments to produced uniformity of usage of the word "joint" were made but were never advanced to the levels required for decision.

After the Permanent Joint Board on Defense was created, five additional U.S.-Canadian agencies were established, three of them before U.S. entry into the war and before the establishment of any of the United Kingdom-U.S. bodies. All were civilian agencies set up to meet needs arising from the conduct of the war.

The first of these, the Joint Economic Committees, was established as the result of a Canadian proposal on 17 March 1941 for the appointment of joint committees of inquiry, which would make studies, after "a great deal of research and analysis," for the dual purpose of effecting a more economic, more efficient, and more co-ordinated utilization of the combined resources of the two countries in the production of war requirements, and of minimizing the probable postwar economic disequilibrium consequent upon the changes the economy in each country was then undergoing.[67]

Some of the detailed subjects proposed for exploration were supplies and use of raw materials, co-ordination of production programs, use of transportation and power resources, and exchange of information in these areas. The United States accepted the proposals, and the agreement completed 17 June 1941 established the following committees:

United States Committee	*Canadian Committee*
William L. Batt	R. A. C. Henry
Harry D. White	W. A. Mackintosh
Alvin H. Hansen	D. A. Skelton
E. Dana Durand	J. G. Bouchard
A. A. Berle, Jr.—as desired	H. L. Keenleyside—as desired
L. D. Stinebower—liaison with Department of State	To be designated—liaison with Department of External Affairs

[67] EAS, 228; Privy Council 4500, 20 Jun 41.

The establishment of the Joint Economic Committees actually was the second step taken by the two countries in the area of economic co-operation, the first step having been the Hyde Park Declaration of 20 April 1941, issued while the agreement on the committees was being worked out.[68] The Joint Economic Committees made many recommendations on diverse subjects. A typical recommendation was one, approved by the President and Prime Minister on 10 April 1942, providing for increased U.S. production of oil-bearing crops and Canadian production of oats, barley, and flax.[69] Another, approved simultaneously, provided for easier movement of agricultural machinery and laborers across the boundary. Co-operation in this matter continued on into postwar years.[70] Still another recommendation, of 9 August 1941, called for equal consideration of civilian and defense shipping requirements of the two countries.[71]

During 1941 the establishment of a Material Co-ordinating Committee, United States and Canada, was announced by William S. Knudsen, Director General of the U.S. Office of Production Management, with the primary purpose of making possible the free exchange of vital information relating to supplies of strategic raw materials required for defense production.[72] Although officially designated the Material Co-ordinating Committee, the title was in some documents prefixed by the word "Joint."[73] Membership comprised two men of Knudsen's staff—William Batt, who was concurrently designated to serve on the Joint Economic Committees, and Howard Sykes—together with Canadian counterparts from the Wartime Industries Board. The U.S. members were later to assume additional duties as U.S. member and executive secretary, respectively, of the Combined Raw Materials Board, upon its establishment.

By 19 September 1941 the Joint Economic Committees had concluded that the existing agencies did not adequately provide for the co-ordination of the defense production capacities of the two countries, and recommended establishment of a Joint Defense Production Committee "to the end that, in mobilizing the resources of the two countries, each country should provide for the common defense effort the defense articles which it is best able to produce." This purpose was a reaffirmation of one of the objectives of the Hyde Park Declaration and was generally similar to the objectives designated for study by the Joint Economic Committees. However, the objective of

[68] See Ch. X, below.
[69] Department of State *Bulletin,* April 11, 1942, VI, 313–15.
[70] *Ibid.;* CTS, 1947, No. 42.
[71] Rosen, *The Combined Boards,* p. 85.
[72] Department of State *Bulletin,* January 16, 1943, VIII, 76.
[73] For an example, see Department of State *Bulletin,* November 8, 1941, V, 360.

360-477 O - 70 - 7

minimizing postwar economic disequilibrium was now to be sought only "as far as possible and consistent with the maximum defense effort." [74]

The President and Prime Minister approved the recommendation, and the new committee was set up with the following membership: [75]

United States

Milo Perkins, Executive Director, Economic Defense Board, Chairman
J. V. Forrestal, Under Secretary of the Navy
W. A. Harrison, Director, Production Division, Office of Production Management
R. P. Patterson, Under Secretary of War
E. R. Stettinius, Jr., Lend-Lease Administrator
H. L. Vickery, Vice Chairman, U.S. Maritime Commission

Canada

G. K. Sheils, Deputy Minister, Department of Munitions and Supply, Chairman
J. R. Donald, Director General, Chemicals and Explosives Branch
J. H. Carmichael, Director General, Munitions Production Branch
R. P. Bell, Director General, Aircraft Production Branch
H. R. MacMillan, President, Wartime Merchant Shipping, Limited
Walter Gordon, Department of Finance

Redesignated the Joint War Production Committee after Pearl Harbor, the committee, which did not hold its first meeting until 15 December 1941, functioned principally through ten technical subcommittees made up of U.S. and Canadian production and procurement officers. The ten subcommittees were designated tank-automotive, artillery, artillery ammunition, small arms and ammunition, chemicals and explosives, communications, conservation, aircraft, naval vessels, and merchant vessels.[76]

United States entry into the war was also the occasion for a joint declaration calling for an all-out war production effort. Approved by the Canadian Cabinet War Committee and by President Roosevelt, who directed appropriate U.S. agencies "to abide by its letter and spirit so far as lies within their power," the declaration stated:

1. Victory will require the maximum war production in both countries in the shortest possible time; speed and volume of war output, rather than monetary cost, are the primary objectives.

2. An all-out war production effort in both countries requires the maximum use of the labor, raw materials, and facilities in each country.

3. Achievement of maximum volume and speed of war output requires that the production and resources of both countries should be effectively integrated, and directed towards a common program of requirements for the total war effort.

---

[74] *Ibid.;* Privy Council 8441, 31 Oct 41.
[75] *Ibid.*
[76] Privy Council 22, 2 Jan 42.

4. Each country should produce those articles in an integrated program of requirement which will result in maximum joint output of war goods in the minimum time.

5. Scarce raw materials and goods which one country requires from the other in order to carry out the joint program of war production should be so allocated between the two countries that such materials and goods will make the maximum contribution toward the output of the most necessary articles in the shortest period of time.

6. Legislative and administrative barriers, including tariffs, import duties, customs, and other regulations or restrictions of any character which prohibit, prevent, delay, or otherwise impede the free flow of necessary munitions and war supplies between the two countries should be suspended or otherwise eliminated for the duration of the war.

7. The two Governments should take all measures necessary for the fullest implementation of the foregoing principles.[77]

It may be noted that this joint declaration of production policy objectives, issued after U.S. entry into the war, did not express concern over the need to minimize postwar economic disequilibrium as had earlier joint declarations. This shift in emphasis is perhaps another indication of one of the differences between the U.S. and the Canadian approach to wartime problems. Short-term wartime need was the primary U.S. motivation, while Canada tended to give weight as well to long-term aspects.

A detailed examination of the operations and achievements of these joint agencies is outside the scope of this study. It should be noted, however, that during 1941 neither the committees nor the Hyde Park Declaration had been successful in achieving their objectives. The several announcements had in turn restated the same objectives or added committee on top of committee with overlapping responsibilities, as if seeking the catalytic restatement of objectives or that combination of committee members which would produce the desired results. It appears probable that Canada, which provided the initial impetus to collaboration in the production and proceurement areas, had not thus far been able to attain the objectives it sought.[78] Apart from their accomplishments, these prewar committees and their efforts were important in that they were the precursors of similar U.S.-United Kingdom "combined" organizations set up after Pearl Harbor.

The U.S.-United Kingdom combined boards and committees did not replace any of the joint U.S.-Canadian committees, which not only continued their work but also were augmented by the creation of two more agencies. In March 1943 a Joint Agricultural Committee was established to keep under continuous study and review joint food production and distribution, in order to further developments that might be of help in solving wartime agricultural and food problems. The enactment by the Canadian Parliament of a

[77] Department of State *Bulletin*, December 27, 1941, V, 579.

[78] For data concerning results achieved under the Hyde Park Declaration, see below, Chapters X and XII.

mutual aid program generally similar to the U.S. lend-lease program motivated establishment of the last wartime joint committee. During the 1943 Quebec Conference, President Roosevelt and Prime Minister King established a Joint War Aid Committee, United States and Canada, as a means of co-ordinating the two arms assistance programs and of eliminating duplication of requests and deliveries.[79]

In addition to these joint U.S.-Canadian committees, Canada and the United States collaborated in varying degrees through a number of the combined agencies. On the purely military side there was the Combined Chiefs of Staff committee. One of its nominally subordinate bodies, the (Combined) Munitions Assignments Board, enjoyed a special status. Segments of this board sat in London and in Washington, and both groups came within the framework of the Combined Chiefs of Staff organization. The Munitions Assignments Board in Washington had as its chairman the President's special assistant and confidant, Harry Hopkins. This board recommended allocation policies and priorities, which, after review by the Combined Chiefs of Staff and approval by the President (as to U.S. resources), became the basis for matériel allocations made by the board.[80]

Canada, which became the third largest munitions producer among the United Nations (exclusive of the Soviet Union), sought direct representation on the board in May 1942. The request was taken up by Mr. King with the President, and, in the Canadian view, his approval was obtained. Yet when the proposal came to Hopkins' attention, he succeeded in rejecting it, and Canadian participation did not materialize.[81]

A full pooling arrangement under which the Washington and London bodies allocated from the total output of the United States and the British Commonwealth never materialized. Later in 1942 Munitions Assignments Committees were established in Canada, Australia, and India, and, in practice, each of the five bodies allocated from the residue available after the producing country's own requirements were met. Under such a procedure Canada's prime interest in the Washington body was to be heard as a claimant, and Canada was able to work out informal arrangements under which Canadian representatives appeared before the Munitions Assignments Board subcommittees to submit and defend Canadian bids. Both U.S. and British members sat on the Munitions Assignments Committee in Ottawa. In addi-

---

[79] Privy Council 2044, 15 Mar 44; Elizabeth H. Armstrong, "Canadian-American Co-operation in War and Peace, 1940–1945," Department of State *Bulletin*, October 28, 1945, XIII, 676.

[80] Department of State *Bulletin*, January 31, 1942, VI, 87–88. Lord Beaverbrook was chairman of the London agency.

[81] Memo, Cdn Leg to Hopkins, 2 Jul 42, D/S 800.24/609; Memo/Conv, Moffat and Pearson, 29 May 42, Moffat Diary; James, *Wartime Economic Co-operation*, p. 234.

tion, War Supplies, Limited, the government corporation established to receive U.S. production orders and place them in Canada, also acted as a claimant in behalf of the United States before the Ottawa committee.[82]

Four other combined boards, civilian in composition, were established to meet wartime needs. The Combined Raw Materials Board and the Combined Shipping Adjustment Board, both created in January 1942, comprised only United Kingdom and U.S. personnel. No Canadians were included, although the U.S. member of the Combined Raw Materials Board was also a member of the United States-Canadian Material Co-ordinating Committee. Canada made several applications for formal membership on the Combined Raw Materials Board, but they were not successful.[83]

In June 1942 the last two boards were created by the United States and the United Kingdom. Neither included direct Canadian representation initially, but both did ultimately. The joint statement issued on 9 June 1942 by Roosevelt and Churchill established the Combined Production and Resources Board and charged it with combining the production programs of the United States and the United Kingdom into a single integrated program, adjusted to strategic guidance from the Combined Chiefs of Staff. On 7 November 1942 Canada was made a member of the Combined Production and Resources Board, and the revamped board was assigned the same task with regard to the pooled production resources of all three countries. The joint statement also established the Combined Food Board. Its purpose was to consider, investigate, inquire into, and formulate plans concerning the supply, production, transportation, disposal, allocation, and distribution of food. The Combined Food Board was also to work in collaboration with others of the United Nations toward the best utilization of their food resources. This board had had a predecessor in the Anglo-American Food Committee, which emerged in May 1941 after passage of the Lend-Lease Act.

The Combined Food Board worked through ten Commodity Supply and Allocation Committees, seven of which included Canadian representatives, although Canada was not then formally a member of the food board itself. Another subordinate agency of the board was the London Food Committee, which comprised representatives of most of the British Commonwealth countries, but not Canada. The London Food Committee was the mechanism through which Commonwealth resources and requirements were reported to the board and board recommendations were transmitted to the Commonwealth members.

[82] Army Service Forces, International Division, *A Guide to International Supply*, pp. 13–14, 28–29, 46; Lingard and Trotter, *Canada in World Affairs*, III, 236–37.

[83] James, *Wartime Economic Co-operation*, pp. 236–37. Rosen, *The Combined Boards*, has been the main source for the remainder of this chapter.

According to one authority, United Kingdom partnership in this Combined Food Board rested, in the view of some Americans, on dubious grounds. Not itself a contributor of significant food resources, the United Kingdom was a major claimant for U.S. and other supplies, yet it had the prerogative of sharing equally in the decisions as to supply allocations.[84] On the other hand, Canada, a major producer of food resources, was not a formal member of the Combined Food Board. Formal Canadian efforts to become a member were made in July, when the board was only a little over a month old. Both the United States and the United Kingdom looked unfavorably on these efforts. After several months of discussion, Canada accepted as a solution formal membership on several of the commodity committees and participated effectively on this level in the work of the board. Nevertheless, Canada continued to press for formal membership in the board itself.[85]

Formal Canadian membership finally materialized in October 1943. In August the U.S. War Food Administrator recommended admission of Canada, Australia, and New Zealand to the Combined Food Board in the light of the large food resources contributed by those countries. The proposal was approved by President Roosevelt and, for Canada only, by the United Kingdom. At London's request, Australian and New Zealand representation continued through the London Food Committee. On 29 October, Canadian acceptance of the Roosevelt-Churchill invitation was announced.[86]

With the exception of agencies established to deal with relief and postwar problems, the foregoing steps were the last involving the establishment of the international machinery for the conduct of the war and providing for Canadian representation in the various agencies.[87]

Throughout the greater part of World War II, the problem of Canadian representation in the war councils was a major irritant in U.S.-Canadian politico-military relations. On the U.S. side, Churchill's view that it was impossible to admit each of the other associated powers was shared. It was not a simple problem of Canada's being the third vertex of a "North Atlantic triangle," for many other participating allies were anxious to hold a corner of this polygon. Obviously the more voting members in the war councils,

[84] Rosen, *The Combined Boards,* p. 225.

[85] Cdn Leg Note 491, 15 Jul 42, D/S 800.5018/22-1/2; James, *Wartime Economic Co-operation,* pp. 332-39.

[86] See Rosen, *The Combined Boards,* pp. 232-33, for a more detailed account of the negotiations.

[87] The committees in which Canada participated in some degree were dissolved as follows: Joint War Production Committee and Material Co-ordinating Committee, 31 December 1945; Joint Economic Committees, 14 March 1944; Joint War Aid Committee, 25 October 1945; Joint Agricultural Committee, not formally dissolved; Combined Food Board, 1 July 1946; Combined Production and Resources Board and Combined Raw Materials Board, 31 December 1945 (except for certain commodity committees).

the more difficult became the direction of the war effort. There was merit in this view, yet the matter of some appropriate relationship to the war councils was one of great import to Canada. Canada soon became a major contributor of resources among the Allies, and as such, and apart from considerations of pride and prestige, merited some means of regularly expressing its views. The long struggle for real recognition of Canadian sovereignty had made Canadians particularly sensitive on this score, especially to attempts to treat Canada as a not fully autonomous member of the British Commonwealth. Maintaining an exclusive U.S.-United Kingdom arrangement was essential for the directing bodies only. There was no valid reason why Canada and the other powers could not join in pairs with the United States, or collectively, in consultative and similar arrangements lacking powers of decision. This was finally done, and met the needs of Canada and the other powers reasonably well without interfering with the agencies for strategic direction of the war.

The U.S. reluctance to accept such arrangements until the fruit of Canadian resentment was overripe unfortunately was matched by an unnecessary maladroitness in dealings of interest to Canada within the North Atlantic triangle. In some instances matters clearly of interest to Canada were resolved by the United States with the United Kingdom without consultation with Canada. Where such consultation took place, a plain lack of tact occasionally occurred to the irritation of Canadians. Another irritation to Canadians was the U.S. tendency to deal with the United Kingdom on matters relating to the Commonwealth as a whole, as in the allocation of U.S. arms production, at the same time permitting the United Kingdom to ignore, override, or inadequately consider Canadian needs. In such situations the United States in failing to insure adequate consideration of the Canadian requirements shared with the United Kingdom the Canadian resentment. It is probable that the minor savings to the United States in administrative effort and convenience resulting from the too-long and too-rigid insistence on exclusive U.S.-United Kingdom arrangements were more than offset by the development, in Canadian dealings with the United States, of a Canadian wāriness whose mark on postwar joint collaborative efforts was apt to be indelible.

CHAPTER IV

Joint Defense Planning

The Permanent Joint Board on Defense, Canada-United States, made its initial studies on 26–27 August 1940 and submitted seven formal recommendations based thereon. These recommendations, which set forth the action needed to meet the most urgent joint defense problems facing Canada and the United States, were sufficiently comprehensive so that, by and large, additional recommendations were needed thereafter principally to solve "spot" defense problems that arose.[1] The first called for a full and complete exchange of information. Other recommendations provided for certain troop deployments and defensive installations needed to insure adequate defense of Newfoundland and the Maritime Provinces. As slightly longer-range measures, the Board recommended steps to assure adequate allocations of matériel, to improve transportation and communication facilities in the more threatened areas, and to stimulate materiel production. The last recommendation of the seven provided that the "Service Members of the Board should proceed at once with the preparation of a detailed plan for the joint defense of Canada and the United States and keep the Board informed of the progress of the work."

The Board's adoption of the first six recommendations in effect prejudged the content of such a plan, since the requirements set forth in those recommendations for operational and logistical facilities should, in theory at least, have emerged from the forces and operations that the plan set forth as needed to carry out the assumed defense tasks. But awaiting the completion of an approved plan would have delayed work in the field at least several weeks, and the urgency of the situation induced the Permanent Joint Board to recommend appropriate measures on the basis of informed estimates of the situation.

Initial Defense Plans

At the request of the Board, the service members undertook the drafting of the defense plan, working closely with the Board as a whole. Work was advanced considerably during the 9–11 September 1940 Board meeting. At

[1] For texts of all the wartime recommendations of the Permanent Joint Board, see Appendix A, below.

the session on 9 September the Canadian members presented a paper entitled "Defense of the Northern Half of the Western Hemisphere." The study, whose geographic scope conformed to that of the terms of reference of the Board, concluded that the defense of the area must provide, *inter alia,* for "important strategic areas such as the Panama Canal Zone." The Board referred the Canadian paper to its service members for use in connection with their planning.[2]

By the time the Board met on 11 September, a joint draft based on an initial U.S. draft was ready.[3] The Board considered the draft and concluded that further revision was necessary. The service members completed a second joint draft on 25 September 1940, and the final joint draft on 10 October 1940.[4] There was no significant difference in the basic assumptions, general concept, or defense tasks set out in each of the three drafts. In the successive drafts, however, more detailed aspects of the plan were augmented and refined. They pertained to the allocation, by country and service, of the responsibilities connected with each task, and to the logistic, garrison, and defense facilities to be provided by each country.

The Joint Canadian-United States Basic Defense Plan—1940, dated 10 October 1940 and frequently called the 1940 Plan, proposed to "provide for the most effective use of Canadian and U.S. Naval, Military and Air Forces for the joint direct defense of Canada, Newfoundland and the United States (including Alaska)." The plan was what U.S. planners called a "capabilities" plan (as opposed to a "requirements" plan), since it was based on the use only of forces actually available. The joint mission of those forces was "to defend Canada and the United States against direct attack by European and/or Asiatic Powers." In the situation assumed, British forces had been either destroyed or neutralized, thus permitting German and Italian offensive operations in the western Atlantic. Alternately or concurrently, Japan was assumed to have initiated hostilities in the Pacific.[5] The plan was designed for a war in which enemy capabilities were conceived as including seizure of a base in northeastern North America; hit-and-run submarine, surface, or air attacks; feints or minor attacks anywhere from Greenland to eastern Brazil; fomenting of internal disturbances in Latin American countries; sabotage and subversion; surface or submarine attacks on shipping in the Pacific; and raids on Pacific coastal objectives.[6]

[2] PDB 133-1.
[3] Copies filed at WPD 4330-5 and PDB 133-3.
[4] Copies at PDB 133-5 and -7, respectively.
[5] PDB 133-7.
[6] *Ibid.*

The joint mission was to be carried out through execution of the following joint tasks:

a. Insure the safety of Canadian, United States, and friendly shipping on the high seas.

b. Defend Newfoundland and protect its vital sea communications.

c. Defend the east coast of Canada and the northeastern United States and protect vital sea communications.

d. Defend Alaska and protect its vital sea communications.

e. Defend British Columbia and the northwestern United States and protect vital sea communications.[7]

For the execution of each of these tasks, certain responsibilities were allocated to the Army, Navy, and Air arms of each country. The plan, in addition, set forth the base and defense facilities that were to be provided by each country.[8]

From the statement of joint defense tasks, it is readily apparent that the geographic scope of the 1940 Plan was narrower than either the terms of the Ogdensburg Declaration or the approach of the Canadians in the initial planning paper they presented at the Board meeting on 9 September 1940. Even the statement of the over-all joint mission, "to defend Canada and the United States," was overambitious. As one adviser to the U. S. Army Chief of Staff pointed out, although the joint mission was so written "out of deference to the feelings of the Canadian members of the Board, actually, there can be no serious acceptance of the idea that the defense of other portions of the United States than the areas immediately contiguous to Canada can be considered a joint mission in the execution of which Canada could be expected to afford material contribution." [9] The plan as finally drafted provided for the defense of Newfoundland, Canada, adjacent portions of the United States, and Alaska. Greenland, which had already been the subject of U.S.-Canadian discussions at the political level, was, at the request of the U.S. planners, excluded from the plan.[10]

The last (10 October) draft of the 1940 Plan contained a number of glaring planning gaps. No statement of availability of forces or allocation of detailed tasks was provided. The plan thus failed to show the correlation, if any, between the tasks to be carried out and the forces available for the

[7] *Ibid.*

[8] *Ibid.* These responsibilities and base requirements appear in the First Report of the Permanent Joint Board (reproduced below at Appendix B) substantially as they were stated in the 1940 Plan.

[9] Memo, WPD for CofS, 17 Sep 40, WPD 4330-5.

[10] See Ch. VI, below.

purpose. A second omission presaged a major planning difficulty that was to plague the joint planners many times in the future. This was the question of organization and command, which went completely unmentioned. In reviewing the plan in the War Department General Staff, the War Plans Division viewed the absence of such provisions as its greatest weakness. It proposed the addition of specific provisions, one of which would have vested over-all direction of forces in Newfoundland and Canadian areas in the United States. Another would have vested local military command of troops in Newfoundland and the Maritime Provinces initially in Canada but subsequently in the United States when its forces became preponderant.[11]

Neither the service members of the Permanent Joint Board nor the Board itself seems to have been particularly concerned with the proposed additions, or with further revision of the 1940 Plan. During early 1941 the planners did draft an operational plan based on the concepts of the 1940 Plan, but as a consequence of the British-U.S. staff talks they soon devoted themselves to the preparation of a new plan based on new assumptions. The 1940 Plan was apparently not formally acted upon by the service departments of the two governments, and it remained neither approved nor disapproved. However, the 1940 Plan did retain a recognized status in the Permanent Joint Board on Defense as the initial joint plan and the plan designed for the contingency of British collapse. As time passed this contingency became more remote, and the planners occupied themselves with plans designed to meet new situations.

While the 1940 Plan as such was not approved or otherwise acted upon, the substance thereof was approved by both governments through a separate action. The heart of the 1940 Plan was its statement, for each of the five joint tasks, of the allocation of specific defense responsibilities to each country. The specific defense responsibilities, such as those of the Canadian Army to "provide ground, anti-aircraft and coastal defenses in the Maritime Provinces and the Gaspé Peninsula," were to become effective when the joint plan was placed in effect "by joint direction by the responsible heads of the Canadian and United States Governments." [12]

In order for the 1940 Plan to be put into effect when required, the plan pointed out, it would "be necessary to initiate at once the preparation and provision of the various facilities and resources as set forth." [13] These facilities involved construction of air bases, installation of harbor defenses, and similar measures. When the Board met on 2–4 October 1940, it found that

[11] Memo, WPD for SUSAM, 9 Nov 40, WPD 4330–5.
[12] PDB 133–7.
[13] *Ibid.*

its service members had already produced two joint drafts during the preceding month but had yet to reach full agreement on the plan. When the service members could produce an agreed joint draft of the plan, there still remained the need for its approval by the service departments and then by the two governments before the recommendations could be acted upon. Review and examination of controversial questions, such as the command problem, could be prolonged.

At the October meeting of the Permanent Joint Board the Canadian Section proposed, as a means of shortening this procedure, that the Board draft a report to the two governments embodying the recommendations of the plan under consideration by the service members of the Board. This proposal was adopted, and on 9 October Mr. LaGuardia presented the First Report of the Board to President Roosevelt, while Mr. Biggar took similar action in Ottawa. At the Board meeting of 14 November 1940, the Canadian Section was able to report approval by the Canadian Government.[14] President Roosevelt approved the report on 19 November.[15] These actions in effect approved the provisions of the 1940 Plan for implementation by the two countries, since the report had incorporated them practically verbatim.

The U.S. action on the First Report pointed up a situation fraught with potential difficulties for the War and Navy Departments. The report was submitted to the President by the U.S. chairman without reference to the two departments. Fortunately, through their review of the drafts of the 1940 Plan, it was apparent that the War and Navy Departments were substantially in accord with the contents of the First Report. Direct access by the U.S. chairman to the President permitted a quick cutting of red tape. On the other hand, unless such actions were first fully explored by the service members within their departments, unsound recommendations lacking the support of the departments could go forward to the President. Approval of recommendations made them binding on the departments and would necessitate the awkwardness and complication of an appeal if the departments deemed them unworkable. Continuing close co-ordination by the service members with the War and Navy Department staffs minimized the dangers of this situation.

Early Supply Assistance

Shortly after Dunkerque and the fall of France, and even as the United States was in the midst of denuding itself of military equipment drawn from reserve stocks to aid the United Kingdom, Canada turned to the United

[14] Journal, PDB 124.

[15] WPD 4330–12. For text of the First Report, see Appendix B, below.

States for help in meeting its greatly increased matériel requirements. The initial Canadian approach, made through diplomatic channels in June 1940, was followed up by the presentation on 12 July in Washington by the visiting Canadian staff officers of a list of requirements. This list included the following items: [16]

280,500 Enfield M1917 rifles
20 37-mm. antitank guns
200 Machine guns, caliber .30
600 Lewis machine guns
500 Submachine guns, caliber .45
20 155-mm. field guns
Ammunition for the above

Later the same month a request was made for over a thousand naval guns of calibers up to four inch. At the Ogdensburg meeting on 18 August Prime Minister King presented President Roosevelt with another "List of Urgent Requirements Which It Is Understood May Be Available," on which appeared these items: [17]

150 3-inch antiaircraft guns
250 Light tanks
150 75-mm. field guns
24 155-mm. field guns
10 8-inch railway guns
15 Flying boats
Ammunition for the above

At the first meeting of the Permanent Joint Board on 26–27 August 1940, a restatement of the more urgent Canadian needs was also discussed. Priorities were listed in the following order: antiaircraft artillery, coast and harbor defense matériel, and mobile artillery for the Canadian Army, and patrol and fighter planes for the Royal Canadian Air Force. New requirements, added to the previous lists, included sixty-six searchlights and sixty-six sound locators.

The Canadian Section of the Board was informed at the next meeting, 9 September, of the nature of the available matériel. Thirty-six 3-inch antiaircraft guns were reported to be available, but the Canadian request for these guns was withdrawn later when it was found they were so obsolete as to be virtually useless and had no ammunition. By November the only transfers the United States had been able to make from its depleted stocks totaled

[16] PDB 103–3.
[17] D/S 842.24/72A.

80,000 Enfield rifles, 250 obsolete 6-ton M1917 light tanks, and a few aircraft. Also, Canada had received from the United Kingdom six of the fifty destroyers transferred by the United States under the destroyer-bases agreement. A few other items, notably naval and coast defense guns, were under discussion. But most of the items requested by Canada bore the notation on the consolidated request that had been compiled in the War Department: "no surplus" or "none available." [18] In the light of the limited assistance received from the United States, Prime Minister King was generous in his appreciation when he told the House of Commons, on 12 November 1940, "how much . . . the Canadian war effort owes to the co-operation of the United States. Aircraft and tanks for training purposes, and destroyers for active service, are outstanding among the many essentials of warfare." [19]

The meagerness of U.S. assistance was due, in some measure, to legislative obstacles. An act of Congress of 2 July 1940 had authorized the Secretary of War to dispose of deteriorated, unserviceable, obsolescent, or surplus matériel in a manner that would permit its replacement by other needed matériel.[20] However, an act of 28 June 1940 required that, before any matériel could be disposed of in any manner, the Chief of Staff of the Army or the Chief of Naval Operations must "first certify that such matériel is not essential to the defense of the United States." [21]

The manner in which the United States overcame these barriers was evidenced during the augmentation of the defenses of Newfoundland and the Maritime Provinces. On 28 November 1940 the Canadian Government presented, through the British Purchasing Commission, a request for eight 10-inch disappearing-mount coast defense guns that had been reported at the September Board meeting as being surplus and available. These guns were to be mounted in pairs as part of the defenses at St. John's, Botwood, Shelburne, and Gaspé.[22] Since these guns were considered surplus, the necessary certificate was readily made by Chief of Staff Marshall, and a directive was issued on 14 January 1941 authorizing the transfer.[23]

Attempts at about the same time to augment antiaircraft artillery defenses in Newfoundland did not as easily clear the legal hurdles. Having found it necessary to cancel its request for the thirty-six available 3-inch M1918

[18] Journals, PDB 124 and 103-3.

[19] *H. C. Debates,* 12 Nov 40, p. 53. Another United States measure, the sale of machine tools to Canada, has been credited by one Canadian authority as alone making possible the rapid expansion of Canadian defense production during 1940. (Dawson, *Canada in World Affairs: 1939–1941,* p. 61.)

[20] PL 703, 76th Congress.

[21] PL 671, 76th Congress.

[22] Memo, for President's Liaison Committee, WPD 4323-15.

[23] Memo, SW for USW, WPD 4323-15.

antiaircraft guns because of their obsoleteness and lack of ammunition, Canada sought modern guns of the same type. Such guns were in short supply in the United States, and their transfer would have been in clear violation of Public Law 671. Fortunately, the U.S. Army was concurrently sending its initial garrison of troops to defend the new base at St. John's, and this garrison was to include a battery of antiaircraft artillery. On 6 December 1940 the Chief of Staff approved the recommendation that the equipment of this battery be augmented by the balance of the equipment for an antiaircraft artillery regiment. The additional equipment, which included eight guns, twenty .50-caliber machine guns, ten searchlights, ammunition, directors, and other auxiliary equipment, was loaned to the Canadian Army "for training" and only technically remained in the custody of the handful of U.S. soldiers that accompanied it.[24]

This precedent proved useful, for soon afterward, on 8 January 1941, the Canadian Army member of the Board made an "unofficial suggestion" that the equipment going to Newfoundland also include "a couple of . . . 155-mm. guns and a spot of ammunition" to fill the gap at St. John's while the 10-inch coast defense guns were being installed.[25] Two days later, on 10 January 1941, he was informed that the equipment would include four 155-mm. guns and the ammunition. Such incidents indicate how, within the limits of severe shortages and legislative restrictions, the United States made sincere efforts to accede to Canadian requests.

A similar procedure was effective in providing U.S. matériel to augment Canadian defenses at the Juan de Fuca Strait in the Puget Sound boundary waters area, but in this case an additional problem required solution. On 22 November 1940 Canada informally requested the transfer of four 8-inch railway guns. General Marshall considered this request in conjunction with the one for antiaircraft matériel for Newfoundland. Since no American troops were to be sent to the Canadian west coast, the dispatch of an armed detachment by the neutral United States to a belligerent Canada as custodian for the guns presented complications that did not exist in the Newfoundland situation. Marshall's advisers recommended a declaration of obsolescence. But the Chief of Staff felt that, for the guns in question, such a certificate would be dishonest and asked instead if legal transfer could not be made on the basis of a certificate that such transfer was "in the interest of National Defense of the United States." [26] Since his legal advisers declared this would

---

[24] WPD 4323-9. This matériel was returned near the end of 1942, by which time it had been replaced by Canadian equipment.

[25] Ltr, to SUSAM, 8 Jan 41, PDB 104-4.

[26] Longhand Note, on Memo, ACofS WPD for CofS, 27 Nov 40, WPD 4323-8.

not be legal, the only feasible solution appeared to be the dispatch of U.S. soldiers as custodians. On 18 December 1940 General Marshall and Secretary Stimson approved this solution, which Canada after some discussion accepted. Meanwhile, as a result of U.S. planning for installation of a 16-inch battery whose field of fire would cover part of the Canadian waters, Canada formally requested only two guns.[27] They were shipped soon afterward, accompanied by a few U.S. soldiers acting ostensibly as instructors but actually as custodians.

After Pearl Harbor, when Canada desired further to improve its west coast defenses, a second pair of 8-inch railway guns was loaned for the defense of Prince Rupert, British Columbia. The urgency of the new situation, with the United States now a belligerent and the war expanded into the Pacific, had made for speedy action on the request with a minimum of red tape. On 15 March 1942, two days after the request, the guns were en route.[28]

The scale of U.S. assistance in the pre-Pearl Harbor period and immediately thereafter would appear small unless one considers that the United States was trying to fill tremendous deficiencies in its own rapidly mobilizing Army. At the same time it was trying to meet some of the urgent priority needs of the United Kingdom in order to help the British survive the Battle of Britain. Among additional items supplied to Canada during 1941 were the following:

20,000 M1917 Enfield rifles
25 37-mm. M1916 guns
50 4-inch naval guns
34 3-pounder naval guns
16 155-mm. artillery howitzers
Ammunition, accessories, and spare parts

Within the limits of a more stringent supply position, Canada reciprocated with assistance where possible. After Pearl Harbor the U.S. Army found serious deficiencies in its radar installations at the vital Panama Canal. At the suggestion of Mr. Watson-Watt, a visiting British scientist, Secretary of War Stimson requested of Canadian Minister of National Defense Ralston four early-warning and ground-controlled interception radar sets from Canadian production as a matter of the greatest urgency.[29] The four sets were supplied and installed soon afterward.

[27] Memo, SUSAM for ACofS WPD, 16 May 41, WPD 4323-9.
[28] *Ibid.*
[29] Ltr, 13 Feb 42, PDB 123-1.

Strengthening the Garrisons

After the fall of France had brought the Axis threat appreciably closer to North America, Canada in the summer of 1940 initiated the steps it could, consistent with its commitments and involvement in the European war, to improve defenses in North America. As an early step an infantry battalion, the Black Watch of Montreal, was deployed to Newfoundland Airport (later redesignated Gander Airport) in June 1940 to protect that operational transatlantic ferry base. This measure was the first significant overt expression of the natural Canadian vital concern in the defense of Newfoundland, an interest that before the first Permanent Joint Board meeting was to mature into a general agreement with the Newfoundland Government on questions of defense co-ordination.

Part of the initial Canadian garrison at Newfoundland Airport was a flight of five Digby reconnaissance aircraft. By August a pair of 4.7-inch guns was en route to Bell Island for manning by Newfoundland personnel, and plans were in hand for the establishment of an advanced naval operating base at St. John's. At its 27 August 1940 meeting the Permanent Joint Board on Defense reviewed these dispositions and concluded that they were inadequate. To correct the situation, the Board agreed on its Second Recommendation calling for an increase in the strength of the Newfoundland garrison, an augmentation of its patrol and fighter aircraft forces, the preparation of air bases for garrison by U.S. air units "when and if circumstances require," and such additional measures as examination showed to be necessary.[30] It is significant that the Board did not recommend immediate reinforcement by U.S. forces. The next day the Canadian Government, pursuant to the Board's recommendation for augmentation of the Newfoundland garrison, decided to send an additional infantry battalion and to install 4.7-inch batteries at St. John's and Botwood.[31]

From its inception the Permanent Joint Board was aware that negotiations were in hand for the leasing of bases in Newfoundland to the United States. It took no official notice of them other than in the Second Recommendation until the 11 September meeting, after the signing of the destroyer-bases agreement. The Eighth Recommendation, approved at that meeting, asked the United States expeditiously to initiate such measures under the Second Recommendation as fell "within the limits of the bases . . . being acquired by the United States." [32]

[30] Text at Appendix A, below.
[31] Journal, 9–11 Sep 40 PJBD meeting, PDB 124.
[32] Appendix A, below.

360-477 O - 70 - 8

At the 2 October 1940 Board meeting the decision of the United States to send a regiment, less one battalion of infantry, with supporting troops to Newfoundland was made known to the Canadian Section. Winter weather handicapped construction of quarters, and the initial force of 58 officers and 919 enlisted men that arrived at St. John's on 29 January 1941 was quartered aboard the USAT *Edmund B. Alexander* (formerly the *America*) until May or June. By that time tent camps had been completed, barracks construction was under way, and the Fort Pepperrell garrison, consisting of the 3d Battalion, 3d Infantry, a battery of the 57th Coast Artillery (Harbor Defense), and a battery of the 62d Coast Artillery (Antiaircraft), came ashore to stay.

The U.S. Navy had meanwhile begun construction of the naval air station at Argentia in December 1940, and, on 25 January 1941, a detachment comprising 3 officers and 108 men of the 3d Provisional Marine Company landed there. The Argentia facility, which was presently expanded to include a naval operating base, was commissioned on 15 July 1941. As early as two months before that date, two seaplane tenders and four destroyers were based at Argentia.

The U.S. Army had also desired to establish an air garrison in Newfoundland, but was faced with the difficulty of doing so before the construction of an airfield could be completed on one of the leased sites. Although the President had earlier rejected the Air Corps' plea to include Gander Airport as one of the leased areas, the War Department with the support of Mayor LaGuardia renewed its request on 28 November 1940, this time for the lease of land adjacent to the airport so that it could be used for urgently needed training of a composite group of U.S. Army aircraft. At the urging of the President the War and Navy Departments restudied the problem and, on 30 January 1941, recommended that a lease not be sought but that an informal basis for stationing an air unit at Gander be worked out with Canada through the Permanent Joint Board. The President approved this recommendation and the suggestion that appropriate language be included in the leased-bases agreement to provide for the status of forces stationed outside the areas of the leased bases. This action was apparently the genesis of Article XIX of the leased-bases agreement.[33]

Although the informal arrangements worked out provided that Canada would make available facilities for two U.S. squadrons by 1 May 1941 and

[33] Ltr, SW to President, 28 Nov 40, WPD 4351-9; Ltr, LaGuardia to President, 29 Nov 40, and Memos, President for SW and Secy Navy, 30 Nov 40, all in Roosevelt Papers, Official File 4101; Ltr, SW and Secy Navy to President, 30 Jan 41, Roosevelt Papers, Secy's File, Box 78; JPC Rpt, 8 Jan 41, WPD 4404-2; Ch. VII, below.

the balance of the facilities by early autumn, it soon became evident that these facilities would not materialize on schedule. The delay appeared to be connected with the unanswered question of responsibility for the defense of Newfoundland.

The first joint effort to resolve the question of defense responsibilities in Newfoundland had been in the First Report of the Permanent Joint Board, approved at the 2-4 October 1940 meeting. In the report, Canada had been assigned the responsibility for the "initial" defense of Newfoundland "except insofar as the United States . . . [might] be in a position to participate in such initial defense."[34] Subsequent discussions of the command question revealed that U.S. willingness to accept the assignment of the "initial" defense responsibility to Canada was based on the expectation that, as soon as U.S. forces outnumbered Canadian forces, the responsibility would pass to the United States.

On 27 March 1941, the same day that the detailed leased-bases agreement between the United Kingdom and the United States was signed, a protocol was signed at Canadian instance by these two governments and Canada delineating the Canadian role in the defense of Newfoundland. According to the protocol, the signatories (a) recognized that Newfoundland defense was an integral part of the Canadian defense scheme, (b) agreed that Canadian defense interests would be respected, (c) continued in effect existing arrangements made through the Permanent Joint Board on Defense, and (d) provided for inclusion of Canada in certain consultations under the leased-bases agreement.[35] Canada in requesting that the protocol be signed signified its unwillingness to have the defense of Newfoundland become a U.S. responsibility or to allow the United States to assume the leading role in that defense.[36]

The United States, on the other hand, was apparently not entirely satisfied with the defensive scheme and with the progress of the Gander Airport arrangements. Immediately after the leased-bases agreement was signed, the United States under the authority of Article XIX asked the United Kingdom to approve the dispatch of U.S. air forces to Gander Airport on a temporary basis until such time as U.S. air-base construction was completed. The United Kingdom gave its approval on 8 April 1941 and undertook to inform the governments of Canada and Newfoundland.[37]

[34] Appendix B, below.

[35] EAS, 235; CTS, 1941, No. 2.

[36] D/S Telg 973, to London, 22 Mar 41, PDB 107-9; *H. C. Debates*, 27 Mar 41, p. 1904; Dawson, *Canada in World Affairs; 1939–1941*, p. 217.

[37] WPD Memo/Conv, Col Crawford and Hickerson, 11 Apr 41, which cites telegram of 9 April from London, PDB 107-9. The United States request also sought authority for similar emergency deployments to Bermuda and Trinidad.

The arrangement came as a surprise to Canada, and at the 16–17 April 1941 meeting of the Permanent Joint Board the U.S. Section explained the "sequence of events which led to the decision," pointing out that the arrangement made by Prime Minister Churchill and President Roosevelt envisaged that the action would be taken in consultation with the Board.[38] The arrival in Newfoundland on 1 May 1941 of the reinforcements, the 21st Reconnaissance Squadron of six B–18 medium bombardment aircraft, two 8-inch guns, and miscellaneous small units, raised the garrison by 646 to a total of 1,666 officers and enlisted men.[39]

In keeping with the tripartite protocol, the mission and responsibility of the U.S. garrison (designated the Newfoundland Base Command) was defined to include the defense of the U.S. bases, co-operation with Canadian and British forces in defending Newfoundland and adjacent Canada, the support of U.S. Navy forces, and the destruction of any German or Italian forces encountered.[40] Although the assigned missions of U.S. and Canadian forces technically did not overlap, had enemy attack on Newfoundland actually occurred, operations by the two sets of forces would have been substantially the same in nature and scope. A critical need for co-ordinated command would have existed. The need was recognized and was long a preoccupation of the commanders in Newfoundland and of higher-level staffs.[41]

The United States continued to reinforce its ground and air garrison in Newfoundland, which had reached a strength of 2,383 by 1 December 1941. In August the 41st Reconnaissance Squadron of eight B–17B Flying Fortress aircraft had replaced the 21st Squadron, and on the eve of Pearl Harbor another squadron of B–17B aircraft was preparing to move to Newfoundland. The first attack by these units on Axis submarines had occurred on 27 October 1941, two days after the initial RCAF attack. With the intensification of submarine warfare in the western Atlantic after 7 December, air attacks on submarines became more numerous.[42]

The Canadian Army defense garrison in Newfoundland by mid-July 1941 had increased to 2,389, and included two infantry battalions and antiaircraft and coast defense artillery units. Additional deployments totaling 1,298

[38] Memo/Conv, Robertson and Moffat, 10 Apr 41, Moffat Diary; Journal, PDB 124.

[39] The Canadian Government had itself increased the RCAF garrison by moving to Newfoundland on 11 April, apparently as a countermove upon learning of the U.S. plan, No. 10 Bomber Reconnaissance Squadron, which had had a flight of five aircraft in Newfoundland since June 1940.

[40] Craven and Cate (eds.) *Plans and Early Operations*, p. 156.

[41] See Ch. V, below.

[42] Craven and Cate (eds.), *Plans and Early Operations*, p. 157; Memo, E. M. Watson for President, 27 Oct 41, Roosevelt Papers, Secy's File Box 78.

were planned by 1 September 1941 in order to increase the Canadian infantry garrison to three battalions—Les Fusiliers de Sherbrooke at St. John's, the Lincoln and Welland Regiment at Gander Airport, and the Prince Edward Island Highlanders at Botwood. The Royal Canadian Air Force concurrently operated a bomber reconnaissance squadron of B-18 aircraft from Gander Airport.

The Maritime Provinces, according to the Permanent Joint Board's Third Recommendation, had a strategic importance "similar to that of Newfoundland."[43] Here, too, the defenses were designed to meet enemy capabilities which, until such time as Britain might fall, were estimated to include bombardment by one or two naval vessels, minor submarine or surface raids, and occasional nuisance air attacks. The Maritime Provinces were more heavily defended than Newfoundland. The garrisons there, unlike those in Newfoundland, included not only the operational defensive deployments of the Canadian Army Atlantic Command and the Royal Canadian Air Force Eastern Air Command but also additional units in various states of mobilization and training. The Royal Canadian Navy Atlantic Coast command was also based on ports in the Maritime Provinces. As the Second Recommendation indicates, the required additions to the Maritime Provinces defenses were not infantry or artillery ground defense forces but special harbor defense and similar measures.

In February 1941 Canadian Army Atlantic Command forces in the Maritime Provinces included the 3d Infantry Division and four infantry and two machine gun battalions, while substantial additions to the coastal defense establishments were under way. The Eastern Air Command concurrently based approximately three bomber reconnaissance squadrons in the Provinces, plus a number of other units in varying states of formation and equipment. Ten months later, on 17 December 1941, the Canadian Army Atlantic Command garrisons included the following numbers and units:[44]

Total	27,628
Maritime Provinces	10,839
5 infantry battalions	
2 machine gun battalions	
14 coast and antiaircraft artillery batteries	
4 searchlight batteries	
Newfoundland	3,975
3 infantry battalions	
3 artillery batteries	
General reserve	12,814
1 infantry division (less certain units)	

[43] Appendix A, below.
[44] Memo, SUSAM for ACofS WPD, 27 Jan 42, PDB 135-2.

The United States provided no part of the garrisons in the Maritime Provinces, but it had been given the responsibility of reinforcing them in the event of a major attack.[45]

On the North Pacific littoral, the defense of Alaska was primarily the concern of the United States. For more than a year Permanent Joint Board recommendations with regard to Alaska were limited to two relating to the air staging route. This is probably a reflection of the state of affairs up until Pearl Harbor. During this period Canada, which was using the recommendations made in the Board as a means of achieving its immediate military objectives, had only a secondary interest in Alaska. However, the 1940 Plan and the First Report based thereon both included provisions for Alaskan defense. These provisions were probably the result of the necessarily over-all approach of the strategic planning studies. Through the medium of the Board, Canada maintained an active interest in U.S. defensive preparations in Alaska, and these preparations were reported on regularly at Board meetings. Naturally, interest was intensified after the beginning of the war with Japan.

The fall of France had given impetus to the development of U.S. defensive installations in Alaska, but considerable time was required before appropriations could be converted into facilities and garrisons. At the time of the establishment of the Permanent Joint Board, U.S. Army forces in Alaska numbered about 1,200 officers and enlisted men.[46]

The First Report of the Board charged Canada with the development of air staging facilities between Alaska and the United States and the United States with the completion of Army bases at Anchorage and Fairbanks, Navy bases at Sitka, Kodiak, and Dutch Harbor, and air bases at Ketchikan, Yakutat, Cordova, Anchorage, Bethel, Nome, and Fairbanks. The United States was assigned the responsibility of providing the necessary defense forces, while Canada was to support these forces if required. Unlike the Permanent Joint Board recommendations for the east coast, those for the west coast did not specify the strength of the Alaska garrisons. But the Board did monitor regularly the reports submitted at Board meetings on the progress of construction and the reinforcement of the garrisons. By the end of 1940, reinforcements had increased the strength of U.S. Army units in Alaska to over 4,000.

During 1941 a build-up of the garrisons at the U.S. bases in Alaska occurred as rapidly as the construction of facilities permitted. By 30 No-

[45] First Report, Appendix B, below.

[46] For accounts of the pre-Pearl Harbor development of Alaskan defenses, see Watson, *Chief of Staff: Prewar Plans and Preparations*, pp. 454–58; Morison, *The Battle of the Atlantic*, pp. 163–65; and Craven and Cate (eds.), *Plans and Early Operations*, pp. 166–70.

vember 1941 an Army and Air Forces strength of 21,945 was reached, of which the major elements were two infantry regiments, four infantry battalions, one pursuit squadron, and two bomber squadrons.[47]

The pre-Pearl Harbor story was generally the same for the Canadian Pacific coast and the U.S. Atlantic and Pacific coasts. The formal recommendations of the Permanent Joint Board virtually ignored the defensive requirements of these areas. The broader approach of the 1940 Plan, and of the First Report framed thereon, had made some provision for these areas:

a. On the Atlantic coast, the United States was to reinforce the Maritime Provinces in case of major attack and to develop the transportation facilities necessary to permit such action.

b. On its Pacific coast, the United States was to provide coast defense and air bases in the boundary waters area, to control and protect shipping, and to provide a one-division mobile reserve for employment in the boundary area.

c. Canada, on its Pacific coast, was to provide coast and air defense facilities, naval and coastal defense in selected areas, and the initial ground, antiaircraft, coast, and air defense of British Columbia.[48]

The U.S. drafters apparently attached the same significance to the word "initial" in the requirements for British Columbia as they did in the case of Newfoundland.

Ten days after Pearl Harbor the strength of the Canadian Army Pacific Command garrisons on the west coast totaled 9,473 and included three infantry battalions, eight artillery battalions, and a general reserve of one infantry brigade, one field artillery regiment, and one reconnaissance battalion. Although the United States nominally established Northeast and Western Defense Commands for its east and west coasts on 17 March 1941, the defense requirements of the western portions of both countries remained in a lower priority than the eastern portions until after the Japanese attack on 7 December.

ABC-1 and ABC-22

When the service members of the Permanent Joint Board prepared the first joint draft of the 1940 Plan on 11 September 1940, they based it on "strength actually existing" and indicated a need for subsequent plans, including a 1941 plan based on the estimated strength as of 1 May 1941.[49] By the time of the 20 January 1941 meeting, the Board noted that the 1940 Plan

[47] Western Defense Command, History of the Western Defense Command, Vol. I, Annex D, OCMH.

[48] See Appendix B, below.

[49] First Joint Draft of 1940 Plan, WPD 4330-5.

was obsolete and that a 1941 plan was already being discussed by the service members. But the planning process was complicated by events that were taking place. The first of the British-U.S. staff meetings was held a few days after the January Board meeting, and these meetings continued during the next two months.[50]

During this period work on a new U.S.-Canadian plan marked time, and on 27 February the Board was informed at its meeting in Buffalo that preparatory work on the 1941 plan had not progressed sufficiently far for a meeting of the service members to be useful. Nevertheless, the Board, in the absence of General Embick who was the senior U.S. Army representative in the British-U.S. conversations, discussed at length the need for further plans. It recognized that in addition to planning for the contingency of a British collapse, a plan was needed that would provide for the contingency of U.S. entry into the European war.[51] This recognition was probably the initial impact on the views of the Board of the U.S.-British conference, whose entire effort was devoted to planning for that contingency.

Between 27 February and 27 March the British-U.S. planners drafted their report at informal sessions on the basis of the exchange of views during the preceding plenary sessions. The report stated that Canadian military representatives were associated with the United Kingdom delegation throughout the course of these conversations but were not present at joint meetings.[52] Neither the minutes of the joint meetings nor pertinent U.S. working papers cast any light on the character of the association.[53]

Whatever the nature of the United Kingdom-Canadian association during the conversations, the report thereon had several significant effects on the development of U.S.-Canadian planning:

a. The conference agreed that the "High Command of the United States and United Kingdom . . . [would] collaborate continuously in the formulation and execution of strategical policies and plans which . . . [should] govern the conduct of the war." The fuller significance of this assumption of supreme direction is apparent in the word "Command," whose singular form was a change from the plural of an earlier draft.[54]

b. The strategic concept and the principal policies for achieving the objective of "the defeat of Germany and her Allies" were offensive in nature, although the detailed war plan provided for the many defensive tasks that

[50] See Ch. III, above.
[51] Journal, PDB 124.
[52] *Pearl Harbor Attack*, Pt. 15, p. 1485.
[53] These minutes and papers are filed in several folders in WPD 4402-89.
[54] BUS(J)(41)22, OPD Exec 4, Item 11.

would also need to be performed. United States-Canadian planning had been entirely defensive in its approach.

c. Upon entering the war, the United States was to assume responsibility for the strategic direction of U.S., British, and other associated military forces in the Western Hemisphere except "the waters and territories in which Canada assumes responsibility for the strategic direction of military forces, as may be defined in the United States-Canada joint agreements."[55]

d. The report agreed on "principles of command" that envisaged a superior commander of one country commanding troops of other countries through their own national commanders.

The final editing of the report took place on 27 March 1941, although the minutes of the fourteenth and last meeting on 29 March record formal approval as of 29 March. At this meeting the short title "ABC-1" was assigned to the document, whose full title was "United States-British Staff Conversations, Report." There appears to be no evidence to support a theory that Canada alone among the other associated powers was singled out for inclusion in the short title, in which the letters A and B stood for American and British, despite the fact that the ABC usage was soon adopted by the United States and Canada, which gave the short title ABC-22 to their next defense plan.[56]

By the time the British-U.S. meetings ended, the service members of the Permanent Joint Board had prepared two distinct joint draft plans. Plan 1, which had already passed through several joint drafts, was an implementation of the 1940 Plan and was based on the concept of a joint U.S.-Canadian war effort without outside aid. Plan 2 was based on a different concept and different assumptions and envisaged the contingency of U.S. entry into the war alongside Great Britain, as contemplated in ABC-1.[57]

The Senior U.S. Army Member of the Permanent Joint Board submitted the draft of Plan 1, which was in the more advanced state, to the War Plans Division of the War Department General Staff. In commenting on this draft the War Plans Division, by that time apparently confident of British success in the Battle of Britain, expressed the principal criticism that a greater

[55] *Pearl Harbor Attack*, Pt. 15, p. 1485 *et passim*.

[56] The "C" in ABC stood for conversations or conference (or possibly Commonwealth). The statement of General of the Army H. H. Arnold, wartime commander of the Army Air Forces, in *Global Mission* (New York: Harper & Brothers, 1949), p. 255, that the ABC plan referred to America-British-China is inaccurate. Besides ABC-22, another offspring of ABC-1 was the ADB report of the American-Dutch-British conversations in Singapore in April 1941. This detailed plan for the conduct of Far East operations is reproduced in *Pearl Harbor Attack*, Pt. 15, pp. 1551-84.

[57] Memo, SUSAM for CofS, 31 Mar 41, PDB 135-2.

need existed for a plan based on the hypothesis that the United States might find it necessary to enter the war and fight with Great Britain. The War Plans Division also felt that matters of strategic direction and command were not adequately covered.[58]

As a result of lack of War Department support for further planning based on Plan 1, no more work was done on it. A few days after War Plans Division criticized Plan 1, the Senior U.S. Army Member of the Permanent Joint Board was able to respond by submitting a new draft of Joint Canadian-United States Basic Defense Plan 2, dated 10 April 1941 and bearing the short title "ABC-22."[59] Although this draft was based on the pertinent assumptions in ABC-1, War Plans Division also took exception to Plan 2, again because of the provisions on strategic direction and command.[60]

By this time the questions of command and strategic direction had become a major issue in the Board, the service departments, and to some extent, the political departments of the two countries.[61] United States service proposals for vesting in the United States the strategic direction of forces in Newfoundland and certain Canadian areas were not acceptable but were argued for over a month while planning ceased. Agreement in principle was reached in the Board at the 28-29 May 1941 meeting. This agreement permitted the service members on 4 June to agree on a revised joint draft of ABC-22. The War Plans Division still considered the command arrangements defective but was willing to interpose no objection to the acceptance of the new draft.[62] On 11 June the Senior Canadian Army Member of the Board submitted a number of amendments to Plan 2, one of which called for the establishment of a Canadian military mission in Washington. This new proposal was followed on 1 July by a formal Canadian request for a mission, and, from that time until the United States replied on 25 July, ABC-22 planning languished.[63] Thereafter, although Canada failed to get its military mission in Washington and the United States failed to get the arrangement it desired for strategic direction of forces in Newfoundland and certain Canadian areas, the questions were resolved, at least for the time being, and at the 29-30 July 1941 Board meeting the service members could report agreement on Plan 2.

[58] Memo, for SUSAM, 7 Apr 41, WPD 4330-21.

[59] This was the first use of the designation ABC-22. The meaning of the number "22" and its relation, if any, to the numbers assigned to the two reports of the ABC conversations, ABC-1 and ABC-2, are not recorded in U.S. files.

[60] Memo, for SUSAM, 2 May 41, WPD 4330-22.

[61] A full account is contained in Chapter V, below.

[62] 1st Ind, to SUSAM, 17 Jun 42, PDB 135-2.

[63] See Chapter III, above, for an account of the negotiations and their bearing on the question of command.

ABC-22 was formally reviewed in the U.S. War and Navy Departments and was approved by the Secretary of the Navy on 16 August and by the Secretary of War on 18 August 1941. The two Secretaries transmitted the plan to President Roosevelt on 20 August 1941 recommending that he approve it, and he did so on 29 August. The President's action on ABC-22 contrasted sharply with that on ABC-1, which he saw fit only to note and to instruct that it be returned for approval if the United States should enter the war.[64] Review of the plan proceeded more slowly in Canada, where "supplementary questions" were still being asked in early October. On 15 October 1941 the Cabinet War Committee finally gave the government's approval to ABC-22.[65]

In its broad outlines ABC-22 differed only slightly from the aborted Plan 1 and its predecessor, the 1940 Plan. The ABC-22 tasks were those required for the defense of northern North America (less Greenland) in an offensive war against Germany. Whereas the 1940 Plan called for protection of only such overseas shipping as was on the high seas when the plan was put into effect, ABC-22 included as a major task the continuing protection of overseas shipping throughout the western Atlantic and the Pacific areas. The defensive tasks were otherwise substantially the same. Naturally, under the different assumptions of the two plans, different estimates of enemy capabilities called for different defensive deployments and strengths. Both plans were capabilities plans, rather than requirements plans, and set forth only the forces actually available for execution of the necessary tasks.

Command, which had not been specifically touched upon in the 1940 Plan, was in ABC-22 to be co-ordinated through mutual co-operation, except where special agreements were made for unified commands. With one exception, the defense responsibility, in each land area, and presumably the command responsibility as well, was assigned to the sovereign country. In Newfoundland, where neither Canada nor the United States was sovereign, the defense was made a common task of the U.S. and Canadian Armies and the Royal Canadian Air Force. In the only other area where the two countries had equal juridical status, the defense responsibility was assigned, in consonance with the *status quo,* to the United States. This was on the high seas, in the northern portions of the Pacific and western Atlantic Ocean areas, where the United States was made responsible for the protection of shipping. One clause in the plan provided that, if circumstances warranted,

[64] Memo, Secy GS for CofS, 29 Aug 41, PDB 135-2; Matloff and Snell, *Strategic Planning for Coalition Warfare, 1941-1942,* p. 46. The memorandum is contained in *Pearl Harbor Attack,* Pt. 3, p. 997; see also pp. 993-96.

[65] Ltr, Pope to Embick, 16 Oct 41, PDB 135-2.

the forces of one country might temporarily extend their operations into the other country.

The plan was to go into effect when directed by the two governments. As a war plan, most of its provisions would be acted upon only when it was placed in effect. Like the 1940 Plan, ABC-22 included a statement of the facilities to be provided by each country. In the Annex to ABC-22, the planners had found it necessary only to list these facilities, since arrangements for their provision had already been agreed upon in the First Report of the Permanent Joint Board or in subsequent recommendations. ABC-22 was the last joint U.S.-Canadian defense plan prepared by the service members of the Permanent Joint Board on Defense during World War II.

Putting Plans Into Action

Even before ABC-22 was completed the preparation of the subordinate plans necessary to translate its broad allocations of missions into detailed operating plans for field commands had already been begun. In the United States, the joint Army-Navy RAINBOW plans provided the approved basis for detailed service planning. While ABC-22 was being drafted, the U.S. Joint Planning Committee was given new direction in its work on Joint Army and Navy Basic War Plan—RAINBOW 5, which was now to be based on ABC-1 and ABC-22.[66] As a matter of fact, when ABC-22 was completed, it was appended as Annex II to RAINBOW 5, which had been approved by the Secretaries of War and the Navy on 2 June and 28 May 1941, respectively. The joint Army-Navy plan RAINBOW 5 became the basis of the more detailed War Department Operations Plan—RAINBOW 5, and the Navy Basic War Plan—RAINBOW 5. These in turn were the basis for plans of the defense commands, departments, naval coastal frontiers, and other subordinate Army and Navy commands. All of these plans therefore reflected the basic allocations and provisions of ABC-22. In a few instances implementation of ABC-22 took the form of preparation of local joint U.S.-Canadian plans in boundary areas of mutual interest. But in the area in most urgent need of such a plan, Newfoundland, no co-ordinated planning took place until after Pearl Harbor.

The first local plan had been drafted for the Puget Sound-Juan de Fuca Strait area in Washington State and British Columbia many months before the drafting of ABC-22. The problem of co-ordination of defenses there occasioned an inspection trip to the area in September 1940 by Brigadier

[66] Matloff and Snell, *Strategic Planning for Coalition Warfare, 1941–1942*, pp. 40–46. For an account of RAINBOW planning, see Cline, *Washington Command Post: The Operations Division*, pp. 55–59, and Matloff and Snell, Ch. I.

Stuart, the Canadian Army Board member, and Colonel McNarney, the U.S. Army Air Corps officer on the Permanent Joint Board. After conferring with the harbor defense commanders of the two countries in the area, Stuart and McNarney recommended to their departments that a joint plan for the area be prepared. Accordingly, the War Department on 28 September 1940 directed the Commanding General, Fourth Army, to initiate the planning.[67] On 21–22 October a joint board of five U.S. and Canadian officers made a complete study of the problem on the ground, discussed it with the local commanding officers, and drafted an International Joint Defense Plan for Strait of Juan de Fuca and Puget Sound Area.[68] The conclusions and recommendations of this plan called for installation of certain additional armament, improvement of communications, preparation of joint codes, exchange of liaison officers, and other measures. Most of the recommendations, modified in some instances after review in Washington and Ottawa, were placed in effect and became the first co-operative measures between commands of the two countries on tactical levels.

Subsequent to the U.S. approval of ABC–22, a joint area plan based thereon was prepared for all of the U.S.-Canadian west coast, including Alaska, as a result of War Department instructions issued on 29 September 1941.[69] A defensive plan, with short title "ABC(Pacific)–22," was completed and approved as of 22 January 1942 (for the United States) by the Commanding General, Western Defense Command, and the Commander, Pacific Northern Naval Coastal Frontier, and (for Canada) by the General Officer Commanding-in-Chief, Pacific Command; Commanding Officer, Pacific Coast (Royal Canadian Navy); and the Air Officer Commanding, Western Air Command.

The real and more important implementation of ABC–22 was the action on the measures it set forth as necessary to permit the carrying out of the plan. These measures called for construction or installation of certain defensive works, operational bases, and logistical facilities. Although ABC–22 was presumably not in effect until so ordered, work on these essential measures listed in the plan was put under way at once, long before the plan was officially placed in effect.

Once the Canadian Government had, on 15 October 1941, matched the earlier action of the U.S. Government in approving ABC–22, this plan had not long to remain on the shelf of war plans before it was put into effect. The Japanese struck Pearl Harbor at 1:25 P.M. (Washington time) on 7 December 1941. At 10:25 A.M. the next morning, General Embick, the

[67] WPD 4330–9.
[68] Copy filed at WPD 4330–9.
[69] History of the Western Defense Command, I, 10.

Senior U.S. Army Member of the Permanent Joint Board, telephoned Brigadier Pope, his opposite number in Ottawa, that the United States had placed ABC-22 in effect "as it applies to Japan," and requested similar action by the Canadian Government. A telephone call the same afternoon between these two officers reported that the same action had been ordered by the Canadian Minister of National Defense.[70] At 4:10 P.M. that afternoon President Roosevelt approved the joint resolution of Congress declaring the existence of a state of war between the United States and Japan. Canada, already at war with two of the Axis Powers, formalized the existence of a state of war with Japan by an order-in-council of 7 December.[71]

On 11 December Congress passed, and the President approved at 3:05 P.M., similar joint resolutions regarding Germany and Italy.[72] Four hours earlier the Chief of Staff had issued orders to his subordinate field commanders placing Joint Army and Navy Basic War Plan—RAINBOW 5, and the corresponding War Department Operations Plan, in effect. The ABC-22 plan, as Annex II to RAINBOW 5, went into general effect at that time. The comparable Canadian action was reported on 22 December, when the U.S. Section of the Board was advised that the Canadian Government had instructed the Canadian Chiefs of Staff "to place ABC-22 in effect without qualification.[73]

[70] Confirming Memos, 8 Dec 41, PDB 135-2.
[71] PL 328, 77th Congress; Privy Council 9592.
[72] PL 331, and 332, 77th Congress.
[73] Ltr, Pope to U.S. Section, PDB 135-2.

CHAPTER V

Organization and Command

The several joint strategic defense plans whose preparation was undertaken pursuant to the Seventh Recommendation of the Permanent Joint Board on Defense necessarily concerned themselves with problems of co-ordination and command jurisdiction. Divergent U.S. and Canadian points of view regarding the solution of these problems were intensified after Pearl Harbor had brought the war to the threshold of the United States. This was due to U.S. unwillingness to leave in the hands of another power the defense of contiguous border areas whose adequate defense was vital to the security of the United States.

Other factors added to the complexity of the problem of U.S.-Canadian co-ordination after Pearl Harbor. Until then the joint relationship involved a common defense problem to be worked out on a mutual basis using newly developed patterns and precedents. After 7 December 1941 certain important continental defense requirements continued to exist, but the principal foci of U.S. military interest shifted from North America to Europe and North Africa, and to Alaska and the mid-Pacific islands. Canada thus became to the United States primarily a territory astride or bordering on essential ground, air, and sea lines of communications to the areas in which the major engagements with the Axis forces were to take place.

Within Canadian territory a vast complex of logistical facilities became necessary for the support of friendly forces in combat zones. The United States, with its preponderance of resources, undertook the development of the greater part of the logistical facilities required in Canada and in the North American areas. The development work took on, to a large extent, the appearance of a U.S.-directed unilateral operation on Canadian territory, with Canada providing rights of way, auxiliary facilities, and the like. Logistical tasks, although of joint interest, did not lend themselves to joint direction as did defense tasks, since they were undertaken primarily by the United States and principally with its own resources.

As more logistical tasks were undertaken, the movement into Canada of U.S. construction, communications, and other organizations mushroomed rapidly. The functioning of this quickly growing establishment presented many new problems of co-ordination, political and military, from the governmental level to the lowest operating echelons.

Unity of Operational Command

Disagreements between Canada and the United States over the command question had begun when the first joint defense plan, the 1940 Plan, was drafted. No direct command provisions were incorporated in it, although allocations of territorial responsibilities were made that presumably included command responsibility. The 1940 Plan set forth the following allocation of defense responsibilities: [1]

a. All Canadian territory, to Canada.

b. All U.S. territory, including Alaska, to the United States.

c. Newfoundland—to Canada, the "initial . . . defenses, except in so far as the United States . . . [might] be in a position to participate in such initial defense"; to the United States, the defense of U.S. bases.

d. Control of shipping in the Atlantic approaches to North America, to Canada. (The Royal Canadian Navy was already handling the task.)

e. Canadian coastal waters, to Canada.

f. United States coastal waters and all North American offshore sea approaches, to the United States, except for air patrol of approaches to Newfoundland and eastern Canada by the Royal Canadian Air Force.

In U.S. and Canadian territorial waters and land areas, the assignment of responsibilities was strictly along lines of national sovereignty. In Newfoundland, governed by the United Kingdom through a Royal Commission and soon to be garrisoned by U.S. as well as Canadian forces, the responsibilities overlapped. In addition, the provision of the plan allocating initial over-all defense responsibility for Newfoundland to Canada implied subsequent allocation of the responsibility to the United States.

The allocation of responsibilities in the North Atlantic approaches to North America reflected the close liaison that was developing among the naval services of Canada, the United Kingdom, and the United States. A big factor in the agreement on command arrangements based on military principles that U.S. officers considered soundest was the fact that arrangements on the high seas were not inhibited by considerations of national sovereignty or by historic U.S. and Canadian psychological attitudes.[2]

The U.S. service members of the Permanent Joint Board had foreseen the need for guidance on the command question immediately after the first Board meeting and before the drafting of the 1940 Plan. The Chief of Staff on 9 September agreed that the United States should propose to assume pri-

[1] The 1940 Plan is filed at PDB 133-5.

[2] For a brief account of the joint naval operations in the North Atlantic, see Chapter IX, below.

mary responsibility for the defense of the Maritime Provinces through their inclusion in the New England Sector of the frontier coastal defense system. For the time being, no defense or command responsibility was to be sought in Newfoundland or British Columbia.[3] Actually, as each of the drafts of the 1940 Plan was prepared, including the last (10 October 1940), no command provisions whatever were included.

The War Department General Staff, in reviewing the plan in November 1940, felt that the lack of provisions as to organization and command should be corrected, since the task of co-ordinating the five separate forces involved (two armies, two navies, and one air force) by mutual co-operation would present "a most difficult problem." The War Plans Division proposed that the Maritime Provinces, Newfoundland, and British Columbia be included as sectors of the U.S. North Atlantic and Pacific Coastal Frontiers. The sectors would remain under Canadian tactical command except that the United States would assume command in the Maritime Provinces or Newfoundland sectors when its forces in either had reached certain levels that would make them preponderant.[4]

There were several other requirements for command and co-ordination arrangements for which the 1940 Plan failed to provide:

a. Co-ordination of the U.S. and Canadian garrisons in Newfoundland and of their overlapping responsibilities.

b. Establishment of a unified defense command in the Strait of Juan de Fuca area, where the boundary divided into two parts, and thereby weakened, a defense that was militarily a single entity.

c. Co-ordinated direction of forces on adjacent sides of the boundaries in other border areas.

d. Some means of over-all direction or co-ordination of the multiplicity of commands involved in the defense of northern North America.

With the establishment of the U.S. Army defense commands in 1941, the principal commanders whose co-operation and co-ordination were required were as follows:[5]

Canada	*United States*
	East Coast
Commodore Commanding Newfoundland Force (Royal Canadian Navy)	Commander in Chief, United States Atlantic Fleet (U.S. Navy)
Commanding Officer, Atlantic Coast (Royal Canadian Navy)	Task Force Commander, United States Atlantic Fleet (U.S. Navy)

[3] Memo, SUSAM for CofS, 7 Sep 40, approved by the Chief of Staff 9 Sep 40, WPD 4330-4.
[4] Memo, WPD for SUSAM, 9 Nov 40, WPD 4330-5.
[5] The commanders are listed in ABC-22, reproduced in *Pearl Harbor Attack,* Pt. 15, p. 1588.

360-477 O - 70 - 9

Canada	*United States*
East Coast	
Air Officer Commanding, Eastern Air Command (Royal Canadian Air Force)	Commander, North Atlantic Naval Coastal Frontier (U.S. Navy)
General Officer Commanding-in-Chief, Atlantic Command (Canadian Army)	Commanding General, Northeast Defense Command (and the subordinate Newfoundland Base Command) (U.S. Army)
	Commanding General, General Headquarters (U.S. Army)
West Coast	
Commanding Officer, Pacific Coast (Royal Canadian Navy)	Commander in Chief, United States Pacific Fleet (U.S. Navy)
Air Officer Commanding, Western Air Command (Royal Canadian Air Force)	Task Force Commander, United States Pacific Fleet (U.S. Navy)
General Officer Commanding-in-Chief, Pacific Command (Canadian Army)	Commander, Pacific Northern Naval Coastal Frontier (U.S. Navy)
	Commanding General, Western Defense Command (and the subordinate Alaska Defense Command) (U.S. Army)

In the conversations between United Kingdom and U.S. service representatives in early 1941, it was agreed that in any given area unified direction of all forces should be exercised by whichever of the two countries was assigned responsibility for the area. This agreement was not intended to prejudice such arrangements as Canada and the United States might make in their joint plans, but it undoubtedly strengthened the U.S. resolve to press for what it considered a sound military solution of the command question.

When joint planning with Canada was resumed in March 1941, the U.S. service members of the Permanent Joint Board incorporated the U.S. views on command and organization in a draft U.S.-Canadian joint defense plan for ground and air operations.[6] The provisions of the plan called for the addition to the U.S. Northeast and Western Defense Commands of three sectors, comprising the Maritime Provinces, Newfoundland, and British Columbia. United States officers were to control the defense commands and the U.S. sectors thereof. The three sectors to be added would be commanded by Canadian officers, and command of the Newfoundland sector would pass to the United States when prescribed levels had been reached by U.S. forces. Liaison between the two countries in regard to the strategic direction of the two defense commands would be effected through military missions to be exchanged between Ottawa and Washington.

In their first counterproposal, of 14 April, the Canadian planners proposed that instead of control by defense commanders, the strategic direction

[6] Prepared in WPD and forwarded to SUSAM by Memo, 20 Mar 41, PDB 133.

of the sectors be vested jointly in the Chief of Staff, U.S. Army, and the Canadian Chiefs of the General and Air Staffs. This direction would be exercised through the missions to be exchanged.[7]

The following day, 15 April, the service planners of the two countries met and produced a "Montreal Revise" of the Canadian draft. The agreed revision contained the following changes:

a. Responsibility for strategic direction of the three sectors was to be vested in the Chief of Staff, U.S. Army, who would be required to consult with the Canadian chief of staff concerned before issuing a directive affecting the Canadian forces.

b. Canada would retain command of the Newfoundland sector regardless of the strength of U.S. forces stationed there.[8]

The revised draft appeared to satisfy U.S. desires and to give the Canadians the military mission in Washington which they sought. Within a week of the planners' agreement on the draft, the Canadian Chiefs of the General and the Air Staffs approved it, subject to minor additions.[9] But the command debate, to all appearances settled, was soon to become more active than ever.

During the Permanent Joint Board meeting on 16–17 April, immediately after the service members had reached agreement on the Montreal Revise, progress made in planning had been discussed. The command arrangements of the plan, even though they were to be approved a few days later by the Canadian Chiefs of the General and the Air Staffs, had been considered unsatisfactory by Mr. Biggar, the Canadian chairman. Subsequently, in a letter of 29 April to Mr. LaGuardia detailing his views, he objected to the uncertainty as to (a) the scope of the strategic direction to be exercised by the Chief of Staff, U.S. Army, and (b) the character of the prior consultation. He transmitted at the same time a draft report embodying his views and proposed that, after it had been refined, the Permanent Joint Board submit it to the two governments for approval as its Second Report.[10] From the U.S. point of view, his proposals represented a step backward, for they not only failed to provide some means of higher strategic co-ordination but also definitively assigned the defense responsibility for Newfoundland to Canada.

LaGuardia replied that he would have the proposals studied but that he feared, frankly, they were "getting dangerously apart." The War Department General Staff, after studying the proposals, found them unacceptable and recommended that the United States stand firm on the agreed Montreal

[7] Draft Plan, PDB 133.
[8] Montreal Revise, PDB 133.
[9] Ltr, Pope to Bissell, 21 Apr 41, WPD 4330–24.
[10] Ltr, 29 Apr 41, WPD 4330–25.

Revise. LaGuardia then addressed the President on 7 May, outlining the problem. He cited the command principle that had been accepted in ABC-1 and stated his "personal conviction that the situation . . . [had] been created for political reasons" as a result of discussions in the Cabinet War Committee. The U.S. chairman recommended that the President personally lay before Prime Minister King the need for vesting strategic direction in the United States.[11]

After an exchange of memorandums with the Secretaries of War and the Navy, the President advised LaGuardia that he agreed with his position and suggested that he outline the matter of responsibility to the Canadians along the following lines:

a. Although not a belligerant, the United States was virtually ready to undertake the defense of eastern Canada and Newfoundland.

b. Canada had neither the men or the matériel for this task except as a participant on a smaller scale than the United States.

c. The Canadian war effort was designed primarily to send men and materials overseas.

d. Since the defensive effort would fall nine-tenths to the United States, the strategic responsibility should be vested in that country.[12]

LaGuardia, in turn, informed the Canadian chairman that the U.S. Government completely supported the U.S. chairman's insistence on the need for U.S. strategic control and proposed an early Board meeting to resolve the issue.

At this point the air began to clear, and Mr. Biggar replied to Mr. LaGuardia by recounting a parable of how two good-natured superintendents employed by touchy owners of two farms of disproportionate sizes and resources worked out means of joint supervision of an attack on a common problem.[13] At the 28-29 May Permanent Joint Board meeting the "good-natured superintendents" and their assistants discussed, during three half-day sessions, the preparation of a new plan and command relationships under it. A terse twelve-line Journal of Discussions and Decisions covered all three sessions and merely reported that "as no mutually acceptable solution of the problem of command relationships was found after a full discussion of this subject, it was agreed that it would be desirable for the question of command

[11] Ltr, 2 May 41; Memo, WPD for SUSAM, 7 May 41; Ltr, 7 May 41; all at PDB 135-3. The last letter does not state the basis of LaGuardia's conviction.

[12] Memos, 14, 15, and 16 May 41, PDB 135-3. The memorandum dated 14 May to the Secretaries of War and the Navy is reproduced in Elliott Roosevelt (ed.), *F. D. R., His Personal Letters, 1928-1945* (New York: Duell, Sloan and Pearce, 1950), II, 1155-56. The four-point answer had been suggested by the President to the Secretaries of War and the Navy and was endorsed verbatim by them in their reply.

[13] Ltr, 21 May 41, PDB 135-3.

relationship under Plan No. 2 to be considered on the basis of command by co-operation.[14]

Although the action is not recorded in the journal, the Permanent Joint Board apparently approved, at least in part, a draft Second Report on the subject of command arrangements.[15] This draft, as had Biggar's, differentiated between the command requirements for the 1940 Plan (premised on British collapse) and for Plan 2 (ABC-22, which assumed U.S. entry into the war alongside the United Kingdom).[16] In regard to the 1940 Plan, the draft report provided for strategic direction by the United States, with full consultation between the two governments on matters of joint war policy and with Canadian representation on the agency that might be created for that purpose. Several drafts were proposed for the portion of the report that concerned Plan 2, as were amendments to the portion of the draft that had been tentatively approved. Although the report was never completed and command arrangements for Plan 2 (ABC-22) were eventually embodied in the plan itself, the agreed portion of the draft Second Report, which covered command arrangements for the 1940 Plan, apparently continued tacitly to be accepted by the Permanent Joint Board as a valid agreement.[17]

Soon after the 28-29 May 1941 Board meeting, a draft of ABC-22 was agreed upon at staff level. The plan, as subsequently approved, included the following command arrangements:

a. Assignment to the forces of each country of tasks that lent themselves to execution by the forces of a single country.

b. Co-ordination of military effort by mutual co-operation, with each country retaining strategic direction and command of its own forces.

c. Establishment of unified commands where required, upon agreement by the chiefs of staff concerned or upon agreement by local commanders and confirmation by the chiefs of staff.

d. Exchange of liaison officers between commanders at the various levels.

The War Department accepted these arrangements reluctantly, since it continued to believe that command by co-operation was inadequate and ineffective. In recommending approval to the Chief of Staff, the War Plans Division stated: "Considering the difficulties the United States representatives experienced in arriving at an agreement with the Canadian representa-

[14] Journal, PDB 124.

[15] Ltr, Pope to Keenleyside, 9 Jun 41, PDB 135-3, refers to "that portion of the draft 2nd Report of the Board which was agreed to at its meeting in Washington on the 29th May."

[16] See Ch. IV, above. Copy of draft is filed at PDB 135-3.

[17] Memo, SUSAM for CofS, 1 Jun 42, PDB 135-2, reports that, if the 1940 Plan became effective, unity of command would be exercised by the United States.

tives . . . [the plan is] the best that could be evolved . . . [and] should be accepted." [18]

Local Command Arrangements

Although Washington and Ottawa during the latter half of 1941 were of necessity reconciled to the "co-ordination by mutual co-operation" concept of ABC-22, the question of unity of command continued to plague commanders in the field. The problem was probably most complicated in Newfoundland, where forces of both Canada and the United States were disposed. Plan ABC-22 had charged both garrisons with the same responsibility—to defend Newfoundland in co-operation with the other country's forces. But the United States, in line with the allocation of initial responsibility for Joint Task Two (the defense of Newfoundland) in the 1940 Plan, had yielded the over-all responsibility for Newfoundland defense to Canada. Five commands were involved in the local defense problem: the U.S. Newfoundland Base Command (Army and Air); U.S. Navy Task Force 4, Argentia; Royal Canadian Navy Newfoundland Force; Canadian Army Force, Newfoundland; and Royal Canadian Air Force No. 1 Group. The mission actually assigned to the U. S. Newfoundland base commander charged him with (a) the defense of only the U.S. military installations there, and (b) co-operating with Canadian forces in the defense of Newfoundland.[19] Although this mission in theory separated defense responsibilities, an actual attack on the island would probably have found the five commands attempting, in the same general area, to counter the enemy through the same types of operations. Lack of co-ordinated direction would have produced confusion, dissipation of resources, and hazard to the un-co-ordinated defenders. As a basic measure, the exchange of liaison officers between commands as provided for under ABC-22 was readily arranged, but little success was achieved in effecting, pursuant to that plan, local arrangements for unity of command.

The harbor defense of St. John's was a narrowly local problem where divided responsibility existed as a result of U.S. installation of an 8-inch battery after Canada had installed a 10-inch battery supplied by the United States. On 5 September 1941, the Canadian Army commander advised the U.S. Newfoundland base commander that he considered "divided responsibility in this matter unsound." He suggested, as a more satisfactory arrangement, transfer of the manning responsibility for the U.S. battery to the Canadian force.[20] When the United States did not respond to the suggestion, it was dropped.

[18] Memo, WPD for CofS, 14 Aug 41, PDB 135-2.
[19] 1st Ind, TAG to GHQ, 13 Nov 41, PDB 111-6.
[20] PDB 103-12.

Not long after Pearl Harbor, U.S. units stationed at Gander Airport complained about the unsatisfactory defense co-ordination there. Air units of both countries were stationed at the same base, yet no delineation of air defense responsibility had been possible, although urgently needed, particularly for the air warning services.[21] The U.S. Section of the Board found it necessary to reply that the situation could not be altered by action through the Permanent Joint Board, for Gander was a Canadian base and the defense responsibility was therefore Canadian.

A new avenue for effecting co-ordination was opened shortly after Pearl Harbor when the Board agreed on its Twenty-second Recommendation.[22] This recommendation, on the decentralization of functions to local commanders, authorized the commanders named in Paragraph 12 of ABC-22 to work out "by mutual agreements any arrangements they deem necessary for the perfection of preparations for the common defense." The wording gave broad scope to the measures that might be taken under the aegis of this recommendation, subject to the requirement—and this from the U.S. point of view was the fly in the ointment—that the local commanders involved mutually agree to the measures.[23]

With the United States unwilling to press for more satisfactory co-ordination arrangements on higher levels, it remained for the operating echelons in Newfoundland to provide such co-ordination through co-operative measures insofar as application of the Twenty-second Recommendation would permit. Efforts were made through the drafting of joint defense plans, through establishment of local joint defense committees and joint operations centers, and through the exchange of liaison officers. Local joint planning had been initiated as early as November 1941, when the U.S. commander drafted a Joint Defense Plan 1, Newfoundland. He later reported success in getting the support of all the commands involved, except for the RCAF command.[24] In December the three Canadian commanders and the U.S. Newfoundland base commander, all stationed at St. John's, joined to form the Local Joint Defense Committee to review all existing plans and recommend changes, and to function under its senior member. Initially the senior member was the U.S. commander, Maj. Gen. Gerald C. Brant.

Immediately after the establishment of the joint committee at St. John's, the Canadian Army member was replaced by Maj. Gen. L. F. Page, who was senior to General Brant by two weeks. He thus displaced the latter as senior member of the committee. This, in the opinion of the Newfoundland base

[21] Memo, GHQ for WPD, 26 Jan 42, WPD 4330-35.
[22] Memo, for WPD, 7 Feb 42, WPD 4330-35.
[23] Text at Appendix A, below.
[24] Informal Rpt, NBC, 1 Dec 41, PDB 104-5.

commander, was the purpose of the Canadian move.[25] To the U.S. consul general at St. John's, it appeared that the move was part of Canadian policy to keep its political and military representatives ahead of the Americans in relative rank. In support of his thesis the consul general cited the earlier appointment of a Canadian high commissioner to St. John's and the promotion of the naval commander to a rank senior to that of the U.S. Navy station commander at Argentia.[26]

An atmosphere reflecting such U.S. suspicions was not improved by reported differences among the Canadian commanders involved. According to the U.S. Army commander, the RCAF commander was "non-co-operative" and barely on speaking terms with the Canadian Army commander and British Air Ministry representatives at Gander Airport; very little co-operation between forces existed; bitter feeling was rampant; and the situation was far from satisfactory.[27] These differences were complicated further by the fact that the Canadian Army and RCAF commanders could not act without consulting their superior authorities, located outside Newfoundland. This requirement, coupled with a communications system whose inadequacy was compounded by meteorological and other failures, presented a serious barrier to the attainment of a high degree of operational effectiveness.

Despite repeated urging from the U.S. Army commander that unity of command be arranged, the War Department declined to act, even after the Canadian chairman of the Permanent Joint Board had suggested that the United States renew its request for a unified command. Remembering the prolonged and unproductive discussions on the subject during the course of earlier U.S.-Canadian planning, the U.S. Section declined to raise the matter on the ground that such a U.S. proposal, in the absence of a substantially increased threat to Newfoundland, would be unsuccessful and only impair what co-operation existed.[28]

Some measure of unification of the Newfoundland commands was

---

[25] Third Informal Rpt, CG NBC, 28 Dec 41, PDB 104-5.

[26] Rpt, 28 Feb 42, PDB 104-5. Dawson expresses a somewhat similar view in *Canada in World Affairs: 1939-1941,* p. 279.

[27] Ltr, CG NBC to DCofS Eastern Theater of Operations, 29 Oct 41, PDB 104-5. In his dealings with the Newfoundland Government, the U.S. commander found its members generally most co-operative and anxious to assist in the defense of the island. (Ltr, Maj Gen G. C. Brant (Ret.) to author, 12 Aug 52.)

[28] Memo, SUSAM for WPD, 28 Feb 42, PDB 135-2. This reluctance may have been motivated, in part, by the fact that the U.S. armed services' own house was not entirely in order. Although Army-Navy antisubmarine air operations from Newfoundland had earlier been unified under the U.S. Navy commander, the over-all Army-Navy wrangle on the subject of unity of command throughout the North American coastal frontiers with respect to operations for protection of shipping was resolved for the time being on 26 March 1942 after several months of deadlock.

achieved in March 1942, apparently as a result of initiative on the part of the Newfoundland Government. In February 1942 it submitted to the Canadian and U.S. commanders in Newfoundland a proposal for the formation of a joint defense council to include representation of the Newfoundland Government. At about the same time it expressed strong dissatisfaction to the Canadian Government with the existing method of co-ordinating command by co-operation and with the lack of unified command.[29] On 18 March Prime Minister King advised the Canadian House of Commons that, upon the recommendation of the Chiefs of Staff, the Cabinet War Committee had approved establishment of unified Canadian commands on the Atlantic and Pacific coasts, and in Newfoundland.[30] General Page was designated commander of the Canadian forces in Newfoundland and was charged with strategic direction of those forces. In each unified command, the operations rooms of the three services were to be combined into a joint operations center.

Six days after this announcement, the Canadian Government transmitted to the United States, through the Board, extracts from the Newfoundland Government's demand for a unified command. The Canadian Government stated that it had invited Newfoundland authorities to attend the next Board meeting for a discussion of the problem.[31] The journals of the next meeting and of the succeeding meetings do not indicate that such discussions took place. Short of unification of the U.S. and Canadian commands, which Canada had vigorously opposed, the Canadian action went as far in the direction of improving co-ordination as was possible. For reasons that are not clear, the Newfoundland Government apparently chose not to press for further action.

By the end of 1942 co-ordination between the forces of the two countries in Newfoundland had improved considerably. The U.S. Newfoundland Base Command joined the new Canadian operations center at St. John's. The appropriate military authorities of the two countries, including the Canadian Chiefs of Staff, prepared and approved a Canadian-U.S. Joint Defense Plan, Newfoundland. Joint field exercises involving all the forces were held, as were command post and communications exercises for the staffs. On 1 October 1942 the U.S. chairman of the Permanent Joint Board, Mr. LaGuardia, was able to report after a visit to Newfoundland that the command arrangements were satisfactory but that this was so only because of

[29] Extracts quoted in Ltr, Cdn Secy PJBD to U.S. Secy, 24 Mar 42, PDB 135-2. The date of the communication from the Newfoundland Government was not given.

[30] *H. C. Debates*, 18 Mar 42, p. 1411.

[31] Ltr, 24 Mar 42, PDB 135-2.

the excellent co-operation between the individuals involved (Generals Page and Brant). Should they be replaced, he felt that there might be danger to U.S. defense interests in Newfoundland.[32]

Whereas the United States after it entered the war did not feel impelled to force the issue of unity of command in Newfoundland, consideration of possible developments on the Pacific coast as a result of Pearl Harbor motivated such action in the command arrangements for British Columbia. Shortly after Pearl Harbor, the War Department urged President Roosevelt formally to propose to Prime Minister King that the defense of British Columbia be placed under U.S. strategic direction. The President preferred that initial overtures be made through other channels before he approached the Prime Minister.[33] LaGuardia on 2 January 1942 then wrote to Mr. Biggar, Canadian chairman of the Permanent Joint Board, proposing that British Columbia come under U.S. strategic direction in the interests of greater security and better integration of forces, particularly since the U.S. Western Defense Command was already responsible for the defense of Alaska and the western United States.[34] He proposed also that suitable limits be placed on the authority of the over-all commander in Canada.

Biggar replied that the Canadian Section of the Board deemed such a recommendation to the Canadian Government inadvisable since under ABC-22 questions of the kind were now in the province of the Canadian Chiefs of Staff. Mr. Biggar's reply also hinted at renewed Canadian dissatisfaction with U.S. unwillingness to accept a Canadian staff mission in Washington when he pointed out that lack of Canadian Chiefs of Staff representation in Washington had made it more difficult for the Canadian Chiefs to weigh the question.[35] In subsequent correspondence the Canadians expressed the view that the co-operation provisions of ABC-22 were adequate, and asked if there had been any evidence of lack of co-operation. They drew attention to the fact that the Canadian Chiefs of Staff had just conferred with the U.S. Chiefs of Staff and had gained the impression that the latter were satisfied with the present organization. Finally, and apparently in response to intimations of a request on the President-Prime Minister level, the Canadians pointed out that in a parliamentary government the Prime Minister would not be able to ignore the contrary advice of his war ministers.[36]

The U.S. Section of the Permanent Joint Board made a last effort to

[32] Memo, LaGuardia for CG EDC, PDB 135-2.

[33] Undated Memo, Hopkins for Marshall, PDB 135-2.

[34] Ltr, LaGuardia to Biggar, 2 Jan 42, PDB 135-2.

[35] Ltr, Biggar to LaGuardia, 3 Jan 42, PDB 135-2. For the Canadian efforts to establish a military mission in Washington, see Chapter III, above.

[36] Correspondence in PDB 135-2.

obtain the desired unity of command at the 20 January 1942 Board meeting. While it was willing to consider the U.S. proposal, the Canadian Section, being of the opinion that major land operations or invasion in British Columbia were unlikely, displayed no readiness to accept U.S. strategic direction there.[37] No further efforts were made by the United States to obtain unity of command on the west coast.

The United States had hardly stilled its requests for unity of command on the Pacific coast when that area was subjected to enemy attack. On 23 February 1942 a Japanese submarine fired some twenty rounds at coastal targets near Santa Barbara, California. Two days later, on 25 February, the "Battle of Los Angeles" took place, in which some 1,440 rounds of antiaircraft ammunition were fired at apparently imaginary enemy aircraft. Alarm mounted among Pacific coast residents in both the United States and Canada.

The mounting feeling was a factor in a Canadian Cabinet War Committee decision to establish Canadian unity of command over coastal defense forces. The Canadian Chiefs of Staff reluctantly recommended such a plan on 10 March 1942, despite their belief that co-ordination through the existing Joint Service Committee was adequate. When Prime Minister King on 18 March announced the establishment of unified Canadian commands on both coasts, Maj. Gen. R. O. Alexander became the Commander in Chief, West Coast Defenses.

Throughout the war U.S.-Canadian operational co-ordination between the field commands on the Pacific coast was limited to the exchange of liaison officers. Such an exchange had been effected in April 1941, between the headquarters of the Canadian Army Pacific Command and the U.S. Army Ninth Corps Area, with officers serving on a part-time basis. In early March 1942, on request of the General Officer Commanding-in-Chief, Pacific Command, a permanent liaison officer was attached to his command from the headquarters of the U.S. Western Defense Command.[38]

Fortunately, the sporadic and insignificant Japanese attacks on the Pacific coast did not test the adequacy of either U.S.-Canadian co-ordination or intra-Canadian co-operation. Canadian steps to establish the latter were for many months hardly more successful than the U.S. efforts to establish unity of command in the field. Despite the Canadian Prime Minister's announcement of 18 March 1942 that a unified Canadian command was to be set up on the Pacific coast, it was more than a year before the joint service head-

---

[37] Journal, PDB 124.

[38] Ltr, CG WDC to Maj Gen R. O. Alexander, 11 Mar 42, cited in History of the Western Defense Command, I, Ch. 7, 1.

quarters was actually established and even then its effectiveness seemed doubtful to U.S. observers because of un-co-operative service attitudes.[39]

During World War II only one unified command was established for Canadian and U.S. forces performing a joint task under ABC-22. This was for Joint Task One, the protection of overseas shipping. At the time ABC-22 was drafted in the spring of 1941, units of the British and Canadian Navies under the over-all direction of a United Kingdom Commander in Chief, Western Approaches, shared the convoy escort task in the North Atlantic. A few months later, in a reorganization effective on 13 June 1941, an independent Canadian command, Royal Canadian Navy Newfoundland Escort Force, was created with a semiautonomous responsibility for the escort task in the western North Atlantic, under the over-all strategic direction of the Royal Navy.[40]

In drafting ABC-1 early in 1941, the British and U.S. representatives had envisaged that the United States would, when that plan was placed in effect (presumably upon U.S. entry into the war), assume responsibility for control and protection of shipping in the western Atlantic except "the waters . . . in which Canada assumes responsibility for the strategic direction of Military forces, as may be defined in United States-Canada joint agreements." [41]

Subsequently the Canadian and U.S. planners in the joint plan ABC-22 assigned to the United States responsibility for routing and protecting shipping in all western Atlantic waters except within the coastal zones of Canada and Newfoundland. Besides furnishing the necessary vessels in the coastal zones, Canada was to allocate five destroyers and fifteen corvettes to the U.S. Navy escort forces when the plan was put into effect.

In extension of the ABC-1 and ABC-22 planning, representatives of the United Kingdom and Canadian Navies were stationed in the U.S. Navy Department in Washington in June 1941 for further planning and discussions. These representatives participated in discussions of Navy Hemisphere Defense Plan 3 (WPL-50) as it was completed, and reviewed drafts and commented on Navy Hemisphere Defense Plan 4 (WPL-51), which was promulgated on 11 July.[42] Other officers primarily concerned with convoy protection were exchanged between Ottawa and Washington, and they maintained close

---

[39] Intelligence Rpt, U.S. Navy Liaison Officer, Vancouver, 4 Aug 43, ONI Serial 8-43. The only World War II attack on the Canadian Pacific coast took place on 20 June 1942, when a Japanese submarine fired some twenty shells on Vancouver Island. The next night a submarine shelled Fort Stevens in Oregon.

[40] Schull, *The Far Distant Ships*, p. 65.

[41] For text of ABC-1, see *Pearl Harbor Attack*, Pt. 15, pp. 1485-1541. Annex V of ABC-1 set forth the details of the arrangements for control and protection of shipping.

[42] Kittredge Monograph, I, Sec. V, 538-45.

contact with each other and with their British counterparts in an intimate and cordial relationship.

After the promulgation of WPL-51, discussions continued among the naval representatives as to its execution when it became effective. In consequence of the urgings of Prime Minister Churchill and others and of the need for better protection for U.S. shipping, WPL-51 was placed in effect on 26 July 1941, but only with respect to U.S. and Icelandic flag vessels plying between North America and Iceland. United State Atlantic Fleet Task Force 1, established on 19 July, assumed this responsibility and was accorded the use of the Royal Canadian Navy bases at Shelburne and Halifax for service and repair.[43]

The Atlantic Conference between Roosevelt and Churchill and their staffs on 9-13 August 1941 led to a major change in the assignment of convoy responsibility in the western Atlantic. Churchill, Hopkins, and others impressed upon President Roosevelt the need for relieving the United Kingdom of part of the burden of its naval responsibility in the western Atlantic. As a result, the two leaders, apparently without further reference to the Canadian Government, agreed that the United States would assume the entire convoy task for vessels of any flag by placing WPL-51 fully in effect, and that the Canadian forces involved would pass to U.S. Navy command.[44] Although Canadian Government representatives did not participate in the conference, the plans were the outgrowth of the earlier Washington discussions among U.S., British, and Canadian naval staff officers.[45]

On 13 September 1941 the U.S. Navy Hemisphere Defense Plan 4 (WPL-51) went into full effect. Before the end of September a broader plan, Navy Hemisphere Defense Plan 5 (WPL-52), had been promulgated, and under it the United States assumed command of North Atlantic convoy operations west of the 30° west meridian.[46] Seventy-five ships of the Royal Canadian Navy Newfoundland Command came under U.S. direction. Bitter feeling could have existed in the situation. After two years of active participation as a belligerent in the Battle of the Atlantic, these Canadian units

[43] *Ibid.*, 547-51; *Pearl Harbor Attack*, Pt. 5, p. 2294; U.S. Navy Atlantic Fleet, Administrative History of the U.S. Atlantic Fleet in World War II, II, 60, 64. For a fuller narrative account of U.S.-British collaboration in the Battle of the Atlantic in the western Atlantic, see below, Chapter IX. This section is addressed primarily to the joint organizational and command aspects.

[44] Winston S. Churchill, *The Second World War: The Grand Alliance* (Boston: Houghton Mifflin Company, 1950), p. 441.

[45] Kittredge Monograph, I, Sec. V, 538-42. Canadian participation at the Atlantic Conference was supplied by HMCS destroyers *Restigouche* and *Assiniboine*. These Canadian ships together with a United Kingdom destroyer escorted the *Prince of Wales*, which carried the United Kingdom party.

[46] Kittredge Monograph, I, Sec. V, 553.

passed to the command of an officer of a nominally nonbelligerent country. However, excellent relations existed and were further developed between the commanders and staffs of the commands involved—Task Force 1 of the U.S. Atlantic Fleet and Royal Canadian Navy Newfoundland Force.[47]

In the ensuing anomalous situation in which a commander of nonbelligerent forces had authority over a commander of belligerent forces in a war situation, the former exercised caution and restraint in administering his command functions. On 13 September 1941, the Commander in Chief, U.S. Atlantic Fleet (CINCLANT), who was also Commander, Task Force 1, forwarded a personal letter to Commodore L. W. Murray of the Royal Canadian Navy, who had already received a copy of plan WPL-51. The Commander in Chief, U.S. Atlantic Fleet, thought it inappropriate to forward a formal instruction to the Newfoundland Force or to include it in his operating plan, and he hoped the draft instruction he had transmitted to Commodore Murray would be useful in effecting the necessary co-ordination between the two forces. Other operational matters were taken up in similar informal correspondence that followed.[48]

United States Navy Task Force 1 under Navy Hemisphere Defense Plan 5 (WPL-52) became Task Force 4, with its own commander, Rear Adm. A. L. Bristol, to whom CINCLANT delegated "co-ordinating supervision of the operations of Canadian escort units." Admiral Bristol continued the practice of carrying on informal correspondence on operational matters, but he included the Royal Canadian Navy units in his operational plans. His Op-Plan 14-41 of 29 October 1941 included, as Task Group 4.11, the Newfoundland Escort Force which, under Commodore Murray, provided escort services in the Canadian coastal zone, while Task Group 4.19 comprised the U.S. Navy and Royal Canadian Navy escort units on the ocean leg to the longitude of Iceland.

The co-ordination of operations was facilitated by the exchange of liaison officers. A U.S. Navy observer was dispatched to Halifax in August 1941 as a result of prompt Canadian approval of the U.S. request for such an arrangement. Subsequently, as a result of world-wide U.S.-British Commonwealth naval liaison arrangements which were worked out, a U.S. Atlantic Fleet liaison officer was stationed at St. John's in October 1941, while a Royal Canadian Navy officer joined the staff of the U.S. Atlantic Fleet Support Force in January 1942.

Although the unified direction of the naval forces of the two countries under the U.S. Navy materialized simply and directly as a result of the con-

[47] Schull, *The Far Distant Ships*, pp. 96-97.
[48] Administrative History of the U.S. Atlantic Fleet in World War II, II, 78-82.

ference at Argentia, the integration of the air forces available for the air patrol missions did not occur so easily. By November 1941 appropriate instructions had been issued directing the U.S. Army Air Forces in Newfoundland to operate under the U.S. Navy in the execution of Joint Task One.[49] The U.S. Section of the Permanent Joint Board requested that similar instructions be issued to the RCAF forces available for patrol duty.[50] At the next Permanent Joint Board meeting, in December, the Board members concluded that the problem arose from the lack of independent command authority of the RCAF unit in Newfoundland, No. 1 Group, which could not independently and without reference to the Eastern Air Command headquarters at Halifax take immediate action to support the Atlantic Fleet task force when requested to do so. The Board therefore concluded that a decentralization of command was needed to permit local operational control and full co-operation.[51] The necessary decentralization was authorized by Canada, effective 20 January 1942, and the U.S. Navy task force commander at Argentia finally achieved the unified operational control of all the air and naval resources of the two countries available for his task.[52]

After U.S. entry into the war, U.S. Navy strategic direction of the Canadian and United Kingdom forces assigned to Task Force 4 for the execution of Joint Task One continued, despite the fact that all the U.S. ships involved in escorting the merchant convoys were withdrawn except for two Coast Guard cutters. The withdrawals were necessary in order to permit reinforcement of the U.S. Pacific Fleet and to make available escorts for the increasing number of U.S. troop convoys to the United Kingdom. A reorganization effected in February 1942 continued strategic direction of the western North Atlantic under the U.S. Navy but met the situation partially through organization of the British and Canadian ships involved into the Royal Canadian Navy-commanded Western Local Escort and the Newfoundland Escort Forces, which now provided the necessary escort forces for the trade convoys under the over-all command of U.S. Navy Task Force 4.[53]

United States strategic direction of an escort task being executed by forces predominantly Canadian and British continued until 1 March 1943, when the Atlantic Convoy Conference, meeting in Washington, reorganized the command system. The United States withdrew its authority, except for over-all strategic responsibility, from the area north of a line east from New York

[49] U.S. Navy Progress Rpt, at 10-11 Nov 41 PJBD meeting, PDB 124.

[50] Ltr, U.S. Section to Biggar, 11 Nov 41, PDB 135-2.

[51] Journal, PDB 124. It was at this meeting that the Board made its Twenty-second Recommendation.

[52] Journal, 20 Jan 42 meeting, PDB 124.

[53] Schull, *The Far Distant Ships*, pp. 100-101.

City and west of the 47° west meridian, and Canada took over the operational responsibility for this area.[54] At this time Canada was also assigned operational control of the air elements being employed by the United States from Newfoundland for convoy protection and antisubmarine operations, although apparently no similar assignment was made of U.S. air units in the New England states.[55]

Thus materialized the only instance of unified command under ABC-22. It might never have been realized had not Roosevelt and Churchill acted with characteristic vigor and without consulting the Canadian Government. Undoubtedly, the fact that questions of sovereignty were not present, as was the case in land areas, allowed the arrangement to be accepted without serious difficulty. That the task was executed efficiently is ample testimony to the excellent spirit of co-operation and good will that existed between the Canadian and U.S. Navies.

Organization for the Logistical Tasks

Whereas the major operational command and co-ordination problems arose early in the war and were soon disposed of, those connected with logistical tasks mushroomed rapidly after Pearl Harbor and continued to increase in 1942 and 1943. Their solution, one by one, resulted in a complex U.S. military organization whose existence, in turn, gave rise to additional problems. The mission of this organizational machinery was, briefly, to construct, operate, maintain, and service the installations, bases, and facilities needed by the United States in the conduct of the war overseas. Canada constructed certain of these facilities for U.S. account, but the United States provided the greater part of the facilities from U.S. resources.[56]

Throughout Canada the post-Pearl Harbor task of the U.S. Army took the form of providing the necessary facilities on wartime standards for use only for the duration of the war. This was not the case in Newfoundland, where the status of the forces engaged in the logistical task differed as a result of the destroyer-bases agreement signed with the United Kingdom on 2 September 1940, long before Pearl Harbor, and the ninety-nine-year lease which made permanent-type construction desirable.

In Newfoundland, the U.S. Army organization for administration, except for construction and associated real estate matters, was parallel to that for operations. The Commanding General, Newfoundland Base Command, ap-

[54] *Ibid.*, pp. 166–67. An account of the Atlantic Convoy Conference is given in Chapter IX, below.

[55] *Canada at War*, No. 24 (May 43), pp. 3–4.

[56] See below, pp. 000–00, for discussion of Canada's method of co-ordinating the construction of facilities for use by the United States.

pointed in December 1940, was initially directly subordinate to the War Department; after July 1941 he was subordinate to General Headquarters, U.S. Army, at Washington; and after December 1941 to Headquarters, Eastern Theater of Operations, in New York City. In Newfoundland, the base commander exercised command through his own staff at St. John's and through the commanders of the U.S. Army leased bases, Forts Pepperrell and McAndrew, and Harmon Field.

Since in the U.S. Army the Corps of Engineers had generally been responsible for construction activities overseas, the construction operations in Newfoundland were handled through a different chain of command. This passed from the War Department to the Chief of Engineers (through the Commanding General, Services of Supply, after the reorganization of the War Department in March 1942), to the North Atlantic Division Engineer at New York, and finally to the Newfoundland District Engineer at St. John's, who directed and supervised the contractors engaged for the construction projects. An additional subordinate district of the North Atlantic Division, the Hudson Engineer District, was established on 19 December 1942 to carry out CRIMSON program construction in eastern Canada.[57]

A roughly parallel situation existed in the U.S. Navy establishment at Argentia. The operational Navy air and sea forces based there were under the command of the Commander in Chief, U.S. Atlantic Fleet. The naval base itself operated under the Commander, North Atlantic Coastal Frontier, while the U.S. Navy Department Bureau of Yards and Docks directed the base construction activities.

The U.S. logistical organization in western Canada began with the establishment in March 1942 of a Headquarters, U.S. Army Construction Forces for the Alcan Highway, which operated through two subordinate headquarters at Fort St. John and Whitehorse established soon afterward. In the latter part of May these two headquarters were made independent and designated the Northern and Southern Sectors, with each commander reporting directly to the U.S. Army Chief of Engineers in Washington. Soon after, when work was begun on the Canol Project, its commander, who established the headquarters of his Task Force 2600 at Edmonton on 26 May, became a third commander in Canada directly subordinate to the Chief of Engineers.

In March, shortly after initial steps were taken for the construction of the Alcan Highway (later designated the Alaska Highway), the Chief of Engineers enlisted the assistance of the U.S. Public Roads Administration, which undertook to handle the engineering, contracting, and supervision of parts of

[57] OCE GO 52, 19 Dec 42.

360-477 O - 70 - 10

the highway. The Public Roads Administration established a district office in Edmonton, which also reported to Washington.

As the approaching completion of the pioneer road in late 1942 foretold the need for expansion of the U.S. logistical establishment in northwest Canada, steps were taken to reorganize the commands. A Headquarters, Northwest Service Command, under Col. James A. O'Connor, was established on 10 September 1942 at Whitehorse, subordinate to Headquarters, Services of Supply, at Washington. This service command was made responsible for U.S. supply, service, and administrative operations, including support of the Army Air Forces, but excluding construction, maintenance, and repair, in that part of Canada comprising British Columbia, Alberta, Yukon Territory, and the Mackenzie District of the Northwest Territories, and in parts of Alaska. Construction, maintenance, and repair of facilities (including both the Alaska Highway and the Canol Project) remained the responsibility of the Chief of Engineers through a new Northwest Engineer Division under Col. Theodore Wyman, Jr., established on 14 November 1942 at Edmonton.[58]

These two major U.S. commands exercised their functions independently, but co-operatively, through separate organizations. Northwest Service Command operated through the posts of Edmonton, Dawson Creek, Whitehorse, and Skagway. The Northwest Division Engineer operated through the District Engineers of the Whitehorse, Fairbanks, Skagway, Dawson Creek, and Edmonton Districts.

On 18 February 1944 the two organizations were consolidated as the Northwest Service Command, with headquarters at Edmonton, under Brig. Gen. Ludson D. Worsham, who had been the Division Engineer. The post organization of the Northwest Service Command was dropped in favor of a district organization comprising the Fairbanks, Skagway, Whitehorse, Dawson Creek, and Edmonton Districts. The logistical organization in northwest Canada retained this form until the end of hostilities. Its functions included the operations of U.S. supply, transportation, medical, communications, and other administrative facilities in the area, with the major tasks including several construction projects, and the operation of the Alaska Highway, the White Pass and Yukon Route railway, and the Canol Project.

In addition to the U.S. Army organizations established in Newfoundland and northwestern Canada, a third organizational structure was developed in Canada east of the 103° west meridian and in Labrador. This structure was created after the two governments approved the Permanent Joint Board's

[58] WD GO 44, 4 Sep 42; OCE GO 42, 14 Nov 42.

BRIG. GEN. C. L. STURDEVANT *(left)* and *Col. James A. O'Connor ready to board a plane for an inspection flight over the southern section of the Alaska Highway, 1942.*

Twenty-sixth Recommendation, which called for the construction of air bases and auxiliary facilities to provide routes suitable for ferrying short-range aircraft from the United States across Canada to Greenland and thence to the United Kingdom. The Canadian Government approved the Twenty-sixth Recommendation on 12 June 1942, and five days later Brig. Gen. Harold L. George of the U.S. Air Corps Ferrying Command was appointed officer in general charge of the project, which was named the CRIMSON Project.[59] General George's over-all responsibility, which was exercised from Washington, did not displace any part of the normal command structure that had gradually developed. The initial garrisons arrived at Churchill, Manitoba, between 15 and 26 July 1942, and as a result of a directive issued on 27 July a Headquarters, CRIMSON Project, was established subordinate to the War Department.[60]

In Canada the commander of the CRIMSON Project, Col. G. K. Hobbs, who was also the commander of the 330th Engineer Regiment which was to initiate the construction work, was made responsible, for construction operations, directly to the Chief of Engineers in the War Department. The initial organization was further complicated somewhat since the new command did not perform its own supply functions. For these functions, two U.S. Army field logistical agencies had occasion to operate in Canada and Labrador—the Sixth Service Command for the supply of the installations at The Pas, Churchill, and Southampton Island; and the Boston Port of Embarkation for the supply of those at Fort Chimo, Frobisher Bay, Padloping Island, and at Goose Bay in Labrador.[61]

As plans were developed for the displacement of the Engineer troops engaged in the construction of bases by civilian contractors and workers, the Division Engineer of the North Atlantic Division (with division offices located in New York City) of the Corps of Engineers was made responsible for all engineer and construction operations under the CRIMSON Project. This responsibility he exercised through a District Engineer, Hudson District. Under this assignment of responsibilities, the project commander retained responsibility for the administration and operation of the military garrisons at these stations.

The command of the bases in Labrador, Quebec, and on Baffin Island from the project headquarters at Churchill proved to be geographically unsuitable in terms of control and communications. The pattern of available

[59] Ott Leg Desp 3198, 22 Jun 42, PDB 149-1.

[60] TAG Ltr 320.2, 27 Jul 42, sub: Command, Supply and Administration, CRIMSON Project.

[61] TAG Ltr 320.2, 2 Aug 42, sub: Amendment No. 1 to Command, Supply and Administration, CRIMSON Project.

communications had already dictated a split of the supply responsibilities between the eastern and western halves of the project. On 9 March 1943 the CRIMSON Project was divided by the 80° west meridian into Western and Eastern Sectors, with headquarters for the latter at Goose Bay. The Eastern Sector headquarters joined the Churchill headquarters in becoming directly responsible to the War Department. The engineer construction and the supply responsibilities remained as before.[62]

The organizational pattern in the Western Sector, CRIMSON Project, did not subsequently undergo significant change. On 1 July 1943 the command was redesignated the U.S. Army Forces in Central Canada, and soon afterward the headquarters location was moved to Winnipeg, where it remained until the command's inactivation on 1 October 1945.[63]

The 1 July 1943 reorganization, which reflected the general drastic curtailment of CRIMSON Project, included a disbandment of the Headquarters, Eastern Sector, CRIMSON Project, and the interim transfer of the responsibilities for the installations in that area to the Commanding General, North Atlantic Wing, Air Transport Command, with headquarters at Presque Isle, Maine. This commander, who was normally responsible, in turn, to the Commanding Generals, Air Transport Command, and Army Air Forces, for his air transport functions, became directly responsible to the War Department for the administration of these installations. A Headquarters, U.S. Army Forces in Eastern Canada, was soon activated at Presque Isle and existed for a few months, until 15 October 1944. On that date its responsibilities were transferred back to what had now been redesignated the Headquarters, North Atlantic Division, Air Transport Command. This arrangement remained unchanged throughout the rest of World War II.[64]

Organizational Chaos

The main elements of the U.S. logistical and administrative organization in Canada and Newfoundland as of 1 April 1943 are shown in Chart 1. This chart reveals the considerable number of separate agencies in Washington and elsewhere in the United States to which the numerous U.S. headquarters in Canada and Newfoundland reported for various purposes. The lack of any focal point through which all communications, or perhaps even all responsibility, might have been channeled inevitably made it more difficult for the host governments to effect co-ordination with the United States on matters of common interest. Many problems concerning channels of communica-

[62] TAG Ltr 320.2, 9 Nov 43, sub: Command, Supply and Administrative Order, NAF Projects.
[63] TAG Ltrs 322, 25 Jun 43 and 5 Jul 43, sub: Modification of the CRIMSON Project.
[64] Air Transport Command, The CRIMSON Route, p. 56.

CHART 1—UNITED STATES ADMINISTRATIVE AND LOGISTICAL ORGANIZATION IN CANADA AND NEWFOUNDLAND: 1 APRIL 1943

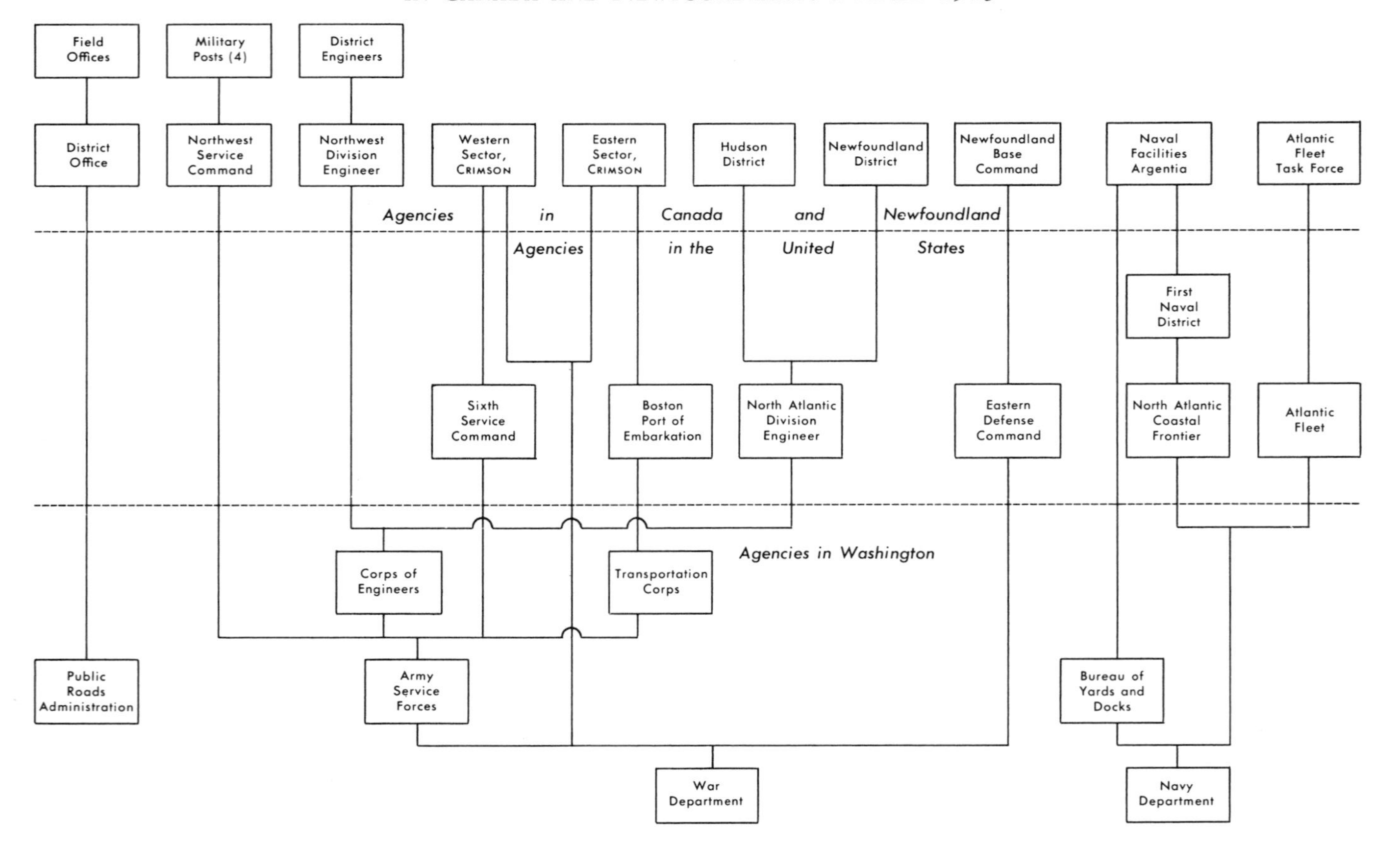

tions and field co-ordination of activities arose and required solution. The situation would have been sufficiently complex if the organization presented in Chart 1 told the entire story. This is far from so. In addition to the main agencies shown thereon, many other command and staff agencies had occasion to operate in Canada and Newfoundland and/or to maintain offices there. In northwest Canada, some of these were the Alaskan Wing, Air Transport Command, U.S. Army Air Forces; Naval Air Transport Service, U.S. Navy; U.S. Army Air Forces contract carriers for Air Transport Command, which included United Airlines, Pan American Airlines, and Western Airlines; Army Air Forces aerial photography mission; Army Air Forces 16th Weather Region (meteorological services); Army Airways Communications Service; Alaska Communications System; Prince Rupert Subport of Embarkation; Quartermaster Market Center and Transportation Corps Regulating Station at Edmonton; and a large number of U.S. civilian contractors on U.S. projects, some of whom established substantial offices in Canada.[65]

Most of these agencies had additional channels of command and communication to other headquarters in the United States. The situation was most complex in northwest Canada, where the major U.S. projects were undertaken. Here, too, American personnel, civilian and military, were introduced in far greater numbers and were necessarily stationed in many instances in populated localities. The situation also existed on a smaller scale in the rest of Canada and in Newfoundland. The North Atlantic Wing, Air Transport Command, operated at air-base facilities in those areas in providing air transport services independently of the Newfoundland Base Command, and was supported by appropriate elements of the AAF communications and meteorological services. In central and eastern Canada, facilities at Montreal and Quebec were used as subports by the Boston Port of Embarkation, and an ordnance testing center was established at Camp Shilo by the U.S. Army Ordnance Department.

Chart 1 and the foregoing additional listings of operating agencies still do not present the full complexity of the American organizational structure in Newfoundland and Canada, or of the patterns of its command and communications channels. Many other agencies of the War Department, although not having a directly subordinate operating agency in those areas, had a responsibility for the technical staff supervision of certain operations there. For example, the Chief Signal Officer of the War Department had

[65] The references in Air Transport Command historical monographs to the lack of co-ordination among the extremely numerous agencies in northwest Canada include the following: Alaskan Division, Historical Record Report, II, 198; History of the Northwest Air Route to Alaska: 1942–1945, p. 83; The Northwest Route Under the Ferrying Division: 16 June 1942–1 November 1942, p 49.

responsibility for the technical supervision of the Alaska Communications System. The execution of this type of staff responsibility necessitated some supervisory and operating activity in Canada and Newfoundland by personnel of his staff, and likewise by numerous other U.S. staff agencies on similar grounds.

The problems of co-ordination and of channels of communications took several forms:

a. Clearing U.S. requests for construction permits and real estate.

b. Co-ordinating Canadian construction on U.S. account to meet U.S. requirements and standards.

c. Co-ordinating U.S. construction on U.S. account to meet conditions and criteria established by Canadian authorities.

d. Co-ordinating competing requirements for the use of construction and transportation facilities, and for labor and materials resources.

e. Co-ordinating disciplinary and other administrative problems arising from the large numbers of American military and civilian personnel stationed in Canada.

On the Canadian side, arrangements for channels of communications and co-ordination were less complex but still involved. A half dozen or more departments of the government in Ottawa, and their field agencies, were concerned with the execution of the construction projects, with their use or arrangements therefor, or with the auxiliary administrative problems that arose. The last category of problems, on matters such as taxes, jurisdiction over and discipline of American personnel, and labor competition and conditions, also concerned in many instances the provincial and local governments.

The situation was not improved by the considerable number of parallel channels of communication that existed between Washington and Ottawa. A reasonable system of mutual co-ordination operated for certain of these channels, particularly those involving the Permanent Joint Board members. Nevertheless, this multiplicity of channels could not help but make more difficult the co-ordination of matters involving Canada and the United States.[66] Many *ad hoc* channels were established, principally between the War Department and the departments in Ottawa, which supplemented the more normal and routine channels that existed throughout the war. The principal routine channels were between:

---

[66] Of the wartime members of the U.S. Section of the Permanent Joint Board who reviewed this study, two commented on this point, agreeing that such a problem existed. One felt its magnitude had been overdrawn, while the other averred that it was "one of the most vexatious problems" of U.S.-Canadian collaboration. (Ltr, Maj Gen G. V. Henry (Ret.) to author, 2 Jan 52; Ltr, Rear Adm J. P. Whitney to author, 10 Nov 52.)

a. Washington War and Navy Department agencies and Ottawa service agencies through the service attachés in Ottawa.

b. The same agencies through the service attachés in Washington.

c. The same agencies through the Canadian Joint Staff in Washington.

d. The pairs of opposite numbers of the Permanent Joint Board sections, that is, the chairmen, the secretaries, and the Army, Navy, and Air members.

e. The Department of State and the Department of External Affairs through the Canadian Legation (later Embassy) in Washington.

f. The same agencies through the U.S. Legation in Ottawa.

The questions of co-ordination and command channels first came up for discussion immediately after the initiation of work on the Alaska Highway and as a consequence of the resulting increase of U.S. agencies in Canada. At the beginning of April 1942, J. A. Wilson of the Canadian Department of Transport discussed with U.S. Minister Moffat the need for centralized control of U.S. operations. Wilson felt that "the utmost good will . . . [was] being shown, but difficulties . . . were bound to crop up and multiply." He suggested that one of the U.S. service attachés in Ottawa "act as co-ordinator and contact man with the Canadians."[67] Two months later the situation was still unsatisfactory, and the Canadian Government appointed C. D. LeCapelain of the Department of Mines and Resources as liaison officer with the U.S. Army forces constructing the Alaska Highway.[68] By the spring of 1943 the Canadian Government had expanded this liaison arrangement to include four officers:[69]

a. C. D. LeCapelain at Whitehorse, for the Alaska Highway and other projects in the vicinity.

b. J. S. Stewart, for the Canol Project.

c. Mr. Urquhart, the district agent at Fort Smith, for projects in that vicinity.

d. L. E. Drummond, with the Northwest Division Engineer at Edmonton.

In the meantime, the Canadian Government complemented this field liaison arrangement by establishing in Ottawa a panel charged with collecting and presenting to the Cabinet War Committee periodic progress reports on the projects under construction. Mr. J. Baldwin of the Privy Council office acted as secretary and as a center for distributing information within Cana-

[67] Ltr, U.S. Secy PJBD to SUSAM, 3 Apr 42, PDB 105-3.
[68] Ltr, U.S. Leg Ott to Hickerson, 2 Jun 42, D/S 842.154 Seattle-Fairbanks Highway/409.
[69] Ltr, Moffat to Hickerson, 22 Jan 43, D/S 811.24542/B.

dian Government circles in Ottawa. At that time Canadian responsibilities for the various projects were assigned as follows: [70]

Project	*Canadian Agency*
North Atlantic Ferry Routes..........	Department of National Defense for Air
Alcan Highway.......................	Department of Mines and Resources
Canol Project.........................	Northwest Territories Council
Alaska railway survey.................	Department of Transport
Aerial mapping project...............	Department of Mines and Resources
Weather and communications stations..	Department of Transport

By the spring of 1943 the Canadian liaison system was not fulfilling its purpose because the "frequent changes in . . . personnel and fields of responsibility . . . [of the] four or five United States authorities . . . operating in the Northwest . . . [made it] increasingly difficult to distinguish the actual sources of authority in the United States organizational setup." The Department of External Affairs requested that it be furnished a chart showing the organization and the various responsibilities and lines of authority for U.S. activities in Canada.[71]

The request, its handling by the United States, and the data furnished the Canadians in reply involved a confusion within the U.S. Government that illustrates the over-all complexity and lack of understanding of the situation. Mr. Hickerson, secretary of the U.S. Section, Permanent Joint Board, referred the request to the Corps of Engineers, the U.S. Army construction agency. This agency was concerned with only part of the U.S. activities in northwestern Canada and was two staff levels below the War Department General Staff, which should have been called upon for an over-all presentation of the U.S. organization. As a result, the reply to the Canadian request constituted an exposition, during meetings in Ottawa 17–18 May, of authorization and construction procedures for "Corps of Engineers Construction Division Activities in Canada." Only indirectly during the exposition did the Canadians learn anything of the responsibilities and organization of the Air Transport Command, Northwest Service Command, and other U.S. agencies operating in the area.

Concurrently, the Canadian Government took several steps designed to resolve certain of the problems of co-ordination that existed. The first of these was the establishment on 19 February 1943 of a crown company, North West Purchasing Limited, whose object was to facilitate the acquisition of supplies in Canada by the various U.S. agencies there in such a manner as

[70] Ott Leg Desp 3198, 22 Jun 42, PDB 149–1.
[71] Ltr, Hickerson to Maj Gen Thomas M. Robins, OCE, 21 Apr 43, PDB 111–12.

to minimize interference with Canadian price controls and controlled materials measures. Initially, U.S. Army procurement officers and contractors avoided the use of the new crown company because of their conviction, to some extent fostered by local merchants, that the company was merely a profit-making organization for the Canadian Government.[72] With the realization that the failure fully to utilize the company was costing the United States considerable sums of money, and, after other demonstrations of the value of the company's services, the antagonism to it disappeared. By August 1943 U.S. procurement regulations required that all supply contracts be made with the company.[73]

During the early weeks of the company's life, when its services were being used hesitantly if at all, the Canadian Government considered another mechanism for co-ordinating the use not only of materials but also of labor resources. The Canadian Section of the Permanent Joint Board proposed for discussion at the 1-2 April 1943 meeting a "Joint Authority in the Northwest Area on Labor and Supplies." Before the meeting took place, this agenda item was withdrawn, the Canadian Government apparently having decided to accomplish the same ends by means other than a joint authority.[74] In an effort harmoniously to satisfy the competing U.S. and Canadian demands for labor resources, the government appointed a Western Labor Board at Edmonton and gave it "jurisdiction over wage and employment conditions on defense projects (Canadian and U.S.) in Alberta, British Columbia, Yukon Territory, and the Northwest Territories." [75]

A third Canadian action was the establishment of the office of Special Commissioner for Defense Projects in Northwestern Canada, within the Privy Council office.[76] To head the office, which was located at Edmonton, the Canadian Government appointed Brigadier (later Major General) W. W. Foster, who was made responsible to the Cabinet War Committee. The creation of a Special Commissioner was intended to provide a focal point and single channel for Canadian co-operation and co-ordination with U.S.

---

[72] Privy Council 2082, 16 Mar 43; John de Navarry Kennedy, *History of the Department of Munitions and Supply: Canada in the Second World War* (Ottawa: E. Cloutier, King's Printer, 1950), I, 380.

[73] Ltr, U.S. Chargé Lewis Clark to Hickerson, 23 Jun 43; Kennedy, *History of the Department of Munitions and Supply,* I, 381-82; Chapter XXXI contains a full account of the work of the company. Food purchases during 1943 averaged $750,000 monthly, while other purchases added $500,000 to that amount.

[74] Ltr, Hickerson to SUSAM, 9 Apr 43, PDB 108-6.

[75] Progress Rpt, 1-14 Jul 43 PJDB meeting, PDB 124. The report cites the establishment as under the authority of Privy Council 3870, 17 May 43.

[76] Privy Council 3758, 6 May 43. Other orders-in-council relating to the staff of this office are Privy Council 4224, 21 May 43, and 5465, 7 Aug 45.

MAJ. GEN. W. W. FOSTER *(left) with Col. J. P. Glandon at Dawson Creek, British Columbia, January 1944.*

authorities in northwest Canada, to centralize the authority of Canadian field agencies, and to decentralize certain authority from Ottawa through its delegation to that office.[77] This action apparently helped satisfy the Canadian requirement for closer co-ordination with U.S. activities in northwest Canada. By this time the situation was also improved by the increased stability of the U.S. organizational structure. Delegation by the Canadian Government to General Foster, whom U.S. commanders found to be most co-operative, of certain authority was also responsive to the U.S. desire for such an arrangement, which had found expression some weeks earlier in a Permanent Joint Board recommendation. The office of the Special Commissioner was to prove particularly useful in prosecuting the expanded program of construction on the Northwest Staging Route that the United States initiated in July 1943.[78]

No further deficiencies were noted or adjustments of significance occa-

[77] Progress Rpt, 1-14 Jul 43 PJBD meeting, PDB 124. Lingard and Trotter, *Canada in World Affairs,* III, 71, call General Foster's office a "Canadian military command." However, he apparently neither reported through military channels nor exercised such command over any Canadian military field agencies except in regard to certain administrative and logistical measures.

[78] Par. 10, Twenty-ninth Recommendation, text at Appendix A, below. See Ch. VIII, below.

sioned in this over-all co-ordination machinery in northwestern Canada. One development of interest did occur in March 1944. By that time a number of precedents had established a pattern for consideration of problems concerning U.S.-Canadian co-operation through joint committees. At a meeting held on 20 March, under the chairmanship of General Foster, to consider co-ordination of the services operating along the Northwest Staging Route and Mackenzie River air route, joint committees of representatives of the agencies concerned were set up for construction and engineering, communications, security of commuications, weather, transportation, supply, and flying control. These U.S.-Canadian committees met from time to time to discuss and agree on solution of problems within their spheres of interest.[79]

Not only were the organizational structures complicated, but the procedures by which projects were reviewed within those structures were often equally or more complicated. The procedures followed for authorization and construction of U.S. projects in Canada are an excellent example. Until the beginning of 1943, all projects were approved on the governmental level. The Permanent Joint Board felt that it should review such projects before governmental action was taken. But approvals were in fact being granted as a result of recommendations based on Board reviews of the projects, direct arrangements on the service level, direct arrangements on the diplomatic level usually involving an exchange of notes, or a combination of these actions.[80] By early 1943 it became apparent that a requirement for Permanent Joint Board review of all projects was impractical, and the Board concluded that decisions on minor projects, particularly those related to approved projects, could be effected between local commanders.[81]

On 17-18 May 1943 meetings were held in Ottawa in response to a Canadian request for clarification of the U.S. organization and responsibilities in Canada. At the meeting the procedures for authorizing and constructing major U.S. projects were outlined in detail and accepted. The meeting was attended by the Permanent Joint Board members, Canadian Government representatives, including General Foster, the Special Commissioner, and by Maj. Gen. Thomas M. Robins, Assistant Chief of U.S. Army Engineers for construction, and Brig. Gen. L. D. Worsham and Brig. Gen. Beverly C. Dunn, Division Engineers, respectively, of the Northwest Engineer Division and the North Atlantic Engineer Division.[82]

---

[79] Progress Rpt, 12-13 Apr 44 PJBD meeting, PDB 124.
[80] Journal, 3 Nov 42 PJBD meeting, PDB 124.
[81] Journals, 24-25 Feb and 6-7 May 43 meetings, PDB 124.
[82] Minutes, PDB 111-12.

To illustrate the complexity of the procedures, the agencies that needed to act in connection with the authorization and initiation of construction of a U.S. Army Air Forces project in Canada were as follows: [83]

Authorization for the project
War Department General Staff
U.S. Section of the Permanent Joint Board
Permanent Joint Board
Canadian Government
Permanent Joint Board secretaries
War Department General Staff

Site selection and approval
Army Service Forces
Chief of Engineers
Division Engineer
Chief of Engineers
Permanent Joint Board secretaries
Canadian Government
Permanent Joint Board secretaries
Chief of Engineers

Directive to construct
Division Engineer
District Engineer
Civilian contractor

For other projects in Canada, the procedures were slightly modified. It should be noted that the procedure included none of the steps involved in the formulation of a project, or in its co-ordination during construction. Additionally, the simple one-line entry shown only for the Canadian Government as a whole undoubtedly involved review by the Special Commissioner for projects in his area and by one or more departments or other agencies.

The development of the U.S. logistical and administrative organization in Canada and the problems of co-ordination that confronted Canada suggest that the early establishment of a unified U.S.-Canadian logistical and administrative command would have been to the advantage of Canada. In such a command, the fact of Canadian sovereignty would have justified an adequate Canadian role. But a unified command might have been objectionable to the United States in that it could have meant less freedom of action.

[83] Minutes, 17–18 May 43 meeting, PDB 111–12.

It is not apparent that Canada took any direct action along this line, perhaps because it would have been inconsistent with the earlier stand on unity of operational command. In fact, in the step-by-step effort to produce order from the organizational chaos, Canada moved, insofar as it could unilaterally, in the direction of unified co-ordination and direction. The joint committees established by the Special Commissioner give support to this hypothesis as do other joint control and staff agencies that were established, as for example the Joint Travel Control Board and the JAN-CAN Committee.[84] The early establishment of a unified logistical command would have paid additional dividends in eliminating some of the duplicate services the two countries developed within Canada such as communications, weather, and airway control facilities.

An alternate solution might have obviated Canadian difficulties with organizations, responsibilities, and channels. This solution would have required the United States to establish a single communications zone type logistical headquarters similar to those the U.S. Army set up overseas to support combat commanders. Such a headquarters could have been charged with the responsibility for all U.S. military activity in Newfoundland and Canada. An integral Canadian office comparable to that of the Special Commissioner would have provided a focal point for contacts with Canadian agencies. A command of such scope might have been inherently unacceptable to the Canadians because of their sensitivity to anything remotely resembling encroachment on Canadian sovereignty. In any event, apparently neither government ever broached such a scheme. Instead, the patterns of U.S. administrative organization developed largely in geographic extension of those already existing within the adjacent establishments in the continental United States. From simple origins the organizations grew "like Topsy" and soon became a Hydra-headed monster.

[84] See below, pp. 224, 302–03.

CHAPTER VI

Hemisphere Defense Problems

The Ogdensburg Declaration directed the Permanent Joint Board on Defense to make studies of the military problems involved in "the defense of the north half of the Western Hemisphere." As has been pointed out, a strict interpretation of this phrase would have resulted in planning embracing Central America, the Caribbean area, and South America to approximately the Amazon River. But in practice the Permanent Joint Board declined to take cognizance of the defense problems of any of Latin America and of much of the United States. Its studies were in fact limited to about that part of North America, excluding Greenland, north of a line through New York City and Portland, Oregon. Common military problems in other parts of the Western Hemisphere were discussed and acted upon in other forums and through other channels.

In the U.S.-Canadian diplomatic discussions soon after the fall of France but long before the United States entered the war as a formal belligerent, Prime Minister King took up with U.S. Minister Moffat the need to prevent Germany from establishing bases in Greenland, Iceland, and the West Indies and the possibility that U.S. action might be desirable. Canada had already, as a consequence of the disastrous events of May 1940, sent forces to Iceland and an infantry battalion, the Winnipeg Grenadiers, to Jamaica. At the time of these discussions the United Kingdom was pressing for more Canadian troops to reinforce Iceland and to replace the British troops that had been sent to the Dutch oil-refining island of Aruba, off the coast of Venezuela. King was dubious about the latter action and proceeded to clear it with Washington, but he was even more concerned about the idea of sending so much of Canada's military strength out of Canada. Nevertheless, in accordance with the United Kingdom request, King was at first prepared to send troops to Aruba by transferring the Canadian battalion from Jamaica.[1]

On 5 July Moffat, who had just returned from Washington, reported to King on the Aruba matter. The United States, he said, was developing a method for establishing trusteeships over territories in the Western Hemisphere that might be threatened with transfer from one non-American state

[1] Memo/Conv, Moffat and King, 27 Jun 40, Moffat Diary; Cdn Leg *aide-mémoire*, 28 Jun 40, D/S 856B.01/43.

to another. The trusteeship plan was to be considered by the conference of foreign ministers of the American states which was to be held later in July at Havana to consider the needs of the new situation in Europe. King welcomed the trusteeship plan, for it promised to relieve Canada of the need to provide garrisons such as that for Aruba.[2] Canada thus looked with interest to the proceedings at Havana, and after the conference it limited Canadian garrisons in the Caribbean to those in British possessions.

The Twenty-second Chair

At the beginning of World War II, the Pan American Union included twenty Latin American republics and the United States. Traditionally, the Pan American Union had long anticipated the possibility of Canadian membership and, for the reason, had maintained in storage a twenty-second chair, identical with the other twenty-one chairs, to seat the Canadian representative. In addition, when the Pan American Union Building in Washington was constructed in 1910, a frieze bordering the patio was installed that included the coat of arms of Canada with those of the twenty-one member states.

Proposals for Canadian membership in the Pan American Union made before World War II were unsuccessful at least in part because of U.S. opposition. The U.S. delegation to the 1928 international conference of American states had been instructed to oppose membership for Canada or any European dependency or colony on the ground that it would inject the influence and policies of a European state into a forum devoted to problems of the Western Hemisphere.[3] At the 1933 conference, Canadian membership had been proposed and approved in subcommittee, but the proposal was dropped after the U.S. delegation asked for a reconsideration.[4] For the same reasons advanced in 1928, the United States continued to oppose Canadian membership up until, and after, the beginning of World War II.[5] Canadian interest in membership, which persisted until the eve of World War II, appears to have been based largely on geographical grounds and on the increasing importance of Canadian-Latin American trade relations.

---

[2] Memo/Conv, Moffat and King, 5 Jul 40, Moffat Diary.

Secretary of State Hull had been disturbed by the earlier British action in occupying Curaçao and Aruba after the invasion of the Netherlands. (Hull, *Memoirs*, I, 814.) He feared such actions would encourage similar steps in the Pacific by an aggressive-minded Japan, which could cite the actions as precedents.

[3] Department of State, *Foreign Relations of the United States, 1928* (Washington: Government Printing Office, 1942), I, 583.

[4] Policy Recommendation, to Norman Armour, 2 Oct 44, D/S 710.001/10-244.

[5] Ltr, Welles to Armour, 24 Feb 36, and Ltr, Clark to Hickerson, 6 Dec 43, both in D/S 710.001/1068-1/2.

360-477 O - 70 - 11

With the outbreak of war the inter-American organization became vitally concerned with defense measures. In September 1939 the foreign ministers of the American republics met at Panama and acted on measures relating to defense and neutrality. After the fall of France a second similar conference was scheduled at Havana.

Announcement of the Havana Conference aroused anew discussions in Canada of proposals for Canadian membership in the Pan American Union. Despite Canada's desire to attend the meeting, the United States discouraged Canadian participation in the Havana Conference. When questioned about it in the House of Commons, Prime Minister King frankly stated his belief that official Canadian participation "would be embarrassing to the United States and to the South American republics" and would be construed as a sign of Canadian weakness.[6] Canada sent Professor Percy Corbett to the Havana meetings as an unofficial observer, and he discussed the possibility of Canadian membership with many of the officials present. Corbett found a sympathetic attitude among those officials but no feeling that formal Canadian participation in inter-American proceedings was important. On the other hand, he encountered considerable comment on Canada's status as a belligerent and a member of the British Commonwealth.[7]

Although the United States had opposed Canadian membership in the Pan American Union, President Roosevelt and State Department officers during 1941 urged Canada to play a greater role in Latin America. They encouraged Canada to co-operate in the war effort by extending Canadian diplomatic representation in that area and by taking other measures. Between September 1941 and January 1942 Canada exchanged diplomatic missions with Argentina, Brazil, and Chile, and it also signed trade agreements with those countries in the interest of expanding trade relations in the postwar period.[8]

When a third meeting of the foreign ministers of the American states to be held at Rio de Janeiro in January 1942 was announced, considerable Canadian press comment in favor of formal Canadian participation appeared.[9]

[6] *H. C. Debates*, 31 Jul 40, p. 2195, and 6 Aug 40, pp. 2540–41. For an excellent account of wartime Canadian press and political party attitudes on the Pan American Union, and of the political, military, geographic, and economic aspects of proposals for Canadian participation, see Eugene H. Miller, "Canada and the Pan American Union," *International Journal*, III (Winter 1947–48), 24–39.

[7] Memo/Conv, Moffat and Corbett, 7 Aug 40, Moffat Diary. Corbett's appraisal of the situation is presumably set forth in his article "Canada in the Western Hemisphere," *Foreign Affairs*, XIX (July 1941), 778–89.

[8] Memo/Conv, King and Moffat, 23 Jun 41, Moffat Diary; *H. C. Debates*, 27 Feb 42, pp. 893–95.

[9] Miller, *op. cit.*, pp. 31–32.

The Canadian Government clearly indicated to the United States on several occasions during December and January its desire to participate or, alternately, to become a member of the Pan American Union. Several of the other American republics had offered to propose that Canada be invited to participate, but the Canadian Government first wished to be assured of U.S. support. Despite his recent encouragement of closer Canadian-Latin American relations, President Roosevelt told Mr. King that he felt bringing in a member of the Commonwealth would be a mistake. The Prime Minister, who had hoped that the United States would welcome Canadian participation, accepted Roosevelt's decision.[10]

As to the attitude of other American states, Sumner Welles reported as the consensus of his discussions with all of the key delegates at Rio de Janeiro the conclusion that nothing official should be done until the end of the war.[11] Yet two months later Canada again raised the question of closer Canadian collaboration with the inter-American machinery, on the ground that it was continuing to receive expressions of interest, particularly from the larger Latin American countries, in seeing such collaboration. United States officials could only explain the contradictory reports by suggesting that the Latin American countries were talking differently to Canada and to the United States.[12]

It was at their January 1942 meeting that the foreign ministers established the Inter-American Defense Board, to comprise service representatives of the twenty-one member countries. This board was to have its seat in Washington and was to study and make recommendations concerning necessary defense measures.[13] In military as well as in other collective measures in the prosecution of the war effort, the hemisphere machinery was to continue to lack the cog representing one of the most important American states.

Sections of the Canadian press took the government to task for what they concluded was Canadian reluctance or outright refusal to accept membership

---

[10] U.S. Leg Ott Telg 4, 7 Jan 42, D/S 851A.01/40; Ltr, Moffat to Duggan, 6 Jan 42, D/S 710.001/953; D/S Telg, to Welles, 13 Jan 42, D/S 710 Consultation (3)/312B; Memo/Conv, Moffat and King, 16 Dec 41, Moffat Diary; Memo/Conv., Welles and Wrong, 18 Dec 41, Roosevelt Papers, Secy's File, Box 75.

[11] Memo, Welles for Duggan, 17 Feb 42, D/S 710.001/957-1/2.

[12] Memo, Duggan for Welles, 3 Apr 42, reporting on inquiry of Hume Wrong, D/S 710.001/971; Memo, Moffat visit to Washington 4-11 Apr 41, Moffat Diary. Welles, who was apparently opposed to Canadian entry, makes only guarded reference to the question of Canadian participation in the Pan American system in his lectures printed as *Co-operation Between Canada and the United States in the Search for World Peace* (Winnipeg: J. W. Dafoe Foundation, 1946), p. 16.

[13] "Final Act of the Third Meeting of Foreign Ministers," Department of State *Bulletin*, February 7, 1942, VI, 137.

in the Pan American Union.[14] The Prime Minister hinted at the truth when he informed the House of Commons: "There have been times quite recently when we might have expected invitations but were given reasons why it would not be advisable to have an invitation extended. That position still exists to a certain extent, for reasons which I cannot publicly explain." [15]

United States policy both before and after the Rio de Janeiro meeting apparently was based on concern over the possible intrusion of the United Kingdom into Pan American affairs through a Canada subservient in foreign policy matters. The Department of State could cite a number of incidents that appeared to support such a possibility. In one instance, after the establishment of the Permanent Joint Board on Defense, a senior Canadian Army officer had suggested that British representatives should participate in the Board, since the Canadian Government had no secrets from the British Government.[16] In another, the St. Pierre-Miquelon affair, Canada more or less openly agreed that the suggested United Kingdom solution would be acceptable.[17] United States concern over United Kingdom intrusion into Pan American affairs may have also been strengthened by the offer, made by British Ambassador Halifax to Sumner Welles, of assistance through the British diplomatic missions in South America in helping the United States to realize its objectives at the Rio meeting. Welles received the offer coolly, stating that he would notify Lord Halifax if British assistance appeared useful.[18] Whatever the intended purpose of the approach to Welles, it appears likely that it did not encourage a favorable U.S. attitude on the question of Canadian participation.

After the Rio de Janeiro Conference the question of Canadian participation in inter-American affairs remained dormant for over a year, until the latter half of 1943. At that time several speeches by Canadian officials suggested that the Canadian people would like to see Canada in the Pan American Union and pointed out that Canada's position in the Commonwealth should not be a barrier since her policy was no longer determined in Downing Street.[19] In analyzing the speeches, the U.S. chargé d'affaires agreed that Canadian policy was not determined by the British where questions affected vital Canadian interests, but he felt that, when this was not the case, Canada still tended to follow British guidance.[20]

[14] Miller, *op. cit.*, p. 32.
[15] *H. C. Debates*, 1 Aug 42, p. 5146.
[16] Memo/Conv, Moffat and Lt Gen H. D. G. Crerar, 12 Oct 40, D/S 842.20 Def/42.
[17] Ltr, Clark to J. G. Parsons, 3 Sep 43, D/S 710.001/1054–1/2.
[18] Memo/Conv, 27 Dec 41, D/S 710 Consultation (3)/368.
[19] Miller, *op. cit.*, p. 33.
[20] Ltr, Clark to Parsons, 3 Sep 43, D/S 710.001/1054–1/2.

In view of the speeches by Canadian Government officials and of the increasing press interest in Canadian membership in the Pan American Union, especially in Quebec, newly accredited Ambassador Ray Atherton initiated a redefinition of the U.S. position at the beginning of 1944.[21] On the advice of Secretary of State Hull, the new ambassador outlined to Prime Minister King the U.S. Government's doubt as to the feasibility of bringing up the question in the light of wartime conditions and its conclusion that the question could be discussed fully after the war. King confirmed these views as exactly his own, since it appeared to him to be a time for considering global rather than regional problems.[22] The flurry of speeches by Canadian Government officials had nevertheless indicated a real interest in Latin America, for during 1944 Canada resumed the expansion of Canadian diplomatic representation in that area.[23]

During the last year of the war the Department of State seemed somewhat more sympathetic toward Canadian membership in the inter-American system. Also, the necessary support from the Latin American countries appeared assured.[24] But during the inter-American conference held at Mexico City in February–March 1945, when Chile sponsored a resolution calling for Canadian admission to the Pan American Union, it was transformed, at U.S. instance, into a resolution (XXII of the Final Act) that paid tribute to the Canadian war effort and expressed the wish that Canadian collaboration with the Pan American system should become ever closer.[25]

By that time the tide of Canada's Pan American aspirations was ebbing. A public opinion poll taken in Canada in January 1944 had indicated that only 28 percent of those polled knew what the Pan American Union was, although the great majority of them favored Canadian membership. As

---

[21] Ltr, Atherton to Hull, 12 Jan 44, D/S 710.001/1106. For a study on Pan American sentiment, see Iris S. Podea, "Pan American Sentiment in French Canada," *International Journal,* III (Autumn 1948), 334–49.

[22] Ltr, Atherton to Hull, 28 Jan 44, D/S 710.001/1102. Hull in his *Memoirs,* II, 1481, states that the Pan American Union question was not much discussed or specially urged by either government, since both had in mind that Canada got into war if the United Kingdom did. He felt that the co-operation that existed was to every practical extent the same that would have occurred had Canada been a member.

[23] Canada, Department of External Affairs, "Canada and Latin America," *External Affairs,* I (May 1949), 26.

[24] A lengthy study resulted in a "Policy Recommendation," dated 2 October 1944, that the United States should assist in bringing about Canadian membership, but the recommendation was apparently not approved. (D/S 710.001/10–244.) A subsequent survey of the United States diplomatic missions in ten American republics confirmed that a broad basis of support existed, subject to assurances as to Canada's position in the British Commonwealth. (Memo, by L. J. Halle, Jr., 23 Nov 45, D/S 710.001/11–2345.)

[25] Ltr, Under Secy State Joseph C. Grew to President, 8 Mar 45, Roosevelt Papers, Secy's File, Box 150; *Report of the U.S. Delegation* (Department of State Publication No. 2497 [Washington: Government Printing Office, 1946]), p. 95.

official Canadian interest cooled, King was able to cite the need for wider general appreciation in Canada of the purposes and responsibilities of the Pan American Union as a condition precedent to active Canadian interest in membership.[26]

The adoption of the Act of Chapultepec at Mexico City in March 1945 may have helped produce a further change in the Canadian attitude. In the light of the new obligations that Canada would assume under the United Nations charter, the additional obligations entailed under the Act of Chapultepec received careful study. Opinions in government and other informed circles in Canada were widely divided on the question of Canadian participation in the inter-American system. Press comment on the question diminished considerably after March 1945, and it ceased to be a political issue.[27]

The question of Canadian admission to the Pan American Union during World War II seems to have been considered by both countries primarily in terms of considerations other than military. The U.S. War and Navy Departments never urged Canadian participation as advantageous in dealing with hemisphere defense problems, and the Permanent Joint Board on Defense recorded no discussions on the subject. As for Canada, a 1949 official publication cited the growth of Canadian interest in Latin America as one of the significant developments in the expansion of Canada's international relations. This publication described the wartime growth of direct Canadian diplomatic representation replacing the earlier representation through United Kingdom representatives. It pointed out the very considerable increase in the volume of trade and the emphasis that had been placed upon cultural relations. Insofar as security problems were concerned, it made no comment on Canadian interest in the over-all defense requirements of the hemisphere. In the postwar period, the article stated, Canada should keep under review the defense requirements of the northern part of the hemisphere through the Permanent Joint Board on Defense and the North Atlantic Treaty Organization. Through the United Nations, Canada could keep in close contact and regularly exchange views with Latin American delegations on problems affecting their security.[28]

---

[26] *Public Opinion Quarterly*, VIII (Spring 1944), 146; *H. C. Debates*, 4 Aug 44, p. 5912. Months later, in February 1945, a government publication was to refute the importance of the poll results as a reason why Canada should not be a member. (Department of External Affairs, Information Division, Reference Paper 34, p. 16.)

[27] U.S. Emb Ott Desp 2884, 1 Aug 45, D/S 710.001/8-145; U.S. Emb Ott Desp 2886, 7 Aug 45, D/S 710.001/8-745.

[28] Canada, Department of External Affairs, "Canada and Latin America," *External Affairs*, I (May 1949), 25-34.

Although the available evidence is far from complete, it suggests that Canadian interest in participating in the inter-American system during World War II was based on economic and political motives, rather than on the possibility of a greater or more effective Canadian contribution to over-all hemisphere security. Partly because it had discouraged a greater Canadian defense contribution in Latin America before Pearl Harbor, the United States found it necessary to supply most of the defense needs that could not be met by the Latin American countries themselves.[29]

Securing Greenland

In May 1939, when the U.S. Senate considered a resolution calling for initiation of negotiations with Denmark for the purchase of Greenland, the War Department in commenting on the proposal stated that any "strategic advantage as would accrue . . . would be negligible, and in any event unnecessary." It also held that Greenland was so undeveloped and so far on the flank of sea and air routes that its possession by a hostile power would not constitute a significant threat.[30] Events were not to support the War Department's appraisal, and before long both Canada and the United States became actively interested in Greenland on three counts:

a. Protection of the cryolite mines at Ivigtut. These mines represented the only important natural source of cryolite, which was essential in the production of aluminum.

b. Use of air-base and weather and communications stations there in connection with ferrying aircraft across the North Atlantic.

c. Denial of its use, for weather and communications purposes, to the Germans.

The German occupation of Denmark on 8–9 April 1940, after the many months of lull in the "phony war," focused attention on the fate of Greenland. Secretary of State Hull, on 13 April, informed Canadian Minister Loring Christie (and the British Embassy as well) that the United States did not recognize the right of any third government, even Canada or the United

[29] Apart from forces in Newfoundland and Labrador, the Canadian Army deployments at the end of the war included a battalion (786 strong) in Jamaica, 163 troops in the Bahamas, and 181 in Bermula. In addition, a detachment of the Veterans Guard of Canada had served in British Guiana, protecting bauxite shipments. (Stacey, *The Canadian Army, 1939–1945*, p. 43n.) Of interest is the fact that the U.S. deployments included forces sent just after Pearl Harbor to Aruba, the Dutch possession that had been the subject of proposed similar action by Canada in June 1940. The U.S. deployments to Aruba and neighboring Curaçao had been arranged with the United Kingdom in March 1941 as part of the ABC–1 report arrangements.

[30] Ltr, Harry H. Woodring, SW, to Bureau of Budget, 16 May 39, WPD 4173–7, Sec. 1. The above comments, prepared at staff level, were reviewed and approved by the head of War Plans Division and by Chief of Staff Malin Craig, as well as by Woodring.

Kingdom, to occupy or otherwise interfere in Greenland. A few days later the Canadian Government, which had been requested to do so by the United Kingdom, advised the United States that it was concerned over the security of the cryolite mines, the danger that Germany might establish bases in Greenland, and the relief needs of the Greenland inhabitants, who had been deprived of their export markets. Canada, Ottawa told Washington, was therefore considering dispatch of a small defense force for the duration of the war, during which time Canada would act "as a trustee for a restored and independent Danish Government." Canada gave assurance that it would not send the force without notifying, or before receiving the views of, the United States. But it would not commit itself not to send the force if such action appeared necessary.[31]

The U.S. Government was extremely anxious that no action of this kind be taken by Canada since it might offer an excuse to other large countries for taking over colonial territories of occupied European countries. Canada accepted the U.S. view on the condition that the United States would assume the responsibility of meeting the threats that might arise. The American Red Cross at the same time began a study of the relief problem in Greenland.[32]

Concurrently, the Danish Minister in Washington, Henrik de Kauffmann, was suggesting to Secretary Hull that a U.S. protectorate be established over the island. Hull opposed the action on the same grounds he had voiced to Canada. The local governments in Greenland, the Greenland Councils, were likewise concerned over the security of the island and, on 3 May 1940, also sought U.S. protection. The United States declined to furnish it but instead arranged for the installation of a consul and vice consul at Godthaab.[33]

The worsening military situation in Europe, together with conflicting U.S. views on the defense responsibility for Greenland, impelled the Canadians to act. Whereas Department of State representatives had stated that the United States would take any action needed in Greenland, President Roosevelt had told Prime Minister King that he expected the British Navy to repel a German attack.[34] Still confused as to U.S. policy after a further inquiry, Canada

[31] Memo/Conv, Hull and Christie, 13 Apr 40, D/S 859B.01/140; Memo/Conv and *aide-mémoire*, 16 Apr 40, D/S 859B.01/155; Memo/Conv, Hickerson and Escott Reid, 17 Apr 40, D/S 859B.01/147. Repeated requests from London reportedly pressed Canada to take prompt action to prevent Greenland from falling into German hands. (Memo/Conv, J. K. Penfield and Dunbar, 27 Dec 41, D/S 859B.00/64.) See also Langer and Gleason, *The Challenge to Isolation*, pp. 429–33, 683–87, for an account of discussions concerning Greenland.

[32] Memo, J. C. Dunn to Secy State, 19 Apr 40, D/S 859B.01/152.

[33] Memo/Conv, 19 Apr 40, D/S 859B.01/154; Hull, *Memoirs*, I, 756; Ltr, Secy State to Minister Kauffmann, 7 Apr 41, EAS, 204; Department of State *Bulletin*, May 4, 1940, II, 473.

[34] Memo/Conv, Christie and Berle, 1 May 40, D/S 859B.01/193.

on 19 May informed the United States of the dispatch of a Hudson's Bay Company ship, the RMS *Nascopie,* to call in Greenland and land a Canadian consul there.

The *Nascopie* had arrived at Ivigtut when, on 3 June, the Governments of North and South Greenland, already disturbed by this event, learned of the approach of the Danish vessel *Julius Thomsen* under control of a British prize crew and formally requested the United States to establish a garrison at Ivigtut to protect the cryolite mines. In discussions with the United States, Canada, too, indicated its concern over the vulnerability of the mines to attack by raiding parties and offered assistance in defending them.[35]

To some U.S. officials, the Canadian interest in Greenland seemed to be related, at least in part, to a desire to expand the Canadian economic position in Greenland and to oust U.S. commercial interests at Ivigtut in favor of the Aluminium Company of Canada. Meetings for the purpose of working out an equitable arrangement for disposition of the output of cryolite had already been held in New York City by representatives of the Departments of State and External Affairs, the Greenland Governments, the Aluminium Company of Canada, and the Pennsylvania Salt Manufacturing Company, the American processor of the cryolite. It was the conduct of these meetings that had served to arouse U.S. suspicions.[36]

In any event and in response to the Greenland request, the USS *Campbell* was dispatched to Greenland. Its arrival on 7 June apparently served to allay the concern of the authorities in Greenland, where no change in the *status quo* took place. A few months later Secretary of State Hull nevertheless considered it necessary, because of British operations designed to eliminate and insure against German activities on the east coast of Greenland and in adjacent waters, to reaffirm to Canada and the United Kingdom the position he had stated on 13 April.[37]

By the summer of 1940, interest was developing in air-base sites in Greenland for use in transatlantic flight operations. Definite proposals were initially made in August 1940. During that month, Capt. J. K. Lacey of the U.S. Army Air Corps made a survey seeking suitable sites. On 27 August the Canadian Government informed the United States of a British desire to establish an air base for use in ferrying short-range aircraft and asked if there

---

[35] U.S. Consulate Godthaab Telg 22, 3 Jun 40, D/S 859B.01/199; Cdn Leg Note, to State Department, 27 May 40, D/S 859B.20/49.

[36] Memo/Conv, Berle and Mahoney, 3 Jun 40, D/S 859B.01/210. Months later, a Canadian official stated that the Aluminium Company of Canada had originally proposed and practically organized "the unfortunate *Nascopie* expedition." (Memo/Conv, 27 Dec 41, D/S 859B.00/64.) Memo for Record, 21 May 1940 meetings in New York City, D/S 859B.01/206.

[37] Ltrs, Hull to Christie and Lothian, 23 Sep 40, D/S 859B.01/293A.

was any objection to an approach to the Greenland authorities for approval of a survey by Canada. Although the War Department had no objections, the Department of State suggested that the Canadian survey be delayed until the U.S. Army survey report was completed. This had the practical effect of delaying a Canadian survey until the following spring.[38] During October 1940, the U.S. Coast Guard cutter *Northland* made an additional survey of potential air-base sites.

In January 1941 the Canadian Government renewed the British and Canadian proposal, stating that it was prepared to construct the desired facilities, to have the United State construct them, or to have the Greenland authorities construct them with U.S. assistance.[39] In presenting the problem to the President and the Secretary of State, Assistant Secretary of State Adolf A. Berle, Jr., expressed the conviction that Canada would seize the Greenland sites unless the United States acted. His recommendation that the Greenland authorities be asked to establish the facilities needed with U.S. assistance was approved.[40]

The United States advised Canadian authorities of this decision and of its relation to the Monroe Doctrine, to the neutral status of Greenland, and to inter-American defense. Since Canada was a nation of the Western Hemisphere and provided a vital part of the hemisphere's defenses, facilities that would be built could be used by that country under the usual neutrality rules. The Canadian officials, when informed also that the problem was already under discussion with the Greenland authorities, expressed their satisfaction with the solution.[41]

While the necessary arrangements were being negotiated with the Danish and Greenland authorities, U.S. interdepartmental committees studied the problem. They concluded that, because of the complexity of considerations of defense, jurisdiction, and operation and maintenance of the facilities, construction by the Greenland authorities was impracticable and should be undertaken by the United States.[42] The Department of State presented to and discussed with Greenland authorities a draft agreement based on that approach. It was signed in Washington on 9 April 1941 by Secretary of State Hull and Minister Kauffmann, who, although he had been repudiated

[38] Memo, H. Cumming for Berle, 27 Aug 40, D/S 859B.7962/2; Memo, G. C. Marshall for Secy Navy, 28 Aug 40, WPD 4330-3.

[39] Memo/Conv, Cumming and Reid, 6 Jan 41, and Cumming and F. R. Hoyer Millar, 13 Jan 41, D/S 859B.7962/3.

[40] Memo, 7 Feb 41, D/S 859B.7962/18.

[41] Memo/Conv, Berle and Mahoney, 13 Feb 41, D/S 859B.7962/13.

[42] Summary of Points Respecting the Establishment of Landing Fields in Greenland Agreed Upon at a Meeting Held on March 5, 1941, WPD 4173-11.

HARBOR CAMP AREA OF THE GREENLAND BASE COMMAND. *Photograph taken June 1943.*

by the new Danish Government after the German occupation of Denmark, was still recognized by the United States as the representative of the King of Denmark. In the agreement, the United States related its acceptance of responsibility for the status of Greenland to the Act of Havana of 30 July 1940. Declaration XX of the Act of Havana had authorized emergency action by any of the American republics to forestall threatened transfer of territory in the Western Hemisphere.[43] The agreement also provided for use of the facilities to be constructed by "airplanes and vessels of all the American Nations for purposes connected with the common defense of the Western Hemisphere." The use of the term "American Nations," rather than the usual Pan American Union usage of "American Republics," brought Canada within the scope of this provision.[44]

[43] EAS, 199. Mr. Hull's note of 7 April also made reference to the Monroe Doctrine and "the traditional policies of this Government respecting the Western Hemisphere," but the agreement signed made no mention of them. It is also of interest to note that the ABC-1 report on the British-U.S. military staff meetings, signed 27 March, had made the defense of Greenland east of 30° west longitude a responsibility of the United Kingdom.

[44] The agreement and notes exchanged before its signing are in EAS, 204. For an examination of the unusual circumstances attending the conclusion of this agreement, see Herbert W. Briggs, "The validity of the Greenland Agreement," *American Journal of International Law,* XXXV (1941), 506–13.

In announcing the agreement, the Department of State revealed that German bomber reconnaissance aircraft had flown over the east coast of Greenland on several occasions not two weeks before the signing. German activity on the island had on the whole diminished after the British seized the German-controlled but Norwegian-manned weather stations in the summer of 1940. Nevertheless, sporadic air reconnaissance thereafter had indicated continued German interest.[45]

In anticipation of the signing of the agreement a South Greenland Survey Expedition had left Boston on 17 March to make the detailed surveys. The Secretary of War had received an allocation of $5 million from the President's emergency fund to permit work to be started at the beginning of the short construction season.[46] As a result of the work of the South Greenland Survey Expedition, the U.S. Army dispatched a force of 473 officers and men, mostly Engineer construction troops, which arrived on 8 July 1941. By the end of 1941 the garrison totaled approximately 700, and the airfield at Narsarssuak was usable by all types of aircraft. Eventually, military development included five installations on Greenland's east coast and eight on its west coast.[47]

Prompted by the *Bismarck* affair and other enemy activity in the Greenland area, Canada made one more approach to the United States, in May 1941, requesting immediate consideration of the need for reinforcement of the defenses at the cryolite mines. The Canadians indicated that, as before, they were ready to provide a Canadian garrison immediately and in other ways to co-operate in strengthening the defenses. The United States declined the Canadian offer of assistance with appreciation and made arrangements to disclose the military measures planned by the United States to Canadian officials through military channels.[48]

The arrival in Greenland of the initial U.S. garrison and its subsequent reinforcement apparently allayed Canadian concern. Other developments served to reduce the security requirements for Greenland. The strengthened Allied military position in the North Atlantic, at least insofar as German

[45] Department of State *Bulletin,* April 12, 1941, IV, 444. For an account of the continuing German activities in Greenland throughout the war and of U.S. countermeasures, see U.S. Coast Guard, *The Coast Guard at War: Greenland Patrol* (Washington: 1945).

[46] Memo, Acting CofS for SW, 10 Apr 41, WPD 4173-25.

[47] The east coast facilities were given the code designations of BLUIE EAST (or BE) 1 to 5; those on the west coast, BLUIE WEST (or BW) 1 to 8. BW-1 and BW-8, the airfields at Narsarssuak and Søndre Strømfjord, became the major bases. See Morison, *The Battle of the Atlantic,* pp. 60-62; Watson, *Chief of Staff: Prewar Plans and Preparations,* pp. 486-90.

[48] Cdn Leg *aide-mémoire,* 27 May 41, WPD 4173-72. A proposal to provide the information in the PJBD was rejected since the Canadian Section had "been given to understand that the defense of Greenland . . . [was] not a matter for consideration by that Board." (Memo, WPD for G-2, 17 Jul 41, WPD 4173-99.)

surface operations were concerned, reduced the German threat. By mid-1942 the U.S. domestic output of synthetic cryolite had reached the rate of 35,000 tons annually, which about equaled the U.S. share of the annual cryolite output in Greenland. Although increasing needs fully absorbed the additional amounts, at least total Allied dependence on the sole natural source was ended.[49]

The Defense of Iceland

German occupation of Denmark after the 8–9 April 1940 invasion raised the question of what action Germany might take vis-à-vis Iceland, which under the Act of Union of 1 December 1918 was a sovereign kingdom joined with Denmark through their common sovereign, His Majesty the King of Iceland and Denmark. The Department of State, in studying courses of action possible if Germany were to lay claim to Iceland and/or Greenland, examined the applicability of the Monroe Doctrine to these and other European territories. A study by one of the State Department's experts concluded that the doctrine could be considered applicable, since it had referred to "this Hemisphere" and since it was "held by authoritative geographers" that the part of the island west of the 20° west meridian was "definitely in the Western Hemisphere." [50] The United States did not find it necessary to take any military steps, for in May 1940 the United Kingdom occupied Iceland and established a garrison of several thousand troops there. This garrison was steadily increased until a year later it exceeded 25,000.

The British garrison had been in Iceland only two months when the Icelandic Government, which had established direct relations with the United States in April 1940, asked on 12 July "whether the United States would include Iceland in the Western Hemisphere and put it under the protection of the Monroe Doctrine." This request received no encouragement, nor did a similar request made in September.[51]

When the Permanent Joint Board on Defense initiated its studies of the "north half of the Western Hemisphere," it either excluded Iceland from its purview or found no need, in the light of the British garrisons already established there, to consider the defense of Iceland. Whatever the case, the records of the Permanent Joint Board do not mention Iceland. The agreements reached by the U.S.-United Kingdom planners during January–March 1941, in

[49] Although aluminum production is feasible using only synthetic cryolite, the process is more efficient and economical if a certain proportion of natural cryolite is used.

[50] Study by H. Notter, Applicability of the Monroe Doctrine if Germany Should Lay Claim to the Possessions of Denmark in the Western Hemisphere, 9 Apr 40, D/S 859.01/43.

[51] Memo/Conv, Berle and Consul General V. Thor, 12 Jul 40, D/S 710.11/2551; Memo/Conv, Hull and Thor, 5 Sep 40, D/S 859A.014/9.

which the defense of Iceland was assigned to the United Kingdom, further moved Iceland from the area of Western Hemisphere problems that might be solved jointly by the United States and Canada.

Although the initial garrison was British and the defense of Iceland was a United Kingdom responsibility, there was some indirect U.S.-Canadian collaboration in meeting the security requirements of Iceland during World War II. On 10 May 1940, when the defenses of France were crumbling, Canada invited British suggestions as to action it might take to be of assistance. As a result of the British reply, Canada offered an infantry brigade of the 2d Canadian Division as part of the garrison for Iceland. Designated Z Force, the initial Canadian elements reached Iceland on 16 June. By 17 July three Canadian battalions, the Royal Regiment of Canada, Les Fusiliers Mont-Royal, and the Cameron Highlanders of Ottawa, formed part of the British garrison.[52] The Canadian garrison reached a peak strength of about 2,700. Around the first of November two battalions left for England, leaving in Iceland the third battalion and a small detachment of special troops.

By the spring of 1941 the United Kingdom was encouraging the United States to provide forces for the defense of Iceland in order to release the substantial British forces there. On 25 March Hitler declared Iceland to be in the war zone, and U.S. interest in that island began to increase. Its usefulness for air bases and convoy protection was pointed out to President Roosevelt, who authorized a reconnaissance of the island. An initial survey was completed in early April. Further surveys were planned but were delayed, and no further action took place until early June.[53]

On 2 June 1941 Harry Hopkins, the Secretaries of War and the Navy, and General Marshall and Admiral Stark met to discuss recommendations of Ambassador John G. Winant brought from London as to ways and means of relieving the pressures on the United Kingdom. They considered a proposal, among others, for U.S. replacement of the garrison in Iceland. In interdepartmental discussions during the next few days the proposal received general support. On 5 June the President decided to send a force to Iceland as soon

[52] Stacey, *The Canadian Army, 1939–1945*, pp. 24–25. Colonel Stacey states that the British War Office wanted the entire 2d Canadian Division in Iceland, although the Canadian Government would have preferred to keep the bulk of the division in Canada. Churchill had still another plan and was surprised to learn from Lt. Gen. A. G. L. McNaughton that the whole 2d Canadian Division was destined for Iceland. "No one was told anything about this. We require two Canadian divisions in England to work as a corps as soon as possible." (Memo, 7 Jul 40, quoted in Churchill, *Their Finest Hour*, p. 268.) Canada, too, preferred to have the entire division concentrated in the United Kingdom, rather than split between Iceland and some other place, and the Churchill plan was carried out. General McNaughton became the Canadian Corps commander.

[53] Morison, *The Battle of the Atlantic*, p. 57.

as the government there requested U.S. protection, and he ordered a Marine force made ready within fifteen days.[54]

The British Government suggested that for military and tactical reasons Iceland be given no advance notice of the dispatch of U.S. troops, and that the United States instead present the Icelandic Government with a *fait accompli.* President Roosevelt rejected this suggestion as inconsistent with the basic U.S. hemisphere nonagression policy and insisted that a request from the Icelandic authorities would be necessary.[55] Despite efforts of the British Minister in Reykjavik, who had been virtually instructed to see to it that a request was made, the Icelandic Government refused explicitly to request or invite U.S. protection because a majority of the Parliament had recently opposed such a request. In the end, the Icelandic Government admitted that the introduction of U.S. troops was in the interest of Iceland and therefore entrusted the protection of that counry to the United States.[56]

In anticipation of a satisfactory arrangement President Roosevelt, on 16 June, had ordered the Chief of Naval Operations to carry out Operation INDIGO for the relief of the British garrison. On 7 July about 4,000 troops of the 1st Marine Brigade (Provisional) landed in Iceland and joined British forces in the Iceland garrison. No Canadian troops were present at that time since their transfer to the British Isles had just been completed. At the end of 1941, approximately 10,000 U.S. Army and Marine troops were in Iceland. During early 1942 the U.S. Marines and most of the British forces were withdrawn and replaced by U.S. Army troops. Command of the island garrison passed in April 1942 from the British to Maj. Gen. Charles H. Bonesteel, U.S. Army, who had arrived the preceding September.[57]

---

[54] Conn and Fairchild, *The Framework of Hemisphere Defense,* pp. 121–29.

[55] Memo, Halifax for Secy State, 16 Jun 41, D/S 859A.20.17; Memo/Conv, Welles and N. M. Butler, 18 Jun 41, D/S 859A.20.20–1/12. Although the President indicated that he was willing to provide a garrison because of American determination to defend the Western Hemisphere, he was not convinced, despite the counsel of some of his advisers, that Iceland should be considered in that hemisphere. Dr. Isaiah Bowman had examined the point for him and concluded it should be excluded since only a doubtful case could be made. A few years later Roosevelt stated, in toasting the President of Iceland, that he had steered clear of a proposition to put Iceland in the Western Hemisphere. (Memo, Bowman for President, 19 Mar 41, Roosevelt Papers, Secy's File, Box 77; Rosenman (compiler), *The Public Papers and Addresses of Franklin D. Roosevelt,* XIII, 236–37.

[56] Memo/Convs, Welles and Halifax, 26 and 28 Jun 41, D/S 859A.20/20–3/12 and /20–4/12. Message, Prime Minister to President Roosevelt, 1 Jul 41, EAS, 232.

[57] Accounts of the garrisoning of Iceland are to be found in Morison, *The Battle of the Atlantic,* pp. 74–78, and Watson, *Chief of Staff: Prewar Plans and Preparations,* pp. 487–90. The most detailed account including the reasons for the inability of the United Kingdom to reduce its garrison during 1941, is given in Stetson Conn, Rose C. Engelman, and Byron Fairchild, Guarding the United States and Its Outposts, a volume in preparation for the series UNITED STATES ARMY IN WORLD WAR II.

St. Pierre and Miquelon

One of the most widely publicized international tempests during World War II involved St. Pierre and Miquelon, two small islands just off the southern coast of Newfoundland. Subsequent to the fall of France, control of the two islands had remained with the Vichy Government. The existence on St. Pierre of a high-powered radio transmitter capable of transmitting meteorological and other information that could be of great value to Germany constituted a serious danger to Allied operations in the Atlantic.

As early as July 1940, the Newfoundland Government had requested Canada to occupy the islands or take other action. Canada discussed the matter with the United States and indicated that it would consult the United States before taking any action.[58] Nothing was done, and the problem remained quiescent until the spring of 1941, when the convoy loss rate in the northwest Atlantic began to climb sharply.

During May 1941 Prime Minister King told Pierrepont Moffat, the U.S. Minister in Ottawa, that Newfoundland had renewed its request on several occasions and that President Roosevelt himself had also asked King what he intended to do. The Canadian Government concluded that the only action needed was to send a Royal Canadian Mounted Police officer to confer with the island's authorities and render a report. Canada also reaffirmed its promise not to act without consulting the United States. The State Department was particularly sensitive to the situation because of its bearing on U.S. policy with respect to administration of European colonies in the Western Hemisphere. In addition, the State Department did not wish to jeopardize the arrangement under which Vichy French fleet units, notably the aircraft carrier *Bearn,* remained neutralized at Martinique. Moffat was accordingly instructed to make clear in Ottawa the need for Canadian co-operation in the matter.[59]

Beginning in July 1941 the United Kingdom made repeated suggestions to Canada that Free French forces be allowed to proceed to St. Pierre and Miquelon to induce them to align themselves with the Free French movement and General Charles de Gaulle. London did not approach the State Department with these proposals, which the Canadian Government had discouraged.[60]

At its 10–11 November 1941 meeting the Permanent Joint Board on Defense reviewed the problem of St. Pierre and Miquelon and agreed that "the

---

[58] Memo/Conv, Moffat and King, 5 Jul 40, Moffat Diary.

[59] Memo/Convs, Moffat and Robertson, 12 and 28 May 41, 15 and 31 Jul 41, Moffat Diary; Ott Leg Telg 188, 17 May 41, D/S 851A.01/10; Ott Leg Desp 1731, 16 Jul 41, D/S 851A.014/8.

[60] Memo/Convs, Moffat and Robertson, 15 and 31 Jul 41, 3 Nov 41, Moffat Diary.

existence on the Islands of an uncontrolled and high-powered wireless transmitting station constituted a potential danger to the interests of Canada and the United States."[61] The problem was also being discussed through diplomatic channels, and the Canadians suggested joint U.S.-Canadian sponsorship of a team of civilian technicians that would proceed to St. Pierre to monitor the radio station operations. Canada solicited the views of both Washington and London. King's query to the British Prime Minister remained unanswered by Churchill, who advanced an alternate plan. General de Gaulle himself, heading the French Committee of National Liberation, had by now also proposed to Churchill that the Free French seize the islands. Churchill saw no objection but asked the Canadian Government to ascertain the attitude of the United States. Roosevelt strongly disapproved the proposed Free French action and asked instead that the proposal to send a small group of civilian technicians be carried out by Canada alone. On learning of the U.S. objections, the United Kingdom asked the French Committee not to take action.[62]

De Gaulle nevertheless ordered his commander of the Free French naval force at Halifax to act without informing the Allies. Ostensibly sailing for St. John's, the force of three corvettes and the giant submarine *Surcouf* instead proceeded to St. Pierre, where it established control on 25 December 1941. The same day a plebiscite produced a 98 percent vote in favor of rallying to the Free French in preference to collaboration with the Axis.[63]

The U.S. Army Newfoundland base commander recommended on 28 December that the islands be left in Free French control. But on the day of the seizure Secretary of State Hull had issued a statement condemning as aribtrary, contrary to the agreement of the parties concerned, and without prior knowledge or consent of the United States, the action of the "so-called Free French" ships.[64] Hull took up with Canada the feasibility of restoring the *status quo ante* through establishment of a commission of Canadian experts to supervise the radio traffic and the withdrawal of the Free French. Canada was unwilling to challenge the Free French action and suggested that the United States and United Kingdom agree on a solution. Canada would be willing to co-operate in the execution of any agreement reached

[61] Journal, PDB 124.

[62] Ott Leg Telg 282, 3 Nov 41, D/S 851A.74/4; Memo/Conv, Moffat and Keenleyside, 14 Nov 41, Moffat Diary; Memo, Wrong for Secy State, 5 Dec 41, D/S 851A.74/12-541; Memo/Conv, Moffat and Robertson, 16 Dec 41, Moffat Diary; Churchill, *The Grand Alliance*, p. 667.

[63] The U.S. consul estimated that even a more neutrally worded choice would have given the Free French a 75 percent majority. (Desp 79, 26 Dec 41, D/S 851A/00/48.)

[64] Informal Rpt, NBC, 28 Dec 41, PDB 104-5; Department of State *Bulletin*, December 27, 1941, V, 580.

360-477 O - 70 - 12

by them.[65] Churchill, then in Washington, said he would be agreeable to any arrangement that would be acceptable to General de Gaulle. But Churchill's attitude, as exemplified by his speech in Ottawa on 30 December extolling de Gaulle's followers, did not appear to be designed to induce co-operative concessions from de Gaulle. After President Roosevelt let it be known that he would not back up State Department demands that the Free French be evicted and the *status quo ante* be restored, a solution acceptable to Churchill, Hull, and de Gaulle appeared impossible.[66]

Secretary Hull's attitude and his reference to the "so-called" Free French came under heavy public attack, even in the United States. In Canada it evoked considerable unfavorable publicity. In part, this was due to an accumulation of resentment over the U.S. attitude on a number of questions, including U.S. failure to discuss Pacific problems with the Canadian Government before the Pearl Harbor attack and U.S. opposition to Canadian participation at the Rio de Janeiro inter-American meeting.[67]

Although the Canadian Government was embarrassed by the Free French action, for the contrary assurances given by the Free French commander in Ottawa had been relayed to Washington through the Department of External Affairs, it took no positive position. To State Department officers, the Canadian attitude appeared to be casual and unconcerned. As for King, he had had nothing to do with the matter and only wanted it settled. By the end of January Hull had decided that the wisest course was to let the matter rest.[68]

Summary

Despite the hope of President Roosevelt and Prime Minister Mackenzie King, as expressed in the Ogdensburg Declaration, that defense problems could be jointly examined on a hemisphere basis, such joint examination was faced with complications in regard to the defense needs of the two countries themselves, let alone the contiguous areas of North and South America. There were several reasons for these complications. One was the simple fact that before Pearl Harbor Canada was a belligerent while the United States was a neutral. A second was Canada's membership in the British Commonwealth, which would not permit an unqualified allegiance to a hemisphere standard.

[65] Memo/Conv, Moffat and Dunn, 25 Dec 41, Moffat Diary; Memo/Conv, Hull and King, 27 Dec 41, D/S 581A.00/50.

[66] See Conn and Fairchild, The Framework of Hemisphere Defense, Ch. VII.

[67] Ott Leg Telg 4, 7 Jan 42, D/S 851A.01/13.

[68] Ott Leg Telg 313, 25 Dec 41, D/S 851A.01/17; Memo/Conv, Berle and McCarthy, 3 Jan 42, D/S 851A.01/65; Hull, *Memoirs*, II, 1137. A number of accounts of this problem are available. See Hull, *Memoirs*, II, 1127–38; Sherwood, *Roosevelt and Hopkins*, Ch. XXI; Langer and Gleason, *The Challenge to Isolation*, pp. 212–26; Churchill, *The Grand Alliance*, pp. 666–67.

Before Pearl Harbor the United States' front line of defense was the coast line of the Americas and their offshore waters. With Canadian troops deployed overseas, Canada considered its front line to be in Europe. From the military point of view, the United States saw merit in efforts designed to increase the military strength and programs of the Latin American countries. In considering the wishes of the United States that Canada join in encouraging these efforts, Canada was inclined to view expenditures of military resources in Latin America as diversions of critical means to a secondary area. Only from a political and longer-range economic point of view could the development of Canada's relations with the Latin American states make sense to Canada.

The neutral United States also considered Canadian and Commonwealth defensive measures in the Western Hemisphere in terms of their impact on the U.S. policy of neutrality, whereas British and Canadian plans vis-à-vis areas such as Greenland, St. Pierre and Miquelon, and other European possessions in the Western Hemisphere were based on the needs of their belligerent status. Because of this fundamental pre-Pearl Harbor split, it was impossible for the two countries to unite in the establishment of a common policy that would motivate jointly desired actions throughout the hemisphere.

After Pearl Harbor the encouragement of closer Canadian relations with Latin America ceased to be useful to the United States, which could either offer to Latin America the material support needed to carry out the desired military measures or take them itself. Under these circumstances, and from the longer-range point of view, the growth of Canadian and Commonwealth interest in Latin America would not accord with U.S. political and economic objectives, and it was therefore not encouraged.

CHAPTER VII

Operations in the Eastern Areas

In the pre-Pearl Harbor period the primary focus of military co-operation between the United States and Canada was on Newfoundland and adjacent northeastern North America. Although the Japanese threat was not disregarded, the operational requirements of the European war and the Battle of the Atlantic after the fall of France were immediate and absorbed most of the modest ground and air forces available to the two countries. For Canada this meant that forces had to be deployed to coastal areas, Iceland, and Great Britain. For the United States it meant that mobile reserves had to be held in readiness to meet and repel the first signs of aggression anywhere in the Western Hemisphere.

The defense needs of the British territory of Newfoundland, the North American outpost on the sea and air approaches to eastern Canada and the adjacent United States, were a matter of great concern to Canada. On the eve of Canadian entry into the European war Prime Minister King told the House of Commons that the integrity of Newfoundland and Laborador was essential to the security of Canada and that he had already obtained British agreement to Canadian participation in the defense of Newfoundland. Not long after the Canadian declaration of war on 10 September 1939, Canada took initial steps to aid in Newfoundland's defense.[1]

Although U.S. joint war plans had earlier recognized the need for offshore bases in the Caribbean and other Atlantic areas, U.S. interest in the Newfoundland area developed only after the fall of France. During the summer and fall of 1940 the British-American destroyer-bases negotiations resulted in the interjection of the United States into the Newfoundland defense scheme.[2] The fall of France also gave considerable impetus to the scope of Canadian participation in the defense of Newfoundland.

The Lease and Construction of Newfoundland Bases

While the French and British armies on the Continent were crumbling before the German blitzkrieg and the British defensive situation was deteriorating rapidly, Prime Minister Churchill on 15 May began his efforts to

[1] *H. C. Debates,* 8 Sep 39, p. 35. See Ch. IV, above.
[2] See Ch. I, above.

induce the United States to transfer some of its World War I destroyers to the British. During the next few months, as Britain and its Atlantic lines of communications lay exposed to the German war machine, repeated requests were to be made by Churchill to U.S. Ambassador Kennedy in London and to President Roosevelt himself. The question whether or not the destroyers should be loaned or transferred was debated at length in the United States.[3]

One arrangement examined at the suggestion of President Roosevelt, and of particular interest to this study, would have provided for sale of the destroyers to Canada on condition that they be used only in the Western Hemisphere. This arrangement would have aided Britain since it would have released Commonwealth ships for other purposes. In addition, it would have relieved the United States of some of its naval patrol responsibilities.[4]

The fall of France also resulted in more active consideration in U.S. military and political circles of the need for Atlantic bases in the defense of the Western Hemisphere. On 29 May 1940 Army Chief of Staff Marshall discussed with Under Secretary of State Welles the desirability of quickly establishing U.S. forces in the British possessions of the Western Hemisphere, "exclusive of Canada and Labrador," should the German victory threaten their surrender or cession. He proposed that the matter be discussed with Great Britain.[5] On 24 June General Marshall, accompanied by Chief of Naval Operations Stark, presented a joint estimate of the situation to President Roosevelt that reiterated the need for strategic bases in the Caribbean and Latin American areas. Even at this time the War and Navy Departments did not foresee the need for U.S. bases in Newfoundland or Canada.

With the services pressing for bases on the one hand and Churchill pleading for destroyers on the other, President Roosevelt at the beginning of August decided to tie the two propositions together. A renewed plea by Churchill on 31 July for the destroyers gave the President the opportunity to propose a trade to the British Prime Minister and in addition to seek new assurances concerning the British Fleet as part of the arrangement. Churchill responded favorably and expressed a willingness to grant limited rights to

---

[3] For accounts of negotiations and debates, see Conn and Fairchild, The Framework of Hemisphere Defense, Ch. II, and Langer and Gleason, *The Challenge to Isolation*. Ch. XXII. See also Kittredge Monograph, Vol. I, Sec. II, and Edward R. Stettinius, Jr., *Lend-Lease: Weapon for Victory* (New York: The Macmillan Company, 1944), pp. 33–43. Mr. Churchill's account is in *Their Finest Hour*, pp. 24–25, 188–89, and 401–14.

[4] Memo, for Secy Navy, 22 Jul 40, in *F. D. R., His Personal Letters*, II, 1049.

[5] The quotation is from WPD Memo, 27 May 40, WPD 4175–9, on which General Marshall noted: "Proposed to Mr. Welles in person, GCM." See also Ch. I, above.

utilize portions of selected air and naval bases.[6] On 13 August the President met with Mr. Welles and Secretaries Stimson, Knox, and Morgenthau and worked out a detailed plan, which was sent to Churchill, proposing the transfer of fifty destroyers and other matériel in return for the right to (a) acquire land by purchase or ninety-nine-year lease for the establishment of bases, and (b) utilize the bases at once for training purposes and, in event of attack on the Western Hemisphere, for operational purposes.[7] Two days later, on 15 August, Churchill indicated his agreement to ninety-nine-year leases subject to consultation with Newfoundland and Canada about the Newfoundland base, in which he said, Canada had an interest.[8]

The proposals continued to be studied in London and Washington while the necessary consultations took place. In Washington, some of the President's close advisers again suggested an initial transfer of the destroyers to Canada rather than directly to the United Kingdom, but Secretary of War Stimson pushed aside this idea as a discreditable subterfuge. In London, the Prime Minister discussed the provisions of the arrangement in the Parliament and with his Cabinet. On 22 August Churchill advised the President that his government wished to offer the base facilities without strings, and not as a trade for the destroyers. Since Roosevelt felt he had no authority to give the destroyers without compensation, discussions continued for a few days on this point until a formula satisfying both governments was found. The final agreement, embodied in an exchange of notes on 2 September 1940, provided that the base rights in Newfoundland and Bermuda were given "freely and without consideration." The other base rights, in the Caribbean area, were granted in exchange for the fifty over-age American destroyers.[9]

Another aspect of the transaction involved the U.S. request for assurances that, should the waters surrounding the British Isles become untenable, the British Fleet would in no event be either surrendered or sunk but would be sent overseas for the defense of other parts of the British Empire. The Prime Minister had already given such a pledge in Parliament on 4 June, and he objected initially, for psychological reasons, to a public reiteration. Nevertheless, since Roosevelt felt that concurrent assurances were a necessary adjunct to the arrangement, the British gave them by answering in the

[6] Morison, *The Battle of the Atlantic*, pp. 33–34; Churchill, *Their Finest Hour*, pp. 403–06; Memo, Lothian for Secy State, 8 Aug 40, D/S 811.34544/1-6/12.

[7] Stimson and Bundy, *On Active Service*, p. 356; D/S Telg 2316, to London, 13 Aug 40, D/S 811.34544/1-6/12.

[8] Churchill, *Their Finest Hour*, pp. 406–07.

[9] Stimson and Bundy, *On Active Service*, p. 357; Churchill, *Their Finest Hour*, pp. 408–13. The exchange of notes is in EAS, 235. According to Secretary of State Hull, the successful formula was proposed by Green H. Hackworth, his legal adviser.

affirmative the U.S. inquiry as to whether Churchill's 4 June statement represented "the settled policy of the British Government." [10]

The delivery of the destroyers began at once. British crews took over the first eight at Halifax on 6 September. The fifty 1,200-ton destroyers plus ten "Lake" class Coast Guard cutters well suited for escort work were delivered by 10 April 1941. Shortly after delivery began, it was announced that six of the destroyers would be commissioned in the Royal Canadian Navy. Named after rivers along the U.S.-Canadian border (*Annapolis, Columbia, St. Croix, St. Clair, St. Francis,* and *Niagara*), they brought the strength of the Canadian destroyer fleet to thirteen. A seventh destroyer, the *Hamilton,* was transferred to the Royal Canadian Navy after some service with the Royal Navy. [11]

Concerning the bases, the 2 September agreement provided that

a. The Newfoundland bases would be on the southern coast and on the Avalon Peninsula.

b. The bases would be on land leased for ninety-nine years free from all rent and charges except for compensation of private property owners. [12]

c. The exact location and bounds of the bases and the adjustment of the U.S. jurisdiction within the leased areas with that of the Newfoundland Government would be worked out by common agreement.

d. The United States would have all the rights and authority, within the bases and the adjacent waters and airspace, necessary to provide access thereto, and defense and control thereof. [13]

Before the exchange of notes, the consultations between London, Ottawa, St. John's, and Washington had gone into the question of the locations of the Newfoundland bases. United States service planners had recommended the lease of existing naval air facilities at Botwood and Gander Lake, naval facilities at St. John's, and the Newfoundland (Gander) Airport, plus sites at St. John's, and on the southeast coast for an Army and a Navy base re-

[10] Department of State *Bulletin,* September 7, 1940, III, 195. The assurances were sought by the President to help make the strongest case for the destroyer transfer since he was being severely criticized by many as having exceeded his authority. Sherwood (*Roosevelt and Hopkins,* p. 274) believes that the President considered impeachment to be a possible consequence. Some of the pro and con views on the transaction are set forth in the following articles in the *American Journal of International Law.* XXXIV (1940): Edwin Borchard, "The Attorney General's Opinion in the Exchange of Destroyers for Naval Bases," 690–97; Herbert W. Briggs, "Neglected Aspects of the Destroyer Deal," 569–87; and Quincy Wright, "The Transfer of Destroyers to Great Britain," 680–89.

[11] Morison, *The Battle of the Atlantic,* pp. 34–36; Schull, *The Far Distant Ships,* p. 56.

[12] In August 1943 the British Government offered to assume even these costs as a reverse lend-lease charge, and the offer was accepted.

[13] EAS, 235; Department of State *Bulletin,* August 14, 1943, IX, 97.

spectively. As a result of British and Canadian representations, Newfoundland Airport, already garrisoned by a Canadian Army infantry battalion and an RCAF flight of reconnaissance aircraft, was specifically excluded by President Roosevelt, who instead designated the areas that appeared in the agreement.[14] The Canadian and Newfoundland Governments approved the proposed locations and arrangements, although the Newfoundland Government actually granted approval on the day after the exchange of notes, 3 September.

By this time a board of U.S. service officers headed by Rear Adm. John W. Greenslade had been organized to work out with British experts the exact locations at all the ninety-nine-year-lease base sites. The Greenslade Board proceeded to Newfoundland, arriving there on 16 September, made its broad survey, and submitted its recommendations to Vice Adm. Walwyn, Governor of Newfoundland, on 20 September. It recommended a joint Army-Navy base on Placentia Bay, naval facilities and an Army base at St. John's and an air base near Stephenville for staging aircraft through the Maritime Provinces to eastern Newfoundland. The Greenslade Board also recommended that the lease agreement authorize the United States to use all harbors, anchorages, and airfields in Newfoundland. Admiral Walwyn accepted the proposals in principle, with generous reservations to meet British and Canadian observations that might be forthcoming.[15] On the recommendation of the Greenslade Board a team of thirty engineers of the U.S. Army Corps of Engineers, designated the Newfoundland Engineer District Office, arrived at St. John's on 13 October to make the detailed hydrographic and topographic surveys of the designated base sites.

By the beginning of 1941 the surveys, general and detailed, had been completed in Newfoundland and at all the other base sites, and a team of U.S. officials proceeded to London to work out the technical aspects of the leases. The technical discussions began on 25 January. During the ensuing weeks it was necessary for the negotiators to bridge an initially wide gulf. The approval of the Lend-Lease Act on 11 March had a beneficial effect on the negotiations, which were concluded on 27 March by the signing of a second leased-bases agreement setting forth the details of the leases.[16]

The agreement granted the United States, *inter alia,*

a. All the rights, power, and authority within (1) the leased areas

[14] JPC Rpt, 28 Aug 40, sub: Base Sites and Facilities, WPD 4351-5; Memo, SUSAM for ACofS WPD, 28 Feb 42, WPD 4351-9; Note for Record, 8 Jul 41, PDB 107-17.

[15] Journal, 27 Aug 40 PJBD meeting, PDB 124; Telg, from U. S. Consul General, St. John's 4 Sep 40, D/S 811.34544/14; Rpt, Board of Experts to Secy Navy, 24 Sep 40, WPD 4351-9; Ltr, to Greenslade, 21 Sep 40, WPD 4351-9.

[16] For an account of these negotiations, see Conn, Engelman, and Fairchild, Guarding the United States and Its Outposts.

necessary for the establishment, use, operation, and defense thereof, or appropriate for their control, and (2) the limits of territorial waters and adjacent airspaces necessary to provide access to and defense of the leased areas, or appropriate for control thereof.

b. When at war or during other emergency, all such rights, power, and authority as might be necessary for conducting military operations throughout Newfoundland and surrounding waters or airspaces.

c. Jurisdiction over all persons committing military offenses within the areas and over non-British subjects committing such offenses outside them.

d. Miscellaneous corollary rights as to the use of public services, conduct of surveys, immigration customs and other duties, postal facilities, and taxation.

e. The same rights and status for U.S. forces outside the leased areas under the agreements enjoyed by forces within these areas.

f. The right to acquire such additional areas as necessary for the use and protection of the bases.[17]

Pursuant to the 2 September 1940 and 27 March 1941 agreements, the Commission of Government for Newfoundland on 14 June 1941 leased to the United States 3,392 acres at Argentia (this parcel was to become Fort McAndrew and the adjacent naval base); 198.36 acres at Quidi Vidi, adjacent to St. John's (Fort Pepperrell); 27.57 acres at White Hills (near Fort Pepperrell for a radio tower area); 2.5 acres on St. John's harbor for a U.S. Army supply dock; and 867 acres at Stephenville (Harmon Field).[18]

Even before the leases were signed, construction at the Newfoundland bases had been initiated under authority granted by the United Kingdom on 11 November 1940. As a matter of fact, the U.S. Army, using local labor, had begun in October the construction of temporary housing, including barracks for 1,000 troops, and of administrative facilities at Fort Pepperrell. Permanent construction was begun on 30 December 1940 under the direction of the District Engineer. On 8 February 1941 the U.S. Army concluded a contract with Newfoundland Base Contractors, a company comprising three U.S. concerns as joint contractors, which assumed the responsibility for the Fort Pepperrell work on 19 May. Temporary construction was started at Harmon Field and Fort McAndrew on 10 and 18 March 1941, respectively, and the Newfoundland Base Contractors took over the work at these bases on 7 April and 5 May 1941.[19]

---

[17] EAS, 235; CTS, 1941, No. 2.
[18] The data in this and the next few paragraphs are from Corps of Engineers, North Atlantic
[19] Ltr, Neville Butler to Knox, 11 Nov 40, Roosevelt Papers Secy's File, Box 59.
Division, U. S. Army Bases: Newfoundland.

The initial plan for the three Army bases called for accommodations for garrisons of 3,500 troops at Fort Pepperrell, 2,000 at Fort McAndrew, and 250 at Harmon Field where an emergency landing field was to be built. The cost of the planned housing, auxiliary buildings, and utilities was estimated in 1940 as approximately $28,000,000. In early 1942 the plans were changed to provide accommodations for 5,500, 7,500, and 2,800 troops respectively, and to include a permanent landing field at Harmon Field comprising three concrete runways 150 feet wide and from 5,000 to 6,000 feet long. A large part of the augmentation was the result of the decision to retain and utilize the temporary housing that had been constructed. Work was completed at Fort Pepperrell on 15 March 1943, at Fort McAndrew on 3 March 1943, and at Harmon Field on 1 March 1943. The actual final cost of construction for the Army bases (including Harmon Field) totaled $60,300,212.

On 1 September 1943 Harmon Field entered upon a new phase. On that date the airfield passed to the jurisdiction of the Air Transport Command, which began to use it as a major base for its North Atlantic operations. A new development program was undertaken that lasted through most of 1944, the principal features of which were construction of two large hangars and extension of the existing runways. The enlarged base played a prominent role in Air Transport Command operations.

At Argentia, adjacent to Fort McAndrew, the U.S. Navy Department had begun construction of a naval air station on 29 December 1940.[20] Civilian contractors completed the air station in early 1942, when the decision was made to construct a complete naval operating base. Until housing could be erected for the 1,500 Americans and 4,000 Newfoundlanders who were ultimately to be engaged on this project, the SS *Richard Peck,* after its arrival on 9 January 1941, had housed some of the former, while the initial local labor force had lived in fishing schooners anchored in the harbor. In October 1942 a Navy construction battalion was sent to Argentia, and, after an additional battalion had arrived, the civilian contractors were relieved in May 1943. The major facilities developed at Argentia included three airfield runways 5,000 feet long (later lengthened), storage for 15,000,000 gallons of gasoline and oil, over 2,000 feet of wharf, a 7,000-ton floating dry dock, hangars, workshops and supply storage buildings, and the housing and other administrative facilities required for the garrison.

Construction undertakings of such magnitude naturally had a major im-

[20] For a full account of the development of the U. S. Navy facilities in Newfoundland, see U. S. Navy Department, Bureau of Yards and Docks, *Building the Navy's Bases in World War II* (Washington: Government Printing Office, 1947), II, 47–54.

pact on the native Newfoundlanders and their economy. Some effects were adverse. One early unhappy effect was the need in the fall of 1941 to evacuate the civilians occupying the Harmon Field base to permit runway construction to proceed. Other effects were beneficial. To the limited extent permitted by the relatively undeveloped state of Newfoundland resources and industry, materials were procured locally. The projects did provide extensive employment for Newfoundlanders, principally in the common labor category. At the peak of Army base construction, 82 percent of the workers were Newfoundlanders. They were paid at lower rates than the Americans, the pay scales having been established in co-operation with the Newfoundland Commissioner of Public Works and in conformity with the prevailing local rates. From the contractor's point of view, local labor was less satisfactory than U.S. labor for several reasons. Newfoundlanders were less skilled, and also made work scheduling difficult through their proclivity for long week ends and their unwillingness to work during the summer fishing season and the bad winter weather. Nevertheless, their employment at the lower pay scales resulted in lower costs for the construction. By August 1941 the rate of additional income for the island was estimated at $3,000,000 per month.

The establishment of the bases and the influx of almost 10,000 Americans brought other problems, too. Difficulties arose in the application of the jurisdiction and customs and taxes provisions of the bases agreement. These difficulties were worked out with the Newfoundland Government Commissioners in good spirit. Some excesses on the part of Americans took place as well as some price gouging by Newfoundlanders. But on the whole excellent relationships prevailed. The Americans participated and co-operated in the social and cultural activities of St. John's and established many friendships with local families. The activities of U.S. Public Health Service officers, together with those of medical officers of the Canadian and U.S. forces, contributed to a rise in the general health level, which had suffered from widespread dietary deficiencies, tuberculosis, and other factors.

As U.S. requirements at the bases became clearer, advantage was taken of Article XXVII of the 27 March 1941 agreement to obtain additional land areas through supplemental leases. The negotiations were carried on between Washington, London, and the Newfoundland Government in St. John's, with Canada playing only a minor and indirect role. A first supplement, filed in early 1941 and signed on 14 July 1942, added 2,142 acres to the original 4,487. The United States submitted a second supplement providing for approximately 10,000 additional acres just before the first supplement was signed. Because of introduction of changes and differences between State and War Department officers as to the scope of the supplement, the U.S. requirement did not become firm until early 1944. Thereafter negotiations languished for numerous reasons, including criticism by the Newfoundland Government of the 1 October 1944 ninety-nine-year lease arrangement with Canada and the postwar uncertainty as to the status of Newfoundland. The second supplement was finally approved on 21 August 1948. With this approval, wartime negotiations in connection with the leased-bases agreement ended and no further changes were required.[21]

Defending Newfoundland

In the pre-Pearl Harbor period when Canada and the United States deployed forces to Newfoundland the troops of both countries became, in effect, tenants on the territory of a third state. This fact presented some complications, at least from the U.S. point of view, in the timely establishment of the garrisons and provision of operating facilities. The Canadian military position in Newfoundland had developed progressively from the outbreak of the European war until August 1940, when informal but broad arrangements were worked out by Canadian authorities with the Newfoundland Commission. Under these and the earlier arrangements, Canada had disposed forces in Newfoundland and had undertaken the construction of such facilities as were necessary. Since the Canadian forces were stationed at locations such as Newfoundland Airport and St. John's harbor, where the major essential installations like runways and docks were already in existence, they could immediately become operational, and the construction requirements were largely in augmentation of the existing basic facilities.[22]

---

[21] With the addition of Newfoundland to Canada as a new province on 1 April 1949, the provisions of the leased-bases agreement and the supplemental leases were after that date to become the subject of extensive discussions between Ottawa and Washington.

[22] Subsequent Canadian construction in Newfoundland included a naval base at St. John's and a subsidiary naval repair base at Bay Bulls, a short distance to the south, the latter on land leased for ninety-nine years. Title to the St. John's base, which was built at Canadian expense and administered by the Royal Canadian Navy, was vested in the British Admiralty. Under the Air Bases Agreement concluded on 17 April 1941, Canada built a fighter base at Torbay, near St. John's, seaplane bases at Botwood and Gleneagles, and additional facilities at Newfoundland Airport. Under the postwar agreement disposing of the air facilities, Canada transferred control and operation of Botwood, Gleneagles, and Newfoundland Airport to the Newfoundland Government. Canada was paid one million dollars for the facilities constructed at Newfoundland Airport, and it retained the right to recapture this base in event of hostilities. Canada retained title in fee simple to the Torbay fighter base, as had been provided in the April 1941 agreement, with a view to using it as a commercial airport between Canada and Newfoundland. (See CTS, 1946, No. 15, and Heather J. Harvey, *Consultation and Co-operation in the Commonwealth* (New York: Oxford University Press, 1952), pp. 373–78). The 1946 postwar disposition ceased to have significance after the union of Newfoundland with Canada on 31 March 1949. Goose Bay Airport, whose construction was undertaken by Canada in August 1941, was covered by arrangements other than the Air Bases Agreement of 1941. The Goose Bay arrangements are discussed later in this chapter.

Since President Roosevelt had acquiesced in the Canadian and British requests that none of the available facilities be included within the U.S. leased areas, the sites leased to the United States were completely undeveloped. In order to garrison and utilize the leased bases the United States had first to construct the operational and administrative facilities required. Because of construction difficulties, the development of the air and naval facilities would require one to two years or more, thus denying to the United States the operational use of the bases for that period. Even before the base-agreement notes had been signed in September 1940, the Permanent Joint Board on Defense had on 27 August approved its Second Recommendation, which included provisions for construction of facilities for use by U.S. forces that would be deployed to Newfoundland only when and if circumstances required. Under these provisions, which accorded with the Canadian concept as to the need for U.S. forces in Newfoundland, Canada was to undertake to prepare facilities for forty-eight U.S. patrol seaplanes and seventy-three land planes.[23]

At the time the Board approved its First Report on 4 October 1940, no action had been initiated pursuant to the provisions of the Second Recommendation, and it therefore incorporated similar provisions in the report.[24] Although the First Report had been approved, action had not yet been taken toward preparing base facilities when, on 30 November, the Secretary of War requested that the base sites under negotiation with the United Kingdom be increased to include land adjacent to the Newfoundland Airport for the purpose of deploying a tactical air group, with a strength of seventy-three aircraft, as soon as facilities could be constructed.[25]

This arrangement was discussed at the Permanent Joint Board meeting on 17 December 1940, together with the alternative (preferred by Canada) of having Canada (a) provide the facilities, and (b) allow their use on an informal basis for operational training. When advised by U.S. Chairman LaGuardia that this alternative was acceptable, President Roosevelt approved it and directed the War Department to submit its requirements. The facilities requirements, submitted to and discussed with RCAF officers in the latter half of January 1941, comprised twelve hangars, twenty 136-man barracks, and auxiliary construction, the estimated cost of which totaled $4,569,670 (U.S.). The Canadian authorities estimated that housing for two squadrons would be available by 1 May 1941 and the balance of the facilities by early autumn.[26]

[23] Appendix A, below.

[24] Appendix B, below.

[25] Ltr, SW and Secy Navy to President, 30 Jan 41, WPD 4404.

[26] *Ibid.*; Memo, Bissell to Embick, 26 Dec 40; Ltr, SW to LaGuardia, 17 Jan 41; Ltr, Lt Col H. L. Clark to ACofS WPD, n.d., reporting on conferences 26–31 Jan 41; all in WPD 4404.

The circumstances of the actual deployment of U.S. air elements to Newfoundland Airport have already been recited.[27] By autumn 1941, the facilities constructed by Canada for the United States exceeded the requirements of the U.S. forces actually there. A minor hiatus occurred when Canada expressed a desire to use these surplus facilities until they were needed by the United States. The latter replied that they could not be made available since additional forces were being readied for dispatch to the airport and would require the facilities upon arrival. Nevertheless, according to the U.S. commander, the RCAF not only converted many such buildings to its own use but also gave the remaining construction for the United States a low priority. The Permanent Joint Board at its November meeting considered the situation and acted to rectify it. Having agreed that the international situation made it desirable that the United States reinforce its air garrison at Gander Airport (as Newfoundland Airport had been redesignated), and having noted that the United States was prepared to do this, the Board concluded that Canada should make available without delay the completed facilities that had been constructed for the United States and should expedite the uncompleted construction. The United States suggested the employment of Army Engineer units to assist in completing the construction, but the RCAF on the advice of labor experts strongly advised against it, and the proposal was dropped.[28] After Pearl Harbor the discussions became academic, since the new situation resulted in the diversion of the squadron of B-17B aircraft originally destined for Gander and in the revision of plans for dispatching additional units to Newfoundland.

In approving the Permanent Joint Board's First Report in the fall of 1940, Canada had also undertaken to provide facilities in Newfoundland for three squadrons of U.S. patrol seaplanes. In January 1941 the Board had recommended that the provision of facilities for at least one squadron at Botwood should be given the most urgent priority. In the following months this work was initiated, and by the summer of 1941 clearing had been completed and construction was in progress. Finally, the Board had, in its First Report, indicated that a new fighter base would be required in the vicinity of St. John's to meet the joint defense needs in Newfoundland. Work had been begun in the spring of 1941 at Torbay, and by the end of that year the airport was operational. Canada extended the use of this airport to the

[27] See Ch. IV, above.

[28] Memo, ACofS WPD for SUSAM, 21 Oct 41, PDB 107-9; Ltr, CG NBC to DCofS, 29 Oct 41, PDB 104-5; Journal, 20-21 Nov and 20 Dec 41 PJBD meetings, PDB 124; Memo/Conv, Moffat and Keenleyside, 12 Aug 41, Moffat Diary. A letter of 25 November 1941 (Heakes to Bissell, PDB 107-9) outlined the measures being taken to make five hangars available to the U.S. Army by the end of December.

United States as expedient and necessary as an alternate airport and for servicing purposes.[29]

Shortly after Pearl Harbor the U.S. Section of the Permanent Joint Board asked if the United States could permanently station its own servicing detachment at Torbay. However, in line with the Canadian determination to retain the predominant role on the Newfoundland defense scene and to limit the U.S. role, the proposal was coolly received; it was made clear that Canada did not wish U.S. personnel stationed there. This position was later modified, and in May 1943 the Canadian Government approved U.S. construction of servicing facilities there, provided that they were placed on land acquired by Canada and that the contracts were approved by the RCAF. These provisos were apparently not to U.S. liking, for the United States withdrew its request, citing as the reason (and thereby contradicting a statement on the subject made one month earlier) the fact that the facilities were no longer a wartime necessity since the U.S. AAF antisubmarine force in Newfoundland would be reduced in the near future.[30]

In the period immediately after Pearl Harbor both Canada and United States continued to enlarge their garrisons in Newfoundland as the construction of facilities and the availability of forces permitted. Canada augmented the infantry defenses of each of the RCAF bases by a special airdrome defense platoon equipped with tracked carriers for high mobility. The Canadian Army likewise provided antiaircraft defense for St. John's and for Torbay and Gander Airports and harbor defenses at St. John's, Bell Island, and Botwood. These augmentations brought the Canadian Army strength to a 1943 peak of approximately 5,700.

During 1942 the U.S. Army added an infantry battalion, four harbor defense artillery batteries, and six antiaircraft gun batteries. Platoons of two 155-mm. guns each were stationed at Harmon Field and Fort McAndrew, those at the latter site augmenting the two 6-inch gun batteries installed by the U.S. Navy. The infantry garrison was principally divided between Forts Pepperrell and McAndrew, with one reinforced company stationed at Harmon. The U.S. Army garrison (including air units) reached its peak strength of 10,882 in 1943.

A draft agreement negotiated after Pearl Harbor provided that the following U.S. forces might be made available on the call of the commander of Canada's Atlantic Command upon approval of the Commanding General, Eastern Defense Command, for reinforcing Newfoundland and the Maritime

[29] Appendix B, below; ABC-22.

[30] Ltr, Bissell to Brant, 30 Dec 41; Ltr, Hickerson to SUSAM, 20 May 42; Ltr, ACofS OPD to SUSAM, 14 Jun 43; all in PDB 107-3.

Provinces: one composite bombardment group and one pursuit squadron for Newfoundland and/or Nova Scotia; one infantry division, reinforced and motorized, and one mobile antiaircraft regiment for eastern Canada.[31] Although the agreement was not formally approved, it at least furnished a planning basis for reinforcing Newfoundland and the Maritime Provinces should such action become necessary. Some minor local liaison and administrative co-operation was carried out, but there was no significant operational co-operation between Canada and the United States in regard to the ground and air defense of the Maritime Provinces, or of New England. Pursuant to the Third Recommendation and the First Report of the Permanent Joint Board, the two countries undertook to develop certain defense and related facilities in this area, including the expansion by Canada of airfields in the Maritimes, so as to provide for the operations of forty-eight patron seaplanes and a composite wing of 200 land planes. Both countries proceeded with the execution of appropriate projects, rendering progress reports thereon at the meetings of the Permanent Joint Board. Insofar as they were planned for joint use in emergency operations in the Maritimes, the projects never came into use.

Enemy activity in the immediate vicinity of Newfoundland and its territorial waters never exceeded nuisance proportions. As the German submarine offensive moved closer to North American shores in the spring of 1942, the patrol and bomber aircraft based on Newfoundland began to assume an increasingly important role in the Battle of the Atlantic, but the rest of the Newfoundland garrisons were not called upon for an active defense role. As early as the spring of 1942, it was believed that German submarines not only were using inlets for night surfacing and battery charging but also making reconnaissances of Conception, Placentia, and St. Georges Bays and adjacent installations. Several attacks on enemy submarines were made by destroyer and aircraft, but no positive successes could be reported.[32]

The vulnerability of the city of St. John's was always a source of concern to the U.S. commander there. The predominantly wooden dwellings and the congestion of shipping in the harbor and of materials and supplies on the docks and in adjacent warehouses presented an excellent target for an in-

---

[31] Memo, ACofS OPD for SUSAM, 8 Apr 42, PDB 135-2.

[32] It was during this period that German submarines penetrated the mouth of the St. Lawrence River, and, in the five months following May 12, torpedoed 23 ships with the loss of 700 lives and 70,000 tons of shipping. For a full account of these forays, which had a substantial psychological impact on the communities along the river banks, see Jack MacNaught, "The Battle of the St. Lawrence," *Maclean's Magazine*, LXII (15 October 1949), 7, 68-70, and (1 November 1949), 22, 47-49.

cendiary attack. Fortunately an attack never materialized. In March 1942 the enemy fired two torpedoes which detonated on either side of the harbor entrance. In September and December of the same year a German submarine ventured into Conception Bay and on each occasion sank two ore boats. A year later, in October 1943, the enemy mined the approaches to St. John's harbor, presumably by submarine, necessitating minesweeping operations over a period of several weeks. One of the effects of enemy activity in adjacent Atlantic waters was the loss through sinkings of construction materials having a value of $550,000 and representing 3 percent of the materials imported for U.S. construction projects.

In mid-1943, with the beginning of a clear trend toward the reduction of German capabilities in the vicinity of Newfoundland, both Canada and the United States began to reduce their garrisons. By the end of 1943, the U.S. force, which had six months earlier exceeded 10,000, was reduced to 5,000. The major unit withdrawn was the 3d Infantry Regiment. Canada, too, on a smaller scale, made initial withdrawals reducing the Canadian Army force from 5,700 to 5,000.

Preparations for the defense of Newfoundland had involved the development and construction of facilities other than the main military bases. As the U.S. garrisons were established and as base construction got under way during the early months of 1941, the Canadian and U.S. commanders acting both unilaterally and jointly carried out reconnaissance of the island. The reconnaissance indicated additional defense needs that included (a) field fortifications for the ground garrison, (b) an aircraft warning system, (c) extensive improvement of the Newfoundland Railway, and (d) construction of a road from St. John's to Argentia.[33]

During the ensuing months the ground garrisons, both Canadian and U.S. proceeded to construct the machine gun nests, strong points, and other field fortications needed to augment the defense of the principal areas around St. John's and Conception Bay. Alternate and reserve firing positions for mobile 155-mm. guns were prepared at various possible landing beaches. In addition, the permanent works necessary for emplacement of coast defense guns and searchlights, together with the necessary housing, power, and communications facilities, were built. The United States built a bombproof command post at Fort McAndrew.

Arrangements between U.S. and Canadian commanders for the establishment of an integrated radar air warning system had to be worked out before actual construction and installation of the stations could begin. It would

[33] Journal, 29 Jul 41 PJBD meeting, PDB 124.

360-477 O - 70 - 13

155-MM. GUN EMPLACEMENT *at Fort McAndrew, Newfoundland, May 1943.*

have been sounder to operate a single system as an integrated unit. But each country desired to operate and control the system, particularly Canada, which wanted to integrate the system with that for the Maritime Provinces. A complicating factor was the fact that, by agreement, the air defense of the north half of the island was a Canadian responsibility, and that of the south half was a U.S. responsibility. The RCAF considered a nine-station net necessary, but it could not immediately provide the required equipment. The United States desired for its purposes a five-station net, of which two stations would be in the RCAF area.[34]

The Air members of the Permanent Joint Board considered the problem and on 13 May 1942 agreed that the United States should install and man its five-station net, with stations at Fogo Island, Cape Bonavista, Cape Spear, Allans Island, and St. Bride's, until such time as the RCAF could make Canadian sets available. The RCAF was to install its available sets in what would make up the balance of the Canadian net. After the installations were made, the RCAF command's No. 1 Group and the U.S. Newfoundland Base Command each operated independent filter centers and operational control organizations, with both systems receiving data from all stations on

[34] Journal, 21 Apr 42 PJBD meeting, PDB 124; Memo, SUSAM for ACofS OPD, 30 Mar 42, PDB 123.

the island.[35] By the end of the summer the Canadian radar equipment had become available, but the U.S. commander, loath to yield operation of his warning net to the RCAF, requested reconsideration of the arrangement previously worked out. No action was taken and the existing arrangement continued until the spring of 1944.

The United States in May 1944 expressed a desire to transfer the stations to Canadian control in order to release U.S. personnel for service in more active theaters. Acceding to the request, Canada assumed control during the succeeding few months under an arrangement whereby the U.S. equipment was retained and the United States supplied the spare parts needed. This arrangement continued throughout the war and into the immediate postwar period, since the system continued to be useful during the demobilization period for air rescue and movement control purposes.[36]

Major deficiencies in transportation facilities in Newfoundland were recognized in the initial surveys of the Greenslade Board in September 1940. Adequate road and rail nets were lacking, and the existing railroad was reported as having small capacity and needing extensive replacement of rolling stock and rehabilitation of repair facilities. Although the roadbed of the 707-mile narrow-gauge railroad, which was owned and operated by the Newfoundland Government, was in good condition, its predominantly 50-pound rail and limited bridge capacities would probably be inadequate for heavy haulage.[37] The scope and condition of the island's transportation facilities became a matter of early concern, since they not only would be a handicap during the time the bases were under construction but also would place definite limitations on the mobility of the defensive garrison.

Early in 1941 steps were initiated in different quarters to improve the condition of the railroad. In January the general manager of the Newfoundland Railway discussed with the U.S. consul general in St. John's the possibility of financing the materials and equipment needed under the pending lend-lease legislation as being related to the construction of the air and naval bases. The U.S. officials who considered the proposal concluded that a sufficiently broad interpretation of the proposed law would not be possible.[38]

[35] Journal, 9 Jun 42 PJBD meeting, PDB 124; Agreement, 12 Sep 42, PDB 123.

[36] Memo, ACofS OPD to CofS, 10 Oct 42; Memo, SUSAM for Cdn Air Member, 15 May 44; both in PDB 123.

[37] Greenslade Rpt, 24 Sep 40, WPD 4351-9. For an account of U. S. Army transportation difficulties to and within Newfoundland, see Joseph Bykofsky and Harold Larson, *The Transportation Corps: Operations Overseas,* UNITED STATES ARMY IN WORLD WAR II (Washington: Government Printing Office, 1957), pp. 9–11.

[38] Ltr, U.S. Consul General, St. John's, to Hickerson, 23 Jan 41; Reply, 15 Feb 41; both in D/S 740.0011EW 1939/7919–3/9.

In April 1941 a representative of the Newfoundland Government appeared before the Permanent Joint Board at one of its meetings to outline the railroad problem and the requirements for its solution. The Board took cognizance of the importance of the rehabilitation work to adequate supply of the U.S. bases and forces in agreeing on its Sixteenth Recommendation. This recommendation called for financial assistance by the United States to Newfoundland as needed for rehabilitating and augmenting the railroad's rolling stock by the amount necessary to meet U.S. military requirements. The rehabilitation requirements were also incorporated into the joint defense plan, ABC-22, which was being drafted concurrently.[39]

In approving the Sixteenth Recommendation, President Roosevelt directed the Reconstruction Finance Corporation to work out the financial arrangements and made $1,250,000 from his emergency fund available for procurement of the rolling stock for the U.S. Army. During the ensuing months several surveys were made in which the cost of railroad rehabilitation to be undertaken with U.S. financial assistance was variously estimated at from $5.5 to $7.0 million (U.S.). Reconstruction Finance Corporation officials conducted an independent survey and discussed the problem with the Newfoundland authorities during August 1941. As a result, a U.S. loan was worked out in principle for $2.1 million, which covered the "absolutely necessary improvements"—five new locomotives, 150 cars of various types, work equipment, and augmentation of repair facilities.[40] The formalities for the loan were completed on 24 November 1941, and the final barrier was cleared with the enactment by the Newfoundland Government on 4 December of the Railway Loan Act.

By this time the U.S. Army had already procured and delivered for operation by railroad authorities the one hundred flat and tank cars it had agreed to provide over and above the rolling stock being obtained under the loan. Title to these cars, and to the five locomotives that were delivered shortly, was retained by the United States. An additional direct U.S. contribution to the railroad rehabilitation was the replacement of the 50-pound rail on the Argentia Branch (supplying Fort McAndrew and the naval base) with 70-pound rail, a project that had been dropped from the curtailed rehabilitation program being financed by the U.S. loan.

Except within the base areas, U.S. forces undertook only one major piece of highway construction in Newfoundland. Harmon Field in southwestern Newfoundland was connected with the Avalon Peninsula by the cross-island

[39] Appendix A; Journal, 23 Apr 41 PJBD meeting, PDB 124.

[40] Ltr, President to SW, 23 Apr 41, PDB 117; Ltr, Commissioner of Defense L. E. Emerson to Hickerson, 23 Aug 41, Department of State Office of Dominion Affairs, PJBD 1941.

railroad. The Argentia-Fort McAndrew base was connected with St. John's by both rail and highway, but the fifty-four miles of highway between the base and Holyrood was inadequate for military purposes. At a meeting of the Permanent Joint Board on Defense on 30 July 1941, Newfoundland Defense Commissioner L. E. Emerson discussed with Board members the highway requirements of Canadian and U.S. forces and possible arrangements for meeting them. Of particular concern to the Newfoundland Government was the maintenance burden being imposed by the heavy military traffic on the island's roads. At the meeting, the Board adopted its Twentieth Recommendation, embodying arrangements suggested by Emerson, which in part authorized both Canada and the United States to construct and maintain such roads as either required. Under the recommendation, the maintenance of such of the roads as the two countries did not see fit to maintain was to be a responsibility of the Newfoundland authorities. Despite the renewed efforts of Newfoundland during the succeeding few months to get Canada and the United States to accept a greater responsibility for maintenance, the positions of the two countries remained firm.[41]

Under the arrangements set forth in the Twentieth Recommendation, the United States proceeded to reconstruct the fifty-four-mile Holyrood–Argentia highway. In the period 1 May–15 December 1942, fourteen miles of highway was relocated and the road was paved with gravel to a 24-foot width along its entire length. The improvements allowed the St. John's–Argentia drive, which formerly required six to eight hours, to be made in two hours.

Communications presented the last major auxiliary facility requirement outside the base areas. By mid-1941 it was apparent to the U.S. authorities that the existing wire line, which paralleled the cross-island railroad, would be inadequate. Even when supplemented by radio networks, the communications were unable to meet the administrative and operational needs of the garrisons. Of particular importance was adequate communications service for the aircraft warning network.

No action had been initiated before the end of 1941, when winter storms began to demonstrate the vulnerability of the wire-line system. Two months of bad weather during January and February 1942 caused extensive breakdown of the wire lines, but the difficulty was climaxed by the damage of a "glitter" storm, involving very heavy ice loads. On the main line some three hundred poles and five hundred cross arms were broken, and hundreds of wire breaks occurred. Two weeks was required to restore telephone service between St. John's and Argentia.

---

[41] Appendix A, below; Journal, 30 Jul 41 PJBD meeting, PDB 124; Ltr, Hickerson to Emerson, 21 Nov 41, Department of State Office of Dominion Affairs, PJBD 1941.

The United States decided to install a telephone cable line adequate to meet the requirements of the several users—the railroad, local officials and police, and the military garrisons of Canada and the United States. The costs were to be borne by the United States, which in turn would be reimbursed on a suitable basis by the users. The telephone cable was expected to be less vulnerable than wire lines. Using a $3.5-million appropriation made available for the purpose, the Newfoundland Base Command in June 1942 contracted with the Bell Telephone Company of Canada for installation of a telephone cable line along the Newfoundland Railway between Whitbourne and Stephenville, the materials to be supplied by the U.S. Army. This project also included the necessary repeater stations and other auxiliary features, and an open wire line from Shoal Harbor to the radar station at Bonavista. Concurrently, a contract was let to the Western Union Telegraph Company for a smaller project involving the construction of a telephone cable between Forts Pepperrell and McAndrew at a cost of $213,000.

In effect, during World War II Newfoundland had two independent sets of defense installations, each with its own defense garrison and under its own defense command. Through the media of joint planning and maneuvers, and of co-ordination of operations on the basis of co-operation between the commanders, a reasonable degree of success was achieved in integrating the garrisons of the two countries. But it was evidently Canadian policy to restrict the scope, or at least the character, of the U.S. defense role in Newfoundland.

Canada's wartime policy toward Newfoundland may have been motivated by both military and political considerations. To Canadian eyes, Newfoundland was a key element of the Canadian defense problem, in the solution of which Canada desired to maintain the predominant position. Likewise, with an eye to the future and a possible revision of the political status of Newfoundland, Canada might naturally be inclined to prevent the development of a situation in which political association with the United States might appear more desirable to Newfoundlanders than other possible courses, such as joining the Canadian Confederation. During the World War II and postwar years, a significant amount of consideration was given by Newfoundlanders in public discussion and the local press to the desirability of political association with the United States as a possible solution to the problem of Newfoundland's political status. To many, this solution promised a brighter economic future than other solutions such as association with Canada. Any encouragement by U.S. officials would probably have increased the sentiment favoring a link to Washington. No such encouragement was offered, and, in consequence of this attitude, Newfoundland became increasingly interested in union with Canada, which saw this step as politically and strategically desirable.

North Atlantic Ferry Operations

One of the major missions of the air bases in Newfoundland was that of supporting the ferrying of aircraft across the Atlantic from North America to the European battle zones. Throughout the war years an ever-increasing number of airplanes staged through these and other bases in eastern Canada and the North Atlantic to help meet the requirements of the Allied air forces. At its full development this operation represented an important joint U.S.-Canadian contribution to the war effort, for the movement of aircraft eastward utilized an integrated network of bases constructed and manned by personnel of both countries.

The first step in building this "Atlantic bridge" was taken in July 1940 when the British Ministry of Aircraft Production arranged with the Canadian Pacific Railway Company for the operation of a ferry service between a western terminal at Dorval Airport near Montreal and an eastern terminal at Prestwick, Scotland. Aircraft were to be delivered by civilian pilots to Dorval from plants of U.S. aircraft manufacturers in California. The first delivery, seven Lockheed Hudsons, took place on 11 November 1940, and involved a 2,100-mile hop from Newfoundland Airport to the United Kingdom. By February 1941 Boeing Flying Fortresses (B-17's) and Consolidated Liberators (B-24's) were also being flown over the route.[42]

On 15 July 1941 the ferrying operation was taken over by the British Ministry of Aircraft Production itself through its ATFERO (Atlantic ferrying organization), and the Canadian Pacific Railway agreement was terminated. At this time 59 percent of the pilots were American, 10 percent Canadian, and 28 percent British. ATFERO was short-lived, for on 1 August the responsibility was assumed by the Royal Air Force Ferry Command, which had been established on 20 July.

United States participation in the ferrying of aircraft produced for the United Kingdom began shortly after approval of the initial lend-lease appropriations on 27 April 1941. In early May 1941 U.S. Army Air Corps and British officials discussed a plan for U.S. assumption of the transcontinental portion of the ferrying. The arrangement appealed to the Air Corps since it would provide additional training opportunities in the coast-to-coast operation of the latest types of aircraft. The British anticipated a reduction in

[42] More detailed accounts of the ferrying operations are to be found in Craven and Cate (eds.), *Plans and Early Operations*, and Great Britain, Central Office of Information, *Atlantic Bridge* (London: His Majesty's Stationery Office, 1945).

the cost of delivery of the aircraft and the release of large numbers of civilian ferry pilots who could then be employed on the transatlantic leg of the delivery route. On 28 May President Roosevelt assigned to the War Department the responsibility for delivery of lend-lease aircraft to the point of ultimate take-off from the United States for the United Kingdom. The next day, 29 May, the Air Corps Ferrying Command came into existence by an order that was formalized on 5 June.[43] In the six months preceding Pearl Harbor, the command ferried 1,350 aircraft to the eastern seaboard for further movement by air or water, financing these operations with over $60,000,000 from lend-lease funds. The scope of the ferrying operation was enlarged during the pre-Pearl Harbor period by a Presidential directive of 3 October 1941, which authorized delivery to any territory within the Western Hemisphere, and by one of 24 November, which expanded the delivery authority "to such other places . . . as may be necessary to carry out the lend-lease program." [44]

Several months before the United States began actively to participate in the transatlantic ferrying operation, the U.S. Army had conducted preparatory studies and discussed the airfield requirements of an expanded operation with British and Canadian officials. It had concluded that additional bases would be needed to permit the ferrying of short-range aircraft, and that because of congestion at the Newfoundland Airport other facilities would have to be provided for long-range aircraft.

Short-range aircraft were to be ferried to the United Kingdom over a route through Greenland and Iceland. In Iceland, the British had constructed airfields at Reykjavik and Kaldaharnes after they established a garrison there in 1940. In Greenland, owing to British and Canadian interest in 1940 and early 1941 in airfields for ferrying operations, the United States proceeded to garrison the island and develop air bases.[45] Construction was begun in Greenland in early July 1941 at Narsarssuak, near Julianehaab, on an airfield having the code designation BLUIE WEST ONE (simplified to BW-1), and in late September 1941 on BW-8 on the Søndre Strømfjord.

The need for airfield facilities to augment those at Newfoundland Airport was first examined by U.S. and Canadian authorities at an Ottawa meeting on 20 March 1941. Canada was asked to survey Labrador for possible sites for staging fields near the village of North West River and also

[43] Army Air Forces, Air Transport Command, Administrative History of the Ferrying Command, 29 May 1941–30 June 1942, pp. 2–8; Ltr, President to SW, 28 May 41, Roosevelt Papers, Secy's File, Box 74.

[44] Administrative History of the Ferrying Command, 29 May 1941–30 June 1942, pp. 58–59.

[45] See Ch. VI, above. On Iceland, additional air-base development was carried out by the U.S. armed forces after their arrival there.

at points farther north. The United States authorities expressed a readiness to undertake surveys as well as development of bases. Canadian authorities after subsequent discussion undertook to make the survey for a site in the vicinity of North West River, Labrador. The United States received authority to make, and concurrently initiated, its own surveys, which it wished to extend northward for possible sites at Hebron, Labrador, and on Baffin Island.[46]

The U.S. surveys were made by a party headed by Capt. Elliott Roosevelt, son of the President and intelligence officer of the 21st Reconnaissance Squadron based at Newfoundland Airport. Its mission was to locate a site in the vicinity of North West River, as well as sites in northern Labrador and on Baffin Island. The latter sites, together with a site to be located in eastern Greenland, would complete the ferry route for short-range aircraft.

In late June, after several weeks' search, the Canadian survey party, under Eric Fry of the Dominion Geodetic Survey, located an eminently suitable airfield site near North West River. On 1 July Captain Roosevelt located the same site and reconnoitered it from the air. The two parties joined at a suitable landing site some distance away and proceeded on foot for a joint ground survey on 4 July 1941.[47] Both parties then returned and rendered favorable reports.

In mid-July the United States proposed, in a letter from Mayor LaGuardia to Colonel Biggar, that an airfield be constructed at once at the North West River site (later designated Goose Bay), and obtained British service support in Washington for urgent action on the proposal. On 28 July word was received in Washington that the RCAF had concluded that development of an airfield would not be possible that summer. The United States then offered aid as a means of expediting construction, and the North West River airfield project was further discussed on 29 July at the meeting of the Permanent Joint Board. As a result, the Board approved its Seventeenth Recommendation, which called upon Canada urgently to construct an air base and auxiliary facilities near North West River. If Canada were unable to do so, construction by the United States was to be arranged.[48] The Cabinet War Committee approved the recommendation on 13 August 1941.

[46] Minutes of Conference, WPD 4173-80; Memo for Record, Conference With General Arnold on 17 Jun 41, WPD 4173-77; Memo, ACofS WPD for SUSAM, 23 Jun 41, WPD 4506-4.

[47] Ltr, Capt Elliott Roosevelt to TAG, 6 Jul 41, WPD 4506-10. For an account of how the data from a 1935 timber survey led Fry to this site, see Kenneth Wright, "How Goose Bay Was Discovered," *The Beaver*, Outfit 277 (June 1946), pp. 42-45.

[48] Appendix A, below; Journal PJBD meetings 29 Jun and 10-11 Nov 41, PDB 124; Ltr, Maj Gen H. H. Arnold to Air Marshall A. T. Harris, 17 Jul 41, and Reply, 28 Jul 41, both in WPD 4506-4.

The Canadians worked rapidly to get construction of the Goose Bay base under way. Detailed surveys were completed by 20 August, a contract was let in early September by the Department of Transport to a Canadian contractor, and the first ship arrived at the site on 19 September. Work was pressed on a twenty-four-hour basis. By 16 November three 7,000-foot runways could receive aircraft, and the following month the airfield was in use. With the closing of the water navigation season, the U.S. Army Air Forces furnished an airplane for transport of materials to the site to permit construction to continue through the winter.[49]

In the meantime, the Roosevelt party had continued its surveys farther north. During the last half July 1941, potential airfield sites were found at Fort Chimo in the Province of Quebec and at upper Frobisher Bay and Cumberland Sound on Baffin Island. Padloping Island was later substituted for Cumberland Sound.[50] The United States soon concluded that the season was too far advanced to undertake airfield construction, but it requested and received, on 22 August, Canadian approval for the establishment of weather stations at the three sites. On 20 September 1941 a ship carrying the weather detachments and construction materials left New York for the three sites, which received the code designations CRYSTAL I (Fort Chimo), CRYSTAL II (upper Frobisher Bay), and CRYSTAL III (Padloping Island). The detachments reached their destinations in October and by the end of the year had constructed the necessary shelter and facilities and were in operation.[51]

The early months of 1942 found major difficulties developing in connection with North Atlantic ferrying operations. As a result of U.S. entry into the war, plans were being laid for the movement of large numbers of tactical aircraft in formations to the United Kingdom. Then, too, the mounting tide of defense production was making increasing numbers of aircraft available for delivery to Great Britain. As if to compound the congestion that would result at Gander and Torbay Airports, spring thaws would render the Goose Bay runways unusable until they could be stabilized or paved for year-round use. Additional, suitably spaced airfields were still needed to permit ferrying of short-range aircraft.

[49] For an account of the development of the base, which was designated Goose Bay, see "Stepping Stone to Europe," *Canada at War*, No. 25 (Jun 43), pp. 3–6. An unofficial account by the senior Royal Canadian Navy officer stationed at the base is to be found in William G. Carr, *Checkmate to the North* (Toronto: The Macmillan Company, 1945).

[50] On 9 August, during the Atlantic Conference at Argentia, the development of these sites as a short-range ferry route was discussed by the President with General Arnold, Captain Roosevelt, and other officers.

[51] Journal, 9 Sep 41 PJBD meeting, PDB 124; Arnold, *Global Mission*, p. 250. An account of the difficulties encountered in transporting materials to those sites is contained in Bykofsky and Larson, *The Transportation Corps: Operations Overseas*, pp. 11–13.

MAYOR FIORELLO H. LAGUARDIA *(second from left) in Newfoundland, September 1942. With him are Hon. L. E. Emerson (left), Brigadier G. P. Vanier, and Capt. Harry DeWolfe (far right).*

The Permanent Joint Board discussed the problem of additional staging airfield requirements at its 27 April and 26–27 May 1942 meetings. At the first of these meetings, the Canadian Section suggested, tentatively and subject to further study, that Canada would be prepared to develop an airfield at Fort Chimo and perhaps at other sites. By the time of the second of the two meetings the War Department had approved a detailed plan, later designated the CRIMSON Project, which the Senior U.S. Army Member outlined to the Canadian Section on 27 May. The Board then recessed to permit its thorough examination.[52]

[52] The ebullient LaGuardia reported to the President on the meeting: "I consider this meeting the most important we have had . . . . The plan itself challenges imagination. It is so gigantic and dramatic. It took our Canadian colleagues by surprise and frankly they have not yet recovered." (Ltr, 28 May 42, Roosevelt Papers, Official File 4090.) A Canadian appraisal of the task had been informally given the U.S. minister a few days earlier by C. D. Howe, who thought that the United States was underestimating the difficulties, such as the long nights and high winds, involved in constructing and operating a base such as the one proposed for Baffin Island. Howe indicated that he would be unwilling to accept such a responsibility for Canada for fear that heavy losses would be incurred. (Memo/Conv, 23 May 42, Moffat Diary.)

The Board on reconvening on 9 June reviewed at length a U.S. AAF presentation on the future requirements for movements over the North Atlantic Ferry Route. The increased traffic was seen as reaching, in 1943, a peak as high as one hundred combat and forty transport aircraft each day. To meet these requirements, a series of airfields 400 to 500 miles apart along three alternate routes was proposed:[53]

a. Eastern route—Fort Chimo, Baffin Island, east coast of Greenland, and Iceland.

b. Western route—Regina, The Pas, Churchill, Southampton Island, thence joining the eastern route at Baffin Island.

c. Central route—Moose Factory, Richmond Gulf, thence joining the eastern route at Baffin Island.

The airfields proposed would not only be adequate to meet foreseeable immediate requirements and provide alternate routes for flexibility to overcome adverse weather conditions but would also be suitable for expansion to meet increased requirements that might arise.

The Permanent Joint Board, after concluding that the aircraft to be ferried over the proposed routes might have a decisive effect in shortening the war, approved its Twenty-sixth Recommendation, calling for the construction by Canada and the United States of nine air bases in Canada and Greenland. The recommendation specified that all existing airfield facilities for ferrying aircraft located in Canada and Newfoundland, including Labrador, were to be considered a part of the project and increased in capacity wherever necessary. Each country was to bear the costs of the airfields it undertook to construct, but all the facilities in Canada were to become the property of Canada six months after the end of the war.[54]

While the two governments were considering the recommendation, the Combined Chiefs of Staff also studied the proposals, the shipping requirements of which would have an impact on those for the build-up of forces in the United Kingdom for the invasion of the European continent. The impact was so great that a Combined Chiefs of Staff committee recommended in mid-June that the project be rejected unless it could be acceptably modified. On 2 July the Combined Chiefs of Staff were able to approve a modified plan requiring water movement of only half the tonnage of the earlier plan. The new plan called for three permanent airfields—at The Pas, Churchill, and Southampton Island—and for airfields with snow-compacted

[53] Journal, PDB 124; U.S. AAF, Appreciation of the North Atlantic Ferry Routes, 6 Jun 42, appended to the journal.

[54] Appendix A, below; Appreciation of the North Atlantic Ferry Routes, cited n.53.

runways, for winter use only, at CRYSTAL I, CRYSTAL II or III, and on the east coast of Greenland. The curtailment involved elimination of the central route and of one airfield on Baffin Island and substitution of winter airfields for permanent airfields at three of the remaining sites.[55]

By the time the Permanent Joint Board on Defense met on 6 July 1942, both governments had approved the Twenty-sixth Recommendation. A week later the Canadian Government reported that, in light of its construction commitments at Goose Bay and elsewhere in Newfoundland and Canada, it could undertake to construct and defend only the airfield at The Pas.[56]

Within the U.S. War Department a special North Atlantic Ferry Route Project Committee, established on 3 June, was at work on an urgent construction program under a directive from the Chief of Staff that the CRIMSON Project "must be thought of in terms of weeks and not years." Although by the latter part of August substantial cargo unloadings were taking place at the airfield sites, the committee found the problem of water transportation and its limitations to be one of the major handicaps to rapid construction. Ice conditions permitted vessels to reach CRYSTAL I (Fort Chimo) only between 10 August and 1 October. Open water was available for a slightly shorter period at CRYSTAL II (upper Frobisher Bay). CRYSTAL III (Padloping Island) was open to shipping only about one month. In varying but usually lesser degrees, a similar handicap was met at all the other sites, including Goose Bay. Where the necessary supplies and equipment could not be landed during the open-water season, the limited capabilities of aerial supply presented the only alternative.

By the end of 1942 remarkable progress on the CRIMSON Project had been made. A civilian contractor under the Canadian Department of Transport had completed a usable 200- by 400-foot snow-compacted runway at The Pas, and two more runways were partially cleared. Housing was 80 percent complete. A U.S. civilian contractor on 1 December took over the work initiated at Churchill on 12 August by U.S. Engineer troops (the 330th Engineer General Service Regiment), and by the end of 1942 a 160- by 6,000-foot concrete runway had been completed, while the grading of two additional runways was more than half finished. Progress at Fort Chimo, Southampton Island, and Frobisher Bay, which were not served by railroads, was slower. Work under U.S. civilian contractors began in late August on all three bases. By 1 January 1943 usable but unpaved runways were available at the three sites and housing was about 50 percent complete.

[55] CCS 81, 14 Jun 42; CCS 81/1, 28 Jun 42, approved 2 Jul 42; Minutes, 30th CCS meeting; Journal, 6 Jul 42 PJBD meeting, PDB 124.

[56] Journals, PDB 124.

During 1942 additional facilities were added to the CRIMSON Project. To meet the need for an emergency airfield between Presque Isle, Maine, the principal U.S. "jump-off" point for the eastern route, and Goose Bay, the United States on 20 October 1942 requested permission to construct a field at Mingan, Quebec. The possibility that the RCAF base at Seven Islands, eighty miles westward, might meet the need was discussed, and a Canadian-U.S. team made a joint survey of the Mingan site. A conclusion in favor of a separate airfield on the direct route was reached, and on 30 October the United States was notified of the approval granted two days earlier by the Cabinet War Committee. The U.S. Army awarded a contract for the work to the McNamara Construction Company, Limited, a Canadian contractor that had released personnel and equipment from the work completed at Goose Bay.[57]

At the Goose Bay base some additional facilities were constructed during the summer and fall of 1942. In April 1942 when a small U.S. detachment had been installed at Goose Bay, it shared the facilities constructed for the RCAF, and minor frictions inevitably developed. To eliminate these frictions, the U.S. garrison sought authority to construct a separate establishment on the opposite side of the airfield. The Canadian Government approved the U.S. request in July, and in November the U.S. garrison, which numbered 325 by the end of the year, moved into its new facilities. In constructing the new facilities, the main elements of which comprised three hangars and housing for 1,000 permanent and 1,200 transient personnel, the U.S. Army Engineer authorities charged with the task had employed the Canadian contractors then at work at Goose Bay.[58]

Canada provided the local defenses for the Goose Bay base, and by March 1943 a Canadian Army garrison of 1,300 was stationed there for that purpose. Three concrete runways, all 200 feet wide by approximately 6,000 feet long, were constructed, together with comparable appurtenant installations, making the Goose Bay base one of the major bases in the area.

The Goose Bay air base enjoyed a special status among the northeastern North American defense installations. Canada, in accordance with the Seventeeth Recommendation of the Permanent Joint Board, had undertaken the construction of the base. In March 1942, as a result of the 1940 and 1941 understandings on defense between Canada and Newfoundland, it had

[57] Ltr, Moffat to Secy State, 31 Oct 42, PDB 105-2. See Table 7, below, p. 324, for the amounts expended by Canada and the United States on the CRIMSON bases.

[58] Journal, 6 Jul 42 PJBD meeting, PDB 124.

With the construction of separate facilities, a large degree of co-operation prevailed between Canadian and U.S. forces at Goose Bay. It extended to official functions, such as the sharing of control tower and radio direction finder and similar facilities, and to unofficial functions, such as the exchange of groups of entertainers and athletic activities.

officially become an RCAF station, on which the U.S. and British detachments were tenants. The Canadian Government in late 1941 had initiated steps to obtain a long-term lease for the base, and discussions with the Newfoundland Government took place over a period of almost three years. On 10 October 1944, a ninety-nine-year lease agreement between the two governments dating from 1 September 1941 was signed at St. John's.[59] It provided that the facilities at Goose Bay would be available for use by U.S. and United Kingdom aircraft "for the duration of the war and for such time thereafter as the Governments agree to be necessary or advisable in the interests of common defense." The provisions of the lease were, on the whole, not as far reaching as the U.S.-United Kingdom lease agreement. One significant difference was that the Goose Bay lease provided that the laws of Newfoundland would remain applicable within the leased area.[60]

In the spring of 1943 changing conditions had caused the War Department planners to reappraise the requirements for the ferrying route. Largely because of the greatly increased range of aircraft and the improved situation in connection with water transportation of aircraft, there was virtually no need for the western ferrying route, and the need for eastern-route airfields had also diminished. At the 6-7 May 1943 meeting of the Permanent Joint Board, the U.S. Section proposed that

a. The airfields at Churchill, Southampton Island, and The Pas be turned over to Canada.

b. The programs at Mingan, Fort Chimo, and Frobisher Bay be expanded to develop these bases more fully as emergency airfields.

c. Meteorological services be curtailed.

d. Canada assume defense responsibility for the base at Southampton Island.[61]

The U.S. proposals were discussed at the May and July meetings of the Board, after which the U.S. Section submitted a modified proposal on 29 July 1943. Under the proposal, which was approved by the Canadian Government, the United States retained the caretaker and defense responsibility for the installations until the end of hostilities.[62] Construction programs at

[59] *Canada at War*, No. 25 (Jun 43), pp. 3-6. The State Department, which was surprised when it learned of the negotiations in October 1943, after they had been in progress for about two years, was apparently unenthusiastic about receiving treatment similar to that given Canada during the negotiations leading up to the March 1941 Newfoundland base agreement signed in London. (D/S Telg 100, to Ottawa, 26 Oct 43, D/S 842.7962/111.)

[60] CTS, 1944, No. 30.

[61] Journals, PDB 124.

[62] Ltr, SUSAM to Keenleyside, and Reply, 8 Sep 43, PDB 150-1. The air bases at Churchill and The Pas were actually transferred to Canadian control before V-J Day. (See Ch. XI, below.)

the sites were meanwhile curtailed, and only the work already under way was completed at Churchill and Southampton Island. At Mingan, Fort Chimo, and Frobisher Bay, the expanded programs provided for the paving of runways that were originally only to be graded.

The development of the air-base system required the parallel creation of a far-flung network of weather and communications stations, of particular importance in northern Canada and over the North Atlantic because of the hazards to flying and to maintenance of communications presented by the arctic and subarctic weather phenomena. The arrival on 9 March 1941 of a weather and communications detachment at Gander Airport had preceded by two months the establishment of the first U.S. air unit in Newfoundland. Even at that early date, the implications for peacetime weather forecasting were appreciated and occasioned some discussion as to the proper role of the U.S. weather services. In April 1941 Canada suggested, through diplomatic channels, that consultations be held among the civilian and service agencies concerned with a view to co-ordinating weather services. At the continuous urging of the Canadian Controller of Meteorological Services over the next two months, an arrangement was worked out under which the Canadian station at Gander Airport provided the official forecasting services for the garrisons of both countries.[63]

The Canadian reluctance to permit the U.S. military to operate a full-scale weather service in Canada and Newfoundland next manifested itself in August 1941 when the United States requested authority to establish the CRYSTAL weather stations. After some discussion as to the scope and details of the U.S. request, Canada granted the authority on 22 August, reserving the right to replace the three U.S. stations with Canadian stations when it was in a position to do so.[64]

A greatly expanded meteorological network was needed for the CRIMSON Project, and under the Twenty-sixth Recommendation of the Permanent Joint Board on Defense the two countries agreed to collaborate in providing it. The requirements for additional service, as presented in a U.S. plan of 7 September 1942, exceeded Canadian capabilities, and on 17 October Canada authorized the United States to establish weather stations at the following points:[65]

[63] Army Air Forces, History of the Army Air Forces Weather Service, III (1941–1943), 212–18.

[64] Ott Leg Desp 1867, 22 Aug 41, D/S 811.9243/27. An account of the early development of the U.S. communications and weather services in Newfoundland and Canada is found in Louis Shores, *Highways in the Sky: The Story of the AACS* (New York: Barnes & Noble, 1947), pp. 33ff., 51ff.

[65] List, U.S. Defense Projects in Canada, 6 May 43, PDB 150–1.

Coral Harbour
Amadjuak Lake
Northern Indian Lake
East Hope Lake, Hudson's Bay Company
Padloping Island
Bowman Bay
Lake Harbour, Hudson's Bay Company
Le Pensie
Ilford
Cape Dorset, Hudson's Bay Company
Churchill
Nueltin Post
Baker Lake
Douglas Harbour
Cormoran
Eskimo Point
Sandy Lake
Cape Low
Sherridon
Herchmer
Repulse Bay
Winter Outpost
York Bay
Etawney Lake
Thicket
Tavani
Stanley
Rat River
Wager Bay
Nuwata

The curtailment of the CRIMSON Project in 1943 produced a corresponding reduction in the meteorological program, most of which had not been put into effect. By an exchange of letters in mid-1943, the authorization for a meteorological network was withdrawn except for the following stations which had actually been put into operation or were still considered necessary: observing and forecasting stations at The Pas, Churchill, Coral Harbour, Frobisher Bay, and Fort Chimo; observing stations at Brochet, Duck Lake, Eskimo Point, Gillam, Hudson Bay Junction, Island Falls, Lake Harbour, River Clyde, Wabowden, Mecatina, and Padloping Island; and additional stations at Foxe Basin, Indian House Lake, Stillwater Lake, and York Bay.[66]

Throughout the war the North Atlantic Ferry Route bases in Newfoundland, including Labrador, and in eastern Canada made possible a large flow of aircraft to the United Kingdom and Europe. Initially, this flow involved principally the delivery of aircraft from the factories of Canada and the United States to the fighting units of the pre-Pearl Harbor Allied Powers. Aircraft deliveries to the United Kingdom via this route increased each year—26 in 1940, 722 in 1941, 1,163 in 1942, and 1,450 in 1943. The 1943 figure was part of a total of 3,280 aircraft ferried for delivery in Europe. The total increased in 1944 to 8,641.[67]

With U.S. entry into the war, the ferry route had assumed a new strategic importance in the staging of U.S. tactical units to the United Kingdom in the preparatory build-up for the planned operations against the European continent. The earliest movements took place in June 1942, when fighter aircraft of the U.S. Eighth Air Force staged from Presque Isle, Maine, to the

[66] Exchange of Ltrs, SUSAM and Keenleyside, 23 Jul–7 Aug 43, PDB 150–1. The existing AAF network, in addition, included stations in Labrador at Hebron and Cape Harrison which were not covered by the exchange with Canada.

[67] Great Britain, Central Office of Information, *Atlantic Bridge*, p. 30; Army Air Forces, Air Transport Command, History of the North Atlantic Division, II (1 Jan 43–1 Apr 44), 131. Additional deliveries were of course made by water transportation and via other air routes.

360-477 O - 70 - 14

United Kingdom via Gander or Goose Bay and Greenland and Iceland. By the end of 1942, 920 aircraft had attempted the crossing and 882 had reached their destinations.[68]

The air transport operations of the Air Transport Command, which had their beginnings in 1942, in 1943 reached major proportions. A fleet of some thirty-five four-engine and thirteen two-engine aircraft, mostly operated by civilian contract carriers, during 1943 carried over 7,600 tons of cargo eastward and 2,200 tons westward, in addition to 15,235 passengers. After 1 September 1943 the transatlantic operations were staged principally through Harmon Field at Stephenville, with Gander and Goose Bay Airports used as alternates. On V-E Day the Air Transport Command's North Atlantic fleet numbered approximately one hundred four-engine and sixteen two-engine transports.[69]

After V-E Day in May 1945, two major movements of aircraft to the United States from Europe took place over the ferry route. The AAF White Project, for the return of tactical aircraft for redeployment to other theaters, involved the movement by 15 July of 3,004 aircraft, which incidentally returned over 50,000 personnel with the loss of only one aircraft and no lives. The Green Project called for the air transport to the United States of personnel eligible for discharge from military service. Under this project, in a ninety-day period ending in Mid-September, 160,000 passengers were transported without a fatality, and by mid-September passengers transported under the White Project had exceeded 80,000.[70]

Throughout these movements the major burden was borne by the main bases at Stephenville, Gander Lake, and Goose Bay, since the increase in range of tactical, as well as transport, aircraft had eliminated the need for the intermediate CRIMSON bases except for emergency purposes. During 1943 and 1944 a total of eighty-five and eighty-seven aircraft landings, respectively, took place at CRYSTAL I (Fort Chimo), and about two-thirds of these landings were the result of Coast Guard PBY (Catalina) ice patrol operations. CRYSTAL II (upper Frobisher Bay) recorded 323 aircraft arrivals in 1943. At

---

[68] An authoritative account of these operations is to be found in Samuel Milner, "Establishing the Bolero Ferrying Route," *Military Affairs*, XI (Winter 1947), 213-22.

[69] History of the North Atlantic Division, II, 308-10, and IV (1 Oct 44-1 Oct 45), 368. Reginald M. Cleveland, *Air Transport at War* (New York: Harper & Brothers, 1946), contains authoritative accounts of the AAF ferrying and air transport operations through the eastern Canada and North Atlantic air bases. Graphic descriptions of difficulties encountered in these operations are to be found in Hugh B. Cave, *Wings Across the World: The Story of the Air Transport Command* (New York: Dodd, Mead & Company, 1945), Ch. II.

[70] History of the North Atlantic Division, IV, 205, 337. Return of U.S. personnel by water at the same time was taking place at the rate of 350,000 per month.

Southampton Island, periods varying from fifty to eighty days occurred during which no aircraft landed at the air base. An insignificant number of ferry aircraft passed through these bases, and air supply, aerial photography, and other miscellaneous operations accounted for most of the aircraft arrivals.[71]

Sault Sainte Marie

The joint U.S.-Canadian defense plans prepared in 1940 and 1941 paid scant attention to defenses for North America except for the coastal areas. It was only in these coastal areas, proximate to the sea power of the enemy and most likely to be reached by air attack, that the U.S. and Canadian planners considered that the Axis Powers had capabilities of any consequence for offensive action. Nevertheless, because of the pressures of public opinion and legislative clamor, the military in both countries were forced to consider measures for the defense of interior locations and areas. The defense of some of these areas, along the U.S.-Canadian boundary, necessitated study and recommendation by the Permanent Joint Board on Defense.

The major interior defense problem along the boundary was protection of the locks, canals, and navigation channels of the Saint Marys River, connecting Lakes Superior and Huron. Through the Sault Sainte Marie locks in the average year passed tonnages exceeding those passing through the Suez, Panama, and Kiel Canals combined. This inland water movement, which was concentrated in the eight months of the year during which the channels were not frozen, was particularly important because it included the transportation of the bulk (90 percent in 1941) of the total iron ore utilized in the United States, as well as large shipments of grain. If through sabotage or conventional attack the enemy could have succeeded in stopping movement of lake traffic through Sault Sainte Marie for a significant portion of the navigable season, major damage might have been done to the Canadian and U.S. military production programs. The nondelivery of ores would have curtailed output of steel and iron or, alternately, the movement by rail of the tonnages of ores involved would have imposed a burden on the already overtaxed rail transportation systems that could only have disrupted other portions of the over-all military support programs.

The Permanent Joint Board on Defense took note of the defense problem as early as 20 January 1941, when it submitted its Thirteenth Recommendation. Approved by the two governments, the recommendation provided for centralization of responsibility for the safety of navigation in a single authority in each country. Each authority was to be adequately empowered

[71] Army Air Forces, Air Transport Command, North Atlantic Division, History of CRYSTAL I, pp. 93–94, and Historical Data: CRYSTAL II, p. 20.

to co-operate in all the necessary precautionary measures with its counterpart.[72]

In addition to sabotage, conventional attack was considered a possibility, however small. Such an attack was usually envisaged as taking the form of submarine penetration of Hudson and James Bays for the purpose of rendezvous with, and resupply of, seaplanes, which could then easily reach Saint Marys River. The Canadian Chiefs of Staff appreciated the U.S. concern over the safety of the locks but felt that the risk of enemy action was slight. Not long after the Board had taken action, President Roosevelt himself expressed fears that the Germans would penetrate Hudson Bay by submarine or raider. Secretary of the Navy Knox was able to reassure him that joint plans for the defense of the Sault Sainte Marie were in preparation and that Canada was watching the Hudson Bay area. The Chief of Naval Operations also pointed out that the Canadians had indicated they would resent any U.S. proposal to patrol Hudson Bay, which they firmly considered to be Canadian territorial waters.[73]

United States entry into the war brought an intensification of interest in the Sault Sainte Marie defense problem. At the 20 January 1942 Permanent Joint Board meeting, it was agreed that each country should review the security situation at the canals and the adequacy and state of the defenses. As a result of the War Department review, the U.S. Section of the Board announced at the next meeting (25-26 February) that a regiment (less one gun battalion) of antiaircraft artillery, equipped with twelve 90-mm. guns, thirty-two 37-mm. guns, and twelve .50-caliber machine guns, and a battery of barrage balloons would be sent to augment canal defense. A general officer

[72] Appendix A, below.

[73] Ltr, to Knox, 23 Apr 41, reproduced in *F.D.R., His Personal Letters*, II, 1145; Undated Memorandum of reply from Secy Navy bearing notation "came to file 28 Apr 41," Roosevelt Papers, Secy's File, Box 77; CNO Memo, for President, 25 Apr 41, same file. Apparently neither the President's suggestion that naval patrols were needed in Hudson Bay nor other deliberations on the problem developed into an occasion for further examination of the question of maritime jurisdiction over these waters, which Canada declared in a statute enacted in 1906 to be Canadian territorial waters. Although the question had not been adjudicated and other countries had not protested the licensing required by the statute, the Department of State privately indicated in the same year that the United States would not accept such a position. (See Green H. Hackworth, *Digest of International Law* (Washington: Government Printing Office, 1940) I, 701.) For examinations of the question reaching divergent conclusions, see V. K. Johnston (who takes the Canadian view), "Canada's Title to Hudson Bay and Hudson Strait," *British Year Book of International Law*, XV (1934), 1-20, and Thomas W. Balch, "Is Hudson Bay a Closed or an Open Sea," *American Journal of International Law*, VI (1912), 409-59, and "The Hudsonian Sea Is a Great Open Sea." *American Journal of International Law*, VII (1913), 546-65. A recent comprehensive study, which examines Canada's Arctic claims in general, including the Hudson Bay question, is the unpublished Ph.D. dissertation (Columbia University, 1952) by Gordon W. Smith, The Historical and Legal Background of Canada's Arctic Claims.

was to be placed in command of the Sault Sainte Marie Military District and charged with the defense responsibility. In addition, Army Engineers were to take steps to assure prompt repair of any damage.[74] The Canadian Section pointed out that an attack was not possible until mid-July, when the navigation season on Hudson Bay normally opened. At the suggestion of the U.S. Section, the Board made its Twenty-fifth Recommendation for measures to complement those already taken by the United States. The recommendation called for (a) a full RCAF study of enemy capabilities for such attack, (b) the deployment of a Canadian antiaircraft battery, and (c) the placing of the Canadian battery under the control of the U.S. military district commander.[75]

Much progress had been made by the time of the Board meeting on 7–8 April 1942. The Canadian Section reported that organization of the Canadian 40th Antiaircraft Battery (Heavy) for the canal defenses had been authorized. By midsummer the unit was in place on the Canadian side and under the operational command of the U.S. military district commander. Until the latter part of 1942, when its own 3.7-inch guns became available, the battery used four 90-mm. guns loaned by the United States. Also, the U.S. Section reported at the same meeting the arrival in the canal area on the U.S. side of the U.S. 100th Coast Artillery Regiment (Antiaircraft) (less one battalion) and the 702nd Military Police Battalion for security duty. United States plans called for the replacement of the military police battalion by the 131st Infantry Regiment, as well as the establishment of a restricted airspace zone over the canals, which would require clearance in that zone of all aircraft movements and would subject unidentified aircraft to interception. The Board noted these plans and agreed that an aircraft warning system should be established at the earliest practicable time with a common system of operational control.[76]

The aircraft warning service requirements in Canada were discussed at a meeting of Canadian and U.S. representatives at Sault Sainte Marie on 5–6 May. The resulting plan for a Central Canada Aircraft Detection Corps was approved by the Canadian Government, and the organization of the corps was put under way by the end of May. By 1 September 266 observation posts, including 215 fire towers plus railway telegraphers and telephone operators, were functioning. Filter rooms were located at Fort Brady, Ottawa, and Winnipeg, in addition to a jointly manned information center at the Sault. By the following summer the system had been expanded to 700 observation points in Canada, manned by 4,740 observers. During November 1942, an

[74] Journals, PDB 124.
[75] Appendix A, below.
[76] Journals, PDB 214.

average of 600 flight plans per week were filed, and 400 observer reports were received.[77]

Although unable to deploy any fighter aircraft to the Sault Sainte Marie canal area because of more urgent requirements in coastal zones, the United States during the summer of 1942 prepared three airfields to receive fighter aircraft in 1943. In furtherance of arrangements approved by Canada on 7 August 1942, the United States also proceeded to establish five radar stations in Canada, at Kapuskasing, Cochrane, Hearst, Armstrong, and Nakina. These stations, along the northernmost route of the Canadian National Railways, provided a screen across the Province of Ontario between the canals and Hudson and James Bays. In addition to providing the sites for this U.S. radar system, Canada also furnished housing facilities for use by portions of the U.S. garrison in the canal area for upward of 50 officers and 2,000 men.[78]

The Permanent Joint Board reassessed the Sault Sainte Marie defense requirements at its July and September 1942 meetings. To Canada, the Sault canals' defense was not of direct and prime importance. Although the Canadians had earlier agreed to watch the Hudson Bay area, they felt that no special patrols should be provided in the bays because of higher priority needs and because existing operations over these waters and Hudson Strait would probably not permit a surface vessel to pass unobserved. Attempt by submarine would offer considerably greater success of penetrating the bays. But if the Canadians had no intention of providing special patrols, they did not encourage the United States to do so. The Canadian Section of the Permanent Joint Board had, in April 1941, made evident a lack of enthusiasm for U.S. Navy patrols in Hudson Bay, which it regarded as Canadian inshore waters. It was the U.S. Section, more sensitive to the possibility, however small, of a Pearl Harbor-type, "long-shot" surprise attack on the canals, that was usually urging a larger scale of defenses in that area. The U.S. Section finally accepted the Canadian view that additional naval patrol in the Hudson Bay would not be justified.[79]

Similar discussion took place on the question of antiaircraft defense, with similar considerations involved. The Canadian Section reported the provisions made for antiaircraft defenses at the Sault canals and at the aluminum plant at Arvida, Province of Quebec. Many other requests for defense of

[77] Journal, 9 Jun 42 PJBD meeting, PDB 124.

[78] Ltr, Air Commodore F. V. Heakes to Douglass, 7 Aug 42, PDB 123-6; the Twenty-second and Twenty-fifth Recommendations were cited by Canada as the basis for the provision of housing facilities for these units. Canadian Rpt, U.S. Defense Projects in Canada, 6 May 43, PDB 150-1. The radar system, operated by the 671st Signal Aircraft Warning Reporting Company with headquarters at Kapuskasing, was manned by nearly 1,000 U.S. troops.

[79] Journals, PDB 124.

similar facilities along the boundary had been made. The Board concluded, in the light of the small prospect of attack at such points, that assignment of defenses thereto was not justified.[80]

As the 1943 navigation season approached, the two countries continued the development of the defenses for the Sault canals. The German submarine menace in the western Atlantic had not yet reached and passed its peak, and the possibility of attack, however small, would be greater in 1943 than in 1942. The United States had already, on 29 September 1942, established the Central Air Defense Zone, a belt some 100–150 miles deep on the U.S. side of the border from the north shore of Lake Superior to 45° north latitude in Lake Huron. Except for local flights, flight plans were required for aircraft movements. By the time of the opening of the 1943 navigation season, Canada had established a prohibited flying zone in Canada with a radius of 100 miles from the canal locks.[81]

By the beginning of 1943 the War Department had also developed plans for the establishment of a military area, pursuant to Executive Order 9066, as had already been done in the U.S. Eastern and Western Defense Commands. By proclamation, the commander of such a military area would become responsible for all defense and internal security activities in the area, including the control of aliens and undesirables, use of radios, codes, and cameras, lighting, and similar activities. The U.S. Section of the Permanent Joint Board suggested that Canada might wish to take similar action. Joint conferences between the officials concerned took place over several months. On the U.S. side, Public Proclamation 1 established the Sault Sainte Marie Military Area effective 22 March 1943. As to similar action by Canada, the question was pursued as far as a joint conference at Toronto on 12 April 1943, when the Canadian conferees presented their conclusions that existing powers were adequate for attaining comparable objectives in Canada and that the establishment of a similar area in Canada was not necessary.[82]

With the passage of the 1943 navigation season, the tide of German naval and air power in the Atlantic, which had already turned, continued to ebb rapidly. The Sault canal defenses were rapidly dismantled. In November 1943 the Permanent Joint Board approved the disbandment of the aircraft detection organizations in the area. The Canadian Observer Corps, then numbering 9,000, was disbanded on 3 January 1944, and the Canadian antiaircraft battery was transferred. In January also, the War Department initiated the inactivation of the Central Air Defense Zone, the withdrawal of

[80] Journal, 1 Sep 42 PJBD meeting, PDB 124.
[81] WD Unnumbered Circular; Journal, 24–25 Aug 43 PJBD meeting, PDB 124.
[82] Journal, 6–7 May 43 PJBD meeting, PDB 124.

the radar stations in Canada, and the redeployment of the ground defenses elsewhere. The security of the canals was left in the hands of the Royal Canadian Mounted Police on the Canadian side and of a military police company on the U.S. side.

Apart from the coastal border areas whose defense was provided for in ABC-22 and the Sault Sainte Marie defense system, only one other border defense problem of major consequence was considered by Canada and the United States jointly. Toward the end of 1942 U.S. Eastern Defense Command planners envisaged the need for siting defense installations such as radar stations and other antiaircraft defenses north of the border in order adequately to defend the defense command sector. In February 1943 a request was forwarded to Ottawa for authority to make reconnaissances and deploy antiaircraft weapons on Canadian territory near Buffalo. The Canadian reply expressed concern that such a deployment would inspire numerous similar demands at other points and suggested that the matter first be discussed in the Board, which had a few months earlier taken a position against such deployments.[83]

From the exchange emerged a U.S. request that (a) the Twenty-second Recommendation be interpreted by the Board as providing authority for joint planning as well as actual emergency action, and (b) appropriate Canadian authorities join in planning for the defense of the Great Lakes-St. Lawrence River valley. The Board agreed to this interpretation, subject to the understanding that such plans would not constitute commitments. On 31 March 1943 Canadian and U.S. officers met at the headquarters of the Eastern Defense Command in New York City and after discussion reached some broad but oral understandings. On the basis of these understandings, Eastern Defense Command planners formulated a plan envisaging a radar network of twenty-three stations and appropriate interception aircraft units and headquarters. The plan was to be placed in effect only when frequent air raids into the Great Lakes-St. Lawrence River valley area became a definite possibility.[84] The U. S. plan, based on the joint discussions, was forwarded in May to Ottawa for review and comment by the Canadian Army and RCAF staff there. It was never revised. By midsummer of 1943 with German capabilities becoming weaker the possibility of such air raids became most unlikely.

[83] Memo, Maj Gen Sanderford Jarman, EDC, for SUSAM, 7 Feb 43, and Reply, 19 Feb 43, both in PDB 126-7.

[84] Memos, ACofS WPD for SUSAM, 15 Feb and 11 May 43, and Reply, 1 Mar 43, all in PDB 135-2.

CHAPTER VIII

Activities in Western Canada

Before 7 December 1941 the Canadian and U.S. military effort in North America reflected an almost complete absorption in the defense problems of the eastern seaboard. This was a natural consequence of the fact that a shooting war was in progress in the Atlantic. The Pearl Harbor attack and the resulting Japanese menace to the west coast and Alaska produced a re-orientation of U.S. military effort in North America. Alaska, whose needs had until then been subordinated to the needs of the Atlantic war and of advanced Pacific bases, found itself enjoying a much higher priority for U.S. military resources. Within a matter of months, a substantial reinforcement of the Alaskan garrison had taken place.

Simultaneously a force of U.S. personnel, both military and civilian, poured into northwest Canada to build the logistical facilities needed to support the defense of that quarter of the continent. United States military strengh in northwest Canada in late 1942 exceeded 15,000, and in the next year, when some of the troops had been replaced by civilian workers, U.S. civilians alone exceeded that figure. On 1 June 1943 the total strength of the American personnel in northwest Canada was over 33,000. In some instances the United States was able to utilize existing air-base and other facilities, expanded by either or both countries to meet wartime requirements. Other projects were carved out of the virgin wilderness, in some cases in areas never before surveyed. It was here in western Canada that the joint U.S.-Canadian war effort left its biggest and most lasting imprint.

It was in western Canada, too, that joint efforts produced the biggest administrative headaches. Shortages of men, materials, and machines were inevitable. Dislocations caused by rapidly changing requirements could not always be avoided. In order to curb competition for available materials, as already noted, the Canadian Government incorporated a crown company, North West Purchasing Limited, on 19 February 1943. Purchases by this company in northwest Canada to meet the requirements of both Canadian and U.S. forces amounted to more than one million dollars a month at the height of construction activity. When the high wage scales paid by U.S. contractors threatened to undermine Canadian wage and price ceilings, the Canadian Government on 17 May 1943 established a Western Labor Board at Edmonton and invited the United States to name a representative to act as a special consultant to the board.[1]

The addition of large numbers of Americans, sometimes less concerned with the amenities of international and human relations than with the compelling urge to get the job done, to communities already overcrowded could not help but produce occasional friction and misunderstanding. However, when the tide of the U.S. influx had receded and the fog of friction and misunderstanding had been dispelled, the solidity of the accomplishments of Canadians and Americans working side by side in the spirit of friendly co-operation gave testimony to the relative insignificance of the discordances.

Throughout most of the war the activities in northwest Canada remained free from any real threat from enemy operations. Except for the planning and other defense measures, Canadian-U.S. co-operation until the end of 1944 related largely to logistical activities. After the first of the "free" Japanese balloons was recovered in California on 4 November 1944, Canada and the United States began to co-operate in measures to meet the new threat. The balloons, 33½ feet in diameter, carried incendiary and antipersonnel bombs in suspended baskets. By the war's end, more than 9,000 had been launched from Honshu Island, althought only a small fraction of that number were known to have reached North America.[2] As the flow of balloons increased in early 1945, full co-ordination between the two countries was established. Information was exchanged in the field on sightings and recoveries, and U.S. military officers at conferences attended by Canadian representatives examined the problem and arranged countermeasures. On the Washington-Ottawa level, too, a full exchange of operational and technical intelligence was maintained, as a part of which the results of the extensive U.S. studies of the balloon equipment were made available to Canada.

The Northwest Staging Route

Of the major wartime logistical projects in northwest Canada, only the Northwest Staging Route was a joint one in the sense that it was developed through the full and active participation and co-operation of the two governments. Unlike the Alaska Highway, the Canol Project, and other projects undertaken after Pearl Harbor, the staging route owed its initial development to Canadian initiative and foresight.[3] Since the early 1920's bush pilots had

[1] *H. C. Debates,* 21 Mar 44, p. 1701; Lingard and Trotter, *Canada in World Affairs,* III, 72; Privy Council 3870, 17 May 43. See also Ch. V, above.

[2] Conn, Engelman, and Fairchild, Guarding the United States and Its Outposts, Ch. III.

[3] The fullest public account of the development of this route is to be found in the historical monograph, History of the Northwest Air Route to Alaska: 1942–1945, which is in the files of the Headquarters, Military Air Transport Service. This official monograph was completed by Maj. Edwin R. Carr and submitted by him to the University of Minnesota as a doctoral dissertation under the title "Great Falls to Nome: The Inland Air Route to Alaska, 1940–1945."

been pioneering airways in the general area, and in 1935 the Canadian Department of Transport initiated a survey of alternate air routes to Alaska. A partial, if not immediate, object of the survey was to seek an air route that might one day form part of the great circle route to the Orient. As a result of the survey, the air route from Edmonton to Alaska was selected as the most favorable.[4]

In 1939 detailed engineering work was authorized and airfields were planned at Grande Prairie, Fort St. John, Fort Nelson, Watson Lake, and Whitehorse. At the outbreak of war in Europe in September 1939, survey parties were in the field. In view of the airfield construction that would thereafter be required for the RCAF training program, Ottawa gave some consideration to terminating the surveys. The Canadians concluded that upon U.S. entry into the war, which was a possibility, this air route would attain real strategic importance and the surveys should therefore be pushed to completion. When the surveys were completed in January 1940, the preparation of detailed plans and specifications was initiated in Ottawa.[5]

The next steps in the development of the air route were not taken until after the establishment of the Permanent Joint Board on Defense, when the United States began to show an interest in the project. The several drafts of the 1940 defense plan, beginning with the very first joint draft prepared by the service members of the Board on 11 September 1940, stated that, in order to execute essential defense tasks, the additional installations that would be needed included aircraft staging facilities between Alaska and the United States.[6] On 4 October 1940 the Board itself, in approving its First Report to the two governments, recommended that Canada develop these facilities as soon as possible.[7]

The First Report was under consideration and had already received Canadian but not U.S. approval when, at the request of its Canadian chairman, Colonel Biggar, the Board was briefed on the Canadian development plans by Squadron Leader A. D. McLean, who earlier as a civilian had been the Canadian Superintendent of Airways. At this meeting, held at Victoria, British Columbia, on 14 November 1940, the Board adopted its Tenth Recommendation, which stated that Canada should provide, as soon as possible, airfields at specified locations and essential facilities to permit rapid move-

[4] *H. C. Debates*, 29 Feb 44, p. 979. For fuller accounts of the pre-Pearl Harbor development of the route, see J. A. Wilson, "Northwest Passage by Air," *Canadian Geographical Journal*, XXVI (March 1943), 107–29, and Lingard and Trotter, *Canada in World Affairs*, III, 30–34, 73–74.

[5] Wilson, *op. cit.*, p. 123n.

[6] Draft Plans at PDB 133–3, –5, and –7.

[7] Appendix B, below.

ment of tactical aircraft to Alaska and northwestern Canada. In addition to the airfields on the staging route to Alaska, the recommendation called for airfields at Prince George and Smithers to facilitate reinforcement of the Prince Rupert-Ketchikan area.[8] The Canadian Government approved the project and on 18 December 1940 released funds for it.

Moves into the field to initiate work on the airfields began on 9 February 1941. The movement of machines and supplies to some of the selected sites was no small task. Whitehorse, Grande Prairie, and Fort St. John, all at or near rail facilities, posed no problem. Materials moved to Fort Nelson from Dawson Creek over a 300-mile frozen winter trail by tractor trains. Materials for Watson Lake moved by steamship to Wrangell, Alaska, thence by boat via the Stikine River to Telegraph Creek, by portage over seventy miles to Dease Lake, and by boat on the Dease River to Lower Post. From the last point they moved over a newly constructed road to Watson Lake.

The Permanent Joint Board on 29 July 1941 in adopting its Nineteenth Recommendation took steps to spur construction. The changed situation in the Far East, the recommendation stated, made early completion of the route a matter of extreme importance. As a result, the tasks of clearing, grading, and paving the runways were pressed during the 1941 summer construction season. Work advanced most rapidly at Whitehorse, where an airfield had already existed, and at Grande Prairie. By the end of the construction season the airway to Whitehorse was usable by daylight in good weather. Radio range stations were in operation at 200-mile intervals from Edmonton to the Alaska boundary by the end of the year.[9]

In Alaska, too, where in 1940 only the airfields at Anchorage, Fairbanks, Juneau, and Nome (on a limited basis) were suitable for military use, the U.S. Civil Aeronautics Authority pushed an airfield program intended to meet military as well as civilian needs. Progress on the Alaskan airfields and the extensions of the staging route was not entirely satisfactory because of difficulties of transportation and operations on the frozen ground. But by the end of 1941 runways had been completed at Nome, Big Delta, Northway, and Juneau; runways were under construction but usable at Gulkana, Bethel, Cordova, Galena, McGrath, and Naknek. In addition, the Alaska Defense Command had improved its fields at Anchorage and Fairbanks and had constructed new ones at Yakutat and Annette Island.

After the Pearl Harbor attack the staging route was sufficiently far advanced to permit its use, and Canada extended the use of its facilities to the United States. In early January 1942 the 11th Pursuit (twenty-five P-40 air-

---

[8] Appendix A, below.

[9] "Canada's Northern Airfields," *The Canada Year Book, 1945*, p. 706. Pages 705-12 of this volume contain a brief account of the wartime development of all of the northern airfields.

craft) and 77th Bombardment (thirteen B-26 aircraft) Squadrons were dispatched to Alaska. A month after their dispatch, thirteen P-40's had arrived, five were still en route, and the rest had crashed; only eight of the B-26's arrived, the balance also crashing at points en route. Causes contributing to this performance were inadequate training of personnel for the winter weather conditions encountered and the limited scale of airway facilities available on the route. The AAF elements en route to Alaska found the route as a whole "usable under optimum conditions," but, since such conditions had not been prevalent during the winter of 1941–42, they made the journey only with considerable difficulty.[10] Throughout the same winter Canada continued the movement of supplies and further developed the route.

During the early months of 1942 a small flow of U.S. tactical aircraft continued to Alaska, and a military transport aircraft began regular supply operations between Edmonton and Fairbanks. To augment the limited military transport operations, the AAF turned to the use of commercial airlines on a contract basis, and during the remainder of 1942 contract operations constituted the major U.S. use of the Northwest Staging Route.[11]

In order to clarify the U.S. need for buildings and facilities on the Canadian portion of the Northwest Staging Route, initial discussions took place in Ottawa between representatives of the two governments on 11–12 March 1942. Short-term (thirty-day) as well as longer-term needs were discussed on a general basis and were then submitted in detail to the Canadian authorities in early April. Under the arrangements made, the Department of Transport was to construct hangars for use by the AAF at Edmonton and Whitehorse, and barracks, fuel storage, and miscellaneous facilities at all the main airfields, while the AAF would assist in the movement of personnel and materials. Meetings in Ottawa on 10 April reviewed and gave approval to the arrangements.[12]

New methods for financing Canadian construction for U.S. use, which had been discussed informally in Washington on 3 March at a meeting between C. D. Howe and Brig. Gen. Robert Olds, came under consideration at the 10 April meeting. Heretofore, Canada had been financing all construction costs on the Canadian portion of the Northwest Staging Route under an arrangement whereby each country took care of the work within its own territory.[13] The Canadian authorities indicated that Canada would in the

[10] See Craven and Cate (eds.), *Plans and Early Operations,* pp. 303–04, 357.

[11] A full account of these contract air services and of the lengthy U.S.-Canadian discussions relating thereto will be found in Chapter XI, below.

[12] History of the Northwest Air Route to Alaska, 1942–1945, pp. 105–07.

[13] *H. C. Debates,* 25 Feb 41, p. 1016; Carr, Great Falls to Nome: The Inland Air Route to Alaska, 1940–1945, p. 109. The United States had already taken cognizance in the exchange of notes on the Alaska Highway (EAS, 246; CTS, 1942, No. 13) of the contribution to overall continental defense by such Canadian expenditures.

future want payment from the United States for certain of the construction to be performed by Canada. The actual decision, taken by the Cabinet War Committee on 22 April, provided that Canada would pay for facilities of continuing value to the route, while the United States should pay for such facilities as were over and above Canadian standards and requirements and needed solely for U.S. military purposes. Regardless of the source of financing, title to all improvements was to be retained by Canada.[14]

Not long afterward, in June 1942, the Japanese penetration of Alaskan defenses brought the staging route into spectacular play. On 3–4 June a Japanese carrier task force attacked Dutch Harbor, and on 9 June it became known that the Japanese had occupied Kiska. To speed urgently needed troop reinforcements and supplies to Alaskan bases, the War Department on 13 June requested eleven U.S. commercial airlines to rush every aircraft that could be made available to Edmonton. Over the next few weeks an emergency airlift of almost fifty aircraft operated around the clock to deliver men and materials to Alaska. Many of the aircraft available were also used to some extent for airlifting materials with which to speed up the work on the Northwest Staging Route.[15] With the emergency over, the more routine air transport operations of the U.S. Army expanded in northwest Canada.

During the first half of 1942 no subordinate field command of the Air Corps Ferrying Command was charged with responsibility for the conduct of transport operations over the Northwest Staging Route. The need for such a step was apparent, and on 16 June the Domestic Wing was charged with the conduct of U.S. ferrying operations. Since the U.S. organization in the field was to be manned by 15 July, personnel movements began at once and detachments arrived at Edmonton and Whitehorse before the end of June. As a consequence of the reorganization of the Air Corps Ferrying Command into the Air Transport Command, and of the completion of plans for ferrying aircraft to Siberia, a new headquarters at Great Falls, Montana—the Northwest Route, Ferrying Division—was established on 14 August 1942. On 17 October in a further organizational change, the Alaskan Wing of the Air Transport Command was activated at Edmonton and assumed the transport responsibility on 1 November, superseding the headquarters at Great Falls. Although further minor organizational changes occurred, the basic pattern remained unchanged and the Alaskan Wing proceeded to

[14] Alaskan Division, Historical Record Report, Nov 42–Dec 43 volume, p. 220; *The Canada Year Book, 1945,* p. 708.

[15] Accounts of the emergency operation are to be found in Craven and Cate (eds.), *Plans and Early Operations,* p. 358; Cleveland, *Air Transport at War,* pp. 163–66; and Cave, *Wings Across the World,* pp. 116–19.

expand to a strength of 1,231 on 1 January 1943, and to a peak of 9,987 in November 1944.

In midsummer 1942 the Army Air Forces was expressing dissatisfaction with the progress of the construction work on U.S. facilities in Canada. At the end of April construction of U.S. facilities had not been started, and a month later little progress toward completion of the thirty-day program had been reported. On 25 June representatives of the two countries met and revised the construction requirements to reflect the new program for ferrying aircraft to the USSR and agreed that both the new and the earlier construction programs should be completed by the end of August. Only two weeks later, on 9 July 1942, Mr. Wilson of the Department of Transport acknowledged that it was doubtful whether even the revised programs could be completed as scheduled.[16]

There were many factors that contributed to the lack of progress. Among them were insufficient transportation and the shortage of competent labor. The need to refer plans to Ottawa, which made U.S. officers chafe, occasioned delays. Overoptimistic or unrealistic construction schedules also appear to have contributed to the situation. Time-consuming organizational and procedural complexities added greatly to delays.[17] Alterations in construction requirements may also have been a factor—for example, U.S. needs at Lethbridge and Calgary, stated on 26 August, were canceled three weeks later. As a matter of fact, the U.S. planners had great difficulty in estimating future needs for aircraft movements over the route. Estimates in 1942 ran as high as 5,000 aircraft per month, in contrast with the planning figures of from 250 to 300 used in May 1943. During the year 1943 a monthly average of over 440 aircraft actually traversed the route.

The War Department would have liked to carry out its own construction program on the Northwest Staging Route, but since it was precluded from doing so by the policy announced in March 1942 by the then Minister of Transport, C. D. Howe, that it was "in the highest degree desirable that . . . [construction of additional facilities needed by the United States] should be undertaken by the Department of Transport rather than by the United States Government," it sought other means to speed up the work.[18] On 25 July 1942 at a conference in Great Falls, Montana, Canadian authorities considered and rejected as impracticable the use of three labor shifts or of overtime work because of the predominance of middle-aged men in the

[16] History of the Northwest Air Route to Alaska: 1942–1945, p. 108; Ltr, to U. S. Military Attache, 9 Jul 42, reproduced in Alaskan Division, Historical Record Report, II, 42.

[17] See above, pp. 131–41.

[18] Ltr, to Brig Gen Olds, 7 Mar 42, PDB 126.

labor force. The U.S. representatives urged that U.S. Army Engineer troops be used. Canada granted authority in August, and U.S. Engineer troops were assigned to the projects. However, because of protests from labor groups, the troops were withdrawn from the projects the same month. In September, when the strength of the Canadian civilian labor force had fallen off considerably, the U.S. Engineer troops were put back on the construction work, only to draw additional protests and be withdrawn.[19]

During these same months the War Department did obtain authority to construct a number of airstrips, in addition to those on the staging route, as an adjunct to the military highway being constructed. There is some evidence that this program was an effort on the part of the AAF to overcome the unsatisfactory situation on the staging route. About 1 June 1942 the U.S. Public Roads Administration, which was preparing to undertake construction tasks on the Alaska Highway, suggested that plans be included for flight strips patterned on a similar program under way along many highways in the United States. In requesting approval of the project, the AAF suggested that the flight strips "would permit the movement of Air Transport Command equipment on a much more dependable basis than . . . [has been] possible with the . . . [existing] system of airports."[20] Canada agreed, on 10 September, to the formal request of 26 August 1942 for the construction of eight flight strips by the United States at points along the Alaska Highway:[21]

Number	*Point*	*Mile Number*
1	Dawson Creek	0
2	Sikanni Chief River	137
3	Prophet River	245
4	Liard River	508
5	Pine Lake	723
6	Squanga Lake	843
7	Pon Lake	1,013
8	Burwash	1,095

[19] History of the Northwest Air Route to Alaska: 1942–1945, pp. 114–15.

This situation aptly exemplified the disparity between the manpower situations of the two countries. Canada, in its fourth year of war, was already plagued by a tight manpower situation occasioned by the requirements of the armed forces, industry, agriculture, and merchant marine. The United States, which in 1942 could pour the flower of its youth into Canada, was not until 1944 faced with manpower difficulties and even then on a lesser scale. The resultant political climate in Canada was not improved by the unwillingness of the Canadian Government to introduce conscription for fear of a repetition of the unhappy experience in World War I, when violent opposition arose in French-Canadian Quebec and elsewhere.

[20] Memo, for CG SOS, 29 Jul 42, Exhibit 4 in Appendix E, House Committee on Roads, 79th Congress, 2d Session, House Report 1705, on House Resolution 255, *The Alaska Highway*, p. 98.

[21] EAS, 381; CTS, 1942, No. 26; House Report 1705, 79th Congress, 2d Session, p. 100.

The flight strips were not to prove of appreciable value to the Air Transport Command as an augmentation of Northwest Staging Route facilities. Because all available construction facilities were being used to push completion of the Alaska Highway, work on the flight strips was begun during 1942 at only one site, Dawson Creek, in late September. The first plane landed on the cleared and graded strip on 29 October, but more work remained to be done in 1943. Work on the other sites did not begin until the late summer and autumn of 1943, by which time the highway had been substantially completed. Flight strips 3, 5, and 6 were completed by the end of 1943, and 2, 4, 7, and 8 were completed in early 1944.

The American Construction Phase

United States dissatisfaction with the progress of construction continued throughout 1942, and by the beginning of 1943 the Commanding General, Army Air Forces, felt that drastic action was necessary to improve the "deplorable" condition of the staging route. He recommended that, in order to prevent serious delays in movement of aircraft to and through Alaska, the U.S. Army take over completion of the work being done by Canada to meet U.S. needs. Maj. Gen. Guy V. Henry, newly appointed Senior U.S. Army Member of the Permanent Joint Board, proceeded cautiously in acting on the request and first sought elaboration of the purported difficulties.[22]

On 12 February 1943 the U.S. Government informally proposed that the United States take over certain unfinished construction at Edmonton, Grande Prairie, Fort St. John, Fort Nelson, Watson Lake, and Whitehorse (Plan A) and be authorized to construct additional facilities at Edmonton and Whitehorse (Plan B). The preliminary Canadian reaction was favorable and included the suggestions that the proposal would be strengthened if the Permanent Joint Board endorsed it, and that a meeting should be held to work out the details.[23]

Meetings of representatives of the RCAF, AAF, and Department of Transport took place in Ottawa on 18, 19, and 20 February. The labor problems arising from the shortage of labor, the competition between Canadian and U.S. contractors, and the different rates paid Canadian and U.S. laborers played a prominent part in the discussions. The conferees agreed that the Department of Transport should complete construction already under way with assistance from U.S. Engineer troops wherever practicable. This included the work at the five original staging route airfields and

[22] Ltr, CG AAF to SUSAM, 7 Jan 43, and Ltr, CG ATC to SUSAM, 5 Feb 43, both in PDB 105-13.

[23] Memo/Conv, Hickerson and Clark, 13 Feb 43, PDB 105-13.

360-477 O - 70 - 15

FLIGHT STRIPS AT THE WATSON LAKE AIRPORT *constructed by U.S. Army Engineers.*

Edmonton, and at certain intermediate strips and facilities that Canada had undertaken to construct at Snag, Aishihik, Teslin, Smith River, Beatton River, and Calgary. Subject to approval of detailed plans and to certain conditions as to the use of U.S. labor, the United States was to be authorized to execute the Plan B construction at Whitehorse and Edmonton. During the meetings the U.S. representatives outlined tentative additional requirements (Plan C) emerging from plans being developed for the defeat of Japan. These requirements included an expansion of facilities at Whitehorse, Watson Lake, Fort Nelson, Fort St. John, Grande Prairie, and a new airfield at Namao, near Edmonton, to relieve possible congestion at the Edmonton airfield. The conferees agreed that subject to similar conditions the United States could initiate the additional construction, even the development of new airfields.[24]

The Permanent Joint Board on Defense at its 24–25 February 1943 meeting considered the recommendations of the conferees and adopted the Twenty-ninth Recommendation, which substantially embodied them.[25]

[24] Minutes of meetings and joint recommendation, 20 Feb 43, by the senior conferees to the PJBD, PDB 105–13.

[25] Appendix A, below.

President Roosevelt approved the Board recommendation on 1 April, but Canadian action was not immediately forthcoming. In addition to pondering the question of whether to depart from the policy of having Canada accomplish all work on the Northwest Staging Route, the Canadian Government was engaged in studies and discussions designed to clarify the intergovernmental procedures for processing project requests, co-ordinating activities, and solving labor and similar problems.

On 27 April the newly designated commanding officer of the Air Transport Command's Alaskan Wing, Col. D. V. Gaffney, met with Department of Transport officers in Ottawa and stated that because of changes made in U.S. development plans, his requirements were being restudied and a revised program would be submitted in place of the one then under discussion.[26] On 18 May 1943, with Canadian approval not yet given to the Twenty-ninth Recommendation, Maj. Gen. Thomas M. Robins of the U.S. Army Corps of Engineers met in Ottawa with C. D. Howe, Minister of Munitions and Supply. They worked out an understanding under which the United States was to take over the work already initiated by Canada on Plan B and at other sites, to continue to utilize the contractors already on the job, and to add others to permit faster execution of the work.[27] The United States on 24 May submitted its proposals to Canada for formal approval, at the same time indicating the possible need for considerable additional expansion of the facilities.

The formal Canadian reply to the U.S. proposals, received on 3 June, appeared to counter the understandings reached at the May meeting since it approved the projects but specified that all work of a permanent character would continue to be done by the Canadian Government using Canadian labor.[28] Somewhat dismayed by the apparent change in policy and concerned over its impact on the supplementary Plan C, which had been developed and awaited submission to the Canadian Government, the U.S. authorities sought informally to clarify the situation. They were advised that some confusion within the Canadian Government was the cause of the reversal, and that the matter could probably be straightened out during consideration of the new Plan C.

The United States on 11 June 1943 submitted the new plan to Canada for approval, and the Cabinet War Committee on 18 June approved it subject to the following provisions:

a. All unfinished construction under Plans A, B, and C, except in the

[26] Minutes of meeting, PDB 105-13.

[27] Minutes of meeting, PDB 111-12.

[28] Ltr, Keenleyside to Clark, 3 Jun 43, PDB 105-13.

Edmonton area, could be completed with U.S. labor. Canadian contractors and labor on such work were to be withdrawn.

b. The United States could complete the work in the Edmonton area, but could use only Canadian contractors and Canadian labor.[29]

The Canadian Government officially notified the United States of the approval on 22 June and a few days later modified the first provision to exclude the work Canada was carrying out at Beatton River, Smith River, Teslin, Aishihik, and Snag, since the projects at these intermediate facilities were almost complete.[30] Except for the limitations on construction work in the Edmonton area, the revised authority conformed to the understandings reached at the 18 May meeting. On the U.S. side, the authorities were willing to give the modified arrangement a trial to see if the solution was adequate.[31]

The tentative departure from the 18 May understandings had apparently been the result of confusion compounded with Canadian reluctance to turn over construction tasks to the United States. There were a number of reasons for the Canadian position. First, although the bulk of the unfinished work was on Plan B projects, over and above the basic U.S. requirements, a transfer of the construction responsibility might make it appear that Canada had failed in its undertakings. Second, Canada naturally preferred to do all permanent work itself and thereby maintain full control rather than risk any trend toward the establishment of a vested U.S. interest. Nevertheless, Canada, when convinced that its construction capabilities were not equal to the expanded requirements for facilities at all points on the staging route, was ready to agree to the use of U.S. troops and labor except in the Edmonton area. In this area the labor situation in general and wages and other difficulties inherent in the operations of Canadian and U.S. contractors side by side were especially complicated. This remaining exception was a logical outgrowth of the local political and economic situation and, in the light of the release of Canadian contractors from other airfields, did no violence to the time limits for the work to be done in the Edmonton area.[32]

The Canadian Government took other concurrent action to help insure that the new arrangement would not allow the United States to intrude unduly upon Canadian sovereignty. On 7 July 1943 the Cabinet War Committee decided that the Canadian Government should (a) take over all

[29] Ltrs, Clark to Hickerson, and Keenleyside to Clark, 22 Jun 43, both in PDB 105-13.

[30] *Ibid.;* Ltr, Keenleyside to Clark, 26 Jun 43, PDB 105-13.

[31] Memo, Robins for Hickerson, 26 Jun 43, D/S 811.24542/51-1/2.

[32] Ltr, Clark to Hickerson, 22 Jun 43, PDB 105-13. For a discussion of criticism in Canada of the government's failure to undertake even greater construction responsibilities than it had, see Lingard and Trotter, *Canada in World Affairs,* III, 72.

existing leases for land used by the U.S. Government, (b) assume the costs of all properties acquired for the United States and make the properties available without charge for the duration of the war, and (c) acquire any additional land required for U.S. Government use. The decision was communicated to U.S. officials in Ottawa on 7 September.[33]

The Canadian Government, having virtually completed the program of construction to meet the basic Canadian and U.S. requirements at the main airfields of the Northwest Staging Route, closed out its contracts and withdrew its construction forces on 12 July 1943. United States Army Engineers undertook a further program of expansion and development of the airfields to meet the increasing volume of air traffic. The major task of this program was the construction of the satellite field at Namao, seven miles north of Edmonton, the contract for which was let to a Canadian company.[34] With the exception of the completion of work at a few intermediate facilities, construction at the six existing main airfields and at Namao continued throughout the remainder of 1943 under U.S. Army control. In general, Plan C, which had been reduced in scope, included repair and expansion of runways, taxiways, and parking aprons and the construction of housing and service and other facilities necessary to raise the capacity of the route to 100 transport and 350 ferried aircraft per month. By the end of the year the work was substantially complete, except at Namao, where the development had started from scratch.

In early 1944 the Air Transport Command desired to expand the capacity of the staging route to 110 transport and 425 ferried aircraft per month. For this purpose, and to provide adequate accommodations for the necessary increase in personnel, a Plan D was advanced and Canadian approval was requested. Construction under the plan consisted of items such as warehouses, gas stations, turnarounds, and warm-up aprons. In addition, approval was requested for a program of repairs to the runways of the main airfields of the route.[35]

These requests reached the Canadian Government shortly after it had

[33] Privy Council 6998, 7 Sep 43. The U.S. officials were able to report in March 1944 that the arrangements were acceptable. (D/S Desp 241, to Ott, 10 Mar 44, D/S 811.24542/76; Privy Council 3869, 23 May 44.) The mechanics of transfer of existing leaseholds and of acquisition of new ones were worked out with U.S. Army representatives at a meeting in Ottawa on 20 October 1944. The conclusions of the meeting, which provided that Canada would assume the payment of rentals dating from 7 September 1943, were formalized in an exchange of notes on 28 and 30 December 1944. (CTS, 1944, No. 34.) Apparently the notes were not published by the Department of State in its Treaties and Other International Acts Series.

[34] Canada, Wartime Information Board, *Defense Projects in Northwest Canada* (Ottawa: 1944, mimeographed), p. 2.

[35] Ltrs, SUSAM to Cdn Air Member, PJBD, 17 Jan 44, 14 and 21 Feb 44, OPD 580.82 Can (27 Jan 44).

again revised its policies with regard to the facilities on the staging route. On 18 December 1943 Canada had notified the United States of its decision to finance all work of permanent value on the northwest route, which embraced work done by or at the request of the United States on items that had originally been considered to be over and above Canadian standards and requirements.[36] The Canadian Government had also decided to reinstitute the use of Canadian contractors and labor in future development work. Its reply to the U.S. requests, while approving the projects, specified that all future construction of a permanent nature would be done by the Canadian Government not only at its expense but also through use of Canadian contractors and labor to the fullest extent possible.[37]

Canada apparently considered the U.S. requests a practicable opportunity to achieve several ends. First, it could re-establish more complete control over the development of the airfields, an objective that was politically desirable for the work to be done at Canadian expense. Second, it could insure employment for Canadian contractors and labor as they were being released from other projects. Too, the execution by Canada of the additional projects would provide useful experience for the postwar development of civil aviation in Canada.

The War Department sought reconsideration of the Canadian reply on the grounds that, since the change-over to Canadian labor would involve loss of at least two months, only prompt action would prevent the airports from being inoperative during the coming summer. Canada reaffirmed its position, although it authorized the United States to complete all work at Whitehorse and Fort St. John.[38]

With the United States at least officially resigned to the new arrangements, the Northwest Service Command found their implementation not entirely to its liking. When that headquarters learned that the design specifications for the repair and rehabilitation work had been changed by the Canadian Department of Transport, it requested opportunity to review and analyze them, citing prior Canadian agreement to consult on any changes that were made to the U.S. plans. On analyzing the Department of Transport specifications, the U.S. Army Engineers took issue with the Canadian plans for work at all four airfields—Grande Prairie, Fort Nelson, Watson Lake, and Edmonton. The report of the U.S. analysis criticized the tech-

[36] EAS, 405; CTS, 1944, No. 19. The policy was announced by Canada on 29 February 1944. (*H. C. Debates*, p. 980.) For data on the expenditures by each country on Northwest Staging Route improvements, see Chapter XII, below.

[37] Ltr, Cdn Air Member, PJBD to SUSAM, 17 Mar 44, OPD 580.82 Can (27 Jan 44).

[38] Ltr, Atherton to Department of External Affairs, 28 Mar 44, and Reply, 3 Apr 44, PDB 105-27.

nical adequacy of the proposed rehabilitation designs and forecast runway failures at three of the sites.[39]

As it turned out, the dire consequences of a change-over to Canadian responsibility predicted by the War Department for the summer of 1944 failed to materialize to the extent of having a serious impact on flight operations, although the technical discussions as to design criteria for the rehabilitation work by Canada at the four airports continued to the end of 1944 and into the spring of 1945. On V-E Day arrangements were in hand for completion of field tests for evaluation of the design criteria, but with the arrival of V-J Day the matter was dropped.

The initial conception of and much of the construction on the Northwest Staging Route were Canadian accomplishments, and only the programs of construction at the main airfields executed from July 1943 into 1944, plus some temporary and limited permanent construction thereafter, were undertaken by the United States. But the U.S. construction programs carried out during the one working season comprised a substantial portion of the total construction at the main bases. United States expenditures on the staging route project of approximately $40 million were about twice the amount of Canadian expenditures on the route during the wartime period. That so much construction could be carried out in the one season was the result of careful planning during the preceding months and of the mobilization of extraordinary resources. The use of construction facilities on a lavish scale was to some extent uneconomical, and therefore the two-to-one ratio of expenditures does not accurately measure the relative accomplishments. Nor does this ratio reflect the handicaps suffered by the Canadians in the earlier years because of the severely limited transportation facilities available.[40] The eight flight strips proposed originally as adjuncts to the Alaska Highway and built by the United States came in practice to fill the need for emergency and alternate landing fields on the staging route. Except for these flight strips and minor construction at the Calgary and Prince George airfields, all facilities supplemental to the main airfields were also developed by Canada.

The wartime construction of another air route in northwest Canada was, on the other hand, almost entirely a U.S.-sponsored contribution to the expansion of the airways system of that area. As with the Northwest Staging Route, U.S. expenditures for improvements of lasting value were repaid by Canada. The development of this route, the Mackenzie River air route,

---

[39] Ltr, CG NWSC to Foster, 4 May 44, and Ltr, SUSAM to Cdn Air Member, PJBD, 20 Sep 44, PDB 105-27.

[40] For details of expenditures by both countries, see Table 7, below, p. 324.

began in September 1942 soon after the initiation of the Canol Project and the construction of facilities for the operation of the water route from Waterways to Norman Wells.

The project was born in a slight fog of misunderstanding. Col. Theodore Wyman, the U.S. Army commander of the Canol Project, initiated the construction of fourteen landing strips during the summer of 1942 without having secured specific authorization from the Canadian Government. Upon learning of the project, the Canadian Government on 17 September asked about the accuracy of reports that the United States intended to construct and operate a chain of airports in the area. The inquiry pointed out that the work had been neither foreseen nor provided for in the diplomatic agreement covering the Canol Project and that the Canadian Government had not been officially informed of the project.[41]

In reply, the United States notified Canada that the fourteen installations would in fact be only landing strips whose construction was incidental to the prosecution of the Canol Project. No special authorization had been considered necessary since it was felt that the original agreement had encompassed essential supply lines and means of communication. The United States pointed out that special authorization had not been necessary for the developments on the water route to the Norman Wells airfields, nor had one been contemplated for the development and use of the winter roads to the same point. The United States indicated a willingness to arrange an agreement if one was considered necessary. Apparently the Canadians accepted the U.S. explanation, for they made no reply and the exchange of correspondence was later cited as the authority for the project.[42]

The airstrips formed a route parallel to the water route from Waterways to Norman Wells. A cutoff from Peace River to Fort Providence paralleled the winter road from the railhead at the former. All were equipped with lighting, and six with radio range beacons. The main strips were at Waterways, Fort Smith, Fort Simpson, and Norman Wells. Those at Peace River, Mills Lake, Wrigley, Embarras, Fort Resolution, Hay River, Fort Providence, and Camp Canol were essentially for emergency purposes. At Waterways and Peace River, the existence of landing facilities reduced the work necessary to develop the sites to the required standards. The work of clearing and grading the strips was for the greater part accomplished by U.S. Army Engineer troops, although civilian contractors did all or part of the work at a few of the sites. Little work was done beyond the clearing and grading

[41] Ott Leg Desp 3614, 17 Sep 42, PDB 110-11.

[42] Ltr, Moffat to Keenleyside, 5 Oct 42, PDB 110-11. See below, pp. 228-35.

and the installation of minimum flying aids. As a result, the expenditures at all sites totaled only $1,264,150.

Proposals to develop part of the Mackenzie River air route and extend it to Fairbanks to provide an alternate air route to Alaska were discussed in Ottawa at the 18–19 February 1943 meeting called to consider the construction program on the Northwest Staging Route. The new route, called the Low-level Route, would originate at Fort Nelson and proceed via Fort Simpson, Wrigley, Norman Wells, Fort Good Hope, Fort McPherson, Old Crow, and Fort Yukon to Fairbanks. Advantages of the new route were that it would provide (1) a means of preventing congestion at Whitehorse, where expansion was limited by physical conditions, (2) an alternate route if the existing route was interrupted at Whitehorse or some other point in close proximity to the coast, (3) facilities capable of handling extraordinary transport operations, (4) alternate weather conditions, and (5) a route for carrying out night operations, which were virtually impossible in winter on the existing route.[43]

The Permanent Joint Board on Defense considered the proposals a few days later. The Board did not adopt a recommendation on the subject, but the Canadian Section undertook to obtain governmental approval of the project.[44] The matter dragged until early April, when Canadian authorities in Washington sought more information on the project. By then it appeared that the Cabinet War Committee, although unenthusiastic about the project, would probably agree to it. At the same time it became evident on the U.S. side that the Army Air Forces had made no definite plans for carrying out the project but had only intended that preliminary inquiries be made of Canada. After re-examining the need for the Low-level Route, the War Department concluded that the Northwest Staging Route would be able to handle all requirements. In consequence, the U.S. Section withdrew its request in the Permanent Joint Board for approval of the project and asked Canada to postpone indefinitely consideration of it.[45] The Canadian Government nevertheless proceeded with a survey of the route with a view to its possible future development.

Traffic Along the Staging Route

From the U.S. point of view, the Northwest Staging Route provided facilities serving three main purposes: (a) the movement of tactical aircraft

[43] Minutes, 18–19 Feb 43 PJBD meeting, PDB 105–13; Memo, ATC for SUSAM, 9 Apr 43, PDB 110–11.

[44] Journal, 24–25 Feb 43 meeting, PDB 124.

[45] Memos, SUSAM for Hickerson, 16 and 19 Apr 43, PDB 110–11; Journal, 6–7 May 1943 PJBD meeting, PDB 124.

to the defense garrisons in Alaska, (b) the delivery of aircraft for the USSR at Fairbanks, whence they continued to the Soviet Union via Siberia, and (c) the administrative and logistical support of the Alaskan garrison and of the U.S. projects in western Canada. The numbers of aircraft delivered over the Northwest Staging Route in the first two categories were as follows:[46]

Year	*Total*	*For USSR*	*For AAF*
Total	8,646	7,930	716
1942	311	148	163
1943	2,776	2,491	285
1944	3,276	3,148	128
1945	2,283	2,143	140

The great bulk of these aircraft were fighter and other short-range types that could not have been delivered to Alaska by air in the absence of the staging airfields.

As is readily apparent from these figures, the movement of aircraft over the route for ferrying to the USSR represented a much greater operation than the movement of aircraft to the Alaskan defense garrison. The ferrying arrangement had first been discussed on 4 August 1941, when Secretary of War Stimson and Soviet Ambassador Constantine Oumansky agreed in principle on the plan. The Russians were not enthusiastic about use of the Siberia route, and it was not until March 1942 that a detailed plan was presented. In April President Roosevelt in a personal message urged Premier Stalin to accept the plan, which he did in July. Under it the Ferrying Division of the Air Transport Command delivered the aircraft to a Soviet detachment at Ladd Field, Fairbanks, Alaska. There Russian pilots tested and accepted the aircraft and then staged them through Nome into Siberia. The first aircraft were delivered to Soviet representatives in Fairbanks on 4 September. Pilots to fly the aircraft away did not arrive until 24 September. Once the program was fully organized, aircraft deliveries took place in steadily increasing numbers.[47]

United States air transport operations to Alaska were largely carried out by the Alaskan Wing of the Air Transport Command, although the Naval Air Transport Service also operated over the route. From mid-1943 on, from thirty-five to forty aircraft were assigned to the Alaskan Wing for these

[46] Special Senate Committee Investigating the National Defense Program, 79th Congress, 2d Session, Hearings on Senate Resolution 46, 80th Congress, extending Senate Resolution 71, 77th Congress, *Investigation of the National Defense Program*, Pt. 39, p. 23470.

[47] For fuller accounts of the arrangements, see History of the Northwest Air Route to Alaska, 1942–1945, and Admiral William H. Standley, "Stalin and World Unity," *Collier's* June 30, 1945. Other sources are The Northwest Route Under the Ferrying Division: 16 June 1942–1 November 1942, and Organizational History of the Ferrying Division: 20 June 1942–1 August 1944.

operations, most of them commercial aircraft operating under contract. The air transport accomplishments of the Alaskan Wing are indicated in the following table:[48]

Year	*Ton-miles*	*Passenger-miles*
1942 (July-December)	6,145,000	13,176,000
1943	19,674,000	86,850,000
1944	30,801,000	153,905,000
1945 (January-September)	23,006,000	116,337,000

The number of total arrivals at the main airfields, including Edmonton, perhaps gives a better layman's appreciation of the scale of activity along the route:[49]

Week	*Total*	*AAF*	*RCAF*	*Civilian*
14-20 August 1943	2,505	782	1,497	226
12-18 August 1944	1,381	990	230	161
11-17 August 1945	867	539	214	114

The Alaska Highway

Of the logistical projects undertaken by the United States in Canada during World War II, two stand out far above the others in magnitude, the complexity of the problems met, and the size of the construction organizations assembled to execute them. These projects were the construction of the Alaska Highway and the related Canol Project.[50] United States governmental agencies had several times since 1930 examined proposals for a highway between the United States and Alaska. Before Pearl Harbor the War Department in commenting on such proposals could find little or no immediate military utility in such a highway. When the proposals of the joint Alaskan International Highway Commission for a highway between British Columbia and Alaska were discussed by the Permanent Joint Board on Defense on 15 November 1940, the Board unanimously agreed that the military value of a road following either of the two routes then proposed would be negligible. The Board, it may be noted, did not rule on the merits of a road to Alaska but only on the two proposed routes, which lay west of the Rocky Mountain Range. At the same meeting the Board did adopt its Tenth Recommendation, calling for the construction of the air staging facili-

[48] Alaskan Division, Historical Record Report, Nov 44–Sep 45 volume, p. 395.

[49] PDB 105-28. These figures include the tactical aircraft deliveries tabulated on page 216. RCAF arrivals for the week 14–20 August 1943 include those incident to operations of No. 2 Air Observers School and Aircraft Repair, Ltd.

Some data on Air Transport Command operations on the route may be found in Cave, *Wings Across the World;* Cleveland, *Air Transport at War;* and Oliver LaFarge, *The Eagle in the Egg* (Boston: Houghton Mifflin Company, 1949).

[50] A fairly voluminous literature on the highway is included in the bibliography. By far the most detailed account is contained in House Report 1705, 79th Congress, 2d Session.

ties between the United States and Alaska, and this action held real significance for the future routing of the Alaska Highway.[51]

During 1941 general interest in a highway to Alaska grew. In January 1941 Dr. Vilhjalmur Stefansson, famous Arctic authority, recommended to the War Department the construction of a highway to Alaska via the Mackenzie and Yukon River valleys.[52] Officials of Alaska, British Columbia, Alberta, and the several U.S. adjacent border states urged routes favoring their own geographic interest.[53] In April 1941 Secretary of State Hull sought the support of Prime Minister King for a highway. King "was not entirely favorable in holding out hope for immediate co-operation," since the Permanent Joint Board had believed the construction of facilities on the air route to Alaska to be more important. In July Mayor LaGuardia, U.S. chairman of the Permanent Joint Board, joined the proponents of a highway, and by October the War Department had declared itself in favor of a highway "as a long-range defense measure." [54]

The Pearl Harbor attack and the subsequent Japanese menace to west coast shipping radically altered the picture. Members of the President's Cabinet at a meeting on 16 January 1942 discussed the possibility that sea communications to Alaska would be interrupted and the desirability of constructing a highway through Canada. The President appointed a committee, comprising the Secretaries of War, the Navy, and the Interior, to study the need for a highway. While this study went forward, Roosevelt took up with General Marshall and Admiral King possible enemy intentions toward Alaska and the state of the defenses there, which the President considered unsatisfactory. Marshall and King anticipated a Japanese raid on Alaska and were troubled by the difficulty of providing air reinforcements.[55] Although Admiral King admitted the vulnerability of the coastal shipping route, he would not agree that it was necessary to construct a highway to Alaska on the basis that the U.S. Navy could not adequately protect coastal shipping, nor would he categorically commit the Navy to insuring uninterrupted sea communications to Alaska under all circumstances. The Army considered Admiral King's position equivocal and unsatisfactory.

---

[51] Journal, PDB 124; see above, pp. 200–207.

[52] House Report 1705, 79th Congress, 2d Session, p. 7.

[53] For a comparison of the various routes proposed, see House Report 1705, 79th Congress, 2d Session. Dr. Vilhjalmur Stefansson supports his proposal in "The North American Arctic," *Compass of the World*, eds. V. Stefansson and H. W. Weigert (New York: The Macmillan Company, 1944), pp. 233–40.

[54] Memo/Conv, 17 Apr 41, D/S 711.42/214; House Report 1705, 79th Congress, 2d Session, p. 8.

[55] Memos, Roosevelt for Marshall and Adm King and for Capt McCrae, 20 Jan 42, Memo, Marshall for President, 21 Jan 42; all in Roosevelt Papers, Secy's File, Box 1. See above, pp. 200–207.

On 2 February the Cabinet committee met with War Department officials and concluded that a highway was needed and that it should follow the line of airports of the air staging route to Alaska. From the military point of view, this alignment had the merits of providing a land route to Alaska, a means of supplying the air bases on the Northwest Staging Route, and a ground guide for pilots flying aircraft over this route. The Army Chief of Staff endorsed the plan, and on 11 February the President approved it, allocating an initial $10 million from his emergency fund and directing that arrangements be made with Canada through the Permanent Joint Board on Defense.[56]

Arrangements with Canada were initiated the next day without awaiting a Board meeting. Minister Moffat in Ottawa, who had warned the Canadians of the impending decision a week earlier, was instructed by the State Department on 12 February to request authority for the dispatch of U.S. survey detachments and for construction of the road. The next day Canada readily granted permission for the "proposed survey," and Moffat reported that Canadian approval of a survey included authority for construction of a pioneer road such as would be needed in connection with the survey.[57] On the basis of the partial approval received, and in anticipation of approval of the entire project, the War Department on 14 February ordered the Chief of Engineers to undertake construction of a pioneer road from Fort St. John to Boundary, Alaska.

The Permanent Joint Board at its 25-26 February 1942 meeting considered the U.S. proposal for the construction of the Alaska Highway.[58] Some of the Canadian members were not entirely satisfied that the project was of sufficient value to justify the diversion of resources needed elsewhere, particularly since by 1 January 1944, the estimated date of completion, they assumed that U.S. sea and air communications to Alaska would be secure. Canadian Department of Mines and Resources officials were even skeptical of the feasibility of constructing a road along the line of airports because of the muskeg areas and winter survey difficulties that would be encountered. Nevertheless, "for reasons of general policy," the Canadian Section supported the Twenty-fourth Recommendation proposed by the U.S. Section.[59] The

---

[56] House Report 1705, 79th Congress, 2d Session, pp. 9-11, 88-89; Memo, CofS for Adm King, 4 Feb 42, and Reply, 5 Feb 42, WPD 4327-27.

[57] Ott Leg Desp 2592, 14 Feb 42, D/S 842.154 Seattle-Fairbanks Hwy/359.

[58] Department of State *Bulletin*, March 21, 1942, VI, 237.

[59] Keenleyside MS; Memo/Conv, Moffat and Hickerson, 7 Feb 42, and Moffat and Robertson, 6 Mar 42, Moffat Diary.

The journal for the Board meeting does not record these Canadian doubts, but only the agreement reached by the Board as a whole on the need for a highway on the basis of a number of military considerations that were discussed in detail.

U.S. ARMY ENGINEERS CONSTRUCTING A PIONEER ROAD *to Alaska through virgin forests, May 1942.*

U.S. Section informed the Board that the United States was willing to assume the responsibility for and the whole cost of constructing and maintaining the highway. In undertaking to meet the cost of constructing the road, the U.S. Section told the Board, the U.S. Government acknowledged the financial burdens Canada had borne since it entered the war in September 1939, especially in connection with the construction on the Northwest Staging Route. The Board then, as its Twenty-fourth Recommendation, proposed that, "as a matter pertaining to the joint defense of Canada and the United States," a highway be constructed along the line of staging route airports and connecting with the existing road systems in Alaska and Canada.[60]

The two governments were not long in approving the Twenty-fourth Recommendation. The Canadian Government approved it on 5 March, and the next day, 6 March, Prime Minister King informed Parliament of the

[60] Extract of Journal at Appendix C, below; see also Appendix A, below. Mayor LaGuardia reported this background to the President in picturesque language: "We encountered more difficulty in giving 'something to somebody' than in collecting a war loan from an ally. . . . The Canadians . . fear a terrific political backfire. . . . I am sure you will agree that all hell will break loose when our Washington and Oregon friends learn of the route." (Ltr, 27 Feb 42, Roosevelt Papers, Official File, Box 1566.) In apparent reflection of the Canadian attitude manifested at the PJBD meeting, the phrase quoted in the text was not included when the recommendation was embodied in the diplomatic notes exchanged later.

project. President Roosevelt on 9 March formally approved the recommendation covering the project to which he had given informal approval several weeks earlier.[61]

In the diplomatic notes exchanged by Canada and the United States on 17 and 18 March 1942 detailing the terms of the agreement, the United States undertook to (1) make the necessary surveys, (2) construct a pioneer road using Engineer troops, (3) arrange for the completion of the highway under civilian contractors, (4) maintain the highway until six months after the termination of the war, and (5) release the highway at that time to become an integral part of the Canadian highway system. On its part, Canada agreed to (1) provide the right of way, (2) waive import duties, taxes, and charges on shipments through Canada and on all equipment and materials to be used in construction and maintenance of the highway, (3) remit income tax of U.S. residents employed on the project, (4) facilitate entry of construction personnel, and (5) permit use of local timber, gravel, and rock for the project.[62]

Only one U.S. proposal occasioned discussion. Canada would not agree to guarantee postwar use of the highway to U.S. military vehicles under conditions to be recommended by the Board. It offered, as an alternative, to "give due consideration" to any recommendation which the Board might make along these lines. The point was simply omitted from the agreement.

Several other points were agreed on or clarified at a later time. In an exchange of notes between Canada and the United States on 4 and 9 May 1942, the Canadian Government agreed that it had been the intent of the Board that the southern terminus of the highway be Dawson Creek, despite the fact that Fort St. John was the southernmost point mentioned in the Twenty-fourth Recommendation. Nearly a year later notes exchanged on 10 April 1943 authorized U.S. use of the highways between Fort St. John and the U.S. border as being in keeping with the language and intent of the original agreement. Finally, at the suggestion of Mr. Anthony Dimond, Alaskan delegate to the U.S. House of Representatives, the highway was officially named the Alaska Highway on 19 July 1943.[63]

[61] House Report 1705, 79th Congress, 2d Session, pp. 91–92.

[62] EAS, 246; CTS, 1942, No. 13. Ltr, Clark to Hickerson, 29 Mar 42, D/S 842.154 Seattle–Fairbanks Hwy/522. The regulations subsequently issued as to exemptions from import duties and taxes are contained in Department of National Revenue order WM No. 75, 9 Oct 42, published in Canada, Privy Council, *Canadian War Orders and Regulations*, III (1942), 155–58.

[63] EAS, 380; CTS, 1942, No. 22. EAS, 381; CTS, 1943, No. 17. EAS, 331; CTS, 1943, No. 10. Concern had been occasioned in Ottawa and in the Department of State by the possibility that the highway might be christened by unilateral U.S. action through Congressional approval of House Joint Resolution 105, introduced by Mr. Dimond on 24 March 1943, rather than by a joint and simultaneous announcement in the two capital cities. However, the announcement was made while the resolution was awaiting committee action. (Memo/Conv, J. G. Parsons and M. Wershof of the Canadian Legation, 30 Apr 43, D/S 842.154 Seattle–Fairbanks Hwy/542–1/2.

Construction on the pioneer road began about a week after President Roosevelt formally approved the Alaska Highway project and after the arrival of the initial contingent of troops at the Dawson Creek railhead on 16 March 1942. The force of Engineer troops was soon built up to seven regiments, reinforced by ponton, survey, and other units, totaling 394 officers and 10,765 enlisted men.[64] On 25 October 1942 the pioneer road was completed, and its 1,523 miles between Dawson Creek and Fairbanks were passable and in use for supply purposes. During succeeding months the pioneer road was developed into a well-graded and well-drained two-lane road 26 feet wide. In the latter half of 1942 the Engineer troops were reinforced by a construction organization (totaling approximately 7,500) under the U.S. Public Roads Administration, which, through arrangements worked out with the Chief of Engineers, undertook to assist in the pioneer road construction and to develop the pioneer road into the final-type highway. The construction of the final-type road by seventy-seven contractors and four management contractors under the Public Roads Administration continued through most of 1943. The work involved a civilian force totaling as high as 15,950 using as many as 11,100 pieces of road-building equipment. By 1 November 1943 construction on the Alaska Highway was 96 percent complete, and, except for certain bridge construction, the remaining work and the maintenance of the highway was taken over by the Army Engineers.

The completed highway between Dawson Creek and Big Delta, Alaska, was a permanent, all-weather road, 1,428 miles long and 26 feet wide, except for the southernmost 75 miles which was 36 feet wide. The link with Fairbanks was provided from Big Delta by the Richardson Highway, which ran from Valdez to Fairbanks. Construction involved 133 bridges 20 feet or more in length. About half the footage was steel bridging. The 2,130-foot suspension bridge over the Peace River was the major structure, and a 2,300-foot, one-lane, pile-trestle bridge over the Nisutlin River was the longest.

The finished highway permitted speeds in safety from 40 to 50 miles an hour and had an estimated normal capacity of 400,000 tons annually, which might be increased to a maximum of 720,000 tons for emergency military purposes. For use as part of a through-road system between the United States and Alaska, the highway capacity was limited by the fact that the road facilities south from Dawson Creek were poor-quality highways, unusable at certain seasons of the year. This limitation could of course be circumvented by use of railroad shipments to Dawson Creek.

---

[64] With passenger shipping in critical supply, Canada contributed to this troop movement by making available between 1 and 19 April, for nine trips between Seattle or Prince Rupert and Skagway, *Prince Rupert*, *Prince George*, *Princess Norah*, and *Princess Charlotte*.

SIKANNI CHIEF RIVER BRIDGE, *one of the first bridges to be completed on the Alaska Highway. Photograph taken in 1943.*

The construction of the Alaska Highway was a tremendous engineering achievement and a tribute to U.S. and Canadian co-operation. Few projects could match the complexity and enormity of the task of putting the highway through virgin forests within established time schedules and in the face of transportation handicaps, muskeg and ice, and thaw, washouts, landslides, freezing temperatures, and other weather handicaps. The cost of the construction work performed on the highway proper was almost $116 million, exclusive of the costs of wartime maintenance, of many auxiliary installations, and of the final job inventory of materials, supplies, and equipment. These two additional categories totaled about $23.5 million. In addition, it has been conservatively estimated that the cost of the Engineer troop labor involved, not included in the above figures, was $8 million.[65]

With the completion of highway construction and the replacement of the initial temporary timber bridges by permanent structures, the required maintenance was easily carried out and was facilitated by the excellent design and construction standards. A steady flow of supplies continued over the highway both in support of the construction operations and of the numerous other U.S. and Canadian activities in northwest Canada. In late 1943 a U.S. Army

[65] House Report 1705, 79th Congress, 2d Session, p. 22.

fleet of over 1,500 trucks (ranging from 2½- to 10-ton capacity) and 27 cross-country-type passenger buses was operating on the highway, and during 1943 moved 134,000 tons of cargo and 42,000 passengers. Hauling for U.S. activities alone totaled over 36,700,000 ton-miles in 1943, and over 30,900,000 in 1944. These figures decreased in 1945 with the closing out of construction activities and the operation of the pipeline along the highway for supply of gasoline to the air bases and other facilities.[66] As early as the spring of 1943 the flow of civilan traffic over the highway had become so heavy that a Joint Travel Control Board was established at Edmonton. The board included representatives of the U.S. Northwest Service Command and of the Canadian Special Commissioner for Defense Projects in Northwestern Canada, who met to deal with applications for civilian travel.[67]

In September 1944, with U.S. need for use of the highway diminishing, the United States suggested in the Permanent Joint Board on Defense the transfer of administration and maintenance responsibility to Canada and indicated its willingness, pursuant to the original agreement, to share the cost of the maintenance operations. The Canadian Section pointed out "certain difficulties which would confront the Canadian Government in accepting this proposal," and, after study and further report, the Board agreed to defer a recommendation on the subject. In notifying the War Department of the action of the Board, the Senior U.S. Army Member thereof stated that the position of the Canadian Section was in line with the previously known attitude of the Canadian Government, which did not desire to assume maintenance responsibility for the Canadian portion of the highway, either with or without U.S. financial assistance.[68]

Upon the termination of hostilities, the United States again sought to transfer the responsibilities to Canada. Canada agreed to assume the responsibility for maintenance and operation of the Canadian portion of the Alaska Highway on 1 April 1946. On that date transfer was effected with appropriate ceremony at Whitehorse, amid general agreement that the highway would be an important factor in the further exploitation of the potential of northwestern Canada.[69]

[66] For an account of transportation operations on the highway, see Bykofsky and Larson, *The Transportation Corps: Operations Overseas,* pp. 57–65. The authors point out that of the total supplies moved along the highway, a net of only 57 tons of supplies had been delivered to the Alaska Defense Command by the end of the campaign in the Aleutians. However, this figure is consistent with the situation in which ocean shipping was the primary means of transportation, with the highway intended for use as an emergency facility.

[67] Journal, 1–14 Jul 43 PJBD meeting, PDB 124.

[68] Journal, 6–7 Sep and 7–8 Nov 44 PJBD meetings, PDB 124. Memo, 15 Nov 44, House Report 1705, 79th Congress, 2d Session, pp. 246–47.

[69] Canada soon redesignated the Alaska Highway as the Northwest Highway System. (Lester B. Pearson, "Canada Looks 'Down North,' " *Foreign Affairs,* XXIV (July 1946), 641.)

The need for road and rail facilities over which to bring freight for the construction of the Alaska Highway involved the U.S. and Canadian Governments in additional negotiations. Freight for the highway was delivered at three points—Dawson Creek, Whitehorse, and Fairbanks. The railhead at and the connecting highway net to Dawson Creek have already been mentioned. For the Alaskan portion of the highway, freight was delivered to Fairbanks principally by the Alaska Railroad after water shipment to either Seward or Whittier. Some freight was transported over the Richardson Highway, which connected the port of Valdez with Fairbanks and also linked the Alaska Highway terminus at Big Delta with Fairbanks. The Glenn Highway, between the Richardson Highway and Anchorage, also linked Anchorage to the Alaska Highway. Another avenue to the northern portion of the Alaska Highway was provided by the Tok cutoff connecting the Alaska and Richardson Highways.

A vital link to the center section of the Alaska Highway was the White Pass and Yukon Route railway, connecting Skagway and Whitehorse and having its origins in 1901 in the Klondike gold rush. Over that railway had passed the supplies for the air base at Whitehorse long before the Alaska Highway was planned. As construction of the Alaska Highway began, the use of this railroad permitted the movement of troops and supplies to a middle point on the proposed highway, from which point construction could advance in two directions. Still later, large rail shipments were to be made to Whitehorse in connection with the Canol Project.[70]

In the fall of 1942 the U.S. need for use of this narrow-gauge (36-inch) railroad made it desirable for the U.S. Army to take over its operation. Of the three segments making up the White Pass and Yukon Route, the two in Canada were owned by companies incorporated in Canada. Arrangements for U.S. lease of these two segments for the duration of the war were worked out in a meeting in Ottawa on 16 October 1942. On the basis of these arrangements, the Canadian Government issued an order-in-council establishing the legal foundation for U.S. lease and operation of privately owned Canadian common carriers. An exchange of notes at Ottawa in February 1943 formalized the agreement.[71]

Operation of the White Pass and Yukon Route railway had been taken over by the U.S. Army Military Railway Service by 19 October 1942. Dur-

[70] The system known as the White Pass and Yukon Route comprises three companies owning the three segments of railroad in Alaska, British Columbia, and the Yukon Territory, and a fourth company operating shipping on the Yukon River and its tributaries. All four companies have but one bank account and common officials and shareholders. (See Carl A. Dawson (ed.), *The New North-West* (Toronto: University of Toronto Press, 1947), pp. 193–98.)

[71] EAS, 390; CTS, 1943, No. 3. The Canadian note also contains the order-in-council, Privy Council 10067, 6 Nov 42.

TRAIN PLOWING THROUGH DEEP SNOW *on the White Pass and Yukon Route railroad.*

ing the ensuing months, the railway battalion assigned to the task completely reconstructed 20 miles of the 111-mile railway, added much new equipment, and rehabilitated the property as a whole. During 1943 the narrow-gauge railway carried up to 40,000 tons of freight per month.[72]

Although the White Pass and Yukon Route offered an excellent means of transportation to Whitehorse, U.S. Army Engineers had examined the need for an alternate transportation route as early as April 1942. At the meeting of the Permanent Joint Board that month, the U.S. Section requested authorization for construction of a highway between Haines, on the Lynn Canal near Skagway, and a point on the Alaska Highway between Kluane and Champagne. The Canadian Section of the Board replied that the Canadian Government would have no objection to a survey but suggested that the question of actual authorization be deferred to a later date. After several months had elapsed, the War Department on 14 October 1942 asked for im-

[72] Bykofsky and Larson, *The Transportation Corps: Operations Overseas*, contains a fuller account of the U.S. Army operations over this railway. The peak figure of 47,000 tons was achieved in August 1943, while the total for 1943 was 284,532 tons in addition to 22,000 passengers.

mediate approval for a survey, and it was granted. Less than a month later the United States requested Canadian approval for construction of the Haines-Champagne cutoff, and the Cabinet War Committee granted it on 18 October. The exchange of notes formalizing the agreement provided that the new section would be considered an integral part of the Alaska Highway and would be constructed under the same arrangements that had been agreed upon for the highway.[73]

Construction was carried forward the same winter by the Public Roads Administration and, beginning in March 1943, by civilian contractor to the U.S. Engineer District. In November 1943 the 159-mile cutoff was completed, but to standards below those of the Alaska Highway proper. Responsibility for the part in Canada passed to Canada on 1 April 1946 along with that for the rest of the Alaska Highway. As in the case of the Alaska Highway, Canada was under no obligation to continue to maintain the Haines cutoff.

Apart from the road construction undertaken in connection with the Canol Project, the road system described was the extent of the highway construction completed in northwestern Canada during World War II. Other highways were proposed but did not materialize. A link between Prince George and Fort St. John was suggested by the Canadian Section of the Permanent Joint Board on Defense at the 7-8 April 1942 meeting, which followed the one at which the Alaska Highway was recommended. After examining a study on this highway link submitted by the Canadian Section, the U.S. Section at the next Board meeting on 27 April reported its view that such a road would have so slight a military value that a sufficiently high construction priority would not be warranted. One other proposal never got past the preliminary survey stage. In December 1942 the United States sought and received authority to undertake a survey for a road from the Mackenzie River near Aklavik to the Yukon River. The road, which never materialized, would have followed the route Peel River-Rat River-Macdougall Pass-Dell River-Porcupine River.[74]

The War Department also examined the feasibility and desirability of constructing a rail route to Alaska. A survey for a route between Prince George and Fairbanks was authorized by Canada in April 1942 and undertaken during the summer. The route surveyed in general followed one of the two that had been proposed by the Alaskan International Highway Commission for a highway. On the basis of the survey the War Department

[73] EAS, 382; CTS, 1942, No. 21.
[74] Journals, 27 Apr and 14 Dec 42, and 13 Jan 43 PJBD meetings, PDB 124.

concluded that a railroad adequate for military purposes could be constructed for $112 million. Although informal discussions between the countries took place in September and October 1942, the War Department in December announced that a military necessity for the railroad did not exist at that time and filed the survey "for possible future wartime use."[75]

The Canol Project

The Canol (from "Canada" and "oil") Project, if not the most spectacular wartime military undertaking in Canada, was surely the most debated and controversial enterprise. The oil was to come from the Mackenzie River field at Norman Wells, where the first oil-producing well had been drilled in 1920. Oil seepages in that vicinity had been reported by Alexander Mackenzie over a hundred years earlier. At the time of the establishment of the Permanent Joint Board on Defense in August 1940, four of seven wells drilled in the general area were producing, and a small refinery was meeting the petroleum products needs of the lower Mackenzie valley.[76]

With Pearl Harbor only a few weeks past, the War Department in January 1942 undertook its initial investigations of the feasibility of using the oil resources at Norman Wells to meet military requirements in Alaska and northwest Canada. At a Cabinet meeting on 16 January 1942, the President indicated to the Secretaries of War and the Navy his concern over the vulnerability of the sea routes to Alaska as well as the critical tanker situation facing the Allies. In the War Department intermittent discussion of the Canol Project took place in the early months of 1942, while tanker losses mounted, the Dutch East Indies oil fields were lost, and Caribbean facilities were shelled by German submarines. On 29 April 1942 War Department representatives outlined the project to officials of the Imperial Oil Company, Limited, of Canada, which owned and operated the oil fields. Action followed quickly. The same day James H. Graham, a technical adviser to Lt. Gen. Brehon B. Somervell, Commanding General, Services of Supply, recommended and received approval for the project. The next day, 30 April, General Somervell directed the Chief of Engineers, U.S. Army, to carry out the project, which at this stage called for the drilling of nine additional wells, the erection by 1 October 1942 of a refinery with a 3,000-barrel daily refining capacity at

[75] WD Press Releases, 4 July and 10 Dec 42; Senate Committee on Foreign Relations, 81st Congress, 1st Session, Senate Report 1131 to accompany H. R. 2186, *Providing for a Location Survey for Railroad Facilities Between the United States and Alaska,* p. 2.

[76] For an account of the prewar development of the Norman Wells field, see Oliver B. Hopkins, "The 'Canol' Project," *Canadian Geographical Journal,* XXVII (November 1943), 238–49. For a detailed account of its wartime development, see Trevor Lloyd, "Oil in the Mackenzie Valley," *Geographical Review,* XXXIV (1944), 275–307.

Whitehorse, and the construction by 15 September 1942 of a 4-inch pipeline between Norman Wells and the refinery. On the following day, 1 May, a contract was let to the Imperial Oil Company for the drilling and operating of the additional wells.[77]

The decision immediately evoked expressions of doubt and criticism. Officers within the War Department and elsewhere in the U.S. Government questioned the soundness of the project as a whole or of parts thereof. Representatives of the Standard Oil Company of California, which the War Department had hired as a consultant on the project, and of the Imperial Oil Company commented unfavorably on the project. The Department of State, in forwarding instructions to the legation in Ottawa, pointedly noted that it had made no examination of the merits of the Canol Project.[78]

Despite the contemporary expressions of doubt, the U.S. decision to undertake the project stood. The United States presented its request for Canadian approval of the project to the Canadian Government informally on 1 May and formally on 8 May. Prodded for a reply on 15 May at the instance of the U.S. Army Engineers who were anxious to utilize the full summer construction season, Canadian officials informally indicated that they were not declining assistance but had serious doubts about the soundness of the proposition. They suggested that the United States give the project additional consideration. The War Department on 18 May reaffirmed its request to the Department of State and indicated that the reconsideration of the Canol Project at Canada's suggestion had confirmed the decision to undertake it, and that the risk involved was justified in terms of the critical situation. The State Department immediately informed Canada of the War Department position, and the same day the Canadian Government signified its approval, which had actually been granted by the Cabinet War Committee on 16 May 1942.[79]

Discussion of the formal diplomatic arrangements followed, and the

[77] An extensive list of literature on the Canol Project is included in the bibliography. The most authoritative and fully documented data result from the investigation by the Senate Special Committee Investigating the National Defense Program. They are contained in Special Senate Committee Investigating the National Defense Program, 78th Congress, 1st Session, Hearings on Senate Resolution 6, *Investigation of the National Defense Program,* Pt. 22; *Investigation of the National Defense Program,* Pt. 39 (cited above, n. 46); and Special Senate Committee Investigating the National Defense Program, 78th Congress, 1st Session, Senate Report 10, *Investigation of the National Defense Program* Pursuant to Senate Resolution 71, 77th Congress, and Senate Resolution 6, 78th Congress, Pt. 14, Additional Report, *The Canol Project.* Minutes of the late April meetings, the recommendation and approval, and the contract are reproduced in *Investigation of the National Defense Program,* Pt. 22, as Exhibits 1095, 1096, 1097, and 1087.

[78] *Investigation of the National Defense Program,* Pt. 22, Exhibits 1097, 1101, and 1141.

[79] D/S Telg 71, 1 May 42, D/S 811.248/486; Memo/Conv, Moffat and Keenleyside, 8 May 42, D/S 842.6363/162; U.S. Leg Ott Telg 80, 18 May 42, D/S 842.6363/168-1/5; Ltr, SW to Secy State, 18 May 42, D/S 842.6363/175.

agreement was effected in an exchange of notes signed in Ottawa on 27 and 29 June 1942. Under the agreement, by which Canada was to provide assistance similar to that for the Alaska Highway, the facilities were to be built by the United States, remain its property during the war, and be disposed of subsequently under an agreed procedure.[80]

Even before the agreement was finalized, the War Department had come forward requesting approval of a supplemental project. This project, suggested by Harold L. Ickes, who as U.S. Petroleum Co-ordinator for War had objected to the original project and had sponsored the new one as an alternative, called for construction of 4-inch pipeline with a 5,000-barrel daily capacity between Skagway and Whitehorse along the White Pass and Yukon Route railroad and of storage and loading facilities at Prince Rupert. The supplemental project, which could be completed in a shorter time, would permit transportation of gasoline to Whitehorse from the United States via the relatively protected and shorter tanker haul along the inside passage from Prince Rupert to Skagway. Canadian approval was given informally in one day, 27 June, and later formalized in an exchange of notes dated 14 and 15 August 1942.[81] The provisions of the earlier agreement were applied to the new one.

Other associated projects were planned and undertaken with the result that the original project became known as Canol 1 and the supplementary project as Canol 2. Canol 3 provided for a 2-inch gasoline pipeline between Carcross, a point on the Canol 2 pipeline, and Watson Lake, with associated storage and other facilities. This line would permit deliveries from Skagway or Whitehorse to installations southward as far as Watson Lake. Canol 4 called for a 3-inch gasoline pipeline from Whitehorse to Fairbanks and related facilities.[82] Canol 5, a gasoline pipeline extension from Fairbanks to Tanana, Alaska, was to be wholly a U.S. project, but it was later abandoned.

None of the proposals in connection with the several Canol programs was processed through the Permanent Joint Board. However, the agreements for Canol 1 and 2 provided that if, at time of disposition of the facilities, there was no purchaser, the problem would be referred to the Board for recommendation. This provision resulted from a War Department suggestion

[80] EAS, 386; CTS, 1942, No. 23.

[81] EAS, 387; CTS, 1942, No. 24.

[82] Canols 3 and 4 had not been specifically authorized before work on them began. They were noted in an exchange of letters in Ottawa, dated 22 September and 5 October 1942, which was the result of Canadian inquiry concerning reports about these projects. They were formally approved for the record on 7 June 1944. (List, U.S. Defense Projects and Installations in Canada, 12 Jan 44 [Canadian origin], PDB 150-1; EAS, 416, and CTS, 1944, No. 16.)

designed to insure against dismantling where such action would be contrary to foreseeable future war needs.[83]

Major logistical tasks faced the U.S. Army even before work at Norman Wells could begin. On 4 June 1942 the vanguard of Task Force 2600 began arriving at Waterways, Alberta, the northernmost railhead in the area, to establish the transportation system to Norman Wells over which could move the civilian construction organization and supplies needed for construction of the pipeline from Norman Wells to Whitehorse. The 1,171-mile route, open only from May to October, involved a 285-mile passage down the Athabasca and Slave Rivers, a 16-mile portage at Fort Fitzgerald, and additional passages of 195, 125, and 550 miles on the Slave River, Great Slave Lake, and Mackenzie River, respectively. By the end of June 1942 a force of over 2,000 troops was constructing the wharfage, warehousing, housing, and other facilities needed at the various terminal and storage points. Available river boats were purchased or hired, others were brought in, and large numbers of prefabricated barges were assembled on the rivers.

By the summer of 1943 more than 39,000 tons of supplies had been moved over this water route. The greater part of the freight moved was delivered by the marine transportation facilities of the Hudson's Bay Company, which carried 50 percent of the tonnage between Waterways and Fort Fitzgerald and 60 percent between Fort Smith and Norman Wells. After mid-1943 an increasing portion of these accomplishments was the result of augmentation of the force operating the route by the civilian organization, Marine Operators, at Edmonton. Pursuant to a contract arranged in February 1943, Marine Operators made extensive preparations for the task, which it took over during the summer of 1943. Task Force 2600 was then withdrawn. By the close of the river navigation season in early October, virtually all the supplies that had been assembled for movement to Norman Wells had reached that destination.[84]

With the waterways frozen during the winter months, alternate routes were sought to permit movement of supplies. Although a network of air bases was constructed which permitted movement of men and supplies by air, the principal means of winter transportation were tractor roads built over the frozen ground, rivers, and lakes.[85] The U.S. Army built such a route during the winter of 1942–43 from the railhead at Peace River to Norman Wells via Hay River and Fort Providence. The 1,000-mile route, sometimes

[83] Memo, by Hickerson, 12 Jun 42, D/S 842.6363/168–4/5.

[84] For an account of the Hudson's Bay Company operations, see "Oil for the Planes of Alaska," *The Beaver*, Outfit 274 (September 1943), pp. 4–14.

[85] See above, pp. 207–15.

referred to as Canol 6, was constructed between 23 October 1942 and 25 February 1943. A shift of the base of operations from the railhead at Waterways to that at Peace River was made because the winter road from the Peace River railhead could to a large extent utilize existing wagon roads and trails as far as Hay River. A route from Fort Smith joined the first at Hay River. A third, from Fort Nelson on the Alaska Highway, joined the first near Fort Simpson. The winter road operation was not successful. An estimated $7.5 million was expended on construction and operation. Of 18,222 tons of supplies that left the Peace River railhead, only 5,293 tons were delivered to Norman Wells. Consumed in the operation were 3,567 tons, while the balance was left along the route, to be delivered by water after the waterway was open. The winter roads were not used after the winter of 1942–43.[86]

The construction of the several pipelines and the erection of the refinery, which were well under way in early 1943, were accomplished by civilian contractor organizations, both Canadian and U.S. The largest of these was Bechtel-Price-Callahan of San Francisco. The Skagway–Whitehorse pipeline, Canol 2, had gone into operation in late 1942. Gasoline reached Watson Lake via Canol 3 on 24 July 1943 and Fairbanks via Canol 4 on 23 February 1944. The crude-oil line from Norman Wells was completed on 16 February 1944, and the first oil was delivered through it on 16 April. Two weeks later, on 30 April 1944, the formal dedication of the refinery at Whitehorse took place and refinery operations began. The construction of the 595-mile pipeline and service road, which at two points reached elevations exceeding 5,000 feet, over the uncharted Mackenzie Range between Norman Wells and Whitehorse was the most difficult of the pipeline tasks, and its execution was a significant step in taming the northwest Canadian wilderness.

At the end of 1942 the War Department in the hope of making available new supplies of oil had decided that additional exploratory well drilling in northwest Canada was desirable. In an exchange of notes dated 28 December 1942 and 13 January 1943, Canada acceded to a U.S. request for a wildcatting program in which exploratory wells would be drilled to seek sources capable of producing from 15,000 to 20,000 barrels of oil daily. Canada authorized the program in the area specified, which included all of the Yukon Territory and that portion of the District of Mackenzie on the mainland and west of the 112° meridian.[87]

Under the initial Canol 1 agreement, producing wells drilled at U.S. expense on land held under prior lease by the Imperial Oil Company became

[86] Bykofsky and Larson, *The Transportation Corps: Operations Overseas*, pp. 64–65.

[87] EAS, 388; CTS, 1943, No. 18. The area was reduced in size by a subsequent agreement published in EAS, 389, and CTS, 1943, No. 19.

the property of that company, which was also to be reimbursed an agreed price for oil delivered to the United States from those wells and from wells already producing at the time the agreement was made.[88] Under the wildcatting program the United States assumed all the costs of the exploratory work, which was carried forward by Imperial Oil Company and by a U.S. company, Noble Drilling Corporation. All the exploratory drilling took place on land for which permits were issued by the Canadian Government to Imperial Oil. Under new regulations issued by the Canadian Government, one-half of any location upon which oil was discovered, together with the wells or other improvements thereon, would remain or become property of the Canadian Government. Imperial Oil Company, as the permittee, became owner of the remaining half of the improvements on crown property, and the two would share equally from the proceeds of oil produced under the new regulations.[89] This arrangement was also applicable to the drilling done under Canol 1 in the Norman Wells area but on ground for which additional permits were needed by and issued to Imperial Oil.[90]

As a result of the exploratory work, new producing wells with a daily output of 3,900 barrels were drilled, and as many as 4,000 barrels of crude oil per day, even in the coldest month of the year, moved through the pipeline to the Whitehorse refinery. The Canadian Government estimated that this proven field contained from thirty to sixty million barrels of oil; U.S. authorities estimated that the oil resources discovered at U.S. expense totaled from sixty to one hundred million barrels, although they admitted that not all of this oil might be obtainable since part of the oil-bearing structure lay under the Mackenzie River. Approximately one-third of the proven field was covered by the old Imperial Oil leases, while the remainder was covered by the new regulations, which gave the crown a one-half interest.[91]

In September 1943 the U.S. Senate Special Committee Investigating the National Defense Program (then commonly referred to as the Truman Committee, after its chairman) began an extensive investigation of the Canol Project. On 26 October the hearings delved into the arrangements effected by the United States with Canada and with the Imperial Oil Company. The committee report, released on 8 January 1944, severely criticized the initial

[88] *Investigation of the National Defense Program,* Pt. 22, Exhibit 1087.

[89] Privy Council 1138, 12 Feb 43; Privy Council 2447, 26 Mar 43; Regulations under Privy Council 742, 28 Jan 43, in Canada, Wartime Information Board, *Defense Projects in Northwest Canada,* pp. 44–64; *Investigation of the National Defense Program,* Pt. 22, Exhibits 1088, 1145, and 1146–A; *H. C. Debates,* 5 May 44, pp. 2721–22.

[90] Privy Council 4140, 18 May 42.

[91] *H. C. Debates,* 5 May 44, p. 2722; WD Press Release, 8 Mar 45; Memo for Record, 20 Nov 43 meeting in War Department, D/S 842.6363/267–4/23.

decision by the War Department to develop the Canol Project. It also criticized subsequent decisions, some made as late as October 1943, to carry the project to completion despite the changing circumstances of the war and the contrary recommendations of the U.S. Petroleum Administrator for War and others, who considered the project to be unsound and excessively costly. The report concluded that the contracts and agreements were unfair and unreasonable, since the question of postwar rights and other U.S. interests had not been properly safeguarded, despite the expenditure of $134 million for the entire project. This failure to safeguard U.S. interests the committee too attributed to improvidence on the part of the War Department, which had prepared the documents. The report also noted that Canada had accepted the U.S. proposal without modification or reservation and that there was no indication that it would not have been possible to obtain a more equitable arrangement from Canada.[92]

Soon after the Truman Committee began to inquire into the Canol contracts and agreements, the War Department, with the cognizance of the committee, initiated action to revise them. As a result of War Department representations to the Department of State a few days earlier, the U.S. Ambassador in Ottawa on 23 November 1943 broached the subject of the renegotiation of the contracts and agreements and arranged a meeting with the Canadians on 2 December. The meeting found Canadians amenable to the idea of making minor adjustments but opposed to any revisions premised on a major oil discovery.[93]

At a second meeting, on 31 January 1944, specific alternate U.S. proposals were discussed. Since the relationship between the Canadian Government and Imperial Oil Company established by an order-in-council had a direct bearing on any changes in the arrangement, it was necessary that this relationship also be amended. The three-way discussions continued at some length, and the arrangements finally worked out were announced publicly on 5 May 1944, five days after the refinery at Whitehorse began operations.

During the period between 1 December 1943 and 30 April 1944, while renegotiation discussions were in progress, the War Department expended $17 million of the $99 million that was the cost of that part of the Canol Project involved in producing and refining oil in Canada. Vigorous War Department action in pushing the project to completion and the protracted

[92] Senate Report 10, 78th Congress, 1st Session, Pt. 14. The report did not criticize that part of the project which called for delivery of petroleum products through Prince Rupert to Skagway and thence through the pipelines to points between Fairbanks and Watson Lake. This portion of the project cost $35 million.

[93] Memo for Record, Hickerson, 30 Nov 43, D/S 842.6363/267-4/23; Minutes, 2 Dec 43 meeting, D/S 842.6363/267-11/23; *H. C. Debates,* 5 May 44, p. 2722.

discussions made it impossible to carry out the Truman Committee recommendation that this project not be completed unless new and equitable arrangements could be worked out with Canada and the Imperial Oil Company.[94]

The Canadian Minister of Mines and Resources explained the arrangements to the House of Commons on 5 May 1944 when he announced the order-in-council, dated 27 April, that established the new relationship between the Canadian Government and the Imperial Oil Company. The new arrangements gave the United States an option to purchase for its own use, at cost plus twenty cents per barrel, an amount up to one-half of the oil recovered in the proven area, not exceeding thirty million barrels.[95]

The agreement formalizing the new arrangements was signed by the two governments on 7 June 1944. As a result of the agreement, the United States gave up all its rights to explore for oil in Canada. The agreement also met the Truman Committee criticism about safeguarding of U.S. interests by providing for (1) application of the disposition arrangements for the Skagway–Whitehorse pipeline to the distribution lines to Watson Lake and Fairbanks, and (2) extension to the postwar lessees or owners of the installations of the rights of way and other rights necessary for their satisfactory utilization.[96]

When it went into operation, the Canol refinery was able to process 3,000 barrels of crude oil per day and produce from this crude 479 barrels of aviation gasoline, 1,018 barrels of motor gasoline, and 525 barrels of fuel oil. This output reflected changes made in the plans to accord with the "anticipated peacetime demand in the territory to be served by it" and still to allow the facilities to "make an important contribution to the wartime demand in the North Pacific region."[97]

The oil-producing and -refining facilities of the Canol Project had not long to operate, for less than a year later, before V–E and V–J Days had arrived, the War Department on 8 March 1945 announced discontinuance of operations as of 30 June. The War Department cited as reasons for its action the improved tanker situation and the improved military situation in Alaska. The system of distribution lines for delivery of petroleum products from the port at Skagway to points between Fairbanks and Watson Lake was not affected and continued to supply that area with petroleum products until after the war ended.[98]

---

[94] Senate Report 10, 78th Congress, 1st Session, Pt. 14.
[95] Privy Council 2904; *H. C. Debates,* 5 May 44, pp. 2722–24; WD Press Release, 5 May 44.
[96] EAS, 416; CTS, 1944, No. 16.
[97] WD Press Release, 5 May 44.
[98] WD Press Release, 8 Mar 45.

Communications and Weather

A major problem for both Canada and the United States in northwest Canada was posed by the extremely limited scale of communications facilities in a region whose size and attendant physical phenomena, such as the aurora borealis, made communications particularly difficult. The need for adequate meteorological data for safe air operations also presented a problem.

As the U.S. troop units and detachments and the civilian elements involved in the construction projects deployed throughout northwestern Canada, the task of maintaining communications for command and administrative purposes was a formidable one. During the initial months of work on the Alaska Highway and Canol projects, the three commands involved (two for the highway, Northern and Southern Sectors) operated independent radio nets. The three networks were also independent of the Canadian facilities serving the airfields of the Northwest Staging Route and other principal locations, except for a brief initial period during which the commanders of both the Northern and Southern Sectors of the highway were linked to Edmonton only by the Department of Transport radio system or by the telegraph line to Edmonton.[99]

Upon the establishment of the Northwest Service Command on 10 September 1942, the need for integrating these three networks and adapting them to new requirements arose. The backbone of the system developed was the telephone and telegraph land line parallel to the Alaska Highway. The construction of this line was considered by the United States to be part of the over-all Alaska Highway project, but it also received specific authorization by the Canadian Government.[100]

Although perhaps dwarfed by other projects under way in that area, the construction of the telephone system was itself no small field engineering feat. Work was begun by the U.S. Army Chief Signal officer with a civilian organization in the late summer of 1942. In November the 843d Signal Service Battalion joined the construction forces on an emergency basis. Reinforced by crews recruited from Canadian and U.S. telephone companies, this battalion by 1 December 1942 had completed the 442-mile line between Edmonton and Dawson Creek, following the highway right of way. Canadian and U.S. contractors continued construction into 1943, and by 1 May they had opened another 900 miles, to Whitehorse; on 14 October the full

[99] Since the Radio Act, 1938, prohibited radio broadcasting except by licensed operators who had to be British subjects, authority for the operation of the U.S. Army stations was furnished, as a war measure, under Privy Council 3363, 28 April 1942.

[100] Ltr, Department of External Affairs to Moffat, 16 Oct 42, cited in List, *U.S. Defense Projects in Canada,* 6 May 43, PDB 150-1.

line between Edmonton and Fairbanks was open. An additional 102-mile line linked Skagway to the system, while 830 more miles was needed to tie in the various air bases, flight strips, and other installations. The line, with a capacity of six voice and thirteen teletype circuits, required the setting of 95,000 poles, the stretching of over 14,000 miles of wire, and the establishing of twenty-three booster stations at from 70- to 100-mile intervals.

With radio communications frequently blacked out, the wire network provided an essential complementary communications link for the many installations in the area. Through its use Fairbanks could be linked directly with Washington, D. C. The system was connected to Helena, Montana, and thence to U.S. commercial networks by Canadian and U.S. commercial circuits leased for military use, and could be linked, through its Edmonton switching center, to Canadian commercial facilities.

Because the wire network was subject to frequent interruption by falling trees, thaws and floods, and fire and winds, radio networks were required not only to link points not served by the line, such as those in the Mackenzie River valley, but also to insure continuous service to points on the line. In June 1943 all U.S. radio nets were consolidated into a single network comprising sixty-five fixed, semifixed, and mobile radio stations that served the Northwest Service Command and the operational and meteorological needs of Air Transport Command operations. Canadian needs for communications continued to be provided independently, through the radio net for the airfields and intermediate fields of the Northwest Staging Route.

Although there was virtually no integration of the communications services by the agencies of the two countries operating in northwest Canada, some such co-ordination was developed in the provision of meteorological services. The Department of Transport had maintained, before the U.S. tenancy on the Northwest Staging Route, a weather system that included hourly observations from each of its radio stations and forecasts every six hours from forecast centers at Edmonton and Whitehorse. The initial U.S. weather services were provided by detachments of Northwest Airlines personnel for the contract transport services that began in March 1942. As the Army Air Forces expanded its air operations along the route in 1942 and 1943, it established its own weather service, which replaced that of the Northwest Airlines and to some extent duplicated that of the Canadian Department of Transport. United States observation stations were established at a number of points along the staging route, only a few of which duplicated Canadian observations. Meetings were held and arrangements worked out for co-ordinating the Canadian and U.S. observation networks so that by and large they supplemented each other. This was also done when Mackenzie

River air operations necessitated the establishment of a reporting system in that area. The Royal Canadian Corps of Signals operated an observing and radio-reporting net of eleven stations, while the AAF operated a net of stations located at the landing strips developed by the United States.

The two countries further collaborated in the collection and dissemination of weather reports. The AAF operated a teletype circuit between Edmonton and Whitehorse to which the Department of Transport stations were linked. Over this circuit were transmitted the reports collected hourly by both Canadian and U.S. stations, in the Mackenzie River valley as well as along the staging route, making all reports available to all agencies.

The U.S. Army saw fit to operate its own forecasting services and established stations at Whitehorse, Calgary, Edmonton, Fort Nelson, Fort St. John, Prince George, and Watson Lake. There undoubtedly was room for economy of operations through better co-ordination of the weather services. However, fundamental differences on the question of airway control and operation made fuller co-ordination infeasible.[101]

The Prince Rupert Port

Although many of the major logistical projects carried out in the Canadian northwest were fully publicized, one of these, the utilization of Prince Rupert as a U.S. Army subport of embarkation, remained officially secret until after the Japanese surrender. Naturally this secrecy was to some extent circumscribed since the operation of the port involved several thousand people and the movement of nearly a million measurement tons of supplies through the port and over the Canadian National Railways line to it.[102]

Surveys of the possible utility of the port in the event of a war had been made by the U.S. and Canadian Armies as early as 1937. As the pre-Pearl Harbor build-up of U.S. bases in Alaska and the Pacific increased the pressure on the ports of Seattle and San Francisco, the desirability of using the port was re-examined. After a survey was made in March 1941, Prince Rupert was declared to be a potentially satisfactory port for the supply of all of southeastern Alaska and for partial supply of western Alaska.[103]

Prince Rupert was desirable for port operations for reasons other than that it would ease the pressures on other west coast ports. The northernmost west coast railhead, the port had rail connections to Vancouver and the west coast industrial areas and through Edmonton to the rest of Canada

[101] See Ch. XI, below.

[102] A summary history of the role of the port in World War II was made public by a War Department press release of 7 September 1945. *The Canadian National Magazine,* XXXI (November 1945), contains an article, "Prince Rupert—Secret City of the War," which expands upon the press release.

[103] Ltr, Commandant 13th Naval District to CNO, 10 Mar 41, Com 13 Serial 122209.

and the United States. Since the port is located 500 miles north of Seattle, a round trip to the Anchorage area would involve only 2,000 miles as opposed to about 3,000 miles from Seattle. In a critical shipping situation the same tonnage of vessels could thus carry 50 percent more cargo by using the shorter route.

At the 20 December 1941 meeting of the Permanent Joint Board on Defense the Canadian Section sought information, on behalf of the Minister of Transport and the Canadian National Railways, on U.S. plans for use of the port.[104] The successful emergency operation of lightering to, and reshipment from, Prince Rupert of the cargo of a grounded U.S. Army Transport Service vessel on 13 January 1942 sparked additional U.S. interest in the port. By the end of the month both U.S. Army and Navy commanders on the Pacific coast had recommended immediate use of the port.[105] The Canadian Government authorized trial shipments, which were handled by the U.S. Army port of embarkation staff at Seattle.

At the 25–26 February 1942 meeting of the Permanent Joint Board, the U.S. Section presented the War Department's request for authority to use the port for supply of Alaska with an estimated daily movement of 2,500 tons and suggested the working out of plans by the local staffs. Canadian willingness to approve the use of the port was indicated at a Board meeting in April.[106] The War Department, apparently anticipating Canadian approval on the basis of the earlier discussions, had on 20 February ordered activation of the port as a subport of the Seattle Port of Embarkation. The port officially opened on 5 April 1942.

The Prince Rupert harbor is rated one of the world's best, but the port facilities were to require considerable augmentation. Canada, with U.S. matériel assistance, assumed responsibility for reinforcing the harbor defenses. The United States expanded the Prince Rupert port facilities to provide a capacity of 50,000 cubic tons of freight per month. Facilities constructed by the U.S. Army Corps of Engineers included 400,000 square feet of warehousing, 54,000 square feet of office space, and a 1,000-ton-capacity cold storage plant. The existing waterfront wharfage was doubled. A complete temporary housing project, which would provide quarters for the majority of the 3,500 military and civilian personnel employed at the subport, was constructed nearby and included theater, gymnasium, medical, and similar facilities. The construction program lasted over the two years from March 1942 to March 1944.

---

[104] Journal, PDB 124.

[105] Ltr, Commandant 13th Naval District to CNO, 14 Jan 42, Com 13 Serial 123003; Ltr, WDC and Fourth Army to ACofS WPD, 28 Jan 42, WPD 323.91.

[106] Journal, PDB 124; Memo, SUSAM for ACofS WPD, 27 Feb 42, PDB 116–1.

360-477 O - 70 - 17

The Corps of Engineers constructed two other major facilities near Prince Rupert. A personnel staging area, accommodating 2,500 personnel, with its own port and rail facilities, was constructed at Port Edward, some ten miles from Prince Rupert. Through this staging area, beginning in March 1943, passed the bulk of the military and civilian personnel en route to or from the U.S. Army projects and garrisons to the north. The other principal operating facility was at nearby Watson Island, which was used as a backup storage dump for ammunition. Shipment of ammunition from this dump was made to bases throughout the Pacific that were supporting the Pacific war.

When the construction in the Prince Rupert area, which was accomplished by civilian contractors under contract to the U.S. Army Engineers, was first initiated, the question arose whether the United States had secured the necessary authority for it. The U.S. Section of the Permanent Joint Board cited the Board's Twenty-second Recommendation. Canada initially questioned whether that recommendation provided the authority but subsequently agreed that it did.[107]

As a result of the U.S. Army construction activities, the population of Prince Rupert increased from a pre-Pearl Harbor 4,700 (excluding 2,300 Japanese that were evacuated) to over 11,000. The subport, which came under the direction of the U.S. Army Seattle Port of Embarkation for port operations, was supported by and reported to the Northwest Service Command for personnel, communications, fiscal, medical, construction and maintenance, and similar purposes.[108] By the time of the Japanese surrender almost a million tons of freight had passed through Prince Rupert.

After V–E Day the War Department sought ways of supplementing the capacity of the Prince Rupert and other west coast ports to permit increased shipment of supplies to the Pacific. In June 1945 U.S. Army authorities initiated investigations and inquiries concerning the use of Ballantyne Pier in Vancouver as an additional subport. They found that the available labor supply would allow the handling of six ships per month at the pier, but that if additional labor were brought in this number could be increased to twenty. The United States formally sought approval of the project in Ottawa in July and readily obtained it.[109] The welcome surrender of Japan prevented fruition of the project.

[107] Appendix A, below; Ltr, Cdn Secy PJBD to U.S. Secy, 24 Apr 42, PDB 147–1.

[108] For a more detailed account of U.S. Army operations at Prince Rupert, see Bykofsky and Larson, *The Transportation Corps: Operations Overseas,* pp. 41–46. Tucker, *The Naval Service of Canada,* II, 233–41, contains an account of the role of Prince Rupert in Royal Canadian Navy operations.

[109] Ltr, SUSAM to Military Attaché, 14 Jul 45, and Reply, 20 Jul 45, both in PDB 126–21.

CHAPTER IX

Comrades in Arms

Although mention of World War II military co-operation between the United States and Canada may first bring to mind the Ogdensburg Declaration and the Permanent Joint Board on Defense or well-publicized projects such as the Alaska Highway and the Canol Project, that co-operation was by no means limited to politico-military and strategic planning or to logistical enterprises carried out in the Canadian northland. On battlegrounds in different quarters of the globe, Canadians and Americans fought and died together as North American brothers-in-arms.[1]

Military units of the two countries inevitably found themselves co-operating on various occasions as the scope and scale of operations in the European theater grew larger. Canadian and U.S. divisions fought side by side in Sicily, in Italy, and during the advance from Normandy. In fact, the U.S. XVI Corps was assigned to the First Canadian Army, commanded by General Henry D. G. Crerar, to assist him in clearing the west bank of the Rhine of the enemy in March 1945.

In the air war, RCAF fighter squadrons teamed up to protect U.S. Eighth Air Force Flying Fortresses on many missions from the United Kingdom against continental targets during 1942 and 1943. Many of the aircraft of Royal Air Force squadrons, furnishing fighter escort in the same way, were manned by RCAF personnel serving in Royal Air Force units. The AAF was able to repay these courtesies many times in Sicily and Italy, where its fighter-bomber and light and medium bomber groups flew hundreds of sorties in direct support of Canadian ground forces.

Still other circumstances found large numbers of Canadians and Americans fighting side by side. Long before Pearl Harbor, a steady stream of Americans had started moving northward across the border to join the Canadian armed forces. By the beginning of 1941 some 1,200 Americans com-

[1] Symbolic of this brotherhood-in-arms was the selection of the sonnet "High Flight" for wide circulation throughout the schools of the British Commonwealth Air Training Plan. This sonnet, which has been viewed as ranking with John McCrae's "In Flanders Fields" and Rupert Brooke's "The Soldier," was penned by an American, Pilot Officer John Gillespie Magee of the RCAF. Magee, who was killed at age nineteen in December 1941, was one of the large number of Americans who enlisted in the Canadian armed forces while the United States was still a neutral. The sonnet begins and ends: "Oh, I have slipped the surly bonds of earth . . . . Put out my hand and touched the face of God."

prised about 10 percent of RCAF officer strength and 3 percent of the other ranks.[2] A U.S. influx totaling about 10 percent of RCAF recruitment continued until, at the time of Pearl Harbor, over 6,000 U.S. citizens were serving in the RCAF, of whom 600 were instructors in the British Commonwealth Air Training Plan. By the same time nearly 10,000 Americans were serving in the Canadian Army.[3] After Pearl Harbor a reverse movement resulted in the absorption of over 26,000 Canadians into the U.S. armed forces during World War II.

Battle of the Atlantic

On 16 September 1939, scarcely two weeks after the beginning of World War II, the first convoy departed Halifax, Nova Scotia, for the United Kingdom.[4] Many others followed, escorted by units of the British and Canadian Navies. The first loss to the submarine enemy did not occur until 14 February 1940, and at the time of the fall of France in June 1940 losses were still few.

The availability of French bases after the fall of France greatly increased German submarine warfare capabilities, and this advantage, coupled with Admiral Karl Doenitz' "wolf-pack" technique, caused losses to mount steadily. Although the U.S.-British destroyer transfer alleviated the situation, by the end of 1940 about 70 percent of the British destroyer fleet was laid up for repairs.

In 1941 the United States took additional steps to support the British. Soon after the approval of the Lend-Lease Act on 11 March 1941 the United States began to finance repairs to British naval vessels in U.S. ports. The U.S.-United Kingdom armed forces liaison, established on an informal basis before August 1940, gradually developed and produced the formal staff conversations that took place in Washington in January-March 1941. From these staff conversations emerged a U.S. undertaking to protect shipping in the western Atlantic, which was to be a U.S. over-all strategic responsibility in the event of U.S. entry into the war.[5] Of greater immediate importance was the fact that the U.S. Navy through this liaison obtained the benefits

[2] Memo for Record, SUSAM, 12 Mar 41, PDB 129-1.

[3] *Canada at War*, No. 8 (Nov 41), p. 46.

[4] For full and authoritative British, Canadian, and U.S. accounts, see Great Britain, Central Office of Information, *The Battle of the Atlantic* (London: His Majesty's Stationery Office, 1946); Schull, *The Far Distant Ships;* Morison, *The Battle of the Atlantic;* Samuel Eliot Morison, *History of United States Naval Operations in World War II*, X, *The Atlantic Battle Won, May 1943–May 1945* (Boston: Little, Brown and Company, 1956); Craven and Cate (eds.), *Plans and Early Operations;* and Wesley F. Craven and James L. Cate (eds.), *The Army Air Forces in World War II*, II, *Europe*—TORCH to POINTBLANK (Chicago: University of Chicago Press, 1949).

The account presented here is limited to the U.S.-Canadian co-operation in the discharge of the convoy escort and antisubmarine responsibilities.

[5] See Ch. IV, above.

of British experience in convoy and antisubmarine operations. This, in turn, permitted the U.S. Navy to accelerate U.S. preparations to undertake such operations. Thanks in part to these benefits, the U.S. Navy, even with its forces deployed for the hemisphere neutrality patrol begun in the fall of 1939, was able to report to the President on 20 March 1941 that it would soon be ready to convoy merchant shipping and lend-lease cargoes across the Atlantic. Surveys had already been made for the necessary naval bases in the British Isles.[6] The next major U.S. step to aid the British was taken on 11 April 1941 when President Roosevelt notified Prime Minister Churchill that the neutrality patrol was to be extended to 26° west longitude, and invited notice of British convoys so that warnings of enemy submarines in the area might be transmitted to them.

Despite the steps taken by the United States, British losses continued to be heavy. In May a convoy lost nine ships well within the patrolled zone. In consequence of such losses, which reached 590,000 tons in June 1941, Great Britain decided to provide convoy escort for the full length of the crossing. To this end, the British Admiralty on 23 May asked Canada to assume the responsibility for protecting convoys in the western zone and to establish the base for its escort force at St. John's in Newfoundland. On 13 June 1941 Commodore L. W. Murray, Royal Canadian Navy, assumed his post as Commodore Commanding Newfoundland Escort Force, under the over-all authority of the United Kingdom Commander in Chief, Western Approaches, whose headquarters was at Liverpool. Six Canadian destroyers and seventeen corvettes, reinforced by seven destroyers, three sloops, and five corvettes of the Royal Navy, were assembled for duty in the force, which escorted convoys from Canadian ports to Newfoundland and from there to a meeting point south of Iceland, where British convoys took over.[7]

During these months both the war and the scale of U.S. precautionary preparations grew at an accelerated pace. In April and July 1941 arrangements were made for dispatch of U.S. garrisons to Greenland and Iceland, respectively.[8] On 27 May, the day on which the German battleship *Bismarck* was sunk, the President declared an unlimited national emergency.[9]

[6] For a detailed account of the development of U. S. policy as to participation in the Battle of the Atlantic, see William L. Langer and S. Everett Gleason, *The Undeclared War* (New York: Harper & Brothers, 1953), pp. 419–64, 742–50.

[7] Churchill, *The Grand Alliance*, pp. 138–42; Schull, *The Far Distant Ships*, pp. 65–75; Sherwood, *Roosevelt and Hopkins*, pp. 291–92.

[8] See Ch. VI, above.

[9] While the *Bismarck* roamed in northwestern Atlantic waters out of range of Canadian aircraft, the RCAF informally proposed to neutral Washington the borrowing of twelve Flying Fortresses, to be ostensibly manned by Canadians, to attack her. War Department officers, including General Marshall and Mr. Stimson, appeared sympathetic but agreed that this would be an act of war and decided against the request. (Note for Record, 24 May 41, WPD 4330–27.)

On 22 June 1941 Germany invaded the USSR. On 15 July the U.S. Navy air and naval base at Argentia was commissioned. It was in this setting that the Argentia meeting of President Roosevelt and Prime Minister Churchill took place on 9–13 August 1941, from which emerged the Atlantic Charter.

Roosevelt and Churchill and their naval chiefs at the Atlantic Conference agreed on new arrangements for convoy escort operations.[10] To the United States, a nonbelligerent, was assigned the convoy escort responsibility in the northwestern Atlantic west of the 30° west meridian. The United Kingdom immediately withdrew its naval vessels from the area, except for a few armed cruisers which it withdrew in October. The Royal Canadian Navy Newfoundland Command was charged with the convoy task in the coastal zone of the new U.S. sector, where it employed five destroyers and ten corvettes. Eight Canadian destroyers and twenty corvettes passed to the direct command of Rear Adm. Arthur L. Bristol, commanding the Support Force of the U.S. Atlantic Fleet, for employment in the escort groups on the ocean leg of the U.S. sector. Where possible each of the escort groups, which usually numbered two destroyers and four corvettes, was made up entirely of ships of one country.[11]

The necessary orders were issued in early September and staff arrangements were completed with British and Canadian naval officers who had established close operational liaison in the Navy Department in Washington in anticipation of an expansion of the U.S. role in convoy escort work. While these preparations were in hand, President Roosevelt on 11 September 1941 issued his "shoot on sight" warning to Germany and Italy, stating that when men-of-war entered waters "the protection of which is necessary for American defense they do so at their own peril." [12]

The first transatlantic convoy to be escorted by the U.S. Navy sailed from Halifax on 16 September 1941, accompanied by a Royal Canadian Navy escort group acting under over-all U.S. direction. The next day, escort of the convoy was taken over by a U.S. Navy group at the "Westomp" (western ocean meeting place), a designated point south of Argentia. The fifty merchant ships, which sailed under a variety of flags and comprised types varying from a 1,500-ton cargo ship to the 17,000-ton *Empress of Asia,* were met at the "Momp" (mid-ocean meeting place) by a British escort group. Here, part of the convoy split off to proceed to Ice-

---

[10] See also Ch. V, above.

[11] Kittredge Monograph, I, Sec. V, 376n; Morison, *The Battle of the Atlantic,* pp. 78–79.

[12] Department of State *Bulletin,* September 13, 1941, V, 196.

land under U.S. escort, while the remainder proceeded to the United Kingdom under Royal Navy escort.[13]

Within the next month convoy escort arrangements were stabilized on the following pattern:

a. Eastbound slow (designated SC) convoys out of Sydney, Nova Scotia, were escorted to the Momp by Canadian escort groups, which on their return voyage escorted westbound slow (ONS) convoys.

b. Eastbound fast (HX) convoys and westbound fast (ON) convoys were escorted to and from the Momp by U.S. Navy escort groups.

c. All convoys proceeding between the Momp and the United Kingdom were escorted by Royal Navy escort groups under the control of the Commander in Chief, Western Approaches.

By the beginning of 1942 naval officers of the three countries had worked out a procedure for routing and controlling convoys. The British Admiralty proposed a convoy route to the Navy Department in Washington, which accepted it after adjustment if necessary. The Navy Department then gave notice of the agreed route to the British Admiralty; the Commander in Chief, U.S. Atlantic Fleet; the British Commander in Chief, Western Approaches; the commander of the U.S. task force that would supply the escort from the Westomp to the Momp; the Commanding Officer, Atlantic Coast command, at Halifax, Nova Scotia; Canadian Naval Staff Headquarters at Ottawa; the Flag Officer, Royal Canadian Navy Newfoundland Command; and the Canadian port director concerned. The Navy Department also notified the port director, who in turn advised the convoy commodore, of the escort arrangements. The convoy departed under its Royal Canadian Navy local coastal escort, to be met at the Westomp by the U.S. Navy ocean escort, which then turned over the escort task and command of the convoy to a Royal Navy escort group at the Momp. West of the mid-ocean meeting place convoys were controlled from Washington, east of it from London. Control from these points was found necessary because of the numbers of convoys often making simultaneous crossings.[14]

The procedures and allocations of responsibilities worked out in the period following the Argentia conference required substantial revision after Pearl Harbor, when the demand for U.S. Navy ships elsewhere became so great that U.S. participation in the escort of merchant ships in the North Atlantic was reduced to two Coast Guard cutters. Under continuing over-all U.S. strategic direction, the Royal Canadian Navy now began to provide

[13] Morison, *The Battle of the Atlantic,* pp. 85–87.
[14] *Ibid.,* pp. 101–02.

the escort groups not only for the coastal leg but also for the ocean leg between the Westomp and the Momp, where, as before, United Kingdom escorts took over.[15]

Canada was able to make other contributions that helped to meet the urgent U.S. need, immediately after Pearl Harbor, for naval vessels for escort and other purposes. In addition to assuming a larger part of the merchant convoy task, the Royal Canadian Navy made twenty-four antisubmarine trawlers available to the U.S. Navy. These trawlers arrived at New York in March 1942, after which they were deployed along the Atlantic coast to assist in escorting the heavy coastal traffic which had become the target of an intensified German submarine effort.[16]

Even when the U.S. Navy was later able to reconstitute its strength in the western Atlantic, it was faced with an ever-increasing demand for escorts for troop convoys to the United Kingdom. These convoys enjoyed a prior claim on the U.S. Navy forces available. Consequently, it remained for the Royal Canadian Navy to provide the bulk of the escort forces for merchant ship convoys in the western Atlantic, although a few U.S. Navy ships were assigned to this duty.

By mid-1942 convoy escort was furnished by escort groups as follows:

a. In the Western Local Area, to a Westomp in locations varying from 45° to 52° west, by eight escort groups of United Kingdom and Canadian destroyers and Canadian corvettes based on Boston and Halifax.

b. In the Mid-ocean Area, to a Momp near 22° west, by fourteen (later eleven) escort groups. The destroyers in three of these groups were U.S., and the three groups were under U.S. command. Seven other groups under United Kingdom command comprised United Kingdom, Canadian, and two Polish destroyers, and Canadian and a few Free French corvettes. The remaining four escort groups were under Canadian command. Ships in all these groups were based on Argentia or St. John's, Newfoundland, and refueled at Londonderry in Ireland.

c. In the Eastern Local Area, by United Kingdom escort groups as before.

d. For the shuttle between Iceland and the Momp, by U.S. escort groups.[17]

The burden of North Atlantic convoying during 1942, in terms of the

[15] *Ibid.*, p. 117; Schull, *The Far Distant Ships*, p. 98.

[16] Canada, Naval Service Headquarters, *Royal Canadian Navy Monthly Review*, No. 2 (Feb 42), p. 6, and No. 3 (Mar 42), p. 7.

[17] Morison, *The Battle of the Atlantic*, pp. 318–20; Tucker, *The Naval Service of Canada*, II, 133.

approximate ratio of ships convoyed to the scale of each nation's escort contribution, was being borne about equally by the United Kingdom, Canada, and the United States, with the Canadian share being somewhat less than one-third.[18] Toward the end of the year the U.S. contribution was reduced sharply by the new demands for convoy escort to North Africa and by other requirements. As a result, as of 27 November 1942, only 3 of the 147 vessels comprising the Western Local Escort and Mid-ocean Escort Forces were U.S., the remainder being contributed about equally by Canada and the United Kingdom.

With the intensification of Nazi submarine warfare in the western Atlantic, air cover from North American and adjacent bases became an important element in the protection of convoys. Although involved with the U.S. Navy in a prolonged jurisdictional dispute over the responsibility for aerial aspects of antisubmarine warfare, the AAF collaborated with the U.S. Navy Atlantic Fleet task force commander at Argentia by placing its air units in Newfoundland at his disposal to augment the U.S. Navy patrol squadron deployed there after Pearl Harbor for the convoy protection task. After discussion of a proposal for similar collaboration by the RCAF, suitable arrangements were finally worked out shortly afterward.[19]

By the spring of 1942 enemy submarines had extended their operations into North American coastal waters and were causing heavy losses. The United States temporarily resolved its own interservice dispute over the control of antisubmarine air operations on 26 March 1942 by making them the responsibility of the U.S. Navy, exercised in U.S. coastal waters by the Eastern Sea Frontier. Immediately thereafter officers of the air and naval air services of Canada and the United States conferred at St. John's, Newfoundland, to improve the co-ordination of air operations for the protection of Allied convoys.

Under the plans worked out, air cover in the ocean convoy sectors was provided as follows:

a. Western Local Area—U.S. Army, Navy, and Civil Air Patrol aircraft based in New England; RCAF aircraft based at Yarmouth, Halifax, and Sydney; and U.S. Navy aircraft based at Argentia.

b. Mid-ocean Area—U.S. Navy aircraft based at Argentia and in Iceland; and RCAF aircraft based at Torbay and Gander Lake, Newfoundland.

[18] Statement by Minister of National Defense for Naval Services A. L. Macdonald, *H. C. Debates*, 7 May 42, p. 2248; Canada, Naval Service Headquarters, *Royal Canadian Navy Monthly Review*, No. 9 (Sep 42), p. 64.

[19] See Ch. V, above.

c. Eastern Local Area—RAF aircraft based in the British Isles.
d. Iceland Shuttle—U.S. Navy aircraft based in Iceland.[20]

Throughout 1942 Allied losses to enemy submarines had continued at a high rate despite intensified countermeasures. Germany had stepped up its submarine production so that it was able in spite of Allied countermeasures to increase steadily the number of submarines at sea on patrol duty. In January 1943, while meeting with President Roosevelt and Prime Minister Churchill at Casablanca, the Combined Chiefs of Staff agreed that "the defeat of the U-boat must remain a first charge on the resources of the United Nations." [21]

Ways and means to this end had already been under discussion, and the Combined Chiefs of Staff took action to improve the situation. The long-range patrol force from Newfoundland comprised four B–17 Flying Fortress aircraft of the Newfoundland Base Command reserve striking force, the 421st Bombardment Squadron, which performed patrol missions for U.S. Navy Task Force 24 as a secondary task. In February 1943 the unit was redesignated the 20th Antisubmarine Squadron, reinforced to a strength of seven B–17's, and assigned to patrol duty as its primary mission. On its part, Canada sought to comply with a request from Prime Minister Churchill that it contribute to the long-range air patrols, as well as to the coastal air patrols, but neither Canada nor the United Kingdom was able to provide the aircraft for enlargement of Canadian responsibility. The Canadian Joint Staff in Washington inquired of the AAF in January 1943 whether fifteen B–24 Liberator aircraft could be supplied for this purpose, but General Arnold, the AAF commander, found it necessary to disapprove the request on the basis that none could be spared.[22]

At the Atlantic Convoy Conference, held in Washington between 1 and 12 March 1943 at the suggestion of Canada, naval officers of the three countries continued to seek solutions to convoying problems. As a result of strong Canadian representations at the conference, a reassignment of the responsibility for the western Atlantic was made. Since September 1941 this area had been under U.S. strategic direction despite the fact that for most of the period the escort of North Atlantic merchant shipping in that sector was being performed in the main by the Royal Canadian Navy and the Royal Navy. As U.S. naval strength in the Atlantic had gradually increased, the requirements for troop convoys and for merchant convoys to the Mediterranean had

[20] Morison, *The Battle of the Atlantic,* pp. 319–20.
[21] CCS 155/1, 22 Jan 43.
[22] AAF Reference History 7, The Army Air Forces Antisubmarine Command, file AAFRH-7, U.S. Air Force Air University, pp. 147–48.

absorbed the additional forces available.[23] Under the new arrangement, which became effective 30 April 1943, the United States retained the broad strategic responsibility for the western Atlantic, but Canada took over the full operational responsibility for surface escort of merchant convoys in an area north of the parallel through New York City and west of the 47° west meridian, except for convoys to Greenland, which remained a U.S. responsibility. The United States and the United Kingdom continued to be responsible for the remainder of the Atlantic convoy task.

Newly promoted Rear Adm. L. W. Murray carried out the Canadian responsibility as Commander in Chief, Canadian Northwest Atlantic. Canadian naval forces were augmented by the transfer of six overage Royal Navy destroyers, by the return of seven corvettes which had been on loan to the U.S. Navy since 1942 for use in the Caribbean, by the return of ships from operations in North African waters, by the commissioning of new ships built in Canada, and by assistance from U.S. escort vessels. Air antisubmarine operations were the responsibility of the Eastern Air Command under Air Vice Marshal George Johnson, and for this task the U.S. military and naval antisubmarine aircraft stationed in Newfoundland were put under his command.[24]

The conference, chaired by Admiral Ernest J. King, Commander in Chief, U.S. Fleet, and Chief of Naval Operations, also agreed on several measures to bring to bear the demonstrated effectiveness of aircraft against submarines. Small escort aircraft carriers were made available in sufficient numbers so that almost every convoy was able to be accompanied by its own air umbrella of twelve carrier aircraft. In response to the conference recommendation that the strength of the land-based VLR (very long range) patrol aircraft covering the ocean legs of the Atlantic crossing be increased, the Combined Chiefs of Staff late in March approved a number of expedients that would allow the assignment of greater numbers of planes and trained personnel to antisubmarine duty. Under these arrangements the British and U.S. services undertook to provide 255 aircraft, by 1 July 1943 if possible:[25]

United States Army Air Forces	75
United States Navy	60
Royal Air Force	105
Royal Canadian Air Force	15

[23] The best public account of the Atlantic Convoy Conference and of the events leading up to it is contained in Tucker, *The Naval Service of Canada,* II, Ch. 14.

[24] Schull, *The Far Distant Ships,* pp. 166–68; *Canada at War,* No. 24 (May 43), pp. 3–4; Tucker, *The Naval Service of Canada,* II, 138–39.

[25] CCS 189/2, approved 29 Mar 43; Minutes, 78th CCS meeting. The fifteen VLR aircraft for the RCAF were to be provided by the Royal Air Force with subsequent attrition made good by the U.S. AAF.

Still another air measure was adopted to reduce the vulnerability of convoys in the mid-ocean region which has been outside the range of land-based aircraft. The conference worked out a plan for shuttle service of the VLR aircraft of the three countries between bases in Newfoundland, the United Kingdom, and Iceland. With the eventual receipt of its Liberator aircraft in June 1943, the RCAF VLR squadron stationed in Newfoundland could now patrol to Iceland or the United Kingdom, refuel, and make the round trip flight. Improved antisubmarine equipment and techniques made the air cover even more effective.

In partial fulfillment of its commitment, the United States in April added two antisubmarine squadrons, the 6th and 19th, to its air forces at Gander, while a headquarters detachment of the 25th Antisubmarine Wing was established in the combined Royal Canadian Navy-RCAF control room at St. John's. In consequence of a decision taken at the Atlantic Convoy Conference, operational control of these forces passed on 30 April to Canada, which exercised a general control through the designation of missions without prescribing tactics and techniques.[26]

Aided by the improvement in flying conditions that came with the spring, the expanded air effort was able to assist in turning the tide of the submarine war by the middle of 1943. The Battle of the Atlantic was by no means over, but the main German submarine effort had shifted away from the North American coastal waters. At the end of August 1943, when the United States had already partly moved its air antisubmarine units from Newfoundland to the United Kingdom, the aircraft based on Newfoundland and Nova Scotia for patrol purposes, both very long range and coastal, numbered as follows:[27]

	Very long range	*Long and medium range*
United States Army Air Forces	12	0
United States Navy	7	0
Royal Canadian Air Force	14	142

Another factor contributing to the shift was the employment, beginning in the spring of 1943, of naval support groups which also contained escort carriers. These groups operated independently of the convoys and their escort groups. Aided by the search capabilities of their aircraft, they could rove at will to seek out enemy submarines, establish and maintain contact

[26] The Army Air Forces Antisubmarine Command, pp. 150–51.
[27] *Ibid.*, pp. 150, 255.

with them, and destroy them. Five such United Kingdom groups, which included U.S. escort carriers, were operating in the spring of 1943. By the end of the year, Canada was contributing the greater part of two such support groups.

Other events in 1943 favored the Allies. The surrender of Italy in September 1943 released additional naval vessels for operations in the Battle of the Atlantic. The following month Portugal agreed to permit establishment of U.S. and British air and naval bases in the Azores. Operations from these bases permitted full air coverage of a mid-Atlantic zone in which enemy submarines had operated with relative impunity.

In early 1944, as a result of the Allied successes of 1943 and the need to assemble and re-equip the naval forces to be employed in the landings in France, operational policies changed. The merchant convoys were made fewer and larger by measures such as the combining of fast and slow convoys. All non-Canadian and some Canadian escort vessels were withdrawn from convoying duty in the North Atlantic and allocated to other tasks. The Royal Canadian Navy assumed in its entirety the task of providing escort groups for the merchant convoys crossing the North Atlantic. In addition, the Royal Canadian Navy assigned two more support groups to the North Atlantic area, making a total of four. By this time, too, RCAF antisubmarine squadron dispositions had been expanded to include a squadron in Iceland.[28]

Canada continued to bear this enlarged convoy escort responsibility until V-E Day. It also took over an increasingly large part of the air antisubmarine effort. At the close of the Battle of the Atlantic, Canada was providing the bulk of the air units engaged, and Canadian commanders and staffs controlled the North Atlantic antisubmarine operations based on the North American mainland, Greenland, and Iceland.[29]

In the course of discharging these and other tasks the Royal Canadian Navy grew from six destroyers and a handful of small craft manned by less than 4,000 active and reserve personnel in August 1939 to a force of over 94,000 personnel and 939 ships of all types. The ships included two cruisers, two escort carriers, and seventeen destroyers. But the core of the naval force, over 200 vessels, consisted of Canadian-built frigates, corvettes, and other miscellaneous craft of the types that made up the major Canadian naval contribution to victory in the Battle of the Atlantic.

---

[28] Royal Canadian Navy Progress Report, 12-13 Apr 44 PJBD meeting, PDB 124; *H. C. Debates*, 29 Feb 44, p. 1032.

[29] Speech by Gen. A. G. L. McNaughton, 12 Apr 48, Department of External Affairs, Statements and Speeches, No. 48/18.

Securing Alaska Against the Japanese

Months before the Japanese actually penetrated the Aleutian Islands, in 1942, Lt. Gen. John L. DeWitt, Commanding General, Western Defense Command, which included the western states and Alaska, sought means of reinforcing the inadequate air defenses of Alaska. On 29 March 1942, after earlier preliminary meetings, he conferred with the senior Canadian commanders in western Canada, who had also formulated proposals for strengthening Pacific air defenses. At this meeting the conferees recommended that the Permanent Joint Board consider the deployment of three additional RCAF squadrons to the area. Two were to be stationed at Smithers in British Columbia, and the third at the U.S. base on Annette Island at the southern tip of the Alaskan panhandle, until such time as a U.S. unit could replace it. From the Canadian viewpoint, the squadron at Annette Island would not only strengthen Alaskan defenses but also those of the Prince Rupert area.[30]

The Permanent Joint Board considered the report on 7 April, and was informed of RCAF plans to increase the Western Air Command from ten to twenty-four squadrons. Concurrently, the War Department approved deployment of a RCAF squadron to Annette Island. The Board also discussed the need for more extensive air reinforcement of Alaska in the event of Japanese attack. A little over a month later, on 26 May, the RCAF member was able to report to the Board that plans for such an eventuality had been completed.[31]

Royal Canadian Air Force No. 115 Fighter Squadron, consisting of fourteen Bolingbroke aircraft, completed its movement to Annette Island on 5 May, the first Canadian forces to enter U.S. territory to assist in its defense. Since the stationing of the unit at Annette Island made it available for the defense of Prince Rupert, the squadron remained under the Canadian operational control of the Officer Commanding, Prince Rupert Defenses. Small detachments of light and heavy antiaircraft and an airdrome defense company of the Canadian Army were later added to the Annette Island force for the protection of the RCAF squadron.[32]

---

[30] History of the Western Defense Command, II, Ch. 7, 4; Journal, 7 Apr 42 PJBD meeting, PDB 124. For authoritative accounts of U.S. AAF and Navy operations in the Aleutians, see Wesley F. Craven and James L. Cate (eds.), *The Army Air Forces in World War II*, IV, *The Pacific—Guadalcanal to Saipan* (Chicago: University of Chicago Press, 1950), and Samuel Eliot Morison, *History of United States Naval Operations in World War II*, VII, *Aleutians, Gilberts and Marshalls* (Boston: Little, Brown and Company, 1951).

[31] Journals, 7 and 27 Apr, and 26 May 42 PJBD meetings, PDB 124.

[32] Journals, 9 Jun and 1 Sep 42 PJBD meetings, PDB 124. In June 1942 the Bolingbrokes were modified for bombing work and No. 115 Squadron was redesignated Bomber Reconnaissance.

In late May 1942 a Japanese attack on the Aleutians was believed to be imminent. General DeWitt discussed with Maj. Gen. R. O. Alexander, commanding the Canadian forces in western Canada, the need for RCAF help in the more forward areas of Alaska. On the basis of this and subsequent discussions, DeWitt believed that a request from him for the deployment of two additional RCAF squadrons to help meet the anticipated attack in the Aleutians would receive Canadian approval. The two squadrons were to be stationed in Alaska at Yakutat, near the southwestern corner of the Yukon Territory, while still another RCAF squadron was to join the one already at Annette Island. As the anticipated time of attack approached, DeWitt, who had presented a firm request to Alexander for the additional squadrons, was informed they could not be made available. The refusal was apparently the result of an Air Force Headquarters conclusion that Canadian aircraft should not be sent north of Annette Island, since to do so would reduce the air forces available for the defense of Prince Rupert. The Air Force Headquarters conclusion also had the support of the Chief of the Army General Staff, Lt. Gen. Kenneth Stuart, who on 30 May arrived in western Canada to assume additional duties as the commander of the Canadian Army Pacific Command and of the triservice West Coast Defenses command.[33]

The disappointed General DeWitt telephoned the War Department and asked it to intercede in Ottawa for loan of the two squadrons for Yakutat at least until 8 June. On 1 June an exchange of telephone calls between the War Department and National Defense Headquarters in Ottawa obtained the approval, and two RCAF squadrons were ordered to proceed to Yakutat.[34]

The RCAF No. 8 Bomber Reconnaissance Squadron of Bolingbrokes landed at Yakutat on 3 June after a 1,000-mile movement from Sea Island, British Columbia, and was after a few days transferred to Anchorage. Detachments were sent to Kodiak and Nome for various periods. Canadian No. 111 Fighter Squadron of P–40's followed by shorter hops from Patricia Bay to Anchorage. Both units undertook patrol missions immediately upon their arrival.

The AAF units had meanwhile moved forward to meet the Japanese task force sighted on 2 June, and engaged Japanese forces which attacked Dutch Harbor on 3 and 4 June. The concentration of the U.S. air units in the critical area had been facilitated by the expected arrival of the RCAF

[33] History of the Western Defense Command, II, Ch. 7, 4; Memo, ACofS OPD for SUSAM, 31 May 42, PDB 106–9; Interview, author with Lt Gen DeWitt, 24 Jan 52.

[34] History of the Western Defense Command, II, Ch. 7, 4.

squadrons in the areas that had been stripped of their U.S. defenses. The emergency over, the two Canadian squadrons moved to Anchorage. In the meantime, the Annette Island force has been reinforced during June by the addition of No. 118 Fighter Squadron so that this force too comprised a fighter and a bomber reconnaissance squadron. During June RCAF "X" Wing Headquarters was established at Fort Richardson, Alaska, and control of the RCAF squadrons in Alaska was assigned to it.[35]

The movement of RCAF squadrons to, and continued support in, Alaska created a problem as to the payment of customs duties on their equipment and supplies. The problem was neatly solved by Secretary of State Hull, who designated all personnel of the Canadian units as "distinguished foreign visitors," thereby granting them free entry of goods.[36]

Canada's No. 111 Fighter Squadron, less a rear base element, was moved in July 1942 from Anchorage to Umnak, the advance AAF base in the Aleutian chain. The base echelon moved to Kodiak in October. Flying elements operated from Umnak and, beginning in late September, from an advance base at Adak. From Adak, elements of this squadron were participating as part of the AAF Alaskan fighter command in strikes against the Japanese garrison at Kiska, 200 miles beyond Adak. The operations of the squadron consisted mainly of bombing and strafing missions against ground targets, since the Japanese air force had evacuated the Aleutian chain, and only occasionally was a submarine sighted. When operating from advance bases without their ground echelons, RCAF elements were furnished the necessary ground support by AAF units. Such operations continued well into the winter.

Shifts took place in the RCAF force late in 1942 and early in 1943. The No. 111 Fighter Squadron in October 1942 moved from Umnak and Anchorage to Kodiak for the defense of that installation, which had also become the rear RCAF base in Alaska. The No. 8 Bomber Reconnaissance Squadron returned to Canada in February 1943. It was replaced by No. 14 Fighter Squadron, which accompanied by its own ground echelon established a main base at Umnak. The No. 14 Fighter Squadron also operated as two echelons, which alternated between Umnak and Amchitka, the advance base the United States had developed only seventy-five miles from Kiska and its Japanese gar-

[35] This and succeeding paragraphs draw upon D. F. Griffin, *First Steps to Tokyo: The Royal Canadian Air Force in the Aleutians* (Toronto: J. M. Dent & Sons, 1944), a brief narrative account of the RCAF role in the Aleutians by a public relations officer attached to units stationed there.

[36] Ltr, SUSAM to CG Alaska Defense Command, 23 Jun 42, PDB 126-7; Hull, *Memoirs*, II, 1182.

rison. By May 1943 the forward element of the RCAF squadron was based at Amchitka and was participating in the strikes against Kiska whenever the weather permitted. Pilots of No. 111 Squadron were also sent forward to participate in these strikes. Both RCAF squadrons were integrated into Task Unit 16.1.1, which as a part of the North Pacific Force of the U.S. Pacific Fleet was commanded by Maj. Gen. William O. Butler of the Army Air Forces. The RCAF force in Alaska thus comprised four squadrons—two fighter squadrons in the Aleutians, and the fighter and bomber reconnaissance squadrons at Annette Island—well into the summer of 1943.

After the successful assault and capture of Attu from the Japanese in the latter half of May 1943, No. 14 Fighter Squadron continued to participate in strikes on Kiska, the lone remaining Japanese garrison in the Aleutians. Since an amphibious force containing Canadian Army units was preparing for the assault of Kiska, the RCAF attacks were supporting not only U.S. forces but also Canadian ground forces. Of the August 1943 invasion of Kiska and of the Canadian participation, more will be said shortly. Aircraft of the RCAF made preinvasion attacks right up to D Day for the amphibious assault. Immediately after the occupation of Kiska by U.S. and Canadian assault forces, the advance party of the Canadian air squadron was withdrawn from Amchitka to Umnak.

When the Japanese had been cleared from the Aleutians, Canada withdrew its air forces. The four RCAF squadrons returned to Canada during August and September 1943. Although the two squadrons at Annette Island were replaced in August by No. 149 Bomber Reconnaissance and No. 135 Fighter Squadrons, by the end of the year these squadrons, too, together with the accompanying Canadian Army defensive detachments, had returned to Canada.

The Royal Canadian Navy was the next of the Canadian armed services to join with U.S. forces in meeting the Japanese threat to Alaska. In May 1942, anticipating the possible need for additional repair facilities as a result of the expected Japanese naval offensive into North Pacific waters, the Royal Canadian Navy placed its Pacific coast base facilities at the disposal of the U.S. Navy. The June 1942 Japanese occupation of Attu and Kiska and the threat of further penetrations toward Alaska and western Canada were soon met by a substantial build-up of U.S. naval forces in Alaskan waters. These U.S. forces were joined by five Royal Canadian Navy vessels which sailed from Esquimalt, Vancouver, for Kodiak on 20 August and participated as part of Task Force Tare, under Rear Adm. Robert Theobald, U.S. Navy, in

360-477 O - 70 - 18

operations for the occupation of Adak on 30 August. Through September and October 1942, these five Canadian vessels—the armed merchant cruisers *Prince Robert, Prince Henry,* and *Prince David,* and the corvettes *Dawson* and *Vancouver*—continued to operate under U.S. Navy command in convoy escort operations between Kodiak, Dutch Harbor, and intermediate points.[37] Although these Canadian naval forces encountered no enemy units, few Canadian ships during World War II encountered such severe conditions of fog and gale as did these forces in the poorly charted, treacherous Aleutian waters. Soon after the return of the five vessels to Canadian Pacific waters, the three merchant cruisers were transferred to the Atlantic. *Dawson* and *Vancouver* remained in the Pacific and made a further contribution to Alaskan operations by aiding in the convoying of forces building up for the Attu and Kiska operations in the spring of 1943.

Meanwhile, the Japanese foothold in the Aleutians was gradually strengthened until in May 1943 enemy forces on Attu numbered 2,500 and on Kiska 5,400. The United States had reacted quickly to this threat of deeper penetrations into northwestern North America. Reinforced air and naval forces bombarded the Japanese garrisons and attempted to cut off their support and prevent reinforcement. United States forces then assaulted Attu, at the end of the chain of islands, on 12 May 1943 and achieved full control of it on 28 May after bloody and bitter fighting. The success of the Attu assault made the isolated Japanese position on Kiska more difficult. But aided by fog and bad weather, the enemy was able to support the garrison, which was strongly established in fortified positions reinforced with mines and wire obstacles.

It was for the reduction of Kiska, the last major enemy foothold in North America, that Canada and the Canadian Army prepared to make major contributions. Canadian participation in the assault operations was first discussed in April 1943 by General DeWitt of the Western Defense Command and Maj. Gen. G. R. Pearkes, commanding the Canadian Army Pacific Command. On 10 May the desirability of such a contribution was informally considered in Washington by the Senior Canadian Army Member of the Permanent Joint Board, Maj. Gen. Maurice Pope, and its U.S. secretary, John Hickerson. The next day, 11 May, Hickerson, in turn, expressed to the Senior U.S. Army Member of the Board his belief that, since the Canadians had as yet had little opportunity to fight, an invitation to participate would be gratefully received. Definite proposals were made and accepted,

[37] Office of Naval Intelligence Combat Narrative, *The Aleutian Campaign* (Washington: 1945), pp. 19, 21; Canada, Naval Service Headquarters, *Royal Canadian Navy Monthly Review,* No. 5 (May 42), p. 8; Schull, *The Far Distant Ships,* pp. 122–23.

and before the end of the month the senior U.S. and Canadian commanders on the Pacific coast were preparing detailed plans.[38]

The plans called for two Canadian forces. The first, comprising an infantry battalion and a light antiaircraft battery, would move to Amchitka or Attu in mid-June for garrison duty. The second would consist of a brigade group (regimental combat team) suitable for amphibious assault operations. Ottawa on 3 June approved the employment of the brigade group in the Kiska operation. The plan for the other force was dropped. Brigadier Harry W. Foster returned to Canada from the United Kingdom to assume command of the Canadian 13th Infantry Brigade, which was reorganized and given the code name GREENLIGHT. The force comprised four infantry battalions (Canadian Fusiliers, Winnipeg Grenadiers, Rocky Mountain Rangers, and Le Régiment de Hull), the 24th Field Regiment, Royal Canadian Artillery, and engineer and machine gun companies and a medical detachment. The battalion Le Régiment de Hull was reorganized and equipped to provide the amphibious engineer support needed.[39]

The original plan for movement of forces for the assault on Kiska, Operation COTTAGE, had called for departure of the 13th Brigade from Vancouver on 1 August, but the entire schedule was advanced a month. The necessary reorganizations and intensive training were urgently pressed. Brigade headquarters adopted the U.S. Army staff patterns. The Canadian weapons of the force were augmented by U.S. 81-mm. mortars and 75-mm. pack howitzers. All other equipment—engineer, signal, medical, and quartermaster, including vehicles—was supplied by the United States. To avoid the Canadian customs difficulties involved in shipping U.S. matériel across the border into Canada for the Canadian brigade, shipment and delivery were made to the U.S. liaison officer with the force, who then turned it over to the Canadians.

Before the Canadian force could leave Canada, the status of many of its members had to be clarified. Large numbers of men in the force had been compulsorily called up for training and home defense military service under the National Resources Mobilization Act of 1940, and they could be employed outside of Canada and its territorial waters only on a voluntary basis

[38] Stacey, *The Canadian Army, 1939–1945,* p. 289; Ltr, Hickerson to SUSAM, 11 May 43, D/S Dominion Affairs Office file, PJBD 1943. Until the invasion of Sicily in July 1943, the Canadian Army force built up in Europe had taken part only in the Dieppe and other smaller raids. For a statement by Minister of National Defense Ralston on this problem, see *H. C. Debates,* 15 Feb 44, pp. 516–18.

[39] The remainder of this account is based on Stacey, *The Canadian Army, 1939–1945,* pp. 233, 289–91; History of the Western Defense Command, II, Ch. 7; and Alaskan Department, Official History of the Alaskan Department, pp. 117–45.

unless the Canadian Government took special action.[40] An order-in-council of 18 June 1943 authorized the use of such personnel in the Aleutian Islands. The Minister of National Defense, in turn, made the order applicable to the conscripted personnel serving in the 13th Brigade.[41]

The brigade sailed from Vancouver Island on 12 July 1943 in four U.S. Army transports, and upon its arrival at Adak on the 19th continued its training, specializing in amphibious operations. Here its staff was thrown into intimate contact with American staffs and planners. The differences in organization and terminology were so great that at times the two groups seemed hardly to speak the same language. Upon its arrival in Alaska for the Kiska operation, the GREENLIGHT force totaled 4,800.

At about the same time that this force departed from Vancouver, another component of the Kiska assault force, also representing a Canadian contribution to the operation, sailed from San Francisco. The First Special Service Force, the unique formation whose three combat regiments were composed of Canadians and Americans intermingled without regard to nationality, was also earmarked to play an important role in the assault.[42]

The combined Canadian and U.S. ground forces for the assault numbered over 34,000 and were organized as Amphibian Training Force 9 under U.S. Maj. Gen. Charles H. Corlett. Units assigned to the Northern Sector were the U.S. 184th Infantry Regiment, the Canadian 13th Infantry Brigade, and the 3d Regiment of the First Special Service Force. Assigned to the Southern Sector were the U.S. 87th Mountain Infantry Regiment, the U.S. 17th Infantry Regiment, and the 1st Regiment of the First Special Service Force. The U.S. 53d Infantry Regiment and the First Special Service Force (less two regiments) comprised the floating reserve. On 13 August, with training and briefing of troops completed and D Day set for 15 August, the force sailed for Kiska. In both sectors, First Special Service Force units had been selected to lead the assaults. In the Southern Sector, the 1st Regiment reached the island at 0120 on 15 August and quickly occupied all objectives. By noon, the southern portion of the island had been scoured and found devoid of the enemy. However, the possibility remained that the Japanese were holding out on the northern half of the island and Northern Sector operations there-

[40] The conscription issue was as much debated in Canada in World War II as in World War I. For accounts thereof, see the volumes on *Canada in World Affairs* by Dawson, Lingard and Trotter, and Soward, particularly the last.

[41] *H. C. Debates*, 11 Feb 44, p. 383. This action added fuel to the conscription debate, since the opposition charged that Kiska was outside the area, that is, "Canada and Canadian territorial waters," intended for employment of National Resources Mobilization Act personnel. Orders-in-council passed during 1942 and early 1943 had already extended such employment to include Newfoundland, Labrador, and Alaska.

[42] The story of this special unit is more fully narrated below, pp. 259–68.

fore proceeded as planned. With the initial objectives achieved, both forces moved out to establish full control over the twenty-five-mile-long island.

When all objectives had been achieved and operations had ended, the reason for the silence that had greeted the initial landings and subsequent operations was apparent. The Japanese had succeeded in evacuating their garrison without detection on 28 July, three weeks before the assault. Fog, coupled with a withdrawal from the area of U.S. Navy forces for refueling, had given the Japanese the opportunity they needed to evacuate their troops. After the intensive preparations that had been made, the assault had proved to be a major anticlimax. Nevertheless, the troops involved were spared what would undoubtedly have been bitter fighting at the cost of many casualties.

The First Special Force immediately returned to the United States, arriving before the end of August, but the Canadian 13th Infantry Brigade was subjected to the bitter Aleutian weather for almost four months. Not until 12 January 1944 did the 13th Brigade depart for British Columbia.

It was particularly fitting that Canada, which had engaged in the defense of North America for twenty-five months preceding Pearl Harbor, should join in the operations that rid North America of its last enemy garrison. Fortunately, Canadian casualties in Alaska were light, numbering 2 killed and 4 wounded in the Canadian Army units and 17 dead or missing and 3 wounded in the RCAF units.

The First Special Service Force

A remarkable facet of Canadian-U.S. military collaboration during World War II was the creation of the First Special Service Force.[43] Unique in its composition, training, equipment, and organization, and outstanding in its fighting ability, the force was an experiment without parallel in the history of the Canadian and U.S. Armies. It had its beginnings in the spring of 1942 when Vice Admiral Lord Louis Mountbatten, British Chief of Combined Operations, succeeded in interesting General Marshall (who was in London to discuss a cross-Channel operation) in a diversionary operation called PLOUGH. The concept underlying PLOUGH was that a force specially trained and equipped to operate over snow could, by its superior capabilities in this "fourth element" of warfare, achieve major strategic gains through sabotage raids on Norwegian and Alpine hydroelectric and Rumanian oil-producing installations, as well as divert German forces from the projected cross-Channel invasion. Since the British were unable to produce in suffi-

[43] For a full history of the force, based on its records and written by one of its officers, see Robert D. Burhans, *The Frst Special Service Force* (Washington: Infantry Journal Press, 1947).

cient time the principal matériel requirement, an oversnow vehicle of superior mobility, Mountbatten offered the entire project to General Marshall, who accepted it.

The War Department, on Marshall's return to Washington, arranged with other government agencies for development work on the snow vehicle. The U.S. Office of Scientific Research and Development and the War Production Board made rapid progress in the design and production of the vehicle, which was named the Weasel.[44] The U.S. agencies also recruited the services of the Canadian National Research Council to assist in the work.

As the officer most familiar with the project, Lt. Col. Robert T. Frederick, who had carried out the War Department studies thereon, was directed on 16 June 1942 to assume responsibility for organizing and commanding the First Special Service Force. His directive contemplated that the force might comprise United Kingdom, Canadian, and Norwegian personnel, as well as American.[45] United Kingdom or Norwegian participation in the force did not materialize, although the expert services of a few ski instructors and intelligence specialists, mostly Norwegian, were used in planning PLOUGH and preparing the force.

Canada began to consider participating in the PLOUGH project during June 1942. Mountbatten, who had been sent by Churchill to Washington in early June, and Frederick had flown to Ottawa to discuss the matter with General Stuart, Chief of the General Staff, and other Canadian officials. On 20 June the Canadian military planning representative in Washington reported to Ottawa the suggestion of Lt. Gen. Joseph T. McNarney, U.S. Army Deputy Chief of Staff, that a request might be made to Canada to supply 500 officers and other ranks for the PLOUGH force. Prime Minister King endorsed Canadian participation, and on 14 July provision of a contingent of 47 officers and 650 other ranks was approved.

While the PLOUGH force was being organized, detailed planning for its employment continued. A decision was reached in favor of an operation in Norway, but it was never to materialize. The plan for a Norway operation received its death blow during a September trip to London of the force commander. There Colonel Frederick learned that lack of aircraft for transporting equipment had required cancellation of the operation.

The Canadian Army General Staff, on being advised on 8 October 1942 of the cancellation of the Norway operation, considered withdrawing the Canadian personnel from the PLOUGH force. But because of a request from

[44] For an account of the Canadian role in the development of the Weasel, see Wilfrid Eggleston, *Scientists at War* (Toronto: Oxford University Press, 1950), pp. 97–100.

[45] Text of the directive is reproduced in Burhans, *The First Special Service Force,* p. 11.

RETREAT CEREMONY AT FORT WILLIAM HENRY HARRISON, *Montana, for members of the First Special Service Force, 1943.*

General Marshall, who now visualized employment of the force in the Caucasus and pointed out the disruptive effect that withdrawal of the Canadian element would have on this highly trained and specialized unit, Canada decided to continue to participate. A condition of Cabinet War Committee approval of continuing participation was the right to review any operational project that might be contemplated.[46]

The First Special Service Force had meanwhile been activated at Fort William Henry Harrison, Helena, Montana, on 19 July 1942. A rapid inflow of Canadian and U.S. personnel had begun, after a careful screening of volunteers from Canadian and U.S. camps had taken place. A Washington-Ottawa press release on 6 August 1942 made public the activation of this unique Canadian-U.S. force of hand-picked volunteers.[47] Each member had

[46] Stacey, *The Canadian Army, 1939–1945,* p. 297.

[47] Canadian officials, who looked upon the force as a joint undertaking, considered as unfortunate the statement in the War Department press release that this was "the first time in history that Canadian troops have served as a part of a U.S. Army unit."

to meet rigid physical requirements, and was to receive specialized training for offensive warfare, including parachute, amphibious landing, and mountain and desert warfare training. The mention of desert warfare in the press release was apparently designed to obscure the real planned role in the Norwegian snows.

The force was organized into a combat element of 108 officers and 1,167 enlisted men, and a service battalion of 25 officers and 521 enlisted men. The service echelon was made up wholly of Americans and provided all supply, administrative, messing, and similar facilities, leaving the combat echelon entirely free of these housekeeping duties. The combat echelon comprised force headquarters and three regiments of two battalions each. Each battalion was divided into three companies, each company into three platoons, and each platoon into two sections, the basic fighting units of nine men each.

Within the combat echelon, Canadians and Americans were integrated without regard to nationality. Officer and noncommissioned officer appointments were initially allotted on a proportionate basis to personnel of both countries. Thereafter, promotions were made on the basis of ability, without regard to nationality. This system proved highly successful and resulted in an approximately equal division of promotions.

When assembled, the conglomeration of former cowhands, miners, and woodsmen who had been recruited for the force undertook an accelerated training program, which included a rigorous program of physical hardening. After early parachute qualification, each member of the force was given intensive training in the use of all types of weapons the force carried, in operation of the Weasel, and in demolitions, rock climbing, skiing, and hand-to-hand combat. Throughout the training process in Montana, a substantial rate of transfers from the force was maintained as individuals showed lack of will, stamina, or other essential qualifications. On 11 April 1943 the force proceeded to Camp Bedford, Virginia, to complete its preparation with a program of amphibious training.

The equipment of the force was as unusual as its composition. After cancellation of the Norway operation, the force's weapons and equipment were augmented so that they included the Weasel, the Browning light machine gun, the submachine gun, the then new 2.36-inch antitank rocket launcher (bazooka), the Johnson automatic rifle, the 60-mm. mortar, and the flame thrower. The additions reflected the change in concept for employment of the force from sabotage to powerful and sustained combat assault.

The two governments in January 1943 formally confirmed the over-all administrative arrangements drafted by the military staffs when the force was formed. The Canadian Government undertook to provide pay for its per-

CANADIAN AND U.S. SOLDIERS OF THE FIRST SPECIAL SERVICE FORCE *at bayonet practice, Fort William Henry Harrison.*

sonnel and transportation costs for their initial move to Helena, and to repay the United States the cost of the rations issued to Canadian personnel. The U.S. Government undertook to house, equip, and clothe the force (less the outfit worn to Helena by Canadian personnel), and to provide the transportation and medical services required.

The matter of the relative pay scales, which favored the Americans, was apparently the only unhappy aspect of the relationship of the force to its two sponsoring governments. Repeated efforts were made to place the Canadian personnel on the same pay scale as the Americans. Every effort was disapproved by the Department of National Defense in Ottawa, which saw no more justification in this situation than in others where Canadians served alongside Americans. Fortunately the different rates, though a source of typical soldier griping, did not affect force morale seriously even when the force moved overseas and U.S. pay scales were augmented by 10 percent for officers and 20 percent for enlisted men.

Administrative details posed no particular problem for the U.S. component, for the force trained and operated within the framework of the logistical and supporting U.S. Army establishment. When the force later moved to Europe, the logistical arrangement increased the administrative complications for the Canadian component, which for Canadian administrative purposes had been designated the 1st Canadian Special Service Battalion. The commander of this formation was the senior Canadian officer present (initially the force executive and later one of the regimental commanders).

Until the First Special Service Force moved from North America, the Canadian component was administered by the Department of National Defense in Ottawa through the Canadian Joint Staff in Washington. Since there would be no guarantee that the force would serve within easy communication of any other Canadian unit after the move from North America, it became necessary to authorize the Canadian battalion to issue certain types of orders, maintain field documents, and perform other functions normally assigned to a higher echelon. On the force's arrival in Italy, where the Canadian Army administrative facilities were available, the Canadian battalion yielded these functions to the higher echelons normally responsible, although the channel of communication continued to run from these echelons directly to Ottawa, instead of through Canadian Military Headquarters in the United Kingdom as was normal for Canadian units in Europe. Use of this channel of communication caused difficulties through considerable delays in reporting casualties and other matters. In August 1944 the personnel records of the battalion were transferred from Ottawa to Canadian Military Headquarters, thus restoring administrative channels of communication to a more normal basis. These administrative complications were in the over-all so small and were handled so competently by the Canadian administrative personnel that they were hardly apparent to U.S. members of the force staff, and they had no practical impact on the force's fighting capabilities.

The thorough integration of Canadians and Americans within the force presented special problems in the exercise of command and administration of discipline. To solve certain of these, an order-in-council authorized (1) every Canadian officer in the force to exercise the disciplinary powers of a detachment commander with respect to Canadian personnel, (2) Canadian personnel to be commanded, but not disciplined or punished, by U.S. personnel of superior rank, and (3) detention of Canadians, if placed under arrest, in places provided by the United States.[48] Disciplinary powers within the Canadian battalion thus remained vested in its Canadian officers. The Canadian commanding officer was given broader powers than those normally granted a battalion commander.

The impending departure of the force from the United States necessitated a grant of the power to convene field general courts-martial and, subject to

[48] Privy Council 629, 26 Jan 43.

certain limitations, to confirm the findings and sentences imposed by them. After the Kiska operation was completed and while the force was preparing to depart for Italy, the powers of the commanding officer were further enlarged by granting him authority to mitigate, commute, or remit punishments and by removing most of the limitations on his power to sentence. In practice, a pattern of uniformity developed in the handling of all but the more serious offenses so that Canadian and U.S. members of the force were hardly aware that they were being disciplined under two different codes of military law.

An additional Canadian administrative difficulty arose from the need to supply trained parachutists from time to time as replacements, once the force was in an advanced state of training. Since there was no other source of trained parachutists, a request in December 1942 for one hundred replacements was filled by taking them from the 1st Canadian Parachute Battalion, with a consequent undesirable effect on its operational readiness and morale. As a result of a recommendation by the Chief of the General Staff on 20 April 1943, the decision was reached to furnish no further replacements on the grounds that the agreed Canadian share had been furnished and that, once committed to a special mission, no reinforcement whatsoever would take place. Nevertheless, a portion of the Canadian deficiency in September 1943 was supplied after the Kiska operation and before the force's departure for Italy.

Once the force was in Italy and committed operationally, the question of Canadian replacements again arose. While the U.S. component drew easily on the U.S. personnel replacement system, the Canadian policy of nonreinforcement in the theater caused the Canadian strength to fall almost 40 percent below normal by May 1944. Because of this situation, the First Canadian Army commander, General Kenneth Stuart, had recommended in January 1944 that the Canadian component be withdrawn. Before a final decision was reached the force became heavily engaged at Anzio, and, in addition, General Dwight D. Eisenhower expressed the opinion that it would be a mistake to withdraw the Canadian component. General Stuart then recommended that Canadian participation be continued but that the U.S. practice of using ordinary infantry replacements be adopted. This practice was followed for the remainder of the time the force was in existence.

A minor element of administrative discord in regard to the Canadian component arose over the matter or awards and decorations. Canadians in the First Special Service Force had been awarded twenty-nine U.S. decorations by October 1944, whereas not a single British award had been received. The difficulty stemmed from the fact that Canadian members of the force competed on the same basis as U.S. troops of the U.S. army to which the force might be assigned for the very small number of British decorations awarded within that army. In October 1944 the Canadian battalion was placed on the same basis for British awards as other British and Canadian personnel in the theater so that its personnel ultimately received seventeen British awards in addition to a total of seventy U.S. decorations.

Only the highlights of the excellent combat record of this unit can be mentioned here.[49] By early June 1943, a number of Canadian and U.S. training inspections had rated the force ready for combat. On 9 June 1943 the War Department directed movement of the force to San Francisco and, on 12 June, obtained the approval of the Canadian Department of National Defense for its use on Kiska. The over-all and broader Canadian participation in the Kiska assault, which unexpectedly found the enemy departed, has already been recounted.

Having returned to San Francisco by 1 September 1943, the force a few weeks later sailed from Hampton Roads, Virginia, for North Africa on 28 October as a result of a request from General Eisenhower, who contemplated using it for raids, sabotage, and guerrilla operations in Italy, southern France, or the Balkans. After only a few days in North Africa the First Special Service Force sailed for Italy to join the Fifth Army. The baptism of fire occurred on 3 December in the Mignano sector in Italy, where the force was engaged for six days in difficult operations to capture Monte la Difensa and Monte la Remetanea. Force casualties totaled 80 killed or missing and 350 wounded. Committed again on Christmas Day, 1943, the force remained engaged until 10 January 1944, capturing several critical hill masses at great cost.

After a move by sea from Naples to Anzio, the force on 2 February took over an 11,000-yard sector along the Mussolini Canal on the east flank of the beachhead. Here, until its relief on 9 May 1944, the force using highly effective raiding tactics played an important role in the beachhead defense. In action again at the breakout, a detachment of the 1st Regiment was, on 4 June, one of the first Allied elements to make a permanent entry into Rome. Two days later, on 6 June, after its brief but costly participation in the breakout operations, the force was relieved to ready itself for operations in southern France as part of the U.S. Seventh Army, which comprised U.S. and French troops.

In the invasion of southern France the First Special Service Force easily accomplished its D-Day task of capturing the two easternmost of the Îles

---

[49] See Burhans, *The First Special Service Force.*

d'Hyéres on 15 August 1944.[50] After transferring to the mainland a few days later, the force advanced rapidly eastward along the Riviera coast and by 9 September had taken up a position behind the Franco-Italian boundary. The force held this position until 28 November, when it was withdrawn to a rear area for inactivation.

Although the possibility that the First Special Service Force might be disbanded had been weighed earlier in 1944 in Ottawa, where by that time Canadian participation was considered an unnecessary dispersion of Canadian resources, serious consideration was not given to the matter until Ottawa on 12 October 1944 received an indication from the War Department that inactivation was being contemplated by the United States. The War Department notified the Canadian Joint Staff in Washington on 28 October of its decision to disband the force, and the Minister of National Defense concurred. Inactivation of the First Special Service Force took place near Villeneuve-Loubet in France on 5 December 1944 with a farewell parade and memorial service. After the force flag was furled, the Canadian component withdrew from the force to form its own battalion and march past the U.S. component. The next day the Canadian battalion of 37 officers and 583 other ranks quit the force bivouac area, and its parachutists were sent to the United Kingdom as reinforcements for the 1st Canadian Parachute Battalion. A month later a large part of the U.S. component moved to northern France as replacements for the 82d and 101st Airborne Divisions. The remaining personnel were assigned to the concurrently activated 474th Infantry Regiment (Separate), which when brought to strength had little resemblance to the original force.

Throughout its combat history, the First Special Service Force engaged but little in the highly specialized types of operations for which it had been trained. Despite its special equipment and training, the force never made a parachute assault or operated in snow country, and, of its two amphibious operations, one was unopposed. Nevertheless, it had proved itself in battle in difficult assault and raiding operations. On the other hand, the force represented a costly expenditure of resources and a complex administrative effort, particularly to Canada because of the force's distance from Canadian administrative machinery. Furthermore, the very nature and status of the force required frequent attention of the Combined Chiefs of Staff to proposals for employment of this group of less than 2,000 men, as well as diplomatic exchanges to obtain Canadian acceptance of proposals—all in all an inordinate

[50] Two Canadian troopships *Prince Henry* and *Prince Baudouin* carried part of the force in the Hyéres landings.

amount of high-level consideration in relation to the size of the force. But from the point of view of Canadian-U.S. relations, the unique experiment was a remarkable success.

Canadian Army Pacific Force

During the last year of the war Canada planned and began to implement a substantial participation in operations against Japan in close association with U.S. forces. During the Second Quebec Conference of the political and military leaders of the United States and United Kingdom in September 1944, the Chief of the Canadian General Staff made known to the visiting chiefs of staff of both countries the desire of the Canadian Government to have its armed forces participate in the war against Japan after the defeat of Germany, not in more remote areas such as Southeast Asia, but in the Central and North Pacific, where they could share in the final assault on Japan proper. Prime Minister Churchill's advocacy of the Canadian aspirations at the last session of the conference won the approval of the President and the Combined Chiefs of Staff, and a brief statement accepting Canadian participation in principle was added to the final report of the conference.[51]

Two months later, on 20 November, the Canadian Cabinet War Committee approved a plan for a force of one division, with supporting troops, to be integrated into the U.S. military commands. The chairman of the Canadian Joint Staff on 9 December 1944 advised General Marshall of the Cabinet War Committee action and of the probable readiness of the force for dispatch from Canada for active operations six months after V-E Day. During this period the force would be organized in Europe, returned to North America, granted a month's leave, equipped, and trained. The Canadian Joint Staff sought the views of the War Department on the strength, composition, and organization of the force and on operational and logistical aspects of its contemplated employment.[52] The Joint Chiefs of Staff, to whom General Marshall referred the Canadian plan, on 21 December 1944 accepted it with the understanding that the force would be available for use in any of the operations to be mounted in the Pacific. In so notifying the chairman of the Canadian Joint Staff, the U.S. Joint Chiefs stated that uncertainty as to the availability date of the force precluded a decision as to its employment.[53]

---

[51] *Aide-mémoire,* given to General Marshall by the Chief of the Canadian General Staff, 16 Sep 44, ABC 384 Canada (15 Sep 44); CCS 680/2, 16 Sep 44; Minutes, 2d Plenary Meeting, OCTAGON Conference Book; *H. C. Debates,* 4 Apr 45, p. 434. The Canadian decision was taken in Cabinet on 6 September 1944.

[52] Ltr, 9 Dec 44, ABC 384 Canada (18 Sep 44).

[53] JCS 1198, 21 Dec 44.

Three months later, on 28 March 1945, Maj. Gen. H. F. G. Letson, head of the Canadian Joint Staff, called on U.S. Army Deputy Chief of Staff General Thomas T. Handy to ask what the next step should be and to suggest a general discussion of the problems arising in connection with the proposed force. As a result of the interview, the Canadian Joint Staff presented specific proposals to General Handy on 23 April. The Canadian Government felt that the force should be organized along U.S. Army lines to facilitate staff arrangements for movement, maintenance, and operation.[54] As a means of expediting the reorganization and training, it was suggested that Canadian cadres be first trained in the United States. These cadres would in turn carry out the necessary training within the force, which would not be trained for amphibious operations. Canada preferred to use its own equipment, but it was prepared to utilize U.S. equipment, except for the distinctive Canadian uniform, to the extent that the War Department considered necessary. Expenses connected with equipping and maintaining the force were to be borne by Canada. The Canadians asked for U.S. views on these proposals in order that their plans might go forward, and they also offered to furnish a planning team to work with the appropriate U.S. authorities.[55]

The War Department outlined the Canadian proposals to General of the Army Douglas MacArthur, who was engaged in planning for the invasion of Japan, and suggested that a Canadian infantry division be accepted for use as a follow-up unit in Operation CORONET, the invasion of Honshu Island. General MacArthur gave his concurrence, and the Canadian plan was then considered by the Joint Chiefs of Staff. On 15 May the Joint Chiefs notified General Letson that the following basis was considered suitable for Canadian participation:

a. The force should comprise a reinforced infantry division totaling 30,000, possibly to include armor, to be employed as a follow-up unit in the invasion of Japan itself.

b. The force should train in the United States and be organized along U.S. lines unless this would delay employment.

c. Equipment, except for uniforms, should be of U.S. types and the force should be supplied in the same manner as the U.S. troops.

---

[54] General A. G. L. McNaughton, Minister of National Defense from November 1944 to August 1945 and a postwar Canadian PJBD chairman, in 1948 stated that a primary reason for this step was to obtain experience with the U. S. system of organization "in view of the obvious necessity for the future to co-ordinate the defense of North America." (Department of External Affairs, Statements and Speeches No. 48/18, 12 Apr 48.)

[55] JCS 1198/1, 15 May 45.

d. The force would be returned from the Pacific in a priority consistent with that applied to all forces.[56]

On 21 May 1945 General Letson was able to report to the Joint Chiefs of Staff not only the agreement of the Canadian Chiefs of Staff but also the fact that a planning team was already at work in Washington.[57]

Immediately after the German surrender on 8 May 1945, Canadian forces in Europe were canvassed for volunteers. Although over 78,000 had volunteered by mid-July, only some 39,000 were accepted as of age and category suitable for the force. This number was far short of the total needed since it had been estimated that, in addition to the 30,000-man force, 33,600 personnel would have to be trained as replacements.[58]

The formation of the 6th Canadian Infantry Division had meanwhile been approved in Ottawa on 1 June 1945, as was a special Pacific campaign pay bonus for members of the force when they departed Canada. Training cadres for the force, which was to assemble at Camp Breckinridge, Kentucky, in early September, were enrolled in appropriate U.S. Army schools and numbered about 325 officers and 1,300 other ranks by mid-August. When Japan surrendered, plans were well in hand to convert the Canadian "brigades" to "regiments," field artillery "regiments" to "battalions," and otherwise mold the Canadian force to the U.S. pattern.[59]

Immediately after the Japanese surrender, the chairman of the Canadian Joint Staff advised the War Department that Canada was canceling the movement of further personnel but would formally notify the United States of its intention to drop plans for the force only when it was certain that hostilities would not be resumed. On 31 August 1945 the formal notification was given.[60] Although the Japanese surrender forestalled participation by Canadian forces in the operations against Japan, Canada expressed no desire to have those forces participate in the occupation that was undertaken immediately by U.S. forces. Nor did Canada join the British Commonwealth Occupation Force, established in Japan the following year, comprising Australian, New Zealand, United Kingdom, and Indian units.[61]

Long before V-J Day Canada also made efforts to have RCAF units participate in the Pacific war in collaboration with the U.S. Army Air Forces. After touring the Pacific combat areas, RCAF Air Vice Marshal L. F. Steven-

[56] *Ibid.* The 30,000 figure comprised the division with supporting and service units and an initial increment of replacements.

[57] JCS 1198/2, 22 May 45.

[58] Stacey, *The Canadian Army, 1939–1945,* p. 292.

[59] *Ibid.; H. C. Debates,* 18 Feb 48, p. 1350.

[60] Memo for Record, 18 Aug 45, OPD 336.2 (18 Aug 45); JCS 1198/4, 4 Sep 45.

[61] Department of State *Bulletin,* February 10, 1946, XIV, 220–22.

son returned reportedly unimpressed by British operations and determined to recommend that the RCAF operate with U.S. forces. As a result of informal discussions between the U.S. military attaché in Ottawa and Air Marshal R. Leckie, the U.S. Ambassador in Ottawa suggested to Washington that here was an opportunity to have the RCAF adopt U.S. equipment if the problem of Canadian inability to purchase the aircraft could be solved.[62]

The Ambassador's suggestion was studied in the War Department, where General Arnold, commanding the Army Air Forces, approved the proposal as being in line with AAF long-range policy to get all the countries of the Western Hemisphere to standardize on U.S. equipment. In replying to the Secretary of State, the Secretary of War suggested that the Canadians submit a formal request for U.S. air force matériel. After the Department of State informally advised the War Department that the RCAF could not, for political reasons, formally submit a request, the two departments sought other means of solving the problem.[63]

On learning that AAF officials were interested in discussing the scheme, Air Marshal Leckie came to Washington in mid-March 1945. There the AAF offered him enough Boston medium bomber (A-20) aircraft to equip several squadrons. Leckie stated he was not interested in equipping RCAF units destined for the Pacific with an outmoded type of aircraft, and the discussions ended.[64] To the Canadians, the offer, almost inevitably doomed to rejection, seemed to be evidence that the AAF wanted to run the air war in the Pacific without any outside help.[65]

Canadian officials discontinued efforts to participate with the AAF and proceeded with plans for a Pacific air effort in co-operation with the RAF. At the time of the Japanese surrender, plans were going forward for the formation of a TIGER Force of eight RCAF heavy bomber squadrons. But with the signing of the act of Japanese surrender, these plans, like those for the Canadian Army Pacific Force, were dropped and the units disbanded.

In the final stages of the Japanese war, Canadian Army participation comprised two small special units and a number of individual observers, while the RCAF was supporting two transport squadrons in Burma and a coastal squadron in Ceylon. The Royal Canadian Navy alone of the Canadian armed forces engaged the enemy in the closing stages of the war

[62] Ltr, 22 Nov 44, to Hickerson, D/S 740.0011 P.W./11-2244.

[63] Ltr, SW to Secy State, 29 Jan 45, D/S Office of Dominion Affairs file, PJBD 1945.

[64] Memo for File, J. G. Parsons, 6 Apr 45, D/S Office of Dominion Affairs file, PJBD 1945.

[65] Memo/Conv, Lewis Clark and Deputy Minister for Air Herbert Gordon, 14 May 45, OPD 336.2 Canada (24 Jun 45). With the RCAF by that date planning to operate with the RAF, Gordon indicated that the Canadian preference still would have been to operate with U.S. forces.

360-477 O - 70 - 19

against Japan in what had become a predominantly U.S. theater of operations.[66]

At the time of the Second Quebec Conference and its endorsement of Canadian participation in the Pacific war, the Royal Canadian Navy had plans in hand for a Pacific force of two cruisers, two light fleet aircraft carriers, appropriate smaller vessels, and 22,000 personnel. In the next month the Cabinet War Committee approved a somewhat modified program which eliminated the carriers and some of the smaller ships.[67] The modified program, calling for sixty ships and 13,500 personnel, was by early 1945 in the early stages of implementation.

Of the Canadian naval forces operating against the Japanese, HMCS *Uganda,* a cruiser, was the only ship actually to take part in the fighting alongside U.S. and other Allied vessels. Having arrived in Australian waters on 9 March 1945, *Uganda* left the forward base at Leyte in the Philippines on 6 April to join British Task Force 57, which was operating under the command of the U.S. Fifth Fleet during the assault on Okinawa. It did picket duty in a force that included four British Fleet aircraft carriers. In subsequent operations against the Japanese, *Uganda* bombarded a Miyako Island airfield and Truk, and participated in strikes against Kure, Kobe, and Nagoya on the main Japanese island of Honshu. Scheduled for duty with the Canadian forces preparing to assist in the final assault on the Japanese home islands, *Uganda* departed western Pacific waters for Canada on 27 July to be remanned by volunteers for Pacific duty. On V-J Day *Uganda* was at Esquimalt, Vancouver Island, and two other Royal Canadian Navy ships were en route to the British Pacific Fleet—*Ontario* in the Red Sea and *Prince Robert* at Sydney, Australia.[68] The war with Japan ended just as Canada's plans for large-scale participation were nearing fruition.

[66] Two Canadian infantry battalions that arrived at Hong Kong shortly before Pearl Harbor were part of the valiant British garrison overrun there at the very beginning of the Pacific war. For this story, see Stacey, *The Canadian Army, 1939–1945,* pp. 273–88.

[67] Tucker, *The Naval Service of Canada,* II, 99–102.

[68] Schull, *The Far Distant Ships,* pp. 408–13; Tucker, *The Naval Service of Canada,* II, 464–67.

CHAPTER X

Co-operation in Other Fields

The web of U.S.-Canadian co-operation during World War II spread its threads throughout many fields other than the activities of the armed services, which themselves involved, over and beyond co-operation in operational and logistical matters, the working out of many common problems in the fields of military administration, discipline, training, and supply. Research and development programs enjoyed a degree of collaboration which guaranteed that the discoveries and advances of each nation were shared by the other in the many fields of investigation. And, as a partner in the combined program for atomic energy research, Canada made significant contributions to the development of the atomic weapon. In the field of arms production, the two countries worked out extraordinary arrangements to see not only that the full Canadian production potential was realized but also that the Canadian economy received enough support to prevent the Canadian war production effort from having harmful effect.

Extensive co-operation also took place on many matters only indirectly related to the main military programs of Canada and the United States, some of which are recorded by other authors or elsewhere in this study.[1] A few examples may be cited. Beginning in 1941, the two countries agreed, for the duration of the war, to permit increased diversions of the waters of the Niagara River, above the Falls, as a means of increasing the electric power supply.[2] For a similar purpose, agreement was reached and repeated annually to provide for the raising of the level of the Lake of St. Francis on the St. Lawrence River.[3] Several measures provided for more effective use of transportation facilities available on the Great Lakes. The two countries agreed in 1941 reciprocally to relax their load-line regulations in order to permit lake shipping to carry increased amounts of ores and other materials.[4]

---

[1] James, *Wartime Economic Co-operation;* R. Dougall, "Economic Co-operation with Canada, 1941–1947," Department of State *Bulletin,* June 22, 1947, XVI, 1185–92, 1246.

[2] EAS, 209, and CTS, 1941, No. 7; EAS, 223, and CTS, 1941, No. 15; Exchange of Notes, 3 May 44, Department of State *Bulletin,* May 13, 1944, X, 455.

[3] EAS, 291; CTS, 1941, No. 19; and CTS, 1942, No. 18; EAS, 377, and CTS, 1943, No. 15; EAS, 424, and CTS, 1944, No. 26. The last extended the agreement for the duration of the emergency, subject to annual review.

[4] CTS, 1941, No. 20; Privy Council 5581, 24 Jul 41.

The United States later lifted its restrictions on the transportation of ores between U.S. lake ports by Canadian vessels, thus permitting over-all improvement of the ore transportation situation through use of shipping resources made available by Canada.[5]

One perennially discussed project, the Great Lakes–St. Lawrence seaway, is notably missing from the catalog of joint undertakings of Canada and the United States during World War II. On the eve of Pearl Harbor an executive agreement on the oft-studied project awaited action on the floor of the House of Representatives. Although a similar treaty signed in 1932 had been rejected by the Senate in 1934, the 1941 technique of approval of an executive agreement by simple majorities in the Congress and Parliament offered promise of success. Although the seaway and power project had been strongly supported by President Roosevelt as a defense measure before Pearl Harbor, with U.S. entry into the war Congress deferred consideration of the project in favor of more urgent undertakings.[6]

Administration and Personnel

Initially, U.S. citizens who enlisted in the Canadian armed forces before Pearl Harbor lost their citizenship by being required to take an oath of allegiance to the British crown. President Roosevelt considered the question and concluded that U.S. citizens could enlist in the Canadian forces without loss of citizenship if they were not obliged to take the oath of allegiance. When this conclusion was conveyed informally to the Canadian Government, it ceased to require the oath from U.S. enlistees.[7]

Immediately after U.S. entry into the war, U.S. authorities received large numbers of requests from U.S. citizens and former citizens serving with Canadian forces for transfer to the armed forces of the United States. The Permanent Joint Board on Defense discussed the problem on 20 December 1941. Although the Canadian members fully agreed that such transfers were desirable from a morale standpoint, they expressed concern over the adverse effects of such a step. For one thing, the instructor staff of the British Commonwealth Air Training Plan, which included several hundred

[5] PL 90, 416, and 695, 77th Congress.

[6] From the extensive literature on this project, only two official sources are cited as briefly covering the background and World War II consideration thereof: Department of State *Bulletin*, November 4, 1945, XIII, 715–19; Department of External Affairs, *External Affairs*, I, No. 2 (February 1949), 3–11.

[7] Hull, *Memoirs*, I, 775; Privy Council 2399, 7 Jun 40; 3294, 20 Jul 40; 3511, 30 Jul 40. At the outbreak of World War II, only British subjects could be enlisted or commissioned in the Canadian forces. By an order-in-council of 14 September 1939 (Privy Council 2677), Canada created the RCAF Special Reserve, which could accept aliens who were, however, required to take an oath of allegiance. A few months later, the Canadian Army made similar provisions to permit the enlistment of Americans and other aliens.

Americans, would be disrupted. For another, several thousand Americans were in the course of being trained, and Canada had already expended many millions of dollars in training them. The active units from which those who had completed training would be transferred would also be impaired. These prospects were not bright ones for Canada, which was already faced with the virtual drying up of the flow of U.S. enlistees as a result of Pearl Harbor.[8] The Permanent Joint Board was unable to agree on a recommendation on the subject at that meeting. A few days later U.S. Chairman LaGuardia obtained President Roosevelt's approval of the U.S. Section's point of view. Canada and the United Kingdom shortly thereafter agreed in principle to a transfer arrangement, and on 17 January 1942 the President announced publicly that arrangements were being made. He pointed out, however, that the need to minimize the impact of transfers on the effectiveness of British and Canadian units would preclude immediate action and necessitate considerable delays.[9]

The armed forces in both Canada and the United States continued to study the technical and administrative problems involved in the transfer. In March 1942 the United States proposed an agreement based on arrangements tentatively worked out for effecting the transfers. Under the proposals, U.S. enlistees were to be given the opportunity to apply for transfer between 6 and 20 April 1942. The United States would then send boards of officers to Canada to interview the applicants, with power to appoint or enlist them. Similar Canadian boards would discharge or release the personnel but would be empowered to postpone transfers "if in their opinion immediate transfer would prejudicially affect the common war effort." The Canadian Government undertook to give effect to the agreement proposed by the United States.[10]

A Canadian-American Military Board, headed by Maj. Gen. Guy V. Henry (retired) who was later to become Senior U.S. Army Member of the Permanent Joint Board on Defense, visited thirty-three Canadian cities between 5 May and 3 June 1942. The board effected the transfer of 2,058 of the approximately 5,000 Americans stationed in Canada of the total of 16,000 Americans in the Canadian forces. The AAF received 1,444 of those transferring, of which 665 were pilots. The transfer of 51 pilots was deferred so as not to interfere with the RCAF training program. Since only a fraction of those eligible made the transfer, the impact on the Canadian

---

[8] Journal, PDB 124; Ltr, Hull to Roosevelt, 15 Jan 42, D/S 841.2221/305a.

[9] Journal, PDB 124; Department of State Desp, 20 Jan 42, to U.S. Diplomatic and Consular Officers in Canada and Newfoundland, D/S 841.2221/306a.

[10] EAS, 245; CTS, 1942, No. 5.

war effort was smaller than had been anticipated, although the training of those who did transfer represented a Canadian investment of about $25 million.[11]

The Canadian-American Military Board on 31 July 1942 became the Inter-Allied Personnel Board and thereafter handled similar matters with other countries. The new board soon developed a voluminous correspondence relating to many of the approximately 3,000 Americans in the Canadian armed forces serving in Canada who claimed lack of opportunity to make the transfer. As a result, transfers from the Canadian Army were reopened in October 1943 and from the RCAF in March 1944. Under the supplementary arrangements, 463 were transferred from the RCAF to the AAF, 137 from the Canadian Army to the U.S. Army, and 338 from the U.S. Army to the Canadian Army.[12]

In early 1942 while examining the problem of transferring these Americans, the authorities of the two countries also discussed the application of compulsory military service requirements of one country to resident nationals of the other country. In the interests of individual morale and each country's war effort, the United States proposed that a Canadian national residing in the United States who had not declared his intention of becoming a U.S. citizen could, if drafted for service under the U.S. Selective Training and Service Act of 1940, elect to serve in the Canadian armed forces instead. Canada was to grant reciprocal treatment to U.S. citizens living in Canada. Canada agreed to this arrangement on 6 April 1942, and in the following months established at seven points in the United States military personnel centers for the purpose of enlisting such of the 91,000 nondeclarant male Canadians who, in place of being drafted into the U.S. armed forces, might choose to serve with the Canadian forces.[13] A few months later, after Canada had amended its compulsory military service regulations to include the conscription of aliens, the arrangement became applicable to U.S. citizens residing in Canada. Since the number of U.S. citizens that might be drafted by Canada was small, the United States did not establish enlisting offices in Canada but adopted a simplified procedure for enlisting these individuals.[14]

Many administrative problems of lesser importance arose and were solved

---

[11] Department of State *Bulletin,* August 22, 1942, VII, 711–13; *Canada at War,* No. 27 (Aug 43), p. 41; Memo, Maj Gen G. V. Henry for Maj Gen B. K. Yount, 16 Jun 42, AG 336.4 Cdn-American Mil Bd (6–11–42).

[12] Memo, Chairman Inter-Allied Personnel Board for CofS, 15 May 46, AG 334 Inter-Allied Personnel Bd (15 May 46).

[13] EAS, 249; CTS, 1942, No. 7; *H. C. Debates,* 28 May 43, p. 3139, and 1 Jun 43, p. 3216.

[14] CTS, 1942, No. 14.

by the two countries in a spirit of friendly co-operation. When in June 1942 Canada suggested that the payment of its forces in Alaska in Canadian dollars presented administrative difficulties and put Canadian soldiers at a disadvantage because of the need to sell their currency at a discount, the United States made arrangements whereby Canadian paymasters were supplied with U.S. currency.[15] In May 1943 a reciprocal arrangement was made under which service personnel of either country could obtain free medical and dental service at a service facility of the other country if facilities of their own were not available.[16] When a requirement arose during the summer of 1944 for hospital facilities for the Canadian armed forces in Edmonton, and empty beds were available in the U.S. Army hospital there, seventy-five beds were made available to Canada.[17] In another instance, to improve the delivery of mail to Canadian forces in Sicily and Italy, the U.S. Army agreed in 1943 to carry some 800 to 1,000 sacks weekly in U.S. ships and invited Canada to place personnel in the U.S. Army Post Office in New York City to assist in handling the mail. Canada, for its part, in 1943 accorded the United States the right to operate six military radio broadcasting stations in Canada for morale and recreation purposes.[18] At the end of the same year, when insufficient shipping was available to return U.S. personnel from Alaska, Canada loaned to the United States the SS *Princess Louise* for use in troop movements.[19]

Personnel of visiting forces who deserted or were absent without leave were a problem in both countries, although the problem was greater in respect to U.S. forces in Canada. The United States established procedures for apprehending, detaining, and transferring Canadian deserters and absentees in the United States. The Canadian Government, at the request of the United States, provided similar arrangements for U.S. deserters and absentees in Canada.[20]

The two governments also made arrangements that effected major savings in administrative effort with respect to claims arising from collisions between government vessels and between vehicles. In several exchanges of notes, the two governments agreed that, in cases where such a collision took place, each government would bear all the expenses arising directly or indirectly from the damage to its own vessel or vehicle and would not make

[15] Disposition Form, to CofS, 20 Jun 42, PDB 111-10.
[16] *Canada at War,* No. 25 (Jun 43), p. 60.
[17] Journal, 6-7 Sep 44 PJBD meeting, PDB 124.
[18] EAS, 400; CTS, 1944, No. 1.
[19] Memo, SUSAM for Chief, Overseas Troop Branch, ASF, 26 Nov 43, PDB 114-6.
[20] WD Cir 258, 1944; Privy Council 6577, 23 Oct 45.

any claim against the other government.[21] Each government quickly made provision for settling claims made by residents of the other country arising from accidents involving vehicles or aircraft of the first. Under the authority of an act of Congress of 2 January 1942, the War Department in 1943 constituted a number of claims commissions within its various commands in Canada to settle such claims. Canada took reciprocal action soon thereafter under authority of an approved minute of the Treasury Board.[22]

Questions of taxation were worked out to the satisfaction of the United States, the government mostly concerned.[23] In the agreements that authorized the two major U.S. projects, the Alaska Highway and the Canol Project, Canada waived (1) the duties, taxes, fees, and similar charges connected with the equipment and supplies or their movement, (2) the income tax of the U.S. residents engaged on the projects, and (3) the royalties on the oil produced by the Canol Project.[24] Canada went even further and agreed that the United States should not be taxed by provincial or municipal authorities. In those instances where it became necessary for the United States to pay such taxes, Canada undertook to make reimbursement for the payments.[25]

Another administrative arrangement agreed upon by the two governments had as its object the simplification of procedures for disposing of prizes captured by the forces of the two countries. Under the agreement, which was reciprocal, a prize captured by the United States in Canadian territorial waters, or captured on the high seas and then brought into Canadian territorial waters, was disposed of through the exercise of jurisdiction by district courts of the United States.[26]

The Rush-Bagot Agreement

One of the cornerstones of Canadian-U.S. friendship, the Rush-Bagot Agreement of 1817, was stretched to its elastic limit through interpretation

[21] EAS, 330, and CTS, 1943, No. 12; TIAS, 1581, and CTS, 1944, No. 10; TIAS, 1582, and CTS, 1946, No. 42.

[22] PL 393, 77th Congress; Army Regulation 25-90, 22 Apr 43; Privy Council 71/3711, 5 May 43.

[23] For a general examination of the problem of taxation of foreign forces, by authors who participated in the development of the U.S. positions, see Chas. Fairman and Archibald King, "Taxation of Friendly Foreign Armed Forces," American Journal of International Law, XXXVIII (1944), 258-77.

[24] EAS, 246, and CTS, 1942, No. 13; EAS, 386, and CTS, 1942, No. 23. See also Department of National Revenue WM No. 75 and WM No. 75 (Revised), published under authority of Privy Council 53/8097. The revised order is in *Canadian War Orders and Regulations*, I (1944), 369-72.

[25] EAS, 339; CTS, 1943, No. 11.

[26] EAS, 394; CTS, 1943, No. 13. Privy Council 6092, 3 Aug 43; Proclamation 2594, 8 FR 13217.

designed to meet World War II needs. Its limitation of three vessels of not more than one hundred tons each on the Great Lakes had hindered World War I programs, and, although modification was studied shortly thereafter, no changes were made.

Even before the start of World War II, the limitation began to hamper the naval training and construction programs of the two countries. Secretary of State Hull was determined to preserve the agreement, which over one hundred twenty years had achieved a symbolic importance. Whereas changes in ship design, the construction of the Welland Canal, and other circumstances had outdated the underlying hypotheses of the treaty, Hull considered the spirit of the agreement to be its essential element. So long as they did no violence to the spirit of the agreement, interpretations that took account of conditions in 1939 would, in his view, better serve the needs of the day. Accordingly, on 9 June 1939, Hull proposed that the following arrangements should, in accordance with this approach, be acceptable:

a. Vessels could be constructed for movement to tidewater immediately on completion, but no armament could be installed until after they had left the Lakes.

b. Five outmoded U.S. Navy vessels of from 1,000- to 2,000-ton displacement could be maintained for training purposes.

c. Armament could be mounted somewhat in excess of the treaty limitations and used for target practice.[27]

These proposed arrangements were accepted by the Canadian Government and made effective.

A year later, with Canada embroiled in the war in Europe and its Atlantic shipyards congested, the Canadian Government sought further liberalization of the agreement. It proposed that installation of armaments on ships be permitted on the Lakes provided that such armaments be rendered incapable of use on the Lakes and that the ships be moved from the Lakes promptly on completion. Each government was to keep the other fully informed as to the nature of its construction program. These proposals were accepted by the United States on 2 November 1940.[28]

The next liberalization of the Rush-Bagot Agreement was proposed in February 1942 by the United States, by then a belligerent, in order to eliminate handicaps imposed by even the 1940 interpretation of the agreement. In order that vessels constructed on the Lakes might be combat ready upon reaching the open sea, the U.S. Government suggested that, for the duration

[27] TIAS, 1836; CTS, 1940, No. 12.
[28] TIAS, 1836; CTS, 1940, No. 12; *H. C. Debates,* 24 Mar 41, pp. 1777–79.

of hostilities, the complete installation and test firing of all armaments on vessels constructed on the Lakes should be permitted there. With the intensification of the German submarine offensive in the northwestern Atlantic putting a burden on the seaboard shipyards, Canada readily acquiesced.[29] This additional interpretation of the agreement adequately met the needs of the wartime situation, and no further arrangements were sought. After V–J Day the 1942 interpretation became ineffective.

In 1946 the two governments again examined the 1817 agreement. They reaffirmed its historic importance as a symbol of the friendly relations between the two countries. In keeping with discussions that had taken place in the Permanent Joint Board on Defense, Canada suggested that the use of vessels for training purposes should be considered within the spirit of the agreement, provided each country kept the other fully informed concerning such training activities. The United States found the proposal acceptable and the Rush-Bagot Agreement, reinvigorated through the new interpretation, continued its role as a symbol of U.S.-Canadian friendship.[30]

Miscellaneous Co-operation

The foundation for a full and complete exchange of military information between Canada and the United States had been laid in the very first recommendation of the Permanent Joint Board on Defense. Procedures for exchanges were developed immediately, the principal mechanism being the Board and the planning teams that drafted the 1940 and 1941 defense plans. The establishment of the Canadian Joint Staff in Washington in July 1942 led to a Canadian request for an improvement in the arrangements for exchange of information. Upon the recommendation of the Joint Staff Planners, the Joint Chiefs of Staff designated the former as its liaison with the Canadian Joint Staff. This liaison was primarily related to strategic planning and military operations.[31]

The mechanics for exchange of intelligence (data concerning the enemy), as distinguished from general military information, had been established long before Pearl Harbor, and in this area actual exchanges of staff officers improved the effectiveness and completeness of the arrangement. These exchanges continued satisfactorily throughout the war except for a period of months in the latter part of 1944, when, because of the heavy turnover of personnel in the War Department, the liaison deteriorated. It soon improved.[32]

---

[29] TIAS, 1836; CTS, 1942, No. 3.

[30] TIAS, 1836; CTS, 1946, No. 40.

[31] JCS 82, 18 Aug 42.

[32] Ltr, Maj Gen H. F. G. Letson to Maj Gen J. E. Hull, 6 Feb 45, and Reply, from Maj Gen H. A. Craig, 12 Feb 45, OPD 336 Canada, Sec. 1–A (7–15–42).

Throughout 1941 the flow of information increased through interchange of observer groups that visited the activities and facilities of the other country. Significant numbers of Canadian personnel also attended U.S. Army motor maintenance, tank techniques and tactics, motorcycle operation, and similar formal training courses.

Reciprocal training assistance took other forms. In October 1941 the United States authorized Canada to use U.S. territorial waters in Puget Sound for an aerial torpedo range. Later the same year, just after Pearl Harbor, Canada offered use of some of its air training facilities to the United States, anticipating that with the cutting off of the flow of U.S. trainees into the RCAF the facilities would be idle. The United States did not avail itself of this offer. It did, however, make use of Canadian facilities at Camp Shilo, Manitoba, during the winter of 1942–43. A detachment of some 900 personnel was sent to Shilo to conduct cold weather tests in the use of tanks and other combat vehicles, trucks, guns and ammunition, and other ordnance. The Shilo arrangement was part of a reciprocal agreement under which Canada sent 600 men to Fort Benning, Georgia, for parachute training, to prepare them for service in the 1st Canadian Parachute Battalion.

Other co-operative training ventures were the cold weather exercises ESKIMO (a 150-mile move by a composite force in the dry cold of central Saskatchewan) and POLAR BEAR (a similar move across the coastal mountains in British Columbia from the interior dry cold to the coastal wet cold) conducted during the winter of 1944–45. In the early spring of 1945 a third similar joint exercise, LEMMING, was carried out near Churchill for the purpose of testing the operation of various types of oversnow vehicles on the "barren grounds" of northern Canada and on the Hudson Bay sea ice. The forces involved were basically Canadian and Canadian equipped, and the United States contributed and benefited by providing observers and assisting specialists and also tractors and other matériel.

One major Canadian proposal for training co-operation was studied over a period of months but failed to materialize. It involved the use by the United States of surplus training facilities of the Canadian-operated British Commonwealth Air Training Plan. The schools established in accordance with the plan, which had been agreed upon in December 1939 by the governments of Canada, Australia, and New Zealand as a result of proposals advanced from London in September 1939, began operation in June 1940. A large proportion of the Americans joining the Canadian forces before Pearl Harbor passed into the British Commonwealth Air Training Plan either as students or as instructors.[33]

---

[33] See above, pp. 241–42.

United States entry into the war threatened to disrupt the Air Training Plan. Not only did many U.S. instructors indicate a desire to transfer to the U.S. armed forces, but also it appeared likely that the flow of U.S. recruits into the system would dry up at a time when the plan had been budgeted for on the basis of an increasing flow of U.S. recruits. As early as 8 December informal suggestions were advanced through displomatic channels that perhaps Canada could, in consequence, lend some of the excess training plant to the United States, which could operate some of its training centers at such Canadian installations.[34]

The general proposition was discussed on 20 December by the Permanent Joint Board, which adopted the recommendation (the Twenty-third) that the two countries should consider a U.S.-United Kingdom-Canadian meeting to study co-ordination of the training programs being conducted in North America. The recommendation was approved by both governments, but it received only desultory consideration by the U.S. military officers during the ensuing months.[35]

In April 1942 Prime Minister King discussed the project with President Roosevelt in Washington and the two announced on 17 April that, at King's invitation, a conference would be held in Ottawa in early May of those Allied nations that had air training programs under way in North America.[36] As conference plans moved forward, the War Department became concerned at the scope of the agenda suggested by Canada, feeling that subjects such as the allocation of U.S.-made training aircraft were outside the competence of the conference. In addition, discussion of subjects such as exchange of air crews between nations and the training of members of the AAF in Air Training Plan schools was precluded by the fact that the War Department, principally at the instance of the Army Air Forces, was firmly opposed to such measures. In the War Department view, the solution to the problem of British Commonwealth Air Training Plan surplus capacity was to concentrate under the plan such training of British Commonwealth air crews as was being done elsewhere, as for example in the United States.[37] On the Canadian side, King was disappointed that the U.S. delegation would include only service representatives. Apparently through his intercession with Roosevelt, the composition of the U.S. delegation was changed on the eve of its departure so that it was headed, not by Lt. Gen. Henry H. Arnold, as

[34] Memo/Conv, Moffat and Robertson, 8 Dec 41, Moffat Diary.

[35] Text at Appendix A, below. The status of action was discussed at the February and 8 April 1942 PJBD meetings.

[36] Department of State *Bulletin,* April 18, 1942, VI, 336–37.

[37] Ott Leg Telg 64, to Department of State, 22 Apr 42, and Ltr, SW to Secy State, 13 May 42, both in PDB 119–6.

had been planned, but by Assistant Secretary of War for Air Robert A. Lovett.[38]

The conference took place in Ottawa from 19 to 22 May 1942, with representatives of fourteen nations present. In an initial speech, Lovett transmitted a glowing tribute from President Roosevelt, in which he had called Canada the "Airdrome of Democracy." The U.S. delegation nevertheless stood fast in its position against commitments for co-ordinated exchange of training capacity. As its final action, the conference recommended establishment of a Combined Committee on Air Training in North America. This committee was to have advisory functions only and concern itself with problems such as the standardization of training methods and most effective use of the air training capacity in North America.[39]

Arrangements for formation of the committee moved slowly. The United States advised Canada of the names of its members in September, but by 1 April 1943 a meeting had not yet taken place. Some discussions did take place within the framework of the committee later in 1943, but these had only minor significance. On the original proposal that the United States utilize Air Training Plan capacity, the War Department position in opposition prevailed.[40]

Except in Alaska and in northeastern United States where the Royal Canadian Navy made use of naval facilities, the Canadian services had only a limited need for use of U.S. installations. When Canadian requests for use of U.S. facilities were made, the United States was able, at least in small measure, to reciprocate for Canadian assistance. In the fall of 1943 the RCAF requested the authority to station a five-man detachment at Millinocket, Maine, and the use of hangar facilities there to assist in handling Canadian service traffic across northern Maine. Instead of constructing a new hangar that would have been needed at Millinocket, the United States provided the needed facilities at nearby Houlton. Similarly, during the summer of 1944, the United States readily granted approval to RCAF training operations at the air base at Bellingham, Washington, under an arrangement that did not involve the provision of any services to the RCAF at the inactive air base.

Internal security of U.S. activities in Canada posed a number of problems that were readily solved through the co-operation of the Canadian au-

[38] Memo/Conv, Moffat and Robertson, 11 May 42, Moffat Diary; WD Press Release, 18 May 42.

[39] Ottawa Air Training Conference, May 1942, *Report of the Conference* (Ottawa: E. Cloutier, King's Printer, 1942), pp. 13, 24–25.

[40] Ott Leg Desp 4306, to Secy State, 1 Apr 43, D/S 800.248/55, and Desp 384, 30 Nov 43, D/S 800.248/64.

thorities. In Canada, as well as in the United States, an evacuation of west coast Japanese took place after Pearl Harbor. Beginning in the spring of 1942 U.S. authorities raised the question of the security of the Canadian National Railways, along which internee camps were located at a number of points. To minimize the threat of sabotage, Canada closed certain of the camps and took additional police measures at others.

Another security problem arose after the construction of the air base at Churchill was initiated as a restricted project. The United States proposed that, in view of the isolated character of the site and of its military activities, travel thereto should be restricted to official purposes. In April 1943 the Canadian authorities acceded to this request and declared the area along the railroad from The Pas to Churchill to be a "controlled area," to which the provisions of the Defense of Canada Regulation 5 applied. At almost the same time, Canada offered to designate all premises in Canada occupied by the U.S. armed services "protected places," thereby excluding unauthorized persons, and it did so upon acceptance of the offer.[41]

A significant U.S. wartime contribution toward the development of the potentialities of northern Canada was the charting of the area by the AAF. The larger part of that area had not previously been photographed aerially, and maps and charts were incomplete and inaccurate. During the summer of 1943 extensive aerial photography projects were executed by AAF aircraft operating from Churchill and Fort Chimo in the east, and Fort McMurray and Norman Wells in the west. The United States shared with Canada the photographs and data obtained.

One of the most spectacular instances of Canadian-U.S. co-operation was the rescue of the personnel of the Hudson's Bay Company post at Fort Ross, Somerset Island. Since the RMS *Nascopie* had been unable to resupply the post for two navigation seasons, it was decided in October 1943 to try to evacuate the personnel by air. The RCAF could not supply an aircraft for the purpose since all suitable aircraft were occupied with urgent patrol work in the Atlantic. The AAF volunteered to provide an aircraft. On 13 November the rescue, which had been regarded by many as impossible since there was no landing strip, was successfully completed.

Research and Development

Participation in the atomic energy development project that produced the atomic bombs dropped on Nagasaki and Hiroshima was perhaps the most spectacular, if not the most important, Canadian contribution in the field of research and development. But other less spectacular Canadian

[41] *Canadian War Orders and Regulations*, II (1943), 184.

scientific contributions to the Allied military effort in World War II also represented substantial Canadian accomplishments.[42]

Canadian-U.S. scientific collaboration was a by-product of a visit to North America, at the suggestion of the United Kingdom, of the British Scientific Mission headed by Sir Henry Tizard in August and September 1940. As a result of the Tizard Mission's visit, the United States, though still a neutral, obtained access to British development work in certain fields such as radar that had far outstripped U.S. research. In return, the United Kingdom gained benefits from the further refinement and production of the new matériel types in the greater engineering and production facilities of the United States. The fruits of further research by U.S. scientists also became available to the United Kingdom. Canada had provided three members (Brigadier Kenneth Stuart, Air Commodore E. W. Stedman, and Dr. C. J. Mackenzie) of the Tizard Mission, and through this membership was drawn into the tripartite scientific co-operation that resulted. Included in the data brought to the United States by the British scientists was full information on advanced radar developments, and, during the mission's visit, programs of further research in the radar and other fields were laid out and responsibilities were allocated to each country.[43]

An urgent need existed for an effective radar in the microwave length band, for only in this band could equipment be made sufficiently small to be readily portable either by aircraft or by motor truck. In October 1940 the Canadian National Research Council began work on a microwave fire direction radar, the GL (gun-laying) Mark III C, and the following month U.S. microwave research began at the Massachusetts Institute of Technology Radiation Laboratory. A staff of six Canadians worked there, and a full exchange of information was maintained between the two projects. By June 1941 the joint effort had resulted in a successful demonstration of the complete GL Mark III C equipment. Canada produced five sets during the rest of 1941, the third of which was furnished to the U.S. Army at its request. Canada then proceeded to mass produce this set, the first of its type to get into large-scale production. Concurrently, the United States developed a similar set, the SCR-584. Both sets incorporated research and design advances worked out in both countries.

[42] Eggleston, *Scientists at War*, gives a full and authoritative account of co-operation on these projects.

[43] For further details on radar development, see two volumes in the series UNITED STATES ARMY IN WORLD WAR II, Dulany Terrett, *The Signal Corps: The Emergency* (Washington: Government Printing Office, 1956), and George Raynor Thompson, Dixie R. Harris, Pauline Oakes, and Dulany Terrett, *The Signal Corps: The Test* (Washington: Government Printing Office, 1957).

In 1942 other advantages in the use of microwave radar induced Canada and the United States to turn to these wave lengths for development of fixed early warning aircraft detection sets. Here, too, close collaboration between the staffs of the two countries by the spring of 1943 had produced a MEW (microwave early warning) radar set of excellent performance. In the field of airborne radar, Canada led the United States. The first radar set mass produced in Canada had been the ASVC (air-to-surface-vessel, Canadian), based on a British prototype. The set was in mass production by the early summer of 1941, and some of the early sets were furnished to the United States for use as models by U.S. manufacturers. The U.S. Army SCR–521 was a close copy of this Canadian set.

Canadians also had a part in the research, engineering, and production of the radio proximity fuze. In its development the Carnegie Institute in Washington, D. C., and the Toronto Group, which attacked the problem in September 1940, maintained close co-ordination. Many features of the fuze represented the integration of the best ideas developed in both Canada and the United States. A particular Canadian contribution was the wet battery idea, in which the electrolytic liquid was contained in an ampoule that broke when the shell was fired, thus completing a live, charged-battery power source, yet one that presented no problem as to self-life during storage.

Another significant contribution Canada made to wartime research was in connection with the military explosive RDX, which has up to twice the power of TNT. The explosive had been known since 1899, but despite its attractive features it had not been used for military purposes because of the high cost of production and other disadvantages. Canada undertook to overcome these disadvantages in the spring of 1940 and soon discovered a new process for producing RDX, which proved to be not fully satisfactory. After the Tizard Mission visited North America, a tripartite RDX Committee was established, and the Canadian data was shared with the U.S. scientists who went to work on the project. As a result of the closest possible collaboration in this committee, a new production process was developed which embraced important contributions of both Canadian and U.S. personnel. Large-scale production of RDX was first initiated in Canada in July 1942.[44]

While the research and devolpment work of Canadian scientists during World War II in other fields was important, it was overshadowed by the significance of Canadian research in the field of atomic energy. When the European war began in September 1939, a few Canadian scientists were en-

[44] The United States and Canada later agreed by an exchange of notes to the mutual interchange of patent rights in connection with RDX and other explosives that had been jointly developed during the war. (TIAS, 1628; CTS, 1946, No. 51.)

gaged in nuclear research in furtherance of the discoveries of Fermi and others relating to the fission of the uranium atom. During 1940 experiments at Ottawa, under sponsorship of the National Research Council, produced encouraging progress toward a chain reaction. By the following year, informal exchanges of technical information on these experiments had taken place with U.S. scientists.[45] On 2 December 1942 the U.S. experiments at the University of Chicago produced the first chain reaction, or self-sustaining pile. As a result of this success, the United States embarked on a full-scale effort to produce the atomic bomb. During these same months in 1942, the Canadian effort also expanded.

With research efforts in the United Kingdom oriented to meet more immediate operational needs and British laboratories threatened with destruction from aerial bombardment, the British Government proposed to the Canadian Government the establishment of a joint atomic energy research project in Canada. The joint effort got under way in September 1942, when a group of British scientists arrived in Montreal. The joint group, financed largely by Canada and administered by the Canadian National Research Council, proceeded with work on a heavy-water pile. United States research was largely utilizing the graphite types.

One factor alone assured Canada a place of importance in the development of atomic energy. In 1930 a large deposit of radium and uranium ores had been discovered on the shores of Great Bear Lake in the Northwest Territories. Important in prewar years as a source of radium, the mine had come to rank in production second only to the source in the Belgian Congo. However, market conditions had forced the mine to close in June 1940. In January 1942 the Canadian Government sought market assurances from the United States as a means of improving the financial condition of the owning company so that it could resume operations. Failure to reopen the mine during the spring of 1942 might have resulted in its permanent impairment because of ground water conditions, and this eventuality nearly materialized, for the Canadian inquiry elicited only a noncommittal reply. Fortunately, the progress of intensified experimentation in the atomic field soon created a substantial demand for uranium ore, and in August 1942 the mine was reopened. The Great Bear Lake mine soon became a critical element in the entire atomic energy development project.[46]

---

[45] For a fuller account of the Canadian role in the development of the atomic bomb, see Eggleston, *Scientists at War*, especially Chapter V. The most authoritative account of the American effort in this field is H. G. Smyth, *Atomic Energy for Military Purposes* (Princeton: Princeton University Press, 1945).

[46] Memo, Cdn Leg to Department of State, 19 Jan 42; Reply, 28 Jan 42, both in D/S 842.6344/4. Stimson and Bundy, *On Active Service*, p. 614.

By mid-1943 it became evident that the various atomic research programs, in the interest of economy of effort, needed to be co-ordinated more closely. As a result of informal discussions during the First Quebec Conference (August 1943), President Roosevelt and Prime Minister Churchill established a Combined Policy Committee, on which they invited Prime Minister King to provide Canadian representation. The committee—Secretary of War Henry L. Stimson, Dr. Vannevar Bush, and Dr. James B. Conant, for the United States; Field Marshal Sir John Dill and Colonel J. J. Llewellin, for the United Kingdom; and Minister of Munitions and Supply C. D. Howe, for Canada—was charged with the broad direction of the programs as between the countries. A technical committee comprising Maj. Gen. L. R. Groves (United States), Sir James Chadwick (United Kingdom), and Dr. C. J. Mackenzie (Canada) was also set up to co-ordinate and correlate the policy decisions and the joint programs.[47]

The importance of the uranium ores at Great Bear Lake was by then fully apparent. In January 1944 the Canadian Government therefore expropriated the stock shares of the company, which was renamed Eldorado Mining and Refining Limited, and began operating it as a crown company. In the following months the shaft was enlarged and deepened and the plant expanded to a capacity of one hundred tons of ore per day. This vital ore source, which was operated on a twenty-four-hour basis, continued to be second in importance only to the Belgian Congo among sources available to the United States and Great Britain. The Combined Policy Committee allocated the ore produced.[48]

By the beginning of 1944 an apportionment of research effort had been made that assigned the heavy-water moderator project to Canada. A site was chosen near Chalk River, Ontario, and the construction of the facility, whose cost together with other costs of the project was to be borne by Canada, moved ahead quickly. Experimentation at Chalk River also progressed rapidly, even while the new laboratories were being completed and the transfer from Montreal was taking place. On 5 September 1945, the Canadian experimental pile was put into operation, the first pile outside of the United States to produce atomic energy. Despite the close tripartite co-operation in atomic research and development, Canada made no attempt to

[47] *H. C. Debates,* 17 Dec 45, p. 3633.

[48] Privy Council 535, 27 Jan 44; *H. C. Debates,* 3 Jun 46, pp. 2106, 2125. Canada consulted the United States as to the desirability of obtaining control of the mines as early as June 1942 and received President Roosevelt's encouragement. (Roosevelt Papers, Secy's Safe File, Dr. V. Bush Folder.) For an account of operations at the uranium mines and of their role in the atom bomb project, see Kennedy, *History of the Department of Munitions and Supply,* Ch. 25.

manufacture the atomic bomb, nor did it seek the necessary information to do so.[49]

When hostilities ended, the three partners in atomic development collaborated in a proposal for international action to prevent the use of atomic energy for destructive purposes. Meeting in Washington on 15 November 1945, President Harry S. Truman and Prime Ministers King and Clement Attlee signed an agreed declaration advancing this proposal and the offer to share information concerning the practical applications of atomic energy as soon as effective safeguards against its use for destructive purposes had been established.[50] Tripartite co-operation was not to continue on any significant scale, however, for the Atomic Energy Act of 1946 enacted by the U.S. Congress necessitated the elimination of Canadian and British participation in the U.S. project except in limited areas of technical co-operation.[51]

The Canadian undertaking in the atomic energy field involved, up to the time of completion of the Chalk River Project, expenditures of approximately $27 million. By comparison with those of the United States in developing the atomic bomb, these Canadian expenditures were modest. But they did produce important results in the heavy-water moderator project, which in turn became the springboard for significant advances in the unilateral Canadian research program initiated in the postwar years.

Arsenals of Democracy

Although the full story of the achievements and contributions to victory of the two countries in the field of munitions production would require a volume in itself, this account would not be complete unless it took brief notice of them. When President Roosevelt on 29 December 1940 labeled the United States an "Arsenal of Democracy," he originated a term that was equally applicable to Canada, whose war production record was all the more remarkable in the light of the industrial base from which it developed.[52] From the mighty arsenals of Canada and the United States poured forth a stream of munitions that supplied Allied forces on seas and battlegrounds

---

[49] Joint Committee on Atomic Energy, 81st Congress, 1st Session, Hearings, *Investigation Into United States Atomic Energy Project,* July 6, 1949, Pt. 19, p. 792; *H. C. Debates,* 14 Jun 46, p. 2490.

[50] TIAS, 1504; CTS, 1945, No. 13.

[51] PL 585, 79th Congress.

[52] For full official accounts of these production accomplishments, see Canada, Department of Munitions and Supply, *The Industrial Front* (Ottawa: E. Cloutier, King's Printer, 1944), U.S. War Production Board, *Industrial Mobilization for War,* I, *Program and Administration* (Washington: Government Printing Office, 1947), and H. Duncan Hall, *North American Supply* (*History of the Second World War: United Kingdom Civil Series* [London: Her Majesty's Stationery Office, 1955]).

TABLE 3—COMBINED CANADIAN-UNITED STATES PRODUCTION OF SELECTED MUNITIONS: 1 JULY 1940–31 AUGUST 1945

[Unit-each, or as designated]

Type	Grand Total	United States	Canada	
			Total	Under U.S. Contract
Airplanes, military types	307, 483	291, 619	15, 864	5, 254
Combat	205, 581	200, 026	5, 555	1, 652
Trainer	64, 061	54, 773	9, 288	2, 850
Cargo and liaison	37, 841	36, 820	1, 021	752
Patrol vessels	2, 438	[a] 2, 158	280	25
Mine craft	1, 164	[a] 966	198	9
Landing vessels, 750 tons and over	1, 085	1, 069	16	0
Ocean-going cargo and supply vessels	5, 504	[a] 5, 113	391	0
Artillery, field, tank and self-propelled	223, 897	207, 988	15, 909	2, 445
Artillery, antiaircraft (Army)	63, 411	49, 909	13, 502	589
Mortars and bomb throwers	186, 234	111, 246	74, 988	46, 567
Small arms (thousands)	21, 808	20, 188	1, 620	299
Ammunition, ground artillery (thousands)	360, 696	324, 897	35, 799	10, 259
Ammunition, mortar and bomb thrower (thousands)	115, 037	102, 413	12, 624	1, 000
Ammunition, small arms (millions)	46, 140	41, 746	4, 394	502
Tanks and tank chassis	108, 941	103, 226	5, 715	0
Scout cars and carriers	132, 416	89, 072	43, 344	6, 783
Military trucks, all types (thousands)	3, 245	2, 472	773	0

[a] Includes conversions; 147 patrol vessels, 104 mine craft, and 349 cargo vessels.

Source: U.S. Civilian Production Administration, *Official Munitions Production of the United States* (Washington, 1947). This report contains a combined U.S.-Canadian supplement.

the world over. The quantities of military items produced, as shown in Table 3, are enough to challenge the imagination.

To reach that level of achievement, Canada and the United States were required to carry out extensive expansion of plant and production capacity. In Canada this expansion was proportionately greater than in the United States and was achieved through the assistance of the United States. The fall of France marked the beginning of the real acceleration of munitions production on both sides of the border. The Canadian production effort was initially severely limited by the available production capacity, and in order to expand capacity there was a critical need for machine tools. Although a large world-wide demand existed, Canada was able to make substantial purchases of machine tools in the United States. Without these tools the expansion of Canadian military production that occurred would not have been possible. Even when U.S. export of machine tools was made subject to licensing by the Act of Congress of 2 July 1940, Canada was still able to obtain the tools it needed without encountering any difficulties.[53] The Canadian production effort also received assistance in other ways, one of which was that U.S. companies having Canadian branches provided the technical experts needed to assist in Canadian expansion.[54]

While Canada and the United States had taken preliminary steps to assist each other in 1940, the real basis for production co-operation was established at Hyde Park on 20 April 1941 by President Roosevelt and Prime Minister King. King and other Canadian officials had earlier been unsuccessfully exploring with U.S. officers in Washington ways and means of meeting the increasing demands for U.S. dollars of Canada's growing production program. By the spring of 1941 these demands had reduced the Canadian holdings of U.S. dollar exchange to dangerously low levels. Just three days after an inconclusive discussion of the problem with Secretary of State Hull, King found the opportunity to present it to the President during a vist to Hyde Park. The two agreed to an arrangement which the President named the Hyde Park Declaration.[55]

The basic purpose of the Hyde Park Declaration was to make it possible for Canada to obtain the U.S. dollar exchange it needed to permit essential purchases from the United States. This was to be accomplished by co-ordinating the production programs of the two countries so that Canada would manufacture, and sell to the United States, the munitions and materials that the Canadian economy was in a better position to supply. This arrangement would permit the United States to delete such items from its production program and to meet its needs through purchases from Canada. In order to facilitate the execution of the co-ordinated program, the United States granted to Canada equal priorities in the assignment of scarce machine tools, raw materials, and shipping allocations.[56]

---

[53] Dawson, *Canada in World Affairs: 1939–1941*, pp. 34, 61, 246.

[54] The *Canadian Geographical Journal*, Vols. XXIV and XXV, contains excellent and authoritative accounts of the development of various of the munitions industries.

[55] Ltr, King to Roosevelt, 24 Apr 41, Roosevelt Papers, Secy's file, Box 74; Memo/Conv, Hull and King, 17 Apr 41, D/S 842.24/110. Full text of the declaration is contained in Appendix D, below.

King rendered an interesting account of the meeting and the formulation of the declaration to the U.S. Chargé d'Affaires, Lewis Clark. King said that during his pleasant visit the two were driving around the Hyde Park estate. Suddenly King remembered a memorandum his financial people had given him, pulled it out of his pocket, and showed it to the President. The President read it and declared that he could agree to it without difficulty. King insisted that he had been taught from childhood that papers involving money should be signed, upon which the President took the memorandum and scribbled on it: "Signed, Franklin and Mackenzie." (Ltr, Lewis Clark to author, 15 Oct 42.) For another version of the meeting, see Bruce Hutchinson, *The Incredible Canadian* (Toronto: Longmans, Green and Company, 1952), pp. 288–89.

[56] Dawson, *Canada in World Affairs: 1939–1941, passim.* See also James' full account of *Wartime Economic Co-operation.*

The dollar exchange objectives of the Hyde Park arrangement were easily achieved. Under the agreement, the United States proceeded to place production orders in Canada in the amounts necessary to cover the Canadian exchange needs. These orders allowed the growing Canadian demands for imports from the United States adequately to be met. The Canadian exchange situation was further improved by a provision of the Hyde Park Declaration that permitted Great Britain to obtain, under lend-lease procedures, component parts the Canadians had theretofore been purchasing in the United States for assembly into equipment being produced in Canada for Great Britain.

The arrangement served its intended purpose perfectly, and, by the end of 1942, new and unexpected sources were supplying U.S. dollar exchange well in excess of Canadian needs. A great expansion of exports, together with large U.S. capital expenditures in Canada, accounted for the unexpected accumulations. In fact, within two years the influx of U.S. dollars into Canada had become so great that it became necessary to put into effect an arrangement to control the size of Canadian holdings of U.S. dollars.[57]

The sale of Canadian-produced matériel to the United States was handled by a crown company, War Supplies, Limited, established on 13 May 1941 to negotiate and receive the U.S. orders expected under the Hyde Park Declaration and to place them in Canada. This company immediately undertook an intensive selling campaign in the War, Navy, and Treasury Departments, War Shipping Administration, Metals Reserve Corporation, and other U.S. agencies. In less than three months, contracts totaling approximately $200 million had been obtained. Initially, purchases were made of types of matériel suitable for transfer to the United Kingdom under the U.S. lend-lease program, but after Pearl Harbor large orders were placed for types of equipment used by the United States.[58]

By 31 March 1946 Canadian cash receipts from U.S. purchases of Canadian matériel under the program amounted to $1,118 million. In addition, over $100 million in orders had been canceled in 1943 as a means of reducing Canadian accumulations of U.S. dollars, and $200 million in contracts had been terminated after V-J Day. The most serious and most criticized

[57] See Ch. XII, below. The U.S. dollar expenditure goals of the Hyde Park Declaration were easily achieved. The volume of sales in each of the years from 1942 to 1944, inclusive, was respectively $275, $301, and $314 million. Canada, Foreign Exchange Control Board, *Report to the Minister of Finance, March 1946* (Ottawa: E. Cloutier, King's Printer, 1946), p. 26. F. A. Knox, in "Canada's Balance of International Payments, 1940–45," *Canadian Journal of Economics and Political Science,* XIII (August 1947), 345–62.

[58] This and the following paragraphs are based on Kennedy, *History of the Department of Munitions and Supply,* Ch. 42. For Canadian use of Lend-Lease Act procedures under this program, see James, *Wartime Economic Co-operation,* pp. 31–42.

TABLE 4—UNITED STATES LEND-LEASE AID: 11 MARCH 1941–31 DECEMBER 1955

(Thousands of U.S. dollars)

Total charged to foreign governments	$48,900,118
Not distributed by foreign governments	1,308,283
Gross lend-lease aid	[a] 50,208,401
Reverse lend-lease aid [b]	7,819,323
Net lend-lease aid	42,389,078
American Republics	493,026
Belgium	156,255
British Empire [c]	31,610,813
China	1,602,249
Czechoslovakia	435
Denmark	4,061
Egypt	2,323
Ethiopia	5,152
France	3,269,936
Greece	81,424
Iceland	4,497
Iran	5,304
Iraq	891
Italy	186,372
Liberia	19,423
Netherlands	246,369
Norway	47,023
Poland	12,452
Saudi Arabia	22,670
Turkey	42,850
USSR	11,054,404
Yugoslavia	32,189

[a] Of this total, $2,343,871,637 of aid was provided during the period 2 September 1945 through 31 December 1955.

[b] The principal contributions, in thousands of dollars, were Belgium $191,216, British Commonwealth $6,752,073, and France $867,781.

[c] This term is apparently intended to embrace those Commonwealth nations that were aid recipients. Canada was the notable exception.

Source: Twenty-seventh Report to Congress on Lend-Lease Operations (Washington: Government Printing Office, 1956).

aspect of the program was the repeated Canadian failure to meet delivery schedules. After the enactment of U.S. contract renegotiation legislation, Canada and the United States agreed on profits to be allowed under the U.S. contracts. United States contracts let to Canadian Government agencies provided for no profit, although amortization of government-owned facilities was allowed at a maximum rate of 25 percent annually. Contracts let to private corporations allowed a profit of 10 percent of cost.

The United States from its war production supplied arms to certain nations through the Lend-Lease Act of 11 March 1941, which provided the authority for ultimate delivery of a net of over $40 billion of munitions and services to countries throughout the world. *(Table 4)* Canada was a

TABLE 5—CANADIAN MUTUAL AID BOARD EXPENDITURES

(Thousands of Canadian dollars)

	Total	1943–44	1944–45	1945–46
Total expenditures	$2, 482, 438	$771, 978	$943, 543	$766, 917
Administrative costs	133	25	53	55
UNRRA administered by Canadian Mutual Aid Board	11, 093	0	11, 093	0
Total mutual aid [a]	2, 471, 212	771, 953	932, 397	766, 862
Australia	91, 325	20, 958	54, 460	15, 907
British West Indies	5, 518	874	3, 883	761
China	39, 742	3, 537	17, 403	18, 802
France	25, 105	0	17, 551	7, 554
Greece	12	0	0	12
India	14, 826	482	14, 431	*87 cr.*
New Zealand	15, 279	0	7, 826	7, 453
United Kingdom	2, 112, 150	722, 821	719, 239	670, 090
USSR	167, 255	23, 281	97, 604	46, 370

[a] These figures include supplies that were not delivered because of the cessation of hostilities and that were later declared surplus.

Source: Canadian Mutual Aid Board, *Final Report, 1946* (Ottawa: E. Cloutier, King's Printer, 1947), p. 9.

notable exception from the list of recipient countries. It felt that as a nation in a favored position, free from the ravages of war, it should meet its own needs and indeed share with the United States in aiding the less fortunate of the Allies.[59]

In line with this policy, Canada adopted a similar program of aid to the Allies. Throughout 1941 and part of 1942, Canadian help initially took the form of loans and other measures which provided the United Kingdom with Canadian exchange in the amount of $1,700 million needed to pay for the munitions the British were procuring from Canada. During 1942 Canada made an outright grant of one billion dollars to the United Kingdom, raising to a total of $2,700 million the Canadian exchange made available to the British. A stream of Canadian supplies, financed by these funds, flowed to the British Commonwealth nations and the USSR through the distribution machinery operated by the United Kingdom.

On 20 May 1943 the "War Appropriation (United Nations Mutual Aid) Act, 1943" was approved and became effective. Under the Mutual Aid Act, Canada proceeded to make arrangements directly with the ultimate recipients of Canadian aid and took the decisions as to what supplies would be provided the countries on the basis of their aid requests. Under the provisions

[59] PL 11, 77th Congress; *H. C. Debates*, 2 Apr 44, p. 2227.

TABLE 6—CANADA'S WAR PRODUCTION DURING THE MUTUAL AID PERIOD: 1 SEPTEMBER 1943–1 SEPTEMBER 1945

(Millions of Canadian dollars)

Major Item Group	Munitions Production		Mutual Aid as Percent of Total
	Total Canada	Mutual Aid Countries	
Total	$4,642	$2,636	[a] 57
Shipbuilding	788	303	38
Aircraft	578	342	59
Transportation equipment	1,124	843	75
Ordnance	272	217	80
Ammunition, chemicals, and explosives	721	574	80
Communications	364	173	47
General supplies	795	184	23

[a] Of this figure, 38 percent was financed by mutual aid, and 19 percent was purchased for cash by the United Kingdom. The remaining 43 percent was divided between Canada's own armed services (29 percent) and purchases by the United States (14 percent).

Source: Canadian Mutual Aid Board, *Final Report, 1946*, p. 16.

of this act and subsequent appropriations, Canada granted additional aid totaling $2,482 million (Canadian) to the Allies during World War II. *(Table 5)* Aid provided under the Canadian Mutual Aid Act differed from lend-lease aid in that, as a general rule, the former was not subject to arrangements for repayment or redelivery. Canada did retain title to the ships it provided. The bulk of U.S. lend-lease aid was also, under the final settlements, provided on a grant basis.[60]

Of particular interest is the fact that, during the period Canada was furnishing assistance under the Mutual Aid Act, only 29 percent of Canadian war production went to meet Canadian needs. As Table 6 indicates, 57 percent went to mutual aid countries; the remaining 14 percent was purchased by the United States. The relationship of the total aid expenditures of the two countries to the total military cost of World War II is also interesting. Canada's total war aid, including mutual aid and the billion-dollar grant to the United Kingdom, amounted to $3,482 million as compared with the estimated total military cost of World War II to Canada of $15,580 million. For the United States, the net lend-lease aid, excluding reverse lend-lease, amounted to $42,389 million, while the total military cost of World War II to the United States was estimated at $330,030 million. It is apparent that Canada like the United States made contributions to Allied victory generally proportionate to its national capabilities.

[60] For a complete account of Canadian aid arrangements, see Canadian Mutual Aid Board, *Final Report, 1946* (Ottawa: E. Cloutier, King's Printer, 1947).

CHAPTER XI

Problems in Jurisdiction

The deployment of large numbers of U.S. troops and associated civilians to Canada during World War II inevitably gave rise to many complex problems vis-à-vis Canadian authorities and the general public. The fact that the areas in which the U.S. personnel operated were never seriously threatened by hostile action added to the complexity of the problems. Had a real threat existed, it would probably have inspired a will to co-operate that would have caused many of the issues which arose to pale into insignificance. The U.S. forces stationed in Canada understandably considered themselves a cog, however remote from the combat zones, in the machine created to fight the enemy. Many Canadians, also understandably, took the view that, since the major combat zones were remote and hostilities were not taking place in Canada, the situation did not call for cessions of Canadian sovereignty or grants of limitless rights and privileges to the U.S. forces.

Canadian attitudes were conditioned by the history of relations with the United States. From 1776 to 1871 Canadians were threatened with annexation, particularly in two actual wars and two long periods of filibustering, and thereafter were promised this fate at intervals by many Americans in responsible positions. Throughout the history of Canadian-U.S. relations most Canadians, and especially French Canadians, have also feared and resisted cultural absorption by the United States. The Canadian Government therefore found it necessary, in considering its position on the various problems that came up for discussion with the United States during World War II, to weigh not only the military needs of the situation but also the force of public opinion, the desires of the provincial governments, and the impact on the position and strength of the Dominion Government itself. Under these circumstances it was a notable achievement that the numberless questions bearing on jurisdiction arising during the war years were all worked out in a manner acceptable to, if not to the full satisfaction of, both countries.

Jurisdiction Over Friendly Foreign Forces

Although the United States deployed troops to Newfoundland a year before the Pearl Harbor attack, it did not send U.S. forces into Canada in significant numbers until after that event. While Canada apparently never issued a clear-cut invitation for the entry of U.S. troops, such entry took place in execution of joint defense projects approved by the Canadian Government after approaches had been made through the Permanent Joint Board on Defense, or through diplomatic or service channels. Although Canadian permission may not have been explicitly stated in the correspondence relating to projects such as the Northwest Staging Route, the Alaska Highway, and the Canol Project, it was implicit in the broader authority granted in each instance. By April 1942 the need for an agreement on questions of jurisdiction over U.S. troops had been informally discussed within the Permanent Joint Board on Defense. Although the Legal Adviser of the Department of External Affairs had recommended such an agreement, the Board members did not feel that one was necessary and no action was taken.[1]

Clarification of the jurisdiction to be exercised by U.S. military authorities over their forces in Canada was accomplished by unilateral Canadian action. The Canadian Government had on 15 April 1941 issued an order-in-council, the Foreign Forces Order, 1941, which provided for limited exercise of jurisdiction in Canada by forces of certain designated countries and of such other countries as might later be designated.[2] On 26 June 1942 Canada issued another order-in-council, "as an interim measure," which made the provisions of the Foreign Forces Order, 1941, applicable to the United States. Before Canada took this step, U.S. service courts, according to the Canadian view, had no right to carry their sentences into effect in Canada. This order stated that U.S. service courts and authorities were empowered to exercise in Canada, in matters concerning discipline and internal administration, all such powers as were conferred by the laws of the United States, except for the offenses of murder, manslaughter, and rape. However, the order also stated that the Canadian civil courts retained concurrent jurisdiction of offenses committed by U.S. military personnel against any law in force in Canada.[3]

Even before this interim step was taken by Canada, the authorities of the two countries had discussed the nature of the U.S. wishes in the matter. The

---

[1] Ltr, Hickerson to LaGuardia, 22 Apr 42, PDB 104–22.

[2] Privy Council 2546.

[3] Privy Council 5484. For an account, from the point of view of international law, of the handling of jurisdictional questions between the United States and Canada and other states during World War II, see Archibald King, "Further Developments Concerning Jurisdiction Over Friendly Foreign Armed Forces," *American Journal of International Law,* XL (1946) 257–79. See also the following articles in the *British Year Book of International Law:* G. P. Barton, "Foreign Armed Forces: Immunity From Supervisory Jurisdiction," XXVI (1949), 380–414, and "Foreign Armed Forces: Immunity From Criminal Jurisdiction," XXVII (1950), 186–235; and M. E. Bathurst, "Jurisdiction Over Friendly Foreign Armed Forces," XXIII (1946), 338–41.

United States was then in the process of negotiating an agreement with the United Kingdom providing for the exclusive jurisdiction by each country over such of its forces as might be stationed in the other. United States authorities indicated that they would like a similar agreement with Canada, the making of which would have resulted in the abandonment of Canada's claim to exclusive jurisdiction of murder, manslaughter, and rape, and to concurrent jurisdiction of other offenses. For their part, the Canadian authorities in early July 1942 indicated a willingness to negotiate for a new agreement along these lines when the U.S.-United Kingdom agreement had been concluded.[4] A short time later the agreement with the United Kingdom was concluded by an exchange of notes dated 27 July 1942, and on 6 August the British Parliament enacted the United States of America (Visiting Forces) Act, 1942, to give effect to the agreement.[5]

During the ensuing months the Canadian Government considered a U.S. request that Canada, too, grant the United States complete criminal jurisdiction over its military personnel serving in Canada. By the beginning of 1943, Canada was contemplating rejecting the request. However, as a result of U.S. argument that Canada should be willing to conclude arrangements similar to those already effected with other nations in the British Commonwealth (Australia and New Zealand, as well as the United Kingdom), joint discussions looking toward an acceptable solution were initiated.[6] The Canadian Government moved cautiously toward satisfying the U.S. requests, for Canadian public opinion was slow to accept the notion of U.S. courts-martial sitting on Canadian soil, especially if the offense to be tried was one against the person or property of a Canadian. This gave the governments of some of the western provinces opportunity to embarrass the Dominion Government by attempting to exercise the concurrent jurisdiction claimed by Canada over U.S. soldiers.[7]

As a result of the discussions with the U.S. authorities, Canada took two steps toward meeting the U.S. requests:

a. It issued a new order-in-council excepting the United States from

---

[4] Ltr, Hickerson to SUSAM, 16 Jul 42, PDB 104-22.

[5] The notes are to be found in EAS, 355, and also as addenda to the Act, which is 5&6 Geo. 6, c. 31. For an account of the development of this agreement and for an examination thereof in terms of World War I and other World War II practice, see Archibald King, "Jurisdiction Over Friendly Foreign Armed Forces," *American Journal of International Law,* XXXVI (1942), 539-67.

[6] Memo/Conv, Hickerson and Pearson, 2 Feb 43, D/S 811.203/252.

[7] For example, in the case of Pvt. William Evans, which aroused public indignation in Dawson Creek, the Attorney General of British Columbia issued a warrant for the arrest of Evans, but his commanding officer refused to surrender him. (Memo/Conv, Hickerson and Clark, 13 Feb 43, PDB 104-22.)

the provision of the Foreign Forces Order that reserved to Canada jurisdiction over the offenses of murder, manslaughter, and rape.[8]

b. It sought an advisory opinion from the Supreme Court of Canada on two questions that looked toward a more liberal attitude on the part of Canada:

> 1. Are members of the military or naval forces of the United States of America who are present in Canada with the consent of the Government of Canada for purposes of military operations in connection with or related to the state of war now existing exempt from criminal proceedings prosecuted in Canadian criminal courts and, if so, to what extent and in what circumstances?
>
> 2. If the answer to the first question is to the effect that the members of the forces of the United States of America are not exempt from criminal proceedings or are only in certain circumstances or to a certain extent exempt, had Parliament or the Governor General in Council acting under the War Measures Act, jurisdiction to enact legislation similar to the statute of the United Kingdom entitled the United States of America (Visiting Forces) Act, 1942.[9]

The Attorney General of Canada filed a factum (brief) urging that both questions be answered in the affirmative. Since the court action was a domestic Canadian matter, the United States could not participate as a party of interest. However, at the request of the Canadian Government, the U.S. officers concerned prepared two unsigned memorandums which examined, from the U.S. point of view, the principles of law involved. These memorandums were printed and laid before the court, as were briefs by four of the nine provinces (Quebec, Ontario, Alberta, and British Columbia) that opposed grants of broader jurisdiction to the United States.[10]

On 3 August 1943 the five justices who considered the case presented four separate opinions, none of which represented that of the court. Concerning the first question, two justices, Kerwin and Taschereau, reached conclusions generally in accord with the U.S. view. The opinion of Chief Justice Duff, concurred in by Justice Hudson, concluded that unless specific legislation so provided, friendly forces visiting Canada enjoyed no exemption from criminal court jurisdiction. The other justice, Rand, took a middle position.[11] As to the second question, all the justices agreed that both the Parliament and the Governor General in Council, acting under the War

[8] Privy Council 2813, 6 Apr 43.

[9] The reference to the Supreme Court was made by Privy Council 2931, 9 Apr 43.

[10] The factum and an accompanying case book by the federal Attorney General of Canada were published by E. Cloutier, King's Printer, Ottawa, in 1943 under the title "Jurisdiction of Canadian Criminal Courts Over Members of the Armed Forces of the United States." Memo/Conv, Clark and R. T. Yingling, 24 Apr 43, D/S 811.203/246-5/6.

[11] The opinions are contained in *Reference re Exemption of U.S. Forces From Canadian Criminal Law* (1943), Canadian S.C.R. 483. For a synthesis of these opinions, see King, "Further Developments Concerning Jurisdiction Over Friendly Foreign Armed Forces," pp. 272-74.

Measures Act, had the authority to enact legislation similar to the United States of America (Visiting Forces) Act, 1942, enacted in the United Kingdom.

These court opinions established both an adequate juridical basis and a suitable political framework in Canada for the next step. In December 1943, in response to repeated U.S. inquiries as to when the action might be forthcoming, the Governor General in Council issued an order which provided that the service courts of the United States would have "jurisdiction to try all members of its forces in Canada in respect of every offense committed by any of its members in Canada." This order met in full the requirements for which the U.S. authorities had been negotiating. The order also authorized various administrative measures, such as the compulsory attendance of Canadian witnesses before U.S. courts-martial in Canada, and the release, upon request, of a member of the U.S. forces detained by any Canadian authority.[12]

Certain points not fully clarified by the order-in-council were discussed in notes exchanged during the ensuing months. In the first of these notes, the Canadian Government stated its assumption that any persons surrendered to the United States by Canadian authorities would be tried. The United States in reply took the position that such persons would be brought to trial only if investigation warranted. However, in the event of a negative finding, the United States agreed to confer with Canadian authorities and to proceed with a trial if they considered one necessary. Other similar questions were harmoniously and satisfactorily worked out.[13]

To the full extent permitted by its system of government, the United States granted to Canada the privileges the Dominion had conferred upon the United States. The United States considered the basic privileges already to be available to Canada without agreement or legislative or other action, since Canadian forces, in the U.S. view, possessed such privileges under international law, which was deemed to be a part of the law of the United States. Apart from the basic privileges of exclusion from the local criminal jurisdiction, certain auxiliary arrangements necessitated enactment of legislation by the Congress. In order to carry out its undertakings to Canada and other governments, the executive branch sought and obtained such legislation. An act of Congress approved on 30 June 1944 provided that, upon

---

[12] Ott Leg Desp 103, to Secy State, 4 Sep 43, D/S 811.203/324; Ltr, Atherton to Hickerson, 5 Oct 43, D/S 811.203/341; Department of State Desp 95, to Ott Leg, 25 Oct 43, D/S 811.203/341; Privy Council 9694, 20 Dec 43.

[13] Department of External Affairs Notes 160 and 26, 27 Dec 43 and 9 Mar 44; U.S. Emb Ott Note 95, 10 Feb 44; all in D/S 811.203/392.

suitable proclamation by the President, arrangements as follows could be effected with designated countries:

a. Arrest and delivery of persons of a foreign force upon request of the commanding officer of that force.

b. Compulsory attendance at courts-martial of friendly forces subject to their having the same privileges and immunities as if before a similar U.S. court.

c. Confinement of prisoners sentenced by a foreign court in a U.S. place of detention.[14]

On 11 October 1944 the President of the United States by proclamation made the provisions of the act of Congress applicable to Canada and the United Kingdom.[15]

On the whole, the arrangements worked very satisfactorily. In Canada, isolated incidents involving Canadian civilians took place in which the Canadian public expressed concern as to the adequacy of the punitive action taken by the U.S. service courts, but such incidents were lost in the over-all pattern of co-operation in handling these problems. In the United States, where the proportion of Canadian service personnel was negligible in comparison to U.S. service personnel in Canada, no problem of any significance arose regarding jurisdiction over criminal offenses.

Airway Traffic Control

As the scope of U.S. activities and the network of U.S. installations in Canada and Newfoundland expanded both before and after Pearl Harbor, and as the volume of U.S. military air traffic in those areas increased, questions quickly arose as to the control of air traffic and airways. In all areas there existed the basic need for co-ordinating the systems employed by the services of the two countries for the regulation of their traffic. There also existed within Canada the fundamental question of sovereignty involving the extent, if any, to which control should be yielded to another government or its agencies over Canadian airways and aircraft movements in the Canadian airspace.

The problem first arose in the latter part of 1941 in Newfoundland, where not only U.S. and Canadian service aircraft but also those of the Royal Air Force operated in connection with Atlantic ferrying operations. By December 1941 the U.S. Newfoundland base commander, Maj. Gen. Gerald C. Brant, had worked out standardized regulations for air traffic control ap-

[14] PL 384, 78th Congress.
[15] Proclamation 2626, 8 FR 12403.

plicable to U.S. Army Air Forces and U.S. Navy aircraft operating in Newfoundland. During December he also submitted proposed regulations to control all aircraft movements in the Newfoundland area.[16] During 1942 the proposal was discussed and reworked by Canadian and U.S. authorities. The RCAF desired to include in the proposed agreement a provision requiring that all aircraft movements be cleared from a central RCAF control station. According to the U.S. base commander, such an arrangement was unacceptable, not only to U.S. Army and Navy units but also to the RAF command in Newfoundland. A protracted controversy took place between the Canadian and U.S. Air commanders concerned, who were unable to agree on standardized regulations. Members of the Permanent Joint Board on Defense discussed the subject briefly in September 1942 and again at their meeting in November. As a result of the latter discussion, an informal meeting of representatives of the two countries took place in Washington on 12 January 1943, but no significant progress materialized from any of these discussions and the problem of co-ordinating airway traffic in Newfoundland and Labrador went, for the time being, unsolved. As a consequence, the air units of each country continued to use their own procedures.[17]

The problems of co-ordinating or controlling airway traffic and of standardizing communications and other procedures in western Canada were examined by the military commands there in early 1943. As a result of U.S.-Canadian service-level discussions at a meeting on 8 January 1943, a joint agreement was concluded for the purpose of establishing "procedures, methods and communications to be used jointly to provide the best exchange of information" on all flights in the area and thus to reduce the number of unidentified aircraft in the air defense zones of western Canada and the adjacent United States.[18]

The procedures governing the movement of aircraft to and from Alaska were re-examined and revised at frequent intervals. At scheduled meetings, the next two of which were held on 15 April and 23 June 1943, representatives of the numerous Canadian and U.S. military commands conducting air operations met and agreed on the revised techniques and procedures to be employed. At the second of these two meetings, at which the agreement acquired the title JAN-CAN (for Joint U.S. Army, Navy-Canadian Agree-

[16] Ltr, CG NBC to CG Eastern Theater of Operations, 23 Feb 42, PDB 104-5.

[17] Memo, E. W. Hockenberry for SUSAM, 11 Mar 43, PDB 126-6.

[18] Appendixes, to Alaskan Division, Historical Record Report, Nov 42-Dec 43 volume, p. 325. The agreement, essentially one for co-ordination and standardization, was effected between representatives of RCAF Western Air Command; Alaskan Wing, ATC; Western Defense Command; and Northwest Sea Frontier. The RCAF had taken over the airway traffic control functions on this route from the Department of Transport in September 1942.

ment), the commands represented were the Western Air Command, RCAF, and six U.S. commands—Western Defense Command, U.S. Army; Alaskan Wing, Air Transport Command, U.S. AAF; Northwest Sea Frontier, U.S. Navy; Naval Air Transport Squadrons, West Coast; Alaska Defense Command; and Fourth Air Force.[19] Similar meetings took place during the rest of 1943, and at the meeting held on 11 November a permanent JAN-CAN Committee, comprising a representative of each of the commanders signatory to the agreement, was established. The RCAF provided a nonvoting secretary for the committee, while the U.S. Navy Northwest Sea Frontier provided office space and administrative assistance.

While the foregoing arrangements were being worked out, the postwar planners of both countries had apparently begun to look at the relationship of the numerous new air bases in northern North America to possible postwar civil air transport operations. This relationship and the wartime impetus given to transport aviation, particularly intercontinental operations, presaged an important Canadian role in international civil aviation. For one thing, the great circle air routes from the United States to northern Europe and to the Orient passed over Canadian territory. For another, bases such as those at Gander in Newfoundland and Goose Bay in Labrador promised to be important stations in the network of postwar civil airports for transoceanic operations. Interest in postwar civil aviation was quickened on the southern side of the boundary, too, where statements and press comment on the subject gave rise to suspicions in Canada that the United States perhaps intended to utilize its wartime position in Canada to its own advantage in the field of civil air transport. The United States, in turn, wondered if Canada was not thinking of gaining a postwar advantage through the Canadian air bases and operations in Newfoundland.[20] In any event, the statement of Prime Minister King in Parliament on 2 April 1943 on the civil aviation policy of the Canadian Government acknowledged publicly the

[19] Progress Rpts, at PJBD meetings of 1–2 Apr and 1–14 Jul, PDB 124.

[20] U.S. Leg Ott Telg 28, 17 May 43, D/S 842.00/690; Memo, Parsons to Hickerson, 5 Apr 43, D/S 840.50/2092; Journal PJBD meeting, 13 Jan 44, PDB 124. See also the exchange of correspondence that took place in October 1943 when the State Department first learned of the Canada-Newfoundland negotiations, which had been in progress about two years, for a ninety-nine-year lease to Canada of Goose Bay air base. (D/S 842.7962/111.) The first comprehensive study on the role of air transportation as a force in national policy had been published only a few months earlier and was indicative of, and perhaps even contributed to, the quickening interest in the subject. See Oliver J. Lissitzyn, *International Air Transport and National Policy* (New York: Council on Foreign Relations, 1942). The Canadian Government had by the end of 1942 set up an interdepartmental advisory committee on international air transport. The United States set up a similar body in January 1943, and some exploratory talks took place subsequently between the two groups.

360-477 O - 70 - 21

decision of Canada to act to take full advantage of Canada's strategic location and to seek a leading place in postwar civil aviation.

The completion of the Alaska Highway and the Canol Project provided the breathing spell that enabled Canada to clarify the question of control of the northern airports and airways constructed and used in collaboration with the United States.[21] Canada had as its objectives (a) to regain full control over the airways and air traffic on them, (b) to establish controls over operations of U.S. civial airlines providing military transport services under contract to the U.S. Army, and (c) to establish adequate controls over the air bases themselves.[22] The initial attack on the problem took the form of raising from the service level to the governmental level discussions on the question of co-ordinating air traffic.

The joint U.S.-Canadian policy was provided by the Thirty-second Recommendation of the Permanent Joint Board on Defense agreed upon at its 24–25 August 1943 meeting. This recommendation, which was approved by the two governments within a month, provided for the allocation of control, as between the two countries, of the wartime air bases of joint interest in Canada and of the airway traffic through them. Canada was assigned control of air traffic through all the airports in northwestern Canada except for the flight strips of the Alaska Highway and Canol Project, which promised to be of little significance to postwar civil aviation except as emergency fields. In the east, Canada yielded control of the more northern of the ferry route bases in Canada, most of which also promised to have no significant place in postwar civil aviation. The air bases of Newfoundland and Labrador were not covered by the recommendation.[23] The recommendation in addition provided that any airway traffic regulations issued should be prepared jointly by the using services.

A joint U.S.-Canadian committee first met in Ottawa on 19 August 1943 to consider the problems emerging from the Thirty-first Recommendation and the Thirty-second then under consideration in draft form. This main committee met again at Ottawa on three subsequent occasions, in December 1943 and in April and October 1944, to work out in detail the many questions that arose in implementing these two recommendations.

A Joint Subcommittee for Canadian Air Traffic Regulations, constituted

---

[21] *H. C. Debates*, 2 Apr 43, pp. 1776–78; *The Canada Year Book, 1945*, p. 703.

[22] Associated objectives of the Canadian program included the execution of all construction on the more important bases by the Canadian Government, and the acquisition of title or the leases to land occupied by official U.S. agencies and installations. They are treated above in Chapter VIII. See also Alaskan Division, Historical Record Report, Nov 42–Dec 43 volume, pp. 214–17.

[23] Appendix A, below.

by the main committee, met in Washington on 23 September 1943. It prepared recommendations as to air traffic regulation in Canada, which were reviewed and approved by the U.S. agencies concerned. The recommendations were then promulgated by Canada in November 1943 in RCAF publication CAP 365, entitled "RCAF Regulations for Control of Aircraft Movement in Canada." CAP 365 was "intended to provide standard regulations for the movement and flight of aircraft on routes and airways through the Royal Canadian Air Force operational areas in the Dominion of Canada, Newfoundland and Labrador, for the purpose of defense. All aircraft which . . . received right of entry to any of the concerned countries . . . [were to] be subject to and governed by these rules and regulations." The regulations were made applicable on the Northwest Staging Route, in Newfoundland and Labrador, and in eastern Canada east of a line twenty-five miles west of Blissville, New Brunswick, and north of a line twenty-five miles north of Quebec City.[24] The over-all flying control plan included (a) airway traffic control on designated airways, (b) route traffic control on certain other RCAF routes, (c) airport traffic control at all airports, and (d) general supervision of all flying in the operational areas to permit integration of the complete traffic pattern.[25]

Canada proceeded to establish the organization required to exercise the airway traffic control envisaged in CAP 365. In western Canada, the JAN-CAN Agreement and Committee were dissolved as of 29 February 1944. To discharge the airway traffic control responsibility on the Northwest Staging Route, a new RCAF command, the Northwest Air Command, was established on 1 June 1944 at Edmonton under Air Vice Marshal T. A. Lawrence. During 1944 thirty-six RCAF officers undertook a course of training at the U.S. Civil Aeronautics Administration School of Airway Traffic Control. As matériel and trained personnel became available, airway traffic control centers were established at Halifax, Vancouver, Edmonton, Prince George, and St. John's.

On the Northwest Staging Route, the inauguration of airway traffic control operations by the RCAF was delayed by the shortage of land-line communication facilities. The AAF had made a through teletype circuit between Edmonton and Whitehorse available to the RCAF, but the circuit was unsuitable for this purpose. The U.S. Army agencies in northwest Canada felt unable, in the light of their own communications requirements, to release

[24] Privy Council 9792, 24 December 1943, declared those portions of Canada through which the Northwest Staging Route passed to be a prohibited area, under the Defense Air Regulations, 1942, thus subjecting them to military control.

[25] Minutes, 15–16 Dec 43 PJBD meeting, PDB 126–10; CAP 365, PDB 126–10.

additional facilities to the RCAF. As a result of discussions of ways and means of meeting the RCAF needs, the U.S. Army at the beginning of 1944 undertook a $2-million project for the installation of the additional voice and teletype circuits and construction of the additional facilities needed by the RCAF. Although construction of these additional facilities which the RCAF had been urging for many months was to be financed as a War Department project, the Morgenthau-Ilsley discussions concurrently in progress provided that Canada would reimburse the United States for the entire landline project, as well as for other construction in Canada.[26]

By midsummer 1944 the installation of the wire circuits was well advanced, but difficulties in procuring certain of the essential signal equipment had been encountered. Despite the best efforts of Canadian and U.S. signal officers, the equipment had not yet been secured by the spring of 1945. Although the RCAF was able to establish full airway traffic controls south and west of Edmonton and along the so-called Interior Staging Route in British Columbia, and partial controls on the Northwest Staging Route, full controls on the latter route were not established after the terminations of hostilities.[27]

Similar equipment deficiencies were encountered for airway traffic control at Gander and Goose Bay air bases. Upon the assumption by the RCAF of airway traffic control in Newfoundland, the AAF proceeded to remove its control tower equipment from the two bases. Since Canada was unable to duplicate the equipment, it requested that the United States sell the equipment to Canada. The removal order was then canceled.[28]

Despite the difficulties encountered in the actual inauguration of control operations Canada succeeded, through the Thirty-second Recommendation and subsequent efforts, in establishing the principle of Canadian control of airway traffic. As hostilities terminated and the U.S. intention to withdraw from Canada as rapidly as possible became fully apparent, the Canadian fears that had been aroused concerning U.S. intentions were completely allayed.

Military Air Services

An early by-product of the Ogdensburg Declaration was the simplification of procedures governing the travel of public vessels and service aircraft of the two countries. An initial agreement, arranged by an exchange of notes in September 1940, gave blanket authority for U.S. service aircraft to fly over Canadian territory and waters between the United States and Alaska

[26] See below, pp. 320–25.
[27] Memo, SUSAM for CG AAF, 20 Sep 44, PDB 105–16.
[28] Journal, 7–8 Nov 44 PJBD meeting, PDB 124.

upon prior notification in each instance to the RCAF Western Air Command and subject to the requirement to avoid prohibited areas. More extensive arrangements worked out in December 1940 provided, upon local notification, for (a) passage by U.S. public vessels through Canadian waters between the United States and Alaska or U.S. bases in Newfoundland and by service aircraft over Canadian territory, (b) exchange visits on joint defense matters, (c) Canadian flights over Maine on the Quebec-Maritime Provinces route in connection with joint defense matters, and (d) U.S. flights between points in the United States over the Ontario peninsula.[29]

The arrangements for local notification were worked out in detail over the succeeding eight months and provided authority adequate for the need for travel of military aircraft between the two countries throughout 1941 and for the first few months after Pearl Harbor. Commercial operations by civilian airlines were covered by a separate agreement that defined the routes over which duly licensed airlines of each country could operate.[30]

By the end of February 1942 a new element had been introduced into the problem of travel by military aircraft. The AAF had for some time planned to use commercial airline aircraft on a contract or charter basis to meet military requirements.[31] Not long after Pearl Harbor, the Canadian Government granted authority for such contract service by Northeast Airlines to the U.S. garrisons in Newfoundland and at Goose Bay. The AAF needed a similar service on the Northwest Staging Route and proceeded on 20 February 1942 to make contract arrangements with Northwest Airlines for the desired military transport services. The U.S. Section of the Permanent Joint Board, at the request of the AAF sought authority at the 25–26 February meeting for an arrangement under which "traffic would be strictly limited to United States Government personnel directly connected with the prosecution of the war" and to military cargoes, and would exclude transportation of commercial passengers or cargo for hire. The Canadian Section undertook to process the request and stated that a favorable reply would probably be received from the Department of Transport.[32]

Before a reply was received from the Canadian authorities, a Northwest Airlines survey aircraft, presumably acting upon instructions, landed at Ed-

[29] Memo, Berle for Christie, 18 Sep 40, and Reply, 19 Sep 40, D/S 811.2342/732 and /738. The exchange of diplomatic notes on 16 December 1940 is in PDB 126–10.

[30] EAS, 186; CTS, 1940, No. 13.

[31] For an excellent account of such operations during World War II, see Cleveland, *Air Transport at War*.

[32] Journal, PDB 124; Memo, Brig Gen Olds for SUSAM, 23 Feb 42, PDB 126; Carr, Great Falls to Nome: The Inland Air Route to Alaska, 1940–1945, p. 26, cites War Department contract No. DA W535ac1763, dated 20 February 1942 and approved 27 February 1942.

monton on 27 February without authority and without undergoing customs processing. The aircraft was detained by the Canadian authorities while the question was examined by Brig. Gen. Robert Olds, commanding the Air Corps Ferrying Command, with Minister of Munitions and Supply C. D. Howe, who chanced to be in Washington. On 2 March the latter orally granted authority for the projected Northwest Airlines operations, and the survey aircraft, which had returned to Minneapolis on 1 March, proceeded to make its survey flight. A few days later Howe in a letter dated 7 March confirmed the grant of authority for use of all airfields and facilities of the Department of Transport by both military aircraft and civilian contract carriers, stating that it was his understanding in regard to the contract carriers that the United States would, "as soon as possible, either enlist the pilots in the Air Corps or replace them by Air Corps personnel." [33]

Northwest Airlines completed its survey flights in March and initiated operations the same month. By mid-May company personnel in Canada and Alaska numbered eighty-eight, mostly located at Edmonton. Until the end of May, the operations were of little consequence and about half the 410 tons of cargo carried (in addition to 889 passengers) comprised Northwest Airlines supplies and equipment. During April two more civilian contract carriers initiated operations for the AAF—Western Airlines from the United States to Edmonton, and United Airlines from the United States through Edmonton to Fairbanks.[34]

The unauthorized Northwest Airlines landing on 27 February had a permanent and unhappy effect on Canadian-U.S. relations locally, and events of the following months produced no improvement. Northwest Airlines employees apparently deliberately emphasized and flaunted the civilian complexion of their operations. Personnel, aircraft, and facilities bore company identifications, and the employees identified their work as a company rather than U.S. Army task. During this period the company operated virtually autonomously and with no local supervision, since the AAF began the gradual introduction of cadres for its organization in Canada only in the latter half of 1942.[35]

The situation displeased Canadians, who saw the Northwest Airlines

[33] The letter to General Olds is in PDB 126. Howe's account of the Edmonton episode is to be found in *H. C. Debates*, 15 May 42, p. 2486. His letter was thereafter cited as the basic authority for U.S. military air operations in Canada.

[34] Carr, Great Falls to Nome: The Inland Air Route to Alaska, 1940–1945, pp. 30–36.

[35] These paragraphs are based on the Carr manuscript and on Alaskan Division: Historical Record Report, II. The president of Northwest Airlines believed that the United States should get its airlines firmly established in Canada and apparently conducted his own company operations with this objective. (Memo/Conv, Moffat and C. Hunter, 14 Dec 42, D/S 811.79642/291.)

actions as designed to create and advertise a privileged position that could be exploited after the war in commercial operations. Misunderstandings developed over the carrying out of agreements for the exchange of meteorological data between the Department of Transport and U.S. Army agencies at the air bases. Reports that Northwest Airlines was carrying passengers for hire were circulated and did not improve the atmosphere.

Finally, at an AAF-RCAF meeting in Ottawa on 25 June 1942, the conferees heard Canadian protests. The Canadians had understood, at similar meetings in Ottawa in March and April as well as in the Howe-Olds exchange, that the AAF had agreed to militarize the civilian contract carriers and to assume ownership of their aircraft.[36] The AAF officers acknowledged this to be so and promised efforts to carry out the Canadian wishes, including the full militarization of the communications and weather personnel.

The AAF took appropriate steps immediately thereafter. It instructed Northwest Airlines to replace its own markings and insignia with those of the Air Transport Command. Personnel were to wear the same uniform as U.S. Army personnel. Army Air Forces personnel were gradually introduced with a view to taking over the communications and weather functions of Northwest Airlines. The change-over to military communications and weather personnel moved slowly and in the face of opposition from Northwest Airlines employees, who resisted relinquishing their jobs. At the beginning of 1943 the transfer was finally effected. A short time earlier the establishment of a Headquarters, Alaskan Wing, Air Transport Command, effective 1 November 1942, had projected military control into the scene of operations over the Northwest Staging Route.

The Canadian Government still remained dissatisfied with the character of the Northwest Airlines operations. In early 1943 Canada claimed that the company was not only continuing to employ its title and conduct its operations as if independent of the AAF, but it was also carrying passengers for hire. To support the last charge, the Canadian Government formally transmitted evidence indicating that the Northwest Airlines had carried personnel for hire and reiterated other grievances.[37]

The Canadian complaints were thoroughly investigated and a comprehensive report was forwarded to Ottawa on 30 March. The report concluded that, although the general Canadian complaints might have been true sev-

---

[36] Extracts of Canadian reports of the meetings are quoted in Memo, SUSAM for CG ATC, 17 Mar 43, and in Ltr, from Hickerson, 27 Mar 43, both in PDB 110-8.

[37] Memo, SUSAM for CG ATC, 17 Mar 43, PDB 110-8. On the other hand, the AAF must have had some degree of success, for the president of Northwest Airlines expressed himself as unhappy about the status of his company and desirous of regaining his company's identity in its operations in Canada. (Memo/Conv, Moffat and Hunter, 14 Dec 42, D/S 811.79642/291.)

eral months earlier, the corrective action pressed continuously by the U.S. Army had eliminated most of the grievances such as the use of airline markings. Although not all the aircraft had become U.S. Government property, most of them had and the others were indistinguishable. Not all the personnel had been militarized, but the civilian employees wore uniforms rendering them almost indistinguishable from military personnel. The Air Transport Command explained the circumstances of the transport-for-hire charges and gave assurances of its earnest desire to extract full compliance from its contract carriers with their instructions in these matters.[38]

Another aspect of the operations of U.S. military air services in Canada that troubled the Canadian Government was their Topsy-like growth. The Northeast and Northwest Airlines contracts had been followed by additional separate grants of approval for similar operations by several other U.S. companies in eastern and northwestern Canada. In addition, the AAF was itself operating military air transport aircraft over a number of routes, some of which had been specifically authorized, others of which had not. During March 1943, as part of its broader program to reassert full Canadian control over air operations and air installations in Canada, the Canadian and U.S. Governments initiated a re-examination of the civilian air transport contract service operations of the AAF. After reviewing its continued dissatisfaction with the character of the operations, the Canadian Government pointed out that some of the operations appeared to have no authority except possibly the December 1940 exchange of notes or the Twenty-second Recommendation of the Permanent Joint Board, both of which appeared to cover only occasional or emergency flights.[39] Canada accordingly proposed to re-establish the authority for all U.S. military transport services in a single over-all agreement to replace the existing piecemeal agreements. Where no specific authority existed, the Canadian Government felt that authorization should first be applied for by and granted to the United States, as a preliminary step to being placed within the framework of the new over-all agreement. The proposal contemplated that the conditions under which the civilian contract services would henceforth be provided could be set forth and made public, thus eliminating misunderstandings which might exist in Canada. An important objective of the proposal was to prevent the U.S. commercial airlines from appearing to have a vested interest in routes that would have postwar commercial significance.[40]

[38] Memo, SUSAM for Cdn PJBD Secretary, 30 Mar 43, PDB 110-8. This memorandum replied to a note from the Canadian secretary, acting in his capacity as Under Secretary of State for External Affairs, to the U.S. Chargé d'Affaires, in Ottawa through the diplomatic channel.

[39] Memo, Under Secy State for External Affairs for U.S. Chargé d'Affaires, 16 Mar 43, PDB 126-10.

[40] Memo, Hickerson for SUSAM, 26 May 43, PDB 126-10.

The proposed over-all agreement, to be effective for the duration of the war, would provide (a) that service aircraft of one country could use the airway facilities of the second on a reciprocal basis for traffic limited as follows: There would be no traffic for hire; goods were to be owned by an Allied government; only diplomatic mail would be carried except in cases where other mail was for delivery outside the second country; and only armed services and other governmental officials and Allied personnel traveling in connection with the war effort would be transported. It also provided (b) that authority would first have to be obtained by appropriate U.S. officials for service aircraft to use routes other than those then in effect, and (c) that commercial aircraft operated on behalf of one country could use airway facilities of the second on a reciprocal basis on routes already approved. Traffic was to be limited as for (a). In addition, commercial aircraft operations were to be replaced within six months by service aircraft operations employing service personnel.[41] The Newfoundland Government, upon Canadian inquiry, stated that it had no objection to inclusion of airway facilities operated by Canada or the United States in Newfoundland territory within the scope of the agreement.[42]

After the War Department had studied a preliminary draft of the Canadian proposal, it prepared a counterproposal for submission to the Canadian Section of the Permanent Joint Board on the occasion of the 6–7 May 1943 meeting. United States diplomatic officials during conversations with their Canadian colleagues had meanwhile obtained the impression that Canada had decided not to press for the agreement inasmuch as the proposal had probably already served its purpose in getting the United States to curb the objectionable commercial airline practices. The U.S. counterproposal was not presented and the matter was not discussed at the Permanent Joint Board meeting.[43]

At the beginning of June Canadian authorities inquired concerning a reply to the Canadian proposal. Three months later Canadian officials again queried the U.S. Section and expressed a hope for an early reply. In the interim, additional Northwest Airlines practices of a kind inconsistent with the intent of the proposed agreement had been reported.[44]

Upon receipt of the June inquiry, State, War, and Navy Department officers had conferred at the working level and had prepared a revised version of the counterproposal drafted earlier. United States reconsideration of

[41] Memo cited above, n. 39.

[42] Ltr, Keenleyside to Chargé d'Affaires Clark, 17 Apr 43, PDB 126–10.

[43] Unused Memo, SUSAM for Keenleyside, 5 May 43; Memo, Hickerson for SUSAM, 12 May 43, both in PDB 126–10.

[44] Memo, Hickerson for SUSAM, 20 Sep 43; Memo, SUSAM for CG ATC, 2 Aug 43, both in PDB 126–10; Ltr, Clark to Hickerson, 4 Jun 43, D/S 811.79642/6–443.

the Canadian proposal moved at a leisurely pace, and the counterproposal, forwarded to the Department of State on 1 October, was further considered there until late November 1943 but was not changed.[45] The counterproposal, finally forwarded to Ottawa on 24 November 1943 for submission to the Department of External Affairs, was an extensive revision of the Canadian proposal, incorporating changes that met the substantive U.S. objections by (a) eliminating the requirement for militarization of commercial contract aircraft as undesirable, and substituting controls designed to meet the Canadian objections, and (b) broadening the categories of traffic to be carried to include, for example, mail for U.S. troops.[46]

Canada undertook a protracted study of the counterproposal. On 17 March 1944 it presented a new draft to the U.S. Embassy at Ottawa. In the main, the suggested changes represented a tightening and clarification of the provisions of the U.S. draft. The major change was the broadening of the definition of U.S. territory to include Hawaii as well as the United States proper and Alaska, looking to the time when the shifting of aircraft to the Pacific after V-E Day might "raise practical problems concerning military air routes across the Pacific."[47]

The United States continued to study this latest draft until early August 1944, when a new aspect of the problem arose. Transoceanic aircraft of the Air Transport Command had begun carrying, on a fill-up basis, fare-paying passengers traveling in connection with the war effort. The U.S. authorities felt that this practice of selling fill-up spaces should be authorized by the agreement, since it was a practice of the British Overseas Airways Company, a crown company operating over the same transatlantic route, and since they considered an intermediate country (Canada) should not dictate terminus to terminus traffic policy. Because Canada opposed such a provision, in late September the United States was prepared to accept a text omitting it.[48]

But before final agreement on the text was reached, the issue was again raised when President Roosevelt signed Executive Order 9492 on 25 October 1944. By this order the President authorized the Air Transport Command to carry passengers for hire under certain conditions. Since it was necessary to take cognizance of this action in the proposed Canadian-U.S. agreement,

[45] Memo, SUSAM for Hickerson, 1 Oct 43; Department of State Desp 123, to U.S. Emb Ott, 18 Nov 43, both in PDB 126-10.

[46] Department of State Desp 123, to U.S. Emb Ott, 18 Nov 43, PDB 126-10.

[47] Department of External Affairs Memo, 17 Mar 44, PDB 126-10.

[48] Memos, Parsons for Berle, 3 and 21 Aug 44, D/S 811.79642/8-344, and /8-2144; Department of State Desp, to U.S. Emb Ott, 26 Sep 44, D/S 811.79642/9-2644.

and Canada considered the carrying of passengers for hire illegal and in violation of Canadian law and treaty provisions, discussions on the problem continued on into January 1945. Finally, at a meeting in New York City in late January, an article in the proposed agreement was redrafted to permit traffic for hire through, but not into or away from, Canada, in connection with Air Transport Command transatlantic operations. With this last point of disagreement resolved, the exchange of notes was effected at Ottawa on 13 February 1945.[49]

When the agreement was made, it included a confidential attachment that listed in detail the routes being operated by each country (a) through use of commercial carriers under military contract, and (b) by its armed forces. Canada operated no route under (a), and only one under (b), the route originally authorized under the 12 December 1940 agreement. The United States was authorized thirteen routes in the first category and seventeen in the second.[50]

Contrary to the originally stated Canadian intention to publish the agreement, it was not made public. Instead, an official press release was issued on 19 February 1945, announcing the substance of the agreement. Actually, the negotiations themselves, lasting over almost two years, had produced the required corrective action on the part of the U.S. authorities so that the Canadian objectives were largely achieved long before complete agreement was reached.[51]

Maintenance and Control of Bases

The establishment of a U.S. Army air garrison at Newfoundland (Gander) Airport in May 1941 using housing and other facilities provided by Canada gave rise to problems that were rapidly to become more numerous and complex as the scale of U.S. activities in Newfoundland and Canada enlarged. The division of responsibility for maintaining and servicing, as well as for operating and defending, the facilities in which there was a joint U.S.-Canadian interest was the subject of negotiations lasting into 1944.

To meet the initial situation, the Permanent Joint Board on Defense on 10 November 1941 adopted the Twenty-first Recommendation, which was promptly approved by both governments. Under it the forces of one country occupying buildings provided by the other were charged with maintaining

---

[49] Memo, from Parsons, 18 Jan 45, D/S 811.79642/1–1845. The agreement is TIAS, 2056; CTS, 1945, No. 1.

[50] TIAS, 2056; CTS, 1945, No. 1.

[51] Department of State *Bulletin*, February 25, 1945, XII, 307. In 1950, when the attachment listing the authorized routes was no longer considered confidential, the text of the agreement was published.

them, as well as the appurtenant buildings within the assigned area, where it was feasible to delineate such an area. Utilities and services were to be provided by the host government on an equitable basis. Where a separate area was assigned and lent itself to the use of an independent system of services and facilities, they could be provided by the occupying forces. The arrangement was to be applicable reciprocally in both countries.[52]

At Gander Airport a separate U.S. area was not delimited. Before long the U.S. Newfoundland base commander concluded that an arrangement by which he was dependent on the Canadian forces for fire and police protection was not desirable. Because of this and the frictions that he cited as being inevitably generated by an arrangement with "two families living in the same house," he continued to press unsuccessfully, during the following months, for designation of a physically separate U.S. area within which responsibility need not be divided.[53]

The same problem soon arose at Goose Bay Airport in Labrador, where forces of both nations also occupied facilities constructed by Canada during the fall and winter of 1941–42. The construction of facilities did not, for diverse reasons, keep abreast of the demand, and, not long after the base was officially established as an RCAF station in March 1942, Canada permitted the U.S. Army to construct an independent group of facilities on the opposite side of the air base from the facilities tenanted by the Canadian and British elements.

The formula embodied in the Twenty-first Recommendation also proved suitable for application to the problems of joint occupancy at the principal bases of the Northwest Staging Route, where U.S. forces used facilities provided by Canada. But it did not cover the air-base facilities constructed by the United States itself in Canada in connection with the North Atlantic Ferry Route and along the Northwest Staging Route and Mackenzie River valley.[54] As these facilities built up and for the United States became operational beginning in the latter months of 1942, new arrangements were needed, since the Twenty-first Recommendation had provided only for tenancy by one country of facilities provided in and by the second country.

The broader questions of control, maintenance, and operation of bases occupied in their entirety by the tenant forces came under discussion at the 24–25 February 1943 meeting of the Permanent Joint Board. The Board agreed that the following arrangement would be suitable:

---

[52] Appendix A, below.
[53] Ltr, CG NBC to Bissell, 16 Dec 41, PDB 107-3.
[54] See Ch. VIII, above.

a. Canada would be responsible for administration, security, traffic con-

b. The United States would assume these responsibilities at air bases used exclusively or mainly by its own forces. Canada might post a liaison officer to each such air base.[55]

The Board agreement was not cast in the form of a recommendation. Shortly after the Board consideration, the Canadian Goverment asked that the agreement be held in abeyance pending further discussion. At the 1 April 1943 Permanent Joint Board meeting, the Canadian Section withdrew its support of the earlier proposal and submitted one that assigned to Canada control of bases which it used substantially and to the United States only those where it was the sole user.[56] The Permanent Joint Board did not settle the matter until its next meeting, on 6–7 May. At this time the Board adopted its Thirty-first Recommendation, which assigned responsibility to the United States for bases of which its forces were the principal or exclusive user. It also provided that defense standards at such bases should be acceptable to the Canadian Chiefs of Staff and that, should Canada desire to assume control of such an airfield, "the necessary arrangements . . . [should] be concerted between the two Governments."[57] The Canadian Government, in reviewing the recommendation, would have preferred that it conform to the Canadian proposal of 1 April. Nevertheless, since the recommendation called for a specific schedule allocating the air-base responsibilities and incorporation of this schedule into a further Board recommendation, the Canadian Government approved the Thirty-first Recommendation.[58]

During the succeeding months the Air members of the Permanent Joint Board worked out on the basis of the Thirty-first Recommendation the allocations of air bases and the details of responsibilities. The results were adopted by the Board on 24–25 August 1943 as the Thirty-second Recommendation. To the United States were allocated the Canol Project and Alaska Highway flight strips; the North Atlantic Ferry Route air bases it had constructed; the air base at The Pas, where it was the principal user; and the Edmonton satellite air base, which was the only one of the major Northwest Staging Route air bases developed from its inception by the United States. Both governments approved the recommendation in September. Approval of the Thirty-second Recommendation represented another step in the

[55] Journal, PDB 124.
[56] Memos, SUSAM for CG AAF, 10 Mar and 5 Apr 43, PDB 113–2.
[57] Appendix A, below.
[58] Alaskan Division, Historical Record Report, Nov 42–Dec 43 volume, p. 225.

Canadian program to reassert Canadian authority over Canada's airways, air bases, and air traffic.[59]

The four meetings of the joint U.S.-Canadian committee that studied problems arising from the Thirty-first and Thirty-second Recommendations, mentioned earlier in the chapter, were also the means for working out further details of the application of the Thirty-second Recommendation. As a matter of fact the greater portions of those meetings were devoted to problems of this type. During the meetings an excellent spirit of co-operation and understanding prevailed, as a result of which suitable arrangements and adjustments were effected as to work specifications, division of labor, and similar questions in a manner best reflecting the availability of resources and the needs of the forces of the two countries.

The Thirty-first Recommendation provided the basis for appropriate shifts of control of air bases to accord with changing circumstances before the general transfer to Canada of control of the entire U.S. system of bases at the end of the war. Control of the Mackenzie River valley flight strips of the Canol Project was transferred to Canada before the end of 1944. Between V-E and V-J Days, it became fully apparent that the air bases at Churchill and The Pas would have no appreciable role in the support of the U.S. effort in either Europe or the Pacific. Since Canada was prepared to take them over and integrate them completely into the Canadian network of civil airports, the transfers were effected on 1 and 2 August 1945, respectively. With Canadian assumption of control and responsibility for these air installations, the general transfer of the entire U.S. air-base system to Canadian control was well under way.[60]

---

[59] Appendix A, below. Despite the provision in the Thirty-first Recommendation for stationing of liaison officers, Minister of Munitions and Supply C. D. Howe revealed a year after approval of the schedule of allocations that there were one or two bases that to his knowledge no Canadian had yet seen, indicating that Canada apparently had not made use of this provision. (*H. C. Debates*, 8 Aug 44, p. 6084.)

[60] See Ch. XII, below.

CHAPTER XII

Mission Accomplished

The tasks assigned to U.S. forces in Canada and related Canadian activities changed frequently as the battle lines receded farther from North America and as the broader logistical requirements and situations shifted accordingly. Certain of the tasks were finished and others were canceled even before the necessary facilities had been fully completed and long before victory was won on the fighting fronts. Still other tasks arose only upon the termination of hostilities in the combat zones. The reduction of the U.S. establishment was thus not an immediate consequence of V-J Day but began long before that date and lasted over a period of years. The arrangements for disposing of U.S. installations and equipment during the U.S. withdrawal differed markedly from the arrangements initiating the activities. Whereas in the early wartime years the military considerations were overriding, many other factors needed to be taken into account in working out the disposal arrangements. This complicating element was compensated for by the fact that, in place of having to reach decisions quickly, those working out the disposal arrangements could take adequate time to study thoroughly the problems involved.

Beginning the American Roll-up

The year 1943 saw the transition from a situation in which northern North America was vulnerable to enemy attack to one of relative security and the use of northern North America principally as a logistical base for overseas operations. By the end of the year the Allied position had improved substantially. The Japanese had been evicted from the Aleutians, the Axis submarine menace was being reduced, and the Allies had seen major successes in the Mediterranean and on the eastern European fronts.

During the latter half of 1943 the United States reduced its garrison in Newfoundland from about 10,000 to half that number. Canada also began to reduce its garrison in Newfoundland. In Canada, Canadian antiaircraft and coastal defense forces were scaled downward. The 7th and 8th Canadian Divisions were disbanded, while the 6th was partially reduced in strength. Similarly, Canadian air base defense detachments were withdrawn from the Northwest Staging Route and other bases. This progressive reduction of the defensive garrisons begun in 1943 continued throughout the remainder of the war.

In the changing situation parts of the U.S. logistical organization and system of installations in Canada for support of the overseas effort became surplus. By mid-1943 the United States was prepared to abandon the uncompleted western route of the CRIMSON Project, together with the supporting meteorological and communications networks, and to curtail the work at other bases of that project. On the Pacific coast, the elimination of 1943 of the Japanese threat to Alaska and the Aleutians reduced certain of the missions and operations of the logistical facilities in that area. Likewise, the completion of the military phase of the construction of the Alaska Highway and Canol Project resulted in the withdrawal, beginning in early 1943, of a large part of the Engineer troop construction force, which had reached a strength exceeding 10,000.

These withdrawals were largely offset by two new developments. The task of completing the projects from which these troops were withdrawn passed to the hands of civilian contractors whose employees had gradually been increased for the purpose. In September 1943 the number of U.S. civilians employed on the Alaska Highway alone reached a peak exceeding 10,000. Throughout the rest of 1943 the civilian force, too, was drastically reduced as the projects neared completion. The second development was the establisment in September 1942, and continued expansion thereafter, of the Northwest Service Command, the logistical organization charged with operating the various U.S. installations, facilities, and services as they were completed or established. By August 1943 the strength of this command exceeded 10,000.

Other circumstances militated against reductions of U.S. forces in the Canadian northwest. The United States assumed an active role in air-base construction during 1943 and 1944 which absorbed a large part of the construction force released from the completed projects. Then, too, operations for ferrying lend-lease aircraft to Alaska for the USSR reached their peak during 1944. Concurrently, the strength of the Alaskan Wing of the Air Transport Command reached its peak of 9,987 in November 1944, and still amounted to 7,032 on V-J Day.[1]

Victory in Europe brought new missions for the forces and facilities in Canada. The North Atlantic Ferry Route was sheduled to play a new role in the movement of air units and personnel in the general redeployment of forces from the European to the Pacific theaters. The Prince Rupert port,

[1] Carr, Great Falls to Nome: The Inland Air Route to Alaska, 1940–1945, pp. 97–98.

on the Pacific coast, was slated to perform a vital function in stepping up the movement of tonnages required in the Pacific area for the intensification of operations against Japan. The early surrender of Japan caused both of these operations to be dropped. In a slightly different form, operations over the North Atlantic Ferry Route did figure importantly in demobilization by speeding return from Europe of Canadian and U.S. fighting forces.[2]

In anticipation of the adjustments and reductions that would be necessary in the U.S. logistical structure in Canada, some consideration had been given to the problem of disposition of surplus property before the end of 1942. The facilities fell naturally into two groups—the fixed and immovable facilities, and the movable facilities, equipment, and supplies. Neither category included such facilities as the Alaska Highway and the Canol Project, for which appropriate arrangements as to disposition had been included in the original agreements.

Shortly after the Canadian Government suggested that the disposition of items not already provided for be arranged, the Permanent Joint Board on Defense examined the problem, at its 3 November 1942 meeting. The Canadian Section of the Board presented a draft recommendation on the subject in furtherance of the Canadian desire that governmental agreement be based upon a formal recommendation by the Board.[3] Why Canada desired the Permanent Joint Board to take up the matter the Canadian Section did not state. The reason may have been that because the disposal operation would undoubtedly be closely examined by the public and legislatures of both countries a background of Permanent Joint Board consideration would minimize the impact on each of the governments. Although the Board unquestioningly accepted the task, the matter of working out disposal procedures appears to have been an administrative problem, to a large extent free of defense considerations, and perhaps properly outside the purview of the Board. In some instances the question of residual military and defense value needed to be considered, but this aspect was only a small part of the larger problem.

One purpose the Canadian Government had in pressing for a Board recommendation on postwar disposition of facilities was the desire to present a recommendation to the House of Commons when it met on 20 January 1943. The Canadian purpose was illuminated on 1 February, when the Prime Minister laid the recommendation before the House. The recommendation and his accompanying statement were an effective method of allaying growing Canadian concern as to the status of U.S. activities in Canada in the

[2] See above, Ch. VII.
[3] Journal, PDB 124; Ltr, Hickerson to Robins, 11 Nov 42, PDB 150-2.

360-477 O - 70 - 22

postwar period. After pointing out that, as a purely wartime arrangement, the United States had provided materials for, or defrayed the cost of, the construction of a number of projects in Canada, he stated:

> It is not contemplated that the contribution which the United States is thus making to the common defense will give the country any continuing rights in Canada after the conclusion of the war. Indeed, with regard to most of the projects that have been undertaken in this country by the United States, agreements have already been made which make the postwar position completely clear.[4]

The Permanent Joint Board's Twenty-eighth Recommendation, based on the Canadian draft and approved on 13 January, was approved by the two governments in an exchange of notes on 27 January. It provided, for facilities or matériel for which no other disposition had been made, that (a) immovable installations would become the property of Canada or of the province, unless other arrangements were agreed within one year after the cessation of hostilities, and (b) movable facilities could be removed from Canada or be offered for sale to Canada during the same period. If these options were foregone, the United States could sell the facilities on the open market, any sale to be subject to approval by both governments.[5] On the surface this arrangement seemed to favor Canada. Unless it agreed to some other arrangement, all immovable installations covered by the recommendation automatically became Canadian property when the year following the termination of hostilities expired. As it turned out, the Twenty-eighth Recommendation was not to be applied in the initial detailed disposition arrangements concluded after its adoption, and, in fact, its provisions were to be amended before it had ever been applied.

The Northern Airfields Settlement

During the first months after Pearl Harbor, when Canada undertook to construct facilities on the Northwest Staging Route at the request of and for use by the United States, it followed the policy set forth in the recommendations of the Permanent Joint Board on Defense by which each government financed the work within its own geographic jurisdiction. In April 1942 Canada modified this position and agreed to pay for the construction of all work requested by the United States when the work was of continuing value to the air route, while the United States was to pay for facilities over and above Canadian standards and needed solely for U.S. military purposes.[6] This policy prevailed for about a year.

---

[4] *H. C. Debates,* 1 Feb 43, pp. 20–21.
[5] Appendix A, below. The exchange of notes is in EAS, 391, and CTS, 1943, No. 2.
[6] See above, Ch. VIII.

In the face of ever-expanding U.S. construction requirements for facilities on the staging route, the Canadian Cabinet War Committee in late March 1943 initially considered reimbursing the United States fully for its payments, but in the next month it decided to withhold such action. After further consideration, the Canadian Government on 31 May 1943 advised the United States that it would no longer submit claims for payment and proposed instead that the whole matter of the settlement of the construction accounts be postponed and worked out at the end of the war.[7] The United States accordingly suspended its payments to Canada on the construction account. Seven months later, on 18 December 1943, the Canadian Government advised the United States that it had again revised its decision. Canada would henceforth bear the cost of construction of all permanent facilities or improvements carried out on airfields in northwest Canada at the request of and for the account of the United States and would reimburse the United States for its expenditures for such construction.[8] The United States would continue to finance such of its projects as had no permanent value.

One factor influencing the decision was the importance Canada attached to the northern airfields. Minister of Munitions and Supply C. D. Howe, in reporting the Canadian decision to the House of Commons on 29 February 1944, pointed out that the Northwest Staging Route was "one of the most important in the world . . . as part of an international air route." Execution of the new policy would make the staging route and its permanent facilities wholly Canadian property, constructed by Canada with the co-operation of the United States but financed entirely by Canada. Still later, in reporting on the final arrangements to the House of Commons, Prime Minister King stated that "it . . . [had been] thought undesirable that any other country should have a financial investment in improvements of permanent value, such as civil aviation facilities, for peacetime use in this country." He cited this factor, together with the Canadian desire to finance the facilities as part of the Canadian contribution to the war effort, as the two considerations prompting Canadian action.[9]

Another factor entering into the Canadian decision was its rapidly mounting U.S. dollar balance, which had by the end of 1942 almost been restored to the September 1939 level and had during 1943 jumped from $319 to $649 million. Because of the rapid rate at which Canada had been accumulating U.S. dollars, the United States in early 1943 had considered it necessary to

[7] Alaskan Division, Historical Record Report, Nov 42–Dec 43 volume, p. 222; Cdn Leg Note 288, to Secy State, 31 May 43, PDB 126.

[8] Cdn Leg Note 643, to Secy State, 18 Dec 43, D/S 842.7962/121.

[9] *H. C. Debates*, 29 Feb 44, pp. 980–81, and 1 Aug 44, pp. 5706–08.

work out an informal arrangement with Canada which would put a limit on Canadian holdings of U.S. dollars. Under the arrangement, called the Morgenthau-Ilsley agreement, the U.S. dollar balance was to be kept within an agreed range through control of the flow of production orders to Canada and other measures. The continued rapid build-up of Canada's exchange position which took place during 1943 prompted the United States to invoke the provisions of the agreement in early 1944. Accordingly, Minister of Finance J. L. Ilsley and Secretary of the Treasury Morgenthau jointly developed a program of measures designed to reduce Canada's current holdings and future receipts of U.S. dollars. Payment to the United States for its expenditures on permanent airport improvements became an important element of the arrangement. Fortunately, this large dollar expenditure was feasible and even desirable at a time when Canada wished to assure its control of the northern airfields. On the U.S. side, no responsible official had envisaged a position of special privilege for the United States in Canada as a result of the wartime operations there, and therefore the offer of unanticipated payment for U.S. expenditures was readily gratefully accepted.[10]

During the months after the December 1943 decision, additional discussions took place between Canada and the United States as to the scope, form, and other details of Canadian payments for construction on the northern airfields. The United States proposed a lump-sum settlement that could be adjusted upon termination of hostilities. Canada preferred to itemize expenditures insofar as possible, leaving a relatively small amount of uncompleted construction for the adjustment process. The United States also requested that, at an appropriate time, discussions take place concerning post-

[10] Ltr, Ilsley to Morgenthau, 24 Mar 44, cited in "Report of Meetings in Washington, D. C. on 25–26 April 1944," PDB 150–4. For the Morgenthau-Ilsley agreement on the dollar balance question, see F. A. Knox, "Canada's Balance of International Payments, 1940–45," *Canadian Journal of Economics and Political Science*, XIII (August 1947), 345–62. Lingard and Trotter, *Canada in World Affairs*, III, p. 215, speculate that the concurrent investigation by the Special Senate (Truman) Committee Investigating the National Defense Program (see above, pp. 233–35) rendered the United States amenable to the Canadian proposition. This appears to be unlikely since in northwest Canada that committee investigated only the Canol Project. Of the total Canol expenditure of about $135 million Canada brought within the airfield agreement only the Mackenzie River flight strips at a cost of $1,264,150, which represented less than 2 percent of the amount finally transferred under the airfield agreement. The validity of the theory is further challenged by the fact that, despite a strong contrary Truman Committee recommendation, the War Department proceeded in the early months of 1944 to expend an additional $19 million on the Canol Project. For Canadian policies and statistics on its U.S. dollar position, see Canada, Foreign Exchange Control Board, *Report to the Minister of Finance, March 1946.* United States figures are to be found in Department of Commerce, Bureau of Foreign and Domestic Commerce, *International Transactions of the United States During the War, 1940–45* (Washington: Government Printing Office, 1948), pp. 122–31.

war use of these and other fields on a reciprocal basis, and Canada acceded to this request.[11]

During the discussions of the airfield settlement and as a consequence of the Morgenthau-Ilsley arrangement, the scope of the proposed agreement was broadened to include (a) the airfields in eastern Canada as well as those in northwestern Canada, (b) the telephone land line that had been constructed as part of the Alaska Highway, (c) Canadian construction on U.S. account at the Goose Bay air base in Labrador, and (d) certain additional construction on the Northwest Staging Route by Canada for U.S. account. The final agreement was embodied in an exchange of notes dated 23 and 27 June 1944.[12] It provided among other things that existing arrangements for the maintenance, operation, and defense of the facilities would continue in effect for the duration of the war. Upon relinquishment of facilities, all items at the installations, nonpermanent as well as permanent, were to be turned over to Canada.

Table 7 presents a summary of the expenditures on the northern airfields by both countries. Of the total U.S. expenditures of $90,683,571 at the installations covered by the agreement, the United States was reimbursed $76,811,551 by Canada for improvements having permanent value. The Canadian expenditures authorized at the same installations amounted to $29,600,643, to which Canada added funds estimated at $5,161,000 to cover the completion of additional construction work desired by the United States.

Not long after the June settlement was concluded the United States began to transfer facilities covered by it to Canada. The Canadian Department of Transport took over the flight strips of the Mackenzie River route on 1 November 1944. In late August and in September the United States had reported its desire to relinquish its facilities at Calgary, Grande Prairie, Fort St. John, Watson Lake, Namao, and Prince George. During October the transfer of facilities at these points began and was completed by the end of 1945. At that time U.S. personnel remained only on the airfields at Edmonton, Fort Nelson, and Whitehorse; the U.S. facilities at these places, together with the telephone land line, were turned over to Canada at a ceremony at

[11] Note, Berle to Cdn Ambassador, 24 Feb 44, and Reply, 20 Mar 44, D/S 842.7962/121 and /134.

[12] EAS, 405, and CTS, 1944, No. 19. Only the latter contains the appendixes that list in detail the Canadian and U.S. expenditures on the facilities covered by the agreement. Accounts of the negotiation are to be found in *The Canada Year Book, 1945*, pp. 705–12, and *Canada at War*, No. 40 (Sep 44), pp. 28–37, as well as in the statement of the Prime Minister, *H. C. Debates*, 1 Aug 44, pp. 5706–08. The statement is also published in Department of State *Bulletin*, August 6, 1944, XI, 139–41. On the broadening of the settlement pursuant to the Morgenthau-Ilsley arrangements, see statement of Ilsley in *H. C. Debates*, 21 Apr 44, p. 2227.

Table 7—Canadian-United States Expenditures on the Northern Airfields, Detailed by Projects

Project	U.S. Expenditures to 24 April 1944 (U.S. Dollars)		Canadian Expenditures (Canadian Dollars)		
	Total	Of Permanent Value	Authorized to 31 March 1944	Expended to 31 March 1944	Balance to Complete Construction
Grand Total	$90, 683, 571	$76, 811, 551	[a] $29, 600, 643	$22, 051, 477	$7, 549, 166
Northeast Staging Route	$39, 494, 300	$31, 631, 310	$11, 240, 690	$7, 516, 406	$3, 724, 284
The Pas, Manitoba	415, 000	415, 000	1, 253, 850	921, 650	332, 200
Churchill, Manitoba	9, 385, 700	6, 206, 800			
Southampton Island, Northwest Territories	7, 043, 200	5, 318, 870			
Frobisher Bay, Northwest Territories	8, 065, 700	6, 833, 190			
Fort Chimo, Quebec	9, 756, 500	8, 686, 470			
Mingan, Quebec	4, 285, 200	3, 627, 980	36, 160	35, 000	1, 160
Goose Bay, Labrador	543, 000	543, 000	9, 950, 680	6, 559, 756	3, 390, 924
Northwest Staging Route	37, 320, 226	31, 311, 196	[a] 18, 359, 953	14, 535, 071	3, 824, 882
Aishihik, Yukon Territory			1, 021, 921	824, 159	197, 762
Beatton River, British Columbia			[a] 941, 407	418, 620	522, 787
Calgary, Alberta	28, 517	28, 517	512, 178	392, 448	119, 730
Edmonton, Alberta, air base	5, 248, 822	2, 836, 835	[a] 3, 634, 759	3, 017, 350	617, 409
Namao, Alberta (Edmonton satellite field)	6, 853, 683	6, 264, 495	200, 000	144, 053	55, 947
Fort Nelson, British Columbia	6, 186, 892	5, 477, 354	[a] 1, 070, 822	649, 535	421, 287
Fort St. John, British Columbia	4, 415, 441	3, 974, 683	1, 297, 132	1, 297, 132	
Grande Prairie, Alberta	1, 968, 015	1, 719, 956	[a] 1, 255, 110	960, 126	294, 984
Kamloops, British Columbia			1, 037, 237	769, 953	267, 284
Lethbridge, Alberta			142, 274	41, 427	100, 847
Prince George, British Columbia	164, 732	164, 732	438, 761	417, 903	20, 858
Regina, Saskatchewan			135, 975	134, 646	1, 329
Smith River, British Columbia			1, 018, 398	813, 130	205, 268
Snag, Yukon Territory			855, 399	645, 095	210, 304
Teslin, Yukon Territory			862, 100	784, 493	77, 607
Watson Lake, Yukon Territory	4, 156, 695	3, 448, 743	[a] 1, 218, 685	1, 035, 374	183, 311
Whitehorse, Yukon Territory	8, 297, 429	7, 395, 881	2, 717, 795	2, 189, 627	528, 168
Flight strips along Alaska Highway	3, 262, 687	3, 262, 687			
Mackenzie–Athabasca route	1, 264, 150	1, 264, 150			
Telephone line, Edmonton to Alaska boundary	9, 342, 208	9, 342, 208			

[a] Additional construction work undertaken by Canada in 1944 on the Northwest Staging Route at the request of the United States is estimated to have cost $5,161,000 in Canadian funds as follows: Edmonton $1,250,000, Grande Prairie $1,500,000, Fort Nelson $1,803,000, Watson Lake $608,000.

Source: Canada at War, No. 40 (Sep 44), p. 37. Details of the above expenditures are to be found in CTS, 1944, No. 19.

Whitehorse on 3 April 1946, at which each government was represented by its chairman on the Permanent Joint Board on Defense. The United States, which had been training Canadian personnel for the land-line operation since November 1945, retained personnel for this purpose with that facility until 1 June 1946.[13] The airfields in eastern Canada, which had been largely constructed, financed, maintained, and controlled by the United States, were released beginning in August 1945.[14]

Disposals Under the Thirty-third Recommendation

The dispositions effected by the June 1944 settlement, together with those provided for specifically as part of project authorizations, reduced considerably the facilities and matériel to which the principles of the general settlement set forth in the Twenty-eighth Recommendation might be applied. In early 1944 questions arose as to the application of the provisions of the recommendation that led to the working out of new arrangements. Canadian authorities had expressed the view that, under the Twenty-eighth Recommendation, within one year after the cessation of hostilities all remaining U.S. immovables would become Canadian property. United States authorities differed with this view on the basis that the recommendation provided for the conclusion of agreements to provide suitable reimbursement for selected facilities and that such agreements had been anticipated for certain of the facilities.[15]

To clarify the disposal arrangements, the U.S Section of the Permanent Joint Board on Defense introduced a new draft recommendation on the subject at the 28–29 June 1944 meeting. At the subsequent Board meeting on 7–8 September, the new recommendation, the Thirty-third and the last agreed upon during the wartime years, was approved.[16] The Canadian and U.S. Governments approved the recommendation in September and November 1944, respectively, and thereafter it was confirmed through an exchange of notes.[17]

---

[13] To meet its continuing requirements for telephone and telegraph communications services in northwest Canada and to Alaska, the United States arranged to lease some of the available channels at a rental of $271,000 annually. (TIAS, 1966; CTS, 1948, No. 6.)

[14] The airfields in eastern Canada were released on the following dates:

Churchill	1 August 1945
The Pas	2 August 1945
Southampton Island	7 September 1945
Mingan	– October 1949
Fort Chimo	– October 1949
Frobisher Bay	1 September 1950

[15] Memo, Parsons for Hickerson, 11 Jul 44, D/S 842.20 Defense/7–844.

[16] Journals, PDB 124.

[17] EAS, 444; CTS, 1944, No. 35. See Appendix A.

According to the recommendation, the United States was to supply within three months after its approval a list of the immovable facilities not already provided for, for which it desired to be reimbursed. The fair market value of these facilities was then to be determined by a joint appraisal, in which an agreed third appraiser was to fix the value if the joint appraisers could not agree. The agreed fair market value was to be paid by Canada to the United States. The remaining facilities not so listed by the United States were to become Canadian property automatically one year after the termination of hostilities. The revised arrangement gave the United States a free hand to determine the immovable facilities for which it should be reimbursed, whereas the Twenty-eighth Recommendation had permitted a reimbursement only when Canada was willing to agree thereto. The new arrangement relieved Canada of the onus of determining the installations for which the United States should be paid, and instead put upon the United States the burden of stating its wishes.

As to movables, Canada had been somewhat concerned over the provision of the Twenty-eighth Recommendation that would under certain circumstances have put the United States into the business of selling surplus property in Canada. This possibility was eliminated by arranging that property not removed from, or purchased by, Canada was to be transferred to a Canadian Government agency for disposal and reimbursement to the United States. To safeguard U.S. interests, a U.S. officer was to have a voice in the disposal of such property. The Canadian Government soon designated the Crown Assets Allocation Committee and the War Assets Corporation, Limited, two governmental agencies, as its agents for carrying out the provisions of the Thirty-third Recommendation. Declarations of surplus were made to the Crown Assets Allocation Committee, and, when portions of such surplus were declared also surplus to the needs of Canadian governmental agencies, they were transferred to the War Assets Corporation, Limited, for sale or other disposition.[18]

Immediately after the governments had agreed to this recommendation, the question was raised as to payment of customs duties on surplus property sold in Canada. Canadian authorities had earlier expressed the view that these duties should be paid and should be assessed on the basis of the value of the property when sold. The U.S. view was that, since the property had

[18] War Assets Corporation, Limited, was established under authority of the Dominion Companies' Act by Privy Council 9108, 29 November 1943, which also authorized establishment of the Crown Assets Allocation Committee. The former agency was succeeded by a new War Assets Corporation established on 12 July 1944 under the statutory authority provided in the Surplus Crown Assets Act, which came into effect 30 June 1944.

been used for the mutual benefit of both countries in the prosecution of the war, the amount recovered by the United States should not be diminished by any duties that would accrue to Canada. At the January 1945 Permanent Joint Board meeting, U.S. Chairman LaGuardia strongly urged that the levies be waived in the interest of good U.S.-Canadian relations. The next month Canada accepted the U.S. view.[19]

The United States, as required by the Thirty-third Recommendation, on 11 February 1945 submitted the list of immovable facilities for which it desired reimbursement on the basis of the jointly agreed fair market value. Even before final agreement had been reached on the Thirty-third Recommendation, the United States had already reported as surplus to its needs the railroad depot at Dawson Creek, and Camp 550 and the Jesuit College at Edmonton. In general, the facilities listed included all U.S. weather stations, command installations, storage and water facilities, and similar installations throughout Canada. The following major items appeared on the list:

Camp 550, Edmonton
Jesuit College, Edmonton
Depot and appurtenances, Dawson Creek
Bechtel-Price-Callahan Building, Edmonton
Military hospital, Edmonton
Railhead and appurtenances, Edmonton
Railhead and appurtenances, McCrae, Yukon Territory
Weather and communications facilities, at 57 sites throughout Canada
Alaska Highway relay stations (14)
Headquarters and base facilities, Whitehorse
Standard Oil Company office and housing facilities, Whitehorse
Prince Rupert Subport of Embarkation, including the Port Edward staging area and Watson Island ammunition storage facilities

An American and a Canadian appraiser proceeded to place valuations upon the immovable facilities that had been listed by the United States. In no instance was it necessary to use a third appraiser, since the two were in each instance able to reach agreement on a fair market value.

Disposition of movable equipment and facilities proceeded concurrently. Large quantities of U.S. equipment and supplies were returned to the United States. Where such matériel was surplus to U.S. needs and was desired by one of the Canadian governmental agencies, transfers were made on a reim-

[19] Journal, PDB 124; Ltr, Hickerson to Pearson, 20 Dec 44, D/S 842.20 Def/12-2044, and Reply, 9 Feb 45, D/S 842.20 Def/2-945.

bursable basis. When there was neither U.S. nor Canadian official need for the surplus matériel, it was put up for public sale with corresponding reimbursement to the United States.[20]

By the beginning of 1946 transfer of a considerable part of the total list had been completed. The United States had been reimbursed $770,000 (U.S.) for the first four items—Camp 550, Jesuit College, the Dawson Creek depot, and the Bechtel-Price-Callahan Building.[21] Disposition of a small number of the minor facilities had also been arranged. Appraisal of the immovable facilities had been substantially completed even though some of the more complex ones, such as the McCrae railhead and the facilities in and near Prince Rupert, had only been declared surplus by the War Department in October 1945.[22]

In early March 1946 Canadian authorities suggested that all remaining U.S. property, movable and immovable, be disposed of under a single agreement at the governmental level, in order to permit completion of the transaction by 31 March, the end of the Canadian fiscal year. This timing would, in turn, permit use of funds available in the old fiscal year, whereas doubt was expressed that funds would be available for the purpose in the new fiscal year. Such an over-all settlement promised greatly to simplify for Canada the task of appraising and taking over the remaining U.S. Government property, which involved, besides the War Assets Corporation, the Departments of National Defense for Air, National Defense (Army), and Transport. In this task Canadians had been encountering administrative difficulties and a considerable duplication of work.[23] Both sides had to make some broad estimates in order to work out an agreement within the time available, but by and large most of the needed basic data was compiled. The notes effecting the agreement were signed on 30 March 1946. The

---

[20] Privy Council 3432, 15 May 45.

[21] Camp 550 was so designated because it was a housing facility having a capacity for 550 persons. The headquarters of the Northwest Division of the U. S. Army Corps of Engineers was located at the Jesuit College, which had been improved and enlarged for that purpose. The Bechtel-Price-Callahan Building had been used for office space by the prime contractor for the Canol Project.

[22] Responsibility for disposition of U.S. property in foreign areas had, by Executive Order 9630, 27 September 1945, been transferred from the War and Navy Departments and the Army-Navy Liquidation Commissioner to the Department of State as of 20 October 1945. The responsibility was discharged by the Foreign Liquidation Commissioner, who established a field organization that included a Deputy Field Commissioner in Ottawa. The actual physical custody of property and administration of the disposal arrangements continued to remain with the U.S. service agencies in Canada. See Department of State, Office of the Foreign Liquidation Commissioner, *Report to Congress on Foreign Surplus Disposal, April 1946,* (Washington: Government Printing Office, 1946), and Department of State *Bulletin,* March 3, 1946, XIV, 350.

[23] Memo/Conv, R. M. Macdonnell and Parsons, 7 Mar 46, PDB 150–2; Privy Council 1189, 29 Mar 46.

arrangement, according to the notes, was based on the underlying principles of the Thirty-third Recommendation, yet it permitted a speedy and expeditious closing out of the bulk of the outstanding disposal problems. By the agreement, the United States was reimbursed $12 million (U.S.) for installations and matériel whose original cost had been as follows: [24]

Total original cost	$58,906,844
Immovable facilities	27,882,825
Movable property	26,674,302
U.S. Navy property lend-leased to the United Kingdom but left in Canada	4,349,717

Under the agreement U.S. forces could recapture or continue to use such facilities and matériel as they needed, subject to the provision that appropriate reimbursement would be made to Canada for any property recaptured. For its part, the United States was not to abandon any property until Canada had been given a reasonable opportunity to arrange for its custody. Under this and earlier agreements, all immovable facilities awaiting disposition had been accounted for.

The 1946 agreement proved a useful tool to Canada in another connection. The Canadian armed forces desired to purchase certain surplus U.S. matériel from stocks outside of Canada. Through use of the agreement and some of the funds available in fiscal year 1945–46, Canada deposited $7 million (U.S.) with the U.S. Government to be used for this purpose. The amount proved to be in excess of the funds needed for the available surplus matériel of the types desired, and of the amount the Canadian Government later decided should be expended for the purpose. On 10 October 1947 Canada requested the return of $1 million of the deposit and, on 24 January 1948, the return of an additional $2.2 million, thus reducing the account to $3.8 million.[25]

Special Dispositions

Separate arrangements were made for two major U.S. undertakings, the Alaska Highway and the Canol Project, in accordance with the terms of the original agreements with Canada authorizing these projects. In the case of the Alaska Highway project, the United States had agreed that it would maintain the highway for at least six months after the termination of the war, and that the portion of the highway in Canada would become an in-

[24] TIAS, 1531; CTS, 1946, Nos. 12 and 31. Lists appended to the notes set forth in detail the facilities and supplies included under this settlement. Canadian Government approval of the transaction was granted in Privy Council 1189, 29 Mar 46.

[25] TIAS, 1981; CTS, 1948, No. 8.

tegral part of the Canadian highway system. No provision was made for reimbursement to the United States for its expenditures.[26]

The terms of the Alaska Highway agreement were applied to other agreements connected with the road. When the construction of the Haines–Champagne cutoff road was authorized, it came under the terms of the basic agreement. Eight flight strips had been authorized and constructed under still another agreement, which also made the strips subject to the terms of the basic Alaska Highway agreement. Constructed under the basic authority of the original Alaska Highway agreement, although not mentioned in the notes exchanged, were many other immovable facilities such as relay stations, construction and maintenance camps, convoy parking sites, and the like.[27] Insofar as disposal arrangements were concerned, auxiliary facilities that were associated with the construction of the highway, such as the construction and maintenance camps, were treated as being covered under the highway disposal plan. Others, which were operational adjuncts to the highway such as the relay stations, were disposed of under the procedures of the Thirty-third Recommendation and the 30 March 1946 exchange of notes.

Arrangements were made for transfer to Canada of the Canadian sections of the Alaska Highway and the Haines cutoff on 1 April 1946. In accordance with the terms of the original agreement, Canada made no reimbursement to the United States, which had expended over $100 million on the highway construction. Perhaps because of policy considerations that were applicable to the northern airfields settlement as a whole, Canada had already elected to bring the eight flight strips of the highway project under the airfields settlement. Accordingly, the United States was reimbursed $3,262,687 (U.S.) for its expenditures on the strips, which would presumably have been transferred to Canada gratis had it insisted on the application of the original highway agreement. The decision probably reflected, in part, the Canadian attitude that the northern airfields would undoubtedly be a significant adjunct to the transportation resources of northwest Canada, whereas no such general conviction then existed about the highway.

Although under no legal obligation to do so, Canada decided to continue to maintain the highway, which was part of the road net redesignated the Northwest Highway System. The Canadian Army was assigned the maintenance responsibility for the system, and it established an organization with headquarters at Whitehorse for the purpose. In December 1946 the Canadian Government decided against further work and maintenance on the

[26] EAS, 246; CTS, 1942, No. 13.
[27] EAS, 381; CTS, 1942, No. 26, and EAS, 382; CTS, 1942, No. 21.

Haines cutoff road, although it proceeded to consult with the United States as to its view in the matter.[28]

The other major unilateral U.S. undertaking in Canada, the Canol Project, had also been covered by special disposal arrangements embodied in the original agreement authorizing the project. This agreement had provided that on the termination of hostilities the pipeline and refinery should be appraised at their current commercial value by two appraisers, one selected by each country, and by an umpire to resolve disagreement if necessary. If the Canadian Government did not act within three months to purchase the facilities, they were to be offered for sale to private companies with the appraised value as the reserve price. In the event that no private company desired to purchase the facilities, their disposition was to be referred to the Permanent Joint Board on Defense for recommendation. That body was also to be consulted in the event either government wished to dismantle the facilities, or to allow them to be dismantled.[29]

As agreements were reached for the construction of the supplementary Canol facilities, somewhat more flexible disposal provisions were incorporated. These arrangements provided only that, upon termination of hostilities, either government could initiate discussions with a view to agreeing to the manner of disposition of the supplementary facilities, which comprised the Prince Rupert storage and loading facilities and the Skagway-Whitehorse, Carcross-Watson Lake, and Whitehorse-Fairbanks distribution pipelines. As with the basic project, no dismantlement of the facilities was to be permitted unless the Permanent Joint Board recommended such action.[30]

The first step in disposing of U.S. Canol installations was taken in April 1944 when the United States negotiated a new contract with the Imperial Oil Company, which was accepted by the two governments in an exchange of notes in June. Under the new contract the United States transferred to the Imperial Oil Company all its facilities, movable and immovable, together with all equipment, machinery, and spare parts in the Norman Wells area and along the Mackenzie River valley transportation routes to that area.[31]

When hostilities terminated, Canada displayed no interest in acquiring the refinery and pipeline installations of the Canol Project, whose wartime utility had been questioned and whose peacetime capabilities were far in excess of foreseeable needs. As a means of simplifying disposal of the Canol

---

[28] House Committee on Foreign Affairs, *Alaska Study Mission*, Committee Print (Washington: Government Printing Office, 1948), p. 7. See also *H. C. Debates*, 13 Mar 47, p. 1326, and 17 Mar 47, p. 1409.

[29] EAS, 386; CTS, 1942, No. 23.

[30] EAS, 387; CTS, 1942, No. 24, and EAS, 416; CTS, 1944, No. 16.

[31] EAS, 416; CTS, 1944, No. 16. See also Ch. VIII, above.

facilities at Prince Rupert, the United States suggested in December 1945 that they be treated together with the Prince Rupert port and staging facilities, which were being processed under the Thirty-third Recommendation and without reference to the Permanent Joint Board. Canada agreed to this proposal.[32]

The remaining Canol facilities were not to be disposed of so easily. Operation of the refinery and the crude-oil line from Norman Wells had been discontinued in March 1945. The United States, desiring to dispose of facilities no longer needed, proposed in February 1945 that the two governments proceed with the appraisal of the commercial value of the facilities, as had been contemplated in the initial agreement on the Canol Project. Canada agreed to the proposal, and the substantial task of inventory, inspection, and appraisal was begun.[33] However, by midsummer the Canadian Government had concluded that it did not desire to exercise its option to purchase the facilities. It consequently suggested to the United States that, since a joint appraisal no longer appeared useful, plans for continuing this appraisal should be dropped. Canada also waived the provision that would then have offered the facilities for sale to private companies with the appraised value as a reserve price. In taking these actions Canada expressed the hope that they would aid in the disposition of the Canol facilities.[34] On 30 June 1946 the last facility of the project still in use, the Skagway-Whitehorse-Fairbanks distribution line, was placed in a nonoperating standby status. But neither this nor the Watson Lake distribution pipeline had yet been declared surplus, so that the only facilities in the surplus category were the refinery and the crude-oil pipeline from Norman Wells. As of 30 June 1946, no disposition of any of the Canol facilities, other than those at Prince Rupert, had been arranged.

In November the United States presented new proposals to facilitate the disposal operation:

a. Since the facilities no longer had defense value, any restrictions as to dismantlement should be lifted.

b. Canada should guarantee such riparian and other rights as might be required by a purchaser for operation of the facilities and waive payment of duties and taxes by a purchaser.

c. The United States or a purchaser could remove any of the facilities from Canada.

[32] TIAS, 1565; CTS, 1946, No. 1. See above, pp. 325-29. As a matter of fact, the five storage tanks had been removed by the United States in November 1944, leaving only the loading dock and other minor facilities.

[33] TIAS, 1695; CTS, 1945, No. 3.

[34] TIAS, 1696.

d. Any facilities not disposed of during a two-year period following agreement on the proposals could be left in place and considered as of no value.

Canada agreed to the proposals, which were made effective 1 March 1947.[35] Armed with the proposals, the United States, which had by this time concluded that dismantlement would be necessary to obtain the maximum monetary return, proceeded energetically through its Foreign Liquidation Commissioner to arrange a disposition.[36]

In August 1947 the refinery and related equipment at Whitehorse, having an original matériel cost of approximately $6 million, were sold to the Imperial Oil Company, Limited, of Toronto, for $1 million. In November the crude-oil pipeline between Norman Wells and the refinery, the parallel telephone line, and road-repair equipment scattered along the pipeline were sold for $700,000 to the L. B. Foster Company of Pittsburgh and the Albert and Davidson Corporation of New York City.[37]

The distribution pipelines from Skagway to Fairbanks and Watson Lake remained under the ownership of the U.S. Government, without being declared surplus. In fact, as the other Canol dispositions were being completed, postwar requirements for fuel deliveries to Alaska began to increase and to justify restoration of the Skagway–Fairbanks pipeline to operational status, which was later done.[38]

One transaction remained to complete the disposal settlements. Under the Thirty-third Recommendation, quantities of surplus movable property had been transferred to Canada for sale by the War Assets Corporation and reimbursement to the United States. Negotiations throughout most of 1948 to settle this account were finally completed as of 31 December. Under the settlement, Canada paid $576,562 for property sold for the United States and purchased a small unsold residue for an additional $4,437.[39]

The final balance sheet for the government-to-government transactions, exclusive of the foregoing final settlement follows: [40]

---

[35] TIAS, 1697; CTS, 1946, No. 41.

[36] Department of State *Bulletin*, February 9, 1947, XVI, 256.

[37] *H. C. Debates*, 18 Feb 48, pp. 1348–49; House Committee on Foreign Affairs, *Alaska Study Mission*, p. 10.

[38] *H. C. Debates*, 18 Feb 48, p. 1439; Department of the Army Press Release, 21 Jan 48.

[39] *Report to Congress on Foreign Surplus Disposal, January 1948*, p. 23, and *January 1949*, p. 16; TIAS, 2352; CTS, 1949, No. 16.

[40] *Report to Congress on Foreign Surplus Disposal, April 1946*, pp. 20–21, and *July 1946*, pp. 25–26. On the basis of the tabulated data, these and other of the quarterly reports cite a return on the order of 40 percent of the cost value of the surplus property. However, if the airfields settlement under which Canada voluntarily paid 100 percent of the cost of permanent facilities is extracted, it would appear that the return in the negotiated settlements was on the order of 13 percent for these transactions.

Transaction	*Original Cost*	*Paid by Canada*
Total	$211,320,000	$93,061,000
The northern airfields settlement	90,683,000	76,811,000
Thirty-third Recommendation transactions		
Army-Navy Liquidation Commissioner	22,696,000	1,251,000
Foreign Liquidation Commissioner	39,034,000	2,999,000
30 March 1946 bulk transaction	58,907,000	12,000,000

All in all, the disposal operation was carried out to the satisfaction of both countries. All U.S.-built or -financed installations were transferred to Canadian control or otherwise disposed of by the United States in a manner that with minor exceptions eliminated the United States as a titleholder to real property and facilities in Canada. Through the disposals and settlements Canada acquired numerous airfields, structures, and facilities, in some instances at only a fraction of their original cost. These capital acquisitions represented a substantial augmentation of the transportation and other resources of northern Canada. The United States also fared well in that it obtained reimbursement on a larger scale than had been anticipated under the original authorizing agreements.

The 12 February 1947 Statement

The collapse of Hitler's Germany in May 1945 signaled the approach of a new phase in the military co-operation between the United States and Canada. Japan had yet to be defeated, but plans for the final operations against Japan were in an advanced state of preparation. And, as the war entered its closing stages, it was apparent that it would be necessary to determine the nature and scope of postwar military co-operation between the two countries. Yet the new situation and the requirements for co-operation in the posthostilities period had not been examined, either by the Permanent Joint Board on Defense or by any other official machinery. Such an examination soon became a matter for active consideration by the Board.

At the June 1945 Permanent Joint Board meeting, not long after V–E Day, General Henry, the Senior U.S. Army Member, outlined his views of the future of defense collaboration. To General Henry, who as a result of his additional responsibilities in the field of military co-operation between the United States and the American republics had had considerable experience with the difficulties stemming from the great diversity of types of matériel, organizational and training methods, and the like, it appeared that Canada should become a member of the "military family of American nations" envisaged in the Act of Chapultepec. Although he recognized that Canadian public opinion might not yet be ready for postwar steps toward standardization of Canadian and U.S. forces and that Canada's Commonwealth ties presented complications, General Henry felt that such steps would have inescapable merit and should be explored. He also recommended that the Board examine the continuing value to continental defense of the facilities developed in northwest Canada during the war.[41]

General Henry's presentation provided the springboard for a full discussion of these problems at the next meeting of the Permanent Joint Board, held in early September soon after the Japanese surrender. On this occasion, the personal and tentative views of the Canadian Section of the Board on the points raised by General Henry were in turn outlined and discussed. As for Canadian participation in inter-American military collaboration, this appeared to be, in the Canadian view, a political question. As to northwest Canada, many of the facilities developed there would certainly have some continuing defense value, the extent of which would be apparent when a military estimate of the situation for northern North America could be prepared.

In the view of the Canadian Section, as outlined by General A. G. L. McNaughton who had succeeded Mr. Biggar as Canadian chairman, a real case for standardization of matériel and organization between the forces of the two countries could not be made. On the other hand, standardization as well as fuller co-ordination of military supply operations between the United States and the British Commonwealth as a whole would be a substantial step toward the common security and international peace. Canada would in the future exert such influence as it could to that end. Thus the Canadian Section made explicitly clear that the dual and sometimes dichotomous position of Canada as a North American state and as a member of the British Commonwealth would continue to be a factor to be taken into account.

On one point the two sections of the Board were agreed. The authors of the Ogdensburg Declaration had used the term "permanent" in the title of the Board advisedly. Military co-operation should be continued within the framework of that declaration. There was no reason why a new appreciation or estimate of the joint defense situation should not be prepared as a step preliminary to revising ABC–22, the basic defense plan, to meet the requirements of the new situation. The Canadian Section suggested that the chiefs of staff of the two countries might on some occasion meet to survey the situation.[42]

Although the Canadian response indicated some receptivity to the pro-

[41] The memorandums are appended to the Journal, 4–5 Sep 45 PJBD meeting, PDB 124.
[42] Journal, 4–5 Sep 45 PJBD meeting, PDB 124.

360-477 O - 70 - 23

posals of the U.S. members of the Board, its tone was cautious and deliberate. Nevertheless, the designation of General McNaughton to chair the Canadian Section of the Board indicated that Canada did not expect the Board to lapse into a subsidiary role. With the addition of this eminent and experienced soldier-statesman-scientist, the Canadian Section was prepared to deal with the highest questions of politico-military policy.

On the U.S. side, the proposal to revise ABC–22, the 1941 plan that had met adequately the requirements of World War II, received the approval of the Joint Chiefs of Staff. In examining the procedure for drafting the new estimate of the situation (appreciation, in Canadian parlance) which would provide the basis for drafting the new joint defense plan, the Permanent Joint Board on Defense and chiefs of staff of both countries felt that the former needed to be supplemented by a similar body on the service level. Whereas the Board, responsible to the President and Prime Minister, was a suitable forum for policy deliberations, a mechanism more closely tied in with the defense departments was needed to co-ordinate the increased amount of consideration that would be necessary. Accordingly, a Military Co-operation Committee was established in February 1946 comprising representatives of the service departments, but also including officers from the Departments of State and External Affairs, and, in addition, the Secretary of the Canadian Cabinet Defense Committee. The sections of the Military Co-operation Committee were made responsible to their respective chiefs of staff. Day-to-day liaison between service authorities was to be maintained through the service attachés in the two capitals and the Canadian Joint Staff in Washington, which continued to operate in the postwar period.[43]

At its very first meeting, held in Washington 20–23 May 1946, the Military Co-operation Committee considered drafts of (a) a study of the requirements for Canadian-U.S. security and (b) a security plan. During the course of succeeding months these documents were finalized and approved and subsidiary plans initiated. These plans were undertaken under the guidance of the Military Co-operation Committee as part of its assigned responsibility of preparing, continuously revising, and submitting recommendations for implementation of the basic security plan and its subsidiary plans.[44]

Concurrently with this joint strategic planning, the earliest measures of practical postwar collaboration were being taken. Exercise MUSKOX, the movement of a mechanized force some 3,000 miles through Arctic Canada

---

[43] JCS 1541, approved 19 Oct 45; Canada, Department of National Defense, *Canada's Defense Program* (Ottawa: E. Cloutier, King's Printer, 1949), p. 38.

[44] U.S. Department of Defense, Organization Manual, *Office of the Secretary of Defense* (Washington: 1952, Processed.), p. 11.15.

during the early months of 1946, was carried out with participation of U.S. observers and use of some U.S. matériel. The experience and test observations obtained on all equipment were made equally available to both countries. During the same period experiments authorized by Canada were carried out by U.S. B–29 aircraft over Arctic Canada in the use of the loran (long range) radio navigation system, which was similar to that which had been used so successfully over ocean areas during the war.[45]

Although the mutuality of the security problem common to the two countries appeared to justify such joint measures, military co-operation with the United States had not yet become a clear-cut facet of contemporary Canadian foreign policy. This policy was fundamentally one of full support for the search for security through the United Nations, and one of minimizing bilateral or multilateral regional arrangements as detracting from the maximum potential of the United Nations for peace. However, during the immediate postwar period, this policy was implemented not actively but passively, and until early 1947 Canada played a retiring role on the international stage.

During 1946 the United States and the USSR came to be increasingly recognized as the protagonists and antipoles of a developing bipolar world situation. A significant body of Canadian public opinion was expressing the view that it was unwise for Canada to act jointly with the United States in measures that might antagonize the USSR. This view had received expression as early as December 1943 at the Montebello Conference of the Canadian Institute of International Affairs, when a substantial number of those present felt that Canada should abandon the Permanent Joint Board in the postwar period as constituting an irritant in relations with the USSR.[46] Canadian attitudes in the postwar period on this point were not improved by occasional injudicious press releases on the part of the U.S. military services in connection with their activities in Canada.

Nevertheless, the undeniable merit and self-evident necessity of further military co-operation prompted official approval of continuing forward planning and modest steps in that direction. As joint strategic planning got under way, the Permanent Joint Board began to consider the areas in which postwar collaboration might be useful, together with the adequacy of the existing mechanisms for that purpose. A recommendation by the Perma-

---

[45] For a full account of actions in the field of defense co-operation in the period immediately after V–J Day, see F. H. Soward, *Canada in World Affairs*, IV, *From Normandy to Paris, 1944–1946* (Toronto: Oxford University Press, 1950), Ch. IX.

[46] Grant Dexter, *Canada and the Building of Peace* (Toronto: Canadian Institute of International Affairs, 1944), pp. 165–67.

nent Joint Board on the principles for continuation of defense collaboration was first considered at the 29 April 1946 Board meeting. During the ensuing months the statement of principles was reviewed and revised, emerging on 20 November as the Board's Thirty-sixth Recommendation. Not long afterward, the approval of the two governments was made known through the release on 12 February 1947 of an agreed statement. The release declared that limited defense collaboration based on the following principles had been authorized:

a. Interchange of personnel.

b. Co-operation in maneuver exercises and development and tests of new matériel.

c. Encouragement of standardization.

d. Reciprocal availability of military facilities.

e. No impairment of control by each country over all activities in its own territory.[47]

Although the principles established could be utilized to provide a basis for broad co-operation, their wording indicated that such broad co-operation could develop only within the limits and restrictions that either country might wish to impose. On the Canadian side particularly, these limitations provided a flexibility that might be used to meet the needs of the domestic and international situations. In presenting the arrangement to be House of Commons, Prime Minister King pointed out that collaboration of this type had long existed between the nations of the British Commonwealth and that Canada's geographical position made it important that such measures should be undertaken with both the United States and the United Kingdom.[48]

The U.S.-Canadian Military Co-operation Committee established a year earlier became the principal mechanism for co-ordinating the actions worked out pursuant to the principles of the 12 February 1947 statement. By this time the revised estimate of the situation and the new security plan had been completed and the committee was able to relate the practical measures to be taken to the detailed requirements, immediate and longer term, that emerged from the plan. These arrangements proved eminently suitable in the light of the contemporary international climate. In addition, they provided a flexibility that allowed for increasing amounts of collaboration as the two countries began to accept the inescapable conclusion that the Soviet

[47] Full text at Appendix E, below.

[48] *H. C. Debates*, 12 Feb 47, pp. 345–48.

strategy left no alternative but to broaden the defensive collaboration designed to guard North America from Soviet aggression.

The Lessons of World War II

With the Allied victory in World War II important changes took place in the power positions of the major nations of the world. The two leading members of the World War II Axis were for the time being eliminated from their positions as foremost military powers. The USSR emerged as the unchallenged single contender against the United States for primacy as the world's most powerful nation. The United States and Canada, despite substantial expenditures of men and treasure, came out of World War II stronger and more vigorous than ever. Other nations, such as the United Kingdom and France, lost in relative power and position. Technological advances, particularly in the fields of electronics and weapons such as the atomic bomb, made far-reaching changes in the military capabilities of the world's powers. But other fundamental factors changed little or not at all.

A salient feature of the relation between the United States and Canada during World War II was the wide disparity in their resources in manpower, material, and productive capacity. From this disparity often flowed U.S. notions that the needs of the United States should be accepted without challenge since the U.S. interests at stake were so much greater, and that the U.S. view should predominate when differences arose. Such a position would of course be unacceptable to the smaller of any pair of sovereign states professing adherence to the tenets of international law. And Canada was free to take an unyielding and divergent stand because it was secure in the knowledge that the United States would never, except under near-catastrophic circumstances, employ forces to impose its will. So long as Canada could, in the given situation, withstand the political, economic, and psychological pressures that might be applied, it remained a free agent.

On the other hand, where Canada was the seeker its relative size left it in a poor bargaining position. Canadian efforts to gain a stronger place in the war councils, for example, could only be successful to the extent that the United States, in consultation with the United Kingdom, would allow. In the case of a problem relating to one of the major war theaters, the Canadian position was even weaker, for the United States considered the United Kingdom to be the principal partner and Canada only a subsidiary of the partner. This stemmed from Canada's position in the British Commonwealth, in which the United Kingdom was exercising war leadership not only because of its historical and material pre-eminence but also because the events of the war had placed it in the most forward positions on the diplomatic and military fronts. Canada's relative size and resources also made it dependent on the United States or the United Kingdom for the supply of much of the matériel with which to equip Canadian forces and for equipment to expand its production base. Finally, the disproportion between the war efforts of the two North American partners sometimes provided occasion for query whether the junior partner was pulling its weight, and for embarrassment in instances where Canadian lack of skills or other resources necessitated a one-sided effort in a project of joint interest.

A second major element of the Canadian experience in North American co-operation in World War II was the extent of the U.S. intrusion on Canadian soil in an area remote from the combat theaters and peopled by Canadians engaged in reasonably normal pursuits. The substantial U.S. garrison operated in Canada independently of Canadian control and legal jurisdiction to an extent considered unwarranted by many Canadians. This garrison constructed, maintained, and operated bases and facilities as if they were on U.S. soil. Command organizations with their independent signal communications systems were established over segments of Canadian territory. Strenuous U.S. efforts were made to have Canadian forces placed under U.S. command on Canadian soil. All these arrangements presented to Canadians serious questions of domestic policy, which were aggravated by sundry accompanying complications—occasional lapses of soldier discipline that outraged the Canadian citizenry, competition for scarce housing and rationed supplies, and concern as to whether U.S. commercial construction, air transport, and similar enterprises might not gain a postwar advantage. Too often it seemed to Canadians that U.S. requests for arrangements that resulted in these intrusions into Canada, as well as U.S. motivations in other dealings, were based exclusively on military requirements, without adequate consideration of the political factors involved.

A perennial state of affairs that conditioned the nature of the U.S.-Canadian relationship was the common amiable ignorance and disinterest on the part of Americans toward Canada. The impact of this ranged from the annoying, when exhibited by individuals in responsible positions, to the serious. There were surely many Americans who failed, or perhaps chose not, to understand that Prime Minister Churchill could in no wise speak for the Canadian Government, and that Canada was fully autonomous and coequal with the United Kingdom within the British Commonwealth. Lack of understanding of the nature of the British Commonwealth, of the nature of the Canadian Confederation, and of some Canadian historical, geographical, and similar background could not fail to introduce errors, discords, or irritations in the policy consideration or operational handling of problems concerning U.S. activities in Canada. Too frequently, such lapses were compounded by an ineptitude on the part of U.S. officials in even the highest positions who violated the basic rules of the "how to win friends and influence people" technique.

A basic factor influencing postwar U.S.-Canadian military collaboration was the impact of advanced weapons and techniques on the Canadian "privileged sanctuary" position. By the end of World War II the development of aircraft, guided missiles, submarine warfare, airborne techniques, and the atomic weapons had advanced warfare to the threshold of a new era. In this new era North America ceased to be relatively immune from assault from other continents. The H-Hour ground assault in Europe could be matched by an H-Hour atomic bombing of Detroit and Windsor or of Washington and Ottawa. The mastery of the Atlantic and Pacific and the barrenness of the Arctic no longer prevented penetration of these barriers, and their value as buffers of time and space had been drastically reduced.

Under these circumstances the utilization of North American resources for and the role of Canada in the defense of the Western Hemisphere as a whole, within the framework of a joint U.S.-Canadian arrangement, assumed increasing importance to Canada. For some time before it entered World War II the United States had a well-developed interest in the defense of Latin America and visualized the danger of military action there as greater than in North Atlantic territories such as Newfoundland, Greenland, and Iceland. After Pearl Harbor the United States allocated substantial military resources to several of the larger Latin American nations. To Canada, the U.S. preoccupation with Latin America and use of resources there probably did not appear warranted by the military situation. Canada learned, too, that dependence on sources of military equipment outside of Canada made dubious the availability of essential supplies in an extreme emergency, such as that resulting from the 1940 German blitzkrieg, when the sources of military equipment for Canada dried up.

Theoretically, two choices were available to Canada in 1940: it could attempt to become self-sufficient in military supplies; or, it could continue to draw upon outside sources for certain items. Within the production base established in Canada by the end of World War II, the first choice might have been feasible. But in 1940, as a practical matter, it was out of the question, and Canada necessarily elected the second choice. In fact, in the working out of the Hyde Park Declaration, Canada strove for adoption and implementation of a concept under which Canada and the United States would correlate their production programs so that each would be completely dependent upon the other for items assigned each country for production. Such an arrangement visualized a balanced mobilization effort with joint production collaboration in the interest of efficient specialization and would, in effect, have bound Canada and the United States into a closely integrated security union at least for the duration of the war.

Actually, the arrangement as conceived by Canada was never carried out. The United States strove to develop the production capacity needed to supply at least some of its requirement of all items, and it utilized Canadian capacity quantitatively to agument its supply of selected items. Canada also departed from the Hyde Park concept. Although it purchased much of its military matériel from the United States and the United Kingdom, Canada broadened its production base and technical know-how until it was producing items in almost every category of military equipment. But with the end of World War II, Canada still remained faced with the question of how it should plan to procure its military equipment in peace and in war, and from what countries the equipment not manufactured in Canada should be procured.

The failure on the part of the United States to take into account political, psychological, economic, and similar factors in dealing with problems relating to Canada made for decisions and actions that were not always in the best U.S. or joint interest. Two examples were the questions relating to unified command and to the Canadian staff mission in Washington. This failure was a basic weakness in the over-all U.S. politico-military conduct of its relations with Canada in World War II.

More problems would have arisen had it not been for the civilian chairmanship of the two sections of the Permanent Joint Board on Defense. This arrangement interposed a civilian between the military of either section and the other government and its Permanent Joint Board representation. Properly selected civilians were competent to act as interpreters and moderators of the needs of their military colleagues and to insure that some account was taken of political and other nonmilitary factors. The civilian chairmen could thus make a useful contribution toward seeing that project requirements were brought within the limits of feasibility. In addition to exerting a moderating influence on the military of his own section, each chairman was in a better position than the military to press the other section harder for acceptance of some project in terms of the nonmilitary as well as the military urgency.

On the other hand, it does not appear from the World War II record that the civilian chairmen of the Permanent Joint Board and other civilian leaders were more inclined than military leaders to commit the two countries to intimate collaboration. To be sure, the basic impetus to U.S.-Canadian military collaboration was given by the civilian heads of the governments when they joined in making the Ogdensburg Declaration. But in practice thereafter civilian officials took the lead in pushing only one major project, the plan backed by Canada for co-ordinated North American aviation training, and then with only indifferent success.

The record of U.S.-Canadian wartime military collaboration shows that the Permanent Joint Board on Defense established at Ogdensburg proved useful beyond the expectations of President Roosevelt and Prime Minister King. It was born more out of political considerations than of military necessity, at least from the U.S. point of view, for neither the War nor the Navy Department was consulted before its establishment, nor had either department indicated a need for such a body. Nevertheless, the Board proved itself an excellent forum for a continuous and informal exchange of views and exploration of common problems, as well as for the conduct of broad studies as contemplated by Roosevelt and King. Through the give-and-take and mutual confidence that marked the functioning of the Board, many problems were solved harmoniously and effectively. Moreover, the Board became useful in handling the day-to-day operational details of a large number of field projects, thereby performing an essential staff function not otherwise provided for.

The problem of integration of the intricate pattern of U.S. activities in Canada and of their co-ordination with the Canadian authorities was a persistent thorn. By dint of continuing adjustment of such organizations as were established, and of extensive liaison between the Canadian and U.S. officials concerned, the problem was kept within manageable bounds. It had several aspects. The foci of the co-ordinating authorities for the numerous U.S. activities in Canada were in Washington and not only physically removed from Canada but also separated by several echelons of command. At few if any of these levels was there an adequate appreciation of Canadian political and other problems that should have been taken into account in reaching decisions and molding troop attitudes.

For lack of better machinery, the Permanent Joint Board on Defense came to have a substantial operational function in the co-ordination of arrangements between the two countries and among the various U.S. agencies involved. The scope of this function was limited, since the U.S. Section could exercise no command authority. Nevertheless, in handing a multitude of routine and administrative details, the Board seemed to fill an essential need in providing some co-ordinated direction to the U.S. projects in Canada.

The Canadian Government, too, experienced such a need and met it by creating the office of Special Commissioner for Defense Projects in Northwestern Canada. Except in the area of major policy, his office provided a Canadian focal point for that part of Canada in the co-ordination of matters of joint interest. This experience suggests that the establishment of a U.S. theater-type headquarters, charged with the conduct of all U.S. activities in Canada and Newfoundland, would have been very useful to both countries. Such a headquarters could have dealt with a single Canadian commissioner for defense projects, and could have provided integrated direction to and supervision of the U.S. activities.

An alternate solution might have been the establishment of a joint U.S-Canadian theater-type headquarters, with appropriately balanced representation from both countries. Such a headquarters, located in or near Ottawa, would have provided a single focus of policy and operational control for the related U.S. and Canadian activities in Canada. Such integrated direction would have made these activities more responsive to the requirements, military and otherwise, of the situation on a continuous basis and would have provided a ready means for joint review of project requirements and implementation of programs. Some faltering steps were taken in this direction. From the Canadian point of view, there were probably as good arguments against as for such an arrangement. On the U.S. side, the many agencies operating in the field in Canada were naturally content without the interposition of such an authority over them. That the need for such a headquarters did not become urgent was probably only the result of the fact that, except in a narrow sense in Newfoundland, the wartime activities in Canada were all of a logistical and not an operational nature. And, although the conduct of those activities involved co-operation between the two countries, the majority thereof were fundamentally unilateral U.S. projects, rather than joint ones in the sense that they were jointly developed and executed to meet a common requirement.

The foregoing conclusions tend somewhat to obscure the full compass of the successful collaboration between the two countries and should not be allowed to do so. For both Canadians and the Americans stationed in Canadian territory the situation was sometimes an awkward one. Both were serving the war effort of their countries, yet within the sphere of their activities, they were far removed from the battle fronts. The many engineering works of permanent value carried out through joint efforts give ample testimony to the success of wartime military co-operation.

There were other and more significant accomplishments that were realized through the efforts of the two partners. Canada is today on the threshold of becoming a world power. In part this emergence is due to the tremendous postwar development of Canadian natural wealth and resources. This development undoubtedly received a major stimulus during World War II as a result of the extensive U.S. operations in Canada, which broadened the knowledge of Canada's northern territories, improved the transportation facilities there, and opened up areas that had been infrequently penetrated by white man. Canada's productive capacity received a substantial boost from the Hyde Park Declaration, which not only generated a flow of orders but collaterally provided for Canadian acquisition of the machine tools and other equipment necessary to fill those orders.

The United States, and to a lesser extent Canada, can take credit for the economic rehabilitation of Newfoundland. In addition, as the question of Newfoundland's political future came to the forefront, the United States and U.S. officials maintained a perfectly correct attitude. Canada was prepared to welcome Newfoundland to the Canadian Confederation. In Newfoundland, there was sentiment for union with the United States, which had been the major fountainhead of its economic well-being, as well as for union with Canada. In no way did Americans try to influence public opinion or take a part in the solution of the problem, which was resolved in favor of admission of Newfoundland to Canada as a new province.

The history of wartime collaboration between the United States and Canada was a record of solid accomplishment with only minor notes of discord. The best testimony to the success of Canadian-U.S. wartime military co-operation is the fact that both countries were prepared, in the immediate postwar period when peace appeared to be a reality and demobilization was proceeding apace, to continue their military co-operation on a revitalized basis.

Appendix A

Recommendations of the Permanent Joint Board on Defense, Canada–United States, 26 August 1940–1 September 1945 [1]

FIRST RECOMMENDATION 26 August 1940

Exchange of Information

It was agreed that there should be a full and complete exchange of military, air and naval information between the two Sections of the Board, with the understanding that each Section would be free to convey to its government any information they received.

Action by U.S. Government: There appears to be no specific evidence in the files of the U.S. Section of approving or disapproving action. However, in the Progress Reports annexed to the Journal of Discussions and Decisions for the 20 21 January 1941 and subsequent meetings, members of the U.S. Section of the Board reported on the progress of action under this recommendation. It is apparent that at least informal approval was implied, or that approval had been taken for granted. This lack of evidence may be accounted for by the fact that the board at its early meetings attacked a large number of substantive problems without concerning itself adequately with procedural and administrative problems.

Action by Canadian Government: Approved, 5 September 1940.[2]

SECOND RECOMMENDATION 27 August 1940

Defense of Newfoundland

A. The Island of Newfoundland occupies a commanding position at the entrance of the St. Lawrence–Great Lakes waterway and on the flank of the sea route between the Atlantic seaboard of North America and Northern Europe. It is on the direct air route between the East Coast of the United States and Northern Europe. It is the point in North America, nearest to Europe, from which, if occupied by an enemy, further operations against the North American continent might be effectively initiated. As such it should be adequately defended.

B. The forces in Newfoundland now consist of one battalion of infantry for the defense of Botwood and the Newfoundland airport, a battery of two 4.7-inch guns now being

[1] Texts of recommendations and dates on which they were made are to be found in the appropriate Journal of Discussions and Decisions for the meeting held on the date indicated. These journals are to be found in file PDB 124.

[2] Memo, Secy, U.S. Section, for Acting Chairman, U.S. Section, 12 Dec 51, PDB 124–1. This list tabulates the dates of approval of the various recommendations by both governments as determined through a co-ordinated study made by the two secretaries in 1951 of the files kept since 1940. It is hereafter cited as the 12 Dec 51 List. At least in regard to action by the U.S. Government, this list is not always accurate, and it is cited only when more authoritative data could not be found.

installed at Bell Island, and a flight of five Digby (Douglas) land planes operating from Newfoundland airport. These forces are considered inadequate for the defense of the island at the present time and the security of Canada and the United States is thereby endangered.

C. The Board considers that the defense of Newfoundland should be materially strengthened by:

(a) Increasing the strength of the Canadian defensive garrisons immediately;
(b) Establishing as soon as practicable, and not later than the spring of 1941, a force of aircraft of suitable types adequate for patrolling the seaward approaches to Newfoundland and Canada and for the local defense of the Botwood area;
(c) Selecting and preparing, as soon as practicable, bases permitting the operation of United States aircraft, when and if circumstances require, in numbers as follows:

(1) A minimum of four squadrons of patrol planes (48 planes).
(2) A minimum of one composite group of land planes (73 planes).

(d) Completing, as early as practicable, and not later than the spring of 1941, the installation of appropriate defense for the port of St. John's, Newfoundland, for Botwood, and for other points as required.
(e) Taking such additional measures as further examination of the defense problem and local reconnaissance show to be necessary.

Action by U.S. Government: See comment on First Recommendation. Insofar as portions of the first eight recommendations related to troop and matériel dispositions which had not been made by 2 October 1940, they were approved as a result of their incorporation in the First Report of the Board to the two governments. This report, reproduced at Appendix B, received formal approval on 19 November 1940. Apparently, because of this action, the 12 December 1951 List arbitrarily assigns that date as the date of United States approval of the first eight recommendations. Such an assignment is not entirely accurate since the First Report encompassed only limited portions of the first eight recommendations.

Action by Canadian Government: Approved, 5 September 1940.[3]

THIRD RECOMMENDATION 27 August 1940

Defense of Maritime Provinces

A. The strategic importance of the Maritime Provinces is similar to that of Newfoundland. However, in addition to providing bases for the operation of aircraft and light patrol craft, the Maritime Provinces must provide secure bases from which major naval operations can be projected.

B. This will require harbors secure from underwater attack, with docking, repair and supply facilities capable of accommodating the major portion of the United States or British fleets; operating facilities for military and naval air forces; and harbor defenses supported by the necessary troop concentrations.

C. The Board finds that some of these requirements have already been met and that steps have been initiated for the accomplishment of others.

D. It is apparent that the following should be undertaken by the Canadian Government:

(a) Early completion of the present projects for underwater defenses at Halifax, Sydney, Gaspé and Shelburne.

[3] 12 Dec 51 List.

(b) Early completion of harbor defenses at these bases.
(c) Early expansion of aircraft operating facilities to include provision for four squadrons of patrol planes (48 planes) and one composite wing of approximately 200 planes.
(d) Such additional measures as further examination of the defense problem and local reconnaissance show to be necessary.

E. The Board also recommends the preparation in Canada and in the United States of adequate strategic reserves of men and materials for timely concentration in the Maritime Provinces if, and when, the need arises.

Action by U.S. Government: See comments on First and Second Recommendations. Portions of this recommendation were included in the First Report.

Action by Canadian Government: Approved, 5 September 1940.[4]

FOURTH RECOMMENDATION 27 August 1940

Allotment of Materials

It was agreed that arrangements concerted between the United States and Canadian representatives of each Service with regard to this material should be passed through the proper channels in order that the proper allocation of the material should be promptly made. It was further agreed that material provided to implement the recommendations of the Board shall not be used for any other purposes. As at present advised, the Board regarded the following classes of material as of special importance, their relative importance being in the order indicated for each Service:

Ground Forces

(a) A.A. armament and ammunition.
(b) Harbor defense armament and ammunition.
(c) General equipment of mobile defense.

Air Force

(a) Patrol planes.
(b) Fighter or pursuit planes with, in each case, armament, ammunition and radio equipment.

As to the Naval Forces the position as reported was that there have already been discussions which have led to arrangements under which it is expected that all present requirements are to be satisfied. These arrangements relate to:

(a) 4″ guns.
(b) .5 machine guns.
(c) Destroyers.

The Board approved of the carrying out of these arrangements for the purpose of the attainment of the objects covered on the Board's previous decisions.

Action by U.S. Government: See comments on First and Second Recommendations.

Action by Canadian Goverment: Approved, 5 September 1940.[5]

FIFTH RECOMMENDATION 27 August 1940

Improving Communications in the Northeast

That the subject of communications between Newfoundland, the Maritime Provinces,

---

[4] *Ibid.*

[5] *Ibid.*

Eastern Canada and the United States, is of high importance, the following subjects requiring to be examined:

(a) Railway facilities.
(b) Water transport.
(c) Roads.
(d) Air transport and communications.

That the establishment of additional commercial airways, complete with landing facilities and aids to air navigation, between these important areas, would be essential to the defense plan.

Action by U.S. Government: See comments on First and Second Recommendations. Portions of this recommendation were included in the First Report.

Action by Canadian Government: Approved, 5 September 1940.[6]

SIXTH RECOMMENDATION 27 August 1940

Production Data

That the Service Members undertake to assemble information on the production in each country of particular items of military equipment in their respective countries, not readily available in the other country, and to exchange information on this subject as data becomes available.

Action by U.S. Government: See comments on First and Second Recommendations.

Action by Canadian Government: Approved, 5 September 1940.[7]

SEVENTH RECOMMENDATION 27 August 1940

Joint Defense Plan

That the Service Members of the Board should proceed at once with the preparation of a detailed permanent plan for the joint defense of Canada and the United States and keep the Board informed of the progress of the work.[8]

Action by U.S. Government: See comments on First and Second Recommendations.

Action by Canadian Government: Approved, 5 September 1940.[9]

EIGHTH RECOMMENDATION 11 September 1940

Defense of Newfoundland

That the United States initiate as expeditiously as practicable such portions of the increased defense of Newfoundland, covered by the Second Recommendation of the Board approved in Ottawa on August 26 and 27, as may be found to fall within the limits of bases now being acquired by the United States.

Action by U. S. Government: See comments on First and Second Recommendations.

Action by Canadian Government: Approved, 7 October 1940.[10]

---

[6] *Ibid.*

[7] *Ibid.*

[8] As reproduced here from the journal for the meeting, the recommendation contains the word "permanent." All U.S. compilations of Board recommendations omit the word "permanent," as do the various drafts of the 1940 Plan, which quote the recommendation as a directive. This omission probably reflects subsequent informal Board agreement to delete the word as inappropriate. Such a plan could hardly have been expected to have been permanent.

[9] 12 Dec 51 List.

[10] *Ibid.*

NINTH RECOMMENDATION 4 October 1940

German Prisoners

The Board learned from Messrs. Emerson and Penson that the Government of the United Kingdom is now arranging to send approximately one thousand captured German airmen to Newfoundland for imprisonment there and that the Newfoundland Government is now beginning the construction of barracks for this purpose about five miles inland from the shore of Conception Bay.

The Board feels strongly that the incarceration of German prisoners in Newfoundland would present a serious military hazard which might jeopardize the Defense Scheme for Newfoundland which the Board is now preparing and thus menace the safety of Canada and the United States.

In these circumstances, the Board earnestly recommends to the Canadian Government that discussions be initiated with the Governments of Newfoundland and the United Kingdom with a view to bringing about an alteration in this plan by the diversion of these German prisoners to some less dangerous destination.

Action by U.S. Government: See comment on First Recommendation.

Action by Canadian Government: Approved, 8 October 1940.[11] *The prisoners were diverted to a camp in Canada, and this fact was reported at the 20–21 January 1941 meeting.*

TENTH RECOMMENDATION 14 November 1940

Air Staging Facilities—Western Canada

The Board recommends that, to implement the recommendation contained in its First Report to the respective governments regarding the development of air staging facilities across Western Canada between the United States and Alaska, suitable landing fields, complete with emergency lighting, radio aids, meteorological equipment and limited housing for weather, communication, and transient personnel be provided at the earliest possible date by Canada at Grand Prairie, Fort St. John, Fort Nelson, Watson Lake, Whitehorse, Prince George and Smithers.

This development will provide means for rapid movement of light bombers and fighter aircraft into Canada, into Centra Alaska via Whitehorse, and into the Ketchikan-Prince Rupert area via Smithers and is considered essential to the defense of Western Canada, Alaska and the United States. Such means are vital to the effective use in joint continental defense of both the rapidly expanding air forces of the United States and the extension of air operating facilities in Alaska.

Action by U.S. Government: See comment on First Recommendation. The First Report of the Board, which contained a less detailed recommendation for the development of such facilities, was approved by the President on 19 November 1940. (See Appendix B.)

Action by Canadian Government: Approved, 28 January 1941.[12]

ELEVENTH RECOMMENDATION 15 November 1940

Ucluelet Airdrome (Vancouver Island)

The Board now recommends that another airdrome be constructed at Ucluelet for the following purposes:

(a) To extend the operational ranges and areas of fighter aircraft and provide more advanced defense to our vulnerable positions.

[11] *Ibid.*
[12] *Ibid.*

(b) To provide bomber and fighter support to the north airdromes and towards the Queen Charlotte Islands and the West Coast up towards Prince Rupert.
(c) To provide an alternative landing place for bombers and fighters in a very variable weather area.

Action by U.S. Government: See comment on First Recommendation.
Action by Canadian Government: Approved, 28 January 1941.[13]

TWELFTH RECOMMENDATION 17 December 1940

War Industry Member

That a war industry member be appointed to the Board by each of the two Governments.

Action by U.S. Government: Approved, 26 December 1940.[14]
Action by Canadian Government: Approved, 20 January 1941.[15]

THIRTEENTH RECOMMENDATION 20 January 1941

Sault Ste. Marie

In view of the vital military importance of the Sault Ste. Marie Canals and the St. Mary's River to the defense program of the United States, and the vulnerability of the navigation channel, the Board agreed that each Government should constitute a single authority to be responsible for the safety of navigation through these waters, and that each such authority be clothed with the necessary powers and required to cooperate with the other in taking all measures necessary for the purpose.

Action by U.S. Government: Approved.[16]
Action by Canadian Government: Approved, 27 March 1941.[17]

FOURTEENTH RECOMMENDATION 21 January 1941

United States Air Units for Newfoundland

That most urgent priority should be given to the provision of facilities for at least one United States squadron of patrol planes at Halifax and one United States squadron in the Botwood area.

Action by U.S. Government: No record of action. See comment on the First Recommendation.
Action by Canadian Government: Approved, 27 March 1941.[18]

FIFTEENTH RECOMMENDATION 16 April 1941

Newfoundland Fuel Storage

The Board reviewed the problem of fuel supply required for aerial operations from the

[13] *Ibid.*
[14] Memo, SUSAM for Bissell, 26 Dec 40, PDB 100. This recommendation was never implemented.
[15] 12 Dec 51 List.
[16] On date unknown according to file PDB 124-1. The President on 17 March 1941 issued a directive to U.S. executive agencies directing co-operation with the War Department in this matter.
[17] 12 Dec 51 List.
[18] *Ibid.*

Newfoundland Airport and in the Lewisporte-Botwood area. Previous estimates contemplated storage for 1,600,000 gallons (of which 600,000 gallons, one month's supply, would be located at Newfoundland Airport) premised on continuous supply by rail from St. John's. It has now been determined that reliance on continuous rail supply during the winter is unsound. Facts were adduced to show that a minimum storage capacity of 2,600,000 gallons will be essential before the close of navigation in the Botwood area next winter. Discussion clearly exposed the urgency of providing the increase in capacity.

It was also pointed out that not only is the increase essential for defense operations but is equally necessary for overseas ferrying of aircraft.

It is recommended that Canada provide the increased storage capacity in accordance with the responsibility accepted by the Canadian Government.

It is further recommended that the United States Government assist in the procurement of the necessary priorities to permit this recommendation to be carried out within the time specified.

Action by U.S. Government: Approved, 22 April 1941.[19]
Action by Canadian Government: Approved, 14 May 1941.[20]

SIXTEENTH RECOMMENDATION 17 April 1941

Rehabilitation of the Newfoundland Railroad

The Board, after consultation with Newfoundland Commissioner; after determination that the present condition and rolling stock (on hand or order) of the Newfoundland railroad are barely adequate for civilian requirements; and after full consideration of the great urgency of adequate supply prior to the winter of 1941 of United States bases and United States forces stationed outside base areas in Newfoundland recommends:

That the United States procure and retain title to such railroad rolling stock as is necessary for its military requirements in Newfoundland including possible operations from the Newfoundland Airport.

That the Newfoundland Government continue to operate the Newfoundland railroad and undertake at once the construction of additional facilities and necessary rehabilitation of the railroad outside of areas leased to the United States.

That necessary arrangements for essential financial assistance be immediately worked out between the United States and Newfoundland Governments.

That both Canada and the United States assist in the procurement of the necessary priorities required to permit this recommendation to be carried out in the time specified.

Action by U.S. Government: Approved, 22 April 1941.[21]
Action by Canadian Government: Approved, 14 May 1941.[22]

SEVENTEENTH RECOMMENDATION 29 July 1941

Northwest River Landing Field

In order to facilitate the ferrying of long and medium range aircraft across the Atlantic, to enhance the effectiveness of plans for hemisphere defense, to prevent congestion at the Newfoundland Airport and to provide greater security for crews and equipment, the Board recommends:

That the Canadian Government should undertake the construction of an air base in

[19] Memo, SUSAM for Brig Maurice Pope, 29 Apr 41, PDB 107-3.
[20] 12 Dec 51 List.
[21] Ltr, President to SW, 23 Apr 41, PDB 143-1.
[22] 12 Dec 51 List.

the vicinity of Northwest River, Labrador, and provide the following facilities *as quickly as possible.*

(a) At least two runways, minimum 150 x 5000 feet, to enable take off and landing into prevailing winds.
(b) Storage facilities for 450,000 gallons aviation gasoline, for 11,250 gallons aviation oil, and for other supplies.
(c) Seven 100 gallon per minute gasoline pumping units for servicing aircraft.
(d) Technical housing and equipment as follows:

1. A direction finder station.
2. An aircraft radio range station.
3. Instrument landing equipment.
4. An airways radio station capable of communication with stations in the U.S., Canada, Newfoundland, and Greenland and with aircraft in flight, for purposes of aircraft control, forwarding and receiving weather data and airplane movement communications.
5. A meteorological station.
6. A maintenance hangar (heated), minimum dimensions 150 x 200 feet.

(e) Housing for personnel.

That if the Canadian Government should decide for any reason that it will not undertake the desired construction immediately, this decision should be made known at once to the Governments of the United States, United Kingdom and Newfoundland and that the Government of the United States be invited to provide the necessary facilities in the area under reference.

That Governments of Canada and the United States should cooperate to make provision for the necessary priorities to permit the earliest possible completion and that the Government undertaking the project should also immediately initiate the necessary measures to insure provision of an installation suitable for safe operations from the ice in the Northwest River area during the winter of 1941–42.

Action by U.S. Government: No evidence of approval in U.S. files.
Action by Canadian Government: Approved, 18 September 1941.[23]

EIGHTEENTH RECOMMENDATION 29 July 1941

Underwater Defenses for Argentia

That the United States proceed with the installation of underwater defenses in the Argentia-Ship Harbor area.

Action by U. S. Government: See comment on First Recommendation.
Action by Canadian Government: Approved, 18 September 1941.[24]

NINETEENTH RECOMMENDATION 29 July 1941

Canadian-Alaskan Staging Fields

On the consideration of the report as to the progress being made with the construction of the Canadian Airway between Edmonton and Whitehorse, attention was directed

[23] The 12 December 1951 List records 18 September 1941 as the date of Canadian governmental approval, although approval was given by the Cabinet War Committee on 13 August 1941.

[24] 12 Dec 51 List.

to the recent change in the Far Eastern situation the effect of which is to make the completion of the airway to Alaska of extreme urgency. It was pointed out that the urgent needs for air strength in Alaska may suddenly increase beyond those heretofore anticipated, that the preparation of airdromes in Alaska is being expedited by the United States as much as possible, but that large numbers of aircraft if sent there would at present be relatively isolated.

In view of this, the Board decided to invite attention to the fact that the completion of both the Canadian and the United States sections of the airway to a point which would permit its use at the earliest possible moment had become of extreme importance and to recommend that other considerations should give way to that of completing as quickly as possible the air route which will permit the rapid reinforcement of the air strength in Alaska.

Action by U.S. Government: See comment on First Recommendation.
Action by Canadian Government: Approved, 18 September 1941.[25]

TWENTIETH RECOMMENDATION 30 July 1941

Newfoundland Roads

(a) That improvement and maintenance of road communications is recognized as essential for effective military operations in the defense of Newfoundland.
(b) That the Newfoundland Government should, without cost to the United States or the Canadian Government, make available the rights of way necessary for such roads as the United States or the Canadian Governments consider must be constructed for military purposes.
(c) That the United States and Canada should be given the right to construct and maintain such roads as each individually requires in Newfoundland for military purposes without obligation either to construct or maintain any roads.
(d) That Newfoundland, Canadian and United States vehicles would have use without tolls of any roads constructed by the United States or Canada in Newfoundland outside of base areas.
(e) That all necessary road maintenance in Newfoundland other than as provided for above should be a responsibility of the appropriate Newfoundland authorities.

Action by U.S. Government: See comment on First Recommendation.
Action by Canadian Government: Approved, 18 September 1941.[26]

TWENTY-FIRST RECOMMENDATION 10 November 1941

Maintenance of Facilities

Attention was directed to the question of the maintenance of the structures, etc., provided by Canada at Gander Lake for occupation by United States Forces and it was recognized that the course of events may make it convenient to permit the use by United States Forces of like facilities in both Newfoundland and Canada and also permit the use of facilities in United States by Canadian Forces. Consideration was accordingly given to the general principles which should govern the responsibilities of each country in respect of the maintenance of structures, etc., built by the Government of either which are occupied by the Forces of the other, and the Board decided to make the following 21st Recommendation:

The Board recommends that when facilities are provided by the Government of either

[25] *Ibid.*
[26] *Ibid.*

country for the occupation of Forces of the other the following principles should apply to the maintenance, upkeep and servicing of such facilities, subject to such local definition and if necessary modification as the circumstances require:

1. Any building constructed by the Government of one country and wholly occupied by Forces of the other should be maintained by the occupying Forces and at the termination of the occupation turned over to the Government of the country by which it was provided in the same condition as when the occupation commenced, ordinary wear and tear, act of God, enemy action, riot, insurrection or fire excepted.

2. The same rule should apply to structures appurtenant to buildings when these are included in an area capable of delimitation and occupied by the Forces concerned which should in these circumstances undertake the policing of the area.

3. The occupying Forces should also be responsible for the heating, lighting and other services relating to any building or area occupied by them in all cases in which the service is derived from a source adapted exclusively to take care of the building or area in question but in other cases the services should be provided on an equitable basis by the Government of the country by which the occupation is permitted.

4. No occupying Forces should make any structural change in existing facilities without the approval of the service by which the area is set aside for occupation or the occupied buildings are provided.

Action by U.S. Government: Approved, 14 November 1941.[27]
Action by Canadian Government: Approved, 26 November 1941.[28]

TWENTY-SECOND RECOMMENDATION 20 December 1941

Decentralization of Functions to Local Commanders

That the United States and Canadian Governments now authorize the Commanders named in paragraph 12 of ABC-22, or their duly authorized representatives, to effect by mutual agreement any arrangements they deem necessary for the perfection of preparations for the common defense including but not limited to, the installations of accessory equipment in the territory of either, the transit of armed forces, equipment or defense materials into or through the territory of either, and the utilization by either nation of the base and military facilities of the other.

Action by U.S. Government: Approved, 24 December 1941.[29]
Action by Canadian Government: Approved, 14 January 1942.[30]

TWENTY-THIRD RECOMMENDATION 20 December 1941

Co-ordination of Aviation Training Programs

That the Canadian and United States Governments should consider the advisability of arranging for a meeting of appropriate representatives of Great Britain, Canada and the United States to make appropriate recommendations for co-ordination of the entire aviation training programs to be conducted in Canada and the United States.

Action by U.S. Government: Approved, 24 December 1941.[31]
Action by Canadian Government: Approved, 14 January 1942.[32]

---

[27] Photostatic copy of text of recommendation bearing the initials "FDR," PDB 107–9.
[28] Ltr, Group Captain Heakes to Lt Col Bissell, 27 Nov 41, PDB 107–3.
[29] Approval reported in Journal, 20 Jan 42 PJBD meeting. See also PDB 135–9.
[30] *Ibid.*
[31] Approval reported in Journal, 20 Jan 42 PJBD meeting. See also PDB 119–3.
[32] *Ibid.*

TWENTY-FOURTH RECOMMENDATION [33] 26 February 1942

Military Highway to Alaska

As its Twenty-Fourth Recommendation, the Board accordingly, as a matter pertaining to the joint defense of Canada and the United States, recommends the construction of a highway along the route that follows the general line of airports, Fort St. John-Fort Nelson-Watson Lake-Whitehorse-Boundary-Big Delta, the respective termini connecting with existing roads in Canada and Alaska.

Action by U.S. Government: Approved, 9 March 1942.[34]

Action by Canadian Government: Approved, 5 March 1942.[35]

TWENTY-FIFTH RECOMMENDATION 25-26 February 1942

Defense of Sault Ste. Marie Against Air Attack

(a) That the Royal Canadian Air Force undertake to make an immediate and comprehensive further study of the data available regarding the danger of air attack to the Sault Ste. Marie area.
(b) That the Canadian Army assign a 4-gun, heavy, antiaircraft battery to Sault Ste. Marie, to protect the Canadian Locks and to tie in with the United States force in order that all-round zone defense may be established. In the event of Canada being unable to provide this equipment within the near future, the United States Army endeavor to lend the necessary guns and stores for manning by the Canadian Army until such time as Canada can meet this commitment from her own production.
(c) That the said Canadian antiaircraft battery come under the operational command of the Commanding General, Sault Ste. Marie Military District, (Michigan).

Action by U.S. Government: Approved, 9 March 1942.[36]
Action by Canadian Government: Approved, 26 March 1942.[37]

TWENTY-SIXTH RECOMMENDATION 9 June 1942

Northeast Short-Range Ferry Routes to United Kingdom

(a) That the airfields in Canadian territory on the ferry routes outlined in the Army Air Forces appreciation dated June 6th be constructed with such variations as the detailed survey, now under way, may determine to be advisable.
(b) That the Canadian Government construct or authorize the United States Government to construct these fields and inform the United States Government as promptly as possible what fields, if any, Canada will construct.
(c) That the existing ferry airdrome facilities in Canada and Newfoundland, including Labrador, form a part of the proposed ferrying project and be increased, wherever necessary, to appropriate capacity.

---

[33] This recommendation, together with other pertinent extracts of the journal of the 25-26 February 1942 meeting, is printed as Exhibit 16, App. C, House Report 1705, 79th Congress, 2d Session, pp. 89-91.

[34] Memo, U.S. Chairman for President, 7 Mar 42, initialed "OK FDR" two days later. This memorandum is printed as Exhibit 17, House Report 1705, 79th Congress, 2d Session, p. 91.

[35] Memo, Stimson for President, 7 Mar 42, printed as Exhibit 18, House Report 1705, 79th Congress, 2d Session, pp. 91-92.

[36] Memo, SUSAM for ACofS WPD, 10 Mar 42, sub: Twenty-fourth and Twenty-fifth Recommendations of the Permanent Joint Board on Defense, PDB 125-2.

[37] 12 Dec 51 List.

(d) That such additional radio weather reporting facilities for these routes be provided and maintained as may be agreed upon by the United States and the Canadian Governments.
(e) That all costs of constructing air fields and other installations in connection with this project be borne by the Government which agrees to undertake that part of the project.
(f) That suitable arrangements be made in Washington and Ottawa to insure the proper centralization of responsibility for and control over the work of construction, and to provide the maximum facilities for instant and effective contact and cooperation between the appropriate authorities of the two countries.
(g) That the proposals relating to defense, to the maintenance of Canadian sovereignty and the postwar disposition of the new installations as outlined in the memoranda under reference be accepted by the two Goverments.
(h) That these airfields and facilities be made available for the use of the Royal Air Force Ferry Command.

Action by U.S. Government: Approved, 3 July 1942.[38]
Action by Canadian Government: Approved, 12 June 1942.[39]

TWENTY-SEVENTH RECOMMENDATION 6 July 1942

Flow of Materials to Canada

That the Governments of Canada and of the United States take immediate steps to eliminate or suspend for the duration of the war every possible formality of customs, import duties, tariffs, and other regulations which prohibit, delay or otherwise impede the free flow between the two countries of munitions and war supplies and of the persons or materials connected therewith.

Action by U.S. Government: Approved, 8 August 1942.[40]
Action by Canadian Government: No formal approval.[41]

TWENTY-EIGHTH RECOMMENDATION 13 January 1943

Postwar Disposition of U.S. Projects in Canada

The Board recommends the approval of the following formula as a generally fair and equitable basis to be used by reference whenever appropriate in the making of agreements in the future and to cover such defense projects, if any, the postwar disposition of which has not previously been specifically provided for:

A. All immovable defense installations built or provided in Canada by the Government of the United States shall within one year after the cessation of hostilities, unless otherwise agreed by the two Governments, be relinquished to the Crown either in the right of Canada or in the right of the Province in which the same or any part thereof lies, as may be appropriate under Canadian law.

B. All movable facilities built or provided in Canada by the Government of the United States shall within one year after the cessation of hostilities, unless otherwise agreed by the two Governments, at the option of the United States Government:

[38] Memo, CofS for President, 3 Jul 42, bearing the notation "OK FDR." Certified copy filed at PDB 149-1.
[39] Ltr, U.S. Secy PJBD to U.S. Chairman, 13 Jun 42, PDB 105-2.
[40] Ltr, Secy State to Secy Treasury, 8 Aug 42, PDB 148.
[41] 12 Dec 51 List.

(1) be removed from Canada: or
(2) be offered for sale to the Government of Canada, or with the approval of the Government of Canada, to the Government of the appropriate Province at a price to be fixed by a Board of two appraisers, one to be chosen by each country and with power to select a third in the case of disagreement.

C. In the event that the United States Government has foregone its option as described in B (1), and the Canadian Government or the Provincial Government decides to forego its option as described in B (2), the facility under consideration shall be offered for sale in the open market, any sale to be subject to the approval of both Governments.

D. In the event of no sale being concluded the disposition of such facility shall be referred for recommendation to the Permanent Joint Board on Defense or to such other agency as the two Governments may designate.

The principles outlined above shall reciprocally apply to any defense projects and installations which may be built in the United States by the Government of Canada.

All of the foregoing provisions relate to the physical disposition and ownership of projects, installations, and facilities and are without prejudice to any agreement or agreements which may be reached between the Governments of the United States and Canada in regard to the postwar use of any of these projects, installations, and facilities.

Action by U.S. Government: Approved, 27 January 1943.[42]
Action by Canadian Government: Approved, 27 January 1943.[43]

TWENTY-NINTH RECOMMENDATION 24 February 1943

United States–Alaska Air Route

1. That the Department of Transport (Canada) be responsible for the completion of all facilities on this route presently in process of actual construction by contractors under contract to the Department of Transport, but that wherever possible and in order to expedite construction, United States Engineer troops be used to assist in such construction.

2. That the construction of the following facilities be approved by the Canadian Government, subject to the submission to the Department of Transport of a detailed plan showing the location of such facilities at the respective airports:

EDMONTON	*PRIORITY*
4 Barracks—68-man capacity each	A
1 Transient Officers Quarters—40-man capacity	B
1 Mess Hall—1,000-man capacity	C
1 Laundry—3,000 capacity	D
2 Hangars—150′ x 200′	E
2 Warehouses—50′ x 400′	F
1 Garage—70′ x 200′	G
1 Recreation Hall & Gymnasium	H
Doors on north end of present #1 Hangar	I

WHITEHORSE	*PRIORITY*
4 Barracks—68-man capacity each	A
2 Transient Officers Quarters—40-man capacity	B
1 Mess Hall—500-man capacity	C

[42] By exchange of notes signed at Ottawa. The notes are contained in EAS, 391, and CTS, 1943, No. 2, and include the recommendation in full.
[43] *Ibid.*

1 Laundry—2,000 capacity . . . . D
1 Hangar and 20,000 sq. ft.—220′ x 200′ office space . . . . E
1 Warehouse—40′ x 200′ . . . . F
1 Garage—70′ x 200′ . . . . G
1 Recreation Hall and Gymnasium . . . . H

3. That the United States Army Air Forces be responsible for the construction of all facilities set forth in 2: (construction to be accomplished by United States Engineer troops or by contract with Canadian or United States contractors, except that at Edmonton airport no construction shall be undertaken by a United States contractor except with the prior approval of appropriate Canadian authorities. If United States contractors are employed, Canadian and United States civilian labor will not be used on the same specific project at Edmonton).

4. That, inasmuch as speed of completion of these projects is of the highest importance, it be understood that contracts with Canadian contractors may require the employment of Canadian labor on a basis of three shifts daily.

5. That if, in the course of construction of the various projects at Edmonton airport, it becomes apparent that United States Engineer troops, or Canadian contractors, or both, are unable to complete any project within the time required, or are unable to undertake the construction of necessary additional facilities, upon appropriate representation the Canadian Government authorize the use of United States contractors, employing United States labor.

6. That the United States Forces be authorized further to expand the facilities, including airports, on this route as may be required subject to the following conditions:

a. The submission of a detailed plan showing the location of the proposed facilities and the approval thereof by appropriate Canadian officials.

b. No United States contractor or labor other than the United States Engineer troops shall be employed at Edmonton without the prior approval of the Canadian Government.

7. That in the construction of any such additional facilities, including airports, at any point north of Edmonton, United States Engineer troops, or Canadian or United States contractors employing United States labor may be employed, except that Canadian and United States contractors be not engaged in the same specific project. (At Edmonton, work to be performed by United States Engineer troops or Canadian contractors, within the limit of the ability of such contractors to perform the services required.)

8. That in all cases where civilian labor is employed, if Canadian contractors are available, their services shall be utilized, within the limit of their abilities, in the construction of these projects.

9. That in any case where Canadian contractors are employed by the United States Forces in the construction of any projects, the United States Forces be responsible for the administration and supervision of the contract.

10. That the Department of Transport (Canada) designate a responsible official to be stationed on this route with authority to make decisions with respect to location of buildings and any other matter which properly may be brought to his attention.

Action by U.S. Government: Approved, 1 April 1943.[44]

---

[44] Ltr, Roosevelt to Chairman, U.S. Section, 1 Apr 43, PDB 105–13. However, this approval apparently was not communicated to the Canadian Government and the recommendation was carried by the U.S. Section as not approved.

Action by Canadian Government: Not approved. However, construction of the projects of this recommendation was approved, subject to certain conditions, by separate action of the Canadian Government on 3 June 1943.[45]

THIRTIETH RECOMMENDATION 1–2 April 1943

Use of Non-Rigid Airships, Eastern Canadian Waters

That the Governments of the United States and Canada, having a mutual interest in the proposal to utilize non-rigid airships in antisubmarine activities in Eastern Canadian waters at the earliest practical date, appoint a Joint Canadian-American Board of officers to investigate, consult and report on the proposal, and on the selection of suitable base sites and facilities, in that area, to support the operation of not more than twelve airships commencing about May, 1944.

Action by U.S. Government: Approved, 13 April 1943.[46]

Action by Canadian Government: Not approved.[47] *Although the Canadian Government was not prepared to approve the recommendation in the form submitted, it had no objection to appointment of the board of officers or to examination of the problem. At its subsequent meeting, 6–7 May 1943, the Board agreed that this qualified action met the essence of the original proposal.*[48]

THIRTY-FIRST RECOMMENDATION 6–7 May 1943

Maintenance and Control of Airdromes in Canada

1. In cases in which the airfield is used principally or exclusively by U.S. forces the United States shall normally be responsible for defense, maintenance and control.

2. In all other cases, unless some special arrangement has been made, Canada shall be responsible for defense, maintenance and control.

3. Provision for the defense of airfields shall, in all cases, be of a standard acceptable to the Canadian Chiefs of Staff.

4. The assignment of responsibilities in respect of any airfield shall remain unchanged during the war except by mutual agreement; provided that should Canada inform the United States that it is prepared to assume such responsibilities in respect of any airfield previously controlled by the U.S. the necessary arrangements shall be concerted between the two Governments.

5. The United States Government may station a liaison officer at any airfield in Canada used by United States forces; and the Canadian Government may station a liaison officer at any airfield in Canada the control of which is exercised by the United States.

It was agreed that upon the acceptance of this Recommendation the Air Members of the Board shall prepare a schedule showing the application of the principles to the airfields affected for submission to the Board as a basis for a further recommendation.

---

[45] See correspondence at PDB 105–13.

[46] Ltr, ACofS OPD to SUSAM, 13 Apr 43, sub: Thirtieth Recommendation, Permanent Joint Board on Defense, Canada-U.S.; and Ltr, Senior U.S. Navy Member to SUSAM, 6 Apr 43, PDB 142–5. This recommendation apparently was not, probably because of its narrow military application, submitted to the President. The date recorded for U.S. approval in PDB 124 is the date on which both War and Navy Department approvals had been submitted.

[47] 12 Dec 51 List.

[48] Ltr, Secy Canadian Section to Secy U.S. Section, 23 Apr 43, PDB 142–5.

Action by U.S. Government: Approved, 3 June 1943.[49]
Action by Canadian Government: Approved, 2 June 1943.[50]

THIRTY-SECOND RECOMMENDATION 24–25 August 1943

Maintenance and Control of Facilities

PART I
Definitions

That for the purposes of this Recommendation, the following definitions apply:

1. *Control:*

Control of airport and airways traffic, and airport administration, provided that regulations applicable to airway and airport traffic control shall be prepared jointly by the using services, and shall be limited to those matters essential to the orderly control of traffic movement, and shall not include ceiling and visability limitation for take-off and landing.

Note: Airport administration, in the military sense, consisting of those functions pertaining to command.

2. *Maintenance:*

a. *Airfields:*

Maintenance of airfield surfaces including runways, taxiways, parking areas, hardstandings, and snow removal according to the standard of the principal user. The priority of such snow removal shall be as prescribed by the principal user.

Maintenance of access roads used solely, or nearly so, for the servicing of the airport and of roads and drainage ditches within and adjacent to the airport area, including snow clearance.

b. *Other Facilities:*

Maintenance of local airport landline communication systems, power, heating, lighting, water, fire-fighting and sewage systems, with the exception of that part of these systems installed in buildings.

c. *Responsibility of Using Service:*

Proper maintenance of all buildings and facilities installed therein is the responsibility of the using service. When facilities are provided by the Government of one country for the occupation of forces of the other, the principles set forth in the Twenty-First Recommendation of the Board apply to the maintenance, upkeep and servicing of such facilities.

d. *Responsibility of Officers Commanding:*

In the discharge of the above responsibilities, Officers Commanding will be authorized to make such definitions or modifications as local circumstances may require.

3. *Defense:*

Defense of the airport area in conformance with standards acceptable to the Canadian Chiefs of Staff.

---

[49] Apparently not submitted to the President. A letter dated 17 June 1943 from SUSAM to the U.S. secretary asked him to notify the Canadian Government of U.S. approval since the War and Navy Departments—"the only two agencies concerned"—had approved it. (PDB 113–2(a).)

[50] Ltr, Secy Canadian Section to Secy U.S. Section, 4 Jun 43, PDB 113–2(a).

Note: Local security of aircraft, technical installations and building areas is the responsibility of the using Service.

PART II
Schedule of Responsibility

1. *Northwest Staging Route:*

a. That Canada be responsible for the *control, maintenance* and *defense* of the following airports:

Feeder: Prince George, Kamloops, B.C.; Lethbridge and Calgary, Alta.; Regina, Sask.

Main: Edmonton, Alta.; Grande Prairie, Alta.; Fort St. John and Fort Nelson, B.C.; Watson Lake and Whitehorse, Y.T.

Intermediate: Beatton River and Smith River, B.C.; Teslin, Aishihik and Snag, Y.T.; (Whitecourt, Alta. when constructed).

b. That the U.S. be responsible for the maintenance, local airport control and defense of the following airports:

Main: Edmonton Satellite

Note: Edmonton Satellite will be subject only to airways traffic control by Canada under mutually acceptable regulations.

2. That the United States be responsible for the *control, maintenance* and *defense* of the following flight strips:

a. *Canol Project (N.W.T.)*
   (i) *Canol #1A*
   Waterways, Alta.; Embarras, Alta.; Fort Smith, Providence, Resolution, Hay River, Fort Simpson, Wrigley, Norman Wells, Canol Camp, N.W.T.
   (ii) *Canol #1 East and West*
   Goodland Lake and Twitya River, N.W.T.; Sheldon Lake, Pelly River and Quiet Lake, Y.T.

b. *Alaska Highway*
   Dawson Creek, Prophet River, Sikanni Chief River, Trout River and Pine Lake, B.C.; Squanga Lake, Pon Lake and Burwash, Y.T.

3. *Northeast Short-Range Ferry Route to U.K.:*

a. That the United States be responsible for the *control, maintenance* and *defense* of the following airports:

Western Sector: The Pas, Churchill, Man.; Southampton Island, N.W.T.

Eastern Sector: Fort Chimo, P.Q.; Frobisher Bay, N.W.T.

Others: Mingan, P.Q.

Note: Mingan will be subject only to airways traffic control by Canada under mutually acceptable regulations.

b. That Canada be responsible for the *control, maintenance,* and *defense* of the follow-airports:

Moncton, N.B.; Dorval, P.Q.

Action by U.S. Government: Approved, 24 September 1943.[51]
Action by Canadian Government: Approved, 22 September 1943.[52]

THIRTY-THIRD RECOMMENDATION[53] 6–7 September 1944

Postwar Disposition of U.S. Projects in Canada

The Permanent Joint Board on Defense recommends that the following formula be applied to the disposition of all defense facilities constructed or provided in Canada by the United States (and *mutatis mutandis* to any defense facilities constructed or provided in the United States by Canada) which have not already been dealt with.

Immovables

A—The Government of the United States shall, within three months from the date of the approval of this Recommendation, supply the Government of Canada with a list of immovables (hereinafter referred to as facilities) which it desires to make subject to the provisions of this Recommendation;

B—In the case of each of the facilities included in the list referred to in A the Canadian Government and the United States Government will each appoint one qualified appraiser whose joint duty it will be to appraise such facility in order to determine the fair market value thereof at the time and place of appraisal. If the two appraisers cannot agree on the fair market value, they will select a third appraiser to determine this value. The amount set by the appraisers shall be paid to the United States Government by the Government of Canada:

Provided that the foregoing paragraphs A and B shall not apply to any facilities heretofore specifically provided for.

C—Any existing facility not included in the United States list shall, within one year after the cessation of hostilities, be relinquished, without cost, to the Crown either in the right of Canada or in the right of the Province in which the same or any part thereof lies, as may be appropriate under Canadian law.

Movables

A—The Government of the United States shall remove from Canada all those items which it desires.

B—The Government of Canada shall arrange through the appropriate governmental agencies for the purchase from the United States of such remaining items as it desires to obtain for its own use or disposition.

C—All other movables shall be transferred to a designated agency of the Canadian Government and shall be sold or disposed of by such agency, the proceeds to be paid to the Government of the United States,

provided that, in connection with the items referred to in Paragraph C, the United States Government shall be represented by an officer designated by it for that purpose, who shall have an equal voice in the setting of prices, the allocation of priorities, the assessment of legitimate sales costs and other details of the sale or other disposal of the items concerned; *and provided further* that any such items remaining unsold at the end of two years from the time they are transferred to the

[51] Telg, Secy U.S. Section to Secy Canadian Section, 28 Sep 43, PDB 113–2(b).
[52] Ltr, Secy U.S. Section to SUSAM, 28 Sep 43, PDB 113–2(b).
[53] Text also contained in EAS, 444, and CTS, 1944, No. 35.

Canadian agency concerned shall either be declared of no value and the account closed or, at the option of the United States, shall be removed from Canada by the United States authorities.

Action by U.S. Government: Approved, 11 November 1944, including the Canadian proviso.[54]
Action by Canadian Government: Approved, 27 September 1944, with the following proviso:

That, as there are certain facilities whose disposal would entail expenses such as custody and demolition, any expense of such a character would be taken into consideration in the final accounting.[55]

---

[54] Ltr, Secy U.S. Section to SUSAM, 13 Nov 44, PDB 150–2. Both governments confirmed their approvals in a subsequent exchange of notes, published in EAS, 444, and CTS, 1944, No. 35.

[55] Ltr, Secy U.S. Section to SUSAM, 3 Oct 44, PDB 150–2. See also n. 54, above.

Appendix B

First Report of the Permanent Joint Board on Defense, Canada-United States [1]

1. The Board has met on three occasions, namely (a) at Ottawa on August 26th, and 27th; (b) at Washington on September 9th, 10th and 11th; and (c) at Boston and Halifax on the 2d, 3rd, and 4th of October 1940.

2. At the first of these meetings the Board made recommendations as to—

(a) The exchange of information.
(b) The strengthening of the forces in Newfoundland.
(c) Certain steps to be taken in respect to the direct defense of the Maritime Provinces.
(d) The allotment of matériel.
(e) Communications.
(f) The collection of information as to facilities for production.
(g) The preparation of a detailed plan for the defense of North America.

Such of the foregoing recommendations as relate to dispositions for defense still to be made are incorporated in the appropriate place in this report.

3. In the interval between the first and second meeting of the Board, announcement was made of the arrangement between the Governments of Great Britain and the United States for the establishment by the United States of bases in Newfoundland, the Bermudas, the Caribbean Area. In the interval between the second and third, the tripartite arrangement between Germany, Italy, and Japan was announced.

4. The present report is directed to indicating the allotment of responsibility as between Canada and the United States for the direct defense of North America so far as that defense may require joint or concerted operations by the two countries and also the steps which should be taken by the two Governments in advance of such joint or concerted operations.

5. In order that joint or concerted operations may be promptly and effectively proceeded with when they become necessary and are ordered to be taken, the Board recommends that each Government should independently, and as soon as possible, take the following steps.

---

[1] This report was approved by the Board on 4 October 1940. It was approved by President Roosevelt on 19 November, and its approval by the Canadian Government was reported at the 14 November 1940 Board meeting. (Journal, PDB 124; Ltr, Acting Secy State Welles to SW, 20 Nov 40, PDB 127.)

EAST COAST

CANADA

(a) Provide facilities in Newfoundland for the operation of United States aircraft in numbers as follows:

(i) A minimum of three squadrons of patrol planes (36 planes).
(ii) A minimum of 73 land planes.

(b) Provide radio and other facilities at Sydney and Newfoundland Airports, for land plane staging.
(c) If physically possible, provide a fighter aerodrome near St. John's.
(d) Complete defenses for the port of St. John's and for Botwood.
(e) Complete the harbor defenses (including underwater defenses) at Halifax, Sydney, Gaspé, and Shelburne.
(f) Expand the aircraft operating facilities in the Maritime Provinces, so as to provide for the operation of United States aircraft in numbers as follows:

(i) Four squadrons of patrol planes (48 planes).
(ii) One composite wing of approximately 200 planes.

UNITED STATES

(g) Select and complete a base or bases in Newfoundland sufficient to permit the operation of at least one squadron of patrol planes (12 planes).
(h) Provide staging facilities in Newfoundland for short-range aircraft between Sydney and the Newfoundland Airport, these to include radio facilities.
(i) Develop airways and other transportation facilities in New England so as to permit the rapid reinforcement of the Canadian Forces in the Maritime Provinces.
(j) Provide ground, anti-aircraft and harbor defenses of United States bases in Newfoundland.

WEST COAST

CANADA

(k) Develop air staging facilities for aircraft en route between Alaska and the Continental United States.
(l) Complete the highway from Terrace to Prince Rupert.
(m) Complete the harbor defenses at Prince Rupert, Vancouver, and Esquimalt-Victoria, including underwater defenses at Esquimalt and Prince Rupert.
(n) If a suitable area can be found, provide an aerodrome at the north end of Vancouver Island so as to permit the operation of defending aircraft therefrom.

UNITED STATES

(o) Complete army bases at Anchorage and Fairbanks, Alaska.
(p) Complete land plane bases at Ketchikan, Yakutat, Cordova, Anchorage, Bethel, Nome, and Fairbanks.
(q) Complete the naval stations (including fixed defenses) at Sitka, Kodiak, and Dutch Harbor.
(r) Complete airways between Ketchikan and Dutch Harbor and between Nome and Bethel.
(s) Provide coast defenses in the Juan de Fuca Straits so as to tie in with the Canadian fixed defenses at Esquimalt.

360-477 O - 70 - 25

(t) Complete aircraft operating facilities at Seattle, Aberdeen, Bellingham, Everett, Olympia, Spokane County, Port Angeles, and Tongue Point.

6. In addition to the foregoing, the Board recommends that

(a) The appropriate civil and military authorities in the two countries make and put into immediate effect reciprocal arrangements from the prompt and continuous exchange of all necessary meteorological information collected by any of them.

(b) The aircraft detection organizations of the two countries on the east coast and on the west coast, respectively, make and put into immediate effect reciprocal arrangements for co-operation between them in their respective areas.

(c) The Governments of Canada and the United States bring about an arrangement to simplify the procedure in connection with the travel of public vessels and service aircraft of the two countries, to include provision for the following:

(1) Passage, upon local notification, of United States public vessels through Canadian Waters and United States service aircraft over Canadian territory while en route between United States ports and Alaska or United States bases in Newfoundland.

(2) Visits of public vessels and service aircraft of either of the two countries to ports of the other country, upon local notification, when engaged on matters connected with the joint defense of Canada and the United States.

(3) Upon local notification, flights of Canadian service aircraft over that part of the State of Maine which lies upon the route between Quebec and the Maritime Provinces when such flights are on matters pertaining to the joint defense of Canada and the United States.

(4) Upon local notification, flights of U.S. service aircraft between points in the United States over the Ontario peninsula, including the prohibited area.

7. The Board recommends that, when joint or concerted operations are directed by the two governments to be undertaken, the responsibilities to be allocated to each country and to be discharged by each through its appropriate land, sea, and air forces, should be as follows:

EAST COAST OPERATIONS

CANADA

(a) To exercise initial control of Canadian, British and friendly shipping on the Atlantic and to inform the United States immediately of the location and routes of all important units.

(b) To undertake the initial ground, anti-aircraft, coast and air defense of Newfoundland and its harbors, except insofar as the United States may be in a position to participate in such initial defense.

(c) To provide for the surface and air patrol of Belle Isle Strait and the initial security of the sea communications between the mainland and Newfoundland.

(d) To provide initial air patrol over other sea approaches to Newfoundland.

(e) To provide for the ground, anti-aircraft, and coast defenses of the Maritime Provinces and the Gaspé Peninsula and the initial air defense of these areas.

(f) To provide for the naval air defense of:

(i) Gaspé and Maritime Provinces harbors;

(ii) The Gulf of St. Lawrence to the line Sydney–Port aux Basques;

(iii) The Bay of Fundy to the line United States-Canadian Border to Yarmouth; and

(iv) The sea area within a thirty-five mile radius from the entrance to Sydney, Halifax, Shelburne, St. John's, Botwood, and any other naval bases operated by Canada.

(g) Provide facilities in aid of the movement, by water, of United States forces from the Maritime Provinces to Newfoundland.

UNITED STATES

(h) To augment its forces in Newfoundland to one reinforced division and a composite air group (73 planes).

(i) To establish off-shore surface and air patrols to seaward of waters to be patrolled by Canada, also in-shore patrols of Placentia Bay.

(j) To control shipping in areas patrolled by the United States.

(k) To augment the mobile ground and air defense of the Maritime Provinces in the event of a major attack.

WEST COAST OPERATIONS

CANADA

(l) To provide for the initial ground, anti-aircraft, coast and air defense of British Columbia.

(m) To provide for the naval defense of Esquimalt-Victoria, Vancouver and Prince Rupert.

(n) To provide naval and air defense for British Columbia coastal waters and naval patrols for such parts of these waters as are enclosed by a line drawn from the Canada-Alaska boundary to Cape Muzon—thence to 3 miles west of Langara—thence 3 miles off the west coast of the Queen Charlotte Islands to Cape St. James—thence to Cape Scott—thence 3 miles off the west coast of Vancouver Island to the meridian of Race Rocks—thence to a position 40° 20′ north 123° west—and thence north along the meridian of 123° west to the shore line in Boundary Bay.

(o) To control shipping in the area in which Canada provides surface patrols.

(p) To concentrate land forces in British Columbia for the initial support of United States garrisons in Alaska, including air support for these, if required.

(q) To provide facilities in aid of the movement by water and air of United States forces to Alaska, including the provision of staging facilities for seaplanes.

UNITED STATES

(r) To provide forces necessary for the defense of Alaska.

(s) To provide for off-shore surface and air patrols to cover the sea approaches south-eastern Alaska, British Columbia, Washington and Oregon, and for protection of shipping in the Gulf of Alaska.

(t) To control shipping in the area patrolled by United States forces.

(u) To provide a mobile reserve of at least one division, with necessary aircraft, for cooperation with Canadian and United States coast defense forces in the British Columbia-Puget Sound region.

360-477 O - 70 - 26

Appendix C

Extract of Journal of Discussions and Decisions for Meeting of Permanent Joint Board on Defense, Canada–United States, on 26 February 1942 [1]

The Board considered the increasing gravity of the military situation in the Pacific and possible developments therein affecting Alaska. The Board was informed that the United States Government believes that the construction of a land route to Alaska as an alternative to the sea route is imperative for the defense of North America and that the United States Government, for military reasons, favors the route that follows the general line of the Canadian airports, Fort St. John–Fort Nelson–Watson Lake–Whitehorse–Boundary–Big Delta, the respective termini connecting with existing roads in Canada and Alaska. The Board shares this belief for the following reasons:

(1) That the effective defense of Alaska is of paramount importance to the defense of the continent against attack from the west, since Alaska is the area most exposed to an attempt by the enemy to establish a foothold in North America.

(2) That sea communications with Alaska in the future may be subject to serious interruption by enemy sea and air action.

(3) That construction of the highway will provide a secure inland route not exposed to attack from the sea, will alleviate the shipping situation, and will provide an alternate route for use in case sea communications are interrupted.

(4) That the air route to Alaska and the defense facilities in Alaska cannot be fully utilized without adequate means of supply for the air route. This can best be provided by a highway along this route.

(5) That the additional line of communications via the inland route will be of great value in the event of an offensive against Japan projected from Alaska.

(6) That there is already on this continent a sufficient supply of land transport vehicles to enable the road to be used to its full capacity for the rapid reinforcement and supply of the forces in Alaska, without adding to the burden of industry, and that the machinery for the construction of the road is already in existence.

(7) Air Transport Service does not offer a practicable substitute for the proposed road because of the shortage of aircraft and of aircraft constructional facilities.

(8) That the use of Skagway as a sea terminal with a road only from Whitehorse to Fairbanks would not be a satisfactory solution of the problem. (It is understood that the Whitehorse–Fairbanks section of the highway would probably be given first construction priority.)

The proposed highway would have its southern terminus on the Edmonton, Dunvegan, and British Columbian Railway, which has available carrying capacity substan-

[1] This extract was published as Exhibit 16, Appendix C, of House Report 1705, 79th Congress, 2d Session, pp. 89–91.

tially in excess of the possible carrying capacity of the road. Its northern terminus would be at a point about 60 miles south of Fairbanks on the Richardson Highway, which connects Fairbanks with Valdez. From Fairbanks there is also a railway connection with Seward. According to information furnished by General Sturdevant of the United States Army Engineers, the estimated approximated length of the road is 1,600 miles of which about 1,200 miles would be in Canada and 400 miles in Alaska; that the cost of a 24-foot gravel road capable of carrying heavy traffic during both summer and winter is likely to average in the neighborhood of $50,000 to $60,000 a mile; and that the total cost might conceivably exceed $100,000,000 and probably would not be less than $75,000,000. The information of the Canadian members in respect to costs was to the same effect.

As its twenty-fourth recommendation, the Board accordingly as a matter pertaining to the joint defense of Canada and the United States, recommends the construction of a highway along the route that follows the general line of airports, Fort St. John–Fort Nelson–Watson Lake–Whitehorse–Boundary–Big Delta, the respective termini connecting with existing roads in Canada and Alaska.

The Board was informed by the United States members that the United States Government, appreciating the burden of the war expenditure already incurred by Canada since her entry into the war in September 1939, and in particular on the construction of the air route to Alaska, and being convinced of the necessity of the road and the urgency of its construction, would be prepared to meet the whole of the cost of its construction, and of its maintenance during the war, without asking Canada to do more than provide certain facilities as indicated below. If this offer on the part of the United States Government were accepted, that Government would—

(A) Carry out the necessary surveys for which preliminary arrangements have already been made and construct a pioneer road by the use of United States engineer troops for surveys and initial construction. (It would expect to complete this work during the current year and is advised that the pioneer road should be sufficiently advanced to be capable next winter of carrying a small amount of emergency traffic.)

(B) Arrange for the highway's completion under contracts made by the United States Public Roads Administration and awarded with a view to insuring the execution of all contracts in the shortest possible time without regard to whether the contractors were Canadian or American. (It expects that the road should be able to carry traffic to its full capacity not later than the end of 1943.)

(C) Maintain the highway until the termination of the present war unless the Government of Canada prefers to assume responsibility at an earlier date for the maintenance of so much of it as lies in Canada.

(D) Agrees that at the conclusion of the war that that part of the highway in Canada shall become in all respects an integral part of the Canadian highway system subject to the understanding that there shall at no time be imposed any discriminatory conditions in relation to the use of the road by Canadian or United States civilian traffic.

In the event of this proposal being accepted, the United States Government would ask the Canadian Government to agree—

(A) To acquire rights-of-way for the road in Canada, the title to remain in the Crown, in the right of Canada or of the province of British Columbia as appears most convenient.

(B) To waive import duties, transit, or similar charges on shipments originating in the United States and transported over the highway to Alaska, or originating in Alaska and transported over the highway to the United States.

(C) To waive import duties, sales taxes, license fees, or other similar charges on all equipment and supplies to be used in the construction or maintenance of the road and on personal effects of the constructural personnel.

(D) To take the necessary steps to facilitate the admission into Canada of such United States citizens as may be employed in the construction or maintenance of the highway, it being understood that the United States will assume the expense of repatriating any such persons if the contractors fail to do so.

Appendix D

Declaration by President Roosevelt and Prime Minister Mackenzie King Regarding Co-operation in War Production [1]

Hyde Park, New York
20 April 1941

Among other important matters, the President and the Prime Minister discussed measures by which the most prompt and effective utilization might be made of the productive facilities of North America for the purposes both of local and hemisphere defense and of the assistance which in addition to their own programs both Canada and the United States are rendering to Great Britain and the other democracies.

It was agreed as a general principle that in mobilizing the resources of this continent each country should provide the other with the defense articles which it is best able to produce, and, above all, produce quickly, and that production programs should be coordinated to this end.

While Canada has expanded its productive capacity manyfold since the beginning of the war, there are still numerous defense articles which it must obtain in the United States, and purchases of this character by Canada will be even greater in the coming year than in the past. On the other hand, there is existing and potential capacity in Canada for the speedy production of certain kinds of munitions, strategic materials, aluminum, and ships, which are urgently required by the United States for its own purposes.

While exact estimates cannot yet be made, it is hoped that during the next 12 months Canada can supply the United States with between $200,000,000 and $300,000,000 worth of such defense articles. This sum is a small fraction of the total defense program of the United States, but many of the articles to be provided are of vital importance. In addition, it is of great importance to the economic and financial relations between the two countries that payment by the United States for these supplies will materially assist Canada in meeting part of the cost of Canadian defense purchases in the United States.

Insofar as Canada's defense purchases in the United States consist of component parts to be used in equipment and munitions which Canada is producing for Great Britain, it was also agreed that Great Britain will obtain these parts under the Lend-Lease Act and forward them to Canada for inclusion in the finished article.

The technical and financial details will be worked out as soon as possible in accordance with the general principles which have been agreed upon between the President and the Prime Minister.

[1] The official text was published in Department of State *Bulletin,* April 26, 1941, IV, 494, and CTS, 1941, No. 14.

Appendix E

Joint Statement on Defense Collaboration [1]

12 February 1947

Announcement was made in Ottawa and Washington today of the results of discussion which have taken place in the Permanent Joint Board on Defense on the extent to which the wartime cooperation between the armed forces of the two countries should be maintained in this postwar period. In the interest of efficiency and economy, each Government has decided that its national defense establishment shall, to the extent authorized by law, continue to collaborate for peacetime joint security purposes. The collaboration will necessarily be limited and will be based on the following principles:

1. Interchange of select individuals so as to increase the familiarity of each country's defense establishment with that of the other country.
2. General cooperation and exchange of observers in connection with exercises and with the development and tests of material of common interest.
3. Encouragement of common designs and standards in arms, equipment, organization, methods of training and new developments. As certain United Kingdom standards have long been in use in Canada, no radical change is contemplated or practicable and the application of this principle will be gradual.
4. Mutual and reciprocal availability of military, naval and air facilities in each country; this principle to be applied as may be agreed in specific instances. Reciprocally each country will continue to provide with its minimum of formality for the transit through its territorial waters of military aircraft and public vessels of the other country.
5. As an underlying principle all cooperative arrangements will be without impairment of the control of either country over all activities in its territory.

While in this, as in many other matters of mutual concern, there is an identity of view and interest between the two countries, the decision of each has been taken independently in continuation of the practice developed since the establishment of the Joint Defense Board in 1940. No treaty, executive agreement or contractual obligation has been entered into. Each country will determine the extent of its practical collaboration in respect of each and all of the foregoing principles. Either country may at any time discontinue collaboration on any or all of them. Neither country will take any action inconsistent with the Charter of the United Nations. The Charter remains the cornerstone of the foreign policy of each.

An important element in the decision of each government to authorize continued col-

[1] The official text was published in Department of State *Bulletin*, XVI (23 Feb 47), 361, and CTS, 1947, No. 43.

laboration was the conviction on the part of each that in this way their obligations under the Charter of the United Nations for the maintenance of internal peace and security could be fulfilled more effectively. Both Governments believe that this decision is a contribution to the stability of the world and to the establishment through the United Nations of an effective system of world-wide security. With this in mind, each Government has sent a copy of this statement to the Secretary General of the United Nations for circulation to all its members.

In August 1940, when the creation of the Board was jointly announced by the late President Roosevelt and Prime Minister King, it was stated that the Board "shall commence immediate studies relating to sea, land and air problems, including personnel and material. It will consider in the broad sense the defense of the north half of the Western Hemisphere." In discharging this continuing responsibility the Board's work led to the building up of a pattern of close defense cooperation. The principles announced today are in continuance of this cooperation. It has been the task of the governments to assure that the close security relationship between Canada and the United States in North America will in no way impair but on the contrary will strengthen the cooperation of each country within the broader framework of the United Nations.

Bibliographical Note

This volume is based primarily upon available official public documents of the United States and Canada and upon the official files of the following U.S. Government agencies: the U.S. Section of the Permanent Joint Board on Defense, Canada-United States, the Department of State, the War Department, the Navy Department, and the Joint Chiefs of Staff. The public documents used in preparing the study are listed below under Published Works.

Official Records

Permanent Joint Board on Defense Papers

These papers were the most concentrated and fruitful source of material for this study. They include the official records of the Board itself, the extensive correspondence exchanged between the various members of the Canadian and U.S. Sections of the Board, and the similar but even more extensive correspondence between the members of the U.S. Section and agencies of the State, War, and Navy Departments.

In theory, the office of the U.S. secretary of the Board in the Department of State was the office of record for the U.S. Section. In fact, the office of the U.S. Army members of the Board was the repository of the most complete records on the subject of U.S.-Canadian wartime military co-operation. There appear to be two reasons for this. First, virtually all matters dealt with by the Board were also within the purview of the U.S. Army members, whereas many matters of narrower scope were worked out between the U.S. Army members and War Department agencies without reference to the secretary of the U.S. Section. Second, the U.S. Army members maintained a separate office of record, whereas the U.S. secretary did not keep distinctly separate records for Board matters. Instead, he incorporated Board papers with the files he maintained as the Canadian-desk officer or as officer in charge of Dominion affairs. In addition, the bulk of the World War II papers of the U.S. secretary has been retired to, and amalgamated with, the general Department of State records. Where the State Department records have been used, they are identified by a Department of State file reference. Permanent Joint Board papers are located in the files of the U.S. Army members of the Board and references thereto are identifiable by the file index PDB.

Department of State Papers

In addition to the papers of the U.S. secretary of the Board, important materials concerning politico-military co-operation in matters outside the area of co-operation through the Permanent Joint Board on Defense are to be found in the Department of State papers. References thereto are identifiable by the file index notation D/S. The papers, carefully classified and indexed, are to be found in the Division of Communications and Records.

War Department Papers

The responsibilities of the War Plans Division, or Operations Division, as it was redesignated in March 1942, were such that the politico-military policy matters, and the major questions of command, strategy, supply, planning, and operations pertaining to U.S.-Canadian co-operation were within its purview. It was necessary to examine the records of those two divisions, particularly for the periods immediately preceding and following the establishment of the Board, in order to obtain materials on those joint problems and transactions that were handled outside the Board.

References to a portion of these papers are identifiable by the file indexes WPD and OPD. Papers relating to problems involving countries other than Canada and requiring consideration by the Combined and/or Joint Chiefs of Staff were maintained by the Operations Division in a separate file identified by the symbol ABC. Most of these records have been retired to the Departmental Records Branch, The Adjutant General's Office.

Navy Department Papers

By and large, the Permanent Joint Board on Defense papers provided adequate material on wartime naval co-operation. In a few instances it was necessary to refer to records of the Chief of Naval Operations on file in the Naval Records and History Division, Navy Department.

Joint Chiefs of Staff Papers

A number of matters bearing on U.S.-Canadian co-operation were acted upon by the Joint Chiefs of Staff. The scope of these matters was severely limited by virtue of the fact that, by the time of the establishment of the Joint Chiefs of Staff in January 1942, the basic U.S.-Canadian plans had been drafted, and the decisions had already been taken concerning the majority of the strategic and logistical measures in which the two countries collaborated.

Documentation from Joint Chiefs of Staff files is identifiable by indexes beginning with the letter "J," as, for example, JCS for Joint Chiefs of Staff, or JPS for Joint Staff Planners.

Private Papers

Significant materials frequently covering matters not of record in the official U.S. Government files were found in the diaries of Henry L. Stimson and Henry Morgenthau, Jr., the World War II Secretaries of War and the Treasury, and of Jay Pierrepont Moffat, the U.S. Minister in Ottawa from 4 June 1940 to 24 January 1943. Messrs. McGeorge Bundy, Henry Morgenthau, Jr., and Joseph C. Grew, respectively, generously granted access to the pertinent data.

The papers of the Franklin D. Roosevelt Library at Hyde Park were an additional valuable source of materials that were not to be found elsewhere. Those papers relevant to this study were examined and, where cited, are identified as from the "Roosevelt Papers."

Interviews

A number of the principal American participants in the events recorded in this volume were interviewed by the author or were queried through correspondence. Their views or comments were sought on points obscure in the official records. In addition, appropriate portions of the draft of the volume were reviewed by the following officers who held positions in the State, War, and Navy Departments during World War II:

Brigadier General Milton W. Arnold, U.S. Air Force (retired)
Brigadier General Henry A. Barber, Jr., U.S. Army (retired)
Major General Gerald C. Brant, U.S. Army (retired)
Lieutenant General Edward H. Brooks, U.S. Army (retired)
Lieutenant Colonel Robert S. Burhans, U.S. Army
Colonel Albert H. Burton, U.S. Army (retired)
Mr. Lewis Clark, Department of State
Colonel C. M. Clifford, U.S. Army
Major General Robert W. Douglass, Jr., U.S. Air Force
Brigadier General Beverly C. Dunn, U.S. Army (retired)
Colonel Parmer W. Edwards, U.S. Army
Lieutenant General Stanley D. Embick, U.S. Army (retired)
Major General Robert T. Frederick, U.S. Army (retired)
Colonel Paul R. Goode, U.S. Army (retired)
Major General Guy V. Henry, U.S. Army (retired)
Vice Admiral H. W. Hill, U.S. Navy (retired)
Colonel E. W. Hockenberry, U.S. Air Force (retired)
Vice Admiral Alfred W. Johnson, U.S. Navy (retired)
Colonel Archibald King, U.S. Army (retired)
Mr. J. Graham Parsons, Department of State
Major General Thomas M. Robins, U.S. Army (retired)
Rear Admiral R. W. Ruble, U.S. Navy
Brigadier General F. S. Strong, Jr., U.S. Army (retired)

Major General C. L. Sturdevant, U.S. Army (retired)
Rear Admiral Frank P. Thomas, U.S. Navy (retired)
Miss Margaret Joy Tibbetts, Department of State
Rear Admiral J. P. Whitney, U.S. Navy
Colonel Kenneth G. Wickham, U.S. Army
Brigadier General Robert J. Wood, U.S. Army
Brigadier General Ludson D. Worsham, U.S. Army (retired)

The comments of these individuals have been appropriately incorporated in this study. The records of the interviews and the correspondence involved are in the possession of the author.

Published Works

The student of the history of U.S.-Canadian relations will find the best collection of studies on the subject to be in the twenty-five volume series on *The Relations of Canada and the United States* sponsored by the Carnegie Endowment for International Peace, Division of Economics and History. The only volume cited below, by John B. Brebner, is in part an over-all summary and provides excellent background reading for this study. It also contains a list of all the volumes in the series.

Books

Baxter, James P., 3d. *Scientists Against Time.* Boston: Little, Brown and Company, 1946.
Bemis, Samuel F. *A Diplomatic History of the United States.* Third edition. New York: Henry Holt and Company, 1950.
Brebner, John B. *North Atlantic Triangle.* (THE RELATIONS OF CANADA AND THE UNITED STATES.) Revised edition. Toronto: Ryerson Press, 1947.
Burhans, Robert D. *The First Special Service Force.* Washington: Infantry Journal Press, 1947.
Bykofsky, Joseph, and Harold Larson. *The Transportation Corps: Operations Overseas.* (UNITED STATES ARMY IN WORLD WAR II.) Washington: Government Printing Office, 1957.
Byrd, Richard E. *Skyward.* New York: G. P. Putnam's Sons, 1928.
California University, Committee on International Relations. *Problems of Hemispheric Defense.* Berkeley: University of California Press, 1942.
Callahan, James M. *American Foreign Policy in Canadian Relations.* New York: The Macmillan Company, 1937.
Canada in World War II. Montreal: Wm. S. Boad and Company, 1945.
Carr, William G. *Checkmate to the North.* Toronto: The Macmillan Company, 1945.
Carter, H. Dyson. *Sea of Destiny.* New York: Greenberg Publisher, Inc., 1940.
Cave, Hugh B. *Wings Across the World: The Story of the Air Transport Command.* New York: Dodd, Mead & Company, 1945.
Chacko, Chirakaikaran Joseph. *The International Joint Commission.* New York: Columbia University Press, 1932.
Churchill, Winston S. *The Second World War.* Boston: Houghton Mifflin Company. (All volumes published through 1951.)
Cleveland, Reginald M. *Air Transport at War.* New York: Harper & Brothers, 1946.

Cline, Ray S. *Washington Command Post: The Operations Division.* (UNITED STATES ARMY IN WORLD WAR II.) Washington: Government Printing Office, 1951.

Coale, Griffith. *North Atlantic Patrol.* New York: Farrar & Rinehart, 1943.

Coe, Douglas. *Road to Alaska.* New York: Julian Meissner, Inc., 1943.

Conference on Canadian-American Affairs: Proceedings at Queen's University, June 23–26, 1941. R. G. Trotter and A. B. Corey (eds.). Toronto: Ginn and Company, 1941.

Craven, Wesley F., and James L. Cate (eds.). *Plans and Early Operations.* (THE ARMY AIR FORCES IN WORLD WAR II, Vol. I.) Chicago: University of Chicago Press, 1948.

———. *Europe—TORCH to POINTBLANK.* (THE ARMY AIR FORCES IN WORLD WAR II, Vol. II.) Chicago: University of Chicago Press, 1949.

———. *The Pacific—Guadalcanal to Saipan.* (THE ARMY AIR FORCES IN WORLD WAR II, Vol. IV.) Chicago: University of Chicago Press, 1950.

Davies, Raymond A. *Arctic Eldorado.* Toronto: Ryerson Press, 1944.

Dawson, Carl A. (ed.). *The New North-west.* Toronto: University of Toronto Press, 1947.

Dawson, Robert M. *Canada in World Affairs: 1939–1941.* Toronto: Oxford University Press, 1943.

Dexter, Grant. *Canada and the Building of Peace.* Toronto: Canadian Institute of International Affairs, 1944.

Dmitri, Ivan. *Flight to Everywhere.* New York: Whittlesey House, 1944.

Eggleston, Wilfrid. *Scientists at War.* Toronto: Oxford University Press, 1950.

843d Signal Service Battalion, U.S. Army Signal Corps. *Alaska Highway Telephone System.* Commercial Printers, Limited, *circa* fall 1945.

Elliott, W. Y., and H. D. Hall (eds.). *The British Commonwealth at War.* New York: Alfred A. Knopf, 1943.

Feis, Herbert. *The Road to Pearl Harbor.* Princeton: Princeton University Press, 1950.

Finnie, Richard. *Canol.* San Francisco: Ryder and Ingram, 1945.

Glazebrook, G. P. de T. *A History of Canadian External Relations.* Toronto: Oxford University Press, 1950.

Godsell, Philip H. *The Romance of the Alaska Highway.* Toronto: Ryerson Press, 1944.

Griffin, D. F. *First Steps to Tokyo: The Royal Canadian Air Force in the Aleutians.* Toronto: J. M. Dent & Sons, 1944.

Griffin, Harold. *Alaska and the Canadian Northwest.* New York: W. W. Norton & Company, 1944.

Hardy, H. Reginald. *Mackenzie King of Canada: A Biography.* Toronto: Oxford University Press, 1949.

Harvey, Heather J. *Consultation and Co-operation in the Commonwealth.* New York: Oxford University Press, 1952.

History of Force 2600. (Unidentified and undated account of Canol Project operations obviously prepared by a U.S. Army agency *circa* 1944.)

Hooker, Nancy H. (ed.). *The Moffat Papers.* Cambridge: Harvard University Press, 1956.

Hull, Cordell. *The Memoirs of Cordell Hull.* 2 vols. New York: The Macmillan Company, 1948.

Humphrey, John P. *The Inter-American System: A Canadian View.* Toronto: The Macmillan Company, 1942.

Hutchinson, Bruce. *The Incredible Canadian.* Toronto: Longmans, Green and Company, 1952.

Ingraham, Rex. *First Fleet: The Story of the U. S. Coast Guard at War.* Indianapolis: Bobbs-Merrill Company, 1944.

James, Robert W. *Wartime Economic Co-operation: A Study of Relations Between Canada and the United States.* Toronto: Ryerson Press, 1949.

Karig, Walter. *The Atlantic War.* (BATTLE REPORT, Vol. II.) New York: Farrar & Rinehart, 1946.

Keenleyside, Hugh L. *Canada and the United States.* Revised edition by Keenleyside and G. S. Brown. New York: Alfred A. Knopf, 1952.

Kennedy, John de Navarry. *History of the Department of Munitions and Supply: Canada in the Second World War.* 2 vols. Ottawa: E. Cloutier, King's Printer, 1950.

King, Ernest J., and W. M. Whitehill. *Fleet Admiral King: A Naval Record.* New York: W. W. Norton and Company, 1952.

King, W. L. Mackenzie. *Canada at Britain's Side.* Toronto: The Macmillan Company, 1941.

———. *Canada and the Fight for Freedom.* Toronto: The Macmillan Company, 1944.

Kizer, Benjamin H. *The U.S.-Canadian Northwest.* Princeton: Princeton University Press, 1943.

La Farge, Oliver. *The Eagle in the Egg.* Boston: Houghton Mifflin Company, 1949.

Langer, William L., and S. Everett Gleason. *The Challenge to Isolation.* New York: Harper & Brothers, 1952.

———. *The Undeclared War.* New York: Harper & Brothers, 1953.

Lanks, Herbert C. *Highway to Alaska.* New York: D. Appleton-Century, 1944.

Leahy, William D. *I Was There.* New York: Whittlesey House, 1950.

Lingard, C. C., and R. G. Trotter. *September 1941 to May 1944.* (CANADA IN WORLD AFFAIRS, Vol. III.) Toronto: Oxford University Press, 1950.

Lissitzyn, Oliver J. *International Air Transport and National Policy.* New York: Council on Foreign Relations, 1942.

Longstaff, F. V. *The Uganda in Action.* Victoria, B. C.: The Author, 1952.

Lower, Arthur R. M. *Canada: Nation and Neighbor.* Toronto: Ryerson Press, 1952.

Lower Post or Freeze: 340th Engineer Regiment on the Alaska Military Highway. Charlotte, N. C.: Herald Press, 1944.

McInnis, Edgar W. *The Unguarded Frontier.* New York: Doubleday, Doran and Company, 1942.

MacKay, R. A. (ed.). *Newfoundland: Economic, Diplomatic and Strategic Studies.* Toronto: Oxford University Press, 1946.

Mansergh, Nicholas. *Survey of British Commonwealth Affairs: Problems of External Policy, 1931 to 1939.* Toronto: Oxford University Press, 1952.

Matloff, Maurice, and Edwin M. Snell. *Strategic Planning for Coalition Warfare, 1941–1942.* (UNITED STATES ARMY IN WORLD WAR II.) Washington: Government Printing Office, 1953.

Morison, Samuel Eliot. *Aleutians, Gilberts and Marshalls.* (HISTORY OF UNITED STATES NAVAL OPERATIONS IN WORLD WAR II, Vol. VII.) Boston: Little, Brown and Company, 1951.

———. *The Atlantic Battle Won, May 1943–May 1945.* (HISTORY OF UNITED STATES NAVAL OPERATIONS IN WORLD WAR II, Vol. X.) Boston: Little, Brown and Company, 1956.

———. *The Battle of the Atlantic, September 1939–May 1943.* (HISTORY OF UNITED STATES NAVAL OPERATIONS IN WORLD WAR II, Vol. I.) Boston: Little, Brown and Company, 1947.

Morton, Henry V. *Atlantic Meeting.* New York: Dodd, Mead & Company, 1943.

Myers, C. V. *Oil to Alaska, Canol Unveiled.* Edmonton: Douglas Printing Company, *circa* 1945.
Nelson, Donald M. *Arsenal of Democracy.* New York: Harcourt, Brace & Company, 1946.
Plumptre, A. F. W. *Mobilizing Canada's Resources for War.* Toronto: The Macmillan Company, 1941.
Polunin, Nicholas. *Arctic Unfolding.* Toronto: Ryerson Press, 1949.
Roberts, Leslie. *Canada's War in the Air.* Third edition. Montreal: Alvah M. Beatty, 1943.
——. *Canada and the War at Sea.* (CANADA'S WAR AT SEA, Vol. II.) Montreal: Alvah M. Beatty, 1944.
——. *The Mackenzie.* New York: Rinehart & Company, 1949.
Roosevelt, Elliott. *As He Saw It.* New York: Duell, Sloan and Pearce, 1946.
Roosevelt, Elliott (ed.). *F. D. R., His Personal Letters, 1928–1945.* 2 vols. New York: Duell, Sloan and Pearce, 1950.
Rosen, S. McKee. *The Combined Boards of the Second World War.* New York: Columbia University Press, 1951.
Rosenman, Samuel I. (compiler). *The Public Papers and Addresses of Franklin D. Roosevelt.* 13 vols. New York: Random House, 1938 (Vols. 1–5), The Macmillan Company, 1941 (Vols. 6–9), and Harper & Brothers, 1950 (Vols. 10–13).
Ross, Richard M. *The History of the 1st Battalion, Cameron Highlanders of Ottawa (M. G).* Ottawa: n.d.
Schull, Joseph. *The Far Distant Ships.* Ottawa: E. Cloutier, King's Printer, 1950.
Sherwood, Robert E. *Roosevelt and Hopkins: An Intimate History.* New York: Harper & Brothers, 1948.
Shores, Louis. *Highways in the Sky: The Story of the AACS. New York: Barnes & Noble,* 1947.
Soward, F. H. *From Normandy to Paris, 1944–1946.* (CANADA IN WORLD AFFAIRS, Vol. IV.) Toronto: Oxford University Press, 1950.
Soward, F. H., *et al. The Pre-war Years.* (CANADA IN WORLD AFFAIRS, Vol. I.) Toronto: Oxford University Press, 1941.
Soward, F. H., and A. M. Maccaulay. *Canada and the Pan American System,* (CONTEMPORARY AFFAIRS, No. 21). Toronto: Ryerson Press, 1948.
Stacey, Charles P. *The Canadian Army, 1939–1945.* Ottawa: E. Cloutier, King's Printer, 1948.
———. *The Military Problems of Canada.* Toronto: Ryerson Press, 1940.
———. *Six Years of War: The Army in Canada, Britain and the Pacific.* (OFFICIAL HISTORY OF THE CANADIAN ARMY IN THE SECOND WORLD WAR, vol. I.) Ottawa: E. Cloutier, Queen's Printer, 1955.
Steffansson, V., and H. W. Weigert (eds.). *Compass of the World.* New York: The Macmillan Company, 1944.
Stettinius, Edward R., Jr. *Lend-Lease: Weapon for Victory.* New York: The Macmillan Company, 1944.
Stimson, Henry L., and McGeorge Bundy. *On Active Service in Peace and War.* New York: Harper & Brothers, 1947.
The Long Trail: 341st Engineers on the Alaska Military Highway. Charlotte, N. C.: Harold Press, 1943.
The War Reports of General of the Army George C. Marshall, General of the Army H. H. Arnold and Fleet Admiral Ernest J. King. Foreward by Walter Millis. New York: J. B. Lippincott Company, 1947.

Tucker, G. N. *The Naval Service of Canada.* 2 vols. Ottawa: E. Cloutier, King's Printer, 1952.

Watson, Mark S. *Chief of Staff: Prewar Plans and Preparations.* (UNITED STATES ARMY IN WORLD WAR II.) Washington: Government Printing Office, 1950.

Welles, Sumner. *Co-operation Between Canada and the United States in the Search for World Peace.* Winnipeg: J. W. Dafoe Foundation, 1946.

Whitaker, Arthur P. (ed.). *Inter-American Affairs.* (Annual surveys 1-5 inclusive for the years 1941-1945.) New York: Columbia University Press, 1942-46. (Contain sections on Canada.)

Public Documents—Canada

Air Force Headquarters, Air Historical Section. *Silver Jubilee of the Royal Canadian Air Force.* Ottawa: E. Cloutier, King's Printer, 1949.

Canada Law Reports. Part VIII, 1943. Ottawa: E. Cloutier, King's Printer, 1943.

Canadian Information Service. Statement, August 15, 1945. (Published as Appendix 8 of H. D. Smyth, *Atomic Energy for Military Purposes,* Princeton University Press, 1946 Edition.)

Canadian Mutual Aid Board. *Final Report, 1946.* Ottawa: E. Cloutier, King's Printer, 1947.

Crown Assets Disposal Corporation (formely War Assets Corporation). *Sixth Annual Report. April 1, 1949–March 31, 1950.* Ottawa: E. Cloutier, King's Printer, 1950.

———. *Seventh Annual Report, April 1, 1950–March 31, 1951.* Ottawa: E. Cloutier, King's Printer, 1951.

Department of External Affairs. *Annual Reports.* Ottawa: E. Cloutier, King's Printer, 1939-1952.

———. "Canada and Latin America," *External Affairs,* Vol. 1, No. 5 (May 1949), 25-34.

———. "Canadian War Data," 1946 Reference Papers Series, No. 4, May 15, 1946.

———. "Joint War Production Committee, Canada and the U.S.A.," Press Release 2, January 12, 1946.

Department of External Affairs, Information Divison. *Background of the Great Lakes-St. Lawrence Waterway and Power Project.* Reference Paper 52. Ottawa: 1950.

———. *Three Power Co-operation on Atomic Energy.* Reference 52. Ottawa: 1949.

Department of Munitions and Supply. *The Industrial Front.* Ottawa: E. Cloutier, King's Printer, 1944.

Department of National Defense. *Annual Reports.* Ottawa: E. Cloutier, King's Printer, 1939-1952.

———. *Canada's Defense.* Ottawa: E. Cloutier, King's Printer, 1947.

———. *Canada's Defense Program.* Ottawa: E. Cloutier, King's Printer, 1949.

———. *Canadian Defense Planning.* Ottawa: E. Cloutier, King's Printer, 1948.

Department of Reconstruction. *Canada's Role in Atomic Bomb Drama.* Ottawa: E. Cloutier, King's Printer, 1945.

Department of Transport, Air Services Branch. *Canada Air Pilot.* 2 vols. Ottawa: Department of Mines and Technical Surveys.

Dominion Bureau of Statistics. "Canada's Northern Airfields," *The Canada Year Book, 1945,* pp. 705-12. Ottawa: E. Cloutier, King's Printer, 1945.

———. "The British Commonwealth Air Training Plan—A Summary of the R.C.A.F.'s Major Role in the War of 1939-45," *The Canada Year Book, 1946,* pp. 1090-99. Ottawa: E. Cloutier, King's Printer, 1946.

———. *The Canadian Balance of International Payments, 1926 to 1948.* Ottawa: E. Cloutier, King's Printer, 1949.

Foreign Exchange Control Board. *Report to the Minister of Finance, March 1946.* Ottawa: E. Cloutier, King's Printer, 1946.
Naval Service Headquarters. *Royal Canadian Navy Monthly Review,* Nos. 1–43 inclusive. Ottawa: 1942–1945.
North Pacific Planning Project. *Canada's New Northwest.* Ottawa: E. Cloutier, King's Printer, 1947.
Ottawa Air Training Conference, May 1942. *Report of the Conference.* Ottawa: E. Cloutier, King's Printer, 1942.
Privy Council. *Canadian War Orders and Regulations.* Ottawa: E. Cloutier, King's Printer, 1942–1945.
———. *Proclamations and Orders in Council Relating to the War.* 8 vols. Ottawa: E. Cloutier, King's Printer, 1940–1942.
Royal Canadian Air Force, Northwest Air Command, Public Relations Office. *The Northwest Staging Route.* Edmonton: 1945.
Supreme Court. "Jurisdiction of Canadian Criminal Courts over Members of the Armed Forces of the United States," *Factum of the Attorney General of Canada* and *Case.* Ottawa: E. Cloutier, King's Printer, 1943. (See also similar factums of the Attorneys General of Quebec, Ontario, Alberta, and British Columbia.)
War Assets Corporation. *Annual Report, July 12, 1944 to March 31, 1945* and Second to Fifth (inclusive) Annual Reports for the four succeeding years. Ottawa: E. Cloutier, King's Printer, 1945–1949.
Wartime Information Board. "Canada and the Inter-American System." Reference Paper 34, February 16, 1945.
———. *Canada at War,* Nos. 1–45 inclusive. Ottawa: E. Cloutier, King's Printer, 1941–45.
———. *Defense Projects in Northwest Canada.* Ottawa: 1944. (Mimeographed.)

Public Documents—Great Britain

Central Office of Information. *Atlantic Bridge.* London: His Majesty's Stationery Office, 1945.
———. *The Battle of the Atlantic.* London: His Majesty's Stationery Office, 1946.
Commander-in-Chief, British Pacific Fleet. *The Contribution of the British Pacific Fleet to the Assault on Okinawa, 1945.* Despatch by Admiral Sir Bruce Fraser, G.C.B., K.B.E., published as a supplement to *The London Gazette* of 1 June 1948. London: His Majesty's Stationery Office.

Public Documents—United States

Army Service Forces, Control Division. *Statistical Review: World War II.* Washington: 1945.
Army Service Forces, International Division. *A Guide to International Supply.* Washington: 1945.
———. *Lend-Lease.* 2 vols. Washington: 1945.
Bureau of the Budget. *The United States at War.* Washington: Government Printing Office, 1946.
Civilian Production Administration. *Official Munitions Production of the United States.* Washington: 1947.
Coast Guard. *The Coast Guard at War: Greenland Patrol.* Washington: 1945. (Processed.)
Department of Commerce. *The St. Lawrence Survey.* 7 vols. Washington: Government Printing Office, 1941.

360-477 O - 70 - 27

Department of Commerce, Bureau of Foreign and Domestic Commerce. *International Transactions of the United States During the War, 1940–1945.* Washington: Government Printing Office, 1948.

Department of State. *Peace and War: United States Foreign Policy, 1931–1941.* Washington: Government Printing Office, 1943.

Department of State, Office of the Foreign Liquidation Commissioner. *Reports to Congress on Foreign Surplus Disposal.* Nos. 1–14, inclusive. Washington: Government Printing Office, 1946–1949.

Finance Department. *Lend-Lease Shipments in World War II.* 2 vols. Washington: 1946.

House Committee on Roads, 79th Congress, 2d Session. House Report 1705, on House Resolution 255. *The Alaska Highway.* Washington: Government Printing Office, 1946.

Joint Committee on the Investigation of the Pearl Harbor Attack, 79th Congress, 1st Session. Hearings on Senate Concurrent Resolution 27. *Pearl Harbor Attack.* Washington: Government Printing Office, 1946.

National Archives. *Federal Records of World War II.* 2 vols. Washington: Government Printing Office, 1951.

Navy Department, Bureau of Yards and Docks. *Building the Navy's Bases in World War II.* 2 vols. Washington: Government Printing Office, 1947.

Northwest Service Command. *First Semi-Annual Progress Report.* Whitehorse: 1944.

Northwest Service Command, Public Relations Branch. *Canol.* Whitehorse: 1944.

——— *The Alaska Highway.* Whitehorse: 1944.

Office of Naval Intelligence. *The Aleutians Campaign.* Washington: 1945.

Office of The Quartermaster General. QMC Historical Study, 9, *Fuels for Global Conflict,* by Erna Risch. Washington: Government Printing Office, 1945.

Special Senate Committee Investigating the National Defense Program, 78th Congress, 1st Session. Senate Report 10. *Investigation of the National Defense Program* Pursuant to Senate Resolution 71, 77th Congress and Senate Resolution 6, 78th Congress. Part 14. Additional Report. *The Canol Project.* Washington: Government Printing Office, 1944.

Special Senate Committee Investigating the National Defense Program, 78th Congress, 1st Session. Hearings on Senate Resolution 6, *Investigation of the National Defense Program.* Part 22. Washington: Government Printing Office, 1944.

Special Senate Committee Investigating the National Defense Program, 79th Congress, 2d Session. Hearings on Senate Resolution 46, 80th Congress, extending Senate Resolution 71, 77th Congress. *Investigation of the National Defense Program.* Part 39. Washington: Government Printing Office, 1947.

War Production Board. *Industrial Mobilization for War,* Vol I, *Program and Administration.* Washington: Government Printing Office, 1947.

Articles

Armstrong, Elizabeth H. "Canadian-American Co-operation in War and Peace, 1940–1945," Department of State *Bulletin,* XIII (October 28, 1945), 674–78.

Balch, Thomas W. "Is Hudson Bay a Closed or an Open Sea," *American Journal of International Law,* VI (1912), 409–59.

———. "The Hudsonian Sea Is a Great Open Sea," *ibid.,* VII (1913), 546–65.

Bartlett, Robert A. "Servicing Arctic Airbases," *The National Geographic, LXXXIX* (May 1946), 602–16.

Barton, G. P. "Foreign Armed Forces: Immunity From Criminal Jurisdiction," *British Year Book of International Law,* XXVII (1950), 186–235.

———. "Foreign Armed Forces: Immunity From Supervisory Jurisdiction," *ibid.,* XXVI (1949), 380–414.

Bathurst, M. E. "Jurisdiction Over Friendly Foreign Armed Forces," *British Year Book of International Law,* XXIII (1946), 338–41.

Batt, William L. "Canada-United States Co-operation," *Industrial Canada,* XLIV (July 1943), 115–18, 131.

Borchard, Edwin. "The Attorney General's Opinion in the Exchange of Destroyers for Naval Bases," *American Journal of International Law,* XXXIV (1940), 690–97.

———. "The St. Lawrence Waterway and Power Project," *ibid.,* XLIII (1949), 411–34.

Brebner, J. B. "A Changing North Atlantic Triangle," *International Journal,* III (Autumn 1948), 309–19.

———. "Canada in North American History," *The Mississippi Valley Historical Review,* XXXIV (March 1948), 653–59.

Brebner, J. B., and R. G. Trotter. "Relations of Canada and the United States," *Canadian Historical Review,* XXIV (1943), 117–35.

Briggs, Herbert W. "Neglected Aspects of the Destroyer Deal," *American Journal of Internationl Law,* XXXIV (1940), 569–87.

———. "The Validity of the Greenland Agreement," *ibid.,* XXXV (1941), 506–13.

Brown, Wilson. "The Allies at Quebec," *Queens Quarterly,* LVI (Winter 1949-1950), 465–78.

Carnegie, R. K. "The Quebec Conference," *Canadian Geographical Journal,* XXVII (September 1943), 96–105.

Claxton, Brooke. "Anglo-American Relations and Canadian Policy," in V. Anderson (ed.), *The United Nations Today and Tomorrow* (Toronto: Ryerson Press, 1943).

Duggan, Stephen. "The Western Hemisphere as a Haven of Peace," *Foreign Affairs,* XVIII (July 1940), 614–31.

Ellis, F. H. "New York to Nome and Back," *The Beaver,* Outfit 280 (September 1949), 28–32.

Ells, S. C. "Alaska Highway," *Canadian Geographical Journal,* XXVIII (March 1944), 104–19.

Evans-Lombe, E. M. "The Royal Navy in the Pacific," *Journal of the Royal United Services Institution,* XCII (August 1947), 333–47.

Fairman, Chas., and Archibald King. "Taxation of Friendly Foreign Armed Forces," *American Journal of International Law,* XXXVIII (1944), 258–77.

Falls, Cyril. "Canada, the United States and the Commonwealth," *Canadian Army Journal,* I (July 1947), 12–14.

———. "Defense of the Commonwealth," *ibid.,* I (June 1947), 14–15, 32.

Fenwick, Chas. G. "Canada and the Monroe Doctrine," *American Journal of International Law,* XXXII (1938), 782–85.

Finnie, Richard. "A Route to Alaska Through the Northwest Territories," *Geographical Review,* XXXII (July 1942), 403–16.

———. "The Epic of Canol," *Canadian Geographical Journal,* XXXIV (March 1947), 136–40.

Glazebrook, G. P. de T. "Canadian Foreign Policy in the Twentieth Century," *Journal of Modern History,* XXI (March 1949), 44–55.

Harrington, Lyn. "The Alaska Highway," *Canadian Geographical Journal,* XLII (June 1951), 239–59.

Harrison, W. E. C. "Canadian-American Defense," *International Journal,* V (Summer 1950), 189–200.

———. "Strategy and Policy in the Defense of Canada," *ibid.,* IV (Summer 1949), 212–43.

Heslop, Barbara. "Arctic Rescue," *The Beaver*. Outfit 274 (March 1944), 8-14.
Hitchins, F. H. "Evolution of the Royal Canadian Air Force," *Canadian Historical Association Report, 1946*, pp. 92-100.
———. "The British Commonwealth Air Training Plan," *The Roundel*, II (December 1949), 5-13.
Hopkins, Oliver B. "The 'Canol' Project," *Canadian Geographical Journal*, XXVII (November 1943), 238-49.
Horner, S. G. L. "Atmospheric Defense," *The Beaver*, Outfit 276 (December 1945), 40-42.
Hunter, Croil. "Northwest Airlines Unfolds Epic of its March to Help Save Alaska," *Air Transportation*, IV (February 1944), 7-10.
Johnston, R. N. "Speeding-Up the Alaska Highway by Aerial-Survey Methods," *Roads and Bridges*, LXXX (November 1942), 17-23, 54.
Johnston, V. K. "Canada's Title to Hudson Bay and Hudston Strait," *British Year Book of International Law*, XV (1934), 1-20.
———. "Canada's Title to the Arctic Islands," *Canadian Historical Review*, XIV (March 1933), 24-41.
King, Archibald. "Further Developments Concerning Jurisdiction Over Friendly Foreign Armed Forces," *American Journal of International Law*, XL (1946), 257-79.
———. "Jurisdiction Over Friendly Foreign Armed Forces," *ibid.*, XXXVI (1942), 539-67.
Knox, F. A. "Canada's Balance of International Payments, 1940-45," *Canadian Journal of Economics and Political Science*, XIII (August 1947), 345-62.
Laing, Lionel H. "Does the Monroe Doctrine Cover Canada?," *American Journal of International Law*, XXXII (1938), 793-96.
Lane, Albert L. "The Alcan Highway," *Military Engineer*, XXXIV (October 1942), 492-500.
Lloyd, Trevor. "Oil in the Mackenzie Valley," *Geographical Review*, XXXIV (1944), 275-307.
———. "The Mackenzie Waterway: A Northern Supply Route," *ibid.*, XXXIII (1943), 415-34.
Lower, A. R. M. "Newfoundland in North Atlantic Strategy," *Foreign Affairs*, XX (July 1942), 767-70.
McCarthy, Leighton. "Canadian-American Relations in War and Peace," *International Conciliation*, No. 398 (March 1944), pp. 200-205.
MacKay, R. A. "The International Joint Commission Between the United States and Canada," *American Journal of International Law*, XXII (1928), 292-318.
McKechnie, L. M., *et al.* "Home War: The R.C.A.F. Guards Our Shores," *Canadian Geographical Journal*, XXVII (October 1943), 150-77.
MacKinnon, M. H. M. "The R.C.A.F. in Newfoundland," *University of Toronto Quarterly*, XV (April 1946), 213-21.
McMillion, Shelby A. "The Strategic Route to Alaska," *Military Engineer*, XXXIV (November 1942), 546-54.
MacNaught, Jack. "The Battle of the St. Lawrence," *Maclean's Magazine*, LXII (October 15, 1949), 7, 68-70, and (November 1, 1949), 22, 47-49.
McNaughton, A. G. L. "Defense of North America," Ottawa: Department of External Affairs, Statements and Speeches, No. 48/18, 1948.
———. "Organization and Responsibilities of the International Joint Commission," *Engineering Journal*, XXXIV (January 1951), 2-4, 12.
Mansergh, Nicholas. "Strains on the Commonwealth," *Foreign Affairs*, XXVII (October 1948), 129-42.

Massey, Vincent. "Canada and the Inter-American System," *Foreign Affairs,* XXVI (July 1948), 693-700.
Miller, Eugene H. "Canada and the Pan American Union," *International Journal,* III (Winter 1947-48), 24-39.
Milner, Samuel. "Establishing the Bolero Ferrying Route," *Military Affairs,* XI (Winter 1947), 213-22.
Mosely, Philip E. "Iceland and Greenland: An American Problem," *Foreign Affairs,* XVIII (July 1940), 742-46.
Neuberger, Richard L. "Highballing at Sixty Below," *Saturday Evening Post,* 27 November 1943, pp. 15, 109-10.
"Oil for the Planes of Alaska," *The Beaver,* Outfit 274 (September 1943), 4-14.
Pearson, Lester B. "Canada and the North Atlantic Alliance," *Foreign Affairs,* XXVII (April 1949), 369-78.
———. "Canada Looks 'Down North'," *ibid.,* XXIV (July 1946), 638-48.
———. "Canada's Northern Horizon," *ibid.,* XXXI (July 1953), 581-92.
Perkins, Dexter. "Bringing the Monroe Doctrine Up to Date," *Foreign Affairs,* XX (January 1942), 253-65.
Pierce, S. D., and A. F. W. Plumptre. "Canada's Relations with Wartime Agencies in Washington," *Canadian Journal of Economics and Political Science,* XI (August 1945), 402-19.
Podea, Iris S. "Pan American Sentiment in French Canada," *International Journal,* III (Autumn 1948), 334-49.
"Prince Rupert—Secret City of the War," *Canadian National Magazine,* XXXI (November 1945), 6-7, 10, 12.
Rainey, Froelich. "Alaska Highway as an Engineering Epic," *National Geographic Magazine,* LXXXIII (February 1943), 143-68.
Richardson, B. T. "Canada-U.S. Relations in the New North," *Canadian Business,* XVII (May 1944), 28-29, 186, 189.
Richardson, Dougall. "Economic Cooperation with Canada 1941-1947," Department of State *Bulletin,* XVI (June 22, 1947), 1185-92.
Ringold, Herbert. "Lifeline to the U.S.S.R.," *Air Force,* XXVII (November 1944), 24-27.
Sage, Walter N. "The Historical Peculiarities of Canada with Regard to Hemisphere Defense," *Pacific Historical Review,* X (March 1941), 15-29.
Stacey, C. P. "The Myth of the Unguarded Frontier, 1815-1871," *American Historical Review,* LVI (October 1950), 1-18.
Standley, William H. "Stalin and World Unity," *Collier's,* June 30, 1945, pp. 17, 75-76.
Stephenson, Wm. "Northern Salvage," *The Beaver,* Outfit 276 (September 1945), 36-39.
Sturdevant, C. L. "The Alaska Military Highway," *Engineering Journal,* XXVI (March 1943), 117-21.
———. "The Military Road to Alaska," *Military Engineer,* XXXV (April 1943), 173-81.
Trotter, Reginald G. "Canada and Pan Americanism," *Queens Quarterly,* XLIX (1942), 252-60.
Tucker, Gilbert N. "Some Aspects of the Battle of the Atlantic," *Report of the Canadian Historical Association, 1946,* pp. 84-91.
Trully, T. J. "The Story of the Alaska Communications," *Signals,* II (May-June 1948), 24-29.
Waters, S. C. "Anzio," *Canadian Army Journal,* II (August-September 1946), 16-23.
Wattsford, G. J. H. "The Strategic Importance of Canada," *Canadian Army Journal,* II (March 1949), 17-21.

Wilcox, F. O. "The Monroe Doctrine and World War II," *American Political Science Review,* XXXVI (June 1942), 433-53.
Wilson, J. A. "Expansion of Aviation into Arctic and Subarctic Canada," *Canadian Geographical Journal,* XLI (September 1950), 130-41.
———. "Northwest Passage by Air," *ibid.,* XXVI (March 1943), 107-29.
Wood, E. P. "Northern Skytrails," *The Roundel,* I, serialized in Nos. 1 (November 1948) to 11 (September 1949), inclusive.
Wright, Kenneth. "How Goose Bay Was Discovered," *The Beaver,* Outfit 277 (June 1946), 42-45.
Wright, Quincy. "The Transfer of Destroyers to Great Britain," *American Journal of International Law,* XXXIV (1940), 680-89.

Manuscripts and Unpublished Monographs

Carr, Edwin R. "Great Falls to Nome: The Inland Air Route to Alaska, 1940-1945." Unpublished Ph.D. dissertation, University of Minnesota, 1947.
Conn, Stetson, and Byron Fairchild. "The Framework of Hemisphere Defense." Manuscript in preparation for publication in the series UNITED STATES ARMY IN WORLD WAR II.
Cressy, Arthur Cheever, Jr. "Canadian-American Co-operation in World War II." Unpublished Ph.D. dissertation, Fletcher School of Law and Diplomacy, 1952.
Keenleyside, Hugh L. "The Canada-U.S. Permanent Joint Board on Defense, 1940-1945." Unpublished manuscript, 1947.
Kittredge, Tracy B. "U.S.-British Naval Co-operation, 1940-1945." Unpublished monograph, Washington, 1947.
Smith, Gordon W. "The Historical and Legal Background of Canada's Arctic Claims." Unpublished Ph.D. dissertation, Columbia University, 1952.

A large number of unpublished official secondary materials in the form of historical reports prepared by unknown authors in the U.S. Government agencies were available, some of which are listed below. Prepared as part of a directed program, these reports were in some cases written by inadequately qualified people. Consequently they vary considerably in quality and utility. The compilations of documents usually appended to the texts of these reports were especially useful.

Alaskan Department. "Official History of the Alaskan Department." Unpublished historical report on file in the Office of the Chief of Military History, U.S. Army.
Army Air Forces. "The Army Air Forces Antisubmarine Command." Reference History 7. Unpublished historical report, 1945, on file in the Department of the Air Force, Air University Historical Liaison Office.
———. "The Army Airways Communication System," Vol. I, "From Activation to Victory." Unpublished manuscript on file at Headquarters, Military Air Transport Service.
———. "History of the Army Air Forces Weather Service." Vols. III-VI, inclusive. Unpublished manuscript in the files of the Air Weather Service Historian, Headquarters, Military Air Transport Service.
Army Air Forces, Air Transport Command. Unpublished official histories, on file at Headquarters, Military Air Transport Service (variously prepared in 1945 and 1946):
"Administrative History of the Air Transport Command: June 1942-July 1944."

"Administrative History of the Ferrying Command: 29 May 1941-30 June 1942."
"Alaskan Division, Historical Record Report."
"Ferrying Command Operations: 29 May 1941-30 June 1942."
"History of the Ferrying Division: 20 June 1942-30 September 1945."
"History of the North Atlantic Division: 1941-1 April 1944."
"History of the Northwest Air Route to Alaska: 1942-1945." (This history was submitted to the University of Minnesota as a Ph.D. dissertation by its author, Edwin R. Carr, under the title "Great Falls to Nome: The Inland Air Route to Alaska, 1940-1945.")
"North Atlantic Wing: 1 April 1944-1 October 1945."
"The Northwest Route Under the Ferrying Division: 16 June 1942-1 November 1942."
"Organizational History of the Ferrying Division: 20 June 1942-1 August 1944."
"The Air Transport Command in World War II."
"The CRIMSON Route."
"The Origins of the Ferrying Division: May 1941 Through June 1942."

Army Air Forces, Air Transport Command, North Atlantic Division. Unpublished official historical monographs, on file at the Air University Research Studies Institute:

"Historical Data: CRYSTAL II."
"History of CRYSTAL I."
"History of the 1383d A.A.F. Base Unit."
"History of the 1387th A.A.F. Base Unit."
"History of the 1388th A.A.F. Base Unit."

Army Service Forces, Control Division. "The Alaska Highway." Report 175. 2 vols. Unpublished report on file in the Office of the Chief of Military History.
———. "The Canol Project." 7 vols. Unpublished report on file in the Office of the Chief of Military History.
Army Service Forces, Seattle Port of Embarkation. "Historical Report: Section V. Expansion and the Subports." Unpublished manuscript on file in the Office of the Chief of Military History.
Bureau of the Budget. "The Canol Project." Report to the Director by the Principal Budget Examiner. Copy in file ASF 65-8 of the Departmental Records Branch, The Adjutant General's Office.
Corps of Engineers, North Atlantic Division. Unpublished official accounts of base development and construction, 1946, on file in the Office of the Chief of Military History:

"U.S. Army Base, District of Keewatin, Canada: Southampton Island."
"U.S. Army Base, Labrador: Goose Bay."
"U.S. Army Bases: Newfoundland."
"U.S. Army Bases, Province of Manitoba, Canada: Churchill, The Pas."
"U.S. Army Base, Province of Quebec: Fort Chimo."
"U.S. Army Base, Province of Quebec: Mingan."

Eastern Defense Command, "History of the Eastern Defense Command." Unpublished manuscript on file in the Office of the Chief of Military History.
U.S. Army Forces in Central Canada. "History of U.S. Army Forces in Central Canada." Unpublished historical report on file in the Office of the Chief of Military History.
U.S. Navy, Atlantic Fleet. "Administrative History of the U.S. Atlantic Fleet in World War II." Vol. II, "Commander, Task Force Twenty-Four." Unpublished official history, 1946, on file in the Naval Records and History Division of the Navy Department.

War Production Board. "History of the Canadian Division of the War Production Board, March 1942–June 1945." Unpublished manuscript, 1945. Copy in War Production Board Records, National Archives.

Western Defense Command. "History of the Western Defense Command." 5 vols. Unpublished historical report on file in the Office of the Chief of Military History.

———. "Military History of the Northwestern Sector." Unpublished manuscript on file in the Office of the Chief of Military History.

Chronology of Statements in the Canadian House of Commons

Although not paralleled in the United States legislature, the Canadian procedure whereby the Prime Minister and his Cabinet Ministers present policy statements and render progress reports on the floor of the House of Commons offers an important source of authoritative material. A list of statements related to the subject matter of this study follows, with the page references to the bound *House of Commons Debates:*

1939	
8 September	Prime Minister W. L. M. King, "Canada Enters the War," pp. 25–41.
1940	
20 May	Mr. King, "Canada's War Effort," pp. 35–50.
21 May	Minister of National Defense Norman McL. Rogers, "Canada's Defense Program," pp. 90–99.
4 June	Mr. King, "Naval Assistance to Britain," pp. 482–85.
18 June	Mr. King, "Emergency War Measures," pp. 853–56.
29 July	Mr. King, "Canada's Defense Policy," pp. 2089–92.
29 July	Minister of National Defense J. L. Ralston, "Our Defense Program," pp. 2093–2103.
29 July	Minister of National Defense for Air C. G. Power, "Air Forces and Naval Services," pp. 2104–11.
30 July	Minister of Munitions and Supply C. D. Howe, "Munitions and Supply," pp. 2113–20.
6 August	Mr. King, "Canadian Participation in the Pan American Union," pp. 2540–41.
12 November	Mr. King, "Canada's War Aims and Efforts and the Ogdensburg Agreement," pp. 48–61.
15 November	Col. Ralston, "Canada's Military Program," pp. 136–53.
18 November	Mr. Power, "The Royal Canadian Air Force," pp. 164–76.
19 November	Minister of National Defense for Naval Services A. L. Macdonald, "The Royal Canadian Navy," pp. 202–08.
20 November	Mr. Howe, "Progress on War Production," pp. 258–72.
1941	
17 February	Mr. King, "Progress of the War," pp. 806–17.
24–25 February	Mr. King, "The Permanent Joint Board on Defense," pp. 980–81, 1015–16.
24 March	Minister of Mines and Resources T. A. Crerar, "Interpretation of the Rush-Bagot Agreement," pp. 1777–79.
25 March	Mr. King, "Canada's War Effort," pp. 1852–54.
27 March	Mr. King, "Defense of Newfoundland," p. 1904.

28 April	Mr. King, "Co-operation in Economic Defense—The Hyde Park Declaration," pp. 2286–89.
3 November	Mr. King, "The United States and the War," pp. 4054–56.
4 November	Mr. Howe, "Canada's Munitions Program," pp. 4081–91.
30 December	Prime Minister Winston Churchill, "Canada and the War," pp. 4479–82.
1942	
26 January	Mr. King, "Canada's War Effort," pp. 30–51.
27–28 January	Mr. King, "Imperial War Cabinet," pp. 58, 105–06.
10 February	Mr. King, "Pacific War Council," p. 598.
18 March	Mr. King, "Unity of Command in Coastal Defense," p. 1411.
25 March	Mr. King, "The Defense of Canada," pp. 1627–32.
25 March	Mr. King, "Co-ordination of United Nations Strategy," pp. 1632–33.
21 April	Mr. King, "Pacific War Council," pp. 1790–91.
10 June	Mr. King, "Canada's War Effort," pp. 3238–44.
23 June	Minister of Finance J. L. Ilsley, "Hyde Park Agreement," pp. 3573–74.
1943	
1 February	Mr. King, "Joint Defense Projects," pp. 20–21.
1 February	Mr. King, "Canada's War Effort," pp. 40–55.
2 April	Mr. King, "Civil Air Transport," pp. 1776–78.
14 May	Col. Ralston, "The Canadian Army in Canada," pp. 2691–94.
21 May	Mr. Power, "The R.C.A.F. Home Establishment and Antisubmarine Operations," pp. 2884–87.
7 June	Mr. Macdonald, "Battle of the Atlantic," pp. 3409–15.
9 July	Mr. King, "Combined Organization and Planning," pp. 4556–58.
12 July	Mr. King, "Relations With Latin American Countries," pp. 4664–68.
1944	
29 February	Mr. Howe, "Northwest Staging Route," pp. 979–81.
16 March	Mr. King, "Canadian Mutual Aid," pp. 1539–41.
21 April	Mr. Ilsley, "Hyde Park Declaration," pp. 2226–28.
5 May	Mr. Crerar, "Canol Project," pp. 2648–52.
26 May	Mr. Crerar, "Canol Project," pp. 3266–95.
1 August	Mr. King, "Financial Settlement for Defense Installations," pp. 5706–08.
4 August	Mr. King, "Canada and the Pan American Union," pp. 5912–13.
1945	
4 April	Mr. King, "The Pacific War," pp. 433–35.
17 December	Mr. King, "Tripartite Declaration on Atomic Energy," pp. 3632–38.
1946	
3 June	Minister of Reconstruction and Supply C. D. Howe, "Atomic Energy," pp. 2105–15.
1947	
12 February	Mr. King, "Defense Co-operation with the United States," pp. 345–48.

List of Abbreviations

AAF	Army Air Forces
ACofS	Assistant Chief of Staff
AG	Adjutant General
ASF	Army Service Forces
ATC	Air Transport Command
Brig	Brigadier
CCAC	Combined Civil Affairs Committee
CCS	Combined Chiefs of Staff
Cdn	Canadian
CG	Commanding General
CINCLANT	Commander in Chief, U.S. Atlantic Fleet
Cir	Circular
CJS	Canadian Joint Staff
CNO	Chief of Naval Operations
CO	Commanding Officer
CofS	Chief of Staff
CTS	Treaty Series (Canada)
DCofS	Deputy Chief of Staff
Desp	Despatch
D/S	Department of State
EAS	Executive Agreement Series (United States)
EDC	Eastern Defense Command
Emb	Embassy
EO	Executive Order
FR	Federal Register
GHQ	General Headquarters, U.S. Army
GO	General Order
GS	General Staff
JAN-CAN	Joint U.S. Army, Navy-Canadian
JCS	Joint Chiefs of Staff
JPC	Joint Planning Committee
Leg	Legation
Ltr	Letter
Maj	Major
Memo	Memorandum
Memo/Conv	Memorandum of conversation
Momp	Mid-ocean meeting place
NBC	Newfoundland Base Command
NWSC	Northwest Service Command
OCE	Office, Chief of Engineers
OCMH	Office, Chief of Military History
OCNO	Office, Chief of Naval Operations
ONI	Office of Naval Intelligence
OPD	Operations Division, War Department General Staff
Ott	Ottawa
PDB	File indicator derived from PJBD

PJBD	Permanent Joint Board on Defense, Canada-United States
PL	Public Law
RAF	Royal Air Force
RCAF	Royal Canadian Air Force
Rpt	Report
Secy	Secretary
SO	Special Order
SUSAM	Senior U.S. Army Member
SW	Secretary of War
TAG	The Adjutant General
Telg	Telegram
TIAS	Treaties and Other International Acts Series (United States)
TS	Treaty Series (United States)
UNRRA	United Nations Relief and Rehabilitation Administration
USW	Under Secretary of War
VLR	Very long range
WD	War Department
WDC	Western Defense Command
WDGS	War Department General Staff
Westomp	Western ocean meeting place
WPD	War Plans Division, War Department General Staff

UNITED STATES ARMY IN WORLD WAR II

The multivolume series, UNITED STATES ARMY IN WORLD WAR II, consists of a number of subseries which are tentatively planned as follows: The War Department, The Army Air Forces, The Army Ground Forces, The Army Service Forces, Defense of the Western Hemisphere, The War in the Pacific, European Theater of Operations, Mediterranean Theater of Operations, The Middle East Theater, The China-Burma-India Theater, The Technical Services, Special Studies, and Pictorial Record.

The following volumes have been published or are in press: *

The War Department
- *Chief of Staff: Prewar Plans and Preparation*
- *Washington Command Post: The Operations Division*
- *Strategic Planning for Coalition Warfare: 1941–1942*
- *Strategic Planning for Coalition Warfare: 1943–1944*
- *Global Logistics and Strategy: 1940–1943*
- *The Army and Economic Mobilization*
- *The Army and Industrial Manpower*

The Army Ground Forces
- *The Organization of Ground Combat Troops*
- *The Procurement and Training of Ground Combat Troops*

The Army Service Forces
- *The Organization and Role of the Army Service Forces*

Defense of the Western Hemisphere
- *The Framework of Hemisphere Defense*

The War in the Pacific
- *Okinawa: The Last Battle*
- *Guadalcanal: The First Offensive*
- *The Approach to the Philippines*
- *The Fall of the Philippines*
- *Leyte: Return to the Philippines*
- *Seizure of the Gilberts and Marshalls*
- *Victory in Papua*
- *CARTWHEEL: The Reduction of Rabaul*

*The volumes on the Army Air Forces, published by the University of Chicago Press, are not included in this list.

European Theater of Operations
The Lorraine Campaign
Cross-Channel Attack
Logistical Support of the Armies, Volume I
Logistical Support of the Armies, Volume II
The Supreme Command

Mediterranean Theater of Operations
Northwest Africa: Seizing the Initiative in the West

The Middle East Theater
The Persian Corridor and Aid to Russia

The China-Burma-India Theater
Stilwell's Mission to China
Stilwell's Command Problems
Time Runs Out in CBI

The Technical Services
The Transportation Corps: Responsibilities, Organization and Operations
The Transportation Corps: Movements, Training, and Supply
The Transportation Corps: Operations Overseas
The Quartermaster Corps: Organization, Supply, and Services, Volume I
The Quartermaster Corps: Organization, Supply, and Services, Volume II
The Quartermaster Corps, Operations in the War Against Japan
The Ordnance Department: Planning Munitions for War
The Signal Corps: The Emergency
The Signal Corps: The Test
The Medical Department: Hospitalization and Evacuation, Zone of Interior
The Corps of Engineers: Troops and Equipment
The Chemical Warfare Service: Organizing for War

Special Studies
Three Battles: Arnaville, Altuzzo, and Schmidt
The Women's Army Corps
Rearming the French
Chronology: 1941–1945
Military Relations Between the United States and Canada: 1939–1945

Pictorial Record
The War Against Germany and Italy: Mediterranean and Adjacent Areas
The War Against Germany: Europe and Adjacent Areas
The War Against Japan

Index

ABC–1. *See* Plans, defense and war, ABC–1.
ABC–2, 104n
ABC–22. *See* Plans, defense and war, ABC–22.
ABC (Pacific)–22, 107
Act of Chapultepec, 148, 334
Act of Havana, 153
Adak, 254, 255–56, 258
ADB, 103n
Admiralty, British, 170n, 243, 245
Aerial photography, 284
Air bases. *See* Bases, air, British; Bases, air, Canadian; Bases, air, U.S.
Air Corps Ferrying Command, U.S., 130, 182, 204, 308
Air cover. *See* Submarines, antisubmarine air operations.
Air defense. *See* Air defense zones, western Canada; Air warning services; Antiaircraft defense; Central Air Defense Zone, U.S.; Central Canada Aircraft Detection Corps; Military Area, Sault Sainte Marie; Newfoundland; Signal Aircraft Warning Reporting Companies, U.S.
Air defense zones, western Canada, 302
Air ferry routes. *See also* Bases, air, British; Bases, air, Canadian; Bases, air, U.S.; CRIMSON Project; North Atlantic Ferry Route Project Committe; Staging fields.
  Alaska-Siberia. *See* Air ferry routes, Northwest Staging Route.
  Interior Staging Route, 306
  Mackenzie River air route, 139, 213–15, 237–38, 322n, 323, 324
  North Atlantic, 46, 53–54, 70, 95, 130, 136, 149, 151, 183, 184, 186, 189, 190, 191–93, 301–02, 314, 315–16, 318, 357–58, 363–64
  operation of, 181–82
  Northwest Staging Route, 53–54, 100, 138, 139, 199–214, 215–18, 219–20, 236, 237–38, 315–16, 317–18, 320–21, 351, 354–55, 359–61, 363–64
    agreements, 203–04, 209–11, 314
    air traffic, 205, 217
    aircraft deliveries, 215–16
    aircraft losses, 202–03
    airway traffic control, 302, 304–06, 309
    airways facilities, 202–03
Air ferry routes—Continued
  Northwest Staging Route— Continued
    commercial airlines, use of by AAF, 307
    design criteria, year-long discussion of, 213
    expenditures on, 213, 324
    RCAF traffic-control delay, and equipment shortages, 305–06
    and U.S. troops in Canada, 296–97
  operation of, PJBD recommendations, 51
  Pacific, 312
Air Force, Department of the, 35n. *See also* Army Air Corps, U.S.; Army Air Forces, U.S.; U.S. Army Air Forces in Newfoundland.
Air Force Headquarters, Canadian, 253
Air forces, Canadian. *See also* Royal Canadian Air Force.
  Annette Island, 252
  Newfoundland, 95, 165–66
Air Forces, U.S.
  Fourth, 303
  Eighth, 191–92, 241
Air Ministry, British, 118
Air Ministry, Canadian, 72n
Air navigation, 337
Air Observers School, Canadian, 217n
Air patrol. *See also* Submarines, antisubmarine air operations.
  Alaska and Aleutians, 253
  North Atlantic, 14–15, 284
Air rescue, Hudson's Bay Company personnel, 284
Air Staff, Canadian, 113
Air strips. *See* Flight strips, Canadian; Flight strips, U.S.
Air Traffic Regulations Subcommittee, Canadian, 304–05
Air transport. *See* Aviation, postwar international operations.
Air Transport Command, U.S., 136, 168, 206, 207, 211, 217n, 237
  Alaskan Wing, 133, 204, 209, 216–17, 302n, 303, 309, 318
  cadres, western Canada, 308
  carrying of passengers for hire, Executive Order, 312
  commercial airlines as contract carriers, 133, 307

Air Transport Command, U.S.—Continued
North Atlantic Division, 131, 192
North Atlantic Wing, 133
and Northwest Airlines, 308–10
Northwest Route, Ferrying Division, 204–05, 216
some routes not authorized, 310
Air warning services, 117, 195–96
Airborne Divisions, U.S.
82d, 267
101st, 267
Aircraft, Canadian
B–18, 99
Bolingbroke, 252, 252n, 253
flights over Maine, 307
production, 295
trainers and flying boats to U.S., 2
Aircraft, cargo, lack of for Norway operation, 260
Aircraft, commercial. *See* Airlines, commercial, contract carriers.
Aircraft, U.S.
A–20 Boston medium bombers, 271
B–17, 181, 241, 243n, 248
B–17B, 98, 172
B–24, 181, 248, 250
B–26, 203
B–29, 337
Canadian requests for, 7, 13–14, 90–91
carrier-based, 249
Catalina PBY, 192
deliveries to Canada, 90–91
deliveries to Soviet Union, 216
deliveries to United Kingdom, 181–82, 184, 191
flights over Canadian territory, 306–07
flying boats not reallocated to Canada, 61
Lockheed Hudson, 181
losses, North Atlantic ferry route, 192
P–40, 202–03, 253
permission to fly over Canada, 306–07
purchase of used planes by Canada, 10
routes in Canada, application for, 310–11
trainers, 282
VLR (very long range) patrol, 249, 250
Aircraft carriers
British, 272
Canadian, 251, 272
Japanese, 204
U.S., 249, 250–51
Aircraft ferrying. *See* Air ferry routes; Green Project, AAF; White Project, AAF.
Aircraft production
U.S., 184
U.S.-Canadian totals, 290
Aircraft Repair, Limited, Canadian, 217n
Airfields. *See also* Airports; Bases, air, British; Bases, air, Canadian; Bases, air, U.S.
authorization for use of Canadian by U.S. planes, 308
northern, cost distribution, 320–21, 322–23
northern, importance to Canada, 321
Airlift of troops and materials by commercial airlines, 204
Airlines, commercial, contract carriers, 133, 310–11, 312–13. *See also* Airlift of troops and materials by commercial airlines; Northeast Airlines; Northwest Airlines.
flights over Canada and U.S., agreement on, 307
Goose Bay and Newfoundland, 307
militarization of, 308, 309–10, 311, 312
Northwest Airlines, and friction with Canada, 307–10
on Northwest Staging Route, 202–03, 216–17, 304, 307–10
Airports
Dorval, 181
Gander, 19–20, 95, 96, 97, 99, 117, 118, 165–66, 173, 181, 182–83, 190. *See also* Bases air, Canadian; Bases, air, U.S.
Goose Bay, 303. *See also* Bases, air, Canadian; Bases, air, U.S.
Newfoundland. *See* Airports, Gander.
traffic control, 304–05.
Airships, nonrigid, in air patrol, 361
Airspace
Canadian, 301
Canadian, restricted zones, 195, 197, 305n, 307
Airway traffic control, 301–03, 304–13. *See also* Air ferry routes, Northwest Staging Route; JAN-CAN (Joint Army, Navy, Canadian).
Airways
facilities, 141, 214–15. *See also* Air ferry routes, Northwest Staging Route.
maintenance and control of facilities, 304–06, 310–16, 355–56, 361–63
Aklavik, 227
Alaska, 40, 48, 50, 53–54, 87–88, 100–101, 107, 109, 110, 120, 128, 199, 201–03, 207, 215–17, 218–20, 225–26, 227–28, 230–31, 235, 238–39, 258n, 277, 283, 302–03, 306–07, 308, 312, 318, 323n, 325n. *See also* Aleutian campaign; and *under* Bases.
defense of, 218, 252
defenses, penetration of by Japanese, 204
Alaska Defense Command, 112, 202, 215–16, 224n, 303

Alaska Highway, 41, 42n, 44, 53-54, 75, 127-28, 135, 200-201, 203n, 206, 207, 213, 217-27, 229-30, 232, 236, 241, 296-97, 304, 318, 319, 323, 327, 357, 363, 370-72. *See also* Flight strips, Canadian; Flight strips, U.S.
agreements, 221, 226-27
civilian traffic, 223-24
gift to Canada, 329
Haines-Champagne road, 226-27, 330-31
military traffic, 223-24
postwar use by U.S. military vehicles, 221
redesignated, Northwest Highway System, 224n
Tok road, 225
transfer to Canada, 224, 227
U.S. expenditures, 223, 330
and use of highways to U.S. border, 221
waiving of duties, taxes, and fees, 278
Alaska Railroad, 225
Alaskan International Highway Commission, 217, 227
Albert and Davidson Corporation, 333
Alberta, 128, 137, 218, 299
Alcan Highway, 136. *See also* Alaska Highway.
Aleutian campaign, 224n, 252-59, 317, 318. *See also* First Special Service Force, U.S.-Canadian.
Aleutian Islands, 252, 253, 256
Alexander, Maj. Gen. R. O., 121, 253
Allied Powers, 289-90, 294-95
postwar positions, 337, 339, 344-45
Aluminium Company of Canada, 151, 151n
Aluminum, 149, 155n, 196
Amadjuak Lake, 191
Amchitka, 254, 255, 257
America, 96
American Nations, use of term, 153
American Red Cross, and relief problem in Greenland, 150
American Republics, 142-43, 293
Act of Chapultepec, 148, 334
Act of Havana, 153
Canada as a member of British Commonwealth, 144, 334-35
defense, 11, 22, 26, 149, 161
defense and neutrality, discussion at Panama, 144
and Greenland bases, use of, 152-53
Inter-American Conference, 1945, 147, 148
Inter-American Conference, 1947, 48
Inter-American Defense Board, 145
liaison officers to, 11
Meeting of Foreign Ministers, First, 1939, Panama, 144
Meeting of Foreign Ministers, Second, 1940, Havana, 11-12, 26n, 143, 144
American Republics—Continued
Meeting of Foreign Ministers, Third, 1942, Rio, 144-46, 160
military co-operation, 334
Treaty of Reciprocal Assistance, 48
Ammunition, 281. *See also* Munitions, Canadian; Munitions, U.S; Munitions, U.S.-Canadian.
Amphibious Training Force 9, U.S.-Canadian, 255, 258
Anchorage, 100, 202, 225, 239, 253-54
Anderson, Air Vice Marshal N. R., 37
Anglo-American Food Committee, 83
Anglo-French Purchasing Board, 60
Annapolis, 165
Annette Island, 202, 252-53, 254, 255
Antiaircraft Battery (Heavy), Canadian 40th 195, 197
Antiaircraft defense
Annette Island, 252
Buffalo, 198
Canada, 317-18
Maritime Provinces, 89
Newfoundland, 92-93, 98-99, 173
Sault Sainte Marie, 194-95, 196
Antilles, 19
Antisubmarine operations. *See* Convoys; Submarines.
Antisubmarine Squadrons, U.S.
6th, 250
19th, 250
20th, 248
Antisubmarine Wings, U.S. 25th, 250
Anzio, 265, 266
ARCADIA Conference, 59, 63-64, 66, 66n, 75
Argentia, 62, 96, 124-25, 168, 178, 179, 184n, 244, 245, 247, 354. *See also* Bases, air, U.S.; Bases, naval, Canadian; Bases, naval, U.S.; Bases, U.S.
Argentina, 144
ARGONAUT Conference, 66n
Armaments, on vessels in Great Lakes, 279-80
Armed forces, Canadian, at outbreak of World War II, 4-5, 5n
Armies, Canadian First, 241, 265
Armies, U.S.
Third, 31
Fourth, 107
Fifth, 266
Seventh, 266
Arms production, Canadian, 273
Army, British, 8-9, 162-63
Army, Canadian, 4-5, 34-35, 89, 105, 118, 173, 198, 241-42, 252, 256-57, 263-64, 274n, 276, 330. *See also* Troops, Canadian.

Army, Canadian—Continued
  active units on V-J Day, 271–72
  Atlantic Command, 20, 30n, 99, 111–12, 173–74
  casualties, Aleutians, 259
  equipment, lack of, 5–6
  General Staff, 113, 260–61
  Newfoundland Force, 116
  Pacific Command, 101, 107, 111–12, 121, 253, 256
  Pacific Force, 51, 268–70, 271–72
  regimental combat team for Kiska assault, 257
Army, French, 162
Army, U.S., 11, 48–49, 105–06, 126, 128–30, 167, 178, 180, 182, 188, 218, 225–26, 231–32, 240, 247, 259, 276, 303, 304, 306
Army Air Corps, U.S., 96, 151–52, 181
Army Air Forces, U.S., 35, 48–49, 51, 128, 131, 140, 184, 203, 205, 206, 207, 215, 217, 241, 248, 249, 276, 282, 284, 302, 305–06, 307, 308–09. *See also* Army Air Corps, U.S.; U.S. Army Air Forces in Newfoundland.
  aerial photography mission, 133
  antisubmarine force, Newfoundland, 173
  antisubmarine units, transfer of, to United Kingdom, 250
  defense of Dutch Harbor, 253–54
  offer to equip RCAF with Boston medium bombers, 271
  and RCAF offer of unit for Pacific, 270–71
  standardization of RCAF on U.S. equipment, 271
  weather forecasting services, 237–38
  Weather Region, 16th, 133
  weather reports, teletype, Canadian northwest, 238
Army-Navy Liquidation Commissioner, U.S., 328n, 334
Army Post Office, New York City, 277
Army Service Forces, U.S., 132, 140
Army Transport Service, U.S., 239
Arnold, General of the Army Henry H., 59, 70, 103n, 248, 271, 282–83
Aruba, 142–43, 143n, 149n
Arvida, 196
Assiniboine, 123n
ATFERO, 181
Athabasca, 324
Atherton, Ray, 147
Athlone, the Earl of, Governor General of Canada, 28
Atlantic Bridge, 181, 191
Atlantic Charter, 62, 69, 244
Atlantic Conference, 62, 123, 123n, 124–25, 184n, 244, 245
Atlantic Convoy Conference, 125–26, 248–50
Atlantic Fleet, U.S., 123, 124–25, 127, 245, 247
  Support Force, 124, 244
  Task Force, 111–12, 132
Atomic bomb, 273, 284, 286–87, 288–89, 339
Atomic bombing, postwar threat to U.S. and Canadian cities, 341
Atomic energy research, U.S.-Canadian, 273, 284, 286–89
Atomic energy tripartite agreement, 289
Atomic weapons, 341
Attachés, air-military-naval. *See* Service attachés.
Attlee, Clement, 289
Attorney General of Canada, 299
Attu, 255–56, 257
Aurora borealis, 236
Australia, 57, 67–68, 70, 72, 82, 84, 235, 281, 295
Avalon Peninsula, 165, 178–79
Aviation, postwar international operations
  airports in Canadian northwest, 304
  Canadian acquisition of airfields at fraction of cost, 333–34
  Canadian fear of U.S. advantages, 340
  civil aviation policy, Canadian Government, 303–04, 321
  U.S. and Canadian advisory committees, 303n
  U.S. and Canadian plans, 303
AWOL problems, 277
Axis, and St. Pierre plebiscite, 159
Axis attack on North America, threat of 47, 87, 95
Axis Powers, 108, 109, 193, 339
Azores, 251

Baffin Island, 183, 187. *See also* Bases, air, U.S., Frobisher Bay (CRYSTAL II), Northwest Territories; Bases, air, U.S., Padloping Island (CRYSTAL III).
Bagley, Vice Adm. D. W., 36
Bahamas, 149n
Baker Lake, 191
Baldwin, J., 135–36
Balkans, 266
Balloons, Japanese, 200
Base Commands. *See* Newfoundland Base Command.
Bases, air, British
  Azores, 251
  Iceland, 182, 251
  Kaldaharnes, 182
  Reykjavik, 182
  United Kingdom, 250

Bases, air, Canadian
  Adak, 254
  Amchitka, 254, 255
  Anchorage, 253-54
  Annette Island, 252-53, 254, 255
  Bellingham, 283
  Botwood, 170n
  Calgary, 324
  Edmonton, 324
  Gander Airport, 170, 170n, 303, 306
  Gander Lake, 247
  Gleneagles, 170n
  Goose Bay, 170n, 188, 303, 306, 314, 324
    99-year lease, 189, 303n
  Grande Prairie, 324
  Halifax, 247
  Houlton, 283
  Kamloops, 324
  Kodiak, 253, 254
  Labrador, 304
  leased bases, 99-year lease, 170
  Lethbridge, 205, 324
  Newfoundland, 304
  Nome, 253
  Nova Scotia, 250
  Patricia Bay, 253
  postwar use, 303
  Prince George, 324
  Regina, 186, 324
  Sea Island, 253
  Smith River, 208, 210, 324
  Smithers, 252
  Sydney, 247
  Torbay, 170n, 172, 173, 184, 247
  Ucluelet Airdrome, 351-52
  Umnak, 254-55
  Watson Lake, 324
  Whitehorse, 324
  Yarmouth, 247
Bases, air, U.S. *See also* CRIMSON Project; Fort Chimo (CRYSTAL I), air base; Fort Nelson, U.S. air base; Fort St. John, U.S. air base.
  Adak, 254
  Alaska, 204, 224
  Amchitka, 254
  Anchorage, 100, 202
  Annette Island, 202, 252
  Antilles, 19
  Argentia, 96, 168, 178, 244, 247
  Azores, 251
  Baffin Island, 183, 185n, 186
  Bermuda, 97n, 164
  Bethel, 100, 202
  Big Delta, 202
  Botwood, 165, 172
  British possessions, 23
Bases, air, U.S.—Continued
  Calgary, 205, 208, 213, 323, 324
  Canada, 49, 52, 53, 75, 89-90, 128, 130, 191, 199, 224, 304
    bases to become Canadian property, 186, 189-90
  Caribbean, 19, 162, 164
  Churchill, Manitoba, 130-31, 186, 187, 189, 189n, 284, 304, 316, 324, 325n
  Cordova 100, 202
  Cumberland Sound, site survey, 184
  Edmonton, 203, 204, 207-08, 209-10, 211, 217, 323, 324
  Edmonton satellite base. *See* Bases, air, U.S., Namao.
  Fairbanks, 100, 202, 215-16
  Frobisher Bay (CRYSTAL II), 130-31, 184, 187, 189, 190, 192-93, 304, 324, 325n
  Galena, 202
  Gander Airport, 19, 97, 171-72, 182, 183, 184, 190, 191-92, 250, 313-14
  Gander Lake, 165, 192
  Goose Bay, 130, 131, 184, 187-89, 192, 307, 314, 323, 324. *See also* Bases, air, U.S., North West River.
  Grande Prairie, 201-02, 207, 208, 211, 212, 323, 324
  Greenland, 149, 182, 183, 186-87, 192
    agreement on bases, 152-54
    Canadian-British proposal of site survey, 151-52
    Canadian use of, 152, 153
    construction by U.S., plan No. 2, 152-53
    construction with U.S. aid, plan No. 1, 152
    site surveys, 151-52
    South Greenland Survey Expedition, 154
  Gulkana, 202
  Harmon Field, 127, 166-68, 169, 173, 192
  Iceland, 156-57, 182n, 186, 192, 248, 250
  Juneau, 202
  Ketchikan, 100
  Kodiak, 253
  Labrador, 128, 186, 191, 304
  McGrath, 202
  Maritimes, proposal of, 49-50
  Mingan, 188, 189, 190, 324, 325
  Naknek, 202
  Namao, 208, 211, 316, 323, 324
  Narsarssuak (BLUIE WEST 1), 154, 182
  Newfoundland, 7, 14, 19-20, 21, 52, 62, 95-96, 97, 164, 181, 186, 187, 191, 250, 304, 307
  Nome, 100, 202, 216
  North West River, 41, 182-83, 353-54

360-477 O - 70 - 28

Bases, air, U.S.—Continued
Northway, 202
Pacific, 199
Padloping Island (CRYSTAL III), 130, 131, 184, 187
postwar use, 303
Presque Isle, 188, 191–92, 247
Prince George, 202, 213, 323, 324
Smithers, 202
Søndre Strømfjord (BLUIE WEST 8), 154n, 182
Southhampton Island, 130, 186, 187, 189, 190, 192–93, 304, 324, 325n
The Pas, 130, 186–87, 189, 189n, 284, 304, 315, 316, 324, 325n
Trinidad, 97n
Umnak, 254
Watson Lake, 201, 207, 208, 211, 212, 323, 324
West Indies, 14–15
Whitehorse, 201–02, 203, 204, 207, 208, 211, 212, 215, 225, 323, 324, 325, 327
Yakutat, 100, 202, 253
Yarmouth, Nova Scotia, proposal of, 23
Bases, Army, U.S. *See also* Fort McAndrew; Fort Pepperrell.
Anchorage, 100
Canada, 52
Fairbanks, 100
St. John's, 166
Bases, naval, British
Azores, 251
Boston, 246, 283
Halifax, 246
Bases, naval, Canadian
Argentia, 118
Bay Bulls, 170n
Boston, 246, 283
Halifax, 123, 246
Kodiak, 255, 283
Maritime Provinces, 99
St. John's 95, 170, 170n, 246
Shelburne, 123
Bases, naval, U.S.
Antilles, 19
Argentia, 116, 118, 127, 132, 167, 168, 178, 244, 246, 247
Azores, 251
British Isles, 243
British possessions, 23
Canada, 52
Caribbean, 19
Dutch Harbor, 100
Greenland, 152–53
Halifax, 49, 123
Iceland, surveys for, 156
Kodiak, 100
Bases, naval, U.S.—Continued
Leyte, 272
Maritime Provinces, 49–50
Newfoundland, 52, 62, 95–96
St. John's, 93, 165–66, 173
Shelburne, 49, 123
Sitka, 100
Sydney, Nova Scotia, 49
Yarmouth, Nova Scotia, proposal of, 23
Bases, U.S. *See also* Destroyers-for-bases; Legislation, U.S.; Miltary planning, U.S.; Prince Rupert.
Alaska, 238
Argentia, 166
Atlantic, need of, 163
Canada, 23, 26, 29, 32–33, 49–50, 69n, 88, 107, 301
Caribbean, 163
Latin America, 163
leased
agreements, 62, 96, 97–98, 164, 165, 166–67, 169–70, 188–89, 189n
Canada, 23–24
Greenslade Board, 166, 177
Newfoundland, 23, 126–27
99-year lease, 164, 165, 166
Newfoundland, 162, 165, 167–73, 177–78, 307
cost of, 168
defense of, 165–66
undeveloped sites and construction delays, 171
U.S. jurisdiction, 165, 166–67
Pacific, 238
Western Hemisphere, need of, 11
Batt, William L., 78, 79
Battle of the Atlantic, 123, 162, 174, 242–51
Battle of Britain, 8, 47–48, 50, 55–56, 94, 103–04
Battle of Los Angeles, 121
Battle of the St. Lawrence, 174n
Bauxite, 149n
Bay Bulls, 170n
Bearn, 158
Beaverbrook, Lord, 70, 82n
Bechtel-Price-Callahan company, 232, 327, 328
Belgian Congo, 287, 288
Belgium, 293
Bell, R. P., 80
Bell Island, 95
Bell Telephone Company of Canada, 180
Bellingham, 283
Berle, Adolf A., Jr., 78
Bermuda, 97n, 149n, 164
Bethel, 100, 202
Big Delta, 222, 225

Biggar, O. M., 32, 34, 37, 90, 113, 114, 115, 120, 183, 201, 335
Bilateral trade agreement, U.S.-Canadian, 4
Bishop, Air Marshal William, 7
Bismarck, 154, 243
Bissell, Lt. Col. C., 36
Black Watch, 95
Blissville, 305
BLUIE WEST 1, 154, 154n, 182
Board of Inquiry for the Great Lakes Fisheries, U.S.-Canadian, 27
Bombardment Squadrons, U.S.
77th, 203
421st, 248
Bomber Reconnaissance Squadrons, Canadian
No. 8, 254
No. 10, 98n
No. 115, 252n, 255
No. 149, 255
Bonesteel, Maj. Gen. Charles H., 157
Boston, 39, 41, 246
Boston Port of Embarkation, 130, 132, 133
Botwood, 92, 95, 99, 165, 170n, 172, 173
Bouchard, J. G., 78
Boundary, Alaska, 219
Bowman, Isaiah, 157n
Bowman Bay, 191
Brant Maj. Gen. Gerald C., 117–18, 118n, 119–20, 301–02
Brazil, 48, 87, 144
Bristol, Rear Adm. Arthur L., 124, 244
British Air Force. *See* Royal Air Force.
British Columbia, 71, 88, 101, 106–07, 111, 112, 120, 121, 128, 137, 217, 218, 225n, 259, 281, 298n, 299
British Commonwealth, 15, 20–21, 49, 55, 56–57, 61, 63, 64, 69, 69n, 82, 83, 85, 144, 145, 146, 147n, 160, 161, 282, 293, 294, 298, 338, 339–40. *See also* British Empire; United Kingdom.
British Commonwealth Air Training Plan, 9–10, 14, 241n, 242, 274–75, 281–83
British Commonwealth Occupation Force, 270
British destroyer fleet, December 1940, 242
British Empire, 1, 3–4, 9, 25, 60, 63–64, 68, 69, 164, 293. *See also* British Commonwealth; United Kingdom.
British Fleet, 3, 49, 272. *See also* Royal Navy.
disposal of, if Britain falls, 8–9, 12–13, 14, 16, 163, 164
British Government. *See* United Kingdom.
British Guiana, 149n
British Isles. *See* United Kingdom.
British Military Mission, 58, 63, 72–73
British Navy. *See* British Fleet; Royal Navy.
British Overseas Airways Company, 312
British Pacific Fleet, 272
British Purchasing Commission, 15, 60, 61, 92
British Scientific Mission, 285, 286
British Supply Council in North America, 61
British West Indies, 9, 295
Brodeur, Rear Adm. V. G., 72, 75n
Buffalo, 39, 41, 102, 198
Burma, 271
Burwash, 206, 207
Bush, Vannevar, 288
Butler, Maj. Gen. William O., 255
Byrd, Lt. Richard E., 2

Cabinet, U.S., 218, 219, 228
Cabinet Defense Committee, Canadian, 336
Cabinet War Committee, Canadian, 34, 42, 70, 71, 75, 80–81, 105, 114, 119, 120, 121, 135–36, 137, 183–84, 188, 204, 209, 210–11, 215, 227, 229, 261, 268, 272, 321
Cadres, for Canadian Army Pacific Force, 269, 270
Cairo-Tehran Conference, 66n
Calgary, 205, 208, 213, 323, 324
Cameron Highlanders, 156
Camp 550, Edmonton, 327, 328
Camp Bedford, 262
Camp Breckinridge, 270
Camp Canol, 214
Camp Pine, 22
Camp Shilo, 133, 281
Campbell, 151
Canadian-American Military Board, 275, 276
Canadian claims
title to all U.S. facilities in Canadian northwest, 203–04
to U.S. bases, 186
to U.S. facilities in Canada, Newfoundland, Labrador, 186
to U.S. radar sets, 71
Canadian Forces in Newfoundland, 118–19
Canadian Fusiliers, 257
Canadian grant to United Kingdom, 294–95
Canadian Military Headquarters in United Kingdom, 264
Canadian military mission to Washington. *See* Joint Staff Mission, Canadian; U.S.-Canadian relations, areas of Canadian discontent, military mission to Washington.
Canadian National Railways, 196, 238, 239, 284
Canadian Pacific Railway Company, 181
Canadian Prime Minister. *See* King, W. L. Mackenzie.
Canadian Special Service Battalion, 1st. *See* First Special Service Force, U.S.-Canadian.

Canadian-U.S. relations. *See* U.S.-Canadian relations, areas of co-operation; U.S.-Canadian relations, areas of Canadian discontent; U.S.-Canadian relations, areas of U.S. discontent.
Canol Project, 52, 128, 135, 136, 200, 214–15, 217, 224, 225, 227, 228–36, 241, 304, 315, 318, 319, 328n, 361–62. *See also* Air ferry routes, Mackenzie River air route; Flight strips, Canadian; Flight strips, U.S.
  agreements, 229–31, 232–33, 234–35
  contracts, revision of, 234
  disposition of, 329, 331–33
  expenditures, 234, 322n
  expenditures and sale price, 333
  and Special Committee of Senate to Investigate the National Defense Program, 233
  Task Force 2600, 127, 231
  and U.S. troops in Canada, 297
  waiving of Canadian royalties, 278
CAP 365. *See* Airways, maintenance and control of facilities.
Cape Dorset, Hudson's Bay Company, 191
Cape Low, 191
Carcross, 230, 331
Cargo transport, intercountry, 51
Caribbean, 7, 19, 48, 142–43, 162, 163, 164, 228, 249
Carmichael, J. H., 80
Carnegie Institute, 286
Casablanca conference, 67n, 248
Caucasus, 261
Central Air Defense Zone, U.S., 195, 197
Central America, 48, 142
Central Canada Aircraft Detection Corps, 195, 197–98
Century Group, 19
Ceylon, 271
Chadwick, Sir James, 288
Chalk River, Ontario, 288
Chalk River Atomic Energy Project, 288, 289
Champagne, 226–27
Chautauqua, 3
Chicago *Tribune*, 18
Chief of General Staff, Canadian, 265, 268
Chief of Naval Operations, U.S., 35, 92, 157, 194, 249. *See also* King, Admiral Ernest J.
  study of Japanese threat, 55n
Chief Signal Officer, U.S. Army, 133–34, 236
Chief of Staff, U.S., 74, 88, 92, 108, 110–11, 113, 115, 187, 219. *See also* Marshall, General of the Army George C.
Chiefs of Staff. *See* Chiefs of Staff, British; Chiefs of Staff, Canadian; Combined Chiefs of Staff, U.S.-British; Joint Chiefs of Staff, U.S.; Joint Staff, Canadian; Joint Staff Mission, British; Joint Staff Mission, Canadian.
Chiefs of Staff, British, 56, 57, 59, 66
Chiefs of Staff, Canadian, 13, 42, 66, 76, 108, 119, 120, 121, 194, 268, 336
Chiefs of Staff, U.S. *See* Joint Chiefs of Staff, U.S.
Chile, 144, 147
China, 3, 58–59, 67, 68, 70, 293, 295
Christie, Loring, 13, 21, 21n, 31, 149
Churchill, Manitoba, 191, 281. *See also* Bases, air, U.S.
Churchill, Winston S., 8–9, 12–13, 19, 20–21, 21n, 24n, 25, 63–65, 65n, 66, 84–85, 123, 156n, 159, 160, 162–65, 248, 260, 268, 340. *See also* Roosevelt and Churchill.
CINCLANT, 124
Citizen action groups
  program for Canadian action, 18, 18n
  U.S. Century Group urges destroyers-for-bases, 19
Civil Aeronautics Administration, U.S., 305
Civil Aeronautics Authority, U.S., 202
Civil Air Patrol, 247
Civil air transport. *See* Aviation, postwar international operations.
Claims, collision, settlement of, 277–78
Clark, Lewis, 291n
Claxton, Brooke, 18n
Coast Artillery Regiments
  57th, 96
  62d, 96
  100th, 195
Coast defense, 317. *See also* Harbor defenses.
  guns, 92, 93–94, 175
  Maritime Provinces, 89
  units, Canadian, 98–99
Coast Guard, U.S., 125, 152, 192, 245
Coast Guard cutters, 165
Coastal Frontier. *See* Naval Coastal Frontier, North Atlantic; Naval Coastal Frontier, Pacific; Sea Frontier.
Cold war, 337, 338
Coldwell, M. J., 19n
Colombia, 48
Colonies, European, in Western Hemisphere
  U.S. policy on, 10, 142–43, 143n, 146, 149–50, 152–53, 158, 163
Columbia, 165
Combined Chiefs of Staff, U.S.-British, 27, 46, 58, 59–60, 62–63, 64, 65n, 66–68, 75, 76, 77–78, 82, 83, 248, 249, 267, 268. *See also* Conferences, politico-military.

Combined Chiefs of Staffs, etc.--Continued
CRIMSON Project review, 186
third powers participate, 65
U.S. personnel, 59, 59n
Combined Civil Affairs Committee, 65-66
Combined Committee on Air Training in North America, 283
Combined Communications Board, 65
Combined Food Board, U.S.-British, 83-84, 84n
Combined versus joint agencies, 77-78
Combined Meteorological Committee, 65
Combined Policy Committee (atomic research), 288
Combined Production and Resources Board, U.S.-British, 83, 84n
Combined Raw Materials Board, U.S.-British, 63, 79, 83, 84n
Combined Shipping Adjustment Board, U.S.-British, 63, 83
Command, unity of, 109, 140-41, 340
in ABC-1 plan, 102-03
antisubmarine operations, under Canadian control, 251
AAF-USN dispute, antisubmarine air cover, 247
in Canada and Newfoundland, 110-22
Canadian antiaircraft battery under U.S. control, 195
in Canadian Armed Forces, 121-22
Canadian insistence on mutual co-operation, 110-11, 356
convoys, eastern Atlantic, under USN and RN, 248-49
convoys, western Atlantic
under Royal Canadian Navy, 125-26, 245-46, 248-49
under U.S. Navy, 123-26, 244, 248-49
U.S. patrol planes, Newfoundland, under RCAF, 249
for Joint Task One, antisubmarine air patrol, 118
lack of, in ABC-22 plan, 103-04, 105-06
lack of, in British Columbia, 120-21
lack of, in Canada and Newfoundland, 74
lack of, in Newfoundland, 97, 98, 104
lack of, in 1940 Plan, 88-90
Newfoundland air patrol, under USN, 247
U.S. antisubmarine aircraft, Newfoundland, under RCAF, 250
U.S. insistence upon, 342
vested in U.S. under 1940 Plan, 115
Commander in Chief, Western Approaches, 122, 243, 245-46
Commodity Supply and Allocation Committees, 83. *See also* Combined Food Board.
Communication channels, multiplicity of, 134
Communication facilities, 86, 130-31, 141, 318
Alaska Communications System, 133-34
Alaska Highway and Canol radio nets, 236, 237
Army Airways Communications Service, 133
Canada, 52, 136, 190, 190n, 349-50
Canadian northwest, 236-37
Greenland, 149
Maritimes, 349-50
Newfoundland, 118, 179, 180, 190n, 349-50
Newfoundland (Gander) Airport, 190
telephone and telegraph line, Edmonton to Alaska, 236-37, 305-06, 323, 324, 325, 325n
White Hills, Newfoundland, 167
Communications agreement, U.S.-Canadian. *See* JAN-CAN.
Communications Committee, U.S.-Canadian, 139.
Compulsory military service for aliens, 276. *See also* Conscription.
Conant, James B., 288
Conception Bay, 174-75
Conferences, politico-military
ARCADIA, Washington, 59, 63-64, 67, 67n, 75
ARGONAUT, Malta-Yalta, 66n
ATLANTIC, Argentia, 62, 123, 123n, 124-25, 184n, 244, 245
OCTAGON, Quebec, 66, 268, 272
Ottawa Air Training Conference, 282-83
QUADRANT, Quebec, 67, 82, 288
SEXTANT-EUREKA, Cairo-Tehran, 66n
SYMBOL (ANFA), Casablanca, 66n, 248
TERMINAL, Potsdam, 66n
TRIDENT, Washington, 66
Congress, U.S., 274, 289, 300-301. *See also* Legislation, U.S.
Conscription. *See also* Compulsory military service for aliens.
French-Canadian opposition to World War I, 206
use of Canadian conscripts outside of Canada, 257-58, 258n
Construction and Engineering Committee, U.S.-Canadian, 139
Construction of facilities. *See also* Engineer Districts; Engineer Divisions; Engineer Troops, U.S.; Engineers, Chief of; Roads, Newfoundland.
Alaska Highway, 218-27
Baffin Island, 184
Canada, bases and facilities, 126-31, 133-40, 304n

Construction of facilities—Continued
Canada, review and authorization of projects, 139, 140
Canol Project, 228-32, 234-35
CRIMSON Project, 184-90
Goose Bay, separate facilities for U.S. forces, 188, 314, 323
Greenland, 182
Labrador, 182-84
Mackenzie River air route, 213-15, 318
Newfoundland bases, 162-63, 166, 167-73
Newfoundland fortifications, radar, roads, 175-80
no continuing rights for U.S. in Canada, 320, 322, 334
Northwest Staging Route, 199-213, 318
Prince Rupert, 239-40
Quebec, 184
telephone-telegraph line, Edmonton to Alaska, 236-37, 305
water route, Waterways to Norman Wells, 231
winter roads, 231-32
Consulates. *See* Diplomatic missions.
Contracts, with Canada
cancellation of, 292-93
revision to allow profits, 293
Controlled areas, railroad, The Pas to Churchill, 284
Controller of Meteorological Services, Canadian, 190
Convoys. *See also* Atlantic Convoy Conference; Command, unity of, convoys, eastern Atlantic, under USN and RN; Command, unity of, convoys, western Atlantic; Newfoundland Escort Force; Task Group 4.19.
Atlantic, U.S. escort, Canada to British Isles, 243
Atlantic coast, 246
Eastern Local Area, 246, 248
with escort aircraft carriers, 249
fast and slow convoys, 245
Greenland, 249
Iceland-Momp shuttle, 246, 248
Kodiak to Dutch Harbor, 256
to Mediterranean, 248-49
Mid-ocean Area, 246, 247
North Africa, 246-47
North Atlantic, 246-47, 251
Pacific, 105-06
routing of, 245
troops for Attu and Kiska operations, 256
troops to Mediterranean, 248-49
troops to United Kingdom, 125, 246
Convoys—Continued
western Atlantic, 48, 49, 88, 105-06, 122-23, 125-26, 242-43, 244, 245-46, 248
loss rate, 158
unified command under U.S., 123-24
Western Local Area, 246, 247
Coral Harbour, 191
Corbett, Percy, 144
Cordova, 100, 202
Corlett, Maj. Gen. Charles H., 258
Cormoran, 191
CORONET, 269
Corps, U.S. XVI, 241
Corps Areas, Ninth, 121
Corps of Engineers. *See* Engineers, Corps of.
Corvettes
British, 243
Canadian, 122, 243, 244, 246, 249, 251, 256
Free French, 246
COTTAGE, 257
Courts, Canadian civil, concurrent jurisdiction over U.S. troops, 297, 298-99
Courts, U.S. military
full jurisdiction over U.S. troops, 300
jurisdiction in Canada, limits to, 297
Courts-martial, in Canada, 298, 300, 301. *See also* Courts, U.S. military.
Craig, Malin, 149n
Crerar, Gen. Henry D. G., 241
CRIMSON Project, 127, 130-31, 132, 190, 191, 192-93, 318. *See also* Air ferry routes, North Atlantic.
bases, 181
preparatory studies, 182-87
review of American plan by JCS, 45-46
urgent construction project, 187, 188
Crops, 79
Crown Assets Allocation Committee, Canadian, 326
Cruisers
British, 244
Canadian, 251, 256, 272
Cryolite
international meeting, New York, on output, 151
mines, 149-50, 151, 154-55
synthetic, 154-55, 155n
CRYSTAL I (Fort Chimo). *See* Fort Chimo (CRYSTAL I), air base.
CRYSTAL II (Frobisher Bay). *See* Bases, air, U.S., Frobisher Bay (CRYSTAL II).
CRYSTAL III (Padloping Island), 130, 131, 184, 187
Cuffe, Air Commodore A. A. L., 17, 32, 37.
Cumberland Sound, Baffin Inland, 184

Curaçao, 143n, 149n
Curtis, Air Vice Marshal W. A., 37
Customs duties, Canadian, 278, 358
avoidance of, on U.S. equipment, 257
on surplus property, 326–27
Customs duties, Newfoundland, 169
Customs duties, U.S., 358
avoidance of, on Canadian equipment, 254
Cutters, U.S. Coast Guard, 245
Czechoslovakia, 293

Dawson, 256
Dawson Creek, 128, 202, 221–22, 225, 236, 298n. *See also* Flight strips, Canadian, Beatton River.
de Gaulle, General Charles, 158–60
Declarations of war
by Canada, 5, 19–20, 69, 107–08, 162
by United Kingdom, 5, 68
by United States, 107–08
Decorations, 265–66
Deerwester, Col. C. H., 36
Defense, Pan American. *See* American Republics, defense.
Defense, U.S.-Canadian. *See also* Military planning, U.S.-Canadian; Permanent Joint Board on Defense; Plans, defense and war.
belligerent Canada, neutral U.S., complications of, 93–94, 160–61, 244
change in emphasis after Pearl Harbor, 109
defense statement, 12 February 1947, 337–39, 374–75
joint defense, demand in Canada for, 21–22
joint defense, necessity of, 1–2, 22
joint planning for, 86–108
military value of facilities in Canadian northwest, 335
Newfoundland, two defense systems, 180
postwar security requirements, 336, 337
and U.S. troops in Canada, 296–97
Defense Commands
Alaska, 112, 202, 215–16, 224n, 303
co-ordination with many commands, 111
Eastern, 132, 173–74, 197, 198
Northeast, 101, 111–12
Western, 100–101, 107, 112, 120, 121, 197, 252, 256, 302–03, 302n
Defense Department, U.S., 50n
Denmark, 149, 153, 293. *See also* Iceland.
Germany, occupation of, 150, 152–53
Dental service, 277
Department of the Air Force, 35n
Department of External Affairs, Canadian, 34, 35, 41, 42, 135, 136, 151, 160, 297, 312, 336. *See also* Keenleyside, Hugh L.
Department of Mines and Resources, Canadian, 135, 136, 219
Department of National Defense, Canadian, 5, 34, 35, 42, 263, 264, 266, 328
Department of National Defense for Air, Canadian, 136, 328
Department of State, U.S., 24, 28–29, 31, 32, 34, 38, 42, 43n, 57–58, 60, 68, 69, 70, 71, 73, 135, 144, 146, 147, 150–54, 155, 158, 159, 160, 169–70, 189n, 219, 221n, 229, 234, 303n, 311, 312, 328n, 336
Department of State *Bulletin,* 28–29
Department of Transport, Canadian, 135, 136, 184, 187, 201, 203, 205, 207–08, 209, 212–13, 236, 237, 238, 302n, 307, 308, 309, 323, 328
Deserters, 277
Destroyers. *See also* Destroyers-for-bases.
British 242, 243, 246, 249
Canadian, 122, 243, 244, 246, 251
Polish, 246
U.S., 246
to Canada, 92
sale of to Canada, proposal, 163, 164
Destroyers-for-bases, 19, 21, 23–24, 29, 32, 49, 62, 69n, 92, 95, 126, 162–65, 165n, 242. *See also* Bases, air, Canadian, leased; Bases, U.S., leased; Legislation, U.S.
delivery of destroyers, 165
DeWitt, Lt. Gen. John L., 41n, 252, 253, 256
Dieppe raid, 257n
Dill, Field Marshal Sir John, 288
Dimond, Anthony, 221
Diplomatic missions
British, in Iceland, 157
British, in South America, 146
British, in Washington, 69, 149. *See also* Lothian, Lord.
Canadian, in Greenland, 150–51.
Canadian, in Latin America, 144, 147, 148, 161
Canadian, in Washington, 31, 42n, 71n, 135, 282. *See also* Christie, Loring.
Danish, in Washington, 150
Icelandic, in U.S., 155
U.S., in Greenland, 150
U.S., in London, 163
U.S., in Ottawa, 135, 234, 271, 282, 291n, 310n, 312. *See also* Atherton, Ray; Moffat, Jay Pierrepont.
U.S., in St. John's, 117–18, 177
U.S.-Canadian, embassy status for, 76
USSR, in Washington, 216
Doenitz, Admiral Karl, 242
Donald, J. R., 80
Douglas Harbour, 191

Douglass, Lt. Col. R. W., Jr., 35
Drummond, L. E., 135
Duff, Sir Lyman, 299
Dunkerque, 7–8, 47–48, 90
Dunn, Brig. Gen. Beverly C., 139
Durand, E. Dana, 78
Dutch East Indies, 103n, 228
Dutch Harbor, 100, 253–54, 256

East Hope Lake, Hudson's Bay Company, 191
Eastern Air Command, 99, 112, 125, 249
Eastern Defense Command, 132, 173–74, 197, 198
Eastern Theater of Operations, 127
Economy. *See also* Pay.
  Canadian, 199, 207, 210, 273
  Newfoundland, 168–69
Edmonton, 127–28, 133, 135, 137, 199–200, 202, 203, 204, 224, 236–37, 238–39, 305, 306, 307–08, 323, 324
Edmund B. Alexander, 96
Egypt, 293
Eire, 16
Eisenhower, General Dwight D., 265, 266
Eldorado Mining and Refining, Limited, 228
Election, U.S. presidential, 55, 56
Embassies. *See* Diplomatic missions.
Embick, Lt. Gen. Stanley D., 31, 32, 36, 102, 107–08
Emergency stations, U.S., in Canada, 70
Emerson, L. E., 41n, 179
Empress of Asia, 244
Engineer Districts
  Dawson Creek, 128
  Edmonton, 128
  Fairbanks, 128
  Hudson, 127, 130
  Newfoundland, 127, 166, 167
  Skagway, 128, 226
  Whitehorse, 128
Engineer Divisions
  North Atlantic, 127, 130, 132, 139
  Northwest, 128, 132, 135, 139
Engineer Regiments, 330th Engineer General Service, 130, 187
Engineer troops, U.S., 172, 214, 221, 223, 318
  Alaska Highway, pioneer road, construction of, 222
  Canol Project, 231
  Greenland, 154
  use of, in Canada, 207
  use of, and withdrawal from Canada, 206
Engineers, Chief of, 127–28, 130, 140, 219, 228
Engineers, Corps of, 127, 130, 132, 136, 139, 166, 188, 195, 209, 211, 222, 226, 229, 239, 240, 328n
England. *See* United Kingdom.
English Channel, 8, 56
Enlistment, of Americans in Canadian Armed Forces, 241–42, 241n, 274–75, 281–82
Enlistment, of Canadians in U.S. Armed Forces, 242
ESKIMO, 281
Eskimo Point, 191
Esquimalt, 255, 272
Etawney Lake, 191
Ethiopia, 3, 293
European Theater of Operations, 241, 317, 318
Evans, Pvt. William, 298n
Exchange. *See also* Morgenthau-Ilsley agreement; Roosevelt, Franklin D., Hyde Park Declaration.
  Canadian, made available to U.K., 294
  Canadian need of U.S. dollars, 291
  Canadian surplus of U.S. dollars, 292–93, 292n, 322
  limits on Canadian holdings of U.S. dollars, 322
Executive Agreement Series, U.S., 29
Executive Agreements
  on Great Lakes-St. Lawrence Seaway, deferral of, 274
  Ogdensburg Declaration, 28–29
Executive Orders, ATC authorized to carry passengers for hire, 312–13
Exercises. *See by name.*
Explosives, 286
Exports, Canadian, to United States, 291–92

Facilities. *See* Airways, maintenance and control of facilities; Construction of facilities; Facilities in Canada; Transportation facilities.
Facilities in Canada
  Alaska Highway, gift to Canada, 329–31
  to become Canadian property: PJBD recommendation, 320, 325
  to become Canadian property after reimbursement to U.S., 326
  disposition of, 44, 54, 317–20, 358–59, 364–65
  negotiated settlement, 333–34
  sale of, to Canada, 327–34
  and surplus property, 328–29
  transfer to Canada, 323, 325
Fairbanks, 100, 202, 215–16, 222, 225, 227, 230, 232, 234n, 235, 237, 308, 331, 332, 333
Far East, 103n, 202
Ferguson, George, 18n
Fermi, Enrico, 287
Fighter Squadrons, Canadian
  No. 14, 254, 255

Fighter Squadrons, Canadian—Continued
No. 111, 253, 254-55
No. 115, 252, 252n
No. 118, 254, 255
No. 135, 255
Financing. *See also projects by name.*
airfields, in eastern Canada, 323
airfields, northern, expenditures on, U.S. and Canadian, 323, 324, 333-34
Alaska Highway, 220, 221, 224
atomic energy research, 287, 288
Canol Project, 230, 232-33
Goose Bay air base, 323
Mackenzie River air route, 213
Northwest Staging Route, 202, 203, 211-12, 213-14, 220, 320-21
Canadian payment for permanent improvements, 322-23
projects in Canada, at U.S. expense, 320
telephone-telegraph line, Alaska Highway, 323
telephone-telegraph line, for RCAF, 306
First Quebec Conference, 66, 82, 288
First Special Service Force, U.S.-Canadian, 51, 258-68
administrative agreements on, 262-63
administrative problems for Canadian personnel, 263-64
and Aleutian campaign, 258-59, 266
awards and decorations, problem of, 265-66
Canadian replacements, problem of, 265
casualties, 266
evaluation of, 267-68
and invasion of France, 266-67
and Italian campaign, 265, 266
training of, 261-62
Fleets, U.S.
Fifth, 272
Pacific, 112, 125, 255
Flight strips, Canadian
Aishihik, 208, 210, 324
Beatton River, 208, 210, 324
Snag, 208, 210, 324
Teslin, 208, 210, 324
Flight strips, U.S. *See also* Fort Simpson; Fort Smith, Northwest Territories.
Alaska Highway, 206, 207, 304, 315, 324, 330
Burwash, 206, 207
Camp Canol, 214
Canol Project, 214, 304, 316
Dawson Creek, 206, 207
Embarras, 214
Fort Providence, 214
Fort Resolution, 214
Fort Simpson, 214
Flight strips, U.S.—Continued
Fort Smith, 214
Hay River, 214
Liard River, 206, 207
Mackenzie River air route, 214, 322n, 323
Mills Lake, 214
Norman Wells, 214
Peace River, 214
Pine Lake, 206, 207
Pon Lake, 206, 207
Prophet River, 206, 207
Sikanni Chief River, 206, 207
Squanga Lake, 206, 207
U.S. alternates for Canadian staging fields, 206, 213, 304
Waterways, 214
weather stations, 237
Wrigley, 214
Flying Control Committee, U.S.-Canadian, 139
Food, purchases in Canada, 137n. *See also* Combined Food Board, U.S.-British; War Food Administrator, U.S.
Foreign Liquidation Commissioner, U.S., 328, 333, 334
Foreign policy, Canadian, and United Nations, 337
Forrestal, James V., 24, 31n, 80
Fort Benning, 281
Fort Brady, Ottawa, 195
Fort Chimo (CRYSTAL I), air base, 130, 184, 185, 186, 187, 189, 190, 192, 284, 304, 324, 325n
Fort Fitzgerald, 231
Fort Good Hope, 215
Fort McAndrew, 127, 167-68, 173, 175, 178, 179, 180
Fort McMurray, 284
Fort McPherson, 215
Fort Nelson, 201, 202, 207, 208, 211, 212, 215, 323, 324
Fort Pepperrell, 96, 127, 167-68, 173, 180
Fort Providence, 214, 231
Fort Richardson, 254
Fort Ross, 284
Fort St. John, 127, 201, 202, 207, 208, 211, 212, 219, 221, 227, 323, 324
Fort Simpson, 214, 215
Fort Smith, Northwest Territories, 135, 214, 231, 232
Fort Stevens, 122n
Fort William Henry Harrison, 261-62
Fort Yukon, 215
Foster, Brigadier Harry W., 257
Foster, L. B., Company, 333
Foster, Maj. Gen. W. W., 137-41, 224, 344

France, 293, 295, 339
fall of, 6, 7–8, 9–10, 18, 20, 47–48, 60, 90, 95, 131, 142, 144, 156, 158, 162, 163, 242, 290
invasion of, 266–67
invasion build-up, 251
matériel aid for, 15
member, Military Representatives of the Associated Pacific Powers, 68
sabotage raids in, 266
Frederick, Lt. Col. Robert T., 260
Free French, 158–59, 160
naval force from Halifax takes St. Pierre, 159
occupation of St. Pierre and Miquelon, 50
French Committee of National Liberation, 159
Frigates, Canadian, 251
Frobisher Bay (CRYSTAL II). *See* Bases, air, U.S.
Fry, Eric, 183

Gaffney, Col. D. V., 209
Gander Lake, 165, 192, 247
Gaspé. *See* Harbor defenses.
Gaspé Peninsula, 89
General Headquarters, U.S. Army, 112, 127
General Staff, Canadian, 113, 260–61
George, Brig. Gen. Harold L., 130
Germany, 8, 10, 11, 102–03, 105, 339. *See also* Declarations of war.
air attacks on Great Britain, 55–56
collapse of, 334
failure to attempt Channel crossing, 56
Greenland, activities in, 154n
Greenland, aerial reconnaissance of, 154
Greenland weather stations, British seizure of, 154
invasion of USSR, 244
naval and air power, Atlantic, 197
naval operations, 154–55
occupation of Denmark, 149, 155
occupation of France, 7
St. Pierre radio-weather station, 158
submarines, increased number on patrol duty, 248
surrender of, 270
threat to bases in Greenland, Iceland, West Indies, 142
threat to Greenland, 150, 151
threat to Iceland, 155
Gleneagles, 170n
Glenn Highway, 225
Godthaab, 150
Goose Bay. *See* Bases, air, Canadian, Goose Bay; Bases, air, U.S., Goose Bay *and* North West River; Newfoundland.
Gordon, Herbert, 271n
Gordon, Walter 80
Governor General, Canada, 28, 299–300
Graham, James H., 228
Grand Prairie, 201–02, 207, 208, 211, 212, 323, 324
Great Bear Lake mine, 287, 288
Great Britain. *See* United Kingdom.
Great Circle Route to Europe, 303
Great Circle Route to the Orient, 201, 303
Great Falls, 204, 205
Great Lakes, 1, 278–80
Great Lakes–St. Lawrence River defense, 198
Great Lakes–St. Lawrence seaway, 50, 274
Greece, 293, 295
Green Project, AAF, 192, 319
Greenland, 14, 48, 50, 87, 88, 105, 142, 154, 155, 161, 182, 341. *See also* Bases, air, U.S.; Plans, defense and war, ABC–1.
American protectorate, suggestion by Denmark, 150
Canadian interest, basis of, 151
Canadian memo to U.S. on security of cryolite mines, 150
cryolite output, and New York City meeting, 151
defense of, 149–55
conflicting American policies on, 150–51
protection for mines, Canadian offers of, 151, 154
German-controlled weather station, 154
German planes, aerial reconnaissance, 154
request for U.S. protection, 150, 151
U.S. opposition to Canadian or U.K. occupation, 149–50, 151
GREENLIGHT. *See* Infantry Brigades, Canadian 13th.
Greenslade, Rear Adm. John W., 166
Greenslade Board, 166, 177
Groves, Maj. Gen. L. R., 288
Guided missiles, 341

Hackworth, Green H., 164n
Hague Convention, 10
Haines, 226
Haines–Champagne road, 226–27, 330–31
Halifax, Lord, 59, 146
Halifax, Nova Scotia, 39, 41, 49, 123, 124, 125, 159, 165, 242, 244, 245, 246, 247, 305
Hamilton, 165
Hampton Roads Port of Embarkation, 266
Handy, General Thomas T., 269
Hansen, Alvin H., 78
Harbor defenses. *See also* Coast defense.

Harbor defenses—Continued
  Argentia, 354
  Bell Island, 95, 173
  Botwood, 92, 95, 99, 173
  Canadian, 89-90
  Gaspé, 92
  Juan de Fuca Strait, 93, 107
  Prince Rupert, British Columbia, 94, 239
  Puget Sound, 93, 106
  St. John's, 92, 93, 95, 96, 99, 116, 173
  Shelburne, 92
Harmon Field, 127, 166-68, 169, 173, 178, 192
Harrison, W. A., 80
Havana, 11, 26, 143, 144
Hawaii, 312
Hay River, Alberta, 231, 232
Heakes, Group Capt. F. V., 37
Hebron, 183
Helena, 237, 261
Henry, Maj. Gen. Guy V., 36, 207, 334-35
Henry, R. A. C., 78
Hepburn, Rear Adm. A. J., 41n
Herchmer, 191
Heuvelton, New York, 23, 28n
Hickerson, John D., 32, 36, 136-37, 256
Highways. *See* Roads; *and by name.*
Hill, Capt. Harry W., 31, 32, 36
Hiroshima, 284
Hitler, Adolf, 8, 156, 334
Hobbs, Col. G. K., 130
Hockenberry, Lt. Col. E. W., 36
Holyrood, 179
Hong Kong, 71n, 272n
Honshu Island, 200, 272
Hopkins, Harry, 48, 82, 123, 156
Hospital facilities, for Canadian troops in U.S. Army hospital, 277
Houlton, 283
House of Commons, British, 8, 13
House of Commons, Canadian, 15n, 18, 23, 24, 28, 92, 119, 144, 146, 162, 235, 319, 321, 338
House Joint Resolution 367, 11
House of Representatives, 274
Howe, C. D., 61, 185n, 203, 205, 209, 288, 308, 309, 316n, 321
Hudson, Albert B., 299
Hudson Bay, 194-95, 196, 281
  U.S. policy on, 194n
Hudson's Bay Company, 151, 231, 284
Hull, Cordell, 12, 13, 14, 15, 19, 35, 55, 59, 62, 68, 71n, 75, 143n, 149-50, 151-53, 153n, 159, 160, 164n, 218, 254, 279, 291. *See also* Department of State, U.S.
Hyde Park, 29
Hyde Park Declaration. *See* Roosevelt, Franklin D., Hyde Park Declaration.

Hydroelectric plants
  Lake of St. Francis, power increase, 273
  Niagara Falls, power increase, 273
  Norwegian and Alpine, 259
Hydroelectric projects, 50, 274

Iceland, 9, 48, 49, 50, 123, 124, 162, 182, 243, 244-45, 250, 293, 341. *See also* Bases, air, British; Bases, air, U.S.; Bases, naval, U.S.
  American troops in, 156, 157
  British troops, occupation by, 155
  defense of, 14, 155-57
  Denmark, Act of the Union with, 155
  and Denmark, King of, 155
  German bases, threat of, 142
  Hitler declares island in war zone, 156
  President of, 157n
  refusal to request U.S. troops, 157
  request for Monroe Doctrine protection, 155
Ickes, Harold, 230
Ilford, 191
Ilsley, J. L., 322
Imperial Oil Company, Limited, 228, 229, 232-33, 234-35, 331, 333
Imperial War Cabinet, London, 64
Imports, Canadian, from United States, 292
Income tax, Canadian, 278
India, 67, 82, 295
INDIGO, 157

Industry, Canadian, 14. *See also* Munitions, Canadian; Munitions, U.S.; War production.
  matériel production program, 5, 86
  need of U.S. dollars, 291
  and U.S. machine tools, 92n, 290-91
Industry, U.S.-Canadian. *See also* Munitions, Canadian; Munitions, U.S.; War production.
  joint production program, proposal, 341-42, 350
  production capacity, wartime expansion, 290-91, 342
Infantry Battalions, Canadian, 95, 99, 142, 257
Infantry Brigades, Canadian 13th, 257-58, 259
Infantry Divisions, Canadian
  2d, 156, 156n
  3d, 99
  6th, 270, 317
  7th, 317
  8th, 317
Infantry Regiments, U.S.
  3d, 96, 175
  17th, 258
  53d, 258

Infantry Regiments, U.S.—Continued
87th Mountain, 258
131st, 195
184th, 258
474th (Separate), 267
Installations. *See* Communication facilities; Construction of facilities; Facilities in Canada; Flight strips, Canadian; Flight strips, U.S.; Weather stations, U.S.; *under* Bases; *and by name.*
Institute of International Affairs, Canadian, 337
Intelligence
exchange of, 347
and exchange of staff officers, 280
Intelligence Division, U.S. War Department General Staff, 17
Inter-Allied Personnel Board, 275, 276
Inter-American Defense Board, 145
Interior Staging Route, British Columbia, 306. *See also* Air ferry routes.
International Conference of American States, 143
International Fisheries Commission, U.S.-Canadian, 27
International Joint Commission, U.S.-Canadian, 27
International Joint Defense Plan for Juan de Fuca Strait and Puget Sound, 106–07
International law, 339
and Canadian jurisdiction over its forces in U.S., 300–301
jurisdiction over friendly foreign forces, 297n
International Pacific Salmon Fisheries Commission, 27
Iran, 293
Iraq, 293
Iron ore, 193, 273, 274
Isolationism, U.S., 2
Italy, 10, 241, 264, 265, 266, 293
declaration of existence of state of war, by U.S., 108
surrender of, 251
Ivigtut, 149, 151

Jamaica, 49, 142, 149n
James Bay, 194, 196
JAN-CAN (Joint Army, Navy, Canadian), 302–03
communications and air traffic control, 302
dissolved February 1944, 305
JAN-CAN Committee, U.S.-Canadian, 141
Japan, 10, 87, 94, 100, 107–08, 143n, 162, 252, 317, 334, 335, 339. *See also* Aleutian campaign; Attu; Kiska.
Japan—Continued
attack on Dutch Harbor, 253
Attu, occupation of, 255
build-up on Attu and Kiska, 256
Canadian desire to participate in final assault on, 268
Canadian attitude toward occupation of, 270
carrier task force attack on Dutch Harbor, 204
diplomatic discussions with, 70
Kiska, evacuation of, 259
Kiska, occupation of, 204, 255
Kiska garrison, attacks on 254–55
surrender of, 270, 271, 319
task force off Aleutians, 253
threat to Alaska, 252, 255
threat of attack on Aleutians, 253
threat in Pacific, 55, 70
threat to west coast, 199, 318
threat to west coast shipping, 218
threat to western Canada, 255
Japanese, evacuation of, from west coast, 284
Japanese balloons, 200
Japanese population, Prince Rupert, evacuation of, 240
Jesuit College, Edmonton, 327, 328
Jeter, Capt. T. P., 36
Johnson, Vice Adm. A. W., 36
Johnson, Air Vice Marshal George, 249
Joint Agricultural Committee, U.S.-Canadian, 81, 84n
Joint Army and Navy Munitions Board Priorities Committee, U.S., 61
Joint Basic Defense Plan, Newfoundland, 117, 119
Joint Basic Defense Plan—1940. *See* Plans, defense and war, Joint Basic Defense Plan—1940, U.S.-Canadian.
Joint Basic Defense Plans 1 and 2, 89, 101–02, 103–04, 105, 112–15
Joint Board, U.S., 45, 46
Joint Chiefs of Staff, U.S., 10, 45, 46, 56, 59n, 66, 76, 106, 120, 268, 269, 270, 280, 336
Joint Declaration by the United Nations, 69
Joint Defense Production Committee, U.S.-Canadian, 79
Joint Economic Committees, U.S. and Canadian, 78–80, 84n
Joint Material Coordinating Committee, 79, 83, 84
Joint Service Committee, Canadian, 121
Joint Staff, Canadian, 34, 51, 52, 76, 135, 268, 269, 270, 280
Joint Staff, U.S. *See* Joint Chiefs of Staff, U.S.

Joint Staff Mission, British, 58, 63, 72, 73
Joint Staff Mission, Canadian, 72–76, 104, 112, 113, 248, 260, 264, 267, 268, 280, 336, 342
Joint Task One (protection of overseas shipping), 122, 125. *See also* Submarine, antisubmarine operations.
Joint Task Two (defense of Newfoundland), 116
Joint Travel Control Board, U.S.-Canadian, 141, 224
Joint War Aid Committee, U.S. and Canada, 82, 84n
Joint War Production Committee, U.S.-Canadian, 80, 84n. *See also* Joint Defense Production Committee, U.S.-Canadian.
Jones, Rear Adm, G. C., 37
Juan de Fuca Strait, 106–07, 111
Julianehaab, 182
Julius Thomsen, 151
Jurisdiction, 134, 165–67, 169, 189, 296–301
  U.S.-Australian and U.S.-New Zealand agreements, 298
  U.S.-British agreement, 297–98
  U.S.-Canadian agreements, 299–301

Kaldaharnes, 182
Kamloops, 324
Kauffmann, Henrik de, 150, 152–53
Keenleyside, Hugh L., 2n, 12, 18n, 21n, 31, 32, 33n, 34, 35, 37, 78, 310n
Kennedy, Joseph P., 8, 163
Kenny, Air Commodore W. R., 71–72
Kerwin, Patrick, 299
Ketchikan, 100, 202
Kiel Canal, 193
King, Admiral Ernest J., 59, 59n, 249
King, W. L. Mackenzie, 3, 4, 9, 12, 13–15, 18–19, 20, 21, 21n, 22, 23, 25, 34, 42, 59, 60, 62, 64–65, 65n, 66, 68, 69n, 70–71, 71n, 73, 76, 92, 114, 119, 120, 121, 142, 143, 144, 145, 146, 147, 148, 150, 159, 160, 162, 218, 220–21, 260, 288, 289, 303–04, 319–20, 321, 336, 338. *See also* Roosevelt and King.
Kingston, Ontario, 3, 24
Kiska, 254–56, 265, 266
  assault on, 256, 257, 258–59
  assault force, 255, 258
  occupation of, 255
Klondike gold rush, 225
Kluane, 226
Knox, Frank, 19, 32, 164, 194. *See also* Secretary of the Navy, U.S.
Knudsen, William S., 79
Kodiak, 100, 253, 254, 255, 283
Kure, 272

Labor, Canadian, 134. *See also* Western Labor Board, Canadian.
  co-ordination of, 137
  inadequacy of, 205–06, 207, 209, 210
  Northwest Staging Route, 209, 210, 212
Labor, U.S.
  Alaska Highway, 221, 222, 227, 318
  Argentia, 168
  Canadian northwest, 199
  Canadian projects, 296
  Canol Project, 318
  Northwest Staging Route, 208, 209–10
  telephone-telegraph line, 236–37
Labrador, 20, 48, 130–31, 149n, 162, 163, 182–83, 258n, 302, 303, 304, 305. *See also* Bases, air, U.S., Goose Bay, Labrador, *and* North West River; CRIMSON Project.
Lacey, Capt. J. K., 151
Ladd Field. *See* Bases, air, U.S., Fairbanks.
LaGuardia, Mayor Fiorello H., 22n, 31–32, 31n, 34, 36, 38n, 41, 42, 50, 52n, 90, 96, 113–14, 119–20, 171, 183, 185n, 218, 220n, 275, 327
Lake Harbour, Hudson's Bay Company, 191
Lake Huron, 193
Lake of St. Francis, 273
Lake Superior, 193
Landing strips. *See* Flight strips, Canadian; Flight strips, U.S.
Latin America, 7, 87, 142, 144, 145, 147, 148, 149. *See also* American Republics.
  defense of, 161, 341
  U.S. policy, in connection with Canadian and Commonwealth interest, 161
Laurier, Sir Wilfred, 2
Lawrence, Air Vice Marshal T. A., 305
Le Pensie, 191
Le Régiment de Hull, 257
Leahy, Admiral William D., 59n
Leased bases. *See* Destroyers-for-bases; Legislation, U.S.; *and under* Bases.
LeCapelain, C. D., 135
Leckie, Air Marshal R., 271
Legations. *See* Diplomatic missions.
Legislation, British, United States of America (Visiting Forces) Act, 1942, 298, 299, 300
Legislation, Canadian
  Defense Air Regulations, 305n
  Dominion Companies' Act, 326n
  Foreign Forces Order, 297, 298–99
  full jurisdiction for U.S. service courts, 300
  Mutual Aid Act, 295
  National Resources Mobilization Act, 1940, 257–58
  oil industry, partial government ownership, 233, 235

Legislation, Canadian—Continued
Surplus Crown Assets Act, 326n
uranium mines, government ownership, 288
U.S. jurisdiction, removal of exceptions to, 299
War Appropriation (United Nations Mutual Aid) Act, 1943, 81-82, 294
War Measures Act of 1914, 5, 299-300
Legislation, U.S.
aircraft, equipment and munitions, 6
Alaska Highway, designation of, 221n
Atomic Energy Act, 1946, 289
claims commissions, 278
contract renegotiation, 293
critical matériel, transfer of, 92-93
jurisdiction over friendly foreign forces, 300-301
Lend-Lease Act, 82, 83, 166, 177, 181-82, 242, 293
limits on transfer of critical supplies, 15
machine tools, export licensing, 290-91
military and naval assistance to American republics, 11
Naval Expansion Act, 1938, 6
Neutrality Act, 1937, 68
Selective Service and Training Act, 1940, 276
surplus matériel, sale of, 92
LEMMING, 281
Lend-lease. *See also* Bases, U.S., leased; Destroyers-for-bases; Legislation, Canadian, War Appropriation (United Nations Mutual Aid) Act; Legislation, U.S., Lend-Lease Act; Mutual Aid program, Canadian.
40-billion-dollar program, 293
aircraft deliveries, 182, 318
component parts for Canadian-built equipment, 292
convoy of lend-lease cargoes, 243
matériel in Canada, 329
purchases in Canada for transfer to U.K., 292
repairs to British naval vessels, 242
summary of, 293
total cost, 295
Les Fusiliers de Sherbrooke, 99
Les Fusiliers Mont-Royal, 156
Lethbridge, 205, 324
Letson, Maj. Gen. H. F. G., 72, 269, 270
Leyte, 272
Liaison, Canadian. *See also* Service attachés.
with Combined Chiefs of Staff, 65
with U.S. construction projects, 135, 343
Liaison, U.S.-British, 20-21, 20n, 58, 110, 122, 124, 242-43, 244. *See also* Combined Chiefs of Staff; Military planning, U.S.-British; Service attachés.
Liaison, U.S.-Canadian, 32, 51, 58n, 71-73, 75-76, 110, 121, 122, 136, 244, 280. *See also* Permanent Joint Board on Defense.
Liaison officers, Canadian, at U.S. air bases, 315, 316n
Liard River, 206, 207
Liberia, 293
Lincoln and Welland Regiment, 99
Liverpool, 243
Llewellin, Col., J. J., 288
Load-line regulations. *See* Transportation facilities, Great Lakes, load-line regulations.
Locomotives, 178
Logistical and administrative command, U.S.-Canadian, feasibility of, 140
Logistical headquarters, U.S.
communications zone type, feasibility of, 141
theater-type, feasibility of, 344
Logistical headquarters, U.S.-Canadian, theater-type, feasibility of, 344
Logistics. *See also* Construction of facilities; North West Purchasing, Limited; Western Labor Board, Canadian.
Canol Project, 231
facilities in Canada, 107, 109, 318
North America as logistical base, 317
organization for, 126-41
London, 55n, 77
leased bases technical discussions, 166
prewar military staff meetings, 58
London Food Committee, 83, 84
Londonderry, Ireland, 246
Loran (long range radio navigation), 337
Lothian, Lord, 10, 13, 14, 19, 55
Lovett, Robert A., 283
Low Countries, 6-7, 11
Lower, R. M., 18n
Low-level Route, Canada, proposed, 215. *See* Air Ferry routes.
Luftwaffe, 8
Lynn Canal, 226

MacArthur, General of the Army Douglas, 269
McCrae, John, 241n
Macdonnell, R. M., 37
Machine tools, 290-91, 345
Mackay, R. A., 18
Mackenzie, Alexander, 228

Mackenzie, C. J., 285, 288
Mackenzie, Ian A., 7
Mackenzie District, 232
Mackenzie King, W. L. *See* King, W. L. Mackenzie.
Mackenzie Range, 232
Mackenzie River, 218, 227, 231, 233, 237
Mackenzie River air route, 314, 316. *See also* Air ferry routes.
Mackenzie River valley, 228, 331
Mackintosh, W. A., 78
MacMillan, H. R., 80
McLean, A. D., 201
McNamara Construction Company, Ltd., 188
McNarney, Lt. Gen. Joseph T., 32, 36, 107, 260
McNaughton, Gen. A. G. L., 37, 41n, 156n, 269n, 335, 336
Magee, John Gillespie, 241n
Mahoney, Merchant, 10
Mail
  for American troops in Canada, 312
  to Canadian forces, 277
  diplomatic only, carried in Canada, 311
Maine, 307
Maintenance and control of bases. *See* Airways.
Maintenance of facilities. *See* Airways.
Malta-Yalta conference, 67n
Manila, 55n
Mapping, aerial, northern Canada, 284
Marine Companies, U.S., 3d Provisional, 96
Marine Operators, 231
Marines, U.S.
  Iceland, 156–57
  Marine brigades, 157
  withdrawn from Iceland, 157
Maritime Provinces, 2, 14, 15, 17, 30n, 49–50, 53, 86, 89, 92, 99–100, 101, 110–11, 112, 166, 176, 307
  defense of, 173–74, 348–49
Marshall, General of the Army George C., 10, 11, 11n, 14, 15–16, 56, 59, 59n, 92, 93, 94, 156, 163, 218, 243n, 259, 260–61, 268, 268n. *See also* Chief of Staff, U.S.
Martinique, 158
Massachusetts Institute of Technology, 285
Material Coordinating Committee, U.S. and Canada, 79, 83, 84n
Materials, allotment of, 349
Matériel, allocations of, by PJBD, 86
Matériel, Canadian
  to British Commonwealth nations, 294
  dollar receipts under Hyde Park program, 292
Matériel, Canadian—Continued
  purchases for lend-lease and for U.S., 292
  to U.K. after Dunkerque, 8
  to USSR, 294
Matériel, U.S. *See also* British Purchasing Commission; Combined Production and Resources Board, U.S.-British; Combined Raw Materials Board, U.S.-British; Combined Shipping Adjustment Board, U.S.-British; Munitions Assignments Board, U.S.-British.
  Canadian needs, supply of, 60–61
  Canadian request for, 13, 49
  direct purchases by Canada, 60, 61
  U.K. study of U.S. production, 285
Mayors, U.S. Conference of, 34
Medical service free for U.S. and Canadian troops, 277
Mediterranean Theater of Operations, 317
Metals Reserve Corporation, U.S., 292
Mexico City, 148
Mid-ocean Escort Force, 247
Mid-Pacific islands, 109
Mignano, 266
Military Area, Sault Sainte Marie, 197
Military Cooperation Committee, U.S.-Canadian, 336, 338
Military District, Sault Sainte Marie, 195
Military enlistment centers, Canadian, in U.S., for enlistment of nondeclarant male Canadians, 276
Military hospital, Edmonton, 327
Military planning, Canadian
  base for British Fleet, July 1940, 13
  defense of Newfoundland and British and French territories, May 1940, 9, 9n
  disposal of British fleet, discussion of, with Washington, June 1940, 12
  Joint Basic Defense Plan—1940, 110
  studies on impending fall of France, June 1940, 9
  troops to Greenland if necessary, April 1940, 150
Military planning, United Kingdom
  British fleet to U.S. or Canada, June 1940, 9
  Canadian Army Corps in England, July 1940, 156
Military planning, U.S. *See also* Plans, defense and war.
  ABC–1 as basis, March 1941, 58
  Alaskan defense, January 1942, 218
  arms and liaison officers to Latin America, May 1940, 11
  bases in Canada, need for, June 1940, 10, 11

Military planning, U.S.—Continued
Canadian air trainees, none in U.S. schools, May 1940, 10
change from defense to support of Britain, October 1940, 55-56
for defeat of Japan, February 1943, 208
defense of the hemisphere, April 1940, 7
estimate of U.S.-Canadian situation, July 1940, 16
estimate of world situation, June 1940, 11, 163
for Europe, North Africa, Alaska, Pacific, December 1941, 109
Greenland not strategically important, May 1939, 149
increased planning with Britain, 1941, 58-59
invasion of Japan, 1945, 269
lack of urgency, September 1939, 6
occupation of European colonies in South America, proposal of, May 1940, 10
orientation toward Caribbean, June 1940, 7, 162, 163, 341
1,200 Canadian trainees in U.S., July 1940, 16
Military planning, U.S.-British. *See also* Combined Chiefs of Staff; Plans, defense and war, ABC-1 *and* ABC-2.
and CRIMSON Project, June 1942, 186, 187
informal talks in London, August 1940, 20, 55, 77, 242
invasion build-up, 1942-44, 186, 191-92, 251, 259
Japanese threat, British proposal of talks on, October 1940, 55
military missions, first meeting of, June 1941, 58
staff talks, British request for, June 1940, 14
staff talks, Washington, January-March 1941, 55-57, 102, 112, 123, 153n, 155-56, 242-43
U.S. troops for Iceland, June 1941, 156-57
Military planning, U.S.-Canadian. *See also* Plans, defense and war; Permanent Joint Board on Defense.
Aleutian campaign, May 1943, 256-57
Alaska, defense of, April 1942, 252
Alaska, and west coast defense, December 1941, 199
defense, Newfoundland and north Atlantic coast, 1941, 162
estimate of world situation, 1946, 336
estimate of world situation, 1947, 338
Greenland, July 1940, 142
Iceland, July 1940, 142
Military planning, U.S.-Canadian—Con.
Montreal Revise, April 1941, 113-14
postwar collaboration, 1946, 337-38
Prince Rupert port, March 1941, 238
Security plan, 1947, 336, 338
staff talks, defense of North America, July 1940, 13-18
state of readiness at time of Pearl Harbor, December 1941, 53
and U.S.-British talks, January-March 1941, 57
U.S. troops allotment to Canada, April 1942, 173-74
West Indies, July 1940, 142
Military planning, U.S.-Dutch-British, 103
Military Police Battalions, U.S. 702d, 195
Military Railway Service, U.S. Army, 225-26
Military Representatives of the Associated Pacific Powers, 68
Millinocket, 283
Mingan, 188, 189, 190, 324, 325n
Minister of Mines and Resources, Canadian, 235
Minister of National Defense, Canadian, 108, 258, 267
Minister of Transport, Canadian, 239
Ministry of Aircraft Production, British, 181
Miquelon (off Newfoundland), 14, 50
Miyako Island, 272
Moffat, Jay Pierrepont, 13-16, 18, 22-23, 24, 24n, 28, 60, 73-74, 135, 142-43, 158, 219
Momp (mid-ocean meeting place), 244, 245, 246
Monroe, James, 48
Monroe Doctrine, 2-3, 4n, 26n, 48, 153n
applicable to 20° west longitude, 155
and Iceland, 155-56, 155n
in relation to Greenland, 152
Monte la Difensa, 266
Monte la Remetanea, 266
Montebello Conference, 337
Montreal, 39, 41, 181, 287, 288
Montreal Revise, 113-14
Montreal Subport of Embarkation, 133
Moose Factory, 186
Morgenthau, Henry, Jr., 15, 16, 60, 164, 322
Morgenthau-Ilsley agreement, 306, 322, 322n, 323
Mountbatten, Vice Admiral Lord Louis, 259, 260
Munitions, Canadian, 342
Canada third largest producer, 82, 341
expansion of industry, 6, 6n
to Newfoundland, 20, 162
shipments to U.S., World War I, 2

Munitions, U.S.
to Canada, 91–92, 94
Canadian requests for, 15, 16, 31, 90–91, 92–94
heavy weapons for Canadian 13th Infantry Brigade, 257
loans to Canada, 93–94
purchase of, by Canada, 7
shipments to Canada, World War I, 1–2
to United Kingdom, 8, 90, 94
Munitions, U.S.-Canadian
complementary production programs, proposal of, 341–42
production, 289–90, 291–92
Munitions Assignments Board, U.S.-British, 63, 64, 82
Munitions Assignments Committees, 82. *See also* Munitions Assignments Board, U.S.-British.
Murray, Rear Adm. L. W., 17, 32, 37, 124, 243, 249
MUSKOX, 336–37
Mussolini Canal, 266
Mutual Aid program, Canadian, 295

Nagasaki, 284
Nagoya, 272
Namao, 208, 211, 316, 323, 324
Naples, 266
Narsarrssuak, 154, 182
Nascopie, 151, 284
Nascopie expedition, 151n
National Defense Headquarters, Ottawa, 253
National Research Council, Canadian, 260, 285, 287
Naval Air Transport Service, USN, 133, 216–17
Naval Air Transport Squadrons, West Coast, 303
Naval Coastal Frontier, North Atlantic, 111, 112, 127, 132
Naval Coastal Frontier, Pacific Northern, 107, 111, 112
Naval support groups, Canadian, 251
Naval support groups, U.K., 251
Navy, British. *See* Royal Navy.
Navy, Canadian. *See* Royal Canadian Navy.
Navy, U.S., 3, 48, 49, 96, 98, 123, 124–26, 173, 218, 244, 247, 248, 249, 250, 302–03
British convoy training, 242–43
build-up in Alaskan waters, 255–56
convoys. *See* Convoys.
Eastern Sea Frontier, command of antisubmarine air operations in, 247
escort forces. *See* Convoys; Task Force 4; Task Group 4.19.

Navy, U.S.—Continued
liaison officers to South America, 11
neutrality patrol, 243, 244
patrol duties, 163
patrol of Hudson Bay, proposal of, 196
ships withdrawn from North Atlantic escort, 125, 245
training vessels on Great Lakes, 279
troop escorts, 246, 248–49
Navy Department, U.S., 7, 10–11, 17, 29, 31, 34, 35, 38, 42, 46, 50, 56, 72, 73–74, 76, 90, 96, 105, 122, 127, 132, 135, 148, 163, 168, 244, 245, 292, 311, 328n, 343
Netherlands, 58–59, 67, 68, 70, 142, 143n, 293
Neutrality, U.S., 2, 9, 68–69, 161
Neutrality patrol, 243, 244
New England, 247
air units in, 126
defense of, 174
New York, 39, 41
New York City, 151, 313
New Zealand, 67, 68, 72, 84, 281, 295
Newfoundland, 11, 50, 52, 53, 126–27, 133, 162–81, 243, 250, 258n, 304, 313, 317, 341, 344. *See also* Communication facilities; Pay; Plans, defense and war; Radar, stations; Railways; Roads; Troops, Canadian; U.S. Army Air Forces in Newfoundland; *and under* Bases.
airway traffic control, 301–02, 305, 306
aviation, postwar, 303
Canadian defense mission, 29–30, 170, 188–89
command problem, 30n, 74, 89, 97, 98, 101, 104, 111, 113, 116, 117, 118–19, 120, 133, 141
defense, 86, 87–88, 92–94, 95–96, 98n, 99, 105, 110, 111, 112, 114, 122, 125, 162, 164, 175–76, 180, 347–48, 350
economic rehabilitation of, 345
fuel storage, 352–53
German prisoners of war to, plan, 351
Protocol, Canadian, 98
Newfoundland a part of Canada for defense purposes, 62, 97
strategic importance to Canada, 19–20, 99, 180
union with Canada, 170n, 180–81, 345
union with U.S., discussion of, 180–81, 345
U.S. air forces to, 98, 172, 352
Newfoundland, Governor of, 166
Newfoundland Base Command, 98–99, 112, 116, 117–18, 119, 126–27, 132, 133, 159, 176–77, 180, 248, 301–02, 314

Newfoundland Base Contractors, 167
Newfoundland Escort Force, 122, 124, 125, 243, 244–46
Newfoundland Government, 21, 41n, 95, 118n, 119, 311
  Air Bases Agreement with Canada, 170n
  Bay Bulls, 99-year lease to Canada, 170n
  Goose Bay, 99-year lease to Canada, 170, 189
  and large American population, 169
  and leased bases, 165, 167
  and maintenance of roads, 178–79
  and Newfoundland Railway, 177–78
  Railway Loan Act, 178
  request that Canada occupy St. Pierre, 158
  Royal Commission, 19, 110
Newfoundland Railway, 53, 175, 177–80, 353
Niagara, 165
Niagara River, 273
Nisutlin River bridge, 222
Noble Drilling Corporation, 233
Nome, 100, 202, 216, 253
Norman Wells, 214, 215, 228, 229, 231–33, 284, 331, 332, 333
Normandy, 241
North Africa, 109, 249, 266
North Atlantic Ferry Route Project Committee, 187
North Atlantic Naval Coastal Frontier, 111, 112, 127, 132
North Atlantic Treaty Organization, 148
North Atlantic triangle, 59–68, 84, 85
North Pacific Force, USN, 255, 259
North West Purchasing, Limited, 136–37, 199
North West River, Labrador, 183. *See also* Bases, air, U.S., Goose Bay *and* North West River.
Northeast Airlines, 307, 310
Northeast Defense Command, 101, 111–12
Northern Indian Lake, 191
Northland, 152
Northwest Air Command, 305
Northwest Airlines, 237, 307, 308
  ATC insignia and Army uniform, 309, 310
  and friction with Canada, 307–11
  militarization, 310
Northwest Highway System, 330. *See also* Alaska Highway.
Northwest Service Command, 132
Northwest Staging Route. *See* Air ferry routes; CRIMSON Project; Flight strips; Canadian; Flight strips, U.S.
Northwest Territories, 128, 137
Northwest Territories Council, Canadian, 136
Norway, 259–60, 262, 293
Nova Scotia, 174, 250
Nuclear research, 286–87
Nueltin Post, 191
Nuwata, 191

O'Connor, Col. James A., 128
OCTAGON Conference, 66, 268, 272
Office, Chief of Engineers, 45n
Office of Scientific Research and Development, U.S., 260
Ogdensburg, 21n, 22, 24, 25, 26n, 27–28, 29, 31, 48, 69, 69n, 91
Ogdensburg Agreement, 27–29. *See also* Ogdensburg Declaration.
Ogdensburg Declaration, 22–26, 27–29, 30, 32, 47, 72, 88, 142, 160, 241, 306, 335, 343
Oil, royalties on Canol production, waiving of, 278. *See also* Aruba; Canol Project.
Oil fields
  Canadian reserves, 233
  Dutch East Indies, 228
  Mackenzie River, 228
Oil industry, Canadian, partial government ownership, 235
Oil pipelines, 224, 229, 230–31, 232, 233, 234n, 235, 331, 332, 333
Oil refineries, 228
  Rumanian, 259
  Whitehorse, 228–29, 232, 233, 234, 235, 331, 332, 333
Oil well drilling, 232–33
Okinawa, assault on, 272
Old Crow, 215
Olds, Brig. Gen. Robert, 203, 308, 309
Ontario, 299, 307
Ontario, 272
Orders-in-council. *See* Legislation, Canadian.
Ordnance, testing center, 133
Ordnance Department, U.S. Army, 133
Oregon, 220n
Ores. *See* Cryolite; Iron ore; Radium ore; Uranium.
Organizations, U.S., multitude of in Canada, 131–34, 343, 344
Ottawa, 39
  Air Training Conference, 283
  Churchill speech on Free French, 160
  leased lands, transfer of, discussion on, 211
  maintenance and control of facilities, talks on, 304
  Munitions Assignments Committee, meetings of, 82
  North Atlantic route, fields needed, talks on, 183
  Northwest and Low-level routes, PJBD talks on, 215

Ottawa—Continued
  Northwest Staging Route, AAF–RCAF talks on, 203–04, 309
  Northwest Staging Route, construction, talks on, 207–08
  PJBD meetings, 33, 40
  U.S. organizations in Canada, delineation of, 136, 139
Oumansky, Constantine, 216

Pacific, air defense, 252
Pacific Fleet, USN, 112, 125, 255
Pacific Northern Naval Coastal Frontier, 107, 111, 112
Pacific Theater of Operations, 318
Pacific War Council, in London, 66–67
Pacific War Council, in Washington, 67
Padloping Island (CRYSTAL III), 130, 131, 184, 187, 191
Page, Maj. Gen. L. F., 117–18, 119, 120
Pan American Airlines, 133
Pan American defense. *See* American Republics, defense.
Pan American Union, 153
  Canadian interest, basis for, 143, 144n, 148, 149
  and Canadian membership, 26n, 143–49
  U.S. opposition to Canadian membership, 143–48
Panama, 144
Panama Canal, 7, 87, 94, 193
Parachute Battalions, Canadian 1st, 265, 267, 281
Parachutists, Canadian, 267. *See also* First Special Service Force, Canadian replacements, problem of; Parachute Battalions, Canadian 1st.
Parliament, British, 164, 298
Parliament, Canadian, 5, 23, 24, 28n, 44, 220–21, 274, 299–300, 303–04
Parliament, Icelandic, 157
Passengers, fare-paying. *See also* Air Transport Command, U.S.; Northwest Airlines.
  agreement on, 312–13
  Canadian opposition to, 309, 311, 312, 313
Patricia Bay, 253
Patrols. *See* Air patrol; Submarines, antisubmarine air operations.
Patterson, R. P., 80
Pay
  overseas increment, U.S., 263
  Pacific campaign bonus, Canadian, 270
  U.S. and Canadian, First Special Service Force, 263
  for U.S. and Canadian laborers, 207
  U.S. dollars for Canadian troops in Alaska, 277
Peace River, 231
Peace River bridge, 222
Pearkes, Maj. Gen. G. R., 256
Pearl Harbor, 58, 71n, 75, 107, 109, 120, 126, 241, 242, 245, 259
  state of U.S.-Canadian readiness, 52–53
Pearson, Lester B., 63
Pennsylvania Salt Manufacturing Company, 151
Perkins, Milo, 80
Permanent Joint Board on Defense, 21n, 22n, 25–27, 28, 29–30, 31–54, 55, 58, 61, 70, 71, 72, 73, 74, 75, 76–78, 86–90, 91, 96, 98, 101–02, 103, 104, 106–07, 112, 113–14, 115–16, 118, 119–20, 120–21, 125, 135, 136, 137, 140, 148, 172, 175, 207, 215, 218, 219, 224, 226–27, 228, 230, 239, 241, 252, 256–57, 274–75, 280, 297, 302, 307, 311, 319, 325, 331, 334–36, 337. *See also* Military Co-operation Committee; Military planning, U.S.-Canadian.
  areas not discussed, 50, 142, 154n, 155
  bases, construction and operation, 49–50, 52, 139
  British as members, 146
  civilian chairmen, 38, 342
  command problem, 110–11
  co-ordination between U.S. and Canadian organizations, 343
  and CRIMSON Project, 185–86
  defense projects, not offense, 50–51
  as executive agency, 34, 45, 45n, 343
  geographical limits, 23, 24, 26, 46, 48–49, 50, 87, 105, 111, 142
  interior air defense, 193–98
  meetings of, 39
  membership of, 36–37
  Newfoundland air bases, construction by Canada, 171–72
  no solution to command problem, 114
  offices of, 38
  as operating agency, 45, 51
  operational planning, 52, 103–04
  procedures of, 41, 90
  radar facilities, Newfoundland, 176
  recommendations, 33, 34, 42–44, 42n, 43n, 45, 46, 49, 51, 52–53, 54, 86, 90, 95, 99, 100, 109, 117, 125n, 128, 130, 138, 171, 174, 178–79, 183, 186, 187, 188, 190, 193–94, 195, 196n, 201–02, 208–09, 217–18, 219, 220–21, 240, 282, 304, 306, 310, 313–16, 320, 325–26, 327, 329, 330, 332, 333, 337–38, 347–75
  Report, First, 43, 43n, 44, 48, 48n, 49, 50, 52, 88n, 90, 97, 100–101, 106, 171, 172–73, 174, 201, 366–69

Permanent Joint Board on Defense—Con.
  Report, Second, 43n, 113, 115
  reports unpublished, 44
  responsibilities of, 46-48, 50-51
  St. Pierre and Miquelon, discussion of, 158-59
  standardization of U.S., British Commonwealth forces, 335
  standardization of U.S., Canadian forces, proposal, 334-35
  transfer of bases to Canada, 189
  war industry members, proposal, 352
Petroleum Administrator for War, U.S., 234
Petroleum Coordinator for War, U.S., 230
Philippine Commonwealth, 67, 272
Pilots
  transfer of, from RCAF to AAF, 276
  world-wide training requirements, 51
Pine Camp, New York, 22
Pine Lake, 206, 207
Placentia Bay, 166, 174
Plans, defense and war
  ABC-1 (Joint Basic War Plan, U.S.-British), 46, 49, 57, 58, 58n, 65, 72-73, 101-04, 104n, 105, 106, 112, 114, 122, 149n
    British responsibility for east Greenland defense, 153n
    British responsibility for Iceland defense, 155-56
    U.S. protection of shipping, western Atlantic, 243
  ABC-2 (Joint Basic War Plan, U.S.-British), 104n
  ABC-22 (Joint Canadian-U.S. Basic Defense Plan 2), 46, 48, 52, 57n, 65, 72n, 73, 74, 89, 101-02, 103-08, 114, 115, 116, 117, 120, 122, 126, 178, 198, 280, 335, 336
  ABC (Pacific)-22, 107
  ADB (U.S.-Dutch-British plan for Far East operations), 103
  International Joint Defense Plan for Juan de Fuca Strait and Puget Sound, 106-07
  Joint Basic Defense Plan—1940, U.S.-Canadian, 48, 86-90, 100, 101, 105, 111, 115, 116, 201, 280, 350
  Joint Basic Defense Plans 1 and 2, 1941, U.S.-Canadian, 89, 101-02, 103-04, 105, 112-15
  Joint Defense Plan, Newfoundland, 117, 119
  RAINBOW 1, 11-12
  RAINBOW 4, 10, 13
  RAINBOW 5, 106, 108
  security plan, 338
  WPL-50 (Navy Hemisphere Defense Plan 3), 122
Plans, defense and war—Continued
  WPL-51 (Navy Hemisphere Defense Plan 4), 122-24
  WPL-52 (Navy Hemisphere Defense Plan 5), 123, 124
PLOUGH, 259-60. *See also* First Special Service Force.
Poland, 5, 68, 293
POLAR BEAR, 281
Pon Lake, 206, 207
Pope, Maj. Gen. Maurice, 36, 74n, 75, 108, 256
Port Edward staging area, 240, 327, 332
Ports. *See individual ports by name.*
Ports of Embarkation. *See* Boston Port of Embarkation; Hampton Roads Port of Embarkation; Prince Rupert Subport of Embarkation; Quebec Subport of Embarkation; San Francisco Port of Embarkation; Seattle Port of Embarkation.
Portugal, 251
Potsdam conference, 66n
Power, C. G., 14, 24n, 30
President, U.S., 336. *See also* Roosevelt, Franklin D.; Roosevelt and Churchill; Roosevelt and King.
President's emergency fund, 154, 178, 219
Presque Isle, 131, 188, 191-92, 247
Prestwick, 181
Prime Minister, Canadian, 120, 336. *See also* King, W. L. Mackenzie; Roosevelt and King.
Prince Baudouin, 267n
Prince David, 256
Prince Edward Island Highlanders, 99
Prince George, British Columbia, 202, 213, 227, 305, 323, 324
Prince George, 222n
Prince Henry, 256 267n
Prince Robert, 256, 272
Prince Rupert, 133, 202, 222n, 252-53, 328, 331-32. *See also* Harbor defenses; Prince Rupert Subport of Embarkation.
Prince Rupert, 222n
Prince Rupert defenses, Canadian, 252
Prince Rupert Subport of Embarkation, 222n, 230, 234n, 238-40, 318-19, 327, 332
Prince of Wales, 123
Princess Charlotte, 222n
Princess Louise, 277
Princess Norah, 222n
Prisoners of war, Germans, 351
Privy Council, Canadian, 28, 37-38, 135-36, 137, 137n
Prizes of war, disposal of, 278

Proclamations, presidential
jurisdictional law, application to Canada and U.K., 301
limited national emergency, 6
Procurement regulations, U.S., 137
Production. *See* Industry; Munitions; War Production.
Program of Immediate Canadian Action, 18, 18n
Prohibited areas. *See* Prohibited flying zones.
Prohibited flying zones, 195, 307
Northwest Staging Route, 305n
within 100 miles of Sault Sainte Marie locks, 197
Prophet River, 206, 207
"Protected places," U.S. premises in Canada, 284
Protocol, Canadian, 98
Proximity fuze, 286
Public Health Service, U.S., 169
Public opinion, Canadian, 296, 298, 299, 301, 334–35. *See also* U.S.-Canadian relations, areas of co-operation.
little co-operation with U.S., no antagonism toward USSR, 337
and Pan American Union, 147
Public opinion, U.S. *See also* U.S.-Canadian relations, areas of co-operation.
on defense of Canada, 25
on involvement in war, 25, 26, 55
on Permanent Joint Board on Defense, 25
Public Roads Administration, U.S., 127–28, 132, 206, 227
Puget Sound, 93, 106-07, 281.
Pursuit Squadrons, U.S. 11th, 202–03
Purvis, Arthur B., 60

QUADRANT Conference, 66, 82, 288
Quartermaster Market Center, 133
Quebec (City), 39, 305
Quebec (Province), 30n, 130, 299
Quebec conferences. *See* Conferences.
Quebec Subport of Embarkation, 133
Quidi Vidi. *See* Fort Pepperrell.

Radar
airborne, 286
ASVC (air-to-surface-vessel, Canadian), 286
British advanced developments to U.S., 285
equipment, Canadian, 94, 177
equipment, U.S., 71, 286
microwave, 285, 286
stations, 52, 71, 94, 175–77, 179, 180, 188n, 196, 197–98
Radio
proximity fuze, 286
stations, St. Pierre, 158, 159
U.S. military broadcasting stations in Canada, 277
Radium ore, 287
Railway guns, 91, 93, 94
Railways. *See also* Canadian National Railways; Canadian Pacific Railway Company; Newfoundland Railway; White Pass and Yukon Route Railway.
northern Canada, 187, 222, 225, 231, 232, 284
sale of railheads and depots to Canada, 327, 328
U.S. to Alaska, proposed, 228
RAINBOW 1, 11–12
RAINBOW 4, 10, 13
RAINBOW 5, 106, 108
Ralston, J. L., 14, 94
Rand, I. C., 299
Rat River, 191
Raw materials, equal U.S.-Canadian allocations, 291
RDX, research on, 286
RDX Committee, 286
Real estate, 126, 134
Canada to acquire land needed by U.S., 211, 304n
Canada to take over titles and leases, 210–11, 304n
Reconnaissance Squadrons, Canadian No. 8, 253
Reconnaissance Squadrons, U.S.
21st, 98, 183
41st, 98
Reconstruction Finance Corporation, 43n, 178
Regina, 186, 324
Reid, Capt. H. E., 37
Replacements, 267
Canadian policy of nonreinforcement in the theater, 265
U.S., 265, 267
Repulse Bay, 191
Research and development, U.S. *See* Atomic energy research, U.S.-Canadian; Radar; Radio, proximity fuze; RDX, research on.
Research and development, U.S.-British, 285–89
Restigouche, 123n
Restricted zones. *See* Central Air Defense Zone, U.S.; Controlled areas, railroad, The Pas to Churchill; Prohibited flying zones; "Protected places."

Reykjavik, 157, 182
Rhine River, 241
Richard Peck, 168
Richardson Highway, 222, 225
Richmond Gulf, 186
Rio de Janeiro, 144–46, 160
Riviera, 267
Roads. *See also* Alaska Highway; Alcan Highway; Glenn Highway; Richardson Highway; Winter roads.
  Canadian, south of Alaska Highway, poor quality, 222
  Canol Project, 227
  Newfoundland, 53, 175, 177, 178, 179, 355
Robins, Maj. Gen. Thomas M., 139, 209
Rocky Mountain Range, 217
Rocky Mountain Rangers, 257
Rome, 266
Roosevelt, Capt. Elliott, 183, 184
Roosevelt, Franklin D., 7, 8, 10–13, 14, 15, 16, 21, 22, 23, 26, 29, 31n, 32–33, 34, 38, 41–42, 43n, 46–47, 50, 56, 59, 59n, 63, 64, 65, 65n, 66–67, 68, 69, 70, 71n, 82, 90, 96, 105, 108, 114, 120, 144, 150, 152, 156–57, 163, 166, 171, 178, 182, 185n, 194, 209, 216, 218, 219, 221, 222, 228, 268, 275, 283, 288n, 289, 301, 312, 336. *See also* Roosevelt and Churchill; Roosevelt and King.
  Americans in Canadian forces, no loss of citizenship, 274
  arms supply policy for American Republics, 12
  Chautauqua pledge of defense assistance, 3
  destroyers-for-bases plan, 19, 164–65
  and Free French on St. Pierre, 159, 160
  Hyde Park Declaration, 79–80, 291, 292, 341, 342, 345, 373
  Iceland not in Western Hemisphere, 157n
  Kingston pledge of defense solidarity, 3–4, 24, 26n, 28
  "shoot on sight" warning to Germany and Italy, 244
  no troops to Iceland without invitation, 157
  unlimited national emergency, declaration of, 58, 243
  at Victoria, British Columbia, 3
Roosevelt and Churchill, 55, 63, 75, 83, 84, 98, 123, 126, 242, 244 248, 288
  ARCADIA Conference 59
  Atlantic Conference, 62
  OCTAGON Conference, 66
  QUADRANT Conference, 66
  TRIDENT Conference, 66
Roosevelt and King, 22, 22n, 24, 25–28, 30, 31, 35, 44, 46, 48, 49, 62, 78, 79, 82, 145, 158, 160, 282, 291, 343
  Atlantic coastal defense talks, 4
  Ogdensburg Declaration, 22–24
  Ogdensburg meeting, 91
  Pacific staff discussions, 3
  staff talks, request for, 21–22, 21n
  at Warm Springs, 4, 7
  Washington talks, 4
Royal Air Force, 241, 248, 249, 301, 302
  Ferry Command, 181
  VLR aircraft for RCAF, 249n
Royal Canadian Air Force, 5, 6, 17, 32, 34, 35, 51, 91, 98, 105, 110, 117, 118, 166, 171–73, 176, 177, 183, 188–89, 195, 198, 201, 207, 217, 241–42, 241n, 247, 255, 275, 276, 281, 283, 284, 309. *See also* Air forces, Canadian.
  antisubmarine squadrons, 251
  casualties, Aleutians, 259
  Eastern Air Command, 99, 112, 125, 249
  ground support, AAF, 254
  inability to purchase aircraft, 271
  Newfoundland air traffic, RCAF desire to control, 301–02
  Northwest Air Command, 305
  No. 1 Group, Newfoundland, 98n, 116, 125
  offer to operate with AAF in Pacific, 270–71
  operation with RAF in Pacific, 271, 271n
  Ottawa meetings, 203
  personnel in Alaska, distinguished foreign visitors, 254
  planes and pilots to England, 10
  Regulations for Control of Aircraft Movement, 305
  request for Flying Fortresses for *Bismarck* attack, 243n
  Special Reserve for Americans and others, 274n
  squadrons, withdrawal from Alaska, 255
  squadrons in Alaska, 252–55
  squadrons in Burma and Ceylon, V–J Day, 271
  Tiger Force, proposed, 271
  U.S. construction of facilities for, 306
  VLR aircraft, 249, 250
  Western Air Command, 107, 112, 252, 302n, 303, 307
  "X" Wing Headquarters, Fort Richardson, Alaska, 254
Royal Canadian Artillery, 24th Field Regiment, 257
Royal Canadian Corps of Signals, 238
Royal Canadian Mounted Police, 158, 198

Royal Canadian Naval Air Service, 2
Royal Canadian Navy, 5, 32, 34, 35, 110, 123, 124, 126, 165, 170n, 184n, 242, 243, 245–46, 248, 250, 272, 283. *See also* Newfoundland Escort Force; Western Local Escort Force.
  Atlantic Coast Command, 99, 111–12, 245
  Atlantic Command, 20
  convoy escort, 244
  engagements in Japanese war, 271–72
  growth of, 251
  Naval Staff Headquarters, 245
  Newfoundland Command, 123–24, 244, 245
  Newfoundland Force, 111, 116
  Northwest Atlantic Command, 249
  Pacific Coast Command, 107, 112
  Pacific coast facilities at disposal of U.S. Navy, 255
  proposals for Pacific force, 272
  vessels in Alaskan build-up, 255–56
Royal Flying Corps, 1
Royal Navy, 122, 150–51, 165, 242, 245, 248
Royal Navy escort group, 244
Royal Regiment of Canada, 156
Ruble, Capt. R. W., 36
Rush-Bagot Agreement, 1, 278–80
Russia. *See* Union of Soviet Socialist Republics.

Sabotage raids, 259, 262
St. Clair, 165
St. Croix, 165
St. Francis, 165
St. Georges Bay, 174
St. John's, 30, 39, 41, 119, 124, 127, 174–75, 179, 243, 247, 305. *See also* Bases, Army, U.S.; Bases, naval, Canadian; Bases, naval, U.S.; Harbor defenses.
  Local Joint Defense Committee, 117–18
  U.S. Army Supply Dock, 167
St. Lawrence River, 23, 174n, 273
St. Lawrence Valley, 2
Saint Marys River, 193, 194
St. Pierre, 14, 50
  Hull, on Free French seizure, 159
  plebiscite for Free French, 159
St. Pierre and Miquelon, 146, 158–60, 161
San Francisco, 39, 41
San Francisco Port of Embarkation, 238, 258, 266
Sandy Lake, 191
Santa Barbara, California, 121
Saskatchewan, 281
Saudi Arabia, 293
Sault Sainte Marie, 352
  defense of, 193–98, 357
Scientists, British. *See* British Scientific Mission.
Sea Frontier, Northwest, 302n, 303
Sea Island, British Columbia, 253
Seattle Port of Embarkation, 222n, 238–39, 240
Second Quebec Conference, 66, 268, 272
Secretary of the Interior, 218
Secretary of the Navy, U.S., 46, 58, 74, 105, 106, 114, 156, 218, 228. *See also* Knox, Frank.
Secretary of State, 271. *See also* Hull, Cordell.
Secretary of War, U.S., 46, 58, 74, 92, 105, 106, 114, 154, 156, 171, 218, 228, 271. *See also* Stimson, Henry L.
Security of Communications Committee, U.S.-Canadian, 139
Security measures, U.S.-Canadian
  evacuation of Japanese from Canadian Railway line, 284
  evacuation of Japanese from west coast, 284
  restricted zone, railroad, The Pas to Churchill, 284
Senate, Special Committee of, to Investigate the National Defense Program, 52, 233–34, 235, 322n
Senate, U.S., 29, 274
  purchase of Greenland, consideration of, 149
Service attachés, 51, 71–73, 76, 135, 271, 336
Service Commands
  Northwest, 128, 136, 212, 224, 236, 237, 240, 318
  Sixth, 130, 132
Services of Supply, U.S., 127, 128, 228
Seven Islands (Sept Isles), 188
Seward, 225
SEXTANT-EUREKA Conference, 66n
Sheils, G. K., 80
Shelburne, 49, 92, 123
Sherman, Commander Forrest P., 32, 36
Sherridon, 191
Shipbuilding
  on Great Lakes, 279
  Canadian, 249, 295
  U.S.-Canadian, 290
Shipping. *See also* Transportation facilities.
  civilian and defense, requirements for, 79
  equal U.S.-Canadian allocations, 291
Shipyards, Atlantic, Canadian, 279
Shoal Harbor, 180
Siberia, 48, 204, 216
Sicily, 241, 257n
Signal Aircraft Warning Reporting Companies, U.S. 671st, 196n

Signal equipment, shortage of, 306
Signal Service Battalions, U.S. 843d, 236
Sikanni Chief River, 206, 207
Singapore, 55, 103n
Sitka, 100
Skagway, 128, 222n, 225, 226, 230, 232, 234n, 235, 237, 331, 332, 333
Skelton, Alexander, 18n
Skelton, D. A., 78
Ski troops. *See* First Special Service Force.
Sloops, British, 243
Smith, Maj. Gen. J. P., 36
Smith River, 208, 210, 324
Smithers, 202, 252
Somerset Island, 284
Somervell, Lt. Gen. Brehon B., 228
Søndre Strømfjord, 154n, 182
South America, 26, 48, 142
South Greenland Survey Expedition, 154
Southampton Island. *See* Bases, air, U.S., Southampton Island.
Southwest Pacific, 63
Sovereignty, Canadian, 140-41
  and U.S. forces in Canada, 296
  and U.S. planes on Canadian airways, 301
Special Commissioner for Defense Projects, 137-41, 224, 344
Squanga Lake, 206, 207
Staff organization
  differences in U.S. and Canadian units, 258
  U.S. Army type for Canadian Army Pacific Force, 269, 270
  U.S. Army type for Canadian brigade, 257
Staging area, Port Edward, 240, 327, 332
Staging fields, 185. *See also* Air ferry routes, North Atlantic; Air ferry routes, Northwest Staging Route; CRIMSON Project; Fort Nelson; Fort St. John; Prestwick; and *under* Bases.
Staging routes. *See* Air ferry routes; CRIMSON Project; Northwest Staging Route.
Stalin, Joseph V., 216
Standard Oil Company, Whitehorse, 327
Standard Oil Company of California, 229
Stanley, 191
Stark, Admiral Harold R., 10, 11, 14, 15-16, 56, 59, 59n, 156
Stedman, Air Commodore E. W., 285
Stefansson, Vilhjalmur, 218
Stephenville, 180. *See also* Bases, air, U.S., Harmon Field.
Stettinius, Edward R., Jr., 80
Stevenson, Air Vice Marshal L. F., 270-71
Stewart, J. S., 135
Stimson, Henry L., 23, 24, 32, 94, 164, 216, 243, 288. *See also* Secretary of War, U.S.
Stinebower, L. D., 78
Strong, Brig. Gen. George V., 17
Stuart, Lt. Gen. Kenneth, 17, 30n, 32, 37, 106-07, 253, 260, 265, 285
Submarine warfare, 341
Submarines. *See also* Joint Task One.
  antisubmarine air operations, 247-48, 249-51, 361. *See also* Aircraft carriers.
    Canadian command of, 251
    co-ordinated plan, 247
    and USN command problem, 118
  antisubmarine equipment, 250
  antisubmarine operations, 2, 98, 126, 173, 174, 242-47, 248-49
    in 1940 plan, 87
  antisubmarine trawlers, Canadian loan to U.S., 246
  French, *Surcouf*, to St. Pierre, 159
  German
    Hudson Bay, threat of entry, 194, 196
    losses to, in Atlantic, 158, 174, 175, 197, 242, 243, 246, 247, 248, 280
    losses to, Conception Bay, 175
    losses to, in St. Lawrence River, 174n
    reconnaissance of Newfoundland bays, 174
    St. John's harbor, mining of approaches, 175
    shelling of Caribbean oil facilities, 228
    shifted from North American coastal waters, 250
    warfare in western Atlantic, 247
    wolf-pack technique, 242
  Japanese
    in Aleutians, 254
    shelling of west coast, 121, 121n
    reduction of menace, 317
    tanker losses to, 228
Suez Canal, 193
Superintendent of Airways, Canadian, 201
Supplies, 137
  acquisition of, in Canada, 136-37
  in Canada. *See* North West Purchasing, Limited; War Supplies, Limited.
Supply Committee, U.S.-Canadian, 139
Supreme Court, Canadian, opinion on jurisdiction, 299-300
Supreme war council, proposal of, 59
Surcouf, 159
Surplus property
  in Canada, disposition of, 44, 317, 319-20, 326-29, 326n, 333, 358-59, 364-65
  in U.S., purchase of by Canada, 329

Sydney, Australia, 272
Sydney, Nova Scotia, 2, 49, 245, 247
Sykes, Howard, 79
SYMBOL (Casablanca) Conference, 66n, 248

Tanana, 230
Tanks, 92, 281
  production totals, U.S.-Canadian, 290
Taschereau, Robert, 299
Task Force 1, USN, 123, 124. *See also* Atlantic Fleet.
Task Force 4, USN-RCN-RN, 116, 124, 125
Task Force 24, 248
Task Force 57, RN, 272
Task Force 2600, 127, 231
Task Force Tare, 255-56
Task Group 4.11. *See* Newfoundland Escort Force.
Task Group 4.19, USN-RCN, 125, 244, 245
Task Unit 16.1.1, AAF-RCAF, 254, 255
Tavani, 191
Taxes, Canadian
  American personnel, 134
  reimbursement of, 278
Taxes, Newfoundland, 169
Taxes, U.S., 278
TERMINAL Conference, 66n
Tests, cold weather, Camp Shilo, 281
The Pas. *See* Bases, air, U.S.
Theobald, Rear Adm. Robert, 255-56
Thicket, 191
Thomas, Capt. F. P., 36
Tizard, Sir Henry, 285
Tizard Mission, 285, 286
TNT, 286
Tok road, 225
Torbay, 170n, 172, 173, 184, 247
Toronto, joint conference on Military Area, 197
Toronto Group, 286
Trade, Canadian
  with Latin America, 143, 148, 161
  agreements with Argentina, Brazil, and Chile, 144
Training. *See also* Air Observers School, Canadian; British Commonwealth Air Training Plan; Pilots, world-wide training requirements; U.S.-Canadian relations, areas of co-operation.
  air, in Canada, for U.S. personnel, proposal of, 42n, 281-83, 343, 356
  assistance, request for by Canada, 13
  British air crews, in U.S., 282
  Canadian personnel in U.S. Army schools, 281
Training—Continued
  cold weather. ESKIMO, POLAR BEAR, LEMMING exercises, 281
  naval, on Great Lakes, 279, 280
  parachute, for Canadian personnel, Fort Benning, 281
  RCAF, at Bellingham, 283
  RCAF officers at U.S. airway traffic control school, 305
  specialized for First Special Service Force, 261-62
Transfers
  of Americans from Canadian to U.S. forces, 274-76, 282
  of Canadians from U.S. to Canadian forces, 276
Transportation Committee, U.S.-Canadian, 139
Transportation Corps Regulating Station, Edmonton, 133
Transportation facilities, 86, 186, 189, 191n, 193. *See also* Air Transport Command; Alaska Highway; CRIMSON Project; Northwest Staging Route; Railways; Roads; Water routes; White Projects.
  air, to Alaska, 219
  Canada, 350
  Canadian, U.S. improvement of, 345
  Great Lakes, load-line regulations, 273
  Maritimes, 349-50
  Newfoundland, 177-79, 349-50
  to northern air bases, 187
  northern Canada, improvements by U.S., 333-34
  ore carriers, Canadian, in U.S. domestic shipping, 274
  river routes, 202
  shipping to Alaska, 239
  U.S. Army truck fleet, Alaska Highway, 223-24
  water, to Alaska, 219
  water route, Waterways to Norman Wells, 214, 231
  winter roads, 202
  winter roads, Peace River-Fort Providence, 214
  winter roads, Peace River-Norman Wells, 214, 231, 232
Treasury Board, Canadian, 278
Treasury Department, U.S., 292
Treaties
  Great Lakes-St. Lawrence Seaway, rejection of, 274
  U.S.-Great Britain, on boundary with Canada, 27
Treaty of Ghent, 1

Treaty of Reciprocal Assistance, 48
Treaty Series, Canadian, 29
TRIDENT Conference, 66
Trinidad, 97n
Troops, Australian, 270
Troops, British, 50, 270
  Aruba, 142
  Iceland, 155
  relieved in Iceland, 157, 157n
Troops, Canadian, 47
  Aleutian campaign, 257
  Bahamas, 149n
  Bermuda, 149n
  British Guiana, 149n
  British West Indies, 9
  Caribbean, 143
  England, 156n
  Fort Benning, 281
  Goose Bay, 188
  Great Britain, 162
  Hong Kong, capture by Japanese, 71n, 272n
  Iceland, 9, 142, 156, 162
  Iceland garrison transferred to British Isles, 157
  Jamaica, 49, 142, 149n
  Labrador, 149n
  LEMMING exercise, 281
  Maritime Provinces, 99, 162
  Newfoundland, 9, 20, 20n, 95, 98–99, 149n, 166, 170, 173, 175
  west coast, 101
Troops, India, 270
Troops, Netherlands, 63
Troops, New Zealand, 270
Troops, U.S. *See also* Air forces, U.S.
  Alaska, 100–101, 199, 204, 277
  Argentia, 168
  Aruba, 149n
  Canada, 134, 199, 296–97, 317–18
    withdrawal from, after V-J Day, 306
  to Canada only if attack imminent, 16–17
  Curaçao, 149n
  Greenland, 154, 243
  Iceland, 156–57, 243
  mobile reserves to repel aggression, 162
  Maritimes, 16–17
  Newfoundland, 16–17, 93, 170, 173, 175, 296, 317–18
Troopships
  Canadian, 222n, 267n, 277
  U.S., 258
Truk, 272
Truman, Harry S., 289
Truman Committee. *See* Senate, Special Committee of, to Investigate the National Defense Program.
Trusteeships. *See* Colonies, European, in Western Hemisphere.
Turkey, 293

Uganda, 272
Umnak, 254–55
Uniform, Army, for contract airline personnel, 309, 310
Union of Soviet Socialist Republics, 58–59, 205, 216, 244, 293, 294–95, 318, 337, 338–39
United Airlines, 133, 308
United Kingdom, 3, 5, 6, 8, 10, 12, 15, 18–20, 21, 23, 24–25, 27, 48, 49, 55, 56–58, 60, 61–62, 64, 65, 66, 67, 68, 69, 70, 72, 77, 83–84, 85, 90, 94, 97, 99, 102, 103–04, 110, 112, 115, 123, 126, 130, 142, 146, 148, 149–50, 149n, 151, 153n, 155–57, 159, 162, 163, 164, 167, 171, 181, 182, 184, 186, 241, 242, 243, 244, 245, 246, 248, 250, 260, 267, 275, 281, 282, 285, 287, 288, 292, 294–95, 298–99, 300, 329, 338, 339. *See also* Battle of Britain; Commander in Chief, Western Approaches.
  Free French occupation of St. Pierre and Miquelon, suggestion of, 158
  government in exile, if Britain falls, 9
  occupation of Iceland to prevent German use, 155
  pressure on Canadians to occupy Greenland, 150
  war leadership, 340
United Nations, 148, 337
U.S. Army Air Forces in Newfoundland, 98, 125, 126, 172, 190, 247, 313
U.S. Army Construction Forces for the Alcan Highway, 127
U.S. Army Forces in Central Canada, 45n, 131
U.S. Army Forces in Eastern Canada, 131
U.S.-British agencies. *See* Anglo-American Food Committee; Combined Chiefs of Staff, U.S.-British; Combined Civil Affairs Committee; Combined Communications Board; Combined Food Board, U.S.-British; Combined Meteorological Committee; Combined Policy Committee (atomic research); Combined Production and Resources Board, U.S.-British; Combined Raw Materials Board, U.S.-British; Combined Shipping Adjustment Board, U.S.-British; Munitions Assignments Board, U.S.-British.
U.S.-Canadian agencies. *See* Alaskan International Highway Commission; Board of Inquiry for the Great Lakes Fisheries,

U.S.-Canadian agencies—Continued
U.S.-Canadian; Canadian Air Traffic Regulations Subcommittee; Communications Committee, U.S.-Canadian; Construction and Engineering Committee, U.S.-Canadian; Flying Control Committee, U.S.-Canadian; International Fisheries Commission, U.S.-Canadian; International Joint Commission, U.S.-Canadian; International Pacific Salmon Fisheries Commission; JAN-CAN Committee, U.S.-Canadian; Joint Agricultural Committee, U.S.-Canadian; Joint Defense Production Committee, U.S.-Canadian; Joint Economics Committee, U.S. and Canadian; Joint Travel Control Board, U.S.-Canadian; Joint War Aid Committee, U.S. and Canadian; Joint War Production Committee, U.S.-Canadian; Material Coordinating Committee, U.S. and Canada; Military Cooperation Committee, U.S.-Canadian; Permanent Joint Board on Defense; Security of Communications Committee, U.S.-Canadian; Special Commissioner for Defense Projects; Supply Committee, U.S.-Canadian; Transportation Committee, U.S.-Canadian; Weather Committee, U.S.-Canadian.

U.S.-Canadian relations. *See* U.S.-Canadian relations, areas of co-operation; U.S.-Canadian relations, areas of Canadian discontent; U.S.-Canadian relations, areas of U.S. discontent; Public opinion, Canadian; Public opinion, U.S.

U.S.-Canadian relations, areas of Canadian discontent. *See also* U.S.-Canadian relations, areas of co-operation; U.S.-Canadian relations, areas of U.S. discontent
- AAF offer of outmoded bombers for use in Pacific, 271
- ABC-1 report, 57
- American attitude on Canada, 340
- attitude on Canadian independence, 68-70, 335, 339, 341
- British-American staff liaison in London, 20-21
- control over contract airlines, 308-10
- construction sites, 200, 296
- failure to consult, 85
- inadequacy of voice in Commonwealth strategy, 5n
- leased-bases agreement on Newfoundland, 62
- matériel procurement difficulties, 60-61
- military mission to Washington, 72-76, 104, 120, 342
- Pacific problems, 70-71, 160

U.S.-Canadian relations, etc.—Continued
- reference to First Special Service Force as a U.S. unit, 261
- representation on Combined Food Board, 83, 84
- representation in war councils, 57, 59-60, 62-64, 68, 73-74, 84-85, 102, 339
- Rio de Janeiro meeting, 160
- Roosevelt-Churchill meeting off Newfoundland, 62
- Secretary Hull's reference to "so-called" Free French, 160
- unity of command, 342
- U.S. postwar advantage, 340
- U.S. troops and civilians on Canadian soil, 340

U.S.-Canadian relations, areas of co-operation, 24-25, 319-20. *See also* Military planning, U.S.-Canadian; Permanent Joint Board on Defense; Plans, defense and war; U.S.-Canadian relations, areas of Canadian discontent; U.S.-Canadian relations, areas of U.S. discontent; *and projects by name.*
- aerial mapping of northern Canada, 284
- aerial torpedo range in Puget Sound, 281
- air training in Canada for U.S. personnel, proposal, 281-83
- apprehension of AWOL's and deserters, 277
- on the battlefield, 241-42
- cold-weather exercises ESKIMO, POLAR BEAR, LEMMING, 281
- cold-weather tests, U.S., at Camp Shilo, 281
- compulsory military training for nondeclarant males, 276
- construction of facilities, 344
- dental and medical services, 277
- enlistments and transfers in Armed Forces, 274
- exchange of intelligence, 280-81
- hospital facilities, 277
- Lake of St. Francis, 273
- Lend-Lease, 293-94
- mail service, 277
- MUSKOX exercise, 336-37
- Niagara River, 273
- parachute training at Fort Benning, 281
- payment of Canadian troops in U.S. dollars, 277
- prizes of war, 278
- rescue of Hudson Bay Company personnel, Fort Ross, 284
- research and development, 273, 284-89
- Rush-Bagot Agreement, 278-80
- security measures, 283-84
- settlement of claims, 277-78
- shipping facilities on Great Lakes, 273
- troopships, Canadian, loan of, 222n, 277

U.S.-Canadian relations, etc.—Continued
U.S. military broadcasting stations in Canada, 277
use of air and naval facilities, 283
waiving of Canadian duties, taxes, royalties, 278
before World War II, 1-3, 296
U.S.-Canadian relations, areas of U.S. discontent. *See also* U.S.-Canadian relations, areas of co-operation; U.S.-Canadian relations, areas of Canadian discontent.
air defense, Gander Airport, 117
airway control and operation, 238
authority and interservice discord in Newfoundland, 118
changes in design specifications for staging fields, 212
communications in Newfoundland, 118
control of U.S. air bases and traffic in Canada, 304, 306
construction sites, 200, 296
delays on Northwest Staging Route fields, 205, 207, 209
inadequate labor force and refusal to permit use of Engineer troops, 205
limited use of proposed Canadian Army Pacific Force 268
local defense, necessity of agreement among commanders, 117
Newfoundland air facilities, 96-97, 171
proposed tax on surplus property used in the war, 327
radar installation in Canada, 71
reassignments to obtain seniority, 117-18
refusal of U.S. servicing detachment at Torbay, 173
repeated failure to meet delivery schedules, 292-93
reversal to Canadian construction on Staging Route, 212, 304
RCAF desire to control air traffic in Newfoundland, 302
RCAF use of U.S. buildings, Gander Airport, 172
unity of command, 74, 89, 90, 98, 104, 121-22
U.S. urgency versus Canadian study of postwar effects, 71, 235, 340
U.S. Department of State. *See* Department of State, U.S.
U.S. Joint Board. *See* Joint Board, U.S.
University of Chicago, 287
Unlimited national emergency, U.S., 58
UNRRA, 295
Uranium, 287, 288
Urquhart, Mr., 135

Valdez, 222, 225
Vancouver, 39, 41, 238, 240, 305
Vancouver, 256
Vancouver Island, 122n, 257, 258
Vandenberg, Arthur, 29
Vanier, Lt. Col. George P., 35, 37
Venezuela, 48
Vessels
Canadian commercial, on Great Lakes, 274
military, on Great Lakes. *See* Rush-Bagot Agreement.
Mutual Aid program ships, Canadian title to, 294-95
U.S., passage through Canadian waters, 307, 310
U.S.-Canadian construction totals, 290
U.S., and Icelandic flag, 123
Veterans Guard, 149n
Vichy French Fleet, 158
Vichy Government, 158
Vickery, H. L., 80
Victoria, 39, 41, 201
Villeneuve-Loubet, 267
V-J Day, 317

Wager Bay, 191
Wagner, Capt. F. D., 36
Walsh, Air Vice Marshal G. V., 75n
Walwyn, Vice Adm., 166
War Assets Corporation, Limited, 326, 326n, 333
War Cabinet, British, 56
War debts, 2
War Department, U.S., 7, 10-11, 17, 29, 31, 34, 35, 38, 42, 42n, 43n, 45-46, 50, 56, 72-74, 76, 90, 92, 96, 104, 105, 107, 115-16, 118, 120, 127, 130-31, 132, 133-35, 148, 149, 152, 163, 169-70, 171, 182, 185, 187, 189, 194, 197, 204, 205, 206, 212, 213, 215, 217, 218, 219, 224, 226-31, 232, 234-35, 239, 240, 252, 253, 260, 266, 267, 268-70, 271, 278, 280, 282, 283, 292, 306, 311-12, 322n, 328, 328n, 343
War Department General Staff, 17, 35, 89, 111, 113-14, 136, 140
War of 1812, 1
War Food Administrator, U.S., 84
War Office, British, 156n
War Office, Canadian, 72n
War Plans Division, WDGS, 17, 52, 89, 103-04, 111, 115-16, 149n
War production. *See also* Industry, Canadian; Industry, U.S.-Canadian; Joint War Production Committee, U.S.-Canadian; Munitions, Canadian; Munitions, U.S.;

War production—Continued
Munitions, U.S.-Canadian; Roosevelt, Hyde Park Declaration.
amortization, on Canadian-owned facilities, 293
distribution of, 295
Canadian, 295
U.S., 292–94
U.S. and Canadian, 339
U.S.-Canadian joint declaration on, 80–81
U.S.-Canadian totals, 289–91
War Production Board, U.S., 260
War Shipping Administration, U.S., 292
War Supplies, Limited, 83, 292
War Supply Board, Canadian, 60
Warm Springs, 4
Wartime Industries Board, Canadian, 79
Wartime Information Board, Canadian, 26n
Washington
Atlantic Convoy Conference, 125, 248–49
Canadian air traffic regulations, talks on, 304–05
Inter-American Defense Board, seat of, 145
meeting, Permanent Joint Board on Defense, 39, 40
Military Cooperation Committee meeting, 336
Newfoundland air traffic control, talks on, 301–02
staff talks, January–March 1941. *See* Military planning, U.S.-British.
staff talks, prewar, announcement of, 58
tripartite agreement on atomic energy, 289
Washington State, 106, 220n
Water route, Waterways to Norman Wells, 231, 331
Waterways, Alberta, 231–32
Watson Island, 240, 327
Watson Lake, 201, 202, 207, 208, 211, 212, 230, 232, 234n, 235, 323, 324, 331, 333
Watson-Watt, Robert, 94
Weapons, advanced, and Canadian privileged sanctuary position, 341
Weapons, atomic, 341
Weasel, 260, 262, 281
Weather, meteorological services, Canadian northwest, 236, 237–38, 309
Weather Committee, U.S.-Canadian, 139
Weather stations, U.S., 318, 327
Brochet, 191
Calgary, 338
Canada, 52, 70, 136, 141, 189, 190–91
Canadian hindrances to U.S. weather services, 190
Cape Harrison, 191n
Churchill, 191
Weather stations, U.S.—Continued
Coral Harbour, 191
Duck Lake, 191
Edmonton, 238
Eskimo Point, 191
Fort Chimo, 184, 190, 191
Fort Nelson, 238
Fort St. John, 238
Foxe Basin, 191
Frobisher Bay, 184, 190, 191
Gander, Canadian forecasts for U.S. garrison, 190
Gillam, 191
Greenland, 149
Hebron, 191n
Hudson Bay Junction, 191
Indian House Lake, 191
Island Falls, 191
Lake Harbour, 191
Mecatina, 191
Newfoundland (Gander) Airport, 190
Padloping Island, 184, 190, 191
Prince George, 238
River Clyde, 191
Stillwater Lake, 191
The Pas, 191
Wabowden, 191
Watson Lake, 238
Whitehorse, 238
York Bay, 191
Welland Canal, 279
Welles, Sumner, 10, 11n, 14, 15, 21–22, 31, 145, 145n, 146, 163, 164
West Indies, 14–15, 142
Western Airlines, 133, 308
Western Defense Command. *See* Defense Commands, Western.
Western Hemisphere, 10, 11, 19, 23, 24, 26, 40, 46, 48, 49, 50–51, 142, 143, 153, 153n, 161, 163, 164, 271, 341. *See also* American Republics; Colonies, European, in Western Hemisphere; Military planning, U.S.; Monroe Doctrine; Permanent Joint Board on Defense, geographical limits.
and Iceland, 155–56, 157n
U.S. convoys to 30° west, 123, 244
U.S. neutrality patrol to 26° west, 243
Western Labor Board, Canadian, 137, 199–200
Western Local Escort Force, RCN-U.K., 125, 245–46, 247
Western Union Telegraph Company, 180
Westomp (western ocean meeting place), 244 246
Whitbourne, 180
White, Harry D., 78

White Hills. *See* Fort Pepperrell.
White Pass and Yukon Route Railway, 128, 225, 225n, 226, 230
  U.S. lease of, 225–26
White Project, AAF, 192, 318
Whitehorse, 127, 128, 135, 224, 226, 228–29, 230–31, 232, 235, 236, 237, 238, 305, 323, 324, 325, 330, 332. *See also* Bases, air, U.S., Whitehorse.
Whitney, Rear Adm. J. P., 36
Whittier, Alaska, 225
Wilson, J. A., 135, 205
Winant, John G., 156
Winnipeg, 45n, 131, 195
Winnipeg Grenadiers, 142, 257
Winter Outpost, Canada, 191
Winter roads, 202, 214, 231, 232
Woodbridge, 4
Woodring, Harry H., 149n
World War I, 1–2, 59
  conscription, French-Canadian opposition to, 206n
  U.S.-Canadian relationships, 2
World War II
  cost, military, to Canada, 295
  cost, military, to U.S., 295
Worsham, Brig. Gen. Ludson B., 128, 139
WPL–50 (Navy Hemisphere Defense Plan 3), 122
WPL–51 (Navy Hemisphere Defense Plan 4), 122–24
WPL–52 (Navy Hemisphere Defense Plan 5), 123, 124
Wrangell, 202
Wrigley, 215
Wyman, Col. Theodore, Jr., 128, 214

Yachts, for conversion, purchase of by Canada, 7
Yakutat, 100, 202, 253
Yarmouth, 23, 247
York Bay, 191
Yugoslavia, 293
Yukon River, Yukon-Alaska, 218, 225n, 227
Yukon Territory, 128, 137, 225n, 232

U. S. GOVERNMENT PRINTING OFFICE : 1970 O - 360-477